Pietro Metastasio's Operatic Storm

Centre d'études supérieures de la Renaissance de Tours
Université de Tours, UMR 7323 du CNRS

Collection « Épitome musical » dirigée par Philippe Vendrix & Philippe Canguilhem

Editorial Committee: Hyacinthe Belliot, Vincent Besson, Camilla Cavicchi, David Fiala, Daniel Saulnier, Solveig Serre, Vasco Zara

Advisory board: Vincenzo Borghetti (Università di Verona), Marie-Alexis Colin (Université Libre de Bruxelles), Richard Freedman (Haverford College), Giuseppe Gerbino (Columbia University), Inga Mai Groote (Universität Zürich), Andrew Kirkman (University of Birmingham), Laurenz Lütteken (Universität Zürich), Pedro Memelsdorff (Centre d'études supérieures de la Renaissance de Tours), Kate van Orden (Harvard University), Yolanda Plumley (University of Exeter), Massimo Privitera (Università di Palermo), Jesse Rodin (Stanford University), Emilio Ros-Fabregas (CSIC-Barcelona), Katelijne Schiltz (Universität Regensburg), Thomas Schmidt (University of Manchester).

Thanks to Valentina Anzani and Tatiana Aráez Santiago for their editorial assistance.

Cover illustration: *Le Triomphe du goût moderne, Dedié alla Signora Faustina Bordoni* (s.l.: s.n., 17.), Bibliothèque nationale de France EST-204' (5), available at <https://gallica.bnf.fr/ark:/12148/btv1b525077207>

© 2022, Brepols Publishers n.v., Turnhout, Belgium.
This is an open access publication made available under a cc by-nc 4.0 International License: https://creativecommons.org/licenses/by-nc/4.0/. No part of this publication may be reproduced, stored in a retrieval system, or transmitted, in any form or by any means, for commercial purposes, without the prior permission of the publisher, or as expressly permitted by law, by licence or under terms agreed with the appropriate reprographics rights organization.

D/2022/0095/314
ISBN 978-2-503-60436-7
E-ISBN 978-2-60437-4
DOI 10.1484/M.EM-EB.5.132181
ISSN 2565-8166
E-ISSN 2565-9510

Printed in the EU on acid-free paper.

Pietro Metastasio's Operatic Storm

Texts and Musics for Metastasio's *Didone abbandonata, Alessandro nell'Indie, Artaserse, Demofoonte,* and *Adriano in Siria*

Edited by
Ana Llorens

Centre d'études supérieures de la Renaissance
Collection « Épitome musical »

BREPOLS

Contents

Contributors — 7

Foreword — 9
Acknowledgements — 11

List of Abbreviations — 13
List of Institutions — 17

Introduction — 33

Didone abbandonata (1724–1832) — 41
    Ana Llorens and Gorka Rubiales Zabarte
Alessandro nell'Indie (1730–1831) — 111
    Ana Llorens and Valentina Anzani
Artaserse (1730–1850) — 189
    Ana Llorens and Gorka Rubiales Zabarte
Adriano in Siria (1732–1828) — 271
    Ana Llorens and Tatiana Aráez Santiago
Demofoonte (1733–1836) — 315
    Ana Llorens, Gorka Rubiales Zabarte and Nicola Usula

Bibliography — 375
Bibliographic Tools — 385

Index Ia. Chronological Index: by Year — 395
Index Ib. Chronological Index: by Date and Title — 407
Index II. Index of Names: Composers — 437
Index III. Index of Names: Printers — 445
Index IV. Theatres — 463

Contributors

Valentina Anzani is a postdoctoral researcher within the ERC Didone Project. She earned her PhD in Musicology and History of Music at the University of Bologna in 2018. Her research focuses on the production and consumption of eighteenth-century opera theatre and castrato opera singers. Her first book, on the life and career of the castrato Antonio Bernacchi (1685–1756) was published in 2022. email: vanzani@iccmu.es

Tatiana Aráez Santiago is Lecturer in Musicology at the Universidad Complutense de Madrid and former 'Juan de la Cierva–Formación' postdoctoral fellow at the Instituto Complutense de Ciencias Musicales. PhD in Musicology (2019), degrees in piano (2006), Philology (2009) and History and Sciences of Music (2013). Her research interests include Spanish music and musicians; Franco-Spanish cultural transfers and the historical, analytical and intertextual study of music; migration and artistic interactions; associations and musical institutions. email: tarez.santiago@ucm.es

Ana Llorens holds a PhD in Music from the University of Cambridge. She is Lecturer in Music Theory and former 'Juan de la Cierva–Incorporación' postdoctoral fellow at the Universidad Complutense de Madrid, as well as the scientific director of the ERC Didone Project, within which the research contained in this volume has been carried out. She is specialised in the analysis of large corpora and, since 2019, board member of the Spanish Society of Musicology. email: allorens@ucm.es

Gorka Rubiales Zabarte earned a PhD in Musicology from the Universidad Complutense de Madrid with a dissertation on short-format dramatic genres in Spain in the early eighteenth century. After working as a research assistant in the ERC Didone Project, he currently is a 'Margarita Salas' postdoctoral fellow at the Universidad de Salamanca. His work focuses on musical iconography, organology, and eighteenth-century stage music. email: gorka.rubiales@usal.es

Álvaro Torrente is Professor in Musicology at the Universidad Complutense de Madrid and Head of the ICCMU. He is the principal investigator of the ERC Didone Project. His research focuses on the sacred villancico and Italian opera from the seventeenth and eighteenth centuries.

He is associate editor of *The Operas of Francesco Cavalli* (Bärenreiter), and his editions have been performed in Munich, London, and Amsterdam. email: atorrente@iccmu.es

Nicola Usula is a senior post-doc researcher on Italian opera and oratorio in the seventeenth and eighteenth centuries. At the core of his production are works on dramaturgy of music, philology of music and libretto, together with codicology and music iconography. In 2020 he was awarded the prize 'Antonio Feltrinelli Giovani' in the category 'Storia e Cultura della musica' by the Accademia Nazionale dei Lincei in Rome. email: nicola.usula@unifr.ch

The Sources of an Operatic Storm

Álvaro Torrente (Universidad Complutense de Madrid)

Publishing a printed catalogue of literary and musical sources of Metastasian opera may look slightly awkward in the twenty-first century, after several decades of critical musicology flagging hermeneutics as the primary purpose of the discipline. It may appear to be like going back to the origins of music research, when biographies, catalogues, and critical editions were the main concern of the forerunners of musicology. Yet, we should never forget that no hermeneutics is reliable unless grounded on consistent evidence. We can embrace critical musicology because librarians, archivists, and scholars keep working tirelessly to clear the thick forest of evidence in order to provide faithful testimonies.

The present catalogue is one of the preliminary tasks undertaken by the team of the Didone Project, funded by an ERC Advanced Grant. The main goal of Didone is to explore the expression of emotions in *opera seria*, focusing on a selection of *drammi per musica* by Pietro Metastasio that enjoyed great success for more than a century. And this is the richest corpus one could find, as Metastasio was doubtlessly the most important and the most influential dramatist for music in the eighteenth century, and possibly in the whole history of opera. It is hard to find any other creator that had such a profound, intense, wide, and lasting influence in the field. *Didone abbandonata*, his first *dramma*, was premiered in Naples in 1724 with music by Domenico Natale Sarro, and soon attracted the attention of other theatres and composers, who wrote new music for the same text —sometimes adapted— in the following decades. Surviving evidence compiled in this volume reveals that, by the early 1830s, there had been beyond 230 productions of more than 100 different musical settings. And *Didone* was by no means an exception in its sheer popularity: *Alessandro nell'Indie*, premiered in Rome in 1730, enjoyed a similar fortune, with more than 210 productions of some 110 settings, while *Artaserse*, premiered the same year, was even more successful, with further 250 productions of around 130 musical settings, mostly before 1800 but with few examples as late as 1850. These three titles were the most successful dramas written by the *poeta cesareo*, yet a comprehensive list should also include *Adriano in Siria* and *Demofoonte*, with around 100 settings each, as well as *Olimpiade* and *Demetrio*, with slightly lower figures. Only five of the 26 dramas by Metastasio, all written after 1750, had less than 20 musical versions, even though a work penned as late as 1756, *La Nitteti*, enjoyed enough popularity to be set to music beyond 40 times. In total, we can estimate that Metastasio's 26 dramas were set to music more than 1,000 times by not less than 400 composers throughout more than one century.

These figures are shocking to any modern observer and are still needing to receive a suitable explanation. Yet, this massive popularity presents a challenge for any researcher precisely because of its enormous dimension, which can only be embraced with the joint work of a team such as the one lead by Ana Llorens for this volume.

Many bibliographic resources were available when the project started, including reference works such as *New Grove* or *MGG*, together with comprehensive bibliographical catalogues such as Sartori or online resources like Corago. The combined strength of all these provided an initial picture of the wideness of the sources of Metastasian opera. However, detailed exploration of other documents, such as printed and online catalogues of libraries and archives, as well as on-site exploration of many collections, together with the help of dozens of generous librarians —listed next in the Acknowledgements page—, soon revealed that the number of testimonies related to each of the titles was substantially higher than the figures provided by the classical tools. For example, the number of new editions of librettos identified in this catalogue represents around an additional 10% of the sources registered in Corago, and *ca.* 25% more than the ones indicated by Sartori. If the surviving copies of librettos are considered, we have located about 50% more than the ones registered in either Corago or Sartori. The evidence about new musical settings is even more relevant. On the whole, we have identified 554 different settings of the five dramas, of which 208 (38%) survive. This represents 71% more versions than the ones reported in the otherwise outstanding article by Don Neville, 'Metastasio, Pietro', in *The New Grove Dictionary of Music and Musicians* (2001), and an additional increase of 17% and 11% with respect to the ones reported in Sartori and Corago respectively.

Sources are just a pale shadow of Metastasio's popularity in European theatres, but they are also the cornerstone for any attempt to understand and explain the phenomenon, as well as the linchpin to enjoy as intensely as possible the aesthetic experience of the *dramma per musica*. No catalogue is ever complete, but it is true that this comprehensive volume represents an extraordinary update of the evidence about Metastasio's rule. They are the surviving material traces of an operatic storm that broke through European theatres during the eighteenth century to dramatically —in the double sense of the word— transform European music. No meaningful hermeneutics of Western music can be properly undertaken without considering these positive testimonies.

Acknowledgements

This volume would not have been possible without the generous help of friends and colleagues who, over the last three years, shared unpublished research, gave invaluable advice, checked catalogues and holdings all around the globe, and made pictures of numerous materials. Especially in times of the COVID-19 pandemic, this made our work much easier and allowed us to provide in-person verified information. To all of them, our most sincere gratitude:

Dr Anna Agostini (I-PS), Angela Anselmo (I-Pl), Mark Bainbridge (GB-Owc), Ana Barata (P-Lcg), Lucia Baroni (I-PIu), Luciana Battagin (I-Vnm), Gerhard Beck (D-HR [D-Au]), Guido Bellando (I-Gl), Prof. Lorenzo Bianconi (Università di Bologna), Dr Juan José Carreras (Universidad de Zaragoza), Dr Gherardo Casaglia, Alessandra Cesare (I-VCc), Francesco Cignoni (I-CRg), Cesare Corsi (I-Nc), Dr Jiří David (CZ-R), Norbert Delestowicz (PL-Ptp), María Teresa Delgado Sánchez (E-Mn), Mateja Demšar (SI-Lsk), Elga Disperdi (I-MOe), Dr Katarína Dobrotková (SK-KRE), Dr José María Domínguez (Universidad Complutense de Madrid), Amanda DuBose (US-SY), Reinhard Ellensohn (A-Wu), Prior Michael Eppenschwandtner (A-MB), Marcello Eynard (I-BGc), Emanuela Ferro (I-Gc), Charlene Fündgens (D-KNth), Dr Federico Gallo (I-Ma), Brigitte Geyer (D-LEm), Paola Gibbin (I-Fc), Giustina Giusto (I-CATu), François-Pierre Goy (F-Pn), Stefano Grigolato (I-BRq), Rosina Harrer (A-Gu), Alison Hinderliter (US-Cn), Sophie Hoffmann (D-MÜu), Dr Johannes Hofinger (Salzburg Stadtarchiv), Carol Houghton (US-PRu), Matej Hreščak (National Museum of Slovenia), Gerlinde Iser (D-Eu), Juliana Jenkins (US-LAum), Anne Ørbæk Jensen (DK-Kk), Joanna Jutrznia (PL-Kj), Janine Klemm (D-Dl), Brigitte Knödler (D-KA), Ina Köhn (D-B), Guido Kraus (RISM), Veronika Kraus (D-KNu), Padre Laffai (I-Rss), Dr Carlo Lanfosi (I-Mr), Vita Lerner (I-LDEsormani), Dr José Máximo Leza (Universidad de Salamanca), Sven Limbeck (D-W), Natalie LoRuso (US-SY), Claudia Lubkoll (D-Dl), Piotr Maculewicz (PL-Wu), Maike Manske (D-KIl), Michela Marangoni (I-RVI), Dr Roberto Marcuccio (I-REm), Isabelle Mattart (B-Bc), Dave McMullin (US-NYp), Carlo Arborio Mella (I-Tf), Prof. Rafaele Mellace (Università di Genova), Dr Alessandra Mercantini (I-Rdp), Elena Mikhailova (RUS-SPtb), Dr Balázs Mikusi (RISM), Dr Jürgen Neubacher (D-Hs), Don Marianno dell'Omo (I-MC), Joachim Ott (D-Ju), Brunella Paolini (I-PESo), Dr Massimiliano Pavoni (I-MAC), Jarosław Pawlik (PL-LZu), Giovanni Piccirilli (I-VEc), Dr Cristina Pinto Basto (P-La), Franca Porticelli (I-Tn), Dr Johannes Prominczel (A-Wgm), Chamisa Redmond (US-Wc), Giovanni Ricci (I-La), Dr Juliane Riepe (Marthin-Luther-Universität Halle-Wittenberg), Dr Miguel Ángel Ríos Muñoz

MC | Acknowledgements

(Universidad Complutense de Madrid), Elena Rosano (I-FOsc), Dr Ana Ruiz Rodríguez (Universidad Complutense de Madrid), Miriam Roner (D-Dl), Matteo Sartorio (I-MS), Rito Saveria (I-Rn), Dr Uta Schaumberg (D-Mbs), Alexandra Schebesta (D-W), Dr Dieter Schmidt-Hensel (D-B), Lisa Schoblaskyl (US-Cn), Kerstin Schulze (D-Wa), Mario Setter (I-Rc), Dr Irmgard Siede (D-MHrm), Maria José Silva Pereira (PL-Cug), Alessandra Sirugo (I-TSci), Dr Andrea Sommer-Mathis (Österreichische Akademie der Wissenschaften), Annarita Soraci (I-Rsc), Dr Jana Spáčilová (Palacký University Olomouc), Maridina Spincich (I-LI), Paulina Stark (PL-MO), Prof. Reinhardt Strohm (University of Oxford), Dr Peter Styra (D-Rtt), Monika Sulejewicz-Nowicka (PL-LZU), Elisa Superbi (I-OS), Birgit Suranyi (A-Wn), Dr Konrad K. Szymański (PL-WRzno), Dr Michele Tagliabracci (I-FAN), Angela Tagliavia (I-PLcom), Sara Taglietti (I-Mb), Rita Tartivita (I-LOcl), Fiametta Terlizzi (I-Ra), Letizia Tombesi (I-IE), Fabio Uliana (I-Tu), Matthew Vest (US-BEm), Julijana Visočnik (SI-Lna), Cheryl Wegner (US-Cn), Michael Werthmann (D-MÜs), and Hans-Peer Zimmer (A-Wn).

We also want to thank Amaya Rico, head of the Interlibrary Loan Services of the Geography and History Faculty at the Universidad Complutense de Madrid, for her immense patience and indefatigable hunts.

Last but not least, our gratitude to Prof. Philippe Vendrix, editor-in-chief of this collection, for supporting our project from the beginning, and Prof. Álvaro Torrente, for always trusting and encouraging us.

** These catalogues are results of the research project 'DIDONE. The Sources of Absolute Music: Mapping Emotions in Eighteenth-Century Italian Opera', funded with an Advanced Grant no. 788986 by the European Research Council, led by Prof. Álvaro Torrente Sánchez-Guisande and based at the Instituto Complutense de Ciencias Musicales, the Universidad Complutense de Madrid, and the Universidad Carlos III de Madrid. This research has also been conducted with funding from Spain's Ministry of Science and Innovation (IJC2020-043969-I / AEI / 10.13039/501100011033 and FCI2019-039058-I / AEI / 10.13039/501100011033).

List of Abbreviations

* Immediately after the library sigla = composer's autograph
* After an aria title = the music setting for the given poem was reused in the following version by the composer

a.	after	Mar.	March
A	act	Mich.	Michaelmas fair
adap.	adapted	modif.	modified
add.	additions	mus.	music
Apr.	April	n	note
arr.	arrangement	NA	not available
Asc.	Ascension Fair	Nap.	Naples
Aug.	August	no.	number
aut.	autumn	nos	numbers
b.	before	Nov.	November
bc	*basso continuo*	NP	not performed
Bs	bass	n/s	no signature
C.	Città	lib.	libretto
Candl.	Candlemass	Mar.	March
carn.	carnival	mus.	music
cf.	confer	Ob.	oboe
Dan.	Danish	Oct.	October
Dec.	December	past.	pasticcio
dir.	directed	Port.	Portuguese
ed.	edition/edited	pr.	premiere
eds	editors	recit.	recitatives
En.	English	Rus.	Russian
Feb.	February	rvl	revival
fl.	flute	S	scene
Fr.	French	S.	San
Ger.	German	Sept.	September
incl.	including	s.d.	*sine data*
It.	Italian	s.l.	*sine loco*
Jan.	January	s.n.	*sine nome*
Jul.	July	Spa.	Spanish
Jun.	June	spr.	spring

MC | List of Abbreviations

St	Saint	**win.**	winter
rev.	revised	**ver.**	version
summ.	summer	**x2**	two different productions in the same season
T.	Teatro		
trans.	translated	**x3**	three different productions in the same season
Vn	violin		
Va	viola	**x4**	four different productions in the same season
vol.	volume		
vols	volumes		

Superscripts

A	aria collection, no recitatives
P	parts
IP	instrumental parts
R	reduction for voice and keyboard

BA	Printed catalogue of the music manuscripts preserved in the Palácio Nacional da Ajuda, Lisbon: Machado Santos, Marianna Amélia, ed., *Biblioteca da Ajuda: Catálogo de Música Manuscrita* (Lisbon: Biblioteca da Ajuda, 1958).
BASE	Online Base Nacional de Dados Bibliográficos <http://porbase.bnportugal.pt> [accessed 21 April 2022].
BL	British Library online catalogue <http://searcharchives.bl.uk> [accessed 3 May 2022].
BnF	Online catalogue of the Bibliothèque Nationale de France <https://catalogue.bnf.fr> [accessed 14 May 2022].
C	Corago <http://corago.unibo.it> [accessed 24 June 2022].
CA	Casaglia, Gherardo. *L'Almanacco di Gherardo Casaglia* <https://almanac-gherardo-casaglia.com> [accessed 7 May 2022].
E	English Short Title Catalogue <http://estc.bl.uk> [accessed 13 May 2022].
GVK	Online Gemeinsamer Verbundkatalog <https://kxp.k10plus.de/DB2.1> [accessed 28 April 2022].
MGG	*Die Musik in Geschichte und Gegenwart* online <https://www.mgg-online.com [accessed 17 May 2022].
NG	*Grove Music Online*, including *The New Grove Dictionary of Music and Musicians* and *The New Grove Dictionary of Opera* <https://www.oxfordmusiconline.com/grovemusic> [accessed 29 May 2022].
NP	Not performed.
PM	Progetto Metastasio, dir. by Anna Laura Bellina <http://www.librettodopera.it> [accessed 7 May 2022].
RISM	Online Catalogue of the Répertoire International de Sources Musicales <https://opac.rism.info> [accessed 21 June 2022].
S	Sartori, Claudio, *I libretti italiani a stampa dalle origini al 1800. Catalogo analitico con 16 indici*, 7 vols (Cuneo: Bertola & Locatelli Editori, 1990–1994).
SBN	Online Catalogue of the Servizio Bibliotecario Nazionale <https://www.iccu.sbn.it> [accessed 20 June 2022].

SB	Online Catalogue of Switzerland's institutional libraries <https://www.swissbib.ch> [accessed 24 April 2022].
IC	Catalogue of the relevant institution, other than those listed above; see the list of main bibliographic tools at the end of this volume.

List of Institutions

A – AUSTRIA
A-Gl	Graz, Steiermärkische Landesbibliothek
A-Gu	Graz, Universitätsbibliothek
A-HALn	Hall in Tirol, Pfarrkirche St Nikolaus
A-KR	Kremsmünster, Benediktiner-Stift Kremsmünster, Regenterei oder Musikarchiv
A-LA	Lambach, Benediktiner-Stift Lambach, Bibliothek
A-MB	Michaelbeuren, Benediktiner-Abtei Michaelbeuren, Bibliothek und Musikarchiv
A-Sfr	Salzburg, Franziskanerkloster
A-Sm	Salzburg, Internationale Stiftung Mozarteum, Bibliotheca Mozartiana
A-Ssp	Salzburg, Stift St Peter, Musikalienarchiv
A-Su	Salzburg, Universitätsbibliothek
A-SCH	Schlägl, Prämonstratenser-Stift, Bibliothek
A-SF	Sankt Florian (Linz-Land), Augustiner-Chorherrenstift, Bibliothek und Musikarchiv
A-ST	Stams, Zisterzienserstift, Bibliothek und Musikarchiv
A-Vpk	Vils, Pfarrkirche, Musikalienarchiv
A-Wgm	Vienna, Gesellschaft der Musikfreunde, Bibliothek
A-Wmi	Vienna, Musikwissenschaftliches Institut der Universität
A-Wn	Vienna, Österreichische Nationalbibliothek, Musiksammlung
A-Wst	Vienna, Wienbibliothek in Rathaus
A-Wu	Vienna, Universitätsbibliothek
A-WIL	Wilhering, Zisterzienserstift, Bibliothek und Musikarchiv

B – BELGIUM
B-Bc	Brussels, Conservatoire royal de Musique, Bibliothèque
B-Br	Brussels, Bibliothèque royale de Belgique
B-D	Diest, St Sulpitiuskerk
B-Nimep	Namur, Institut de Musique et de Pédagogie

BR – BRAZIL
BR-Rn	Rio de Janeiro, Biblioteca Nacional

MC | List of Institutions

CDN – CANADA
CD-HNu	Hamilton, Ontario, McMaster University, Mills Memorial Library
CD-Lu	London, Ontario, University of Western Ontario Library System, Music Library
CD-Mlr	Montréal, McGill University, Humanities and Social Sciences Library McLennan-Redpath
CD-Ttfl	Toronto, University of Toronto, Thomas Fisher Rare Book Library

CH – SWITZERLAND
CH-A	Aarau, Aargauische Kantonsbibliothek
CH-AR	Salenstein, Napoleonmuseum
CH-Bk	Basel, Bibliothek von Musikakademie der Stadt Basel
CH-Bm	Basel, Musikakademie der Stadt Basel, Bibliothek
CH-Bu	Basel, Öffentliche Bibliothek der Universität Basel, Musiksammlung
CH-BEb	Bern, Burgerbibliothek
CH-BEl	Bern, Schweizerische Lasndesbibliothek
CH-BEms	Bern, Universität Bern, Institut für Musikwissenschaft
CH-BM	Beromünster, Musikbibliothek des Stifts
CH-E	Einsiedel, Kloster Einsiedeln, Musikbibliothek
CH-EN	Engelberg, Kloster, Musikbibliothek
CH-Gc	Genève, Conservatoire de Musique, Bibliothèque
CH-Gmu	Genève, Bibliothèque musicale de la ville de Genève
CH-Gpu	Genève, Bibliothèque de Genève
CH-Lz	Luzern, Zentral- und Hochschulbibliothek
CH-N	Neuchâtel, Bibliothèque publique et universitaire de Neuchâtel
CH-SAf	Sarnen, Benediktinerinnen-Abtei St Andreas
CH-SGd	St Gallen, Domchorarchiv
CH-SO	Solothurn, Zentralbibliothek, Musiksammlung
CH-Zz	Zürich, Zentralbibliothek, Musikabteilung

CZ – CZECH REPUBLIC
CZ-Bm	Brno, Moravské zemské muzeum, oddělení dějin hudby [The Moravian Museum, Department of Music History]
CZ-Bu	Brno, Moravska zemská knihovna v Brně [The Moravian Library]
CZ-BER	Beroun, Státní okresní archiv [State Archive]
CZ-BRE	Březnice, Římskokatolická farnost Březnice, Kostel sv. Ignáce [St Ignaz Castle]
CZ-KR	Kroměříž, Knihovna arcibiskupského zámku [Library of the Archbishop Castle]
CZ-KRa	Kroměříž, Arcibiskupský zámek, Hudební sbírka [Archibishop's Castle, Music collection]
CZ-KU	Kutná Hora, Oblastní muzeum [Regional Museum]
CZ-LIT	Litoměřice, Státní oblástní archiv v Litoměřicích [State Regional Library]
CZ-NH	Nové Hvězdlice, Farní kostel svatého Jakuba [Parish Church of St James]
CZ-NYd	Nymburk, Děkanský úřad římskokatolický v Nymburce [St Jiljí Castle]
CZ-OLu	Olomouc, Vědecká knihovna [University Library]
CZ-OP	Opawa, Slezské zemské muzeum [Silesian Museum]

MC | List of Institutions

CZ-OSm	Ostrava, Český rozhlas, hudební archiv [Czech Radio, Music Archive]
CZ-Pak	Prague, Archiv Pražského hradu [The Archive of the President's Office]
CZ-Pdobrovského	Prague, Národní muzeum, Dobrovského (Nostická) knihovna [National Museum, Dobrovského Library, Department of Early Prints]
CZ-Pk	Prague, Knihovna Pražské konzervatoře, specializovaná knihovna [Prague Conservatory, Special collections]
CZ-Pkřiž	Prague, Rytířský řád křižovníků s červenou hvězdou, hudební sbírka [Knights of the Cross with the Red Star, Music collection]
CZ-Pn	Prague, Knihovna Národního muzea [National Museum Library]
CZ-Pnm	Prague, Národní muzeum-České muzeum hudby, hudebně-historické oddělení [Czech Museum of Music]
CZ-Pr	Prague, Český rozhlas, Fond hudebnin [Czech Radio, Music Archive]
CZ-Pu	Prague, Národní knihovna České republiky [National Library of the Czech Republic]
CZ-R	Rajhrad, Knihovna benediktinského kláštera [Benedictine Abbey, Library]
CZ-TEk	Teplice, Děkanský kostel sv. Jana Křtitele [St John the Baptist Church]

D – GERMANY

D-Aab	Augsburg, Archiv des Bistums Augsburg
D-As	Augsburg, Staats- und Stadtbibliothek
D-Au	Augsburg, Universitätsbibliothek
D-AM	Amberg, Staatliche Bibliothek
D-ASh	Aschaffenburg, Schloß Johannisburg, Hofbibliothek
D-B	Berlin, Staatsbibliothek zu Berlin Preußischer Kulturbesitz, Musiabteilung
D-Bga	Berlin, Geheimes Staatsarchiv, Stiftung Preußsischer Kulturbesitz
D-Bhm	Berlin, Universität der Künste, Universitätsbibliothek
D-Bs	Berlin, Stadtbibliothek, Musikbibliothek
D-Bsa	Berlin, Sing-Akademie
D-Bsommer	Berlin, Hans-Sommer-Archiv
D-Bu	Berlin, Freie Universität Berlin, Universitätsbibliothek
D-BAd	Bamberg, Archiv des Erzbistums Bamberg, Diözesanarchiv
D-BAs	Bamber, Staatsbibliothek
D-BAR	Bartenstein, Fürst zu Hohenlohe-Bartensteinsches Archiv
D-BAUd	Bautzen, Domstift und Bischöfliches Ordinariat, Bibliothek und Archiv
D-BDk	Brandenburg, St Katharinenkirche, Notenarchiv
D-BFb	Steinfurt, Fürst zu Bentheimsche Musikaliemsammlung Burgsteinfurt; in D-MÜu
D-BHu	Bayreuth, Universitätsbibliothek der Universitäts Bayreuth
D-BNu	Bonn, Universitäts- und Landesbibliothek
D-BS	Brunswick, Stadarchiv und Stadtbibliothek
D-BSSp	Bad Soden-Salmünster, Katholische Kirchengemeinde St Peter und Paul, Stifts- und Pfarrarchiv Salmünster
D-BÜ	Büdingen, Fürstlich Ysenburg- und Büdingensche Bibliothek
D-Dl	Dresden, Sächsische Landesbibliothek – Staats- und Universitätsbibliothek Dresden
D-DEl	Dessau, Anhaltische Lansdesbücherei, Abteilung Sondersammlungen

MC | List of Institutions

D-DEsa	Dessau, Stadtarchiv
D-DI	Dillingen an der Donau, Kreis- und Studienbibliothek
D-DO	Donaueschingen, Fürstlich Fürstenbergische Hofbibliothe
D-DS	Darmstadt, Universitäts- und Landesbibliothek Darmstadt
D-Es	Eichstätt, Staat- und Seminarbibliothek
D-Eu	Eichstätt, Universitätsbibliothek der Katolischen Universität Eichstätt-Ingolstadt
D-ERu	Erlangen, Universitätsbibliothek
D-ERP	Landsberg am Lech, Katolische Pfarrkirche
D-EU	Eutin, Eutiner Landesbibliothek
D-F	Frankfurt am Main, Universitätsbibliothek Johann Christian Senckenberg
D-Fsg	Frankfurt am Main, Philosophisch-Theologische Hochschule Sankt Georgen, Bibliothek
D-FUl	Fulda, Hochschul- und Landesbibliothek Fulda
D-Gs	Göttingen, Niedersächsische Staats- und Universitätsbibliothek
D-GOl	Gotha, Forschungs- und Landesbibliothek
D-GZbk	Greiz, Staatliche Bücher- und Kupferstichsammlung, Bibliothek
D-Hhg	Hamburg, Hasse-Gesellschaft Bergedorf e. V.
D-Hmg	Hamburg, Museum für Hamburgische Geschichte
D-Hs	Hamburg, Staats- und Universitätsbibliothek Carl von Ossietzky, Musikabteilung
D-HAh	Halle an der Saale, Händel-Haus
D-HAmi	Halle an der Saale, Martin-Luther Universität, Universitäts- und Landesbibliothek Sachsen-Anhalt, Institut für Musikwissenschaft, Bibliothek
D-HAu	Halle an der Saale, Martin-Luther Universität, Universitäts- und Landesbibliothek Sachsen-Anhalt
D-HEms	Heidelberg, Musikwissenschaftliches Seminar der Ruprecht-Karls-Universität
D-HEu	Heidelberg, Universitätsbibliothek
D-HEI	Heide, Klaus-Groth-Museum
D-HER	Herrnhut, Unitätsarchiv der Evangelischen Brüder-Unität
D-HR	Harburg, Fürstlich Öttingen-Wallerstein'sche Bibliothek, Schloß Harburg
D-HVl	Hannover, Niedersächsische Landesbibliothek, Gottfried Wilhelm Leibniz Bibliothek
D-HVs	Hannover, Stadbibliothek, Musikabteilung
D-Ju	Jena, Thüringer Universitäts- und Landesbibliothek
D-Kdma	Kassel, Deutsches Musikgeschichtliches Archiv, Bibliothek
D-Kl	Kassel, Landesbibliothek und Murhardsche Bibliothek der Stadt Kassel
D-KA	Karlsruhe, Badische Landesbibliothek, Musikabteilung
D-KIl	Kiel, Schleswig-holsteinische Landesbibliothek
D-KIu	Kiel, Universitätsbibliothek
D-KNmi	Kiel, Musikwissenschaftliches Institut der Universität
D-KNh	Köln, Staatliche Hochschule für Musik, Bibliothek
D-KNth	Köln, Theaterwissenschaftliche Sammlung der Universität
D-KNu	Köln, Universitäts- und Stadtbibliothek
D-LB	Langenburg, Fürstlich Hohenlohe-Langeburg'sche Scholoßbiliothek
D-LEm	Leipzig, Städtische Bibliotheken, Musikbibliothek

MC | List of Institutions

D-LEmi	Leipzig, Universität, Zweigbibliothek Musikwissenschaft und Musikpädagogik
D-LEu	Leipzig, Universitätsbibliothek, 'Bibliotheca Albertina'
D-LÜh	Lübeck, Bibliothek der Hansestadt Lübeck, Musikabteilung
D-Mbs	Munich, Bayerische Staatsbibliothek, Musikabteilung
D-Mms	Munich, Musikwissenschaftliches Seminar der Universität
D-Mth	Munich, Theatermuseum, Bibliothek
D-Mu	Munich, Universitätsbibliothek
D-MEIr	Meiningen, Staatliche Museum, Abteilung Musikgeschichte, Max-Reger-Archiv
D-MH	Mannheim, Wissenschaftliche Staadtbibliothek
D-MHav	Mannheim, Mannheimer Altertumsverein, Bibliothek
D-MHrm	Mannheim, Städtisches Reiß-Museum
D-MHu	Mannheim, Universitätsbibliothek
D-MT	Metten, Abtei Metten, Bibliothek
D-MÜs	Münster, Santini Bibliothek
D-MÜu	Münster, Universitäts- und Landesbibliothek
D-MÜG	Mügeln, Evangelisch-lutherisches Pfarrant St Johannis, Kantoreiarchiv
D-NEhz	Neuenstein, Hohenlohe-Zentralarchiv, Landesarchiv Baden-Württemberg
D-NEZkpn	Neuzelle, Katolische Pfarrgemeinde Neuzelle, Musiksammlung
D-OB	Ottobeuren, Benediktiner-Abtei, Bibliothek
D-Pu	Passau, Universitätsbibliothek
D-Rp	Regensburg, Bischöfliche Zentralbibliothek, Proske-Musikbibliothek
D-Rs	Regensburg, Staatliche Bibliothek
D-Rtt	Regensburg, Fürst Thurn und Taxis Hofbibliothek und Zentralbibliothek
D-RH	Rheda, Fürst zu Bentheim-Tecklenburgische Musikbibiotheñ Rheda; in D-MÜu
D-ROmi	Rostock, Universitätsbibliothek, Fachbibliothek Musikwissenschaften
D-ROu	Rostock, Universität Rostock, Universitätsbibliothek, Fachgebiet Musik
D-RT	Rastatt, Bibliothek des Friedrich-Wilhelm-Gymnasiums
D-Sl	Stuttgart, Württembergische Landesbibliothek
D-Sla	Stuttgart, Landeskirchliches Archiv
D-SDOk	Schorndorf, Evangelische Kirchengemeinde, Musikbibliothek und Archiv
D-SWa	Schwerin, Mecklenburgisches Landeshauptarchiv
D-SWl	Schwerin, Landesbibliothek Mecklenburg-Vorpommern, Musikaliensammlung
D-Tl	Tübingen, Schwäbisches Landesmusikarchiv
D-Tmi	Musikwissenschaftliches Institut der Eberhard-Karls-Universität
D-Tu	Tübingen, Eberhard-Karls-Universität, Universitätsbibliothek
D-TEGha	Tegernsee, Herzogliches Archiv
D-TRb	Trier, Bistumsarchiv
D-TRp	Trier, Priesterseminar
D-W	Wolfenbüttel, Herzog August Bibliothek, Musikabteilung
D-Wa	Wolfenbüttel, Niedersächsisches Staatsarchiv
D-WO	Worms, Stadtbibliothek und öffentliche Büchereien
D-WRgs	Weimar, Stiftung Weimarer Klassik, Goethe-Schiller-Archiv
D-WRha	Weimar, Hochschule für Musik Franz Liszt, Hochschularchiv, Thüringisches Landesmusikarchiv

MC | List of Institutions

D-WRl	Weimar, Thüringisches Hauptstaatsarchiv Weimar
D-WRz	Weimar, Herzogin Anna Amalia Bibliothek
D-WWW	Wolfegg, Stifts- und Pfarrbibliothek, Verein zur Erhaltung des Xanterer Doms
D-ZL	Leutkirch, Fürstlich Waldburg-Zeil'sches Archiv

DK – DENMARK
DK-Ch	Christiansfeld, Brødremenigheden [The Moravian Church]
DK-Kc	Copenhagen, Carl Claudius musikhistoriske Samling
DK-Kk	Copenhagen, Det Kongelige Bibliotek på Slotsholmen [The Royal Library of Denmark]
DK-Ku	Copenhagen, Det Kongelige Bibliotek Fiolstræde [University Library]
DK-Sa	Sorø, Sorø Akademi, Biblioteket

E – SPAIN
E-Bbc	Barcelona, Biblioteca de Catalunya
E-Bcapdevilla	Barcelona, Felipe Capdevilla Rovira, private collection
E-Bim	Barcelona, Consejo Superior de Investigaciones Científicas, Institut Milà i Fontanals
E-Bu	Barcelona, Universitat de Barcelona, Biblioteca
E-E	El Escorial, Real Biblioteca del Monasterio de San Lorenzo del Escorial
E-LPAu	Las Palmas de Gran Canaria, Biblioteca de la Universidad de Las Palmas de Gran Canaria
E-Mba	Madrid, Real Academia de Bellas Artes de San Fernando, Archivo de Música
E-Mlg	Madrid, Fundación Lazaro Galdiano
E-Mmh	Madrid, Biblioteca Histórica Municipal
E-Mn	Madrid, Biblioteca Nacional de España
E-Mp	Madrid, Palacio Real, Biblioteca y Archivo, Real Biblioteca
E-Mresad	Madrid, Real Escuela Superior de Arte Dramático
E-Msi	Madrid, Universidad Complutense, Biblioteca de San Isidoro
E-Mtnt	Madrid, Consejo Superior de Investigaciones Científicas, Archivo del Centro de Ciencias Humanas y Sociales, Biblioteca Tomás Navarro
E-ME	Maó, Menorca, Biblioteca-Arxiu Fernando Rubió Tudurri
E-MO	Montserrat, Arxiu Històric Musical de l'Abadia de Montserrat
E-PAp	Palma de Mallorca, Biblioteca Provincial
E-SC	Santiago de Compostela, Catedral Metropolitana
E-Tp	Toledo, Biblioteca Pública Provincial
E-TAu	Tarragona, Universita Rovira i Virgili
E-VAu	Valencia, Biblioteca Universitaria
E-VALm	Valldemosa, Museo de Fryderyk Chopin y George Sand

F – FRANCE
F-A	Avignon, Bibliothèque municipale Livrée Ceccano
F-AIXm	Aix-en-Provence, Archives diocésaines
F-BO	Bordeaux, Bibliothèque municipale
F-CO	Colmar, Bibliothèque municipale

MC | List of Institutions

F-Dc	Dijon, Bibliothèque du Conservatoire
F-G	Grenoble, Bibliothèque municipale
F-Lm	Lille, Bibliothèque municipale
F-Lu	Lille, Université de Lille III, Bibliothèque centrale
F-LM	Le Mans, Bibliothèque municipale
F-MOa	Montpellier, Archives départementales de l'Hérault
F-MOc	Montpellier, Conservatoire National de Région
F-Nm	Nantes, Bibliothèque municipale
F-Pc	Paris, Bibliothèque du Conservatoire
F-Pm	Paris, Bibliothèque Mazarine
F-Pn	Paris, Bibliothèque nationale de France, Département de Musique
F-Po	Paris, Bibliothèque-Musée de l'Opéra
F-Ps	Paris, Bibliothèque de la Sorbonne
F-Sgs	Strasbourg, Grand Séminaire, Bibliothèque musicale
F-Sim	Strasbourg, Institut de Musicologie de l'Université
F-Sn	Strasbourg, Bibliothèque Nationale et Universitaire
F-Susc	Strasbourg, Union Sainte Cécile

GB – GREAT BRITAIN

GB-ABu	Aberystwyth, University of Wales, Old College Library
GB-AY	Aylesbury, Bucks, County Record Office
GB-Bp	Birmingham, Public Libraries
GB-Cfm	Cambridge, Fitzwilliam Museum
GB-Cu	Cambridge, University Library
GB-CDp	Cardiff, Public Libraries, Central Library
GB-CDu	Cardiff, University College of South Wales and Monmouthshire
GB-DRu	Durham, University Library
GB-En	Edinburgh, National Library of Scotland
GB-Ge	Glasgow, Euing Music Library
GB-Lam	London, Royal Academy of Music, Library
GB-Lbl	London, The British Library
GB-Lcm	London, Royal College of Music
GB-Lfm	London, Faber Music
GB-Lfom	London, The Foundling Museum
GB-Lgc	London, Gresham College
GB-Lu	London, University of London, Senate House Library
GB-Lucl	London, University College London, Library
GB-Mp	Manchester, Central Public Library
GB-NOr	Nottingham, Archive Office
GB-Ob	Oxford, Bodleian Library
GB-Owc	Oxford, Worcester College
GB-SA	St Andrews, University Library
GB-SMleatham	Stamford, Brughley House, Lady Victoria Leatham, private collection
GB-WMl	Warminster, Longleat House Old Library
GB-WWrp	Warwick, Warwickshire County Record Office

MC | List of Institutions

H – HUNGARY

H-Ba	Budapest, Magyat Tudományos Akadémia Könyvtára [Hungarian Academy of Sciencies, Old Boks and Manuscripts Division]
H-Banc	Budapest, Magyar Tudományos Akadémia Népzenekutató Csoport Könyvtára [ungarian Academy of Sciences, Folk Music Research Group Library]
H-Bn	Budapest, Országos Széchényi Könyvtár [National Széchényi Library]
H-Bu	Budapest, Eötvös Loránd Tudományegyetem Egyetemi Könyvtár [Loránd Eötvös University Library]
H-Gk	Győr, Székesegyházi Kottatár [Chapter Private Archive, Music Collection]
H-KE	Keszthely, Helikon Kastélymúzeum Könyvtára [Museum of the Helikon Castle]
H-PH	Pannonhalma, Szent Benedek Rend Központi Főkönyvtára [Benedictine Chief Central Library, Music Collection]
H-VEs	Veszprém, Székesegyházi Kottatár [Musica Archive of the Cathedral]

HR – CROATIA

HR-Dha	Dubrovnik, Povijesni arhiv [Historical Archives]
HR-Dsmb	Dubrovnik, Franjevački samostan Male braće [Franciscan church and monastery]
HR-OSm	Osijek, Muzej Slavonije (zbirka Prandau) [Museum of Slavonia]
HR-PORzm	Poreč, Zavičajni muzej Poreštine [Poreč Heritage Museum]
HR-Sk	Split, Glazbeni arhiv katedrale [Musical archive of the Cathedral]
HR-Sm	Split, Muzej grada Splita [Vity Museum of Split]
HR-Zha	Zagreb, Zbirka Don Nikole Udina Algarotti [Udina-Algarotti Collection]

I – ITALY

I-ASs	Asti, Seminario Vescovile, Biblioteca
I-AT	Atri, Basilica Cattedrale di Santa Maria Assunta, Biblioteca Capitolare e Museo
I-Baf	Bologna, Accademia Filarmonica, Biblioteca
I-Bam	Bologna, Collezioni d'Arte e di Storia della Cassa di Risparmio (Biblioteca Ambrosini)
I-Bas	Bologna, Archivio di Stato, Biblioteca
I-Bc	Bologna, Museo internazionale e biblioteca della musica di Bologna
I-Bca	Bologna, Biblioteca Comunale dell'Archiginnasio
I-Bda	Bologna, Università degli Studi di Bologna, Dipartimento di Musica e Spettacolo, Biblioteca
I-Bl	Bologna, Conservatorio Statale di Musica G. B. Martini, Biblioteca
I-Bsf	Bologna, Biblioteca S. Francesco (Convento dei Frati Minori Conventuali)
I-Bu	Bologna, Biblioteca Universitaria
I-BDG	Bassano del Grappa, Museo Biblioteca Archivio (Biblioteca Civica)
I-BEc	Belluno, Biblioteca Civica
I-BGc	Bergamo, Biblioteca Civica Angelo Mai e Archivi storici comunali
I-BGi	Bergamo, Civico Istituto Musicale Gaetano Donizetti, Biblioteca
I-BRc	Brescia, Conservatorio Statale di Musica A. Venturi, Biblioteca
I-BRmd	Brescia, Museo Diocesano

MC | List of Institutions

I-BRq	Brescia, Biblioteca Civica Queriniana
I-BRs	Brescia, Seminario Vescovile Diocesano, Archivio Musicale
I-BZf	Bolzano, Convento dei Minori Francescani, Biblioteca
I-CATu	Catania, Biblioteca Regionale
I-CBp	Campobasso, Biblioteca Provinciale Pasquale Albino
I-CDGbm	Castellammare del Golfo, Biblioteca Multimediale
I-CF	Cividale del Friuli, Archivio capitolare del Duomo (S. Maria Assunta)
I-CHc	Chioggia, Biblioteca Comunale Cristoforo Sabbadino
I-CHf	Chioggia, Archivio dei Padri Filippini
I-CHRc	Chieri, Biblioteca Comunale
I-CMbc	Casale Monferrato, Biblioteca Civica Giovanni Canna
I-COLbarcella	Colombaro, Biblioteca Privata Luigi Barcella
I-CRg	Cremona, Biblioteca Statale (ex Governativa)
I-E	Enna, Biblioteca e Discoteca Comunale
I-Fc	Florence, Conservatorio di Musica Luigi Cherubini, Biblioteca
I-Fm	Florence, Biblioteca Marucelliana
I-Fn	Florence, Biblioteca Nazionale Centrale
I-FAN	Fano, Biblioteca Comunale Federiciana
I-FEc	Ferrara, Biblioteca Comunale Ariostea
I-FEu	Ferrara, Università degli Studi di Ferrara, Facoltà di Magisterio, Cattedra di Storia della Musica, Biblioteca (Biblioteca Amleto Bassi)
I-FEwalker	Ferrara, Biblioteca privata Thomas walker
I-FOLc	Foligno, Biblioteca Comunale
I-FOSc	Fossano, Biblioteca Civica
I-FPfanan	Fratta Polesine, Giorgio Fanan private library
I-FZc	Faenza, Biblioteca Comunale Manfrediana
I-Gc	Genoa, Biblioteca Civica Berio
I-Gl	Genoa, Conservatorio di Musica Niccolò Paganini, Biblioteca
I-Gsl	Genoa, S. Lorenzo (Duomo), Archivio Capitolare
I-GRA	Gravina in Puglia, Biblioteca Capitolare
I-GOl	Gorizia, Biblioteca musicale e musicologica 'Maestro Rodolfo Lipizer'
I-GOp	Gorizia, Biblioteca Provinciale (Archivio Storico Provinciale)
I-GOs	Gorizia, Biblioteca Statale Isontina e Civica
I-Ibborromeo	Isola Bella, Borromeo private library
I-IE	Jesi, Biblioteca Communale 'Planettiana'
I-La	Lucca, Archivio di Stato
I-Lg	Lucca, Biblioteca Statale (ex Governativa)
I-Li	Lucca, Istituto Musicale Luigi Boccherini, Biblioteca
I-LDEsormani	Lurago d'Erba, Sormani Verri di Lurago private library
I-LEpastore	Lecce, Biblioteca privata Giuseppe Pastore
I-LI	Livorno, Biblioteca Comunale Labronica Francesco Domenico Guerrazzi
I-LOc	Lodi, Duomo, Archivio Capitolare
I-LOcl	Lodi, Biblioteca Comunale Laudense
I-LOVbc	Lovere, Biblioteca Comunale Tredici Martiri
I-Ma	Milan, Biblioteca Ambrosiana
I-Mafb	Milan, Accademia dei Filodrammatici, Biblioteca

MC | List of Institutions

I-Mb	Milan, Biblioteca Nazionale Braidense
I-Mc	Milan, Conservatorio di Musica Giuseppe Verdi, Biblioteca
I-Mcom	Milan, Biblioteca Comunale Sormani
I-Mfil	Milan, Teatro Filodrammatici, Archivio
I-Mgentili	Milan, Biblioteca privata Massimo Gentili-Tedeschi
I-Mr	Milan, Biblioteca della Casa Ricordi
I-Ms	Milan, Biblioteca Teatrale Livia Simoni, Museo Teatrale alla Scala
I-Mt	Milan, Biblioteca Trivulziana e Archivio Storico Civico
I-MAav	Mantua, Accademia Nazionale Virgiliana di Scienze Lettere ed Arti, Biblioteca
I-MAc	Mantua, Biblioteca Comunale
I-MAC	Macerata, Biblioteca Comunale Mozzi-Borgetti
I-MACgiochi	Macerata, Biblioteca privata Filippo Giochi
I-MATts	Matera, Biblioteca Provinciale Tommaso Stigliani
I-MC	Montecassino, Monumento Nazionale di Montecassino
I-MFad	Molfetta, Archivio Diocesano
I-MOc	Modena, Biblioteca Civica di storia dell'arte Luigi Poletti
I-MOe	Modena, Biblioteca Estense
I-MTa	Montecatini Terme, Accademia d'Arte
I-MTc	Montecatini Terme, Biblioteca Comunale
I-Nc	Naples, Conservatorio di Musica S. Pietro a Majella, Biblioteca
I-Nf	Naples, Biblioteca Oratoriana del Gerolamini (Filippini)
I-Nn	Naples, Biblioteca Nazionale Vittorio Emanuele III
I-Nragni	Naples, Biblioteca privata Sergio Ragni
I-Nsn	Naples, Società Napoletana di Storia Patria, Biblioteca
I-NOVa	Novara, Archivio di Stato
I-NOVc	Novara, Biblioteca Comunale Negroni
I-OS	Ostiglia, Opera Pia Greggiati, Biblioteca
I-Pca	Padua, Biblioteca Antoniana con Archivio Musicale
I-Pci	Padua, Biblioteca Civica
I-Pl	Padua, Conservatorio di Musica Cesare Pollini, Biblioteca
I-Pmc	Padua, Museo Civico, Biblioteca
I-Psaggiori	Padua, Saggiori private library
I-PAc	Parma, Biblioteca Nazionale Palatina, Sezione Musicale presso il Conservatorio di Musica Arrigo Boito
I-PAp	Parma, Biblioteca Nazionale Palatina
I-PAt	Parma, Archivio Storico del Teatro Regio, Biblioteca
I-PAVbcb	Pavia, Biblioteca del Collegio Borromeo
I-PCc	Piacenza, Biblioteca Comunale Passerini Landi
I-PEc	Perugia, Biblioteca Comunale Augusta
I-PEsf	Perugia, Congregazione dell'Oratorio di S. Filippo Neri, Biblioteca e Archivio
I-PEsp	Perugia, Biblioteca Benedettina di San Pietro, Biblioteca e Museo della Badia
I-PEA	Pescia, Biblioteca Comunale Carlo Magnani
I-PESo	Pesaro, Biblioteca Comunale Oliveriana
I-PIu	Pisa, Biblioteca Universitaria
I-PLcom	Palermo, Biblioteca Comunale
I-PLcon	Palermo, Conservatorio di Musica Vincenzo Bellini, Biblioteca

MC | List of Institutions

I-PLn	Palermo, Biblioteca Centrale della Regione Sicilia (ex Nazionale)
I-PLpagano	Palermo, Roberto Pagano private library
I-PLZc	Palazzolo sull'Oglio, Biblioteca Comunale Giacinto Ubaldo Lanfranchi
I-PS	Pistoia, Biblioteca dell'Archivio Capitolare
I-PSbsg	Pistoia, Biblioteca San Giorgio
I-PSrospigliosi	Pistoia, Rospigliosi private collection
I-Ra	Rome, Biblioteca Angelica
I-Rac	Rome, Villa Medici, Accademia di Francia, Biblioteca
I-Raf	Rome, Accademia Filarmonica Romana, Biblioteca
I-Rama	Rome, Accademia Nazionale di S. Cecilia, Bibliomediateca
I-Rb	Rome, Biblioteca e Raccolta Teatrale del Burcardo della S.I.A.E.
I-Rc	Rome, Biblioteca Casanatense
I-Rcagli	Rome, Bruno Cagli private library
I-Rdp	Rome, Archivio Doria Pamphilj
I-Ria	Rome, Istituto d'Archeologia e Storia dell'Arte
I-Rig	Rome, Istituto Storico Germanico di Roma, Sezione Storia della Musica, Biblioteca
I-Rmassimo	Rome, private library of the Massimo Princes
I-Rn	Rome, Biblioteca Nazionale Centrale di Roma
I-Rrai	Rome, RAI-Radiotelevisione Italiana, Archivio Musica
I-Rsc	Rome, Conservatorio di Santa Cecilia, Biblioteca Musicale Governativa
I-Rsg	Rome, Basilica di San Giovanni dei Fiorentini, Archivio
I-Rss	Rome, Curia Generalizia del Domenicani (S. Sabina), Biblioteca
I-Ru	Rome, Biblioteca Universitaria Alessandrina
I-Rvat	Rome, Città del Vaticano, Biblioteca Apostolica Vaticana
I-REas	Reggio Emilia, Archivio di Stato
I-REm	Reggio Emilia, Biblioteca Municipale Antonio Panizzi
I-REt	Reggio Emilia, Teatro Municipale Romolo Valli, Biblioteca
I-RVE	Rovereto, Biblioteca Civica Girolamo Tartarotti
I-RVI	Rovigo, Accademia del Concordi, Biblioteca
I-Sc	Siena, Biblioteca Comunale degli Intronati
I-SAa	Savona, Seminario Vescovile, Biblioteca
I-SML	Santa Margherita Ligure, Biblioteca Comunale Francesco Domenico Costa, Biblioteca Comunale Modena Achille e Amalia Vago
I-SORmde	Sogliano al Rubicone, Museo del disco d'epoca
I-SPEbc	Spello, Biblioteca Comunale Giacomo Prampolini
I-Tac	Turin, Archivio Storico della Città di Torino
I-Tbcc	Turin, Biblioteca Civica Centrale
I-Tbnb	Turin, Biblioteca Norberto Bobbio dell'Università degli Studi di Torino
I-Tci	Turin, Biblioteca Civica Musicale Andrea della Corte
I-Tco	Turin, Conservatorio di Musica Giuseppe Verdi, Biblioteca
I-Tbgg	Turin, Biblioteca di Storia e Cultura del Piemonte 'G. Grosso'
I-Tmnr	Turin, Biblioteca e Archivio del Museo Nazionale del Risorgimento Italiano
I-Tn	Turin, Biblioteca Nazionale Universitaria
I-Tp	Turin, Biblioteca Storica della Provincia
I-Tstrona	Turin, Strona private library

MC | List of Institutions

I-Tt	Turin, Teatro Regio, Archivio Musicale
I-TLp	Torre del Lago Puccini, Museo di Casa Puccini
I-TRc	Trento, Biblioteca Comunale
I-TRsf	Trento, Biblioteca dei Padri Francescani di S. Bernardino (Fondazione S. Bernardino)
I-TSci	Trieste, Biblioteca Comunale Attilio Hortis
I-TSmt	Triste, Civico Museo Teatrale di Fondazione Carlo Schmidl, Biblioteca
I-UDc	Udine, Biblioteca Comunale Vincenzo Joppi
I-Vc	Venice, Conservatorio di Musica Benedetto Marcello, Biblioteca
I-Vcg	Venice, Casa di Goldoni, Biblioteca
I-Vgc	Venice, Istituto di Lettere, Musica e Teatro della Fondazione Giorgio Cini, Biblioteca
I-Vire	Venice, Istituzioni di Ricovero e di Educazione (IRE), Biblioteca e Archivio
I-Vivs	Venice, Istituto Veneto di Scienze, Lettere e Arti
I-Vlevi	Venice, Fondazione Ugo e Olga Levi, Biblioteca
I-Vmc	Venice, Museo Civico Correr, Biblioteca d'Arte e Storia Veneziana
I-Vnm	Venice, Biblioteca Nazionale Marciana
I-Vqs	Venice, Fondazione Querini-Stampalia, Biblioteca
I-Vt	Venice, Teatro La Fenice, Archivio Storico-Musicale
I-Vverardo	Venice, private library Pietro Verardo
I-VAc	Varese, Biblioteca Civica
I-VCc	Vercelli, Biblioteca Civica
I-VEas	Verona, Archivio di Stato
I-VEc	Verona, Biblioteca Civica
I-VEcon	Verona, Conservatorio di Musica Evaristo Dall'Abaco, Biblioteca
I-VIb	Vicenza, Biblioteca Civica Bertoliana
I-VIc	Vicenza, Conservatorio di Musica A. Pedrollo, Biblioteca

IRL – IRELAND

IRL-Dn	Dublin, National Library of Ireland
IRL-Dtc	Dublin, Trinity College Library

J – JAPAN

J-Tk	Tokio, Kunitachi Ongaki Daigaku [Kunitachi College of Music Library]
J-Tn	Tokio, Nanki Ongaku Bunko [Nanki Music Library, Ohki Collection]

M – MALTA

M-Vnl	Malta, National Library of Malta

NZ – NEW ZEALAND

NZ-Wt	Wellington, The Alexander Turnbull Library [in The National Library of New Zealand]

MC | List of Institutions

P – PORTUGAL

P-Cug	Coimbra, Biblioteca Geral da Universidad
P-La	Lisbon, Biblioteca do Palácio Nacional da Ajuda
P-Laa	Lisbon, Academia de Amadores de Música
P-Lcg	Lisbon, Fundação Calouste Gulbenkian
P-Ln	Lisbon, Biblioteca Nacional de Portugal
P-Lt	Lisbon, Teatro Nacional de Teatro de São Carlos
P-VV	Vila Viçosa, Biblioteca do Palácio Real

PL – POLAND

PL-CZ	Częstochowa, Klasztor OO. Paulinów Jasna Góra [Archive of the Jasna Góra Monastery]
PL-GD	Gdansk, Polska Akademia Nauk Bibliotheka Gdańska [Polish Academy of the Sciences]
PL-Kc	Krakow, Muzeum Narodowe w Krakowie, Biblioteka Książąt Czartoryskich [National Museum in Cracow, Czartoryski Library]
PL-Kj	Krakow, Biblioteka Jagiellońska [Jagiellonian Library]
PL-Kp	Krakow, Biblioteka Naukowa Polskiej Akademii Umiejętności i Polskiej Akademii Nauk [Polish Academy of Sciences]
PL-KI	Kielce, Biblioteka Wyższego Seminarium Duchownego [Higher Theological Seminary Library]
PL-KŁwnm	Kłodzko, Parafia Rzymskokatolicka Wniebowzięcia Najświętszej Maryi Panny [Archive of the Church of the Assumption of the Virgin Mary]
PL-ŁA	Łańcut, Muzeum – Zamek w Łańcucie, Biblioteka i Archiwum [Castle Musem, Library and Archive]
PL-ŁZu	Łódź, Biblioteka Uniwersytetu Łódzkiego, Sekcja Muzykaliów w Oddziale Zbiorów Specjalnych [Łódź University Library, Music Collections]
PL-MO	Kraków-Mogiła, Opactwo Cystersów, Archiwum i Biblioteka [The Sanctuary Of The Holy Cross of The Cistercian Abbey In Mogiła]
PL-OPsm	Opole, Uniwersytet Opolski, Wydział Teologiczny [University of Opole, Theology Section]
PL-Pa	Poznań, Archiwum Archidiecezjalne [Archdiocesan Archives]
PL-Ptp	Poznań, Biblioteka Poznańskiego Towarzystwa Przyjaciół Nauk [Library of the Poznań Society for the Advancement of Arts and Sciences]
PL-R	Raków, Kościół św. Trójcy w Rakowie, Archiwum [Holy Trinity Church, Archive]
PL-SA	Sandomierz, Biblioteka Diecezjalna w Sandomierzu [Higher Theological Seminary Library]
PL-STAb	Staniątki, Biblioteka Opactwa Sióstr Benedyktynek p. w. św. Wojciecha [Library of the Benedictine Abbey of St Adalbert]
PL-Wn	Warsaw, Biblioteka Narodowna [National Library]
PL-Wu	Warsaw, Biblioteka Uniwersytecka [University of Warsaw, Library]
PL-WRzno	Wrocław, Zakład Narodowy im. Ossolińskich [The Ossolinski National Institut]

MC | List of Institutions

RUS – RUSSIA
- RUS-Mk   Moskow, Naučnaja muzykaľnaja biblioteka im. S. I. Taneeva Moskovskoj gosudarstvennoj konservatorii im. P. I. Čajkovskogo [Moskow Conservatory, Sergey Taneyev Music Library]
- RUS-Mrg   Moskow, Rossijskaja Gosudarstvennaja biblioteka [Russian State Library]
- RUS-SPit   St Petersburg, Rossijskij institut istorii iskusstv [Russian State Institute of History]
- RUS-SPsc   St Petersburg, Rossijskaja nacionaľnaja biblioteka [Russian National Library]
- RUS-SPtob   St Petersburg, Centraľnaja muzykaľnaja biblioteka Mariinskogo teatra [Mariinski Opera Theatre, Central Library]

S – SWEDEN
- S-HÄ   Härnösand, Murberget Länsmuseet Västernorrland [Västernorrland County Museum]
- S-L   Lund, Universitetsbiblioteket [University Library]
- S-N   Nörrköping, Stadsbiblioteket [City Library]
- S-Sk   Stockholm, Kungliga biblioteket [Royal Library]
- S-Skma   Stockholm, Musik- och teaterbiblioteket [Music and Theatre Library]
- S-Sm   Stockholm, Musikmuseet [Music Museum]
- S-Sn   Stockholm, Nordiska museet, Arkivet [Nordic Museum, Archive]
- S-St   Stockholm, Kungliga teaterns bibliotek [Royal Theatre, Library]
- S-SK   Skara, Stifts- och landsbiblioteket [Diocese and National Library]
- S-STr   Strängnäs, Roggebiblioteket
- S-Uu   Uppsala, Universitetsbibliotek, Carolina Rediviva [Carolina Rediviva, Upssala University Library]

SI – SLOVENIA
- SI-Ln   Ljubjana, Narodna in univerzitetna knjižnica, glavni knjižni fond [National and University Library]
- SI-Lna   Ljubljana, Nadškofijski arhiv [Archiepiscopal archive]
- SI-Lsk   Ljubljana, Semeniška knjižnica [Seminar Library]
- SI-Mpa   Maribor, Pokrajinski arhiv [Provincial archive]

SK – SLOVAKIA
- SK-BRnm   Bratislava, Slovenské národné múzeum [Slovak National Museum]
- SK-KRE   Kremnica, Štátny archív v Banskej Bystrici [State Archiv]
- SK-J   Svätý Jur, Okresný archív Bratislava-vidiek

UA – UKRAINE
- UA-Knbuv   Kiev, Nacionaľna biblioteka Ukrajiny imeni V. I. Vernadsʼkoho, viddil muzyčnych fondiv [Vernadsky National Library of Ukraine, Music Department]

MC | List of Institutions

US – UNITED STATES

US-AAu	Ann Arbor (MI), University of Michigan, Music Library
US-AM	Amherst (MA), Amherst College, Vincent Morgan Music Library
US-AUS	Austin (TX), University of Texas at Austin, The Harry Ransom Humanities Research Center
US-Bl	Boston (MA), Grand Lodge of masons in Massachusetts, A. F. & A. M. Library
US-Bp	Boston (MA), Boston Public Library, Music Department
US-Bu	Boston (MA), Boston University, Mugar Memorial Library, Special Collections
US-BAu	Baltimore (MD), John Hopkins University Libraries
US-BEm	Berkeley (CA), University of California, Music Library
US-BER	Berea (OH), Baldwin-Wallace College, Riemenschneider-Bach Institut, Emilie and Karl Riemenschneider Memorial Bach Library
US-BL	Bloomington (IN), Indiana University Library
US-Ccrl	Chicago (IL), Center for Research Libraries
US-Cn	Chicago (IL), Newberry Library
US-Cu	Chicago (IL), University of Chicago, Joseph Regenstein Library, Special Collections
US-Cum	Chicago (IL), University of Chicago, Music Collection
US-CA	Cambridge (MA), Harvard University, Harvard College Library
US-CAe	Cambridge (MA), Harvard University, Eda Kuhn Loeb Music Library
US-CAh	Cambridge (MA), Harvard University, Houghton Library
US-CAt	Cambridge (MA), Harvard University, Theatre Collection
US-CAward	Cambridge (MA), John Milton Ward, private collection
US-CHum	Charlottesville (VA), University of Virginia, Music Library
US-CHH	Chapel Hill (NC), University of North Carolina, Music Library
US-CLp	Cleveland (OH), Cleveland Public Library, Fine Arts Department
US-COu	Columbus (OH), Ohio State University, Music Library
US-DMu	Durham (NC), Duke University Libraries
US-E	Evanston (IL), Garrett Biblical Institute
US-Eu	Evanston (IL), Northwestern University Libraries
US-FAy	Farmington (CO), Yale University, Lewis Walpole Library
US-HA	Hanover (NH), Dartmouth College, Baker Library
US-HG	Harrisburg (PA), Pennsylvania State Library
US-I	Ithaca (NY), Cornell University Music Library
US-LAgri	Los Angeles (CA), Getty Research Institute
US-LAuc	Los Angeles (CA), University of California, William Andrews Clark Memorial Library
US-LAum	Los Angeles (CA), University of California, Music Library
US-LAur	Los Angeles (CA), University of California, Special Collections Dept, University Research Library
US-LOu	Louisville (KY), University of Louisville, School of Music, Library
US-MAu	Madison (WI), University of Wisconsin
US-MAL	Malibu (CA), Paul Getty Museum
US-NH	New Haven (CT), Yale University, Music Library

MC | List of Institutions

US-NHub	New Haven (CT), Yale University, Beinecke Rare Book and Manuscript Library
US-NHs	New Haven (CT), Yale University, Sterling Memorial
US-NO	Normal (IL), Illinois State University, Milner Library, Humanities/Fine Arts Division
US-NYcu	New York (NY), Columbia University, Music Library
US-NYcub	New York (NY), Columbia University, Butler Library, Rare Book and Manuscript Library
US-NYp	New York (NY), Public Library, Performing Arts, Music Division
US-NYpm	New York (NY), Pierpont Morgan Library
US-PHu	Philadelphia (PA), University of Pennsylvania Libraries
US-PRu	Princeton (NJ), Princeton University Library
US-PRV	Provo (UT), Brigham Young University
US-R	Rochester (NY), University of Rochester, Eastman School of Music, Sibley Music Library
US-SFsc	San Francisco (CA), San Francisco State University, Frank V. de Bellis Collection
US-SM	San Marino (CA), Henry E. Huntington Library & Art Gallery
US-STum	Stanford (CA), Stanford University, Music Library
US-SY	Syracuse (NY), Syracuse University Music Library
US-U	Urbana (IL), University of Illinois at Urbana-Champaign, Music Library
US-Wc	Washington (DC), Library of Congress, Music Division
US-WS	Winston-Salem (NC), Moravian Music-Foundation, Peter Memorial Library

Introduction

Pietro Trapassi (1698–1782), better known as Pietro Metastasio, can be considered as the most renowned operatic libretto writer of eighteenth-century Europe. His *drammi per musica* contributed in the reform of the structure and the style of the opera of his time and remain the most premiered and revived operatic texts over time. Born in Rome, where he spent the first half of his personal and professional life gaining success and influence as a poet, in 1730 he was appointed *poeta cesareo* by Emperor Charles VI in Vienna. At the imperial court he continued to produce a great number of operatic librettos, which, departing from the poet's original conception, travelled all around Europe —and beyond— throughout the eighteenth century and the early years of the nineteenth.[1] They experimented modifications, changes, and, importantly, various dramatic and artistic situations in which they were revered. Traces of such travels and transformations are the numerous poetic and musical sources that have survived: on some occasions, full materials for a given performance, including the orchestral parts, bear witness of the operatic incarnation of a given *dramma* in a specific place and time; on others, only just some excerpts or the modified Metastasian text can help us reconstruct what was a full dramatic experience; and, sometimes, we know of Metastasian *drammi*'s landing on a given theatre only through contemporaneous accounts. All these situations sketch an unprecedented —and unrepeated— dramatic fever that took both court and commercial opera productions by storm.

To fulfil one of the aims of the European Research Council Didone Project, i.e., to study how the emotions contained in the closed numbers of some Metastasian *drammi per musica* were expressed through music during the eighteenth century, part of our research has been dedicated to the localisation and the retrieval of their sources, both poetical and musical, allowing us to compile catalogues for five of his *drammi per musica*. The first, dedicated to *Demofoonte* (1733), has already been published by Ana Llorens, Nicola Usula, and Gorka Rubiales.[2] Now, we are publishing the catalogues of four others: *Didone abbandonata* (1724), *Alessandro nell'Indie* (1726),

---

1. On Metastasio, see Sommer-Mathis, Andrea and Elisabeth Theresia Hilscher, eds, *Pietro Metastasio – uomo universale (1698–1782): Festgabe der Österreichischen Akademie der Wissenschaften zum 300. Geburtstag von Pietro Metastasio* (Vienna: Österreichische Akademie der Wissenschaften, 2000); Mellace, Raffaele, '*L'autunno del Metastasio.' Gli ultimi drammi per musica di Johann Adolf Hasse* (Florence: Olschki, 2007); and Sala di Felice, Elena, *Sogni e favole in sen del vero. Metastasio ritrovato* (Rome: Aracne, 2008).
2. Llorens, Ana, Gorka Rubiales, and Nicola Usula, 'Operatic Sources for "Demofoonte": Librettos and Scores after Metastasio's "figliuolo"', in *Demofoonte come soggetto per il dramma per musica: Johann Adolf Hasse ed altri compositori del Settecento*, ed. by Milada Jonášová and Tomislav Volek (Prague: Academia, 2020), pp. 271–317.

MC | Introduction

Artaserse (1730), and *Adriano in Siria* (1734), along with an updated version of the *Demofoonte* one, which is now unified to the new catalogues' criteria. Not insubstantially, many entries have now been updated with sources which were not accessible during the COVID-19 pandemic lockdown.

This publication aims at being not only the most complete catalogue of the surviving textual and manuscript sources related to the abovementioned operatic librettos, but also a chronology of the musical settings of their different versions. Nevertheless, it is important to underline that, even though we have included all the sources we could find, there could be some missing ones. Similarly, all our assertions are valid at the moment of preparation of this volume and, for instance, when we hypothesise that previously referenced sources are lost, we are aware that other scholars may be able to locate them in the future in the corresponding institution or elsewhere.

In our quest for libretti, we departed from the catalogue that Claudio Sartori published in 1994–1997, as well from as its digital 'heir', the well-known online database Corago.[3] Similarly, the research for music sources started with the database of the Répertoire International des Sources Musicales – RISM, and with the works and composer' lists in their respective entries in *The New Grove Dictionary of Music and Musicians* and *Die Musik in Geschichte und Gegenwart*. In all cases, we acknowledge such information thorough relevant superscripts. With further research for sources through other OPACs, meta-OPACs, printed and card catalogues and library stacks, we have significantly updated and completed the information given on such catalogues.

As a result of our research, we give for each opera a list of sources to date as exhaustive as possible. To do so, the catalogues tabulate all known representations of the aforementioned Metastasian titles in chronological order: the entries are organised by the date of the premiere of the first version of each composer —or composers in case of *pasticcios* and multi-author settings.[4] All the subsequent versions and revivals of a single composer(s) follow this first one. In the first column of each entry, we indicate the season in which the performance took place. For instance, for Carnival season, which usually started a few days before the end of the year and continued for the following ones, we give the following year (e.g., 1735 would stand for 26/12/1734). For each entry we also indicate the occasion for which the musical version was commissioned (mostly carnival seasons, fairs and courtly celebrations of monarch's weddings and birth and name days), but we do not indicate dedicatees.

The lists of the literary —that is, all the surviving libretto— and the musical sources are subsequently given. Each source is followed by indications relating to the library location —using

---

3. Sartori, Claudio, *I libretti italiani a stampa dalle origini al 1800. Catalogo analitico con 16 indici*, 7 vols (Cuneo: Bertola & Locatelli, 1990–1994); *Corago. Repertorio e archivio di libretti del melodramma italiano dal 1600 al 1900*, ed. by A. Pompilio (Bologna: Università di Bologna) <http://corago.unibo.it> [accessed 24 June 2022]. For our main bibliographic tools, see the List of Abbreviations at the beginning of this volume.

4. We follow the criterion in Llorens, Ana and Álvaro Torrente, 'Constructing *Opera Seria* in the Iberian Courts: Metastasian Repertoire for Spain and Portugal', *Anuario musical*, 76 (2021), 73–110 <https://doi.org/10.3989/anuariomusical.2021.i76>, according to which two performances two months apart – or more – are treated as separate productions.

the RISM sigla[5]— and the call number in each institution. Call numbers of both libretti and music manuscripts are arranged in alphabetical order. In case of multi-piece volumes and printed sources, we indicate the position of the piece in question with an Arabic numeral inside square brackets. When possible, we include hyperlinks to all the sources that are freely available online at the moment of completion of the catalogues.[6]

All through the catalogues —and the indices—, the titles of the operas are unified; therefore, we do not list all variants of the opera titles (e.g., *Adriano in Siria* vs. *L'Adriano in Siria*) except in cases when the differences are notable (e.g., *Cleofide* instead of *Alessandro nell'Indie*). If a libretto is bilingual, we indicate the two languages in parenthesis and with abbreviatures (e.g., It./Ger.), and if a translated version of the title appears on the source, we add it (e.g., title *Alexander in Indien*).

The treatment of the musical sources is very specific. Except in cases in which the differences between the music of a premiere and its subsequent revival(s) are marked, we do not distinguish between the musical sources for the premiere and those used in later revivals, as in most cases drawing such a distinction is not feasible. In the few cases in which such a distinction is drawn, we explain our criteria. In any case, when we can establish a relation between a musical source and a given performance other than the premiere of its corresponding musical version, we offer the data in a footnote. Moreover, we draw a distinction between musical versions as such and later *pasticcios* in which the composer did not personally contribute and which, accordingly, are not to be considered as authorial.

For each musical version we classify the musical sources as follows:
- *complete scores*;
- *excerpts*, among which we include closed numbers (arias, duets, trios, and choirs) but not the overture and recitatives. We list the excepts normalising the titles of the closed numbers based of the 1st edition of the librettos and following alphabetical order;
- *printed sources*. We only consider printed sources close to the performance date of the relevant version; we acknowledge that the list of later prints is not complete;
- *contrafacta*, for which we give the title of the original poem first, followed by the title of the later textual setting between square brackets; in cases of multiple textual adaptations, those are also listed alphabetically;
- *parodies*, that is, settings of the original music adapted to a different profane text. We follow the same criteria as in the sacred contrafacta.
- *arrangements*, in very few —but meaningful— cases; and
- *doubtful sources*, for which, in all cases, we expound our reservations.

Some aria collections contain all the closed numbers for a given musical setting. In such cases, we list them among the *complete scores* followed by the corresponding superscript (^{A}). Other aria

---

5. See the List of Institutions at the beginning of this volume.
6. All hyperlinks are operational as of 6 March 2023, the last day of consultation.

collections, on the contrary, just contain some of the closed numbers of the version. For those sources, we list the separate arias among the *excerpts*. When we list *particellas*, we distinguish parts in general (^{P}), i.e., those containing the vocal line too, from instrumental parts (^{IP}), i.e., those not including the voice(s). We mark their presence with the corresponding superscript after the musical manuscript call number; the inclusion of such superscript does not necessarily indicate that no orchestral score is preserved under that call number.

Through our research we noted a marked variability on the key (tonality) —and sometimes the *tempo* marking— in which the Metastasian poems were set through time. To list such divergences, we take the complete source as the model and indicate the variants in a footnote; when no complete source is available, we follow the source(s) that is/are believed to be the closest to the premiere or, when such relation cannot be established, the majoritarian setting.

The difficulties in compiling these catalogues arose above all due to the extremely fluid conception of eighteenth-century opera authorship (both regarding text and music), especially for revivals,[7] knowing that text and music in most of the cases was manipulated on each occasion in order to comply with the necessities of each production: for complex theatrical seasons, such as the London ones, in some cases there are difficulties in attributing the authorship of the music, or in establishing whether a libretto manipulated in almost every scene could nevertheless be considered 'by Metastasio'.[8] We have carefully evaluated case by case, indicating the relative assumptions in the footnotes. Even more particular cases are the *pasticcios*, of which the authorships are listed in the catalogues only when certain.[9]

Deciding what to include in these catalogues inevitably led to some exclusion criteria. In respect of the poetic sources, the Italian so-called 'literary' editions, not directly related to any per-

---

7. On the shared responsibility of authorship between operatic composers and singers, see Calella, Michele, 'Zwischen Autorwillen und Produktionssystem. Zur Frage des "Werkcharakters" in der Oper des 18. Jahrhunderts', in *Bearbeitungspraxis in der Oper des späten 18. Jahrhunderts. Bericht über die internationale wissenschaftliche Tagung von 18. bis 20. Februar in Würzburg*, ed. by Ulrich Konrad and others (Tutzing: Schneider, 2007), pp. 15-32; Strohm, Reinhard, 'Wer entscheidet? Möglichkeiten der Zusammenarbeit an Pasticcio-Opern', in *'Per ben vestir la virtuosa'. Die Oper des 18. und frühen 19. Jahrhunderts im Spannungsfeld zwischen Komponisten und Sängern*, ed. by Daniel Brandenburg and Thomas Seedorf (Schliengen: Argus, 2011), pp. 62-79.
8. '[…] what London – and, indeed, other centres around Europe – saw performed in the theatre as texts by Metastasio, had, in fact, little to do with the poet at all, for his operas, when they reached the London stage, were always in more or less "pasticcio" versions'. The author continues: 'London —like almost everywhere else— never saw Metastasio's "real text"; the text and story were not established before it appeared as a "pasticcio", and every version performed in England afterwards —whether a musical "pasticcio", a new setting, or simply a version for London— was different from Metastasio's original, and that there was precious little Metastasian poetry included in some of those stagings. […] It should not be forgotten that Metastasio's plots and text were a drawcard'; see Burden, Michael, 'Metastasio's "London Pasties": Curate Egg or Pudding's Proof?', in *Pietro Metastasio - uomo universale (1698-1782): Festgabe der Österreichischen Akademie der Wissenschaften zum 300. Geburtstag von Pietro Metastasio*, ed. by Andrea Sommer-Mathis and Elisabeth Theresia Hilscher (Vienna: Österreichische Akademie der Wissenschaften, 2000), pp. 290-390.
9. See Strohm, Reinhard, 'Italian Pasticcio Opera, 1700-1750: Practices and Repertoires', in *Operatic Pasticcios in 18th-Century Europe. Context, Materials and Aesthetics*, ed. by Berthold Over and Geza Zur Nieden (Bielefeld: Transcript, 2021), pp. 45-67. For the most updated overview on *pasticcios*, see the *Introduction* to the same volume, pp. 9-25.

formance of the Metastasian *drammi*, were discarded. Examples of these are the Venetian libretti printed by Giuseppe Antonelli and Antonio Curti at the end of the eighteenth century. In the case of the musical sources, we do not include vocal pieces with piano accompaniment or other —normally later— settings by a composer who did musicalise the whole *dramma,* as we consider them to be a different genre despite their being based on a text by Metastasio. We nonetheless include reductions for voice and thorough bass which undoubtedly reflect an operatic practice ([R]). We similarly discard dramatic representations, normally in the vernacular tongue, performed without music. These include, for instance, José de Nebra's *Más gloria es triunfar de sí* (1737), on *Adriano in Siria*, or the German and Polish adaptations that were on vogue around the middle of the eighteenth century.

A very special case are the versions fully set in languages other than Italian: differently from bilingual libretti which bear witness of an Italian interpretation, we grant these translated versions a dedicated entry, but we do not offer complete lists of performances or sources, as they represent a different genre. These normally refer to English and French adaptations dating from the end of the eighteenth century or the beginning of the nineteenth.

Nevertheless, all kinds of translation, modification, and elaboration are fundamental to understand the monumental size and scope of Metastasio' impact on the European operatic landscape. With this volume, which attests to the recurrence of only five of the twenty-six his renowned *drammi per musica*, we hope to have given an exemplary and as accurate as possible portrait of the phenomenon across time and space.

Catalogue

Didone abbandonata (1724–1832)

Ana Llorens, Lecturer, Department of Musicology, Universidad Complutense de Madrid; scientific director, ERC Didone Project, email: allorens@ucm.es

Gorka Rubiales Zabarte, 'Margarita Salas' postdoctoral researcher, Universidad Complutense de Madrid–Universidad de Salamanca, email: gorka.rubiales@usal.es

Complete operas

1724	mus. by Sarro, Domenico Natale	
1724 Naples	Teatro di S. Bartolomeo (carn., 01/02/1724) 1st version	(1)
1727 Turin	Teatro Regio (carn.)	(2)
1730 Venice	Teatro Grimani di S. Giovanni Grisostomo (24/11/1730) text altered by G. Boldini 2nd version	(3)
1734 Brno	Teatro della Taverna (aut.)[1]	(4)
1741 Arezzo	Teatro Nuovo (29/10/1741) pasticcio[2] opening of the theatre	(5)
Librettos	(1) Naples: Ricciardo, 1724 F-Pn YD-5243 [2];[3] I-MOc MOR E 121; I-Rvat Stamp.Ferr.V.7836 [1]; US-Wc ML 50.2.D55S2 (2) Turin: Gattinara,[4] [1727] I-Rsc Vol. Carv.138 [3]; I-Tac Simeom L 16; I-Tci L.O.0060	

1. December according to Over, Berthold, 'Dido Abandoned? Shifts of Focus and Artistic Choices in *Didone* Pasticcios of the Mingotti Opera Troupe', in *Operatic Pasticcios in 18th-Century Europe: Contexts, Materials and Aesthetics*, ed. by Berthold Over and Gesa zur Nieden (Bielefeld: Transcript, 2021), pp. 285–328.
2. A pasticcio according to <https://www.pasticcio-project.eu/database/work/P102A65> [accessed 25 May 2022].
3. Microfilm copy: F-Pn MICROFILM M-2402.
4. 'Nella stampa di Gio. Radix'.

MC | *Didone abbandonata* (1724–1832)

(3) Venice: Buonarigo, [1730]

I-Bc Lo.05031; I-Mb Racc.dramm.0435; I-PAc F. Libretti, sc.III [102]; I-RVI Silv., op. 662; I-Vcg LIBRETTI S.GIO.GRISOSTOMO 151; I-Vnm DRAMM.1421 [6]; I-Vnm DRAMM.1240 [2]; I-Vnm DRAMM.3556 [9]; SI-Lsk AE 57 [1]; US-LAum ML48 .R114 1730 [13]; US-Wc ML48 [S9422]

(4) Brno: Swoboda, [1734] (It./Ger.)

CZ-Bu CH-0003 [525]; CZ-Bu ST1-0242 [152]

(5) [Arezzo?: s.n., 1741][5]

Music sources

1st version: 1724, Naples

[complete scores] D-MEIr Ed 147v[RISM]; I-Nc 18.4.2[IC,MGG,NG,RISM,SBN] [Act I]; I-Nc 31.3.19[NG,RISM,SBN,6]

[excerpts] *Ah, non lasciarmi, no* (D-Kdma ms. 895 [1][IC]); *Cadrà fra poco in cenere* (GB-Lbl R.M.23.e.2 [3][RISM]; I-MC 5-B-11 [50][RISM]; I-Nc 22.3.13[SBN]); *Chiamami pur così* (D-Kdma ms. 895 [9][IC]); *Dirò che fida sei* (D-Kdma ms. 895 [11][IC]; I-Nc 31.3.19[SBN]); *Infelice e sventurato* (D-Kdma ms. 895 [8][IC]); *Leon, che errando vada* (D-Kdma ms. 895 [10][IC]); *Nel duol che prova* (D-Kdma ms. 895 [7][IC]; I-Nc Cantate 3[RISM,7]; I-Nc 33.4.22 [2][SBN]); *Non ha ragione ingrato* (D-Kdma ms. 895 [5][IC]; I-Nc S.7.21 [17][SBN]; I-Rc Mss. 2222 [55][SBN]; I-Vqs MS CI.VIII.14 (1128)[RISM,SBN;R]); *Ogni amator suppone* (D-Kdma ms. 895 [6][IC]); *Quando saprai chi sono* (D-Kdma ms. 895 [3][IC]); *Son quel fiume che gonfio d'umori* (D-Kdma ms. 895 [4][IC]; I-MC 5-B-11/5 [11][RISM]); *Va lusingando amore* (D-Hs ND VI 1078 [1/17][RISM]; D-Hs ND VI 1078 [2/28][RISM]; D-Kdma ms. 895 [2][IC]; I-Rc Mss. 2222 [39][SBN])

[doubtful] *Cadrà fra poco in cenere* (CH-Gc R 232 [35][RISM]); *Già si desta la tempesta* (CH-Gc R 232 [44][RISM])[8]

[contrafacta] *Va lusingando amore* ([*Ad Deum suspirando*] CZ-Pak 1422 [1][RISM])

2nd version: 1730, Venice

[complete scores] I-Nc 32.2.20[IC,MGG,NG,RISM]

---

5. See ^S7775.
6. Given as I-Nc 31.3.12 in [IC].
7. This and the following source, misattributed to Tomaso Albinoni.
8. The music of these two sources is different from that in D-MEIr Ed 147v and I-Nc 32.2.20.

MC | *Didone abbandonata* (1724–1832)

Sources of doubtful identification

[complete scores] I-PESo Cod. 2007[RISM,9]

[excerpts] [inserts] Galuppi, Baldassare, *Se ti lagni sventurato* (I-Vqs MS CI.VIII.14 (1128)[RISM,SBN;R]); *Son qual cervetta su verde sponda*[10] (<u>D-KA Don Mus. Hs. 74</u>[RISM]; <u>D-KA Don Mus. Hs. 1040</u>[RISM]; I-IBborromeo Ms. Misc. 18[RISM]; I-Vqs MS CI.VIII.14 (1128)[RISM,SBN;R])

1724	mus. by Scarlatti, Domenico[11]
1724 Rome	NA
1724 Palermo	Teatro di Santa Cecilia[12]

Music sources [excerpts] *Già si desta la tempesta* (D-Hs ND VI 24 [94][13])

1725	mus. by Albinoni, Tomaso Giovanni	
1725 Venice	Teatro Tron di S. Cassiano (carn., 26/12/1724)	(1)
1726 Crema	Teatro di Crema (Sept. & Oct. Fair, 24/09/1726)	(2)
1726 Wrocław	Teatro Ballhaus (11/1726)	(3)
	Dido	
	with one aria by A. Bioni[14]	
1729 Milan	Teatro Regio Ducale (carn., 26/12/1728)[15]	(4)

9. This source does not correspond to any of Sarro's supposedly authorial versions (Naples 1724 and Venice 1730); Hucke, Helmut, 'Die beide Fassungen der Oper "Didone abbandonata" von Domenico Sarri', in *Gesellschaft für Musikforschung Kongreßbericht* (Hamburg: [s.n.], 1956), pp. 113–17. For a complete discussion of the source and its relation to the performances of Sarro's *Didone*, see Gialdroni, Teresa M., 'I primi dieci anni della *Didone abbandonata* di Metastasio: il caso di Domenico Sarro', *Analecta Musicologica*, 30 (1998), 437–500.
10. The aria is inserted into A2-S14 of the libretto, yet in I-Nc 32.2.20 it is substituted by *Veggio la sponda*. I-IBborromeo Ms. Misc. 18 has the inscription 'Sig. Sarri', while the three other sources attribute the music to Galuppi; in I-Vqs MS CI.VIII.14 (1128) one finds the inscription 'S. Gio. Gris.mo P.ma | del Sig.r Baldissera Galuppi'. This might indicate that: a) in the 1730 version arias by composers other than Sarro were inserted and b) I-Nc 32.2.20 was not used in that performance. For a detailed discussion of these arias and the manuscript in I-Vqs, see Gialdroni, 'I primi dieci anni', pp. 454–56.
11. Clement, Felix and Pierre Larousse, *Dictionnaire lyrique ou Histoire des operas* ([s.l.]: Keissinger, 1869); Hugo Riemann attributes it to Alessandro, and Bruno Brunelli, to Domenico; cf. Riemann, Hugo, *Opern-Handbuch* (Hildesheim: Olms, 1887) and Brunelli, Bruno, *Tutte le opere di Pietro Metastasio* (Milan: Mondadori, 1943). See also Kirkpatrick, Ralph, *Domenico Scarlatti* (Princeton: Princeton University Press, 1983) and Pagano, Roberto, *Scarlatti Alessandro e Domenico: due vite in una* (Milan: Mondadori, 1985).
12. Sorge, Giuseppe, *I teatri di Palermo nel secoli XVI-XVII-XVIII* (Palermo: Industrie Reiunite Editoriali Siciliane, 1926).
13. Lost according to Charteris, Richard, 'The Music Collection of the Staats- und Universitätsbibliothek, Hamburg: A Survey of its British Holdings prior to the Second World War', *Royal Musical Association Research Chronicle*, 30 (1997), 1–138 <https://doi.org/10.1080/14723808.1997.10540978>.
14. Over, 'Dido abandoned?', p. 288.
15. Tintori and Schito relate this version to Albinoni's setting. The 'Pasticcio' Project gives Geminiano Giacomelli as the composer (<https://www.pasticcio-project.eu/database/work/P130540> [accessed 25 May 2022]) and Strohm hypothesises that the pasticcio was set up by Giacomelli; cf. Tintori, Giampiero and M. Maddalena Schito, eds, *Il Regio Ducal Teatro di Milano (1717–1778): cronologia delle opere e dei balli con 10 indici* (Cuneo: Bertola & Locatelli, 1998) and Strohm, Reinhard, 'Italienische Opernarien des frühen Settecento', *Analecta Musicologica*, 16.1–2 (1976).

MC | *Didone abbandonata* (1724–1832)

	pasticcio	
1730 Pesaro	Teatro del Sole (carn.)	(5)
1730? Linz[16]	Teatro Arciducale (Fair, 04/05/1730)	(6)
1731 Prague	Teatro Spork (spr.)	(7)
	pasticcio[17]	
1733 Ferrara	Teatro Bonacossi da S. Stefano (carn.)	(8)

Librettos

(1) Venice: Rossetti, [1725]
F-Pn 8-YTH-52040; I-Bc Lo.00069; I-Mb Racc.dramm.2850; I-Pmc[S]; I-Rig Rar. Libr. Ven. 585 [1]; I-RVI Silv., op. 595; I-Vnm DRAMM.1031 [1]; I-Vnm DRAMM.1230 [3]; I-Vnm DRAMM.3546 [4]; I-Vcg LIBRETTI S. CASSIANO 14; US-Wc ML48 [S89]

(2) Venice: Rumieri, [1726]
I-BRq 10a.Y.VI.18m3; I-Mb Racc.dramm.3737

(3) [Wrocław?: s.n., 1726] (It./Ger.)
US-Wc ML48 [S90]

(4) Milan: Malatesta, 1728
F-Pn LIV IT-3516 [16]; I-LDEsormani 297/6/19; I-Mb Racc.dramm.6040 [2]; I-Mc Coll.Libr.091; I-Mr Libr. 04300; I-Rn 40.9.C.13.5

(5) Pesaro: Gavelli, 1729
I-PESo G-09-B-18 [5]

(6) [s.l.: s.n., *c.* 1730] (It./Ger.)
NA[18]

(7) Prague: Wessely, [1731] (It./Ger.)
CZ-Pu 65 E 3207; SK-KRE 3192 [2]

(8) Venice: Stamparia Nova, [1733]
I-Rsc Carv.4375

Music sources [doubtful] *Se resto sul lido* (B-Bc 15180 [1])[RISM,19]

1725   mus. by unknown composer(s)

1725 Florence   Teatro della Pergola (carn.)[20]

---

16. 1731–1734 according to Over, 'Dido abandoned?', p. 285.
17. A pasticcio according to <https://www.pasticcio-project.eu/database/work/P1042C5> [accessed 25 May 2022].
18. [C,S] refer to a copy in D-DO [D-KA], yet, as confirmed by the library staff, the information is not correct; see [S]7733 and <http://corago.unibo.it/libretto/DRT0013967> [accessed 24 June 2022].
19. Probably by Albinoni according to [RISM], based on the years of performance of the other arias in the collection, all of which come from stage works created in Venice between 1724 and 1725.
20. It might be by Sarro or a pasticcio based on Sarro's *Didone abbandonata*. See Holmes, William C., 'Vivaldi e il Teatro la Pergola a Firenze: nuove fonti', in *Nuovi Studi Vivaldiani: edizione e cronologia critica delle opere*,

MC | *Didone abbandonata* (1724–1832)

Librettos Florence: Verdi, [1725]
I-Bc Lo.06208; I-Fc E.V.1723

1725	mus. by Porpora, Nicola	
1725 Reggio Emilia	Teatro Pubblico (Fair, 19/04/1725)[21]	(1)
1731 Hamburg	Oper am Gänsemarkt (05/11/1731)	
	Der Streit der Kindlichen Pflicht und der Liebe, oder Die Flucht des Aeneas nach Latien (Ger. only)	
	recit. and arr. by G. P. Telemann; lib. by G. Hamann	
1734 Brunswick	Teatro Ducale (summ. Fair)	(2)
	with some recit. by G. F. Händel[22]	
1745 Parma	Teatro Ducale (carn.)	(3)

Librettos (1) Reggio Emilia: Vedrotti, 1725
I-Bc Lo.04320; I-MOe 83.H.30 [1]; I-MOe 83.I.41 [3]; I-REm 19.K.124

(2) Wolfenbüttel: Bartsch, [1734]
D-HVs Op. 1, 151a;[23] D-W Textb. 349

(3) Parma: Salaroli, [1745]
I-Mb Racc.dramm.4158

Music sources [complete scores] GB-Lbl* Add. 14119[MGG,NG,RISM] [Acts II&III]

[excerpts] *Ah, non lasciarmi, no* (GB-Lbl Add. 31595[RISM,24]; I-Rama A.Ms.3709 [26][RISM]); *Chiedi in vano amor da me* (D-W Cod. Guelf. 301 Mus. Hdschr [9][RISM,25]); *Infelice e sventurato* (I-Rama A.Ms.3709 [20][RISM]); *Non lascia il ben che brama* (I-Rama A.Ms.3709 [27][RISM,26])

[doubtful] *Agitata è l'alma mia* (D-B Mus.ms. 30237 [25][RISM,27])

---

ed. by Antonio Fanna and Giovanni Morelli (Florence: Olschki, 1988). Identified in the Ryom catalogue as a pasticcio: RV Anh. 118. See also Holmes, William C., *Opera Observed: Views of a Florentine Impresario in the Early Eighteenth Century* (Chicago: University of Chicago Press, 1993), pp. 117–30.

21. Date given in [C]. [CA] gives 10/05/1725.
22. Händel's recitatives *Scoglio d'immota fronte* (from *Scipione*, London, 1726) and *L'armi implore del tuo figlio* (from *Alessandro*, London, 1726), as well as Porpora's *Son fra l'onde in mezzo al mare* (from *Gli orti speridi*, Naples, 1721), were inserted. For a detailed analysis of this and the previous revival of Porpora's *Didone*, see Voss, Steffen, 'Musica di Nicola Porpora al teatro d'opera di Amburgo: *Siface*, *Didone abbandonata*, *Gli orti esperidi* ad alcuni pasticci', in *Nicola Porpora musicista europeo: le corte, i teatri, i cantanti, i librettisti. Atti del Convegno Internazionale di Studi / Reggio Calabria, 3–4 ottobre 2008*, ed. by Niccolò Maccavino (Reggio Calabria: Laruffa, 2001), pp. 95–120.
23. Microfilm copy: D-HVs MASTER 511.
24. From a *Didone abbandonata*, either by Porpora or a pasticcio performed in 1732 in Rome. See Hughes-Hughes, August, *Catalogue of Manuscript Music in the British Museum* (London: Clowes, 1906–1909).
25. Text from Metastasio's *Endimione*.
26. According to [RISM], performed during the carnival of 1732 in Rome, Teatro delle Dame.
27. Strohm attributes the authorship of this aria to Vivaldi since it had been included in a performance of the opera *Farnace* RV 711. In TVWV it is wrongly attributed to G. P. Telemann. See Strohm, Reinhardt, *The Operas of Antonio Vivaldi* (Florence: Olschki, 2008).

MC | *Didone abbandonata* (1724–1832)

1726	mus. by Vinci, Leonardo lib. rev. by Metastasio[28]	
1726 Rome	Teatro delle Dame (carn., 14/01/1726)	(1)
1726 Vienna	Kleines Hoftheater (carn., 21/02/1726)[29]	(2)
1729 Lucca	Teatro Pubblico[30]	(3)
1734 Perugia	Teatro del Pavone (carn.)	(4)
1736 Jaroměřice	Count's Adam of Questenberg's castle (aut.) *pasticcio*[31]	(5,6)
1737 Jaroměřice	Count's Adam of Questenberg's castle (carn.)[32]	(7)

Librettos

(1) Rome: Bernabò,[33] [1726]
B-Bc 19902; D-Mth 001/8 18949 [1]; F-Lu A-3043; F-Pn LIV IT-3758 [3]; F-Pn YD-3531;[34] H-Banc 564.480/koll. 4.; I-Bc Lo.05512; I-Fm Mel.2259 [13]; I-IE PLAN LIBR MUS 047; I-Mb Racc.dramm.2297; I-MAC 7.II.A.69; I-NOVa Biblioteca Teatro Coccia 65; I-PEc ANT Misc. II.N 81 [5]; I-Rb FS3 34.01.29; I-Rc Misc.Dramm.A.25 [10]; I-Rn 35.9.L.23.02; I-Rn 35.10.A.10.04; I-Rvat Stamp.Chig.V.2374; I-Rvat Stamp.Ferr.V.8049 [5]; US-CHH IOLC.00134; US-Wc ML50.2.D55V4

(2,7) NA

(3) Lucca: Ciuffetti, 1719 [i.e., 1729]
I-Bc Villa.Lo.056

(4) Perugia: Costantini, [1734]
I-AT BVA.A.21

(5) Vienna: van Ghelen, 1735 [i.e., 1736][35]
CZ-NH 1437

(6) Vienna: van Ghelen, 1736 (Ger.)
A-Wst 70701 A

---

28. Roberts, John H., 'Handel and Vinci's "Didone Abbandonata": Revisions and Borrowings', *Music & Letters*, 68.2 (1987), 141–50.
29. Klein, Rudolf, 'Die Schauplätze der Hofoper', *Österreichische Musikzeitschrift*, 24 (1969), 371–422; see also Pitarresi Gaetano, ed., *Leonardo Vinci e il suo tempo* (Reggio Calabria: Iiriti, 2005); Markstrom, Kurt S., *The Operas of Leonardo Vinci, Napoletano* (Hillsdale, NY: Pendragon, 2007).
30. Pitarresi, ed., *Leonardo Vinci*, p. 316.
31. Spáčilová, Jana, *Catalogue of the Italian Opera Libretti in Central Europe in the 1st Half of the 18th Century* (Prague: KLP, forthcoming).
32. Pečman, Rudolf, 'Schloß Jaroměřice und seine Musikkultur im 18. Jahrhundert', *Musicologica Brunensia*, 45 (1996), 5–11.
33. 'Si vendono à Pasquino nella libraria di Pietro Lioni'.
34. Microfilm copy: F-Pn MFICHE YD-3531.
35. Microfilm copy of a (lost?) copy in PL-Kj: CDN-Lu ML48.M47H383 1761a.

MC | *Didone abbandonata* (1724–1832)

Music sources [complete scores] A-Wn Mus.Hs.17710[IC,MGG,NG] [Acts I&II]; D-MÜs SANT Hs 4242[MGG,NG,RISM]; US-Cn MS VM1500.V77d[MGG,NG,RISM]

[excerpts] *Ardi per me fedele* (B-Bc 4936[RISM]; I-Rama A.Ms.3705 [11][RISM]; US-LAur MS 170/389 [5][RISM]); *Cadrà fra poco in cenere* (I-Tf 2 IV 3 [12][RISM]); *Chiamami pur così* (B-Bc 4939 [1][RISM]); *Dirò che fida sei* (D-Hs M A/679 [1/2][RISM]; D-Hs M A/1243 [8/1][RISM]; I-PEsp M.CXXVIII [17/1][SBN]; I-Rama A.Ms.3705 [15][RISM]; S-Skma T-SE-R[RISM,36]); *Dovrei... ma no* (D-Hs A/679 [1/1][RISM]); *L'augelletto in lacci stretto* (B-Bc 4939 [2][RISM]); *Non ha ragione ingrato* (B-Bc 4944[RISM]; D-Hs M A/1243 [8/2][RISM]; F-Pn VM7-14[BnF]; GB-Cfm [GB-Cu] MU.MS.49[IC]; GB-Lam MS 134 [8b][RISM]; GB-Ob Ms. Mus. 33.7 [15][RISM]); *Prende ardire e si conforta* (B-Bc 4948[RISM]; D-Hs M A/1243 [20] [13][RISM]); *Quando saprai chi sono* (D-Hs ND VI 1078 [2][RISM]; I-PEsp M.CXXVIII [17/2][RISM,SBN]); *Se resto sul lido* (B-Bc 4951[RISM]); *Son qual fiume che gonfio d'umori* (GB-Ob Ms. Mus. d.4 [8][RISM]; I-Rama A.Ms.3705 [6][RISM]); *Son regina e sono amante* (B-Bc 4952[RISM]; GB-Lam MS 134 [8a][RISM]; GB-Lbl Add. 31605[RISM]; I-Rama A.Ms.3705 [12][RISM]; US-NYp JOG 72-29 (vol. 9) [7][RISM]); *Su la pendice Alpina* (US-NYp JOG 72-29 (vol. 9) [4][RISM]); *Vado... ma dove... oh dio!* (B-Bc 4939[RISM])

[contrafacta] *Dirò che fida sei* ([*Non curo voluptates*] PL-Wu RM 4457/18 [1][RISM;P]); *Non ha ragione ingrato* ([*Non tardes cor meum*] CZ-Pak 1461 [20][RISM]); *Quando saprai chi sono* ([*Quando mi Jesu care*] CZ-Pak 1449[RISM])

[inserts] [London, 1737] *Quel pastor che*, by G. A. Ristori (GB-Cfm [GB-Cu] MU.MS.258[IC])

[doubtful] *Amor che nasce con la speranza*[37] (B-Bc 4935[RISM])

1727	mus. by unknown composer(s)
1727 Livorno	Teatro da S. Sebastiano (carn., 26/12/1726)
Librettos	Florence: Paperini, 1727
	<u>US-CHH IOLC.00135</u>

---

36. It seems highly probable that the source comes from a later revival of the opera, as the aria in the 1726 version is in alto clef and in E major, whereas the actual source is in soprano clef and in G major.
37. The aria was not included in the original libretto.

MC | *Didone abbandonata* (1724–1832)

1727	mus. by unknown composer(s)
1727 Mantua	Teatro Arciducale[38]
Librettos	Mantua: Pazzoni, [1727]
	I-VEc D.708 [2][39]
1728	mus. by unknown composer(s)
1728 Syracuse	Casa Senatoria (13/11/1728)
	solemnity of St Lucia
Librettos	Catania: Bisagni, 1728
	CZ-Pu 9 F 243 [2]
1729	mus. by unknown composer(s)
1729 Vienna	Teatro Privilegiato (08/02/1729)[40]
Librettos	Vienna: Heyinger, 1729
	A-Wn 299204-A
1730	mus. by Sarro, Domenico Natale (2nd version) → see 1724 (p. 43)
1732	mus. by Porpora, Nicola; Broschi, Riccardo; and Duni, Egidio Romualdo[41]
1732 Rome	Teatro delle Dame (carn., 02/01/1732)
Librettos	[Rome: Leone,[42] 1732]
	F-Pn P-YD-174; F-Pn YD-5264 [5]; GB-En RB.s.267 [3]; I-Rsc Libr. n. XIV [9]; I-RVE r-Z 93 31 [2]; US-CHH IOLC.00165; US-Wc ML48 [S11380]
Music sources	[excerpts][43]
	Fini, Michele, *Dirò che fida sei* (I-Fc D.I.209 [16][IC,RISM,SBN]); *Non voglio, non sento* (I-Rama A.Ms.3709 [22][RISM])

---

38. It may be a composition by Vivaldi or an adaption by Vivaldi of an earlier composition. Gallico, Claudio, 'Vivaldi dagli archivi di Mantova', in *Vivaldi veneziano europeo*, ed. by Francesco Degrada (Florence: Olschki, 1980), pp. 77–88. The relation with the 1725 production in Florence and with Sarro's music is not clear. [MGG] identifies it as a pasticcio with arias from Vivaldi's other operas arranged by the composer himself.
39. Pages 2–8 missing.
40. Klein, 'Die Schauplätze', p. 388.
41. Identified composers: Duni, Egidio Romualdo; Porpora, Nicola; Sarro, Domenico Natale; Vinci, Leonardo.
42. 'Si vendono a Pasquino all'insegna di S. Gio. di Dio'.
43. Some of the arias by Porpora included in this pasticcio were taken from the 1725 production in Reggio Emilia → see 1725, mus. by Porpora, Nicola. The arias by Duni were probably taken from his 1739 production for Milan → see 1739, mus. by Duni, Egidio Romualdo. We cannot ascertain which arias were performed in each of the productions.

MC | *Didone abbandonata* (1724–1832)

Broschi, Riccardo, *M'offendi e pur conviene* (I-Rama A.Ms.3709 [21]^{RISM})
Duni, Egidio Romualdo, *Va crescendo il mio tormento* (D-B Mus.ms. 5312$^{\text{RISM,44}}$; D-SWl Mus.1717 [2]^{RISM}; D-SWl Mus.2985 [2]^{RISM}; D-SWl Mus.4167 [2]$^{\text{RISM,45}}$); *Vado… ma dove?… oh dio!* (D-SWl Mus.1717 [1]$^{\text{RISM,46}}$; D-SWl Mus.4167 [3]$^{\text{RISM,47}}$); *Veggio la sponda* (I-Rama A.Ms.3709 [23]^{RISM}); *Vorrei disciogliere le mie catene* (I-Rama A.Ms.3709 [25]^{RISM})

Didone abbandonata, in *Opere drammatiche del signor abate Pietro Metastasio romano, poeta cesareo* (Venice: Bettinelli, 1733), vol. 1, pp. 435–506.

1733	mus. by unknown composer(s)
1733 Messina	Teatro della Monizione (carn.)
Librettos	Messina: Chiaramonte & Provenzano, [1733]
	I-Rsc Carv.4376
1735	mus. by unknown composer(s)
1735 Florence	Teatro della Pergola (carn., 26/12/1734)
Librettos	Florence: Pieri, [1735]
	I-Fc E.V.1436; I-Fn MAGL.21.8.164; US-Cn BLC #625
Music sources	[excerpts] *Ah, non lasciarmi, no* (US-BEm MS 120 [14]$^{\text{IC,RISM}}$); *Non ha ragione ingrato* (US-BEm MS 14 [6]$^{\text{IC,RISM}}$; US-BEm MS 120 [25]$^{\text{IC,RISM}}$)
1735	mus. by Schiassi, Gaetano Maria
1735 Bologna	Teatro Formagliari (31/05/1735)[48]

---

44. The aria is in G minor. We cannot ascertain if the arias belong to this pasticcio or the 1739 production for Milan with music by Duni → see 1739, mus. by Duni, Egidio Romualdo. This applies to the following source too.
45. Not clear if the aria belongs to this production. Kade attributes the aria to Antonio Duni (see D-SWl Mus.1717); the same aria is also recorded under Niccolò Jommelli, with the note: 'Written for Vienna in 1749, revised in Stuttgart on Feb. 11, 1763'. For further discussion, see Kade, Otto, *Die Musikalien-Sammlung des Großherzoglichen Mecklenburg-Schweriner Fürstenhauses aus den letzten zwei Jahrhunderten* (Schwerin: Sandmeyerschen Hofbuchdruckerei, 1893).
46. The aria is in G minor. We cannot ascertain if the arias belong to this pasticcio or the 1739 production for Milan with music by Duni → see 1739, mus. by Duni, Egidio Romualdo.
47. Not clear if the aria belongs to this production. Text from *Didone abbandonata*. See Kade, *Die Musikalien-Sammlung des Großherzoglichen Mecklenburg-Schweriner Fürstenhauses*.
48. Ricci, Corrado, *I teatri di Bologna, nei secoli XVII e XVIII: storia aneddotica* (Bologna: Monti, 1888).

MC | *Didone abbandonata* (1724–1832)

Librettos	Bologna: Stamperia di S. Tommaso d'Aquino,[49] [1735]
	I-Bc Lo.05165; I-Bca 17-ARTISTICA Gb, 017; I-PAc F. Libretti, sc.III [103]
Music sources	[excerpts] *Non ha ragione ingrato* (D-B Mus.ms. 30330 [10][RISM]; F-Pn D-14501 [8][BnF]); *Tacerò se tu lo brami* (B-Bc 4880[MGG,RISM])

1737	mus. by Scalabrini, Paolo and others[50]	
1737 Graz	Theater am Tummel-Platz (carn.)[51]	(1)
1741 Graz	Theater am Tummel-Platz (carn.)[52]	(2)
	Die verlassene Dido	
1741 Strasbourg	NA	(3)
1742 Ljubljana	Palazzo Provinciale (carn.)	(4)
1744 Hamburg	Oper am Gänsemarkt (06/08/1744)	(5)
	pasticcio[53]	
1746 Hamburg	Oper am Gänsemarkt (09/11/1746)[54]	(6)
	pasticcio	
1747 Dresden	Nuovo Teatro Privilegiato? (10/06/1747)[55]	(7)
1747 Leipzig	City hall theatre (Michaelmas, 15/10/1747)[56]	(8)
1747 Hamburg	Oper am Gänsemarkt (25/11/1747)	(9)
1748 Copenhagen	Court theatre – Charlottenborg Palace	(10)
	pasticcio	

Librettos	(1) Graz: heirs of Widmanstadj, [1737] (It./Ger.)
	A-Gl C 10709¹; A-Wn 28534-B
	(2) Graz: [s.n., 1741] (It./Ger.)
	A-Gu I 57634; D-B Mus. Td 363; D-Gs MA 95-III [602]

---

49. According to [NG], libretto edited by Formagliari. See [NG] 'Schiassi, Gaetano Maria'.
50. Composers included: Paolo Scalabrini, Giovanni Battista Lampugnani, Santo Lapis, Baldassare Galuppi, Geminiano Giacomelli, and Domingo Terradellas. For a list of the arias and their composers, see Bärwald, Manuel, *Italienische Opern in Leipzig (1744-1756)* (Beeskow: ortus, 2016).
51. For the attribution of this and the following performance to P. Scalabrini, see Kokole, Metoda, 'Two Operatic Seasons of Brothers Mingotti in Ljubljana', *De musica disserenda*, 8.2 (2012), 57–90. She positions herself against Gialdroni, who claimed that the Ljubljana performance was a remake of Sarro's Brno production of 1732; cf. Gialdroni, 'I primi dieci anni', p. 456 n. 62.
52. Strohm, Reinhard, 'Metastasio at Hamburg: Newly-Identified Opera Scores of the Mingotti Company, with a Postscript on *Ercole nell'Indie*', in *Il canto di Metastasio. Atti del convegno di studi, Venezia (14–16 dicembre 1999)*, ed. by Maria Giovanna Miggiani (Bologna: Forni, 2004), pp. 541–61.
53. For a detailed list of the arias in the Hamburg and Copenhagen productions, see Over, 'Dido abandoned?', pp. 314–19.
54. October according to Over, 'Dido abandoned?', p. 285.
55. For this and the following performance, see Strohm, 'Metastasio at Hamburg'.
56. The production ran for three consecutive performances; see Bärwald, *Italienische Opern in Leipzig*, p. 288.

MC | *Didone abbandonata* (1724–1832)

(3) Strasbourg: Heitz, [1741] (It./Ger.)
A-Wu Dr-1805b; E-Mtnt M-Resid MP1 8611?; CH-Zz MFA 96: 602[57]

(4) Ljubljana: Reichardt, [1742]
SI-Lsk Z VIII 5 [3]

(5) Hamburg: Spiering, 1744 (It./Ger.)
B-Br Fétis 4.520 A IX,11 Mus.; <u>D-B Mus. T 8 [8]</u>; D-DEl HB 29988; D-DEl HB 29989; D-LEm I A 78; D-EU Lp 65 [4]; D-HVl Op. 2,46;[58] <u>D-LEm I.A.78</u>

(6) Hamburg: Spiering, 1746 (It./Ger.)
B-Bc 19903; RUS-Mrg Ит.-4° [50-8419156]

(7–9) NA

(10) Copenhagen: Berling, 1748 (It./Ger.)
DK-Kk 59,-368 8°

Music sources [complete scores] I-MOe Mus. F. 1587[IC,59]

[excerpts] *Ah, si resti, onor mi sgrida* by Andrea Bernasconi[60] (D-ROu Mus.Saec. XVIII: 6 [17][RISM]); *Di quest'alma il fier tormento* (S-Uu Vok. mus. i hs. 164:49[RISM]); *Quando freme altera l'onda* by Domenico Terradellas[61] (D-RH Ms 583[RISM]; P-Ln C.I.C. 116[IC]; S-Skma T-SE-R[RISM]); *Vivi superbo e regna* (F-Pn L-19908[BnF;P])

[doubtful] *Vivi superbo e regna*[62] (DK-Kk mu7502.1738[RISM])

1737 mus. by Vinci, Leonardo and others[63]

1737 London Covent Garden (13/04/1737)
rev. by Händel[64]

---

57. According to the description in [SB], the title pages and four pages of dedication are the only parts belong to this edition; the remaining pages were taken from van Ghelen's.
58. Microfilm copy: D-HVl DE-35 / ZEN <MASTER 513>.
59. For Hamburg 1746 while retaining some arias from the 1744 performance; see Strohm, 'Metastasio at Hamburg', pp. 560–61.
60. From Bernasconi's *Temistocle* (Padua, 1740).
61. Inserted aria from Terradellas' *Merope* (Rome, 1743).
62. The music is different from that in I-MOe Mus. F. 1587.
63. This version contained one aria from each of the following operas: Vinci's *Semiramide* (Rome, 1729), Giacomelli's *Annibale* (Rome, 1731), Vivaldi's *Griselda* (Venice, 1735), and Hasse's *Euristeo* (Venice, 1732), *Issipile* (Naples, 1732), and *Cajo Fabricio* (Rome, 1732). Strohm, Reinhard, 'Händels Pasticci', *Analecta Musicologica*, 4 (1974), 208–67.
64. For this occasion, Händel revised Vinci's *Didone* (Rome, 1726) and inserted arias from other composers; see Strohm, 'Händels Pasticci' and Roberts, 'Handel and Vinci's "Didone abbandonata"'.

MC | *Didone abbandonata* (1724–1832)

Librettos	London: Wood, 1737 (It./En.)
	D-Hs M A/401; GB-Lbl RB.23.a.6966[65]
Music sources	[complete scores] GB-Lbl Add. 31607[BL,MGG,NG,RISM]

1738 — mus. by Paganelli, Giuseppe Antonio

1738 Bayreuth	Court theatre (05/05/1738)[66]	(1)
1739 Brunswick	Teatro Ducale	(2)

Librettos (1) NA

(2) Wolfenbüttel: Bartsch, 1739 (It./Ger.)
D-W Textb. 328

1739 — mus. by Duni, Egidio Romualdo[C,S] or Brivio, Giuseppe Ferdinando[NG]

1739 Milan	Teatro Regio Ducale (carn.)

Librettos Milan: Malatesta, 1739
F-Pn LIV IT-3518 [14]; I-Bc Lo.06209; I-LDEsormani 297/7/16; I-Mb Racc.dramm.6061 [2]; I-Mb Racc.dramm.6076 [4]; I-Mc Coll.Libr.104; I-MATts Luc. O.B.02067; US-CAh h *IC7 M5648 D1739

Music sources[67]

1739 — mus. by Lampugnani, Giovanni Battista

1739 Padua	Teatro Obizzi (Fair, 15/08/1739)	(1)
	1st version	
1742 Alessandria	Teatro Solerio (aut.)	(2)
	pasticcio[68]	
1745 Crema	Teatro di Crema (Fair, 27/07/1745)	(3)
	pasticcio[69]	
1753 Naples	Teatro di S. Carlo (20/01/1753)	(4)
	birthday of Carlo VII, king of Naples	
	2nd version	
1754 Brescia	Teatro degli Erranti (carn.)	(5)

---

65. Microfilm copy: GB-En Mf.134, reel 10307 [2].
66. Pegah, Rashid-S., 'The Court of Brandenburg-Culmbach-Bayreuth', in *Music at German Courts, 1715–1760: Changing Artistic Priorities*, ed. by Samantha Owens, Barbara M. Reul, and Janice B. Stockigt (Woodbridge: The Boydell Press, 2011), pp. 389–412.
67. We cannot ascertain if the arias by Duni belong to this production or to the pasticcio performed in Rome in 1732 → see 1732 mus. by Porpora, Nicola; Broschi, Riccardo; and Duni, Egidio Romualdo.
68. See <https://www.pasticcio-project.eu/database/work/P103EF4> [accessed 25 May 2022].
69. See <https://www.pasticcio-project.eu/database/work/P103E30> [accessed 25 May 2022].

MC | *Didone abbandonata* (1724–1832)

1763 Palermo	Teatro di Santa Cecilia (win.)	(6)

Librettos   (1) Padua: Conzatti, 1739[70]
I-Pmc[S]; I-Rsc Carv.4377

(2) Alessandria: Vimercati, [1742]
I-FPfanan[71]

(3) Brescia: Turlino, [1745]
I-Rsc Carv.4378

(4) [Naples]: Langiano, 1753
E-Mn T/7988

(5) Brescia: Vendramino, [1754]
I-LOVbc MAR.16721

(6) Palermo: Toscano, 1763
US-CAt TS 8154.369 1763

Music sources

1st version: 1739, Padua

[complete scores] E-Mn M/2369/2370[IC,NG] [Acts I&II]

[excerpts] *Cara, l'avverso fato lungi* (D-KA Don Mus.Ms. 1538 [2][RISM]; D-Hs ND VI 1079 [8][RISM]; DK-Kk mu6510.2233[RISM]; CH-SAf Mus. SAf.Ms.846[RISM;P]; D-SWl Mus.3328[RISM]); *Dirò che fida sei* (F-Pn D-6556 [8][BnF]); *Fra lo splendor del trono* (F-Pn D-6556 [7][BnF]); *Quando saprai chi sono* (D-B Mus.ms. 12495 [5][RISM]; D-KNmi R 613 R [3][RISM]); *Son regina e sono amante* (D-B Mus.ms. 12501 [8][RISM]); *Tormento il più crudele* (D-BNu S 2982 [2][RISM]); *Vedi nel mio perdono* (F-Pn VM4-889[BnF])

[contrafacta] *Cara, l'avverso fato lungi* ([*Pater si potes a me transeat calix iste – Quando ah surgit dies*] D-BSSp Mus.ms. Lampugnani 1[RISM;P])

2nd version: 1753, Naples

[excerpts] *A trionfar mi chiama* (F-Pn VM4-873[BnF]; I-Gl B A.1.4 [10][IC,SBN]; *Ah non sai bella Selene* (D-Mbs Mus.ms. 1106[RISM]; I-Nc 57.2.8 [9][SBN,72]); *Dovrei… ma no* (D-Mbs Mus.ms. 1107[RISM]; GB-Lbl Add. 14219 [5][RISM]); *Quando saprai chi sono* (F-Pn D-6556 [10][BnF]; F-Pn* VM4-888[BnF]); *Se resto sul lido* (CH-SAf MusSAf.Ms.844[RISM;P]); *Son regina e sono amante* (D-KNmi R 613 R [4][RISM]); *Tormento il più crudele* (D-KNmi R 613 R [7][RISM])

---

70. According to [NG], libretto edited by Obizzi; see [NG] 'Lampugnani, Giovanni Battista'.
71. According to [C], there was a copy of this libretto in I-FPfanan (previously in Turin), yet the items of the collection were sold independently and can no longer be traced.
72. The aria does not appear in the complete score of 1739. It is usually included in the second act of the drama.

MC | *Didone abbandonata* (1724–1832)

Sources of doubtful identification

[excerpts] *Ah, non lasciarmi, no* (S-Skma T-SE-R[RISM]); *Son regina e sono amante* (B-Bc 40618[RISM]; S-SK 494 [28][RISM,73]); *Tormento il più crudele* (GB-Lbl Add. 31604[RISM])

[contrafacta] *Quando saprai chi sono* ([*Justus in domo, alma florebit sicut palma*] CZ-Pkřiž XXXV E 176[RISM])

1740	mus. by various composers	
1740 Vienna	Teatro Privilegiato (14/05/1740)[74] *Die verlassene Dido*[NP, 75]	(1)
1741 Vienna	Teatro Privilegiato	(2)
Librettos	(1) Vienna: van Ghelen, [1740] (It./Ger.) A-Wn 443714-A[76]	
	(2) Vienna: van Ghelen, [1741] (It./Ger.) A-Gl 135430¹	

1740	mus. by various unknown composers
1740 Lucca	Teatro Pubblico (aut.)
Librettos	Pistoia: Gatti, [1740] I-Bc Villa.Lo.065

1741	mus. by Galuppi, Baldassare	
1741 Modena	Teatro Molza (carn., 26/12/1740) 1ˢᵗ version	(1)
1752 Madrid	Teatro del Buen Retiro (23/09/1752) birthday of Fernando VI, king of Spain lib. rev. by Metastasio[77] rev. version	(2)

---

73. Doubtful date; it may correspond to the 1739 production with a different instrumentation.
74. Klein, 'Die Schauplätze', p. 391.
75. According to Sommer-Mathis, the premiere was scheduled for the autumn 1740, yet it had to be cancelled due to the Emperor's decease on 20 October; see Sommer-Mathis, Andrea, '*Didone abbandonata*–Aufführungen am Wiener Kärntnertortheater in der ersten Hälfte des 18. Jahrhunderts', in *Didone come soggetto nel dramma per musica*, ed. by Milada Jonášová and Tomislav Volek (Prague: Academia, 2018), pp. 213–34.
76. Microfilm copies: GB-Cu Microfilm.Ser.10.Reel 302; US-AAu FILM 17545 no. 3406 reel 602; US-Bl n/s; US-BAu Film no. A. G42 reel 602 no.3406 c.1; US-CAe Film A 440 no. 3406 [602]; US-Phu Microfilm D186 no.3406 [602].
77. Sommer-Mathis, Andrea, 'El tandem Metastasio–Farinelli: producción de óperas y escenografía del *dramma per musica*', *Scherzo*, special dossier: *Metastasio en el Madrid del XVIII*, 384 (May 2022), 64–66.

MC | *Didone abbandonata* (1724–1832)

1752 Madrid	Teatro del Buen Retiro (19/12/1752)[78]	(3)
1753 Florence	Teatro della Pergola (carn.)	(4)
	mus. by B. Galuppi or G. M. Orlandini?[79]	
1753 Madrid	Teatro del Buen Retiro (18/10/1753)	(5)
1754 Madrid	Teatro del Buen Retiro (14/04/1754)	(6)
1754 Madrid	Teatro del Buen Retiro (18/12/1754)	(7)
1755 Madrid	Teatro del Buen Retiro (12/01/1755)	(8)
1755 Madrid	Teatro del Buen Retiro (30/03/1755)	(9)
1755 Madrid	Teatro del Buen Retiro (06/04/1755)	(10)
1764 Venice	Teatro Grimani di S. Benedetto (carn.)	(11)
	2nd version	
1766 St Petersburg	Court theatre – Winter Palace (03/03/1766)	(12)
1770 Naples	NA[NP,80]	(13)
1772 Naples	Teatro di S. Carlo	(14)

Librettos

(1) Modena: Torri, [1741]
I-PAc F. Libretti, sc. III [104]

(2) Madrid: [s.n.], 1752
E-Mn T/24147

(3, 5–10, 13–14) NA

(4) Florence: Pieri, [1753]
GB-Lbl 1342.a.37 [6];[81] I-Bc Lo.06210; I-Fc E.V.0526; I-Fc E.V.1724; I-Fc E.VI.3208

(11) Venice: Fossati, [1764]
D-B Mus. Tg 102; F-LM BL 8° 2747; I-Mb Racc.dramm.4385; I-Vcg LIBRETTI S.BENEDETTO 57 A 14; I-Vgc ROL.0315 [4]; I-Vlevi

---

78. For performances in Madrid, see Casanova Sánchez de Vega, Teresa, 'El intermezzo en la corte de España, 1738-1758' (doctoral dissertation, Universidad Complutense de Madrid, 2019); Leza, José Máximo, 'Metastasio on the Spanish Stage: Operatic Adaptations in the Public Theatres of Madrid in the 1730s', *Early Music*, 26.4 (1998), 623–31; and Llorens, Ana and Álvaro Torrente, 'Constructing *Opera Seria* in the Iberian Courts: Metastasian Repertoire for Spain and Portugal', *Anuario musical*, 76 (2021), 73–110 <https://doi.org/10.3989/anuariomusical.2021.i76>.

79. Doubtful. See *Informazioni e Studi Vivaldiani: Bollettino dell'Istituto Italiano Antonio Vivaldi* (Venice: Fondazione Giorgio Cini–Ricordi, 1984). See also Weaver, Robert Lamar and Norma Wright Weaver, *A Chronology of Music in the Florentine Theatre, 1751-1800: Operas, Prologues, Farces, Intermezzos, Concerts, and Plays with Incidental Music* (Warren, MI: Harmonie Park Press, 1993). Libretto printed by C. M. Pieri, see below. Production for the 1753 carnival season in Florence (premiered on 26 December 1752); it might be by Orlandini.

80. According to [NG], the revival of *Didone abbandonata* for Naples in 1770 was refused by the singers (Insanguine rewrote it); see [NG] 'Galuppi, Baldassare'.

81. Microfilm reproduction: GB-Lbl PB.Mic.13959.

MC | *Didone abbandonata* (1724–1832)

Dramm. 841; I-Vnm DRAMM.1089 [1]; I-Vnm DRAMM.1300 [1]; US-LAum ML48 .R114 1764 [1]; <u>US-Wc ML48 [S3503]</u>[82]

(12) St Petersburg: Imperial Academy of the Sciences, [1766] (It./Rus.) RUS-SPsc Rossica 13.13.1.116

Music sources

1st version: 1741, Modena[83]

[excerpts] *Ah, non lasciarmi, no* (D-KNmi R 614 R [4][RISM]; F-Pn D-4300 [2][RISM]; <u>I-Nc 57.2.8 [4]</u>[SBN]; UA-Knbuv Rozum 120501 [21][RISM]); *Ardi per me fedele* (I-Nc 34.5.29 [1][SBN]); *La caduta d'un regnante* (F-Pn MS-1898[RISM]); *Se resto sul lido* (<u>D-Mbs Mus.ms. 255 [11]</u>[RISM]); *Son quel fiume che gonfio d'umori* (DK-Kc R304[RISM]); *Tacerò se tu lo brami* (<u>D-Dl Mus.2973-F-3 [2]</u>[RISM,84]; <u>D-Mbs Mus.ms. 255 [2]</u>[RISM]); *Vado... ma dove?... oh dio!* (I-MC 2-D-1 [9][RISM]; I-Rc Mss. 2250 [10][SBN]; US-SFsc *M2.1 M126[RISM])

[printed sources] *Non ha ragione ingrato*, in *The Favourite Songs in the Opera call'd Antigono* (London: Walsh, [1746])[85]

rev. version: 1752, Madrid

[complete scores] B-Bc 2097[MGG,NG,RISM;A,86]; P-La 44-VI-69[BA,MGG,NG]; US-Wc M1503.G182 D5[MGG,NG,RISM]

[excerpts] *Ah, non lasciarmi, no* (<u>D-Dl Mus.1-F-21 [1]</u>[RISM,87]; S-Skma T-SE-R[RISM]); *Chiamami pur così* (DK-Kc R305[RISM]); *Dovrei... ma no...* (F-Pn* MS-1897[RISM]); *Son regina e sono amante* (F-Pn* MS-1896[RISM])

[doubtful] [Venice, 1754] *Vado... ma dove?... oh dio!* (S-Skma Alströmer saml. 152 [15][RISM]; S-Skma T-SE-R[RISM])

---

82. Copy: D-KNmi FH 1187.
83. As no complete source has been preserved for Galuppi's 1st setting of *Didone abbandonata*, the excerpts included in this section meet the following criteria that make us discard a later date for them: i) they were included in the original libretto; ii) their music is different from that of Galuppi's 2nd and 3rd versions, or from that included in later revivals; and iii) they have no inscription relating them to other performances.
84. Galuppi inserted this aria into his opera *L'Arminio* (Venice, 1747).
85. Reference to this printed source found in Burden, Michael, 'Metastasio on the London Stage, 1728 to 1840: A Catalogue', *Royal Musical Association Research Chronicle*, 40 (2007), 1–332.
86. The manuscript contains eleven arias, one trio, and one recitative. According to [NG], it is a convoluted source from different periods. It contains the following pieces: *Ah, non lasciarmi, no* [6]; *Ardi per me fedele* [5]; *A trionfar mi chiama* [10]; *Deh resta, deh senti* [12]; *Dirò che fida sei* [1]; *Fosca nube il sol ricopra* [*La sua sorte il suo destino*] [7]; *Io d'amore, oh dio, mi moro* [11]; *La caduta d'un regnante* [9]; *Quando saprai chi sono* [3]; *Se resto sul lido* [4]; *Sinfonia per benvenuto di Iarba* [2]; *Veggio la sponda* [8]. [7]: second Italian text line added above Iarba's line which does not belong to the original aria. Most of the materials belong to the 1752 version, except for the duet *Deh resta, deh senti*, which belongs to the 1764 production.
87. Wrongly attributed to Antonio Aurisicchio in [MGG].

MC | *Didone abbandonata* (1724–1832)

2nd version: 1764, Venice	
	[complete scores] I-Nc 27.6.16/17/18[IC,MGG,RISM,SBN,88]; P-La 44-VI-66/67/68[BA,89]; RUS-SPtob[MGG,NG]
	[excerpts] *Ah, non lasciarmi, no* (D-Dl Mus.2973-F-31 [3][RISM]); *Deh resta, deh senti* (A-Wgm VI 737/1 [Q 2899][IC]; A-Wgm VI 737/2 [Q 2899a][IC]; CH-Gc Rmo 123/12 [2][RISM]; D-Dl Mus.1-F-82,28 [7][RISM]; D-Dl Mus.2973-F-36 [15][RISM]; D-LÜh Mus. Q 198[RISM]; D-Mbs Mus. ms. 20866 [3][RISM]; DK-Kk mu6409.0835[RISM]; DK-Kk mu6409.1830[RISM]; F-Pn D-4303 [13][BnF,RISM,90]; F-Pn D-4307 [14][BnF,RISM]; F-Pn L-17936[BnF]; I-Bc FF.86 [4][IC,RISM,SBN]; I-Nc 34.5.29 [17][SBN]; I-Raf 1.E.4 [5][RISM,91]); *Fosca nube il sol ricopra* (D-LÜh Mus. Q 173[RISM]); *Fra lo splendor del trono* (D-LÜh Mus. Q 179[RISM]); *Quando saprai chi sono* (I-Bc FF.86 [7][IC,RISM]); *Se dalle stelle tu non sei guida* (D-LÜh Mus. Q 186[RISM]); *Son regina e sono amante* (US-CAe Mus 503.601 [7][RISM]); *Tu mi disarmi il fianco* (F-Pn* MS-1903[BnF,RISM]); *Vado… ma dove?… oh dio!* (F-Pn MS-1972 [1][BnF,RISM,92])
	[doubtful] [Venice, 1765] *Ah, non lasciarmi, no* (D-LÜh Mus. Q 190[RISM]); *Non ha ragione ingrato* (D-LÜh Mus. Q 177[RISM]); *Son regina e sono amante* (D-F Mus Hs 452[RISM]; D-LÜh Mus. A 180[RISM]); *Tu mi disarmi il fianco* (D-LÜh Mus. Q 191[RISM]); *Vado… ma dove?… oh dio!* (D-RH Ms 466[RISM;P,93])
	[Naples, 1770 or 1772] *Tremar non sento* (I-Mc Noseda Q.39 [2][SBN]; I-Nc A 205 [18][SBN])
[undated]	[excerpts] *Vado… ma dove?… oh dio* (GB-Lbl Add. 31605[RISM]; GB-Lbl Add. 31632[RISM])
[inserts]	→ see 1751, mus. by Perez, Davide

1741	**mus. by Bernasconi, Andrea**	
1741 Venice	Teatro Grimani di S. Giovanni Grisostomo (carn., 28/01/1741) 1st version	(1)
1743 Cesena	Teatro Spada (19/05/1743) pasticcio[94]	(2)

---

88. For St Petersburg 1766.
89. Xerox copy: US-BEm M2.8.G25 D54.
90. Microfilm copy: F-Pn VM BOB-31989.
91. I-Raf 1.E.4 [5]; D-LÜh Mus. Q 173; D-LÜh Mus. Q 179; and D-LÜh Mus. Q 186: for Venice 1765.
92. Microfilm copy: F-Pn IFN-10024916.
93. The music is similar to the 1764 version and in a different key.
94. A pasticcio according to [MGG,S]; see [MGG] 'Bernasconi, Andrea' and [S]Index I, p. 352.

MC | *Didone abbandonata* (1724–1832)

1756 Munich	Court theatre (carn., 26/01/1756)	(3)
	Die verlassene Dido	
	2nd version	
1760 Munich	Court theatre (carn.)	(4)

Librettos

(1) Venice: Rossetti, [1741]
D-B Mus. T 52; I-Mb Racc.dramm.3782; I-Rsc Carv.4380; I-RVI Silv., op. 761; I-Vcg LIBRETTI S.GIO.GRISOSTOMO 156; I-Vnm DRAMM.1067 [2]; I-Vnm DRAMM.1253 [1]; I-Vnm DRAMM.3569 [4]; US-LAum ML48 .R114 1741 [4]

(2) Bologna: Sassi, [1743]
I-Bc Lo.00489

(3) Munich: Vötter, [1756] (It./Ger.)
D-Au 221/IU 9651 D.55.756; D-Mbs Bavar.4015-18,1 [3]; D-Mbs Slg. Her 360; D-Mu 0001/8 Don. 10-1091; I-Vgc ROL.0162 [25]

(4) Munich: Vötter, [1760]
CZ-Bu ST1-0962 [843]; D-KNth 1372; D-Mbs Bavar.4015-28,1 [6]; D-Mbs Bavar.4015-31,1 [13]; D-Mu 0001/8 Don. 10-1090; D-MHrm T 250; D-Sl Fr.D.oct 5067; US-Cn ML50.2 D47 M47 1760; US-Wc ML48 [S858]

Music sources

1st version: 1741, Venice

[excerpts] *Ardi per me fedele* (B-Bc 3718[RISM]); *Infelice e sventurato* (D-MÜs SANT Hs 183 [17][RISM]); *Veggio la sponda* (D-MÜs SANT Hs 183 [25][RISM,95])

2nd version: 1756, Munich

[complete scores] D-Hs M A/705[RISM] [Act II]; D-Mbs Mus.ms. 207[MGG,NG,RISM]; D-Mbs Mus.ms. 20890[NG,RISM]

[excerpts] *Quando saprai chi sono* (GB-Lbl Add. 5057 [3][RISM]); *Son qual fiume, che gonfio* (D-SWl Mus.1227[RISM,96]; I-Fc D.I.209 [1][IC,NG,RISM,SBN]; I-Mc Mus. Tr.ms.117[RISM])

1741	mus. by Di Capua, Rinaldo
1741 Lisbon[NG]	Teatro de Rua dos Condes
Librettos	Lisbon: Gayo, 1741
	F-BO D 34195 [2]; I-Rsc Carv.4379; P-Cug Misc. 686 [9643]

95. It reportedly belongs to the 1741 production in Venice. However, this aria is not contained in any of the librettos (Venice 1741, Bologna 1743, Munich 1756, or Munich 1760).
96. This and the following source: for Munich 1760.

MC | *Didone abbandonata* (1724–1832)

1742	mus. by unknown composer(s)	
1742 Palermo	Teatro di Santa Cecilia (summ.)	
Librettos	Palermo: Ciché & Gramignani, 1742	
	I-CATu Ant.D.234.3; I-PLpagano n/s	
1742	mus. by Hasse, Johann Adolph	
	lib. rev. by Algarotti, Francesco[97]	
1742 Dresden	Court theatre – Hubertusburg (07/10/1742)	(1)
	Die verlassene Dido	
	birthday of August III, king of Poland	
1743 Dresden	Court theatre (carn., 04/02/1743)[98]	(2,3)
1744 Naples	Teatro di S. Carlo (20/01/1744)	(4)
	birthday of Carlos VII, king of Naples?	
	rev. by N. Logroscino[99]	
1748 London	King's Theatre in the Haymarket (26/03/1748)	(5)
	chiefly by J. A. Hasse, pasticcio	
1752 Dresden	Court theatre	(6)
1753 Berlin	Court theatre (carn., 29/12/1752)	(7)
	Die verlassene Dido[100]	
1753 Paris	Court theatre – Palace de Versailles (28/08/1753)	(8)
	wedding of Marie-Josèphe de Saxony with the Dauphin of France	
	rev. version	
1770 Berlin	Court theatre (22/12/1769)[101]	(9)
	Die verlassene Dido	
1780 Berlin[102]	NA (carn.)[NP]	(10)

97. Algarotti altered the original plot: the burning of Carthage which concludes the original text was replaced by a lengthy recitative and aria. The classical restraint of Algarotti's substitution must have seemed an improvement on Metastasio's youthful libretto of 1724; as late as 1757 Hasse asked Algarotti to send the score of the closing scene so that he could give it to Padre Martini; the score is currently in I-Bc; see [NG] 'Johann Adolf Hasse'.
98. For the differences between this revival and the premiere of Hasse's setting, see Hochstein, Wolfgang, '*Didone abbandonata* in der Vertonung von Johann Adolph Hasse', in *Didone come soggetto nel dramma per musica*, ed. by Milada Jonášová and Tomislav Volek (Prague: Academia, 2018), pp. 185–212.
99. [C] only identifies Francesco Algarotti as responsible for the revision of the libretto.
100. According to [NG], a new revision by Hasse.
101. Schneider, Louis, *Geschichte der Opern und des königlichen Opernhauses in Berlin* (Berlin: Dunker & Humbolt, 1852) and Henzel, *Berliner Klassik* (Berlin: ortus, 2009). The production ran for five consecutive performances.
102. According to [NG]: further revival cancelled on account of the death of Princess Louisa Amalia; see [NG] 'Johann Adolf Hasse'. See also Mangum, John, 'The Repertory of the Italian Court Opera in Berlin, 1740-1786', in *The Oxford Handbook of the Operatic Canon*, ed. by Cormac Newark and William Weber (New York: Oxford University Press, 2020), pp. 75–92 and Schmidt-Hensel, Roland Dieter, '*La musica è del Signor Hasse detto il Sassone…*': *Johann Adolf Hasses 'Opere serie' der Jahre 1730 bis 1745. Quellen, Fassungen, Aufführungen* (Göttingen: V&R unipress, 2009).

MC | *Didone abbandonata* (1724–1832)

Librettos

(1) Dresden: [widow of] Stössel, 1742 (It./Ger.)
D-B Mus. Th 252; D-DI Mag7XVII 475; D-Gs 8 P DRAM I, 6818; F-Pn TH B-2893; RUS-Mrg MK Ит.-8° [50-8419157]; S-Skma Dram. utl. Rar Metastasio; US-Wc ML48 [S4535]

(2) Dresden: [widow of] Stössel, [1743]
D-KNth L 1373

(3) Dresden: [widow of] Stössel, [1743] (It./Ger.)
D-Dl Lit.Ital.D 1240; D-Mth 001/8 17906 [1]; PL-Wu GSD 17.2.13.14 [1]; S-Skma Dram. utl. Rar Metastasio

(4) Naples: Ricciardi, 1744
I-Nragni L117; I-Nsn SALA A MISC.10.E.6 [5]

(5) London: Woodfall, 1748 (It./En.)
CDN-Lu MZ0.055; GB-Lbl 907.i.6 [1];[103] I-Mb Racc.dramm.4508

(6) Dresden: [widow of] Stössel, 1752 (It./Ger.)
NA[104]

(7) Berlin: Haude & Spener, [1752] (It./Ger.)
D-B Mus. T 67 [6]; D-Hs A/34173 [11]; D-MHrm T 16; D-SWa Ob V 5,1020 [19]; GB-Lbl 11714.b.36; PL-Wu GSD 28.20.4.5873 [1]

(8) NA

(9) Berlin: Haude & Spener, 1769 (It./Ger.)
D-B Xq7472 [8]; US-CAh *GC7 A100 B750 [135]; US-Wc ML48 [S4536]

(10) NA

Music sources

[complete scores] A-Wn Mus.Hs.1044[IC,MGG,NG,105]; B-Bc 2145[IC,MGG,NG,RISM,106]; D-B AmB 308[IC]; D-B Mus.ms. 9549/1[IC,MGG,NG,RISM;A,R]; D-B Mus.ms. 9549/4[NG,RISM;A]; D-B Mus.ms. 9549/6[NG,RISM;A,R,107]; D-Bsa* [D-B] SA 1087[MGG,NG,RISM,108]; D-Dl Mus.2477-F-35[MGG,NG,RISM,109]; D-Dl Mus.2477-F-35a/b[MGG,RISM;IP,110]; D-HAmi MS 66[MGG,

---

103. Microfilm copy: GB-En Mf.134, reel 5686 [5].
104. [C] lists a source in RUS-Mrg, yet it is not included in the [IC]; see <http://corago.unibo.it/libretto/0001297056> [accessed 24 June 2022].
105. For Dresden 1743.
106. For Versailles 1753.
107. Overture and nine arias.
108. Possible autograph.
109. The parts (D-Dl Mus.2477-F-35a/b) offer the 1742 version plus the changes incorporated in the later 1743 revival, to which the full score belongs. Since the 1742 and 1743 versions are partly worked into each other, separate page counts cannot be made. Except for the Marcia, it can be assumed that up to A3-S16 the music remained unchanged from one occasion to the other.
110. Microfilm copies: CDN-Lu MZ0.055; US-AUS FILM 26150; US-CHum Micfilm 671.

MC | *Didone abbandonata* (1724–1832)

NG,RISM,111; D-DS Mus.ms 508[MGG,NG,RISM,112]; D-Hmg Bü 3687[NG,RISM;R,113]; D-Hs ND VI 2938[MGG,NG,RISM,114]; D-KNmi H 210 R[RISM;P]; D-LEm Becker III.15.15[RISM;A,115]; D-LEm PM 3300[IC,MGG,NG;A,116]; D-LEm PM 3551[MGG,NG,RISM]; D-MÜs SANT Hs 1979[RISM;A,117]; D-SWl Mus.2477[MGG,NG,RISM;A]; D-W Cod. Guelf 118 [a] Mus. Hdschr.[MGG,RISM;A]; D-W Cod. Guelf 118 [b] Mus. Hdschr.[MGG,RISM;A]; F-Pn D-5947[BnF,NG,118]; F-Pn L-15377[BnF,MGG;A]; F-Pn L-20202[BnF,MGG,NG;P]; F-Pn RES-1351 [1/2/3][BnF,NG,119]; GB-CDu Mackworth Collection vol. 14[MGG,RISM;A,120]; GB-Lbl R.M.22.e.14/15/16[MGG,NG,RISM,121]; I-Mc Noseda F.67 [1–2][MGG,NG,SBN,122]; I-Nc 27.2.17/18/19[MGG,NG,RISM,SBN]; I-Vnm Mss. 9837[MGG,SBN]; S-Skma T-R [I–II][MGG;A,R]; S-Uu Vok. mus. i hs. 56:5[IC,MGG,NG,RISM;A,R]; US-NYp Mus. Res. *MS[IC,MGG]; US-Wc M1500.H35 D43[MGG,NG,RISM,123]

[excerpts] *Ah, non lasciarmi, no* (A-Wn Mus.Hs. 17563 [2][IC]; B-Bc 15184 [2][RISM,124]; D-Dl Mus.1-F-124 [4][RISM;IP]; D-Mbs Mus.ms. 180 [7][IC]; F-Pm Res F7.29[BASE]; F-Pn D-5455 [3][BnF]; P-Ln C.I.C. 14,I [4][RISM]; GB-Lbl R.M.23.d.19 [11][RISM]; I-Mc Noseda I.93 [11][SBN]; I-MC 2-F-15/2 [1][RISM]; I-MOe Mus. F. 1355 [16][IC]; I-Nc 33.2.20 [39][SBN]; I-Nc 33.2.22 [13][SBN]; I-Rc Mss. 2767 [2][NG,SBN]); *Cadrà fra poco in cenere* (B-Bc 5303[RISM;R]; B-Bc 15185 [4][RISM]; D-Dl Mus.2477-F-116 [2][RISM;IP]; GB-Lam MS 137[IC]; I-MC 6-E-3 [2][RISM,125]; I-Nc 33.2.22 [6,6bis][SBN,126]); *Chiamami pur così* (I-Mc Noseda I.93 [7][SBN]); *Dirò che fida sei* (B-Bc 4110[RISM]; B-Bc 15183 [1][RISM]; D-B Am.B 308[RISM]; D-Dl Mus.1-F-123 [1][RISM;IP]; F-Pn D-5465 [15][BnF,127];

---

111. For Dresden 1743, with acts I–III (up to S16) from the original 1742 version. Microfilm copy: US-AAu MICRO-F M45 no. 30.
112. For Berlin 1753.
113. For Berlin 1769.
114. For Dresden 1743.
115. Microfilm copy: US-AAu MICRO-F M45 [30].
116. This and the following source have A1 to A3-S16 from the 1743 version and A3-S17 to S20 from the 1742 version.
117. It also contains other arias from operas by Hasse.
118. For Dresden 1743. Microfilm copy: F-Pn VM BOB-20423.
119. For Versailles 1753. It may be the same source as the one in F-Pc to which [NG] refers. Microfilm copy: F-Pn VM BOB-2006/2007/2008.
120. It may correspond to the source in GB-CDp of which [NG] speaks, but that source has not been found in any of the catalogues consulted.
121. For Naples 1744.
122. This and the following source, for Versailles 1753 according to [NG].
123. [NG] lists a further source in GB-Ob, but it has not been found in [IC].
124. B-Bc 15184 [2]; D-Dl Mus.1-F-124; GB-Lbl R.M.23.d.19 [11]; I-Nc 33.2.22 [13]; and I-Rc Mss. 2767 [2]: in D major instead of E major; same as in the sources corresponding to the 1744 Neapolitan revival.
125. In a minor instead of A flat major; in C-3 instead of C-1 clef.
126. For Naples 1744, as sung by Giovanni Manzuoli.
127. Microfilm copy: F-Pn VM BOB-25743.

I-MOe Mus. F. 1355 [18]^{SBN}; P-Ln C.I.C. 14,I [6]^{RISM}); *Fra lo splendor del trono* (B-Bc 5313$^{RISM;R}$; F-Pn VM7-7353^{IC}; I-Nc 33.2.20 [34]^{SBN}; I-Nc 33.2.22 [7]^{SBN}); *Già si desta la tempesta* (S-Skma SO-R^{IC}); *L'augelletto in lacci stretto* (D-Bsa [D-B] SA 1576^{RISM}; D-Hhg n/s^{IC}; <u>D-Dl Mus.2477-E-504 [5]</u>^{RISM}; F-Pn VM7-7361^{IC}); *Leon, che errando vada* (CZ-Pkřiž XXXVI B 102^{RISM}; P-Ln C.I.C. 14,I [3]^{RISM}); *Nel duol che prova* (B-Bc 4129^{RISM}; B-Bc 5322$^{RISM;R}$; B-Bc 15183 [3]^{RISM}; D-B Mus.ms. 141 [1]^{RISM,128}; <u>D-Dl Mus.1-F-123 [2]</u>$^{RISM;IP}$; D-Mbs Mus.ms. 141 [14]^{IC}; D-Wa 46 Alt 716^{RISM,129}; F-Pn D-5466 [7]^{BnF,130}; GB-Ob Ms. Mus. c.107 [3]^{RISM,131}; <u>I-Nc 33.3.18 [11]</u>^{SBN}; S-Skma T-SE-R^{RISM}); *Non ha ragione ingrato* (A-Wn Mus.Hs.4055^{IC}; B-Bc 4133^{RISM,132}; B-Bc 15185 [1]^{RISM}; <u>D-Dl Mus.2477-F-116 [7]</u>$^{RISM;IP}$; D-Hhg Hg 203^{RISM}; D-MGmi HA IV 66^{RISM}; F-Pn D-5466 [5]^{BnF,133}; F-Pn D-5468 [12]^{BnF}; F-Pn D-5470 [10]^{BnF}; F-Pn D-17652$^{BnF;IP}$; I-Fc D.IV.55^{IC}; I-Mc Noseda I.93 [14]^{SBN}; I-MC 2-F-15/2 [3]^{RISM}; I-MC 2-F-15 [11]^{RISM,134}; I-MC 2-F-16/1 [4]^{RISM}; I-MC 2-F-16/20 [2]^{RISM}; I-Nc 33.2.19 [21]^{SBN}; I-Nc 33.2.20 [36]^{SBN}; <u>I-Nc 33.2.21 [18]</u>^{SBN}; I-Nc 33.2.22 [9]^{SBN}; I-Rc Mss. 2767 [1]^{NG,SBN}); *Ogni amator suppone* (D-RH Ms 360 [2]^{RISM}; I-MC 2-F-15/2 [4]^{RISM}); *Ombra cara, ombra tradita* (B-Bc 5175^{RISM}; B-Bc 15184 [4]^{RISM,135}; D-B Mus.ms. 30341 [8]^{RISM}; <u>D-Dl Mus.1-F-124 [4]</u>$^{RISM;IP}$; <u>D-Dl Mus.2477-F-110 [27]</u>^{RISM}; F-Pm Res F7.29^{BASE}; F-Pn D-5467 [1]^{BnF,136}; F-Pn D-5467 [6]^{BnF}; GB-Lcm MS 2071 [15]^{IC}; I-Bc FF.244 [1]^{IC}; I-Mc Noseda I.93 [13]^{SBN}; I-MC 4-F-8 [18]^{RISM}); *Quando saprai chi sono* (<u>D-Dl Mus.1-F-123 [9]</u>$^{RISM;IP,137}$; GB-Cfm [GB-Cu] MU.MS.167 [6]^{IC}; I-Gl S.B.2.3.V.2.16^{IC}; I-Nc 33.2.20 [42]^{SBN}; I-Vc Torrefranca Ms.B. 10 [1]^{NG,RISM,SBN}); *Se dalle stelle tu non sei guida* (B-Bc 15182 [6]^{RISM}; <u>D-Dl Mus.2477-F-116 [5]</u>$^{RISM;IP}$; GB-Cfm [GB-Cu] MU.MS.167 [6]^{IC}; I-MC 2-F-15/2 [2]^{RISM}; <u>I-Nc 33.2.17 [15]</u>^{SBN}; I-Rama A.Mss.4259^{IC,138}); *Se resto sul lido* (<u>D-Dl Mus.1-F-28,5 [4]</u>^{RISM};

---

128. Wrongly attributed to Benedetto Negri on source; in a different key from Hasse's 1742 version.
129. In A major instead of b minor.
130. Microfilm copy: F-Pn VM BOB-25807.
131. Music without text; in a key different from the original.
132. In c minor instead of b minor; in C-3 instead of C-1 clef.
133. Microfilm copy: F-Pn VM BOB-25807.
134. I-MC 2-F-15 [11]; I-MC 2-F-16/20 [2]; and I-Rc Mss. 2767 [1]: in g minor instead of f minor; probably from the 1744 Neapolitan performance.
135. This and the following two sources: in F major instead of E flat major.
136. Microfilm copy: F-Pn VM BOB-23048.
137. In C major instead of F major.
138. Inserted into Hasse's *Leucippo* (Hubertusburg–Dresden, 1747); see Antolini, Bianca Maria and Annalisa Bini, 'Johann Adolph Hasse nei manoscritti della Biblioteca di S. Cecilia di Roma', *Analecta Musicologica*, 25 (1983), 495–511.

MC | *Didone abbandonata* (1724–1832)

D-Hmg Bü 3687 [1.13]^(RISM;R); D-MÜs SANT Hs 1979 [14]^(RISM,139); D-W Cod. Guelf. 118 [a] [8]^(RISM); D-W Cod. Guelf. 118 [a] [11]^(RISM); F-Pn VM7-7271^(BnF,RISM); GB-Cfm [GB-Cu] MU.MS.167 [6]^(IC); I-Mc Noseda A.34 [24]^(SBN); I-MC 2-F-16/1 [3]^(RISM); I-Nc 33.2.17 [10]^(SBN); I-Nc 33.2.22 [11]^(SBN,140); I-Vc Torrefranca Ms.B. 10 [3]^(NG,RISM); RUS-Mrg Φ.954 N°134–138 [4]^(RISM;IP); S-Skma T-SE-R^(RISM)); *Son regina e sono amante* (B-Bc 4168^(RISM); F-Pn D-5466 [18]^(BnF,141); GB-Cfm [GB-Cu] MU.MS.167 [10]^(IC); I-Mc Noseda A.34 [22]^(SBN); I-MOe Mus. F. 1355 [19]^(IC)); *Tacerò se tu lo brami* (B-Bc 15183 [6]^(RISM); D-Dl Mus.1-F-123 [4]^(RISM;IP); D-Mbs Mus.ms. 141 [12]^(RISM,142); GB-Cfm [GB-Cu] MU.MS.167 [6]^(IC); GB-Lam MS 137^(RISM); PL-SA L 1668 [85]^(RISM;R,IP)); *Tu mi disarmi il fianco* (D-SWl Mus.2484^(RISM;P); I-MC 2-F-16/20 4]^(RISM); I-MC 6-E-10 [29]^(RISM); I-Nc 33.2.20 [19]^(SBN); I-Nc 33.2.22 [8]^(SBN)); *Vado... ma dove?... oh dio!* (F-Pn D-5470 [1]^(BnF)); *Va lusingando amore* (D-Dl Mus.2477-E-504 [3]^(RISM); D-Dl Mus.2477-F-111 [12]^(RISM;IP); I-Mc Mus. Tr.ms. 569(a-b) [575]^(RISM); P-Ln C.I.C. 14,I [5]^(RISM)); *Vedi nel mio perdono* (A-Wgm VI 15385 [Q 3959]^(IC)); *Veggio la sponda* (B-Bc 5322^(RISM;R); B-Bc 5338^(RISM;R); B-Bc 15185 [2]^(RISM); D-Dl Mus.2477-F-116 [2/1]^(RISM;IP); I-Vc Giustiniani B.20 [17]^(IC))

[printed sources] *Dirò che fida sei* [1]; *Nel duol che prova* [3]; *Ombra cara, ombra tradita* [2]; *Va lusingando amore* [4]; *Volgi a me gli affetti tuoi* [5], in *The Favourite Songs in the Opera call'd Didone by Sigr Hasse* (London: Woodfall, 1748)[143]

[contrafacta] *Ah, non lasciarmi, no* ([Consecratus iste orbis] PL-Wu RM 4310 [2]^(RISM;P)); *A trionfar mi chiama* ([In te Domine speravi] D-ERP [D-Aab] 138^(RISM;P); [Omni die dic Mariae, mea laudes anima] PL-Wu RM 4457/20^(RISM); [Voce sonora clamante] CZ-Pak 1459^(RISM;P)); *Chiamami pur così* ([Aspera licet via ad caeli atria] PL-Wu RM 5709 [1]^(RISM;P)); *Fra lo splendor del trono* ([Pater summe majestatis] PL-Wu RM 4457 [24]^(RISM;P)); *Già si desta la tempesta* ([Alma redemptoris mater, quae pervia caeli] CZ-Tek n/s^(RISM;R)); *Leon, che errando vada* ([Ad Jesum volate] PL-SA 456/A VIII 96 [1]^(RISM;R)); *Non ha ragione ingrato* ([Cessa o homo ingrato] CZ-Pak 1431^(RISM); ([Non tardes cor meum] CZ-Pak 1461^(RISM;P); [Veni mi Jesu care, languentem recreare] CZ-Pkřiž XXXVI B 81^(RISM;P)); *Se resto sul lido* ([Natantes Syrenae cantantes] PL-Wu 4310 [1]^(RISM;P)); *Tacerò se tu lo brami*

---

139. In G major instead of D major.
140. I-Nc 33.2.22 [11] and RUS-Mrg Φ.954 N°134–138 [4]: in E major instead of D major; for Naples 1744, as sung by Caffarelli.
141. Microfilm copy: F-Pn VM BOB-25807.
142. In F major instead of A major.
143. Reference to this printed source has been found in Burden, 'Metastasio on the London Stage', p. 154.

MC | *Didone abbandonata* (1724–1832)

([*Non recedam a te care*] CZ-Pak 459[RISM;P]); *Tu mi scorgi al gran disegno* ([*Ave Maria, gratia plena Dominus tecum*] D-Mbs Mus.ms. 5001[RISM]); *Va lusingando amore* ([*Plaude applaude gaude vox canora*] PL-Wu RM 4460[RISM;P])

[arrangements] *L'augelletto in lacci stretto* (F-Pn D-5403 [3][BnF,144])

[doubtful] *Se resto sul lido* (B-Bc 5176[RISM,145])

1745	mus. by various unknown composers
1745 Mantua	Teatro Regio Ducale (carn., 24/01/1745)
	Didone abbandonata da Enea
Librettos	Mantua: heirs of Pazzoni, [1745]
	I-MAc MISC.-.476 [8]; I-Rsc Carv.4400
1745	mus. by unknown composer(s)
1745 Bologna	Teatro Formagliari? (*c.* 18/04/1745)
Librettos	Bologna: Sassi, 1745
	I-Rc 40.9.E.7.6[146]
1745	mus. by Aurisicchio, Antonio and others
1745 Fano	Teatro della Fortuna (Jul. Fair, 04/07/1745)[147]
Librettos	Fano: Donati, 1745
	I-Bc Lo.00360; I-FAN Mus 12 [1] MUS 1360
Music sources	[excerpts] I-FZc[NG]
1747	mus. by Jommelli, Niccolò
1747 Rome	Teatro di Torre Argentina (carn., 28/01/1747)[148] (1)
	1st version
1749 Vienna	Teatro Privilegiato (08/12/1749) (2)
	birthday of Franz I, Holy Roman Emperor
	2nd version

144. Arrangement for two flutes. Microfilm copy: F-Pn VM BOB-26159.
145. Completely different from Hasse's original setting.
146. Front page missing.
147. According to [MGG] and [NG], only some arias are by Aurisicchio; see [MGG,NG] 'Aurisicchio, Antonio'.
148. According to Loewenberg, Alfred, *Annals of Opera, 1597–1940* (Cambridge: Heffer & Sons, 1943), premiered in Vienna in 1749, but the libretto for this production is clear. For the specific date, we follow Franchi, Saverio, *Drammaturgia romana II (1701–1750)* (Rome: Edizione di Storia e Letteratura, 1997). Rinaldi, Mario, *Due secoli al Teatro Argentina* (Florence: Olschki, 1978) gives 04/02/1747 instead.

MC | *Didone abbandonata* (1724–1832)

1751 Stuttgart	Teatro Ducale[149]	(3)
	Die verlassene Dido	
	birthday of the Duchess of Württemberg and Teck	
1763 Stuttgart	Teatro Ducale (11/02/1763)	(4,5)
	Didon abandonnee	
	birthday of the Duke of Württemberg and Teck	
	3rd version	
1777 Stuttgart	Teatro Ducale (10/01/1777)	(6)
1780 Stuttgart	Teatro Ducale (10/10/1780)	(7)
1782 Stuttgart	Teatro Ducale (25/09/1782)[150]	(8)

Librettos

(1) Rome: de' Rossi, [1747]
B-Bc 19904; I-Fc E.VI.4885; I-Rn 35.9.L.18.01; I-Vgc ROL.0392 [2]; US-CHH IOLC.00233

(2) Vienna: van Ghelen, [1749]
F-Pn 16-YD-509

(3) Stuttgart: Cotta, 1751 (It./Ger.)
D-Tu Dk III 27 [4]; US-Wc ML48 [S4854]

(4) Stuttgart: Cotta, 1763 (It./Ger.)[151]
B-Bc 19906; D-BHu 73/LU 39360 D5.763 [1]; D-KNth L 1375; F-Pn 8-RA6-219; I-Bu A.VI.B.V [29]; US-AAu ML 50.2 .D56 J75 1763

(5) Stuttgart, Cotta, 1763 (It./Fr.)
US-Wc ML48 [S4855][152]

(6) Stuttgart; Cotta, [1777] (It./Fr.)
D-Sl W.G.qt.K.1067;[153] F-Pn YD-588[154]

(7) Stuttgart: Cotta, [1780] (It./Ger.)[155]
B-Bc 19908[156]

---

149. Treated as a pasticcio in <https://www.pasticcio-project.eu/database/work/P1036F6> [accessed 25 May 2022].
150. Krauß, Rudolf, *Das Stuttgarter Hoftheater von den ältesten Zeiten bis zur Gegenwart* (Stuttgart: Metzler, 1908).
151. Microfilm copy of unspecified physical item, supposedly in D-Sl: D-Dl R 18 Met 17.
152. Copy: D-KNmi 1189.
153. Microfilm copy: D-Dl R 18 Met 2 (two copies).
154. Microfilm copy: F-Pn MICROFILM M-2657.
155. Microfilm copy of unspecified physical copy: D-Sl R 18 Met 8.
156. Photocopy: CDN-Lu ML48.M47J66 1780a.

MC | *Didone abbandonata* (1724–1832)

(8) Stuttgart: Cotta, [1782] (It./Fr.)[157]
D-As 4 H 159; D-Mth 001/8 18762 [1]; D-MHrm T 324;[158] D-ROu LBN 200; F-Pn 8-RA6-245; RUS-SPsc Rossica 13.21.5.15; US-Cn BLC #260b1

Music sources
1st version: 1747, Rome

[complete scores] D-Dl Mus.3032-F-1[RISM;A]; I-Mc;[159] I-Nc 28.5.6[IC,MGG,NG,RISM,SBN,160]

[excerpts] *Dirò che fida sei* (I-MC 2-D-1/7 [4][RISM]; S-Skma T-SE-R[RISM]); *Fra lo splendor del trono* (D-Dl Mus.3329-J-1 [8][RISM]); *Già si desta la tempesta* (D-MÜs SANT Hs 10 [8][RISM]); *Infelice e sventurato* (D-MÜs SANT Hs 10 [12][RISM]); *Nel duol che prova* (B-Bc 4267[RISM]; D-MÜs SANT Hs 10 [9][RISM]); *Non ha ragione ingrato* (B-Bc 4269[RISM]; B-Bc 5217[RISM]; D-MÜs SANT Hs 10 [10][RISM]; D-MÜs SANT Hs 2270 [13][RISM]; GB-Lbl R.M.23.f.1 [16][RISM]; GB-Lgc G MUS. 427 [17][RISM]; S-Skma T-SE-R[RISM]); *Se il mio cor fra tante pene* (B-Bc 4303[RISM]; D-Mbs Mus.ms. 6314 [15][RISM]; D-MÜs SANT Hs 10 [14][RISM]; D-MÜs SANT Hs 2270 [4][RISM]); *Se resto sul lido* (D-MÜs SANT Hs 10 [13][RISM]); *Son qual fiume che gonfio* (D-MÜs SANT Hs 10 [15][RISM]); *Son regina e sono amante* (B-Bc 5219[RISM]; GB-Lbl R.M.23.f.1 [15][RISM]; GB-Lgc G Mus. 427 [18][RISM]; I-Nc 57.2.4 [7][SBN]; US-BEm MS 326[IC,RISM]); *Tacerò se tu lo brami* (I-Nc 32.2.25 [16][RISM]); *Vedi nel mio perdono* (D-MÜs SANT Hs 10 [11][RISM])

[contrafacta] *Son regina e sono amante* ([*Lauda Sion, salvatorem lauda ducem et pastorem*] D-Mbs Mus.ms. 5044 [3][RISM;P])

2nd version: 1749, Vienna

[complete scores] A-Wn Mus.Hs.18282 [1–3][IC,MGG,NG,161]; D-KNmi J 255 R [1][RISM]; D-LEmi [D-LEu] 8-Mus.31 [1–3][IC]; F-Pn D-6234/6235/6236[BnF,MGG,NG,162]; GB-Cfm [GB-Cu] MU.MS.773[IC,MGG,NG]; H-Bn Ms.mus IV 239[IC]; US-Wc M1500.J72 D5[IC,RISM,163]

---

157. Microfilm copy of unspecified physical copy: D-Sl R 18 Met 9.
158. Photocopy: CDN-Lu ML48.M47D54 1782a.
159. Microfilm copies: US-CHH 55-M1242; US-Eu Film 19992.
160. [MGG] and [NG] list a further complete source in I-Mc, which we have not found in [IC]. It might correspond to the excerpts we list as undated.
161. It contains an aria by Wagenseil (*Cadrà fra poco in cenere*). Microfilm copy: US-PRu MICROFILM 2401.
162. Microfilm copies: US-BEm MICROFILM A1191 M; US-CHH 55-M1249; US-Eu Film 20185; US-STum M/F 180.
163. Transcript of A-Wn Mus.Hs. 18282 [1–3].

MC | *Didone abbandonata* (1724–1832)

[excerpts] *Ah, non lasciarmi, no* (D-Dl Mus.3032-F-4 [13]^{MGG,RISM}; I-Nc 33.2.28 [25]^{SBN}; J-Tk S11-277-5 [2]^{RISM}); *Ah, non sai bella Selene*[164] (GB-Lbl R.M.22.f.8 [12]^{RISM}; I-MC 3-C-3 [4]^{RISM}; I-Nc 33.2.28 [18]^{SBN}); *Ardi per me fedele* (I-Nc 33.2.28 [27]^{SBN}); *A trionfar mi chiama* (I-Nc 33.2.28 [19]^{SBN}); *Fosca nube il sol ricopra* (D-Mbs Mus.ms. 1059 [1]^{RISM}; I-Nc 33.2.32 [11]^{SBN}; S-Skma T-SE-R^{RISM;R}); *Nel duol che prova* (I-Mc Noseda I.160 [3]^{SBN}); *Se resto sul lido* (I-Nc 33.2.24 [24]^{SBN}); *Son qual fiume che gonfio d'umori* (I-Nc 33.2.24 [2]^{SBN}); *Son regina e sono amante* (I-Nc 33.2.24 [10]^{SBN,165}); *Tormento il più crudele* (I-Nc 33.2.25 [19]^{SBN})

3rd version: 1763, Stuttgart

[complete scores][166] A-Wn* Mus.Hs.16488^{IC,MGG,NG}; D-B Mus.ms 11246^{IC,MGG,NG,RISM}; D-Sl HB XVII 242 [a–c]^{MGG,NG,RISM,167}

[excerpts] *Dirò che fida sei* (I-Bc GG.70 [12]^{IC,RISM,SBN}); *Son regina e sono amante* (B-Bc 4314^{RISM}; D-KNmi J 255 R [4]^{RISM})

[undated]

[excertps] *Cadrà fra poco in cenere* (B-Bc 4233^{RISM,168}); *Dirò che fida sei* (F-Pn D-14665 [1]^{BnF}; I-Mc Noseda M.22 [3]^{SBN}); *Nel duol che prova* (I-Mc Noseda M.22 [12]^{SBN}; I-Nc 33.2.30 [14]^{SBN,169}; I-Nc 33.2.30 [22]^{SBN}); *Son regina e sono amante* (I-Mc Noseda M.22 [10]^{SBN}); *Tacerò se tu lo brami* (I-Mc Noseda M.22 [9]^{SBN})

1747	mus. by Adolfati, Andrea
1747 Venice	Teatro di S. Girolamo (carn., 19/02/1747)[170]
Librettos	Venice: Pavini, 1747
	F-Pn 8-YTH-52346; GB-Cu Bute.121; I-Mb Racc.dramm.0337; I-Rsc Carv.4380; I-Vcg LIBRETTI MURANO 241–243; I-Vgc ROL.0392 [2][171]; I-Vnm DRAMM.1067 [9]; I-Vnm DRAMM.1263 [8]; I-Vnm DRAMM.3722 [4]; US-Cn ML50.2.D473 A36 1747; US-Wc ML48 [S57]

---

164. This aria was included in neither the libretto nor the full score of the premiere (A-Wn Mus.Hs.18282 or D-Dl Mus.3032-F-1). However, the following sources clearly state the city, the date, and the premiering singer (Caffarelli), which may indicate that it was a late insertion for the sake of the castrato's on-stage importance.
165. Apparently performed in Vienna in 1754. In a different key from the original.
166. Microfilm copy of unspecified manuscript: US-CHum Micfilm 7446.
167. For Stuttgart 1777.
168. B-Bc 4233 and I-Mc Noseda M.22 [3]: probably from the 1747 version. No collation with other sources has been possible.
169. This and the following two sources: from 1747 or 1749; we had no access to the score or its incipit.
170. Performed with puppets; see ^{NG} 'Adolfati, Andrea' and Selfridge-Field, Eleanor *A New Chronology of Venetian Opera and Related Genres, 1660–1760* (Stanford: Stanford University Press, 2007).
171. Photocopy: I-Vgc PF.

MC | *Didone abbandonata* (1724–1832)

Music sources	[excerpts] *Non ha ragione ingrato* (US-CHH VFM3.1.A36150z [10][MGG,RISM])
1748	**mus. by Bertoni, Ferdinando[172]**
1748 Venice[173]	Teatro di S. Girolamo (carn., c. 22/02/1748)
Librettos	Venice: Pavini, 1748 F-Pn 8-YTH-52346; GB-Cu Bute.121; I-Fm Mel.2158 [1]; I-Rsc Carv.4381; I-Vnm DRAMM.1069 [7]; I-Vnm DRAMM.1264 [4]; I-Vnm DRAMM.3722 [5]
Music sources	[excerpts][174] *Son quel fiume che gonfio d'umori* (I-VId U. 3[RISM;P]); *Son regina e sono amante* (I-PAc Sanv.A.117[NG,RISM,SBN]); *Va crescendo il mio tormento*[175] (HR-Sk LIV/677[RISM]; I-BGc B.II.1[RISM,SBN]; US-R n/s[IC,RISM]) [inserts] *Non ho pace, non trovo respiro*[176] (I-Fn MS MUS 1268[SBN])
1748	**mus. by unknown composer(s)**
1748 Genoa	Teatro del Falcone (carn.)
Librettos	Genoa: Franchelli, [1748] F-Pn 8-YTH-50189; I-PAp BB XI.25664
1748	**mus. by Chiarini, Pietro**
1748 Brescia	Teatro degli Erranti (1)
1756 Cremona	Private theatre (carn.) (2)
Librettos	(1) Brescia: Vendramino, 1748 F-Pn LIV IT-1634; I-Ma S. I. H. III. 8 [1]; I-Vc 1057; US-BEm ML50.2.D5 C5 (2) Cremona: Ricchini, [1756] I-Rsc Carv.4385

---

172. Performed with puppets; see Selfridge-Field, *A New Chronology of Venetian Opera*, p. 625.
173. According to [NG], premiered in 1748; see [NG] 'Metastasio'. Not clear if the music materials by Bertoni belong to this production or to the pasticcio in which he participated together with Rampini and Naumann in 1790 in Venice.
174. The arias were included in the pasticcio performed in Venice in 1790 with music by Bertoni, Rampini, and Naumann → see 1790, mus. by Bertoni, Ferdinando; Rampini, Vincenzo; Naumann, Johann Gottlieb; and Gazzaniga, Giuseppe. We cannot ascertain that there are the same music Bertoni used for his 1748 *Didone abbandonata*. The music for *Va crescendo il mio tormento* in HR-Sk LIV/677 does not coincide with that in US-R.
175. Although the text belongs to Metastasio's *Didone abbandonata*, this aria was included in Bertoni's revival of *Quinto Fabio* (A1-S3) in Padua in 1778. We cannot ascertain that it was first used in the composer's *Didone abbandonata*, or that it is by Bertoni himself. It does not coincide with the music in HR-Sk LIV/677.
176. Inserted into Bertoni's *Artaserse* (Forlì, 1776).

MC | *Didone abbandonata* (1724–1832)

1749	mus. by Jommelli, Niccolò (2nd version) → see 1747	

1750	mus. by Terradellas, Domingo Miguel Bernabé	
1750 Turin	Teatro Regio (carn., 17/01/1750)[177]	
Librettos	Turin: Zappata & son, [1750] I-NOVa Biblioteca Teatro Coccia 95 [1]; I-Rsc Vol. Carv.143 [6]; I-Tac Simeom L 41; I-Tci L.O.0135; I-Tn F VII.357 [4]; <u>I-Tn F XIII.487 [1]</u>; I-Tstrona^S; US-BEm ML48 .C65; US-Wc ML48.A5 [4]; <u>US-Wc ML48 [S10285]</u>	
Music sources	[excerpts] *A trionfar mi chiama* (I-Rsc G.Mss.15 [18]^MGG,NG,RISM,SBN); *Cadrà fra poco in cenere* (I-Rsc G.Mss.15 [19]^NG,RISM,SBN); *Cara, partir degg'io* ([*Cara tra i dolci amplessi*] D-Sla 112^RISM;P,178; I-Rsc G.Mss.15 [17]^MGG,NG,RISM,SBN); *Dirò che fida sei* (I-Rsc G.Mss.15 [10]^MGG,NG,RISM,SBN); *Infelice e sventurato* (I-Rsc G.Mss.15 [13]^MGG,NG,RISM,SBN); *La bella sua calma* (I-Rsc G.Mss.15 [15]^MGG,NG,RISM,SBN); *L'augelletto in lacci stretto* (I-Rsc G.Mss.15 [16]^MGG,NG,RISM,SBN); *Non ha ragione ingrato* (I-Rsc G.Mss.15 [14]^MGG,NG,RISM,SBN); *Se dalle stelle tu non sei guida* (I-Rsc G.Mss.15 [12]^MGG,NG,RISM,SBN); *Son regina e sono amante* (I-Rsc G.Mss.15 [11]^MGG,NG,RISM,SBN)	

1751	mus. by Manna, Gennaro	
1751 Venice	Teatro Grimani di S. Giovanni Grisostomo (carn., 30/01/1751)	
Librettos	Venice: [s.n.],[179] [1751] I-Fm Mel.2183 [3]; I-Ria MISC. Teatrale 7 [4]; I-Rsc Carv.4382; I-Vcg S.GIO.GRISOSTOMO 160; I-Vnm DRAMM.1073 [5]; I-Vnm DRAMM.1269 [2]; US-CAh *IC7 A100 B750 [39]; US-LAum ML48 .R114 1751 [7]; <u>US-Wc ML48 [S5901]</u>	
Music sources	[complete scores] D-Hs^MGG,NG,180; D-MÜs SANT Hs 2469^MGG,NG,RISM [excerpts] *Ah, non lasciarmi, no* (I-MC 3-E-22 [15]^RISM,181); *Ah, non sai bella Selene* (I-VEas Malaspina ms.n.68^RISM,SBN; I-MC 3-E-22 [1]^RISM; S-Skma	

---

177. The production ran for twenty-two consecutive performances; see Bouquet, Marie-Thérèse, Valeria Gualerzi, and Alberto Testa, *Storia del Teatro Regio di Torino: cronologie*, ed. by Alberto Basso (Turin: Cassa di Risparmio di Torino, [1988]).
178. The aria is included with the text 'Cara partir degg'io' in Terradellas' *Didone abbandonata* (A2-S8).
179. 'In Merceria all'insegna della Scienza'.
180. Doubtful; not found in ^RISM.
181. Author identified in ^RISM as Manna, Giuseppe.

MC | *Didone abbandonata* (1724–1832)

T-SE-R[RISM]; US-BEm MS 26 [4][IC,RISM,182]; *A trionfar mi chiama* (A-Wn Mus.Hs.10458[IC]; D-KA Don Mus.Ms. 125[RISM]; <u>D-KA Don Mus.Ms. 1924</u>[RISM;P]; I-PEsf n/s[SBN]); *Dovrei… ma no* (D-MÜs SANT Hs 2469[RISM]); *Non ha ragione ingrato* (US-NYp* Mus. Res. MP (Italian) [35][RISM])

1751	mus. by Fiorillo, Ignazio
1751 Brunswick	Teatro Ducale (win. Fair)
Librettos	Brunswick: heirs of Keitel, [1751] (It./Ger.) D-HVs Op. 1, 210;[183] <u>US-Wc ML48 [S3200]</u>
Music sources	[complete scores] D-Wa* 46 Alt 10[MGG,NG,RISM]
	[excerpts] *Ah, non lasciarmi, no* (D-W Cod. Guelf. 314 Mus. Hdschr. [11][RISM;P]); *Chiamami pur così* (D-W Cod. Guelf. 314 Mus. Hdschr. [13][RISM;P]); *Dirò che fida sei* (D-W Cod. Guelf. 314 Mus. Hdschr. [18][RISM;P]); *Non ha ragione ingrato* (D-W Cod. Guelf. 314 Mus. Hdschr. [17][RISM;P]); *Quando l'onda che nasce dal monte* (D-W Cod. Guelf. 314 Mus. Hdschr. [15][RISM;P]); *Son regina e sono amante* (D-W Cod. Guelf. 314 Mus. Hdschr. [14][RISM;P]); *Tacerò se tu lo brami* (D-W Cod. Guelf. 314 Mus. Hdschr. [12][RISM;P]); *Va lusingando amore* (D-W Cod. Guelf. 314 Mus. Hdschr. [16][RISM;P])

1751	mus. by Perez, Davide	
1751 Genoa[NG]	NA	(1)
1752 Reggio Emilia	Teatro Pubblico (Fair, 29/04/1752)	(2)
1753 Lisbon	Court theatre – Palácio de Salvaterra de Magos (carn.)	(3)
1755 Mantua	Teatro Arciducale (carn.) *pasticcio*[184]	(4)
1757 Faenza	Teatro dei Remoti (carn.)	(5)
1761 London	King's Theatre in the Haymarket (14/03/1761) mus. by D. Perez and B. Galuppi[185]	(6)
1765 Lisbon	Teatro do Bairro Alto (summ.)[186]	(7)

182. Misattributed to Perez on the source.
183. Microfilm copies: D-HVl MASTER 512; D-HVl Mifi 2765.
184. See <https://www.pasticcio-project.eu/database/work/P104217> [accessed 25 May 2022].
185. Burden, 'Metastasio on the London Stage', p. 156 and 'The King's Theatre in London, 1705–1820', in *The Oxford Handbook of the Operatic Canon*, ed. by Cormac Newark and William Weber (New York: Oxford University Press, 2020), pp. 151–30. The production ran for ten consecutive performances; see Petty, Fred Curtis, 'Italian Opera in London, 1760–1800' (doctoral dissertation, Yale University, 1971).
186. According to [NG], some arias were by Avondano; see [NG] 'Avondano, Pedro Antonio'. [C] mentions Perez among the various composers.

MC | *Didone abbandonata* (1724–1832)

Librettos (1) NA

(2) Reggio Emilia: Vedrotti & Davolio, [1752]
D-Mbs L.eleg.m. 3876; I-Mb Racc.dramm.4511; I-MOe 70.I.31 [2]; I-Rsc Libr. n. XVI [50]; I-REm 19.K.119

(3) Lisbon: Sylviana, 1753
I-PAc F. Libretti, sc.III [105]; I-Rsc Carv.4383; P-Ln 5747

(4) Mantua: heirs of Pazzoni, 1755
I-MAc Misc.476/8

(5) Faenza: Archi, 1757
I-FZc RM.N.I.37

(6) London: Woodfall, 1761 (It./En.)[187]
GB-Lbl 11714.aa.21 [3];[188] GB-Oas BX.3.9 [2]; GB-Ob Vet. A5 e.2256 [1];[189] US-CAt TS 8154.428 1761

(7) Lisbon: [s.n., 1765] (It./Port.)
I-Rsc Carv.4362; P-Ln M. 1504 P.

Music sources [complete scores] I-Vnm Mss. 9785/9786/9787[MGG,NG,SBN,190]; P-La 45-V-26/27/28[BA]; P-La* 45-V-48/49[BA,MGG,NG]; S-Skma T-R[MGG,NG,RISM]; US-Wc M1503.P434 D5[IC,MGG,NG,RISM,191]

[excerpts] *Ah, non lasciarmi, no* (A-Wgm VI 15353 [Q 3370][IC]; B-Bc 5177[RISM,192]; D-B N-.Mus. BP 745[GVK]; D-Mbs Mus.ms. 180 [1][RISM,193]; I-MC 6-E-9 [8][RISM]; I-Nc 34.613 [14][SBN]; I-Nc 34.613 [39][SBN]; I-Nc 51.2.51 [1][SBN]; I-Nc 57.2.3 [2][SBN]; I-PAc Sanv.A.181 [1–8][SBN;IP]; I-VEcon MS 308[RISM,SBN]; J-Tk S10-934-3 [3][RISM]; P-La 54-II-71 [71–73][BA;P]; US-SFsc *M2.1 M391[RISM]); *Ah, se dagli occhi tuoi* (D-LÜh Mus. Q 270[RISM]; GB-Lbl R.M.23.e.9 [2][MGG,RISM,194]); *Infelice abbandonata* (A-Wgm VI 6746 [Q 3957][IC]; D-Mbs Mus.ms. 254 [9][RISM]; D-W Cod. Guelf. 314 Mus. Hdschr.[32][RISM;R]; J-Tk S10-613-5 [5][RISM,195]; P-La 54-II-71 [74–80][BA;IP];

---

187. S7820 claims there is another copy in the Hicke private library in London.
188. Microfilm copies: D-Gs MA 89-24:5345 [23]; GB-En Mf.134, reel 5345 [23].
189. Microfilm copy: GB-Ob Films ESTC 18th C., reel 5345 [23].
190. This and the following three sources: for Lisbon 1753.
191. Not totally similar to the 1753 version; perhaps corresponding to the 1751 premiere.
192. Probably for Reggio Emilia 1752.
193. B-Bc 4603; D-Mbs Mus.ms. 180 [1]; D-Mbs Mus.ms. 180 [13]; GB-Lbl R.M.23.d.19 [10]; I-Nc 34.613 [39]; I-VEcon MS 308: for Reggio Emilia 1752.
194. According to the inscription on the source, it was performed in 1752 in Reggio Emilia. As no libretto for the 1751 premiere has been preserved, and as the duet did not appear in the 1753 version, Perez's authorship cannot be ascertained.
195. B-Bc 4603; J-Tk S10-613-5 [5]; P-La 54-II-71 [63–67]; P-La 54-II-71 [68–70]; P-La 54-II-71 [74–80]; P-La 54-II-71 [81–83]: for Lisbon 1753.

S-Skma Alströmer saml. 163 [6]^{RISM}; S-Skma T-SE-R^{RISM}; US-BEm MS 98 [2]^{IC,RISM}); *Non ha ragione ingrato* (P-La 54-II-71 [68–70]$^{BA;IP}$; US-SFsc *M2.1 M387^{RISM}; US-SFsc *M2.1 M392^{RISM}); *Quando saprai chi sono* (D-Mbs Mus.ms. 988 [8]^{RISM}; GB-Lbl R.M.23.e.3 [10]^{MGG,RISM}); *Se resto sul lido* (US-SFsc *M2.1 M393^{RISM}); *Son regina e sono amante* (B-Bc 5178^{RISM}; D-SWl Mus.4172^{RISM,196}; P-La 54-II-71 [63–67]$^{BA;IP}$); *Teneri affetti miei* (P-La 54-II-71 [81–83]$^{BA;IP}$); *Tu mi disarmi il fianco* (D-Mbs Mus.ms. 180 [13]^{RISM}; GB-Lbl R.M.23.d.19 [10]^{MGG,NG,RISM}); *Va crescendo il mio tormento* (B-Bc 5179^{RISM}; B-Bc 4603^{RISM}; D-Mbs Mus. ms. 10419$^{RISM;P}$); *Va lusingando amore* (B-Bc 4604^{RISM,197}); *Vado… ma dove?… oh dio!* (S-Skma T-SE-R^{RISM}; US-SFsc *M2.1 M390^{RISM})

[parodies] *Ah, non lasciarmi, no* ([*Ah, non lasciarmi bell'idol mio*] F-Pn VM7-7289^{RISM,198})

[printed sources] *Ah, non lasciarmi, no* [2]; *Va crescendo il mio tormento* [4]; *Son regina e sono amante* [5], in <u>The Favourite Songs in the Opera call'd La Didone abbandonata</u> (London: Walsh, 1761); *Ah, non lasciarmi, no*, in *Alla Sig. Maria Colomba Mattei […] 1752 a la parte di Didone abbandonata* ([s.l.: s.n., s.d.])

[inserts]

[London, 1761] Galuppi, Baldassare?, *Come potessi, oh Dio!* [3]; *Se non ti moro allato* [1], in <u>The Favourite Songs in the Opera call'd La Didone abbandonata</u> (London: Walsh, 1761)

[Lisbon, 1765] Avondano, Pedro António, *Ah, non lasciarmi, no* (F-Pn MS-63 [2]^{BnF}); *Ah non sai bella Selene* (J-Tk S10-934 [1]^{RISM})

1752	mus. by Poncini Zilioli, Francesco
1752 Livorno	Teatro da S. Sebastiano (carn.)
Librettos	Livorno: Fantechi & co., 1752
	<u>CDN-Ttfl Itp Pam 00765</u>; <u>I-Bc Lo.04313</u>^{199}
1752	mus. by Scolari, Giuseppe
1752 Barcelona	Teatre de la Santa Creu (30/05/1752) (1)
	birthday of Fernando VI, king of Spain

---

196. In C major instead of D major.
197. The aria is not included in the librettos from the 1752, 1753, and 1761 performances.
198. Wrongly attributed to Graun. Microfilm copy: F-Pn VM BOB-14289.
199. Pages 9–10 missing.

MC | *Didone abbandonata* (1724–1832)

1753 Barcelona	Teatre de la Santa Creu (10/1753)	(2)
1763 Ferrara	Teatro Bonacossi [da S. Stefano] (carn.)	(3)
1763 Barcelona	Teatre de la Santa Creu (04/11/1763)[200]	(4)
	name day of Carlos III, king of Spain	

Librettos (1) Barcelona: [s.n.], 1752 (It./Spa.)[201]

(2) Barcelona: Campins, [1753] (It./Spa.)
E-Bbc C400/235; E-Mn T/22340; I-Bc Lo.06211

(3) Ferrara: Fornari, [1763]
I-Vgc ROL.0611 [4]; US-Wc ML48 [S9806]

(4) Barcelona: Generas, [1763] (It./Spa.)
E-Bcapdevilla 850 Met; E-Bu 07 XVIII-3210

Music sources [excerpts] *A trionfar mi chiama* (I-MC 6-A-3/6[RISM]); *Se dalle stelle tu non sei guida* (US-BEm MS 98 [5][IC;RISM])

1752 mus. by Galuppi, Baldassare (rev. version) → see 1741

1752 mus. by Bonno, Giuseppe
1752 Vienna[NG] NA[NP]

1753 mus. by Mazzoni, Antonio Maria

1753 Bologna	Teatro Formagliari (carn.)	(1)
1761 Prague	Teatro Nuovo (carn.)	(2)

Librettos (1) Bologna: successors of Benacci [i.e., Sassi], [1752]
I-Bc Lo.03032; I-Bc Lo.09724

(2) [Prague]: Pruscha, [1761]
A-Wn 407379-A; CZ-Pnm B 4117; CZ-Pu 65 E 2972; D-Hs A/23802

Music sources [excerpts] *Ah, non lasciarmi, no* (I-CHf [I-CHc] C 7 [2][RISM]); *Se resto sul lido* (I-CHf [I-CHc] C 7 [4][RISM]; I-CHf [I-CHc] C 7 [4][SBN]); *Son regina e sono amante* (I-CHf [I-CHc] C 7 [3][RISM]); *Vado... ma dove?... oh dio!*[202] (I-MAav* Cart.7 n.34[RISM;IP])

---

200. Alier y Aixalà, Roger, *L'òpera a Barcelona: orígens, desenvolupament i consolidació de l'òpera com a espectacle teatral a la Barcelona del segle XVIII* (Barcelona: Institut d'Estudis Catalans, 1990).
201. Cotarelo y Mori, Emilio, *Orígenes y establecimiento de la ópera en España hasta 1800* (Madrid, Revista de arch., bibl. y museos, 1917).
202. This aria was inserted into A. Mazzoni's setting of *Demofoonte* (Parma, 1754), sung by the character of Timante in A2-S6.

MC | *Didone abbandonata* (1724–1832)

1753	mus. by Lampugnani, Giovanni Battista (2nd version) → see 1739

1753	mus. by unknown composer(s)	
1753 Pavia	Teatro Omodeo (carn.)	
Librettos	Milan: Ghislandi, [1753]	
	I-LDEsormani^{C,S,203}	

1754	mus. by Ciampi, Vincenzo Legrenzio	
1754 London	King's Theatre in the Haymarket (05/01/1754)	(1)
1754 London	King's Theatre in the Haymarket (03/04/1754)^{CA}	(1)

Librettos (1) London: Woodfall, 1754 (It./En.)
GB-Lbl 11715.g.13 [1];[204] PL-Wu GSD 28.20.4.3849 [1][205]

Music sources [excerpts] *Ah, non lasciarmi, no* (B-Bc 5171^{RISM;R}); *Non ha ragione ingrato* (B-Bc 5172^{RISM;R}); *Ogni amator suppone* (D-MÜs SANT Hs 184 [14]^{RISM}); *Se resto sul lido* (B-Bc 5173^{RISM;R}); *Vado… ma dove?… oh dio!* (D-MÜs SANT Hs 184 [16]^{RISM}); *Veggio la sponda* (B-Bc 5174^{RISM})

[printed sources] unspecified aria, in *Air de Didone abbandonata* ([s.l.: s.n., s.d.]); *Ah, non lasciarmi, no* [1]; *Nel duol she prova* [3]; *Non ha ragione ingrato* [4]; *Se resto sul lido* [2]; *Veggio la sponda* [5], in *The Favourite Songs in the Opera call'd Didone* (London: Walsh, [1754]); *Nel duol che prova*, in *Airs in the Opera of Didone* (London: Lonsdale, [s.d.])

Didone abbandonata, in *Poesie del signor abate Pietro Metastasio* (Paris: widow of Quillau, 1755), vol. 2, pp. 307–403.

1755	mus. by Fioroni, Giovanni Andrea	
1755 Milan	Teatro Regio Ducale (carn., 18/01/1755)	(1)

Librettos Milan: Malatesta, 1755
B-Bc 19905; F-Pn LIV IT-3524 [2]; I-Bc Lo.01738; I-LDEsormani 309/2/11; I-Ma S. I. H. I. 7 [7]; I-Mb Racc.dramm.6076 [4]; I-Nragni L095; US-Cn BLC #754; US-Wc ML48 [S3206]

---

203. Lost?; not found in the library or in its Excel catalogue.
204. Microfilm copy: GB-En Mf.134, reel 10234 [10].
205. Attributed to P. Anfossi in the card catalogue of P-Wu.

MC | *Didone abbandonata* (1724–1832)

Music sources	[excerpts] *Cadrà fra poco in cenere* (F-Pn D-15157[BnF,RISM])
	[contrafacta] *Ardi per me fedele* ([*Veni o sponse care*] CH-E 464,7[RISM;P]); *Chiamami pur così* ([*Quid cupis cor bonum forsam hic caro est*] CH-SAf MusSaf.Ms.632[RISM;P])
1755	mus. by unknown composer(s)
1755 Verona	Teatro Filarmonico (carn.)
Librettos	Verona: Saracco, [1755]
	I-Rsc Carv.4384; US-CAt TS 8154.236 1755
1756	mus. by Bernasconi, Andrea (2nd version) → see 1741

Didone abbandonata, in *Poesie del signor abate Pietro Metastasio* (Turin: Stamperia Reale, 1757), vol. 2, pp. 293–382.

1757	mus. by Traetta, Tommaso	
1757 Venice	Teatro Giustiniani di S. Moisè (aut.)	(1)
	1st version	
1759 Pavia	Teatro Omodeo (carn.)	(2)
1763 Milan	Teatro Regio Ducale (carn.)	(3)
	2nd version	
1764 Naples	Teatro di S. Carlo (20/01/1764)	(4)
	birthday of Carlos III, king of Spain	
	3rd version, with a prologue by Majo	
Librettos	(1) Venice: Fenzo, [1757]
	I-GOl COR/07/0273; I-Mb Racc.dramm.0548; I-Ria MISC. Teatrale 4 [1]; I-Vnm DRAMM.1079 [10]; I-Vnm DRAMM.1278 [4]; US-LAum ML48 .R114 1757 [10]; US-Wc ML48 [S10402]
	(2) Milan: Ghislandi, [1759]
	I-LDEsormani 314/3/11
	(3) Milan: Malatesta, 1763
	F-Pn LIV IT-3527 [2]; I-Bc Lo.05339; I-LDEsormani 309/3/18; I-Ma S. I. H. I. 10 [1]; I-Mc Coll.Libr.133; I-Nc Rari 8.16.1; I-Rn 40.9.D.16.6;[206] I-Rsc Vol. 9 [10]
	(4) Naples: Flauto, 1764
	US-NYp Mus. Res. *MZ, A/27 [11]

---

206. Mutilated on the first [12] and the last pages.

MC | *Didone abbandonata* (1724–1832)

Music sources

1st version: 1757, Venice

[complete scores] D-B Mus.ms. 2002[NG,RISM] [Act I]

[excerpts] *Ah, non lasciarmi, no* (US-SFsc *M2.1 M496[RISM]); *Dovrei… ma no* (S-Skma T-SE-R[RISM]); *Prendi l'estremo addio* (CH-Bu kr IV 355[RISM;P]; D-B Mus.ms. 19178 [27][RISM;IP]; D-KNmi IV, 19R[RISM]; D-MGmi HA IV 141[RISM]; I-MAav Cart.4 n.11 [11][RISM]; US-Wc M1505.A2 T79[RISM]); *Quando saprai chi sono* (I-MAav Cart.9 n.20[RISM;P]; I-MC 6-A-20 [11][RISM]; I-Tf 2 IV 19 [21][RISM]); *Son regina e sono amante* (A-Wn Mus. Hs.10773[IC]; B-Bc 5194[RISM]; S-Skma T-SE-R[RISM])

2nd version: 1763, Milan

[complete scores] F-Pn D-13729[BnF,NG,207]; I-Nc R.8.8/9/10[IC,MGG,NG,SBN; A,208]; P-La 46-VI-38/36/40[BA,NG]; P-La 54-I-54/55/56[BA,NG]

[excerpts] *Ah, non lasciarmi, no*[209] (I-Mc Mus. Tr.ms. 1284[RISM,SBN]); *Ah non sai bella Selene* (I-MC 6-A-17/2 [4][RISM]); *Cadrà fra poco in cenere* (I-Mc Mus. Tr.ms. 1285[RISM,SBN]; I-MC 6-A-17/2 [3][RISM]); *Dirò che fida sei* (B-Bc 4912[RISM]; I-MC 6-A-17/2 [1][RISM]); *Già si desta la tempesta* (I-MC 6-A-17/2 [2][RISM]); *In tanto tormento* (D-GOl Mus. 2° 52b [6][RISM;R]; D-Sla 92[RISM;P]; D-SWl Mus.5454[RISM;P]; I-Mc Mus. Tr.ms. 1280[RISM;P]; S-Skma T-SE-R[RISM]); *Nel duol che prova* (I-Mc Noseda Q.26 [9][SBN]); *Quando saprai chi sono* (I-Mc Mus. Tr.ms. 1282[RISM,SBN]; I-MC 6-A-19/2 [1][RISM]); *Son regina e sono amante* (I-Gl B C.3.23 [6][IC,SBN]; I-Mc Mus. Tr.ms. 1287[RISM,SBN]; I-MC 6-A-19 [4][RISM]; I-Nc 34.5.21 [15][SBN]; I-Nc Arie 599 [9][SBN]); *Vado… ma dove?… oh dio!* (D-KNmi III, 68 R[RISM])

[unspecified] F-Pn MS-9798[BnF]

3rd version: 1764, Naples

[complete scores] P-La 46-VI-35/36/37[BA,NG]; US-Wc M1500.T76 D4[NG,RISM]

1758	mus. by Zoppis, Francesco
1758 St Petersburg	Court theatre – Winter Palace (25/11/1758)
	coronation of Elizaveta Petrovna Romanova, empress of Russia
Librettos	St Petersburg: Imperial Academy of the Sciences, 1758
	RUS-SPsc Rossica 13.16.9.67

---

207. Microfilm copy: F-Pn VM BOB-23122.
208. [RISM] lists another source from I-Nc (I-Nc Rari 7.9.20/21/22), yet it could not be found in [SBN].
209. This aria and *Cadrà fra poco in cenere* are the same as in the 1757 version but in a different key.

MC | *Didone abbandonata* (1724–1832)

Music sources	[excerpts] *Ah, non lasciarmi, no* (I-OS Mss.Mus.B 1337[RISM]); *Tu mi scorgi al gran disegno* (S-Skma T-SE-R[RISM]); *Vivi superbo e regna* (D-Dl Mus.1-F-82,37 [9][RISM])

1759	**mus. by Brunetti, Giuseppe**
1759 Siena	Teatro degli Intronati (carn.)
Librettos	Siena: Rossi, [1759]
	I-Rsc Libr. n. XVI [51]

1759	**mus. attributed to Auletta, Pietro Antonio**[210]
1759 Florence	Teatro della Pergola (26/08/1759)
	orchestra conducted by G. Brunetti, who also composed some of the arias
Librettos	Florence: Stamperia dirimpetto all'Oratorio di S. Filippo Neri, [1759]
	I-Bc Lo.06212; I-Fc E.V.1418; I-Fc E.V.1746; I-Fn B.17.6.272.1.2; I-PS BM.257 [9]
Music sources	[complete scores] I-Fc D.I.55/56/57[NG,RISM,SBN]

1760	**mus. by various unknown composers**
1760 Verona	Teatro Filarmonico (carn.)
Librettos	Verona: Ramanzini, [1760]
	I-VEc D.381 [8][211]

1760	**mus. by Ferradini, Antonio**
1760 Lucca	Teatro Pubblico (23/08/1760)
Librettos	Lucca: Benedini, 1760
	I-Fm Mel.2045 [1]
Music sources	[complete scores] P-La 44-VI-15/16/17[BA,MGG,NG]; P-La 47-VI-22/23/24[BA,MGG,NG]

---

210. [C,S] mention Giuseppe Brunetti as the composer of some of the arias; see [S]Index I, p. 359. On the libretto: 'La Direzione della Musica è del Sig. Giuseppe Brunetti, Maestro di Capella Napoletano, e l'Arie con questo segno * sono di sua composizione'.
211. Microfilm copy: CDN-Lu ML48.M47T38 1787a.

MC | *Didone abbandonata* (1724–1832)

1762	mus. by Sarti, Giuseppe	
1762 Copenhagen	Royal Danish Theatre (12/1762)[212]	(1)
	Den forladte Dido	
	1st version	
1771 Copenhagen	Royal Danish Theatre (spr.)	(2)
1782 Padua	Teatro Nuovo (Fair, 12/06/1782)	(3)
	2nd version	
1784 Esterháza	Court theatre	(4)
1786 Lucca	Teatro Pubblico (05/08/1786)	(5)
1792 Madrid	Teatro de los Caños del Peral	(6)
	birthday of Maria Luisa, queen of Spain	
	mus. by G. Sarti and G. Paisiello	
1793 Mantua	Teatro Arciducale (carn., 26/12/1792)	(7)

Librettos

(1) Copenhagen: Svare, [1762] (It./Dan.)
DK-Kk 56,-370; I-Vnm DRAMM.1121 [4]; US-Wc ML48 [S9432]

(2) Copenhagen: [s.n., 1771] (It./Dan.)
DK-Ku [DK-Kk] Rom. 12300 8°

(3) Padua: Conzatti, [1782]
I-Pci B.P. 2577. XIII; I-Pmc^{C,S,213}

(4) Oldenburg: Siess, [1784]
CZ^{S,214}; H-Bn 208.421

(5) Lucca: Bonsignori, [1786][215]
CDN-Tcfl Itp Pam 00973; I-La Dono Pellegrini – Libretti d'opera, 40; I-Lg B.ta 203 [1]; I-Nragni L119; I-REt TE Lib 0304; I-Vgc ROL.0600 [9];[216] US-AAu ML 50.2 .D564 S25; US-AUS KL-17 238; US-Cn ML50.2.D47 S27 1786; US-CAt TS 8154.598 1786 [B]; US-PRV n/s

---

212. Jensen, Niels Martin, 'Giuseppe Sarti: attività danese e manoscritti sopravvissuti', in *Giuseppe Sarti musicista faentino: Atti del convegno internazionale*, ed. by Mario Baroni and Maria Gioia Tavoni (Modena: Mucchi, 1986), pp. 159–65. For a study of the socioeconomic conditions around Sarti's *Didone*, see Venturi, Simonetta, 'Il periodo danese di Giuseppe Sarti e la "Didone abbandonata"', *Studi e documentazioni: Rivista umbra di musicologia*, 15.1 (2007), 23–38. For a discussion of the costumes used in Sarti's Danish productions and the translations into the vernacular tongue, see, respectively, Jeanneret, Christine, 'Costumes and Cosmopolitanism: Italian Opera in the North', *Cambridge Opera Journal*, 21.1 (2020), 27–51; 'Made in Italy, Tailored for Danes: Giuseppe Sarti and Italian Opera in Copenhagen', *Music & Letters*, 102.2 (2021), 271–93.
213. The library was closed at the time of preparation of this volume and, therefore, we could not check its holdings.
214. One copy in the library of the Radenín palace in the Czech Republic [Radenin zamecke knihovna].
215. According to ^{S}7856, there was a copy of this libretto in I-FPfanan (previously in Turin); see note 71 above.
216. Microfilm copy: CDN-Lu ML48.M47T38 1787a.

MC | *Didone abbandonata* (1724–1832)

(6) Madrid: widow of Ibarra, [1792] (It./Spa.)
E-Bbc C400/292; E-Mn T/24571; I-Nc Rari 15.10.4

(7) Mantua: heirs of Pazzoni, [1793]
I-MAc Misc.360/5;[217] I-OS LIBRETTI 114

Music sources

1st version: 1762, Copenhagen

[complete scores] DK-Kk mu7502.0538[IC,MGG,NG,RISM]

[excerpts] *Fosca nube il sol ricopra* (DK-Kk mu7502.1335[RISM,218]); *Io d'amore, oh dio mi moro* (DK-Sa R320[RISM]; S-Skma T-SE-R[RISM])

2nd version: 1782, Padua[219]

[complete scores] F-Pn D-13729[BnF,MGG,NG]; H-Bn Ms.mus OE-90[IC,MGG,NG]; I-Pl ATVa 12 [I-III][MGG,NG,RISM,SBN;P,220]; P-La 46-IV-15/16/17[BA,MGG,NG]

[excerpts] *Ah, non lasciarmi, no* (D-B Mus.ms. 19503/5[RISM]; I-Vc Correr Busta 5.18[SBN]); *Ah, non sai qual pena sia* (D-Dl Mus.1-F-82,27 [11][RISM]; D-Hs M A/907 [1][RISM]; D-SWl Mus. 186h[RISM;P]; D-WRz Scha Bs Mus Hs 60 [2][GVK]; GB-Lbl Add. 29967[RISM]; I-BGi PREIS.138.1345[SBN]; I-Fc D.IV.427[IC]; I-Mc Noseda Q.12 [6][SBN]; I-MC 5-E-19 [2][RISM]; I-MC 5-F-2 [8][RISM]; I-Nc 57.2.33 [1][SBN]; I-Pca D.IV.1621[SBN]; I-PAc Ms.Tor.72[RISM,SBN]; I-Vc Correr Busta 5.14[SBN]; I-Vc Correr Busta 8.20[SBN]; I-Vnm Mss. 11391[SBN]; US-Eu MSS 992[IC,RISM]; US-Wc M1505.A1 (vol. 241)[RISM]); *Prendi l'estremo addio* (I-Vc Correr Busta 5.15[SBN]); *Quando saprai chi sono* (F-Pn D-14549[BnF,221]; F-Pn D-14907[BnF]; I-OS Mss.Mus.B 2765[RISM,SBN,222]); *Son regina e sono amante* (D-BFb [D-MÜu] S-ar 77[RISM;P,223]); *Vado… ma dove?… oh dio!* (I-Vc Correr Busta 5.19[SBN])

---

217. Photocopy: CDN-Lu ML48.M47G378 1787a.
218. In a different key from Sarti's 1762 original.
219. Sarti's music for this production was possibly included in a pasticcio performed in 1782 in Genoa → see 1782, mus. by Sarti, Cherubini, Anfossi, and Bianchi.
220. Microfilm copy: CDN-Lu M1500.M57S273 1782a.
221. This and the following source were used for the insertion of the aria into Mayr's lyric opera *Che originali — Fedeltà ed amore alla prova* (Turin, 1800).
222. In D major instead of E flat major.
223. In C major instead of B flat major.

MC | *Didone abbandonata* (1724–1832)

[undated]	[excerpts] *Son regina e sono amante* (D-Hs NMC: 5:2a [1]$^{\text{RISM;R}}$)
[unspecified]	[excerpts] In *Journal d'ariettes italiennes*, 252 (Paris: Bailleux, 1782)[224]
[doubtful]	[excerpts] *Son regina e sono amante* (D-Mbs Mus.ms. 10576$^{\text{RISM;P,225}}$); *Va lusingando amore*[226] (D-B Mus.ms. 19508 [9]^{RISM}; D-SWl Mus.4766^{RISM}; S-Skma T-SE-R^{RISM})

1763	mus. by Traetta, Tommaso (2nd version) → see 1757
1763	mus. by Jommelli, Niccolò (3rd version) → see 1747
1764	mus. by Galuppi, Baldassare (2nd version) → see 1741
1764	mus. by Traetta, Tommaso (3rd version) → see 1757

1765	mus. by Schwanenberger, Johann Gottfried
1765 Brunswick	Teatro Ducale (08/1765)
Librettos	[s.l.: s.n., 1765] (It./Ger.)
	D-Wa S. 2537; RUS-Mrg 50-9285813
Music sources	[complete scores] D-Bsa [D-B] SA 1196^{RISM} [Act I]; D-Wa* 46 Alt 323/324/225$^{\text{IC,MGG,RISM}}$
	[excerpts] *Nell'affanno, oh dio, nel pianto* (D-B Mus.ms. 20492/4 [2]^{RISM}); *Son regina e sono amante* (CZ-BER HU 596$^{\text{RISM;P}}$; CZ-BER HU 789$^{\text{RISM;P}}$); *Tacerò se tu lo brami* (D-RH Ms 718^{RISM}); *Va lusingando amore* (B-Bc 4065^{RISM}; <u>D-LB [D-NEhz] La 170 Bü 431</u>$^{\text{IC,RISM}}$; D-RH Ms 715^{RISM}); *Veggio la sponda* (D-RH Ms 717^{RISM}; US-NYp n/s^{IC})
	[unspecified] F-Pn MS-5757^{BnF}

1766	mus. by Zannetti, Francesco	
1766 Livorno	Teatro da S. Sebastiano (carn., 26/12/1765)^{CA}	(1)
1781 Perugia	Teatro Civico del Verzaro (aut.)	(2)
	opening of the theatre	

---

224. Doubtful. The text of the recitative (*Deh taci oh Dio! De grace ah!*) was not found in the librettos of the 1762 and the 1782 versions. It could be linked to the 1782 production in Genoa → see 1782, mus. by Sarti, Giuseppe; Cherubini, Luigi; Anfossi, Pasquale; and Bianchi, Francesco.
225. The music is different from that in DK-Kk mu7502.0538 and P-La 46-IV-15/16/17.
226. The aria was not found in the librettos of the 1762 and the 1782 versions.

MC | *Didone abbandonata* (1724–1832)

Librettos	(1) NA
	(2) Perugia: Riginaldi, [1781]
	D-Mth 001/8 R 00401 [1]; I-Fc E.VI.3210; I-PEc ANT Misc. I.C 51 [5]; I-PEsf[C,S,227]; US-BEm f PQ4717 .D5 1781a; US-Wc ML48.A5 vol. 5 [12][228]
Music sources	[complete scores] P-La 46-VII-50/51/52[BA]
	[doubtful] [excerpts] *Quando saprai chi sono* (D-B Mus.ms. 23483[RISM]); *Vivi superbo e regna* (F-Pn D-14497[BnF])
	[contrafacta] *Quando saprai chi sono* ([*Salve regina, mater misericordiae vita dulcedo*] D-HR [D-Au] III 4 1/2 2° 405[RISM;P,229])

1767	**mus. by unknown composer(s)**
1767 Pavia	Teatro Omodeo (carn.)
Librettos	Pavia: Bolzani, [1767]
	I-Mcom MUS.M MUS.1.-450 [1]

1767	**mus. by unknown composer(s)**
1767 Barcelona	Teatre de la Santa Creu
Librettos	Barcelona: Altés, [1767]
	E-Bu 07 XVIII-3329

1768	**mus. by Boroni, Antonio**	
1768 Prague	Teatro Regio (carn.)	(1)
s.d. Rome?	Teatro di Torre Argentina	(2)
Librettos	(1) [Prague: s.n., 1768] (It./Ger.)	
	CZ-Pnm B 4710; CZ-Pu L 1212; CZ-Pu 65 E 2973	
	(2) NA	
Music sources	[complete scores] D-Dl Mus.3406-F-5[MGG,NG,RISM,230]	
	[excerpts] *Tu mi disarmi il fianco* (F-Pn L-17351[BnF])	
	[doubtful] *Sento che il cor guerriero* (S-Skma T-SE-R[RISM,231])	

---

227. The library was not accessible throughout the preparation of this volume.
228. Microfilm copy: US-AAu FILM M236 [5].
229. The Latin text 'Salve regina' is added under the Italian text by a different hand.
230. Microfilm copy: US-CA 5225311.
231. It corresponds to a supposed revival in Rome. The aria was not included in the original 1768 version; it is probably not by Boroni.

MC | *Didone abbandonata* (1724–1832)

1768	mus. by unknown composer(s)
1768 Cádiz	Teatro Italiano (04/11/1768)
	Dido abandonada
Librettos	Cádiz: Espinosa, [1768] (It./Spa.)
	CH-Gpu Gg 514/3 [2]

1768	mus. by unknown composer(s)
1768 Kassel	Theatre
	Didon abandonée
Librettos	Kassel: Estienne, 1768 (It./Fr.)
	D-BFb [D-MÜu] B-St 112; D-FUl Schw Stift Kf 17

1770	mus. by Celoniati, Ignazio
1770 Milan[232]	Teatro Regio Ducale (carn., 26/12/1769)
Librettos	Milan: Montani, 1769
	F-Pn LIV IT-3529 [1]; I-Bc Lo.00947; I-Fc E.VI.5438; I-LDEsormani 309/4/24; I-Ms MUS. C. LXIII. 1; I-Rsc Vol. 12 [4]; US-CAh *IC7 M5648 D1769
Music sources	[complete scores] F-Pn D-1907/1908/1909[BnF,NG,RISM]; I-Tf[NG]; P-La 47-II-38[BA,NG]

1770	mus. by Di Majo, Gianfrancesco
1770 Venice	Teatro Grimani di S. Benedetto (carn., 26/12/1769)[233]
Librettos	Venice: Fenzo, 1770
	A-Wmi BT-727; I-Rsc Carv.4386; I-Vcg LIBRETTI S.BENEDETTO 190; I-Vnm DRAMM.1097 [3]; I-Vnm DRAMM.1305 [2]; I-Vnm MISC.4004 [2]; US-Wc ML48 [S5855][234]
Music sources	[complete scores] D-Mbs Mus.ms. 20889[MGG,NG,RISM]; P-La 44-XI-52/53/54[BA,NG]

---

232. According to [C], the 1st performance took place in December (not November) 1769. However, the libretto indicates that this version 'fu rappresentato in uno de' Teatri più qualificati della Germania…'. Similarly, [BnF,RISM] refer to revivals in Germany and Milan during the carnival of 1770 [1771?], yet we could not find further information about those performances.

233. De Filippis, Felice and Raffaele Arnese, *Cronache del Teatro di S. Carlo (1737–1960)* (Naples: Edizioni Politica Popolare, 1961) date the premiere of Majo's *Didone* in an unspecified day in 1768 and include no performance in the 1769–1770 season. The libretto is nonetheless clear.

234. Microfilm copy: US-BEm ML50.2.A7062 M3 1768.

MC | Didone abbandonata (1724–1832)

[excerpts] *Se resto sul lido* (US-BEm MS 107 [4][IC,RISM]); *Vado... ma dove?... oh dio!* (D-B Mus.ms. 13399/5[RISM]; F-Pn D-7267 [6][BnF,RISM,235]; US-SFsc *M2.1 M309[RISM])

[doubtful] *Già si desta la tempesta* (UA-Knbuv Rozum 120501 [20][RISM,236])

1770	mus. by Piccinni, Niccolò	
1770 Rome	Teatro di Torre Argentina (carn., 08/01/1770)	(1)
	1st version	
1776 Havana	Teatro Coliseo (12/10/1776)	(2)
	opening of the theatre	
1780 Naples?	Teatro di S. Carlo?[237]	(3)
1783 Paris	Court theatre – Palace de Fontainebleau (16/10/1783)	(4,5)
	Didon (Fr. only)	
	French version of the libretto by J. F. Marmontel	
	2nd version	
1783 Paris[238]	Académie Royale de Musique (01/12/1783)	(4,5)
1785 Paris	Académie Royale de Musique	(6)
1787 Lyon	Theatre	(7)
1799 Berlin	Court theatre (18/05/1799)[239]	(8)
1808 Berlin	Court theatre (c. 04/04/1808)	(9)
Librettos	(1) Rome: Corradi, 1770	
	F-Pn YD-5393 [4];[240] I-Rsc Libr. n. XVII [52]; I-Rvat Stamp.Ferr.V.8059 [2]; I-Vgc ROL.0537 [3]	
	(2,7–9) NA	
	(3) [s.l.: s.n., 1780]	
	(4) Paris: Roullet, 1783 (Fr.)	
	I-Nragni L082	

---

235. Microfilm copy: F-Pn VM BOB-34155.
236. The aria is included in neither the libretto nor the complete score D-Mbs Mus.ms. 20889.
237. Performance date based on the extant sources.
238. According to the libretto, a second performance took place on 1 December 1783. Also referenced by [NG]; see [NG] 'Piccinni, Niccolò' and Liggett, Margaret McGuiness, 'A Biography of Niccolò Piccinni and a Critical Study of his "La Didone" and "Didon"' (doctoral dissertation, Washington University, 1977).
239. According to Hartmann and Schäffer, twenty-five performances until 4 April 1808. As the number of separate productions cannot be specified, we list the first and the last of them; see Hartmann, Carl and Carl Schäffer, eds, *Die königlichen Theater in Berlin: Statischer Rückblick auf die Kunstlerische Thätigkeit und die Personal-Verhältnisse während des Zeitraums vom 5. December 1786 bis 31. December 1885* (Berlin: Berliner Verlag-Comtoir, 1886).
240. Microfilm copy: F-Pn MICROFILM M-2659.

MC | *Didone abbandonata* (1724–1832)

(5) Paris: de Lormel, 1783 (Fr.)
CZ-Pnm B 4175; D-KNth L 1371; I-Bca; US-Cn BLC #182

(6) Paris: Brouhlet [*recte* Roullet], 1785 (Fr.)
I-Vgc ROL.0537 [2]

Music sources

1st version: 1770, Rome

[complete scores] D-HR [D-Au] III 4 1/2 2° 413[RISM] [Act II and parts of I&III]; I-Mc Part. Tr.ms. 331[IC,MGG,NG,RISM,SBN]; I-MC 4-F-26[NG,RISM,241]; I-Nc* 16.4.27/28[IC,MGG,NG,RISM,SBN,242]; I-Nc 32.2.14[IC]; I-Rvat Chig.Q.VII.147-155[MGG,NG;IP,243]; P-La 46-II-1/2/3[BA,MGG,NG]; US-Wc M1500.P58 D42[IC,MGG,NG,RISM]

[excerpts] *Ah, non lasciarmi, no* (D-Dl Mus.3264-F-33 [6][RISM]; DK-Kk mu7502.0736[RISM]; GB-Lbl R.M.22.m.23 [3][RISM]; GB-Lbl R.M.22.m.23 [8][RISM]; GB-Lbl R.M.23.f.11 [2][RISM]; GB-Lbl R.M.23.f.11 [4][RISM]; US-SFsc *M2.5 v.10 [3][RISM]); *Ah, non sai per questo core* (CH-Gc Rmo 123/7 [1][RISM]; D-Dl Mus.3264-F-33 [4][RISM]; D-Dl Mus.3264-F-33 [9][RISM]; GB-Lbl Add. 29966[RISM]; GB-Lbl R.M.23.f.11 [8][RISM]; I-MC 5-A-13 [9][RISM]; I-Nc 57.2.6 [8][SBN]; I-PEsp M.CXXX [20][RISM]; I-Raf 1.E.8 [4][RISM]; US-SFsc *M2.5 v.10 [7][RISM]); *Cadrà fra poco in cenere* (D-BAd EB 524[RISM;P]; I-Fc D.I.205 [7][IC,SBN]; *Chiamami pur così* (GB-Lbl R.M.23.g.5 [3][RISM]; GB-Lbl R.N.23.g.5 [1][RISM]); *Dovrei… ma no* (US-SFsc *M2.5 v.9 [1][RISM]); *L'augelletto in lacci stretto* (GB-Lbl R.M.23.f.11 [8][RISM]; GB-Lbl R.M.23.g.5 [2][RISM]; US-SFsc *M2.5 v.9 [2][RISM]); *Non ha ragione ingrato* (D-Dl Mus.3264-F-33 [7][RISM]; F-Pn D-14500 [5][BnF]; GB-Lbl R.M.23.f.11 [5][RISM]; US-SFsc *M2.1 M408 [7][RISM]; US-SFsc *M2.5 v.10 [4][RISM]); *Quando saprai chi sono* (GB-Lbl R.M.23.f.11 [3][RISM]; US-SFsc *M2.5 v.9 [8][RISM]); *Se resto sul lido* (CH-Bu kr IV 221[RISM;P]; CH-Gc Rmo 123/7 [4][RISM]; D-Dl Mus.3264-F-33 [8][RISM]); *Son regina e sono amante* (I-Mc Noseda O.44 [22][SBN]); *Tacerò se tu lo brami* (GB-Lbl R.M.23.g.5 [4][RISM]); *Tu mi disarmi il fianco* (F-Pn L-19494[BnF]); *Vado… ma dove?… oh dio!* (D-Dl Mus.3264-F-33 [5][RISM])

[inserts] *Se il ciel mi divide*, in *Se il ciel mi divide. Madam Mara's Favorite Song in Didone abbandonata* (London: Longman & Broderip: [s.d.]); in [...] *the Grand Serious Opera of Didone* (London: Lee, [c. 1800])

---

241. For a performance in 1780; part of the music is different from the 1770 version.
242. Possible autograph.
243. Microfilm copy: US-PRu MICROFILM 1826.

MC | *Didone abbandonata* (1724–1832)

1770	mus. by Insanguine, Giacomo
1770 Naples	Teatro di S. Carlo (20/01/1770)[244] (1)
	birthday of Carlos III, king of Spain
1772 Naples	Teatro di S. Carlo (15/02/1772) (2)
Music sources	[complete scores] I-Nc 28.6.14/15[IC,MGG,NG,RISM,245]; P-La 45-II-23/24/25[BA,MGG,NG]; P-La 54-III-15[BA,MGG,NG]
	[excerpts] *Ah, non lasciarmi, no* (I-MC 3-B-4 [4][RISM]); *Ah, non sai bella Selene* (B-Bc 4220[RISM]; I-MC 3-B-5 [6][RISM]); *Dirò che fida sei* (DK-Kk mu6506.1431[RISM]); *Dovrei... ma no* (GB-Lbl Add. 14221 [3][RISM]; I-MC 3-B-6 [6][RISM]; I-MC 3-B-7/2 [3][RISM]; I-MC 3-B-7 [7][RISM]; <u>I-Nc 34.3.15 [12]</u>[MGG,SBN]; <u>I-Nc 34.3.15 [13]</u>[MGG,SBN]; <u>I-Nc 57.2.8 [8]</u>[MGG,SBN]; I-Nc Musicale Strumentale 55 [5–28][SBN;IP]; S-Skma T-SE-R[RISM;IP]; US-CAe Mus 503.601 [2][RISM]); *Non ha ragione ingrato* (GB-Lbl R.M.23.c.19 [1][RISM,246]; I-Nc 34.3.17 [1][MGG,SBN,247]; I-Nc Arie 660 [2][MGG,SBN]); *Ombra cara ombra tradita* (CH-Gc Rmo 123/14 [5][RISM]; <u>F-Pn D-6172 [7]</u>[BnF,248]; I-MC 3-B-4 [10][RISM]; I-MC 3-B-5 [9][RISM]; I-MC 3-B-7/3 [3][RISM]; I-MC 3-D-8/5 [2][RISM]; <u>I-Nc 34.3.15 [14]</u>[MGG,SBN]; I-Nc 34.3.17 [2][MGG,SBN,249]; S-Skma T-SE-R[RISM]); *Sai pur che adorai quel caro sembiante* (US-CAe Mus 503.601 [9][RISM]); *Son regina e sono amante* (B-Bc 4221[RISM]; D-B Mus.ms. 11169[RISM]; I-MC 3-B-4 [8][RISM]; I-Nc 22.2.5 [10][SBN])
	[parodies] *Ombra cara ombra tradita* ([*Justo comm'a franfellicco giallo sicco*] I-MC 3-B-7/4 [1][RISM])
	[doubtful] *Caro figlio, amabil pegno*[250] (I-MC 3-B-5 [1][RISM])
1770	mus. by various unknown composers
1770 Lucca	Teatro Pubblico (25/08/1770)
Librettos	Lucca: Benedini, 1770
	<u>I-Baf FA2.LIB.657</u>

---

244. This commission began as an assignment to revise and direct Galuppi's setting, and only when Galuppi's work proved impossible to adapt to the needs of the S. Carlo theatre was Insanguine asked to set the text anew; see Giovine, Alfredo and Ulisse Prota-Giurleo, *Giacomo Insanguine detto Monopoli: musicista monopolitano* (Bari: Archivio delle tradizioni popolari baresi, 1969).
245. For Naples 1772.
246. In E flat major instead of A major.
247. In G major instead of A major.
248. Microfilm copy: F-Pn VM BOB-28468.
249. I-Nc 34.3.17 [2] and US-CAe Mus 503.601 [9]: for Naples 1772.
250. This aria is not included in P-La 45-II-23/24/25.

1772 1772 Bologna	mus. by various unknown composers Nuovo Teatro Pubblico (carn., 03/02/1772)
Librettos	Bologna: Sassi, [1772] CDN-Ttfl Itp Pam 00496; I-Bam Ambr.Comunale.011; I-Bc Lo.06214; I-Bca 17-ARTISTICA Gd, 007; I-Bu A.III.Caps.097 [62]; I-Rsc Carv.4387; I-Vgc ROL.0680 [11]; US-BEm ML48 .I7 [436]
1772 1772 Florence	mus. by Mortellari, Michele Teatro della Pergola (20/09/1772)
Librettos	Florence: Risaliti, 1772 I-Bc Lo.06213; I-Fc E.V.1747
Music sources	[excerpts] *Ah, non lasciarmi, no*[251] (GB-Lbl Add. 31817[RISM]); *Io ti lascio e questo addio*[252] (CH-Gc X 5 [27][RISM]; D-B Mus.ms. 14796[RISM]; D-Dl Mus.1-F-49,4 [6][RISM]; D-MEIr F 574[RISM]); *Son regina e sono amante* (I-MC 3-E-22 [13][RISM]; I-Vc Correr Busta 123.16[SBN]) [printed sources] → see 1775, mus. by Mortellari; Rauzzini; Sacchini; and Giardini, Felice, as well as → 1786, mus. by Anfossi, Pasquale and others
1772 1772 Florence	mus. by unknown composer(s) Teatro dei Risoluti (18/10/1772) *Enea in Cartagine*
Librettos	Florence: Stecchi & Pagani, 1772 I-Bc Lo.06298; I-Rn 35. 5.K.01.08
1773 1773 Turin	mus. by Colla, Giuseppe Teatro Regio (carn., 23/01/1773)[253]
Librettos	Turin: Derossi, [1773] D-Mbs L.eleg.m. 3937; I-Bc Lo.01246; I-Fm Mel.2096 [7]; I-PAc F.Libretti, sc.III [110]; I-Rsc Libr. n. XVIII [70]; I-Rsc Vol. Carv.152 [4]; I-Tci L.O.0265; I-Tn C.SAN 435 [4]; I-Tn F XIII.305 [3]; I-Tn F XIII.493 [7]; I-Tp P.i.107/2.7; I-Tstrona[S]; S-Uu n/s; US-CAt TS 8154.120 1773; US-Wc ML48 [S2107]

---

251. The aria was inserted into the 1786 London pasticcio → see 1786, mus. by Anfossi and others.
252. From Mortellari's *Arsace*. Later reworked by J.Ch. Bach for his own version of the libretto.
253. The production ran for twenty-three consecutive performances; see Bouquet, Gualerzi, and Testa, *Storia del Teatro Regio di Torino*, pp. 76, 159.

MC | *Didone abbandonata* (1724–1832)

Music sources [complete scores] I-Tf 1 VII 4/5/6[IC,NG,RISM]; P-La 44-V-24/25/26[BA,MGG,NG]; P-La 47-VII-27/28[BA,MGG,NG]

[excerpts][254] *Ah, non lasciarmi, no* (D-BFb [D-MÜu] C-ol 52[MGG,NG,RISM]); *Fosca nube il sol ricopra* (I-Tf 2 IV 4 [2][NG,RISM]); *Non ha ragione ingrato* (I-Tci Mus.Ms.38[NG,RISM]); *Va lusingando amore* (D-B Mus.ms. 3920[RISM;P])

1774	mus. by Anfossi, Pasquale	
1774 Rome	Teatro di Torre Argentina[MGG]	(1)
	1ˢᵗ version	
1775 Cremona	Teatro Nazari (25/05/1775)	(2)
1775 Venice	Teatro Giustiniani di S. Moisè (Asc., 28/05/1775)[255]	(3)
	mus. by P. Anfossi and others[256]	
1775 Lucca	Teatro Pubblico (aut., 23/08/1775)	(4)
1776 Cremona	Teatro Nazari (carn.)	(5)
	mus. by F. Bianchi and others[S,257]	
1776 Warsaw	Radziwiłł palace	(6)
1776 Warsaw	Theatre[258]	(7)
1778 Venice	Teatro Giustiniani di S. Moisè (31/05/1778)[CA]	(8)
1782 Pavia	Teatro dei Quattro Cavalieri Associati (carn.)	(9)
1788 Naples	Teatro di S. Carlo (30/05/1788)	(10)
	name day of Ferdinando IV, king of Naples	
	2ⁿᵈ version	

Librettos (1,2,7,8) NA

(3) Venice: Fenzo, 1775

I-Bc Lo.00206; I-Mb Racc.dramm.4000; I-Rsc Libr. n. XVIII [71]; I-Vcg LIBRETTI S.MOISÈ 57 C 37; I-Vnm DRAMM.1102 [2]; I-Vnm DRAMM.1314 [5]

---

254. [MGG] and [NG] list further sources in D-MH and I-Gl, but we have not been able to locate them.
255. As no libretto for the Roman performance has been preserved, contrarily to [MGG,NG] and Tribuzio, consider the Venetian occasion as Anfossi's premiere; see [NG] 'Anfossi, Pasquale' and Tribuzio, Giovanni, 'Pasquale Anfossi: operista alla moda', in *Il secolo d'oro della musica a Napoli. Per un canone della Scuola musicale napoletana del '700*, ed. by Lorenzo Fiorito (Frattamaggiore: Diana, 2019), vol. 2, pp. 133–48.
256. Liborio, Francesco Maria, *La scena della città: rappresentazioni sceniche nel Teatro di Cremona 1748–1900* (Cremona: Turris, 1994).
257. ˢIndex I, p. 343.
258. Żórawska-Witkowska, Alina, 'The Music Library of the Warsaw Theatre in the Years 1788 and 1797: An Expression of the Migration of European Repertoire', *Arti musices: hrvatski muzikološki zborni*, 47.1–2 (2016), 103–16.

(4) Lucca: Benedini, 1775
I-Fc E.VI.3817; I-Vgc ROL.0137 [15]; US-Cn ML50.2.D47 A54 1775; US-Wc ML48 [S233]

(5) Cremona: Manini & co., [1776]
B-Bc 19907; I-Rn 40.9.G.10.2; I-Rsc Carv.4388

(6) Warsaw: Dufour, 1776
PL-KI[S]; PL-Ptu 23280 II; PL-Wu GSD 143686

(9) Milan: Pirola, [1782]
US-CAh *IC7 A100 B750 [43]

(10) Naples: Flauto, 1788
CDN-Ttfl Itp Pam 00019; F-Pn YD-5466;[259] I-Fm Mel.2215 [1];[260] I-La Dono Pellegrini – Libretti d'opera, 41; I-MC ANT 13C.I 15; I-Nc Rari 10.3.2 [6]; I-Ra E.I.24 [9];[261] I-Rsc Carv.4390; US-NYp Mus. Res. *MZ, A/28 [11][262]

Music sources
1st version: 1774, Rome

[excerpts] *Ah, non lasciarmi, no* (D-MÜs SANT Hs 141 II [10][RISM]; I-Mc Noseda A.17 [6][SBN,263]); *Cadrà fra poco in cenere* (F-Pn D-222 [2][BnF,264]); *Dovrei… ma no* (D-MÜs SANT Hs 141 II [4][RISM]); *Non partir, m'ascolta oh Dio!* (F-Pn D-222 [4][BnF]); *Prendi l'estremo addio* (D-Mbs Mus. ms. 20866 [7][RISM]); *Son regina e sono amante* (F-Pn D-222 [3][BnF]); *Va crescendo il mio tormento* (CZ-Pnm XLII C 306[RISM]; D-Mbs Mus.ms. 8738 [14][RISM;IP,265]; I-MAav Cart.20 n.4 [59][RISM,266])

[printed sources] *Se il ciel me divide*, in *Journal d'ariettes italiennes*, 10 (Paris: Bailleux, 1779)[267]

2nd version: 1788, Naples

[complete scores] F-Pn D-117/118[BnF,MGG,NG,RISM,SBN,268]; I-Nc 24.5.1[MGG,NG,SBN,269]; P-La 44-I-27/28[BA,MGG,NG]; P-La 44-II-1/2[BA,MGG,NG]

---

259. Incomplete.
260. Microfilm copy: CDN-Lu M1500.P272D5 1789.
261. Microfilm copy: CDN-Lu M1500.M57P287 1800a.
262. Microfilm copy: US-NYp *ZB-3266 [3].
263. D-Mbs Mus.ms. 20866 [7]; F-Pn D-222; and I-Mc Noseda A.17 [6]: for Venice 1775.
264. Microfilm copy of all the pieces in F-Pn D-222: F-Pn VM BOB-25903.
265. Fl. and bc parts.
266. In G major. The other sources are in A major.
267. The aria was not included in the 1775, 1776, and 1788 librettos: doubtful.
268. Microfilm copy: F-Pn VM BOB-25678.
269. Microfilm copy: US-PRu MICROFILM 1678.

MC | *Didone abbandonata* (1724–1832)

[doubtful] *Ah, non sai qual pena sia* (A-Wgm VI 19846 [Q 2678]^{IC,270})

1775	mus. by Mortellari, Michele; Rauzzini, Venanzio; Sacchini, Antonio; and Giardini, Felice
1775 London	King's Theatre in the Haymarket (07/11/1775)[271]
Librettos	London: Cadell, [1775] (It./En.) CDN-HNu DIS B116 E37; D-Gs 8 P DRAM I, 6821; GB-Lbl 907.i.15 [4];[272] GB-Ob Harding D 2448 [1]; PL-GD^E; US-SM La 389; US-Wc ML48 [S11321]
Music sources	[excerpts] Sacchini, Antonio, *Ah, tu piangi i casi miei* (US-Wc M1505.S211^{RISM}); *Parto è ver ma son fedele* (D-BFb [D-MÜu] S-ac 14^{RISM}); *Son regina e sono amante* (D-HEI 37.1.340 [6]^{RISM}; D-KA Don Mus.Ms. 1702^{RISM}; F-Pn L-19884 [2]^{BnF})
	[printed sources] *Ah, tu piangi i casi miei* by Sacchini [2]; *Dovrei… ma no* by Rauzzini [5]; *E mi lascio l'ingrato* by Mortellari [3]; *Infelice e sventurato* [4]; *Io ti lascio, e questo addio* by Giardini [9]; *Parto è ver, ma son fedele* by Sacchini [10]; *Quando saprai chi sono* [7]; *Se mai vedi il mio tesoro* [6]; *Sentirsi dire dal caro bene* by Rauzzini [8]; *Son regina e sono amante* by Sacchini [1], in *The Favourite Songs in the Opera Didone* (London: Bremner, 1775); *Son regina e sono amante* by Sacchini, in *Son regina e sono amante. Sung by Madam Mara* (London: Longman & Broderip, 1775)

1776	mus. by Schuster, Joseph Anton	
1776 Naples	Teatro di S. Carlo (12/01/1776)[273] *birthday of Ferdinando IV, king of Naples*	(1)
1779 Venice	Teatro Grimani di S. Benedetto (carn., 20/01/1779)	(2)
Librettos	(1) Naples: Morelli, 1776 CDN-Ttfl Itp Pam 00915; I-Mc Lib.I.090; I-Nragni L100; US-NYp Mus. Res. *MZ, A/31 [5]	

---

270. The rondo was included in neither the 1775 nor the 1788 version.
271. Date given in *The London Stage 1660–1800: A Calendar of plays, Entertainments & Afterpieces together with Casts, Box-Receipts and Contemporary Comments: Compiled from the Playbills, Newspapers and Theatrical Diaries of the Period* (Carbondale, IL: Southern Illinois University Press, 1961–1968). ^{CA,NG} and Petty ('Italian opera in London', p. 186) give 11/11/1775.
272. Microfilm copy: GB-Es Mf.134 reel 5684 [26].
273. ^{CA} wrongly dates it on 12/03/1776.

MC | *Didone abbandonata* (1724–1832)

(2) Venice: Fenzo, 1779
F-Pn 8-YTH-51562; I-Mb Racc.dramm.3800 [1]; I-Vcg LIBRETTI S.BENEDETTO 194; I-Vgc ROL.0610 [9]; I-Vnm DRAMM.1323 [5]; I-Vnm DRAMM.1323 [6]

Music sources [complete scores] D-Dl Mus.3549-F-9[MGG,NG,RISM,274] [Acts II&III]; D-Dl Mus.3549-F-10[MGG,NG,RISM]; I-Nc 31.2.8/9/10[IC,MGG,NG,SBN]; P-La 47-IV-54/55[BA]

[excerpts] *Ah, non lasciarmi, no* (A-Wgm VI 19996 [Q 9521][IC;P]; CH-Zz Mus Ms A 183[SB]; D-B Mus.ms. 20469 [4][RISM,275]; I-MC 6-A-1 [5][RISM]; I-Nc 34.5.15 [4][SBN]; I-Rc Mss. 3217[IC;IP]); *Dovrei… ma no* (D-B Mus.ms. 30134 [13][RISM]; D-Dl Mus.3549-F-35 [6][RISM]; D-KNmi A 4 R[RISM]; I-Nc 34.5.15 [3][SBN]; F-Pn L-4580 [8][BnF]; I-MC 5-F-23 [3][RISM]; I-MC 5-F-25 [1][RISM]; I-MC 5-F-25 [4][RISM]; I-MC 5-F-25 [14][RISM]; I-MC 5-F-25 [18][RISM]; S-Skma T-SE-R[RISM]; US-Wc M1505.A1 (vol. 204) [6][MGG,RISM]); *Io vi lascio, e questo addio* (B-Bc 4881[RISM]; D-Dl Mus.3548-F-35 [7][RISM]; D-KNmi S 697 R[RISM]; I-Mc Mus. Tr.ms. 1238 [A][RISM,SBN]; I-Mc Mus. Tr.ms. 1238 [B][RISM,SBN]; I-MC 4-C-3 [3][RISM]; I-MC 5-F-23 [6][RISM]; I-MC 5-F-25 [2][RISM]; I-MC 5-F-25 [11][RISM]; I-MC 5-F-25 [12][RISM]; I-MC 5-F-25 [15][RISM]; I-MC 6-A-1/13 [1][RISM]; I-Nc 34.3.14 [10][SBN]; I-Nc 34.5.15 [6][SBN]; S-Skma T-SE-R[RISM]; US-SFsc *M2.1 M476[RISM]); *Ombra cara ombra tradita* (B-Br Ms II 4045 Mus Fétis 2624[RISM]; D-Dl Mus.3549-F-508[RISM]; I-MC 3-F-10/5 [9][RISM]; I-MC 6-A-1 [4][RISM]); *Quando saprai chi sono* (I-MC 5-F-23 [7][RISM]); *Se resto sul lido* (D-KNmi A 4 R [8][RISM]; D-KNmi S 695 R[RISM]; F-MOa MS22[BASE]; F-MOc Ms 22[BASE]; F-Pn L-4580 [10][BnF]; I-Mc Mus. Tr.ms. 1237[RISM,SBN]; I-MC 1-E-12 [2][RISM]; I-MC 4-C-3 [4][RISM]; I-MC 5-F-25 [7][RISM]; I-MC 6-A-1 [3][RISM]; I-MC 6-A-1 [12][RISM]; I-Rrostirolla [I-Fn] MS MUS 565 [12][SBN]; I-Rrostirolla [I-Fn] MS MUS 565 [16][SBN]; I-Tf 1 IV 1 [1][RISM]; S-Skma T-SE-R[RISM]); *Son qual fiume che gonfio* (F-Pn D-14462[BnF,276]; F-Pn L-4580 [9][BnF]; F-Pn L-19917[BnF;P]); *Son regina e sono amante* (I-Mc Noseda N.18 [5][SBN]; I-MC 2-F-14/4 [10][RISM]; I-MC 5-F-23 [5][RISM]; I-MC 5-F-25 [3][RISM]; I-MC 5-F-25 [10][RISM]; I-MC 5-F-25 [17][RISM]; I-Nc 34.5.15 [5][SBN]; I-Nc 64.41.3[SBN]; I-Vlevi CF.B.85[RISM,SBN]); *Tu mi disarmi il fianco* (I-MC 6-A-1 [7][RISM]); *Va crescendo il mio tormento* (F-Pn L-4580 [13][BnF]; I-MC 5-F-24 [4][RISM]; US-NH Misc. Ms. 36 [14][RISM]); *Voglio che m'ami ancora* (D-KNmi A 4 R [7][RISM]; D-KNmi S 693 R[RISM]; F-Pn L-4580 [7][BnF]; I-MC

---

274. This and the following source: for Venice 1779.
275. According to [RISM], performed in 1799 in Venice. No further information about this production could be found.
276. Microfilm copy: F-Pn VM BOB-31588.

5-F-23 [2]^RISM; I-MC 5-F-23 [4]^RISM; I-MC 5-F-23 [8]^RISM; I-MC 5-F-25 [4]^RISM; I-MC 5-F-25 [16]^RISM; I-Nc 34.3.13 [11]^SBN; I-Nc 34.5.15 [9]^SBN; I-Nc 64.41.5^SBN; S-Skma T-SE-R^RISM; US-Wc M1505.A1 (vol. 204) [5]^MGG,RISM)

[contrafacta] *L'augelletto in lacci stretto* ([*Precorre regina caeli, corde pio*] D-BAUd Mu II:56 [2]^RISM;P); *Ombra cara ombra tradita* ([*Quando Jesus est in corde*] B-Asj Sj 264^RISM;P); *Se dalle stelle tu non sei guida* ([*Ave Maria gratia plena*] D-NEZkpn 2/42^RISM;P); *Son regina e sono amante* ([*In te Domine speravi*] PL-Wu RM 4971^RISM;P; [*Jesu dulcis memoria, dans vera cordis gaudia*] D-NEZkpn 2/43^RISM;P); *Va crescendo il mio tormento* ([*Redde blandum*] D-BAUd Mu II:56 [1]^RISM;P); *Voglio che m'ami ancora* ([*Ave mundi spes, Maria*] D-BAUd Mu II:56 [3]^RISM;P); *Vorrei disciogliere le mie catene* ([*Maria salus es, O Deus salus es, in vita tota spes*] D-BAUd Mu II:56 [4]^RISM;P)

[doubtful] *Ah, non lasciarmi, no*[277] (D-Dl Mus.3549-F-36 [6]^RISM; D-Dl Mus.3549-F-36 [8]^RISM; D-Dl Mus.3549-F-40^RISM; D-KNmi S 694 R^RISM; GB-Lbl R.M.23.d.3 [5]^RISM; I-Mc Noseda N.18 [6]^SBN; I-MC 6-A-1 [2]^RISM,278; I-Rc Mss. 6217^RISM; I-Rcagli 62^RISM; I-Rrostirolla [I-Fn] MS MUS 1119^RISM;IP,279; S-Skma T-SE-R^RISM); *Di chi mi fiderò* (I-Mc Mus. Tr.ms. 1236^RISM,SBN,280)

1776	mus. by Mombelli, Francesco Domenico
1776 Crescentino	NA

1778	mus. by various unknown composers
1778 Genoa	Teatro da S. Agostino (spr.)
Librettos	Genoa: Gesiniana, [1778]
	NA[281]

1778	mus. by various unknown composers
1778 Florence	Teatro della Pergola (28/10/1778)

---

277. The music of these sources is different from Schuster's original 1776 version. There is no proof that Schuster was involved in the 1779 revival. Furthermore, and although some sources indicate '1779 Venezia', the aria was included in Schuster's *Il marito indolente*, premiered in 1782 in Dresden, as the provenance of some of the preserved sources attests. Therefore, we consider that this aria does not belong to *Didone abbandonata*.
278. Wrongly dated 1776 on source.
279. Va part.
280. Although the source has the inscription '1779 Op.ra 2.a S. Benedetto Del Sig|r Giuseppe Shuster', neither the aria nor the recitativo that precedes it is included in the libretto for such performance.
281. ^C,S list a copy in US-NYp, yet this cannot be found in any of the institution's catalogues; see ^S7745 and <http://corago.unibo.it/libretto/DRT0013991> [accessed 24 June 2022].

MC | *Didone abbandonata* (1724–1832)

Librettos	Florence: Risaliti, 1778
	I-Bc Lo.06215; I-Fc E.VI.3209
Music sources	[excerpts] *Ah, non lasciarmi, no* (CDN-Lu GM/AR 220 [3]^{RISM,282})

1779	mus. by Ottani, Bernardo
1779 Forlì	Teatro Pubblico (spr., c. 08/05/1779)
Librettos	Forlì: Marozzi, [1779]
	I-Bc Lo.03610; US-Wc ML48 [S7364]
Music sources	[complete scores] F-A Ms. 1173[BASE]; I-Tf 1 IV 21/22/23[MGG,NG,RISM,283]
	[excerpts] *Ah, non lasciarmi, no* (CZ-Pnm XLII B 107[RISM,284]; D-Hs M A/831 [2/1][RISM]; I-MC 4-C-2/1 [4][RISM]; US-Wc M1505.A2 O85[RISM]); *Fra lo splendor del trono* (I-MC 4-C-2/3 [4][RISM]); *Son regina e sono amante* (I-MC 4-C-2/3 [2][RISM]); *Vanne a colei che adoro* (I-MC 4-C-3 [9][RISM])

1779	mus. by Holzbauer, Ignaz	
1779 Mannheim	Court theatre (06/07/1779)	(1)
	La morte di Didone	
1784 Mannheim	Court theatre (06/06/1784)[CA]	
	Die Zerstörung von Carthago (Ger. only)	
Librettos	(1) Mannheim: [s.n.], 1779 (It./Ger.)	
	US-Wc ML50.2.M788 H6 1779	
Music sources	[complete scores] D-B Mus.ms. 10781[MGG,NG,RISM]; US-Wc M1500.H77 T5[MGG,NG,RISM,285]	
	[excerpts] *Non ha ragione ingrato* (D-Sla 110[RISM;P]); *Va lusingando amore* (D-B Mus.ms. 10781[NG,RISM;P])	

> *Didone abbandonata*, in *Opere del signor abate Pietro Metastasio* (Paris: widow of Hérissant, 1780), vol. 3, pp. 3–108.

---

282. According to an inscription on the source, it is by Colla, yet music is completely different from his original 1773 version.
283. Microfilm copy: CDN-Lu M1500.M57O774 1779a.
284. Inserted into a revival of Anfossi's *I viaggiatori felici* (Venice, 1780).
285. In German. There was another manuscript score in D-MHmr, lost according to Corneilson, Paul Edward, 'Opera at Mannheim, 1770–1778' (doctoral dissertation, The University of North Carolina at Chapel Hill, 1994).

MC | *Didone abbandonata* (1724–1832)

1780	mus. by Piticchio, Francesco	
1780 Palermo	Teatro di Santa Cecilia (carn.)	(1)
1784 Brunswick	Teatro Ducale (win. Fair)	(2)
	Die verlassene Dido	
Librettos	(1) NA	
	(2) Brunswick: [s.n.], 1784 (It./Ger.)	
	D-BS Brosch. I 20.773; D-HVs S2547,b; <u>I-Bc Lo.04262</u>	
Music sources	[complete scores] D-Wa* 46 Alt 222/223/224[MGG,NG,RISM,286]	

1780	mus. by Astarita, Gennaro
1780 Bratislava	NA
Music sources	[complete scores] <u>A-Wn Mus.Hs.16538</u>[IC,MGG,NG,287]

1780	mus. by unknown composer(s)
1780 Kassel	Theatre
Librettos	Kassel: Hampe, 1780 (It./Fr.)
	B-Br Fétis 4.489 A V,27 Mus.[288]

1782	mus. by Sarti, Giuseppe (2nd version) → see 1762

1783	mus. by Piccinni, Niccolò (2nd version, Fr. only) → see 1770

1783	mus. by Prati, Alessio
1783 Munich[289]	NA

1784	mus. by Andreozzi, Gaetano	
1784 St Petersburg	Court Theatre – Winter Palace	(1)
1785 Pisa	Teatro Prini (30/04/1785)	(2)
1789 Reggio Emilia	Teatro Pubblico?	(3)
1791 Madrid	Teatro de los Caños del Peral (summ., 13/08/1791)	(4)
	Dido abandonada	

---

286. Possible autograph; for Brunswick 1784.
287. Microfilm copy: CDN-Lu M1500.M57A74 1780a.
288. Microfilm copy: CDN-Lu ML48.M47L442 1783a.
289. Doubtful according to [NG]. Cf. [NG]'Prati, Alessio'.

MC | *Didone abbandonata* (1724–1832)

Librettos	(1–3) NA
	(4) Madrid: González, 1791 (It./Spa.)
	E-Mn T/24504
Music sources	[excerpts] *Ah, non lasciarmi, no* (I-PAc Sanv.A.24^RISM); *Ah, non sai qual pena sia* (D-B Mus.ms. 620 [25]^RISM;R); *Cara, deh, frena il pianto* (I-Mc Mus. Tr.ms. 18^RISM,SBN); *Luci amate a voi non chiedo* (D-Dl Mus.1-F-82,33 [2]^RISM); *Se pietà l'affanno mio* (I-Nc 34.2.1 [1]^SBN)

1785	mus. by Guglielmi, Pietro Alessandro
1785 Venice^NG	NA

1786	mus. by various composers; arr. by Madam Mara[290]
	lib. rev. by Badini, Carlo
1786 London	King's Theatre in the Haymarket (14/02/1786)[291] (1)
1787 London	King's Theatre in the Haymarket (29/03/1787)[292] (2)

Librettos	(1) London: Almon, 1786 (It./En.)
	US-NYcub 820.12 Z9329; US-SM La 721
	(2) NA
Music sources	[printed sources]
	Mortellari, Michele, *Ah, non lasciarmi, no*, in *Ah, non lasciarmi, no bell'idol mio Sung by Madame Mara* (London: Longman & Broderip, [1786])
	Piccinni, Niccolò, *Se il ciel mi divide*, in *Madam Mara's Favorite Song in Didone abbandonata* (London: Longman & Broderip, [1786]); in *Se il ciel mi divide Sung by Made Catalani* ([London]: Lee, [c. 1790])
	Sacchini, Antonio, *Son regina e sono amante*, in *Son regina e sono amante sung by Madame Mara* (London: Longman & Broderip, [1786])
	Schuster, Joseph Anton, *Ombra cara, ombra tradita*, in *Ombra cara ombra tradita Sung by Madame Mara* (London: Longman & Broderip, [1786]); in *Ombra cara ombra tradita Sung by Madame Mara* (London: Longman & Broderip, [1790])

---

290. Composers included: Anfossi, Pasquale, with additions by Sacchini, Antonio; Gazzaniga, Giuseppe; Mortellari, Michele; Piccinni, Niccolò; Schuster, Joseph Anton.
291. The production ran for eight consecutive performances; see Petty, 'Italian opera in London', p. 271 and Price, Curtis, Judith Milhous, and Robert D. Hume, *Italian Opera in Late Eighteenth-Century London*, vol. 1: *The King's Theatre, Haymarket 1778–1791* (Oxford: Clarendon Press, 1995).
292. *The London stage 1660–1800*, p. 5:2:963. The production had just one performance; see Petty, 'Italian Opera in London', p. 283 and Price, Milhous, and Hume, *Italian opera in Late*, p. 360.

MC | *Didone abbandonata* (1724–1832)

1786	mus. by various unknown composers
1786 Bergamo	Teatro Riccardi (22/08/1786)[293]
Librettos	Bergamo: Antoine, [1786]
	I-Vcg LIBRETTI BERGAMO 246[294]

1786	mus. by various unknown composers
1786 Florence	Teatro della Pergola (20/10/1786)
Librettos	Florence: Albizziniana, 1786
	I-Bc Lo.06216; I-Fc E.VI.2921[295]

1787	mus. by Sarti, Giuseppe; Cherubini, Luigi; Anfossi, Pasquale; and Bianchi, Francesco
1787 Genoa	Teatro da S. Agostino (carn., 17/02/1787)
Librettos	Genoa: Gesiniana, [1787]
	I-Nragni L070; I-Rsc Carv.4389; I-SML 229 FC 2113 7; I-Tstrona[S]; I-Vnm DRAMM.3261 [8][296]
Music sources	[complete scores] I-Gl B M.7.6/7[IC,MGG,NG,SBN,297]
	[excerpts]
	Sarti, Giuseppe, *Son regina e sono amante* (A-Wgm VI 286 [Q 3895])[IC,NG,298] Bianchi, Francesco, *Agitata è l'alma mia* (I-MC 1-B-23/9 [1])[RISM]; *Ah, non lasciarmi, no* (D-Wa 46 Alt 657[RISM]; I-CHf [I-CHc] B 25 [2][RISM;P]); *Va crescendo il mio tormento* (H-Gk AMC, B. 34[RISM,299]; HR-Dsmb 38/1078[RISM]; I-BGc E.1.2 [12][RISM,SBN]; I-Mc Mus. Tr.ms. 140[RISM,SBN]; I-Mc Noseda C.36 [12][SBN]; I-MC 1-B-23 [7][RISM]; I-MC 1-C-2 [2][RISM]; I-MC 1-C-3 [11][RISM]; I-Raf 1.E.1 [17][RISM])
	[printed sources] *Va crescendo il mio tormento* by Francesco Bianchi, in *Va crescendo il mio tormento* (Venice: Zatta, [s.d.])

---

293. Date in [C, CA] gives 24/08/1786.
294. Microfilm copy: CDN-Lu ML48.M47B53 1787a; photocopy: CDN-Lu ML48.M47D542 1786a.
295. Microfilm copy: CDN-Lu ML48.M47Z54 1786aa.
296. Microfilm copy: CDN-Lu ML48.M47A46 1791a.
297. Opera pasticcio by different composers based on Sarti's *Didone* of 1782, recomposed with pieces copied by different hands at different moments. The 1st volume includes on p. 157: 'Duetto Luigi Cherubini'.
298. The source states: 'Sung in Genova, 1787, by Margheritta Moriggi'. The music of this aria is different from that of the 1762 premiere and the 1782 version. The attribution to Sarti and the performance date provided by the source leads us to identify this production as the pasticcio with music by Sarti, Cherubini, Anfossi, and Bianchi. See also Frassoni, Edilio, *Due secoli di lirica a Genova* (Genoa: Cassa di Risparmio di Genova e Imperia, 1980).
299. In G major; the other sources are in F major.

MC | *Didone abbandonata* (1724–1832)

1787	mus. by Gazzaniga, Giuseppe	
1787 Vicenza	Teatro Eretenio (summ.)	(1)
1789 Venice	Teatro Grimani di S. Giovanni Grisostomo (?)	(2)
1794 Genoa	Teatro da S. Agostino (carn.)	(3)

Librettos   (1) Vicenza: Giusto, [1787]
I-Vcg LIBRETTI VICENZA 57 E 62;[300] I-VIb GONZ.019 [6]
(2,3) NA

Music sources   [complete scores] P-La 44-VIII-11/12[BA]

[excerpts] *Ah, non lasciarmi, no* (D-Hs M a/326 [5][GVK,RISM]; I-BEc Miari AM.ms107[RISM,SBN]; I-MC 2-D-5/3 [2][RISM]; I-MC 2-D-6/3 [2][RISM]; I-Nc 64.21.22 [12][SBN]; US-NHub GEN MSS 23 [I,IV][RISM]; US-Wc M1497.N776 [1][RISM]); *Dovrei… ma no* (I-Mc Mus. Tr.ms. 483[RISM,SBN]); *Va crescendo il mio tormento* (I-FZc A.VI.50[SBN,301]); *Vado… ma dove?… oh dio!* (I-Mc Mus. Tr.ms. 475[RISM,SBN])

[doubtful] *Ah, non lasciarmi, no* (I-OS Mss.Mus.B 3570[RISM,SBN,302]); *Quando saprai chi sono* (F-Pn L-17960[BnF,303]; HR-Zha XLVI-K[RISM;IP,304])

1788	mus. by Anfossi, Pasquale (2nd version) → see 1774	

1790	mus. by Bertoni, Ferdinando; Rampini, Vincenzo; Naumann, Johann Gottlieb; and Gazzaniga, Giuseppe	
1790 Venice	Teatro Grimani di S. Samuele (aut.)	(1)
1791 Bergamo	Teatro Riccardi (Aug. Fair, 24/08/1791)[305] *opening of the theatre*	(2)
1793 Padua	Teatro Nuovo	(3)

Librettos   (1) Venice: Fenzo, 1790
A-Wmi BT-550; F-Pn 8-YTH-51134; F-Pn 8-YTH-51894; <u>I-Mb Racc. dramm.3907</u>; I-Vcg LIBRETTI S.SAMUELE 182[306]

---

300. Microfilm copy: CDN-Lu ML48.M47G39 1787a.
301. In F major instead of G major.
302. The music does not coincide with I-MC 2-D-5/3 [2].
303. Inserted into Gazzaniga's *La vendemmia* (Florence, 1778), reworked as *Quando saprai chi sono sorpresa resterai*.
304. The source includes a reference to a performance in the carnival season of 1779 in the Teatro Grimani di S. Giovanni Grisostomo. The music is different from P-La 44-VIII-11/12.
305. For a complete analysis of the circumstances surrounding this performance, see Labruna, Serena, 'La *Didone abbandonata* al Teatro Riccardi di Bergamo nel 1791: nascita de un teatro stabile ai margini della Repubblica di Venezia', in *Theatre Spaces for Music in 18th-Century Europe*, ed. by Iskrena Yordanova, Giuseppina Raggi, and Maria Ida Biggi (Vienna: Hollitzer, 2020), pp. 387–408.
306. Microfilm copy: CDN-Lu ML48.M47B53 1787a; photocopy: CDN-Lu ML48.M47D54 1790a.

MC | *Didone abbandonata* (1724–1832)

(2) Milan: Bianchi, [1791]
CDN-Ttfl Itp Pam 00495; I-BGc Sala 32 D 1.2.23; I-Fc E.VI.4884; I-SORmde LA.039; I-Vcg LIBRETTI BERGAMO 247;[307] I-Vgc ROL.0108 [3]

(3) NA

Music sources
[excerpts]
Bertoni, Ferdinando, *Va crescendo il mio tormento* (HR-Sk LIV/677[RISM,308])
Naumann, Johann Gottlieb, *Se ti perdo amato oggetto* (CH-Bk [CH-Bm] MAB SCB MFA Fk-72[SB]; D-Mbs Mus.ms. 2373[RISM]; D-Rtt Sammelband 6 [6][RISM]; I-BGi 17302[IC,RISM,SBN,309]; I-Nc 34.3.23 [1][SBN]; I-OS Mss. Mus.B 1205[RISM,SBN]; I-PAc Sanv.A.180[RISM,SBN]; I-Vnm Mss. 11274[SBN])
Paisiello, Giovanni, *Tu mi chiami amato bene* (CZ-Pnm XLII B 280[RISM]; CZ-Pnm XLII C 58[RISM]; D-BFb [D-MÜu] P-ai-34[RISM])
Rampini, Vincenzo, *Non ha ragione ingrato* (D-B Mus.ms. 18110[RISM]; D-BFb [D-MÜu] R-am 50 [1–2][NG,RISM]; F-Pn D-14986[BnF,NG]; I-BGc Mayr 232.97[RISM,SBN]; I-Vc Correr Busta 123 [5][NG,SBN])

1791	mus. by various unknown composers
1791 Padua	Teatro Nuovo (Fair, 15/08/1791)
Librettos	Padua: Conzatti, [1791] I-Pci BP.2555.X;[310] I-Pmc[C,S]; I-Vgc ROL.0680 [12];[311] US-Cn BLC #488
1792	mus. by various composers (Andreozzi, Gaetano; Cimarosa, Domenico; Giordani, Tommaso; Paër, Ferdinando; Rampini, Domenico; Sacchini, Antonio; Salieri, Antonio; Sarti, Giuseppe; Schuster, Joseph; arr. Storace, Stephen)
1792 London	King's Theatre in the Haymarket (23/05/1792)[312] *Dido, Queen of Carthage*
Librettos	London: [s.n.], 1792 (It./En.)[313] GB-Ob Vet. A5 d.961; US-CAe *EC8 H6514 792d; US-FAy 768 H65 792d; US-NYp[E]; US-SM La 948; US-U 782.1 St74d1795

---

307. Microfilm copy: CDN-Lu ML48.M47B53 1787a; photocopy: CDN-Lu ML48.M47G37 1791a.
308. → see comments in 1748, mus. by Bertoni, Ferdinando.
309. Arrangement for piano and mandolin.
310. Lost according to the library staff.
311. Microfilm copy: CDN-Lu ML48.M47T38 1787a.
312. Apparently, a revision of Metastasio's libretto; see [NG] 'Storage, Stephen' and Burden, 'Metastasio on the London Stage', pp. 161–62.
313. Microfilm copy of unspecified copy: US-BL PR1269 .T55 no. S123.

MC | *Didone abbandonata* (1724–1832)

Music sources	[printed sources] *Songs, Duet, Trio, and Chorusses, in the Opera of Dido, Queen of Carthage. With the Masque of Neptune's prophecy. The Music Principally New, and Composed by Mr. Storace; with Selections from the Most Celebrated Works of Sacchini, Salieri, Andreozzi, Giordaniello, Cimarosa, Sarti, Rampini, Schüster, and Paër* (London: [s.n.], 1792)	
1794	**mus. by Paisiello, Giovanni**	
1794 Palermo	Teatro di Santa Cecilia (summ.)	(1)
1794 Naples	Teatro di S. Carlo (04/11/1794)	(2)
	name day of Maria Carolina of Austria, queen of Naples	
1795 Florence	Teatro dei Risoluti (01/07/1795)	(3)
1796 Verona	Teatro Filarmonico (carn.)	(4)
1796 St Petersburg	Teatro Hermitage (19/10/1796)[CA]	(5)
1799 London	King's Theatre in the Haymarket (30/05/1799)[314]	(6,7)
	add. By A. Benelli, V. Federici, and P. Guglielmi[315]	
1808 London	King's Theatre in the Haymarket (26/01/1808)[316]	(8,9)
	add. by S. Buonaiuti	

Librettos

(1) Palermo: d'Affrunti, [1794]
US-BEm ML48 .S5 [143]

(2) Naples: Flauto, 1794
B-Bc 19909; CDN-Ttfl Itp Pam 00671; I-Bc Lo.03932; I-Fm Mel.2337 [7]; I-Nc Rari 10.3.2 [5]; I-Nn S.MARTINO 52.7 24 [1]; I-Ra E.I.06 [8]; I-Ra E.I.24 [9]; I-Vgc ROL.0509 [11]; US-BEm ML48 .I7 [708]

(3) Florence: Pagani & co., [1795]
GB-Lbl 906.c.12 [1]; US-Wc ML48 [S7699]

(4) Verona: Ramanzini, [1796]
I-Vcg LIBRETTI VERONA 57 F 73; I-Vgc ROL.1074 [15]; I-Vnm DRAMM.1122 [15]; I-VEc[S]

(5) NA

(6) London: Pall-Mall no. 5, [1799] (It./En.)
GB-Lbl 639.f.27 [5]; US-CAt TS 8154.502 1799; US-SM La 1259; US-Wc ML48 [S7606]

(7) Dublin: Tyrrell, 1800 (It./En.)
IRL-Dn 1800 [15]

---

314. The production ran for five consecutive performances; see Petty, 'Italian opera in London', p. 365.
315. Burden, 'The King's Theatre in London', p. 130 n. 39.
316. Burden, 'The King's Theatre in London', p. 163, gives 30/05/1808.

MC | *Didone abbandonata* (1724–1832)

(8) London: Zotti, [1808] (It./En.)
GB-Lbl 907.k.9 [10]; GB-Ob Johnson e.658; US-BL; US-CAt TS 8154.502 1808; US-SM La 1537

(9) Dublin: Tyrrell, 1808 (It./En.)
IRL-Dn J 85

Music sources

[complete scores] A-Wgm IV 264341 [Q 1818][IC,MGG,NG]; CDN-Lu GM/AR 24 [7][RISM;P]; D-B Mus.ms. 16608 [50][MGG,NG,RISM]; F-Pn D-10151 [1–2][BnF,MGG,NG,317]; GB-Lbl Add. 32069[MGG,NG,RISM]; I-Fc D.I.485/486[IC,SBN]; I-Nc* 16.8.36/37[IC,MGG,NG,RISM,SBN]; I-Rama A.Ms.377/378[NG,SBN]; I-Vnm Mss. 10183/10184[MGG,NG,SBN]; US-Bp M.51.4[MGG,NG,RISM]

[excerpts] *Ah, non lasciarmi, no* (F-Pn VM4-573[BnF,318]; I-Fc F.P.S.409 [1][RISM,SBN]; I-MC 4-C-15 [5][RISM]; I-Nc 34.6.10 [2][SBN]; I-Nc 64.133.10[SBN]; I-Nc Arie 683 [10][SBN]; S-Skma T-SE-R[RISM]; US-Wc M1505.A1 (vol. 165) [2][RISM]); *Cari accenti del mio bene* (CDN-Lu GM/AR 24 [7][RISM]; D-B Mus.ms. 16609[RISM]; I-Fc F.P.S.409 [19][RISM,SBN]; I-Rsc G.Mss.154 [4][MGG,NG,RISM,319]; I-VEcon MS 289[RISM]; US-Wc M1505.A1 (vol. 172) [4][RISM]); *Morire, oh dio, mi vedi* (F-Pn D-12016 [8][BnF]; I-Fc F.P.S.409 [3][RISM,SBN]; I-MC 4-D-4 [4][RISM]; I-MC 4-D-7 [6][RISM]; I-Nc 34.6.8 [12][SBN]; US-Wc M1505.A1 (vol. 169) [2][RISM]); *Non ha ragion l'ingrato* (D-B Mus.ms. 18110[RISM]; I-Rsc G.Mss.102 [3][MGG,NG,RISM]); *Povero cor tu palpiti* (F-Pn D-14848[BnF]; F-Pn VM4-574[Bn,320]; I-Fc F.P.S.409 [16][RISM,SBN]; I-MC 4-C-13 [1][RISM]; I-Nc Arie 467.A.2[SBN]; S-Skma T-SE-R[RISM]; US-Wc M1505.A1 (vol. 165) [4][RISM]); *So che un sogno è la speranza* (I-Fc F.P.S.409 [2][RISM,SBN]); *Son regina e sono amante* (I-Bsf M.P.IV.14[SBN]; I-MC 4-D-15 [5][RISM]; I-Rsc G.Mss.102 [4][MGG,NG,RISM]); *Vado… ma dove?… oh dio!* (B-Bc 4564[RISM]; I-Mc Noseda O.4 [7][SBN])

[doubtful] *Soccorete o giusti dei* (A-Wgm VI 8742 [Q 3280][IC,321]); *Tu mi chiami amato bene*[322] (CZ-Pnm XLII B 280[RISM]; CZ-Pnm XLII C 58[RISM;IP]; D-BFb [D-MÜu] P-ai 34[RISM,323])

[printed sources] [London, 1808] *Ah non partir spietato*[324] by G. Paisiello, in *Ah non partir spietato, the Favorite Duett Sung by Mad.ᵉ Catalani &*

---

317. Microfilm copy: F-Pn VM BOB-28879/28880.
318. Microfilm copy: F-Pn VM BOB-23836.
319. Fols 381–82 and 411–12 by a different hand.
320. Microfilm copy: F-Pn VM BOB-23836.
321. Despite the inscription on the source, the terzet was not included in Paisiello's 1794 version.
322. The duet was performed in the 1790 revival but was not included in Paisiello's 1794 version.
323. According an inscription on the score, the premiere took place in 1790.
324. Printed for one of the London performances. The duet was not included in Paisiello's original version.

MC | *Didone abbandonata* (1724–1832)

Mad.^e Dussek (London: Kelly, [c. 1805]) *Più non ho la dolce speranza* by A. Sacchini, in *Più non ho la dolce speranza, the Favorite Cavatina Sung by Mad.^e Catalani* (London: Kelly, [c. 1805]); in *Più non ho, the Favorite Songs as Sung by Mad.^e Catalani* (London: Lavenu, [c. 1814]); in *Più non ho la dolce speranza, Sung by Mad.^e Catalani* (London: Birchall, [c. 1808?]); *Se il ciel mi divide* by A. Sacchini, in *Se il ciel mi divide. A Favourite Song Sung by Mad.^e Catalani* (London: Birchall, [c. 1808?]); *Ve come nobile* by G. G. Ferrari, in *Ve come nobile, Cavatina & Duett, as Sung by Mad.^e Caralani & Mad.^e Dussek* (London: Birchall, [1808?])

[doubtful] *Ove son… chi sei?* (F-Pn D-12016 [8])[BnF,325]

1795	mus. by Koželuh, Leopold
1795 Vienna	Teatro Privilegiato[326]

1798	mus. by Marino, Settimino and others (incl. Portugal, Marcos António?) lib. rev. by Caravita, Giuseppe	
1798 Porto	Teatro de São João (summ.)	(1)
1799 Lisbon	Teatro de São Carlos (16/10/1799)	(2)
1803 Lisbon	Teatro de São Carlos (17/12/1803) *birthday of Maria I, queen of Portugal*	(3)
Librettos	(1) NA	
	(2) Lisbon: Ferreira, 1799 (It./Port.) I-Rsc Carv.4364; US-Wc ML48 [S5968]	
	(3) Lisbon: Ferreira, 1803 (It./Port.) I-Rsc Carv.4365; US-Wc ML48 [S8446]	

1810	mus. by Fioravanti, Valentino
1810 Rome	Teatro Valle (spr., 09/06/1810)
Librettos	Rome: Puccinelli, 1810 I-Bc Lo.01702; I-Fc E.VI.3204; I-Nc Rari 10.3.9 [7]; I-Rsc Carv.4366

---

325. Although the catalogue of the French National Library identifies this duet as part of a *Didone abbandonata* by Paisiello, it does not appear in the corresponding libretto. The duet belongs to *Enea e Lavinia* (Naples, 1785) with text by Gaetano Sertor and music by Pietro Alessandro Guglielmi.
326. Lost according to [NG].

MC | *Didone abbandonata* (1724–1832)

Music sources   [excerpts] *Chiamami pur così* (F-Pn L-4569 [2,3][BnF,RISM]; I-PAc Borb.2802 [3][RISM,SBN]; I-Rc Mss. 2533 [12][RISM,SBN]; I-Rsc G.Mss.893[RISM]; US-SFsc *M2.1 M117[RISM]); *Quando saprai chi sono* (S-Skma T-SE-R[RISM]); *Son regina e sono amante* (I-MC 2-C-10 [1][RISM])

1810	**mus. by Paër, Ferdinando**	
1810 Paris[NG]	Tuileries	(1)
	La Didone	
	1st version	
1811 Paris	Tuileries (09/06/1811)	(2)
	Didone abandonée	
	lib. rev. by S. Vestris	
1812 Paris	Tuileries (31/01/1812)	(2)
1812 Dresden	Royal theatre	(3)
1814 London	King's Theatre in the Haymarket (07/07/1814)	(4)
	lib. rev. by S. Vestris	
	2nd version	
1817 Parma	Teatro Ducale (carn., 14/01/1817)	(5)
1817 Florence	Teatro della Pergola (spr.)	(6)

Librettos   (1) NA

(2) Paris: Fain, 1811 (It./Fr.)
CZ-Pnm B 5184; <u>D-Mbs L.eleg.m. 1022</u>; F-Pn GD-9042; F-Pn 8-RA3-332; F-Pn 8-RO-8671;[327] F-Pn 16-EGC-3268;[328] I-Fc E.V.1722;[329] I-Fc E.VI.3211; I-PAc F. Libretti, sc.III [106]; <u>I-Rc COMM 527 [2]</u>

(3) Dresden: [s.n.], 1812 (It./Ger.)
D-B 7 T 28 [7]; <u>D-Dl MT.1650.a</u>; <u>US-Wc ML48 [S7488]</u>

(4) London: Gillet, 1814 (It./En.)
GB-Lbl 970.k.11 [1]; I-Nragni L064; US-SM La 1819[330]

(5) Parma: Rossi–Ubaldi, [1817]
I-Ms MUS. P. IV. 29; I-PAc F. Libretti, sc.112 [107]; I-PAc F. Libretti, sc.112 [108]; I-PAt Fer.Libretti.054; <u>I-Rn 40.10.I.24.2</u>; I-Rsc Carv.4391; I-Vnm DRAMM.3294 [20]; <u>US-Wc ML48 [S7491]</u>

---

327. Microfilm copies: CDN-Lu ML48.M47V54 1820a; F-Pn R117944.
328. Microfilm copy: F-Pn R117944.
329. Microfilm copies: CDN-Lu ML48.M47P344 1811a; I-Rig Film Kf 426 [1].
330. Microfilm copy: US-CLp PR1271 .N56X.

MC | *Didone abbandonata* (1724–1832)

(6) Florence: Fantosini, [1817][331]
CDN-Lu ML48.M47P344 1817a; CDN-Ttfl Itp Pam 00640; I-Bc Lo.03755; I-Fc E.V.0527; I-Fc E.V.1417; I-Fc E.VI.3205; I-Fm Mel.2330 [9]; I-Fn B.17.6.272.8.5; I-Nc Rari 10.3.9 [3]; I-Rsc Carv.4367; I-Rsc Libr. n. XXII [70]; I-Vgc ROL.0505 [6]; US-AUS KL-18 324; US-CAh *IC8.A100.B525 [5]; US-Wc ML48 [S7490]

Music sources   [complete scores] D-Dl Mus.4259-F-513[NG,RISM]; D-Dl Mus.4259-F-513a[NG,RISM;P]; F-Pn CS-2161 [1–2][BnF,332]; F-Pn L-12166[BnF,333]; F-Pn D-19235[BnF;P]; I-Fc F.P.T.372[NG,RISM,SBN,334]; I-MOe Mus. E. 177[IC;P]; I-MOe Mus. F. 861[IC,NG]; I-PAc ML.136/137[NG,RISM,SBN]; I-PAc Ms.M.C.C.21[NG,RISM,SBN]

[excerpts] *Dovrei... ma no* (F-Pn D-17985[BnF,RISM;P]); *Morir oh Dio! mi vedi* (F-Pn D-15006[BnF]); *Povero tu cor palpiti* (I-PAc Ms.M.C.C.7.h[RISM,SBN]); *Sei vinto, e pur non sai* (I-Fc D.I.185 [2][IC,RISM,SBN]; I-Mc Noseda N.31 [3][SBN]; I-Nc 6.2.9.35[SBN]; I-Rama A.Ms.232[SBN]; I-Rama A.Ms.1718[SBN]); *Se resto sul lido* (I-Fc D.I.194 [2][IC,RISM,SBN]; I-PAc ML.143 [2][RISM,SBN]); *Vado... ma dove?... oh dio!* (I-PAc ML.143 [3][RISM,SBN])

[unidentified arias] F-Pn L-19216[BnF]

[doubtful] *Io d'amore, oh Dio! mi moro* (CH-AR Mus Ms A 37[RISM;R,335]; I-Nc Arie 647 [1][SBN])

[printed sources] [London, 1814] *La Didone abbandonata. The much Admired Grand Serious Opera as Performed at The King's Theatre Haymarket* (London: Birchall, [c. 1815])[R]

[excerpts] *Accogli o regina*, in *Accogli o Regina, Duetto, as Sung by Madame Grassini & Sig.r Marzocchi* (London: Birchall, [c. 1814]); *Ah, non lasciarmi, no*, in *Inumano tiranno, Recitativo ed Ah, non lasciarmi, no, the Favorite Rondo, as Sung by Madame Grassini* (London: Birchall, [c. 1814]); *Cari accenti del mio bene*, in *Cari accenti del mio bene, Terzetto, as Sung by Madame Grassini, Signor Marzocchi & Signor Tramezzani* (London: Birchall, [c. 1814]); *Dovrei... ma no*, in *Dovrei, ma no, Cavatina, as Sung by Madame Grassini* (London: Birchall, [c. 1814]); *Morire oh Dio mi vedi*, in *Enea salvo gia sei, Recitativo, e Morire oh Dio mi vedi, as Sung by Ma-*

---

331. Microfilm copy of unidentified copy: CDN-Lu ML48.M47P344 1817a. According to the [IC], the original libretto was held in I-Ms, yet no such source is present in the institution's card catalogue; [C,S] do not include any source there.
332. Microfilm copies: F-Pn BOB-759/760; F-Pn R-107036/107037.
333. Microfilm copy: F-Pn VM BOB-30952.
334. Microfilm copy: CDN-Lu M1500.M57P344 1811a.
335. The aria was not included in the original version. For voice and piano.

dame Grassini & Sig*r* Tramezzani (London: Birchall, [c. 1814]); *Povero cor tu palpiti*, in *Povero cor tu palpiti, Cavatina, As sung by Madame Grassini* (London: Birchall, [c. 1814]); *Sei vinto e pur non sai*, in *Sei vinto, e pur non sai, Duetto, as Sung by Sig*r* Marzocchi & Sig*r* Tramezzani* (London: Birchall, [c. 1814]); *Se resto sul lido*, in *Se resto sul lido, Aria con Coro, Sung Sig*r* Tramezzani* (London: Birchall, [c. 1814]); *Son regina e sono amante*, in *Son regina, e sono amante, Aria con Coro, as Sung by Madame Grassini* (London: Birchall, [c. 1814]); *Vado… ma dove?… oh dio!*, in *Oh Dio! cresce l'orrore, Recitativo, e Vado, ma dove, Cavatina, as Sung by Madame Grassini* (London: Birchall, [c. 1814])

1814	mus. by Paër, Ferdinando (2nd version) → see 1810	
1823	**mus. by Mercadante, Saverio**	
1823 Turin	Teatro Regio (carn., 18/01/1823)	(1)
	1st version	
1823 Milan	Teatro Re in Salvatore (summ.)	(2)
1823 Livorno	Teatro degli Avvalorati (aut., 15/11/1823)	(3)
1823 Lucca	Teatro del Giglio (aut.)	(4)
1824 Genoa	Teatro da S. Agostino (carn.)	(5)
1824 Vicenza	Teatro Eretenio (summ.)	(6)
1824 Palermo	Teatro Carolino	(7)
	9th opera of the 1824 theatrical season	
1825 Mantua	Teatro Nuovo della Società (carn.)	(8)
1825 Florence	Teatro della Pergola (spr.)	(9)
1825 Cremona	Teatro della Concordia (Fair, 13/11/1825)	(10)
1825 Naples	Teatro di S. Carlo (31/07/1825)[336]	(11)
	lib. rev. by A. L. Tottola[337]	
	2nd version	
1826 Ravenna	Teatro Comunale (carn.)	(12)
1826 Udine	Teatro della Nobile Società (10/08/1826)	(13)
1826 Barcelona	Teatre de la Santa Creu	(14)
1826 Gorizia	Teatro di Gorizia	(15)
1826 Venice	NA	(16)
1827 Milan	Teatro alla Scala (carn., 02/01/1827)	(17)

---

336. Date in Ajello, Rafaele, ed., *Il teatro di San Carlo: la cronologia 1737–1987* (Naples: Guida, 1987). De Filippis and Arnese (*Cronache del Teatro di S. Carlo*, p. 64) give 04/08/1724.
337. Seller, Francesca, 'La *Didone abbandonata* di Saverio Mercadante (1825)', in *Pietro Metastasio: il testo e il contesto*, ed. by Marta Columbro and Paologiovanni Maione (San Marcellino: Altrastampa, 2000), pp. 165–70.

1827 Lisbon	Teatro de São Carlos (20/04/1827)	(18)
1827 Venice	Teatro Vernier in S. Benedetto (spr.)	(19)
1827 London	King's Theatre in the Haymarket (05/07/1827)	(20)
1828 Verona	Teatro Filarmonico (carn.)	(21)
1829 Turin	Teatro Regio (carn., 30/01/1829)	(22)
1830 Florence	Teatro Alfieri (spr.)	(23)
1832 Brescia	Teatro Grande (Aug. Fair)	(24)

Librettos

(1) Turin: Derossi, [1823]
CDN-Ttfl Lib 01726; D-Mbs L.eleg.m. 4386; F-Pn LIV IT-3762 [10]; I-Bc Lo.03074; I-Fm Mel 2190 [11]; I-PAc F. Libretti sc.112 [110]; I-PAc F. Libretti, sc.112 [116]; I-Rn 35. 10.F.05.04bis; I-Rn 35. 10.F.06.07; I-Rsc Carv.4392; I-Rsc Libr. n. XXIII [102]; I-Rsc Vol. 128 [15]; I-Tac Simeom L 178 [4]; I-Tn F XIII.507 [6]; I-Tp P.h.405; I-Tp P.h.571 [6.2]; I-Vgc ROL.0456 [1]; I-Vnm DRAMM.3306 [4]; US-AUS KL-18 537; US-CHH IOLC.00524

(2) Milan: Tamburini, [1823]
A-Wn 180468-A; I-Bc Lo.03079; I-Mb Racc.dramm.6079 [5]; I-TRc t-ML 619 [4]; I-Vnm DRAMM.893 [10]

(3) Livorno: Vignozzi, 1823
I-Fc E.VI.2841; I-Fm Mel.2032 [24]; I-Rsc Carv.4393

(4) [Lucca]: Benedini & Rocchi, [1823]
B-Bc 19910;[338] CDN-Ttfl Lib 01738; I-Fm Mel.2106 [21]; I-Fn B.17.6.271.1.16; I-La Dono Pellegrini – Libretti d'opera, 81; I-PAc F. Libretti, sc.112 [109]; I-Rsc Carv.4394; I-Rsc Libr. n. XXIII [101]

(5) Genoa: Pagano, [1824]
D-BHu 76/LQ 53000 D763-2 [5]; I-Fm Mel.2321 [1]; I-PAc F. Libretti, sc.112 [111]; I-Rn 40.8.A.17.10

(6) Vicenza: Parise, [1824]
I-Bl FS.W.993; I-Mb Racc.dramm.6125 [19]; I-PAc F. Libretti, sc.112 [112]; I-Vnm DRAMM.0886 [5]; I-VIb GONZ.030 [20]

(7) Palermo: Società tipografica, 1824
D-Mbs L.eleg.m. 4394; US-AUS KL-18 560; US-BEm ML48 .S5 [S396]

(8) [Mantua]: Branchini, [1825]
I-MAc MISC.-.358 [15]; I-Mb Racc.dramm.6302 [14]; I-Mb Racc.dramm.6145 [16]; I-Vnm DRAMM.0854 [7]; US-NYp *MGTY-Res., E/1825/26 [9]

---

338. Photocopy: CDN-Lu ML48.M47M483 1823a.

(9) Florence: Fantosini, 1825
CDN-Ttfl Lib 01727; D-Mbs L.eleg.m. 4431; I-Bc Lo.03075; I-Fm Mel.2153 [6]; I-Ms MUS. M. XXXVII. 180; I-Rb LIB.MUS 094; I-Rn 35.10.G.25.06; I-Rn 35.10.H.01.06; I-Rsc Carv.4368; I-Vgc ROL.1004 [1];[339] US-CHH IOLC.00566

(10) Brescia: Nicoli–Cristiani, [1825]
I-CRg CIV.A.PP.11.13; I-Mcom MUS.M.MUS.1.-450 [2]

(11) Naples: Flautina, 1825
B-Bc 19911;[340] I-Baf FA2.LIB.302; I-Bc Lo.03076; I-Nc Rari 10.3.2 [4]; I-Nn L.P. Libretti A 0118 [8]; I-PAc F. Libretti, sc.112 [113]; I-Vgc ROL.1004 [2]; US-AUS KL-18 591; US-CAh *IC7 A100 B750 [118]; US-NYp Mus. Res. *MZ, E/1825/26 [9]

(12) Ravenna: Roveri & sons, 1825
I-Bu A.V.Caps.217 [55]; I-Fn B.17.7.422.4; I-Ru XIII d.8 19

(13) Udine: Vendrame Liberale, [1826]
I-GOp MISC 00 0001048 FA 8

(14) Barcelona: Torner, [1826]
E-Bbc C400/144; E-Bbc C400/2607; E-Bu F-8/439/9; E-Mn T/26448

(15) Udine: Vendrami, [1826]
I-GOp MISC 00 0001048 FA 8

(16) Venice: Rizzi, [1826]
I-UDc Misc. Joppi 221 [11]; I-Vgc ROL.1004 [4]

(17) Milan: Fontana, 1826
CDN-Ttfl Lib 01728; D-Mbs L.eleg.m. 4470; F-Pn LIV IT-1635; F-Pn LIV IT-3583 [4]; I-Bc Lo.3077; I-Bc Villa Lo.73; I-BGi PREIS.237.3280; I-FEc P 42.24.20; I-Fm Mel.2147 [9]; I-LDEsormani 311/2/44; I-Ma OP. B. II. 24; I-Mb Racc.dramm.6127 [14];[341] I-Mc Lib.C.090; I-Mcom MUS.M MUS.1.-450; I-Mcom MUS.M MUS.1.-450-A; I-Mr Libr. 04301; I-Ms MUS. M. XXXVII. 72; I-Nc Rari 10.3.9 [8]; I-PAc F. Libretti, sc.112 [114]; I-PAc F. Libretti, sc.112 [115]; I-PAt Fer.Libretti.327; I-PLn BIBL.MIR. 109 [10]; I-Ra OP.B.II.24; I-Rsc Carv.4395; I-Rsc Libr. n. XXIII [103]; I-Rsc Vol. 70 [4]; I-Tci L.O.2360; I-Tci L.O.0476; I-TSci L.O. 0476; I-VAc V.A.R.VIII.4.5; I-Vc 1058; I-Vgc ROL.1004 [3]; I-Vnm DRAMM.0863 [25]; I-Vnm DRAMM.3313 [2]; I-Vqs Opus.

---

339. Mutilated on p. 1, probably blank.
340. Photocopy: CDN-Lu ML48.M47M483 1825aa.
341. Microfilm copy: CDN-Lu M1500.M57S227 1788aa.

C. 1167; US-AUS KL-18 644; US-CAt TS 8154.424 1826; US-CHH IOLC.00584; US-HA ML50.M573 D53; US-PRV n/s; US-Wc ML48 [S6319]

(18) Lisbon: Bulhões, 1827
D-KNth L 1374; I-Rsc Carv.4396

(19) Venice: Rizzi, [1827]
I-Bc Lo.03078; I-Mb Racc.dramm.5098; I-Mb Racc.dramm.6127 [4]; I-Nragni L060; I-Rsc Carv.4369; I-UDc Misc. D.T. 63 [3]; I-UDc Misc. Joppi 221 [11]; I-Vcg LIBRETTI S.BENEDETTO 57 B 28; I-Vgc ROL.1004 [6]; I-Vnm DRAMM.1383 [8]; S-Uu n/s

(20) London: Ebers, 1827
GB-Lbl 907.k.16 [5]; US-CAe Mus 570.25; US-U 782.1 M53d1827

(21) Verona: Bisesti, [1828]
F-Pn 8-RO-8597; I-Bl FS.W.320; I-Mb Racc.dramm.6136 [3]; I-Mb Racc.dramm.6306 [4]; I-Nragni L112 [11]; I-Rsc Libr. n. XXIII [99]; I-Vgc ROL.1004 [7]; I-Vnm DRAMM.0887 [8]; US-CAt TS 8154.424 1828; US-NYp *MGTY-Res.

(22) Turin: Derossi, [1829]
D-Mbs L.eleg.m.4557; I-BRq Misc.E.290; I-Fm Mel.2171 [2]; I-FZc RM.N.4.138; I-MOe MD.H.41; I-Nc Rari 10.3.21 [10]; I-Nragni L097; I-PAc F. Libretti, sc.112 [116]; I-Rn 35. 10.F.05.04bis; I-Rn 35. 10.F.06.07; I-Rsc Carv.4397; I-Rsc Vol. 129 [17]; I-Rsc Vol. 134 [13]; I-Tci L.O.0985; I-Tn F XIII.509 [4]; I-Tp P.h.571 [6.13]; I-Vc 1059; I-Vgc ROL.1004 [8]; I-Vnm DRAMM.3317 [12]; I-VCc 20 G 524; US-AUS KL-18 747; US-CAt TS 8154.424 1829; US-CHH IOLC.00638

(23) Florence: Fabbrini, [1830]
I-Fc E.V.0529; I-Fc E.V.0530; I-Fc E.V.1240; I-Fc E.V.3206; I-Fc E.V.3207; I-Ms MUS. M. XXXVII. 179; I-Rsc Carv.4370; I-Rsc Libr. n. XXIII [100]; I-Vgc ROL.1004 [9]

(24) Brescia: Simoncelli, [1832]
I-Fm Mel.2387 [9]; I-Rsc Carv.4398; S-Uu n/s

Music sources [complete scores] F-Pn D-7912[MGG,NG,342]; I-Nc* 14.2.22/23[MGG,NG,SBN]; I-Nc 29.6.3[MGG,NG,SBN]; I-Nc H.3.42[MGG,NG,SBN]; I-Tco*[MGG,NG]; I-PAc Borb.2623 [I–II][MGG,RISM]; US-Wc[MGG,NG,343]

---

342. Microfilm copies: CDN-Lu M1500.M57M474 1823a; F-Pn VM BOB-25107.
343. Microfilm copy: US-PRu MICROFILM 1788.

MC | *Didone abbandonata* (1724–1832)

[excerpts] *Addio felici sponde* (A-Wgm VI 7631 [Q 6980][IC]; I-OS Mss. Mus.B 954[RISM,SBN]); *A Dido il re di mori* (US-Bu BSO Collection, vol. 115[RISM]); *Ah, non lasciarmi, no* (A-Wgm VI 7219 [Q 6979][IC]); *Che mai sento* (A-Wgm VI 7262 [Q6981][IC]; I-Fc* F.P.T.831[MGG,NG,RISM,SBN]); *Dunque lasciarmi vuoi?* (I-Rama A.Ms.534 [7][SBN]; I-Rama A.Ms.534 [8][SBN]); *Non odi consiglio?* (US-Bu BSO Collection, vol. 107[RISM]); *O come rapido fuggi? Il timore* (I-Mc Noseda M.16 [8][SBN]); *Qual rosa in sul matino* (I-Rama A.Ms.534 [9][SBN]); *Quando saprai chi sono* (A-Wgm VI 38794 [Q 6982][IC]); *Vedi mio ben, di Venere* (I-OS Mus.Mss.B 1046 [RISM,SBN]; I-Rama A.Ms.534 [10][SBN]); *Vivi superbo e regna* (A-Wgm VI 7139 [Q 3752][IC]; I-Gl B C.3.29 [7][IC,SBN])

[printed sources] [complete scores] *Didone / dramma posto in musica dal maestro Zaverio Mercadante; ridotto per pianoforte solo da Giuseppe Concone* (Turin: Tagliabò & Mangrini, [c. 1830])[R]

[printed sources] [excerpts] [arrangements for voice and pianoforte]
Addio felici sponde, in *Addio felici sponde: cavatina nell'opera Didone abbandonata / del S.r M.o Mercadante* (Milan: Ricordi, [1823]); in *Cavatina di Enea nella Didone Abandonata, del maestro Mercadante* (Paris: Pacini, [s.d.])

Ah, non lasciarmi, no, in *Ah non lasciarmi no: duetto nell'opera Didone abbandonata / del Sig.r M.o Saverio Mercadante* (Milan: Ricordi, [1823]); in *Ah, non lasciarmi, Duetto, Sung Madᵉ Pasta & Madᵉ Puzzi* ([London]: Mori & Lavenu, [1825?]); in *Duetto per soprano e contralto nella Didone abandonata del maestro Mercadante* (Paris: Pacini, [s.d.])

Che mai sento, in *Che mai sento?: rec.vo e terzetto nell'opera Didone abbandonata / del Sig.r M.o Mercadante* (Milan: Ricordi, [1823])

Il soave del contento, in *Il soave bel contento, aria, composta del Sigʳ Mº Pacini* (Milan: Ricordi, [1824–1827]); in *Il soave bel contento, Cavatina, Introduced by Madame Pasta* (London: d'Almaine, [c. 1835])

Quando saprai chi sono, in *Quando saprai chi sono: duetto nell'opera Didone abbandonata / del Sig.r Maes.o Mercadante* (Milan: Ricordi, [1823])

Si mori, rea, che fo, in *Rondo | Nella Didone Abandonata | Del sig. M.o Mercadante* (Milan: Artaria, [1823–1828])

Vedi mio ben, di Venere, in *Vedi mio ben: cavatina […] nell'opera Didone Abbandonata / musica del Sig. M. Saverio Mercadante; ridotta con acc.to di pianoforte* (Naples: Girard, [s.d.])

Vivi superbo e regna, in *Rondò: Vivi superbo e regna: Nell'Opera Didone abbandonata: Del Sig.r Maes.o Mercadante: Eseguito dalla Sig.a Fanny Ekerlin al R. Teatro di Torino* (Milan: Ricordi, [1823])

MC | *Didone abbandonata* (1724–1832)

Quando saprai chi sono, in *Duetto nella Didone abandonata, musica di Mercadante* (Paris: Pacini, [s.d.])

[unidentified] 2 *Airs à 1 v. et acc. tirés de Didone abbandonate*, in *Journal d'Euterpe*, 12 (Paris, 1824)

1823	mus. by Klein, Bernhard
1823 Berlin[344]	NA (15/10/1823)
	Dido (Ger. only)

1824	mus. by Reissiger, Carl Gottlieb
1824 Dresden	Royal theatre (31/01/1824)
	Die verlassene Dido
Librettos	Dresden: [s.n.], 1824 (It./Ger.)
	D-Dl MT.2560; D-LEmi [D-LEu] Ästh.987-I; D-Mbs Slg.Her 361; I-Rsc Carv.4399; US-Wc ML48 [S8671]
Music sources	[complete scores] D-Dl Mus.4888-F-504[RISM;R,345]; D-Dl Mus.4888-F-504a[RISM;IP]

Arie sciolte

Annibali, Domenico, *Se resto sul lido* (F-Pn VM7-7271[NG,RISM])
Bach, Johann Christian, *Fosca nube il sol ricopra*[346] (US-BER n/s[RISM]; US-CAward [US-CAt] M1497. C813 1765 [1][RISM])
Bindi, *L'augelletto in lacci stretto* (F-Pn VM7-7267[BnF,RISM;P])
Boccherini, Luigi, *Ah, non lasciarmi, no* (P-Po RES-506 [1][RISM])
Böhme, Johann Gottfried, *A trionfar mi chiama* (D-Mbs Mus.ms. 1812 [1][RISM])
Borghi, Giovanni Battista, *Son quel fiume che gonfio d'umori* (GB-Lbl R.M.23.d.16 [10][RISM])
Bresciani, Giovanni Battista, *Quando saprai chi sono* [1794] (I-Mc Mus. Tr.ms. 197[RISM,SBN])
Bucelli, Orazio, *Fosca nube il sol ricopra* (I-Rrostirolla [I-Fn] MS MUS 483[RISM,SBN]); *Fra lo splendor del trono* (I-Rrostirolla [I-Fn] MS MUS 488[RISM,SBN]); *Io d'amore oh Dio! mi moro* (I-Rrostirolla [I-Fn] MS MUS 421[RISM,SBN]); *Quando saprai chi sono* (I-Rrostirolla [I-Fn]* MS MUS 425[RISM,SBN])
Celestino, Eligio, *Ah, non lasciarmi, no* (D-B Mus.ms. 30115[RISM])
Cimarosa, Domenico, *Ah, non lasciarmi ingrato*[347] (D-MÜs SANT Hs 1126[RISM])
Fini, Michele, *Quando saprai chi sono* (US-FAy Quarto 532 MS 6[RISM])
Hertel, Johann Wilhelm, *A trionfar mi chiama* (D-SWl Mus.2781[RISM;P])

---

344. It may have been revived in Cologne. Cf. the articles on Klein by L. Rellstab in *Neue Zeitschrift für Musik* 3 (1835), pp. 5–14, 57–84, 193–202 and also Griffel, Margaret Ross, *Operas in Germany: A Dictionary* (Lanham: Rowman & Littlefield, 2018).
345. Choruses.
346. Inserted into the composer's *Temistocle* (Mannheim, 1772); for the character of Temistocle.
347. The aria is not Metastasio's original but was included in Schuster's 1776 version of his *Didone abbandonata*.

MC | *Didone abbandonata* (1724–1832)

Kraus, Benedikt, *Ah, non lasciarmi, no* (D-OB MO 536[RISM;P]); *Fosca nube il sol ricopra* (D-OB* MO 539[RISM])

Lemner, Thomas, *Ogni amator suppone* (S-Skma T-SE-R[RISM])

Mayr, Johann Simon, *Quando saprai chi sono* (I-BGc Mayr 324.7[SBN]; US-Wc M1613.A2 M475 P[RISM])

Moroni, Filippo, *Son regina e sono amante* (I-PAc Borb.2886[SBN])

Mozart, Wolfgang Amadeus, *Ah, non lasciarmi, no* (CZ-Pu M II 11b Mozarts Denkmal[RISM])

Naselli, Diego, *Quando saprai chi sono* [1772] (I-MC 3-D-7 [2][RISM]; I-MC 6-D-10 [24][RISM]; US-NH Misc. Ms. 33 [5][RISM]; US-Wc M1505.A1 (vol. 245 B) [6][RISM])

Negri, Benedetto, *Nel duol che prova* (D-Mbs Mus.ms. 141[RISM])

Perillo, Salvatore, *Son regina e sono amante* [1763] (CH-Bu kr IV 201[RISM;P]; DK-Kk mu7501.2734[RISM])

Plantade, Charles-Henri, *Va lusingando amore* (F-Pn D-14858[BnF])

Reichardt, Johann Friedrich, *Ah, non lasciarmi, no* (D-B Mus.ms.autogr. Reichardt, J. F. 36[RISM])

Rickert, Aemilius, *Quando saprai chi sono* (D-BAd EB 510[RISM])

Rutini, Giovanni Marco, *Se resto sul lido* (D-Dl Mus.3329-J-1 [4][RISM])

Salieri, Antonio, *Ah, non lasciarmi, no* (I-Vnm Mss. 12649 SBN; I-VIb XII.2013 [6][RISM,SBN])

Sbacchi, Guglielmo, *Veggio la sponda* (D-MÜs SANT Hs 180 [16][RISM])

Selvaggi, Gaspare, *Se resto sul lido* (I-Nc* 32.1.12 [20][SBN])

Sperger, Johannes, *A trionfar mi chiama* [1801] (D-SWl Mus.5129[RISM;P])

Stuntz, Joseph Hartmann [1819], *Se resto sul lido* (D-Mbs* Mus.ms. 4064 [3][RISM]); *Va lusingando amore* (D-Mbs* Mus.ms. 4064 [14][RISM,348])

Tarchi, Angelo, *Dovrei… ma no* [1785] (I-PEsp M.CXXX [14][RISM])

Valeri, Gaetano, *Se resto sul lido* (US-Eu MSS 1002[IC,RISM])

Viotti, Giovanni Battista [c. 1750], *Ah, non lasciarmi, no* (I-Mc Noseda Q.40 [2][SBN]; I-MC 2-F-17 [14][RISM,349]; I-Nc 34.3.14 [16][SBN])

Wolf, Ernst Wilhelm, *Fosca nube il sol ricopra* (D-WRl HMA 3927[RISM])

Zingarelli, Niccolò Antonio, *Ardi per me fedele* [1790] (I-Rama* A.Ms.883 [13][SBN]); *Fosca nube il sol ricopra* (D-B Mus.ms. 23634 [5][RISM,350]); *Son regina e sono amante* [1789] (I-Rama* A.Ms.881[SBN]); *Tormento il più crudele* [1790] (I-Rama* A.Ms.883 [14][SBN])

Arias by unknown composer(s)

Ah, non lasciarmi, no (D-HAh AS-Reichardt A 4[RISM,351])

Ah, non lasciarmi, no (D-Hs ND VI 1078 [1][RISM])

Ah, non lasciarmi, no (GB-Ob Ms. Mus. e.11 [15][RISM])

Ah, non lasciarmi, no (I-Rrostirolla [I-Fn] MS MUS 1209 [9][SBN])

Ah, non lasciarmi, no (I-Rc MS MUS 6217[SBN])

Ah, non lasciarmi, no (US-Bu H. C. Robbins Landon Collection, Box 5, Folder 4[RISM])

A trionfar mi chiama (J-Tk S10-929 [2][RISM])

A trionfar mi chiama (US-BEm MS 26 [6][IC,RISM])

---

348. Arranged for voice and piano in D-Mbs* Mus.ms. 4064 [12].
349. Misattributed to Hasse on source.
350. For the character of Temistocle.
351. Wrongly attributed to Reichard in [RISM]; the music does not coincide with the composer's autograph (D-B Mus.ms.autogr. Reichardt, J. F. 36).

MC | *Didone abbandonata* (1724–1832)

Chiamami pur così (S-Skma Alströmer saml. 171 [24]^{RISM})
Fra lo splendor del trono (US-BEm MS 25 [8]^{IC,RISM})
L'augelletto in lacci stretto (A-Wn Mus.Hs.10873^{IC;P})
L'augelletto in lacci stretto (HR-PORzm ZMP 11921^{RISM;R})
Non ha ragione ingrato (I-MC 1-D-13 [2]^{RISM,352})
Non ha ragione ingrato (I-BGc Mayr 246.5^{SBN})
Ogni amator suppone (D-B Mus.ms. 30359 [3]^{RISM})
Son quel fiume che gonfio d'umori (B-Bc 5386^{RISM})
Quando saprai chi sono (I-PAc Borb.3045 [18]^{RISM,SBN})
Se resto sul lido (P-Ln C.I.C. 14,I [2]^{RISM})
Son regina e sono amante (GB-Ob Ms. Mus. d.9^{RISM})
Tormento il più crudele (US-BEm MS 17 [9]^{IC,RISM})
Tormento il più crudele (US-BEm MS 26 [7]^{IC,RISM})
Tu mi scorgi al gran disegno (A-Wgm VI 15385 [Q 3959]^{IC})
Va crescendo il mio tormento (I-OS Mss.Mus.B 3549^{RISM,SBN,353})
Va crescendo il mio tormento (US-Bu H. C. Robbins Landon Collection, scores x781A Box 7^{RISM})

Unidentified contents

I-MOe Mus. K. 1587[IC,354]
Chiamami pur così (I-Fc D.I.183 [4]^{IC,SBN})
Son regina e sono amante (I-Fc D.I.183 [20]^{C,SBN}; I-Vc Correr Busta 72.18^{SBN;IP,355})

Printed sources

Rutini, Giovanni Marco, *Va lusingando amore*, in *Aria | a Voce Sola | con uno | Violino Principale concertato. | due Violini, Alto Viola, e Cembalo per l'accompagnamento | composte | da Sig: Gio: Marco Rutini Fiorentino* ([s.l.: s.n., s.d.])
[unidentified] *Va crescendo il mio tormento*, in *Rondo* (Venice: Marescalchi, [s.d.])

Contrafacta

Alberti, Giuseppe Matteo, *Non ha ragione ingrato* ([*Quid mili est in caelo*] F-Sgs M 399^{RISM;P})
Dittersdorf, Carl Ditters von, *Va lusingando amore* ([*Adore te devote, latens deitas*] CZ-Pnm XXXVIII A 236^{RISM;P})

---

352. Attributed to Chieti in ^{RISM}, but Chieti is a town East of Rome.
353. Incomplete.
354. Complete version of a *Didone abbandonata* in three acts.
355. Vn part.

Alessandro nell'Indie (1730–1831)

Ana Llorens, Lecturer, Department of Musicology, Universidad Complutense de Madrid; scientific director, ERC Didone Project, email: allorens@ucm.es

Valentina Anzani, postdoctoral researcher, ERC Didone Project, Instituto Complutense de Ciencias Musicales, email: vanzani@iccmu.es

Complete operas

1730	mus. by Vinci, Leonardo[1]	
1730 Rome	Teatro delle Dame (carn., 02/01/1730)[2]	(1)
1731 Livorno	Teatro da S. Sebastiano (carn., 26/12/1730?) *pasticcio*	(2)
1732 Florence	Teatro del Cocomero (carn., 29/01/1732) *pasticcio*	(3)
1733 Brescia	Teatro degli Erranti (carn.)[3]	(4)
1733 Reggio Emilia	Teatro Pubblico (carn.) *pasticcio*[4]	(5)
1734 Urbino	Teatro Pascolini (carn.)	(6)
1734 Vyškov	Theatre	(7)
1735 Munich	Court theatre (carn.) add. by J. A. Hasse[5] and G. B. Ferrandini	(8,9)

1. This setting by Vinci opened the carnival season of 1730 in Rome; for this and the following two productions, see Strohm, Reinhardt, 'L'"*Alessandro nell'Indie*" del Metastasio e le sue prime versioni musicali', in *La drammaturgia musicale*, ed. by Lorenzo Bianconi (Bologna: il Mulino, 1986), pp. 157–76.
2. 26/12/1729 in De Angelis, Alberto, 'I drammi di Pietro Metastasio rappresentati al Teatro Alibert o "Delle Dame"', *Rivista italiana del teatro*, 2.6 (1943), 211–24.
3. Bellina treats this performance as a possible revival of Pescetti's setting → see 1732, mus. by Pescetti, Giovanni Battista; see Bellina, Anna Laura, 'Metastasio in Venezia: appunti per una recensio', *Italianistica: Rivista di letteratura italiana*, 13.1–2 (1984), 145–73.
4. See <https://www.pasticcio-project.eu/database/work/P103E04> [accessed 25 May 2022].
5. Related to this version survives the musical source in D-Mbs Mus.ms. 169. An examination of the score shows that none of the musicalised arias in this manuscript were included in Hasse's 1731 *Alessandro*. *Vede il nocchier*

MC | *Alessandro nell'Indie* (1730–1831)

1736 Parma	Teatro Ducale (carn.)	(10)
	pasticcio[6]	
1740 Lucca	Teatro Pubblico (carn.)	(11)
1745 Faenza	Teatro dei Remoti	(12)
1750 Sassuolo	Teatro Pubblico (aut.)[7]	(13)

Librettos

(1) Rome: Zempel & de Mei,[8] [1730]
CDN-Ttfl Itp Pam 02028; F-Pn LIV IT-3738 [7]; F-Pn YD-3536;[9] F-Pn YD-5234 [3]; F-Pn YD-5368 [1]; F-Pn YD-5448 [5]; GB-En RB.s.2667 [1]; GB-Lbl 905.k.6 [2]; I-Bc Lo.05515; I-Fm Mel.2266 [9]; I-FOLc G B 2-3-7; I-Rvat Stamp.Ferr.V.7836 [6]; I-RVE r-Z93 30 [5]; I-Vgc ROL.0650 [9]; US-Cn BLC #17; US-CAt *2004T-403; US-Wc ML48 [S10742][10]

(2) Lucca: Marescandoli, [1731]
I-Fm Mel.2072 [1]

(3) Florence: Pagani, 1732
I-Nn L.P. Libretti A 0018

(4) Brescia: Turlino, [1733]
I-Mb Racc.dramm.1150

(5) Reggio Emilia: Vedrotti, [1733]
I-REm 19.K.7; I-REm 19.K.206; I-REm Racc. Dramm E. Curti 146 [2]

(6) Urbino: Mainardi, 1734
CDN-Ttfl Itp Pam 00962[11]

(7) Brno: Swoboda, [1734]
CZ-OP ST-A-250

(8) Munich: Vötter, [1735]
US-Wc ML48 [S11297][12]

(9) Munich: Vötter, [1735] (It./Ger.)[13]
D-Mbs Bavar.4015-14,1 [4]; D-Mbs Slg.Her 2478

---

talora comes from Hasse's *Euristeo* (Venice, 1732). Believing that it is improbable that Hasse wrote further musical settings for them, the following arias might thus be by Ferrandini: *Vedrai con tuo periglio* (A1-S2), *Io non venni insino al Gange* (A1-S3), *Di rendermi la calma* (A1-S10), *Agitata da più bande* (A2-S2), *Scoglio alpestre in mezzo all'onde* (A2-S10), *Agitato dal furore* (A3-S1), *Finché rimango in vita* (A3-S7), and *Dov'è? Si affretti* (A3-S9).

6. See <https://www.pasticcio-project.eu/database/work/P104154> [accessed 25 May 2022].
7. Bianconi, Lorenzo and Giorgio Pestelli, eds, *The History of Italian Opera* (Chicago: The University of Chicago Press, 1988). Original edition: *Storia dell'opera italiana* (Turin: Edizione di Torino, 1987).
8. 'Si vendono nella libraria di Pietro Leone'.
9. Microfilm copy: F-Pn S129235.
10. Microfilm copy: US-PRu MICROFILM 00457.
11. Pages 49–72 missing.
12. Photocopy: US-Cn Folio ML50.2.A54 V5 1735°.
13. Photocopies of unspecified copy(s): US-BEm ML50.2.A54 V5 1735a; US-Cn Folio ML50.2.A54 V5 1735a.

(10) Parma: Monti, [1736]
I-Mb Racc.dramm.4507

(11) Lucca: Ciuffetti, [1740]
I-Bc Villa.Lo.063; I-Lg B.ta 208 [3]

(12) Faenza: Ballanti & Foschini, [1745]
US-NYp *MGTY-Res.

(13) Modena: Soliani, 1750
I-Fm Mel.2287 [17]; I-MOe 70.I.24

Music sources   [complete scores] B-Bc 2367[MGG,NG,RISM] [Acts II&III]; D-Mbs Mus.ms. 169[MGG,NG,RISM,14]; GB-Lbl R.M.23.c.8/9/10[MGG,NG,RISM,15]; I-MC 6-B-21[MGG,NG,RISM]; I-Nc 32.4.9[IC,MGG,NG,SBN]; I-Rac Ms. 07[BASE,RISM] [Act I]

[excerpts] *Chi vive amante sai che delira* (F-Pn VM7-7211[BnF]; GB-Lbl MS Mus. 143 [11][BL,RISM]; GB-Lbl R.M.23.f.2 [2][BL,RISM]; I-Rc Mss. 2558 [7][SBN]; US-BEm MS 870 [10][IC,RISM]); *Come il candore* (GB-Lbl MS Mus. 143 [7][BL,RISM]); *Compagni nell'amore* (F-Pn VM4-959 [4][BnF]); *Destrier che all'armi usato* (F-Pn D-3623 [4][BnF,RISM]; F-Pn VM4-959[BnF]; GB-Lam MS 134 [5][RISM]; I-Mc Noseda A.25.11[SBN]; I-PEsp M.CXXXVI [15][RISM,SBN]; I-Rama A.Ms.3702 [14][RISM]; I-Rc Mss. 2558 [19][SBN]; US-BEm MS 870 [11][IC,RISM]; US-FAy Quarto 532 MS 3 [20][RISM]); *Digli che io son fedele* (D-B Mus.ms. 22381 [4][RISM]; D-Hs M A/678 [21][RISM]; D-Hs M A/681 [3][RISM]; GB-Lam MS 134 [4][RISM]; GB-Lbl MS Mus. 143 [10][BL,RISM,16]; GB-Lbl R.M.23.f.2 [6][BL,RISM]; I-PSbsg San Giorgio n/s[SBN]; US-BEm MS 120 [52][IC,RISM]); *Dov'è? Si affretti* (B-Bc 5144[RISM;R]; F-Pn VM4-959 [9][BnF]; I-Rc Mss. 2558 [12][SBN]; I-Rc Mss. 2773 [11][SBN]; I-Rc Mss. 2558 [12][SBN]; US-BEm MS 870 [12][IC,RISM]); *È un prezzo leggiero* (D-Hs M A/681 [1][RISM]); *Non sarei sì sventurata* (GB-Lbl MS Mus. 143 [19][BL,RISM]); *Risveglia lo sdegno* (I-Rc Mss. 2558 [9][SBN]); *Se amore a questo petto* (F-Pn VM4-959 [6][BnF]; GB-Lbl MS Mus. 143 [20][BL,RISM]); *Se è ver che t'accendi* (F-Pn VM4-959 [8][BnF]; GB-Lbl MS Mus. 143 [2][BL,RISM]; GB-Lbl R.M.23.f.2 [9][BL,RISM]); *Se il ciel mi divide* (I-Nc 34.3.14 [15][SBN]; I-Nc 40.2.29[SBN,17]); *Se mai turbo il tuo riposo* (D-Hs ND VI 1078 [1][RISM]; GB-Lbl MS Mus. 143 [6][BL,RISM]; GB-Lbl R.M.23.f.2 [4][BL,RISM]); *Se mai turbo il tuo riposo* [duet] (D-B Mus.ms. 30408 [3][RISM,18]; D-Hs M A/681

---

14. For Munich 1735. Some of the arias are ordered differently from the libretto, e.g., *Di rendermi la calma*; others simply do not appear in the poetic source, e.g., *Agitata da più bande* and *Vede il nocchier talora*.
15. Microfilm copies: US-CAe Mus. 3870.599 [50/5]; US-PRu MICROFILM 00909.
16. Annotated in 3/8, whereas the aria is in 6/8 in I-Nc 32.4.9.
17. In d minor instead of f minor.
18. In A major instead of B flat major.

[2]^{RISM}; GB-Cfm [GB-Cu] MU.MS.13^{IC}; GB-Lbl Add. 31596 [12]^{BL,RISM}; GB-Lbl MS Mus. 143 [14]^{BL,RISM,19}; GB-Lbl R.M.23.e.2 [27]^{RISM}; GB-Lbl R.M.23.f.2 [5]^{BL,RISM}; GB-NOr DD/P/6/15/75^{RISM,20}; I-Fc D.I.210 [7]^{IC,RISM,SBN}; I-Nc 34.5.25 [9]^{SBN}; I-Rama A.Ms.3702 [12]^{RISM}; I-Rc Mss. 2773 [2]^{SBN}; US-AUS Finney 37 [3]^{RISM}; US-BEm MS 869 [5]^{IC,RISM}; US-FAy Quarto 532 MS 3 [29]^{RISM}; US-SFsc *M2.1 M518^{RISM}; US-Wc ML96.H83 [2]^{MGG,NG,RISM}); *Senza procelle ancora* (GB-Lbl MS Mus. 143 [9]^{BL,RISM}; GB-Lbl R.M.23.f.2 [8]^{BL,RISM}; I-Bc KK.308 [1]^{IC,RISM,SBN}; I-Rama A.Ms.3708^{RISM}; I-Rc Mss. 2773 [12]^{SBN}; P-Ln M.M. 395 [4]^{IC}; US-LAur MS 170/389 [4]^{RISM}); *Se possono tanto* (A-Wn Mus.Hs.1075 [16]^{IC}; D-Hs M A/678 [20]^{RISM}; D-Hs ND VI 1078 [1]^{RISM}; GB-Lam MS 134 [5]^{RISM}; GB-Lbl MS Mus. 143 [4]^{BL,RISM}; GB-Lbl R.M.23.f.2 [7]^{BL,RISM}; I-Bc KK.308 [14]^{IC,RISM,SBN}; US-BEm MS 27 [13]^{IC,RISM,21}; US-FAy Quarto 532 MS 3 [21]^{RISM}); *Se troppo crede al ciglio* (A-Wn Mus.Hs.1075 [15]^{IC}; GB-Lbl Add. 31602 [8]^{BL,RISM}; GB-Lbl MS Mus. 143 [8]^{RISM}; GB-Lbl R.M.23.f.2 [1]^{BL,RISM}; S-SK 494 [61]^{RISM}); *Se viver non poss'io* (D-Hs M A/681 [4]^{RISM}; GB-Lbl MS Mus. 143 [13]^{BL,RISM}; I-Rc Mss.2773 [15]^{SBN}); *Son confusa pastorella* (D-Hs ND VI 1078 [1]^{RISM}; F-Pn VM4-959 [10]^{BnF}; GB-Lbl MS Mus. 143 [12]^{BL,RISM}; GB-Lbl R.M.23.f.2 [3]^{BL,RISM}); *Vedrai con tuo periglio* (B-Bc 4955^{RISM}; F-Pn VM4-959 [2]^{BnF}; GB-CDu Mackworth Collection vol. 17 [6]^{RISM}; GB-Lbl MS Mus. 143 [5]^{BL,RISM}; I-Rc Mss. 2558 [10]^{SBN}; US-NH Misc. Ms. 75 [3]$^{RISM;R}$); *Vil trofeo d'un'alma imbelle* (B-Bc 5150 [21]$^{RISM;R,22}$); *Voi che adorate il vanto* (GB-Lbl MS Mus. 143 [21]^{BL,RISM})

[contrafacta] *È prezzo leggiero* ([*Salve Regina*] CH-Lz Mus. 34^{RISM}); *Se mai turbo il tuo riposo* [duet] ([*Quando languentem*] CZ-Pak 1357^{RISM}); *Se possono tanto* ([*Terrena cur amas, o Clemens cor meum*] A-WIL 1333^{RISM})

[doubtful] *Perder l'amato bene*[23] (D-Dl Mus.1-F-82,29 [4]^{RISM})

1731	mus. by Porpora, Nicola	
1731 Turin	Teatro Regio (carn., 01/1731)	(1)
	Poro	

19. Although the vocal part is the same as in I-Nc 32.4.9, this version starts with seven bars of an orchestral ritornello; barlines are annotated differently too.
20. In D major instead of B flat major. Fl. and bc parts only.
21. In F major instead of A major.
22. Annotated in 3/8, whereas the aria is in 6/8 in I-Nc 32.4.9.
23. The aria is not included in the librettos for the 1731 and 1735 versions. We have found only one other aria with the same title, written by Hasse in 1731 for his *Alessandro*, yet its music is different from this one.

MC | *Alessandro nell'Indie (1730–1831)*

1731 Vienna	Teatro Privilegiato (b. 01/07/1731)[24] *pasticcio with music by N. Porpora?*[25]	(2)
Librettos	(1) Turin: Valetta, [1731][26] I-Tci L.O.0080; I-Tci L.O.3403; I-Tn F XIII.519 [1] (2) NA	
Music sources	[excerpts] *Destrier ch'all'armi intorno* (D-B Mus.ms. 30173 [7a][MGG,NG,RISM]); *Digli che io son fedele* (D-Dl Mus.1-F-82,21 [11][MGG,NG,RISM]); *Finché rimango in vita* (I-PAc Sanv.A.270[MGG,NG,RISM,SBN]); *Il vezzoso tuo sembiante* (D-B Mus.ms. 30123 [8c][MGG,NG,RISM]); *Raggio amico di speranza* (D-B Mus.ms. 30123 [7b][MGG,NG,RISM]); *Se è ver che t'accendi* (D-B Mus.ms. 30123 [8b][MGG,NG,RISM]); *Sommi dei, se giusti siete* (B-Bc Bc 4958 [2][RISM],[27]; D-Hs M A/894 [25][RISM]; GB-Lbl Add. 31504 [115][RISM;R]); *Son prigioniera d'amore anch'io*[28] (D-B Mus.ms. 30123 [8a][MGG,NG,RISM]; GB-Lbl Add. 31593[RISM]; GB-Lbl MS Mus. 143 [18][BL,RISM]; I-Nc 34.6.25 [30][SBN]; US-BEm MS 21 [3][RISM]) [inserts] *Se viver non poss'io*[29] (GB-Cfm [GB-Cu] MU.MS.111 [12][IC]; GB-Lbl Add. 31593[RISM]; GB-Lbl Add. 31596[RISM]; GB-Lbl Add. 31603[RISM]; GB-Lbl R.M.23.d.4 [8][BL,RISM]; GB-Lbl R.M.23.d.8 [21][BL,RISM]; GB-Ob Ms. Mus. e.7 [3][RISM]; I-Bas IV 89/749a [3][RISM,SBN]; I-Rama A.Ms.3704 [31][RISM,SBN])	

1731   mus. by Predieri, Luca Antonio

1731 Milan	Teatro Regio Ducale (carn.)	(1)
1732? Genoa?	Teatro del Falcone *mus. by L. A. Predieri?*[30]	(2)
Librettos	(1) Milan: Malatesta, 1731 F-Pn LIV IT-3517 [4]; I-Bc Lo.04440; I-LDEsormani 297/6/27 (2) NA	

---

24. Klein, Rudolf, 'Die Schauplätze der Hofoper', *Österreichische Musikzeitschrift*, 24 (1969), 371–422.
25. Strohm, 'L'"*Alessandro nell'Indie*"', p. 174. The libretto is not listed in [C] and there is no mention to this performance in the Viennese operatic chronologies of Gluxam, Dagmar, 'Verzeichnis der Sänger in der Wiener Opern- und Oratorienpartituren 1705–1711', in *Studien zur Musikwissenschaft. Beihefte der Denkmäler der Tonkunst in Österreich*, ed. by Theophil Antonicek and Elisabeth T. Hilscher (Tutzing: Schneider, 2002), pp. 269–320 and Huss, Frank, 'Die Oper am Wiener Kaiserhof unter den Kaisern Josef I. und Karl VI. Mit einem Spielplan von 1706 bis 1740' (doctoral dissertation, Universität Wien, 2003).
26. According to [S]18965, there was a copy of this libretto in I-FPfanan (previously in Turin), yet the items of the collection were sold independently and can no longer be traced.
27. This and the following manuscript are wrongly attributed to Benedetto Micheli on the sources.
28. GB-Lbl MS Mus. 143 [18] and I-Nc 34.6.25 [30] are in a minor; the other sources, in g minor. US-BEm MS 21 [3] has a Moderato tempo marking; the other sources, Allegro.
29. Inserted into Porpora's *Germanico in Germania* (Rome, 1732).
30. Strohm, 'L'"*Alessandro nell'Indie*"', p. 174. No existing libretto found.

MC | *Alessandro nell'Indie* (1730–1831)

Music sources[31]

1731	**mus. by Händel, Georg Friedrich**	
1731 London	King's Theatre in the Haymarket (02/02/1731)[32] *Poro, re dell'Indie* 1*st* version	(1)
1731 London	King's Theatre in the Haymarket (23/11/1731) 2*nd* version, 3 arias added	(2)
1732 Hamburg	Oper am Gänsemarkt (14/02/1732)[33] *Triumph der Grossmuth und Treue: oder Cleofida, Königin von Indien* arranged and German recit. by G. P. Telemann lib. adap. by C. G. Wendt	(3)
1732 Brunswick	Teatro Ducale (summ. Fair, 25/08/1732) *Poro e Alessandro* probably adap. by G. C. Schürmann (three arias added)[34]	(4)
1736 London	Covent Garden (08/12/1736)[35] 3*rd* version six arias added (one by L. Vinci, two by G. A. Ristori)	(5)
1736 Hamburg	Oper am Gänsemarkt *Triumph der Grossmuth und Treue: oder Cleofida, Königin von Indien* German recit. by G. P. Telemann text adap. by C. G. Wendt	(6)
1743 London	King's Theatre in the Haymarket (15/11/1743)[CA] *Roxana or Alessandro nell'Indie* adap. by G. B. Lampugnani; lib. rev. by P. A. Rolli	(7)
1748 London	King's Theatre in the Haymarket (20/02/1748) *Roxana or Alessandro nell'Indie* adap. by G. B. Lampugnani; lib. rev. by P. A. Rolli	(8)
1748 London	King's Theatre in the Haymarket (08/03/1748) *Roxana or Alessandro nell'Indie* adap. by G. B. Lampugnani; lib. rev. by P. A. Rolli	(8)

---

31. According to Cummings, Graham, 'Reminiscence and Recall in Three Early Settings of Metastasio's *Alessandro nell'Indie*', *Proceedings of the Royal Musical Association*, 109 (1982–1983), 80–104, separate arias for Predieri's setting have been preserved, yet we have not been able to locate them.
32. Händel's *Poro* had sixteen consecutive performances; see Dean, Winton, *Handel's Operas 1726–1741* (Woodbridge: The Boydell Press, 2006). Fassini gives 12/02/1731 as the date of the premiere; cf. Fassini, Sesto, *Il melodramma italiano a Londra nella prima metà del Settecento* (Turin: Bocca, 1914).
33. Fassini, *Il melodramma italiano*, pp. 187–88; Strohm, 'L'"*Alessandro nell'Indie*"', p. 174.
34. Dean, *Handel's Operas*, p. 188.
35. Winton Dean gives 08/12/1736 as the date of this revival, after being postponed from 1 December; see Dean, *Handel's Operas*, p. 186. [C] gives 07/12/1736.

MC | *Alessandro nell'Indie* (1730–1831)

Librettos

(1) London: Wood, 1731 (It./En.)
CDN-Ttfl Itp Pam 00630; F-Pn RES-VS 420;[36] GB-Bp 782.12 Plays B/41; GB-En Bh.Lib.39;[37] GB-Lbl 639.d.19 [2]; GB-Lfom[E]; GB-Ob Vet. A4 e.3343; US-Cn ML50.2.P66 H36 1731; US-Cu PQ4714.A47 1731; US-CAt TS 8010.272 1731; US-LAuc ML50.2.D21 A7*; US-PRu Hall Handel XB83.0184; US-Wc M1500.H13 P55

(2) London: [s.n.], 1731 (It./En.)
F-Pn RES VS-420; GB-Bp 782.12 Plays B/41

(3) Hamburg: Stromer, [1732] (It./Ger.)
D-B Mus. T 7 [23]; D-Hs Ms 640/3 [9]; D-HVl Op. 2, 41; D-KIu Arch4 284; US-Wc ML48 [S4487]

(4) Wolfenbüttel: Bartsch, 1732 (It./Ger.)
D-BS Brosch. I 20.598; D-HVl Op. 1, 144; D-Mbs Slg.Her 2754

(5) London: Wood, 1736 (It./En.)[38]
F-Pn RES VS-421; GB-Ob Harding D 2447 [1]; US-Wc ML48 [S4486]

(6) Hamburg: [s.n., 1736] (It./Ger.)
GB-Lbl Hirsch IV.1347[39]

(7–9) NA

Music sources

1st version: 1731, London

[complete scores] D-B Mus.ms. 9054/5[RISM,40]; D-Hs M A/1042[RISM]; D-Hs M A/1042a[RISM;R]; D-Hs M B/1610[RISM,41]; GB-Lbl* R.M.20.b.13[RISM,42]; GB-Lfom Accession Number 338[RISM,43]; GB-Lfom Accession Number 743[RISM]; GB-Mp MS. 130Hd4v.191/192/193/194/195/196[RISM;IP]; GB-Mp Mp MS. 130Hd4v.236[RISM]; S-Skma T-SE-R[RISM;A]

[excerpts] *Caro amico amplesso* (D-SWl Mus.182 [31][RISM;IP]; GB-Cfm [GB-Cu] MU.MS 56[IC]); *Caro vieni al mio seno* (D-HEms Th Hä 35 [2][RISM;P]; D-SWl Mus.182 [45][RISM;IP]; GB-Cfm [GB-Cu] MU.MS.56[IC];

---

36. Microfilm copies: F-Pn VM BOB-9359; US-CAe 3447.5.83.
37. Microfilm copy: D-Gs Ma 2001-46:11966 [22].
38. According to [C,E,S], there was a further copy in the Theatre Museum, London, closed since 2007; see [S]18969. As the future of the collections is not clear, no [RISM] siglum can be used. Microfilm copies of unidentified copy(s): D-Gs MA 2001-46:12278 [24]; GB-En Mf.134, reel 12278 [24].
39. Microfilm copy: GB-Lbl Mus.Misc.1755.
40. Parts and short score, translated into German.
41. Recitatives in German, arias in Italian.
42. Microfilm copy: US-PRu MICROFILM 1279 [6].
43. Incomplete.

MC | *Alessandro nell'Indie* (1730–1831)

GB-Cfm [GB-Cu] MU.MS.145 [1]^(IC); GB-Lbl Add. 56487^(RISM;P,44); GB-Lbl MS Mus. 143 [3]^(BL,RISM); GB-Lbl R.M.23.d.11 [15]^(RISM;P); GB-Mp BRm710.5Rf31^(RISM;R,IP,45); S-Skma T-SE-R^(RISM;R,P)); *Come il candore d'intatta neve* (GB-Mp MS. 130Hd4v.314 [75]^(RISM;R); US-PHu Curtis 66 [9]^(RISM,46)); *Compagni nell'amore* (D-SWl Mus.182 [43]^(RISM;IP)); *Digli che io son fedele* (D-Bsa [D-B] SA 1560 [12]^(RISM;P); GB-Cfm [GB-Cu] MU.MS.145 [4]^(IC)); *Dov'è? Si affretti* (D-Bsa [D-B] SA 1560 [14]^(RISM;P); US-CAt M1505.H26 A57 1750^(IC)); *Mio ben ricordati* (D-SWl Mus.182 [3]^(RISM;IP); GB-Mp Mp MS. 130Hd4v.314 [76]^(RISM;R); GB-Ob Ms. Mus. c.107 [78]^(RISM;IP); S-Skma T-SE-R^(RISM;P)); *Se amore a questo petto* (D-Bsa [D-B] SA 1560 [11]^(RISM;P)); *Se il ciel mi divide* (GB-Mp Brm710.5Rf31^(RISM;IP); S-L Saml.Engelhart 542^(RISM;P); S-Skma T-SE-R^(RISM)); *Se mai turbo il tuo riposo* (D-Bsa SA 1560 [8]^(RISM;P); D-Bsa [D-B] SA 1560 [10]^(RISM;P); D-SWl Mus.182 [50]^(RISM;IP); GB-Lbl R.M.20.d.2 [9]^(BL,RISM); GB-Lbl R.M.23.d.11/15 [17]^(BL,RISM;P); GB-Lbl R.M.23.d.14^(BL,RISM)); *Se mai turbo il tuo riposo* [duet] (D-SWl Mus.182 [16]^(RISM;IP)); *Senza procelle ancora* (D-Bsa [D-B] SA 1560 [13]^(RISM;P)); *Se possono tanto* (D-Bsa [D-B] SA 1560 [9]^(RISM;P); D-SWl Mus.185 [3]^(RISM); D-SWl Mus.2479 [3]^(RISM;R)); *Se troppo crede al ciglio* (D-SWl Mus.182 [15]^(RISM;IP); D-SWl Mus.182 [44]^(RISM;IP)); *Se viver non poss'io* (S-Skma T-SE-R^(RISM)); *Son confusa pastorella* (D-SWl Mus.182 [15]^(RISM;IP); GB-Cfm [GB-Cu] MS.Add.9448 [12]^(IC,RISM); GB-Lgc G. Mus 362 (vol. II)^(RISM); GB-Mp BRm710.5Rf31^(RISM;R); GB-Mp MS. 130Hd4v.314 [77]^(RISM); I-Bc DD.52 [8]^(IC,RISM,SBN,47); US-NYp Mus. Res. *MN [64]^(RISM;R,IP,48)); *Vedrai con tuo periglio* (D-Bsa [D-B] SA 1560 [7]^(RISM;P); D-SWl Mus.182 [42]^(RISM)); *Vil trofeo d'un'alma imbelle* (D-SWl Mus.182 [14]^(RISM;IP); S-Skma T-SE-R^(RISM;P))

[printed sources] *Porus, an opera, as it is Perform'd at the Kings Theatre in the Hay Market Compos'd by Mr Handel* (London: Walsh, [1731]); *Caro vieni al mio seno; Come il candore; Mio ben ricordati; Digli che io son fedele; Se il ciel me divide; Se mai turbo il tuo riposo; Se possono tanto; Son confusa pastorella*, in *The favourite Songs in the Opera call'd Porus* (London: Walsh, [1731]); *Caro vieni al mio seno*, in *Caro vieni al mio seno. The favourite Minuet Sung in the Opera of Porus* ([s.l.: s.n., s.d.]); in *Return Fair Maid: A Favourite Minuet in Porus*, the Words by T. Brerewood Junr ([London: s.n.,

---

44. In a minor instead of a minor.
45. In d minor instead of b minor.
46. In g minor instead of b minor.
47. Microfilm copy: I-Bc 3462.
48. In G major instead of D major.

1735?]); *Se mai turbo il tuo riposo* [duet], in *Twelve Duets for Two Voices with a Thorough Bass for the Harpsichord or Bass Violin Collected out of All the Late Operas, Compos'd by Mr Handel, to which is Added the Celebrated Trio in the Opera of Alcina* (London: Walsh, [1735]); *Son confusa pastorella*, in *Son confusa pastorella. The Celebrated Song in Porus Sung by Sig.ra Merighi* ([s.l.: s.n., s.d.])

[contrafacta] *Son confusa pastorella* ([*Huc pastores properate*] <u>D-Dl Mus.2410-D-66a</u>[RISM])

[unidentified] GB-Lfom Accession Number 743[49]; S-Skma T-SE-R[RISM;P,50]

[doubtful] *Se mai turbo il tuo riposo* (GB-Lbl* R.M.20.d.2 [9][BL,RISM,51])

2nd version: 1732, Hamburg

[complete scores] D-Hs M B/1610[RISM]

1731	mus. by Hasse, Johann Adolf	
1731 Dresden	Court theatre (13/09/1731)[52] *Cleofide* lib. rev. by M. A. Boccardi	(1)
1732 Milan	NA [Teatro Regio Ducale]	(2)
1736 Venice	Teatro Grimani di S. Giovanni Grisostomo (carn., 28/01/1736)[53] *Alessandro nell'Indie* 2nd version	(3)
1736 Naples	Teatro di S. Bartolomeo (04/11/1736)[54] name day of Carlo VII, king of Naples mus. by J. A. Hasse, prologue by G. di Majo	(4)
1737 Ferrara	Teatro Bonacossi da S. Stefano (carn.) pasticcio mus. by J. A. Hasse, add. by A. Vivaldi	(5)

---

49. No title is given in the catalogue but, according to the singer's name (Annibale Pio Fabri), it is one of the arias for the character of Alessandro.
50. One of the duets included in the opera. Parts for soprano and thorough bass.
51. Composer's autograph, included in an aria collection with pieces only by Händel. However, the music is completely different from that in the 1731 version, and the aria was not included in the 1858 complete works, edited by Chrisander.
52. The production ran for five consecutive performances; see Schmidt-Hensel, Roland Dieter, '*La musica è del Signor Hasse detto il Sassone…*': *Johann Adolf Hasses 'Opere serie' der Jahre 1730 bis 1745. Quellen, Fassungen, Aufführungen* (Göttingen: V&R unipress, 2009).
53. For the three Venetian productions of Hasse's *Cleofide* (1736, 1738, and 1743), see Wolff, Hellmuth Christian, 'Johann Adolph Hasse und Venedig', in *Venezia e il melodramma nel Settecento*, ed. by Maria Teresa Muraro (Florence: Olschki, 1978), pp. 295–308.
54. Treated as a pasticcio in <https://www.pasticcio-project.eu/database/work/P103A74> [accessed 25 May 2022].

MC | *Alessandro nell'Indie* (1730–1831)

1738 Graz	Theater am Tummel-Platz (carn.) mus. by J. A. Hasse, add. by A. Vivaldi	(6)
1738 Venice	Teatro Grimani di S. Giovanni Grisostomo (carn., 15/01/1738) 3rd version[55]	(7)
1739 Klagenfurt	NA (carn.)[56]	(8)
1739 Vicenza	Teatro di Piazza (Fair)[57]	(9)
1740 Verona	Teatro Filarmonico (carn.)	(10)
1741 Bratislava	Teatro Nuovo (06/1741) pasticcio[58]	(11)
1743 Venice	Teatro Grimani di S. Giovanni Grisostomo (carn., 19/01/1743) pasticcio; with arias by C. Pontiamola[59]	(12)
1744 Florence	Teatro della Pergola (carn., 26/12/1743) pasticcio?[60]	(13)
1746 Pesaro	Teatro del Sole (carn., 08/01/1746)[61]	(14)
1746 Genoa	Teatro da S. Agostino (carn.)[62]	(15)
1746 Genoa	Teatro da S. Agostino (aut.)	(16)
1746 Vienna	Burgtheater (11/08/1746) mus. by J. A. Hasse or C. W. Gluck[63]	(17)
1746 Vienna	Teatro Privilegiato (08/12/1746)[64] birthday of Franz Joseph I, emperor of Austria	(18)
1754 Verona	Teatro Filarmonico (carn.)	(19)
1759 Lucca	Teatro Pubblico (18/08/1759)	(20)
1777 Berlin	Court theatre (06/01/1777)[65] *Cleofide* (rvl of 1st version)	(21)

---

55. The performance is listed as a 3rd version in Mellace, Raffaele, *Johann Adolf Hasse* (Palermo: L'Epos, 2004).
56. Doubtfully by Hasse according to Strohm, 'L'"*Alessandro nell'Indie*"', p. 175. Treated as a pasticcio in <https://www.pasticcio-project.eu/database/work/P102B54> [accessed 25 May 2022].
57. For the date of this performance and its attribution to Hasse, see Bellina, Anna Laura, 'Metastasio in Venezia: appunti per una recensio', *Italianistica: Rivista di letteratura italiana*, 13.1–2 (1984), 145–73.
58. See <https://www.pasticcio-project.eu/database/work/P10107X> [accessed 25 May 2022].
59. Selfridge-Field, Eleanor, *A New Chronology of Venetian Opera and Related Genres, 1660–1760* (Stanford: Stanford University Press, 2007).
60. Strohm, 'L'"*Alessandro nell'Indie*"', p. 175.
61. Schmidt-Hensel, '*La musica è del Signor Hasse*', vol. 2, p. 461.
62. For this and the following performance, see Giazotto, Remo, *La musica a Genova nella vita publica e privata dal XIII. al XVIII. secolo* (Genoa: Societa Industrie Grafiche e Lavorazioni Affini, 1951).
63. Klein, 'Die Schauplätze', p. 392.
64. Schmidt-Hensel, '*La musica è del Signor Hasse*', vol. 2, p. 462.
65. The production ran for five consecutive performances; see Henzel, Christoph, *Berliner Klassik* (Beeskow: ortus, 2009).

MC | *Alessandro nell'Indie* (1730–1831)

Librettos

(1) Dresden: Stössel, 1731 (It./Fr.)
CZ-Bu Bib.II.35.2.R.; D-Dl MT.4.119; D-Hhg n/s; <u>D-Mbs 4P.o.it.231d</u>; D-W Textb. 4° 25; US-NYp Mus. Res. *MZ

(2) [Milan: s.n., 1732] (It./Fr.)
US-NYp 597288B.

(3) Venice: Rossetti, 1736
F-Pn 8-YTH-51979; <u>I-Bc Lo.02493</u>; I-Rsc Carv.478; I-Rsc XIV [7]; I-RVI Silv., op. 712; I-Vcg LIBRETTI S.GIO.GRISOSTOMO 154; I-Vnm DRAMM.1051 [3]; I-Vnm DRAMM.1248 [6]; I-Vnm DRAMM.3564 [3]; SI-Lsk AE 87 [5]; US-Cn BLC #813; US-LAum ML48 .R114 1736 [3]; <u>US-Wc ML48 [S4508]</u>

(4) Naples: [s.n.], 1736
B-Bc 19032; <u>I-Mb Racc.dramm.1296</u>; US-NYp Mus. Res. *MZ, A/11 [5]

(5) Ferrara: Barbieri, 1737
US-AUS KL-17 75

(6) Graz: heirs of Widmanstadj, 1738 (It./Ger.)
A-Gl C 7509[I]; A-Gl C 135437[I]; A-Gu[C,S,66]

(7) Venice: Rossetti, 1738
<u>I-Bc Lo.02494</u>; I-Mb Racc.dramm.0510; I-PAc F. Libretti, sc.013 [202]; I-RVI Silv., op. 727; I-Vcg LIBRETTI S.GIO.GRISOSTO-MO 155; I-Vnm DRAMM.1053 [2]; I-Vnm DRAMM.1250 [3]; I-Vnm DRAMM.3566 [2]; SI-Lsk AE 58 [6]; US-LAum ML48 .R114 1738 [1]; US-LAum ML48 .R114 1738 [2]

(8) Klagenfurt: Kleinmayr, [1739] (It./Ger.)
<u>A-Wn 29286-A</u>; <u>I-Mb Racc.dramm.2175</u>

(9) Venice: Rossetti, 1739
<u>I-Mb Racc.dramm.1230</u>

(10) Verona: Ramanzini, [1740]
<u>D-ERu H58/EZ-II 1780</u>; <u>I-Bc Lo.02495</u>; I-VEc D.381 [1]

(11) Bratislava: heirs of Royeriani, [1741] (It./Ger.)
F-Pn 16-YD-177; H-Bn 307.728; <u>US-Wc ML48 [S4509]</u>[67]

(12) [Venice: s.n., 1743]
B-Bc 19033; <u>I-Bc Lo.02496</u>; I-Rsc Carv.479; I-RVI Silv., op. 781; I-Vcg LIBRETTI S.GIO.GRISOSTOMO 157; I-Vmc RAV 103831; I-Vnm

---

66. Not found in [IC]; lost?
67. Photocopy: US-BEm ML50.2.A54 H34 1741a.

DRAMM. 1059 [4]; I-Vnm DRAMM.1256 [1]; I-Vnm DRAMM.3571 [3]; US-LAum ML48 .R114 1743 [4]; US-Wc ML48 [S4593]

(13) Florence: Pieri, [1744]
I-Fc E.V.1486; I-Fn 1264 [5]

(14) Pesaro: Gavelli, [1746]
I-PESo G-09-B-21 [2]; I-Vc 0101

(15–17) NA

(18) Vienna: van Ghelen, [1746]
A-Wn 4919-A; US-Wc ML50.2.A518 W8 1796[68]

(19) Verona: Saracco, [1754]
I-Mb Racc.dramm.4159; I-VEc D.381 [1]; US-NYp *MGTY-Res.

(20) Lucca: Benedini, 1759
B-Bc 19035; I-Fm Mel.2045 [4]

(21) Berlin: Haude & Spener, 1777 (It./Ger.)
PL-Łzu 1002079; US-Wc ML48 [S4573]

Music sources

1st version: 1731, Dresden

[complete scores] B-Bc 2133[IC,MGG,NG,RISM,69]; D-B Mus.ms. 9541[MGG,NG,RISM;A,70]; D-B Mus.ms. 9541/1[IC,MGG,NG,RISM]; D-B Mus.ms. 9541/2[MGG,NG,RISM]; D-Dl Mus.2477-F-9[MGG,RISM,71]; D-Dl Mus.2477-F-9a[MGG,RISM;IP]; D-Dl Mus.2477-F-10[MGG,RISM;A,R]; D-LEm Becker III.15.16a[MGG,NG,RISM]; D-HAmi MS 61[MGG,NG,RISM]; D-Mbs Mus.ms. 213[MGG,NG,RISM;A]; F-Pn D-5424[BnF,72]; GB-CDu Mackworth Collection Vol. 19[IC,MGG,RISM;A]

[excerpts] *Appena amor che nasce* (D-LEm Becker III.11.46a [38][RISM;R]; S-L Saml. Engelhart 432[IC,RISM;P]; S-L Saml. Engelhart 561[IC;P]; S-Skma SO-R[IC,RISM;P]; S-Skma T-SE-R[RISM]); *Cervo al bosco che piagato* (A-Wgm VI 28493 [H 30813] [25][IC]); *Che sorte crudele* (A-Wgm VI 28493 [H 30813] [6][IC]; D-Hs ND VI 2918 [6][RISM]; D-LEm Becker III.11.46a [49][RISM;R]; D-Mbs Mus.ms. 20882 [3][RISM,73]; D-ROu Mus. Saec. XVI-II:40 [14][RISM]; GB-Lbl R.M.23.d.8 [10][BL,RISM]; I-Nc 33.2.23 [4][SBN]);

---

68. Wrongly dated 1796 in [IC].
69. Wrongly related to Hasse's 3rd version in [NG].
70. This and the following two sources: for Berlin 1777.
71. Microfilm copies: CH-Bm MAB SCB MFA Mf-3255[SB]; CH-Bm MAB SCB MFA Mf-3256[SB].
72. Microfilm copy: F-Pn VM BOB-22791.
73. In d minor instead of e minor.

Chi vive amante sai che delira (D-B Am.B 312 [4]^(RISM,74); D-LEm Becker III.8.28^(RISM;R); D-LEm Becker III.11.46a [41]^(RISM;R); S-Skma T-SE-R^(RISM)); *Dagli astri discendi* (D-Bsa [D-B] SA 1004^(RISM)); *Digli che io son fedele* (B-Bc 4109^(RISM); D-B N.-Mus. BP 381^(RISM;P); D-B* Mus.ms.autogr. Friedrich d. Gr. 1 [1]^(RISM;R); D-Dl Mus.1-F-82,21 [11]^(RISM); D-Hs ND VI 2918 [11]^(RISM); D-LEm Becker III.11.46a [48]^(RISM;R); D-MGmi HA IV 61^(RISM); D-MGmi HA IV 62^(RISM); F-Pn MS-76 [27]^(BnF,RISM); GB-Lbl R.M.23.d.8 [11]^(RISM); GB-Ob Ms. Mus. e.11 [25]^(RISM); I-MC 2-F-15/7 [2]^(RISM); S-L Saml.Engelhart 341^(RISM); S-Skma Alströmer saml. 157 [3]^(RISM); S-Skma Alströmer saml. 157 [5]^(RISM); S-Skma SO-R^(RISM;P); S-Skma T-SE-R^(RISM); S-Skma T-SE-R^(RISM;P); S-Uu Leufsta Mus. Ms. 37 [8]^(RISM); S-Uu Vok. mus. i hs. 56:8^(IC,RISM;P)); *Dov'è? Si affretti* (S-L Saml.Kraus 290^(RISM;P)); *È ver che all'amo intorno* (A-Wgm VI 28493 [™ 30813] [10]^(IC)); *Generoso risvegliati, o core* (A-Wn Mus.Hs.4073^(IC); S-Skma SO-R^(RISM)); *Perder l'amato bene* (D-LEm Becker III.11.46a [43]^(RISM;R); F-Pn D-5470 [13]^(BnF); GB-Lbl Add. 14180 [22]^(BL,RISM); GB-Lbl R.M.23.d.8 [1]^(RISM); I-Nc 33.2.17 [14]^(SBN); S-Skma Alströmer saml. 157 [6]^(RISM); S-Skma SO-R^(RISM); S-Skma T-SE-R^(RISM)); *Pupillete vezzossette* (B-Bc 4147^(RISM); D-Hs ND VI 1078 [2]^(RISM); D-LEm Becker III.11.46a [44]^(RISM;R); I-MC 2-F-15 [21]^(RISM); S-Skma T-SE-R^(RISM)); *Quanto mai felici siete*[75] (D-LEm Becker III.11.46a [37]^(RISM;R); F-Pn D-5467 [1]^(BnF); I-Mc Noseda O.41 [39]^(SBN); I-MC 2-F-16/20 [5]^(RISM); S-Skma T-SE-R^(RISM); US-BEm MS 129 [18]^(RISM;R)); *Se costa tante pene* (D-LEm Becker III.11.46a [39]^(RISM;R); D-ROu Mus.Saec. XVIII:40 [10]^(RISM;P); GB-Lbl R.M.23.d.8 [6]^(RISM); S-Skma T-SE-R^(RISM); US-LAum Ms 27 [6]^(RISM)); *Se mai più sarò geloso* [duet] (A-Wgm VI 28493 [H 30813] [7]^(IC); GB-Lbl R.M.23.d.4 [5]^(BL,RISM); I-Mc Noseda Q.7 [2]^(SBN); S-Skma T-SE-R^(RISM); S-Uu Vok. mus. i hs. 56:11 [1]^(IC,RISM); S-Uu Vok. mus. i hs. 56:11 [2]^(IC,RISM)); *Se mai turbo il tuo riposo* (D-LEm Becker III.11.46a [45]^(RISM;R); GB-Lbl Add. 14180 [21]^(BL,RISM); I-Nc 33.2.29 [17]^(SBN); S-L Saml.Wenster M:55^(RISM); S-Skma SO-R^(RISM); S-Skma T-SE-R^(RISM); S-Uu Leufsta Mus. Ms. 37 [2]^(RISM;R)); *Se possono tanto*[76] (D-Dl Mus.2477-E-536^(RISM,77); S-Skma T-SE-R^(RISM)); *Se troppo crede al ciglio* (D-B Am.B 312 [1]^(RISM,78); D-LEm Becker III.11.46a [40]^(RISM;R); GB-Cfm [GB-Cu]

---

74. This and the following source: in A major instead of B flat major. Inserted into *Il trionfo della fedeltà*, pasticcio (Dresden, 1754).
75. Text originally from Metastasio's *Ezio*.
76. For this aria in his *Cleofide*, Hasse reused the music of the aria *Del nobile vanto indegni voi siete* from his *Attalo, re di Bitinia* (Naples, 1728), for the character of Arsinoe in A1-S12.
77. In G major instead of A major.
78. Inserted into the pasticcio *Il trionfo della fedeltà* (Dresden, 1734).

MU.MS.633[IC]; GB-Lbl Add. 14180 [27][BL,RISM]; I-PLcon Pisani 27 [3][IC]); *Son qual misera colomba* (A-Wgm VI 27229 [Q 2916] [18][IC]; A-Wn Mus. Hs.4095[IC]; D-B N.-Mus BP 401[RISM;P]; D-Dl Mus.2477-F-124[RISM;R]; D-LEm Becker III.11.46a [47][RISM;R]; GB-Lbl R.M.22.d.25 [12][BL,RISM]; GB-Lbl R.M.23.d.8 [9][RISM]; I-Mc Noseda Q.8 [19][SBN]; S-Skma T-SE-R[RISM]; S-Uu Leufsta Mus. Ms. 37 [7][RISM]); *Spera sì che amor pietoso* (D-LEm Becker III.11.46a [46][RISM;R]; F-Pn MS-76 [26][BnF,RISM]); *Vedrai con tuo periglio* (D-Dl Mus.2477-E-522a [10][RISM]); *Vil trofeo d'un'alma imbelle*[79] (B-Bc 4158[IC]; GB-Lbl R.M.23.d.8 [12][RISM]; S-Skma SO-R[RISM]); *Vuoi saper se tu mi piaci?* (D-Hs ND VI 2918 [1][RISM,80]; GB-Lbl R.M.23.d.8 [3][BL,RISM]; GB-Lcm MS 687 [2][RISM]; I-Nc 33.2.16 [16][SBN]; S-L Saml.Engelhart 579[RISM;IP]; S-Skma T-SE-R[RISM]; S-Skma T-SE-R[RISM,81])

[contrafacta] *Che sorte crudele* ([Mater Digna Dei] PL-R Rap-62[RISM]); *Chi vive amante sai che delira* ([Beatur ille servus] PL-Wu RM 5577 [2][RISM;P,82]); *Digli che io son fedele* ([Amor mi Jesu care] PL-SA 221/A VI 25 [1][RISM;P,83]; [Auf singt in muntren Chören] D-Dl Mus.2477-E-533a[RISM;P]; [Ave maris stella, Dei mater alma] D-Mbs Mus.ms. 4997 [2][RISM;P]; [Dive Nepomucene, vir sanctitae] D-KA Don Mus.Hs. 635[RISM;P]; [Jesus ist der rechte Freund] D-MÜG Mus.ant.405 [1][RISM;P]; [Lamm Gottes unschuldig ach wie so sehr geduldig] CZ-TEk n/s[RISM]; [Nolo vivere absque caritate] A-WIL 1323[RISM;P]); *È ver che all'amo intorno* ([Huc gentes properate festinate] PL-Wu RM 4457 [4][RISM;P]); *Perder l'amato bene* ([Amor mi Jesu care] CZ-Pak 445[RISM]; [Ave rosa decora formosa] PL-Wu Wu RM 4389[RISM;P]); *Pupillette vezzossette* ([Bone pastor panis vere] A-LA 1769[RISM]); *Quanto mai felici siete* ([Auf und laßt uns eilend laufen] D-MÜG Mus.ant.405 [2][RISM;P,84]; [Omni die dic Mariae, mea laudes anima] PL-Kłwnm A-253 [3][RISM;P]; [Quantum potes cor fidele] CZ-Pkřiž XXXV C 167 [2][RISM;P]); *S'appresti o mai la vittima* ([Volate seraphini docete me] CZ-Pak 453[RISM]); *Se costa tante pene* ([Jesu dulcis memoria] PL-SA 85/A II 25 [2][RISM]; [Te Deus amare] CZ-Pak 1462 [7][RISM;P]); *Se è ver che t'accendi* ([Jam vieta prostrata] A-LA 487[RISM;P]); *Se mai turbo il tuo riposo* ([Ah quam taediosa mora sine Jesu] PL-Wu RM 4452 [5][RISM;P]; [Stora kinung Jesus] S-L Saml. Engelhart 355[RISM;P]); *Se troppo crede al ciglio* ([Laß doch den Kummer

---

79. For this aria in his *Cleofide*, Hasse reused the music of the aria *Pria di darmi sì bel vanto* from his *L'Ulderica* (Naples, 1729), for the character of Ulderica in A1-S8.
80. D-Hs ND VI 2918 [1], I-Nc 33.2.16 [16], and S-L Saml.Engelhart 579: in c minor instead of d minor.
81. In f minor instead of d minor; different from the other copy in S-Skma.
82. In A major instead of B flat major.
83. PL-SA 221/A VI 25 [1] and D-MÜG Mus.ant.405 [1]: in D major instead of E major.
84. In D major instead of F major.

fahren] D-Dl Mus.2477-E-512 [2]^{RISM}); *Son qual misera colomba* ([*Auf mit freudigem Getümmel*] D-Dl Mus.2477-E-536 [1]^{RISM,85}; [*Dominus meus mortuus est*] PL-Wu RM 5536$^{RISM;P}$; [*Mente laeto nec*] SK-BRnm MUS XXV 82 [1]^{RISM}; [*Venit mundi solamen*] CZ-Pak 1462 [4]^{RISM}; [*Virgo gaude quod defrause daemonum*] PL-SA 221/A VI 25 [2]^{RISM}); *Spera sì che amor pietoso* ([*Herr du lässest nach dem Weinen*] D-Dl Mus.2477-E-529$^{RISM;P}$; [*Kom och skåda*] S-L Saml.Engelhart 686^{RISM}); *Vedrai con tuo periglio* ([*Aurora lucis rutillat*] PL-Wu RM 4457 [5]$^{RISM;P}$; [*Im Himmel und auf Erden*] D-Dl Mus.2477-E-505^{RISM}; [*O quanta sit mi Jesu dulcedo*] CH-SAf MusSAf.Ms.700$^{RISM;P}$); [*Quam pulchra es amica mea*] PL-STAb 23c^{RISM,86}); *Voi che adorate il vanto* ([*Justus ut palma, florebit sicut cedrus*] PL-Pa Mus GR III/72^{RISM})

2nd version: 1736, Venice

[complete scores] GB-Lbl Add. 30838^{RISM,87}; D-Hs ND VI 2923$^{MGG, NG,RISM,88}$; HR-PORzm ZMP 8928$^{RISM;A,R}$

[excerpts] *Compagni nell'amore* (B-Bc 4102^{RISM}; B-Bc 4115^{RISM}; F-Pn D-5465 [5]^{BnF,RISM}; F-Pn D-5465 [9]^{BnF,RISM,89}); *Digli che io son fedele* (D-W Cod. Guelf. 301 Mus. Hdschr. [25]^{RISM}; F-Pn D-5465 [14]^{BnF,RISM}; F-Pn D-5470 [2a]^{BnF,RISM,90}; F-Pn D-5470 [3]^{BnF,RISM}; GB-Cfm [GB-Cu] MU.MS 145 [8]^{IC}; GB-Lbl Add. 31604^{BL,RISM}; I-Nc 33.2.17 [12]^{SBN}; I-Nc 33.2.23 [6]^{SBN}; US-FAy Quarto 532 MS 1 [21]^{RISM}); *È prezzo leggiero* (B-Bc 4115^{RISM}; F-Pn D-5465 [19]^{BnF}); *Mio ben ricordati* (SI-Mpa SI_PAM/1857/010 [18]^{RISM}); *Non sarei sì sventurata* (GB-Lbl Add. 31504$^{BL,RISM;R}$); *Se amore a questo petto* (A-Wn Mus.Hs.4050^{IC}; B-Bc 4153^{RISM}; F-Pn D-5466 [17]^{BnF,91}; I-Nc 33.217 [4]^{SBN}); *Se è ver che t'accendi* (B-Bc 4163 [a]^{RISM}; F-Pn D-5466 [22]^{BnF}); *Se il ciel mi divide* (S-SWl Mus.144^{RISM}); *Se mai turbo il tuo riposo* (S-SK 494 [69]^{RISM}); *Se mai turbo il tuo riposo* [duet] (I-Mc Noseda Q.7 [2]^{SBN}); *Serbati a grandi imprese* (F-Pm Res F7.29^{BASE}; F-Pn D-5466 [18]^{BnF}); *Se troppo crede al ciglio* (F-Pn D-5466 [23]^{BnF}); *Se viver non poss'io* (A-Wgm VI 15149 [Q 3016]^{IC}; D-B Mus.ms. 30408 [5]^{RISM}; GB-Lbl Add. 31624 [24]^{BL,RISM}; US-FAy Quarto 532 MS 1 [9]^{RISM}); *Son confusa pastorella* (D-ROu Mus. Saec.

---

85. This and the following source: in G major instead of A major.
86. Wrongly attributed to I. Holzbauer on source.
87. Microfilm copy: US-PRu MICROFILM 1330.
88. Wrongly related to Hasse's 1731 setting in ^{NG}.
89. Microfilm copy: F-Pn VM BOB-25743. It also applies to F-Pn D-5465 [14]; F-Pn D-5465 [19], and F-Pn D-5466 [20].
90. Microfilm copy: F-Pn VM BOB-25125.
91. Microfilm copy: F-Pn VM BOB-25807. It also applies to F-Pn D-5466 [18] and F-Pn D-5466 [23].

XVIII:40[12]$^{RISM;P}$; F-Pn D-5466 [20]^{BnF}); *Vil trofeo d'un'alma imbelle* (D-B Mus.ms. 30408 [7]^{RISM,92}; F-Pn D-5467 [16]^{RISM,93}; GB-Cfm [GB-Cu] MU.MS.111 [8]^{IC}; I-MC 2-F-17 [6]^{RISM,94}; I-Nc 33.2.17 [8]^{SBN}; I-Nc 57.2.3 [3]^{SBN}; S-Skma T-SE-R^{RISM})

[contrafacta] *Digli che io son fedele* ([*Exultet orbis gaudis, caelum resultet laudibus*] PL-Wu RM 4457 [6]$^{RISM;P}$; [*In me si fremant poena*] PL-Kłwnm A-253 [2]$^{RISM;P}$)

3rd version: 1738, Venice

[complete scores] F-Pc [F-Pn]+^{MGG,NG}; GB-CDp^{NG}

[excerpts] *Chi vive amante sai che delira* (I-Vnm Mss. 10002$^{NG,SBN;R}$); *Dov'è? Si affretti* (I-Bc FF.244 [5]^{RISM,SBN}); *È ver che all'amo intorno* (I-Vnm Mss. 10002$^{NG,SBN;R}$); *Non temer, rasciuga il ciglio* (I-Vnm Mss. 10002$^{NG,SBN;R}$); *O su gli estivi ardori* (I-Vnm Mss. 10002$^{NG,SBN;R}$); *Se è ver che t'accendi* (I-Vnm Mss. 10002$^{NG,SBN;R}$); *Senza procelle ancora* (I-Mc Noseda I.93 [8]^{SBN}); *Se possono tanto* (A-LA 795^{RISM,95}; D-Dl Mus.2477-F-112 [2]$^{RISM;IP}$; DK-Kk mu6501.1630 [12]^{RISM}; I-Gl A.1.4 [6]^{IC,SBN})

[doubtful] *Per chi perdo*[96] (D-LEm Becker III.11.46a [42]$^{RISM;R}$); *Se viver non poss'io*[97] (D-MÜs SANT Hs 1982 [2]^{RISM})

1731	mus. by Händel, Georg Friedrich (2nd version) → see 1731

1732	mus. by Pescetti, Giovanni Battista
1732 Venice	Teatro Sant'Angelo (carn., 30/01/1732)
Librettos	Venice: Buonarigo, 1732
	F-Pn LIV IT-3740 [4]; F-Pn 8-YTH-51789; I-Bc Lo.04144; I-Mb Racc. dramm.0411; I-Pmc^S; I-Rig Rar. Libr. Ven. 657; I-Rsc Libr. n. XIV [6]; I-Vcg LIBRETTI S.ANGELO 125; I-Vnm DRAMM.1045 [4]; I-Vnm DRAMM.1244 [1]; I-Vnm DRAMM.3560 [7]; SI-Lsk AE 88 [5]; US-LAum ML48 .R114 1732 [4]; US-Wc ML48 [S7960][98]

92. In C major instead of F major.
93. In E flat major instead of F major. Microfilm copy: F-Pn VM BOB-23048.
94. In E flat major instead of F major.
95. Allegro comodo instead of Lento.
96. The aria was not included in any of the librettos for Hasse's three versions (1731, 1736, 1738).
97. The text is included in the 1736 and 1738 versions as an aria; this manuscript source has it as a duet. It was not included in the 1731 version.
98. Photocopy: US-BEm ML50.2.A54 P47 1732a.

MC | *Alessandro nell'Indie* (1730–1831)

Music sources   [excerpts] *Agitata dal furore* (I-Bas IV 89/749a [18]^{IC,MGG,NG,RISM,SBN}); *Chi vive amante sai che delira* (<u>D-Dl Mus.2967-F-2 [2]</u>^{RISM;P}); *Compagni nell'amore* (<u>D-Dl Mus.2967-F-2 [4]</u>^{RISM;P}); *Di rendermi la calma* (<u>D-Dl Mus.2967-F-2 [8]</u>^{RISM;P}); *Dov'è? Si affretti* (D-Rtt Prota 4^{RISM}); *Mio ben ricordati* (<u>D-Dl Mus.2967-F-2 [3]</u>^{RISM;P}; I-Bas IV 89/749a [14]^{IC,MGG,NG,RISM,SBN}); *Se è ver che t'accendi* (<u>D-Dl Mus.2967-F-2 [5]</u>^{RISM;P}); *Senza procelle ancora* (I-Bas IV 89/749a [19]^{IC,MGG,NG,RISM,SBN}); *Se mai turbo il tuo riposo* (I-Bas IV 89/749a [17]^{MGG,NG,RISM,SBN}); *Se amore a questo petto* (I-Bas IV 89/749a [16]^{IC,MGG,NG,RISM,SBN}); *Se mai turbo il tuo riposo* [duet] (I-Bas IV 89/749a [13]^{IC,MGG,NG,RISM,SBN}); *Serbati a grandi imprese* (<u>D-Dl Mus.2967-F-2 [7]</u>^{RISM;P}); *Senza procelle ancora* (I-Bas IV 89/74 a [19]^{MGG,NG,RISM,SBN}); *Se troppo crede al ciglio* (<u>D-Dl Mus.2967-F-2 [1]</u>^{RISM;P,99}; GB-Lbl R.M.23.d.9 [6]^{BL,RISM}; I-Bas IV 89/749a [15]^{IC,MGG,NG,RISM,SBN,100}); *Se viver non poss'io* (<u>D-Dl Mus.2967-F-2 [6]</u>^{RISM;P})

[doubtful] *Digli che io son fedele* (US-FAy Quarto 532 MS 9 [4]^{RISM}); *Rasserena i mesti rai*[101] (D-Hs ND VI 1079 [3]^{RISM}; D-Mbs Mus.ms. 1105 [10]^{RISM})

Alessandro nell'Indie, in *Opere drammatiche del signor abate Pietro Metastasio romano, poeta cesareo* (Venice: Bettinelli, 1733), vol. 2, pp. 243–322.

1732	mus. by Mancini, Francesco
1732 Naples	Teatro di S. Bartolomeo (carn., 02/02/1732)
Librettos	Naples: [s.n.], 1732 <u>I-Mb Racc.dramm.1212</u>; <u>I-Rig Rar. Libr. Op. 18. Jh. 169</u>; US-NYp Mus. Res. *MZ, A/9 [4]
Music sources	[excerpts] *Chi vuol vedere un petto* (<u>I-Nc 33.3.32 [43]</u>^{SBN}); *Compagni nell'amore* (<u>F-Pn MS-76 [16]</u>^{BnF,RISM}); *Se viver non poss'io* (D-B Mus.ms. 30330 [5]^{MGG,NG,RISM}); *Son confusa pastorella* (<u>F-Pn MS-76 [17]</u>^{BnF,RISM})

1733	mus. by unknown composer(s)
1733 Palermo	Teatro di Santa Cecilia (carn.)
Librettos	Palermo: Felicella, 1733 I-PLn RARI SIC. 197

---

99. In D major.
100. In A major.
101. The aria is not contained in the original libretto from 1732.

MC | *Alessandro nell'Indie* (1730–1831)

1734	mus. by Bioni, Antonio[NG,102]	
1734 Wrocław	Teatro Ballhaus (carn.)[103]	(1)
1734 Prague	Theatre in Malá Strana (aut.)[104]	(2)

Librettos
(1) NA
(2) Prague: Kamenicky, [1734] (It./Ger.)
CZ-Pu 65 E 2445

Music sources
[excerpts] *Se viver non poss'io* (CZ-KRa A 4101[105])

1734	mus. by Schiassi, Gaetano Maria	
1734 Bologna	Teatro Formagliari (carn., 19/02/1734)[106]	(1)
	1st version	
1734 Jesi	Teatro di Jesi (07/1734)	(2)
	pasticcio[107]	
1736 Lisbon	Academy on the Trinità Square	(3)
	2nd version?[108]	

Librettos
(1) Bologna: [Sassi, 1734]
I-Bc Lo.05163; I-Bu A.V.Tab.IX.Caps.XXI [26]

(2) Jesi: de' Giuli, 1734
I-MACgiochi Rac. F.V.12

(3) Lisbon: da Fonseca, 1736 (It./Port.)
I-Lg B.ta 888 [6]; I-Rsc Carv.480; P-Cug 4-3-22-574; P-Ln RES. 975//9 P.

---

102. Strohm, 'L'"*Alessandro nell'Indie*"', p. 174.
103. Mattheson, Johann, 'Verzeichnis aller welschen Opern, welche von 1725 bis 1734 auf dem breslauischen Schauplatz vorgestellt worden sind', in *Grundlage einer Ehrenpforte, woran der Tüchtigsten Capellmeister, Componisten, Musikgelehrten, Tonkünstler etc. Leben, Werke, Verdienste etc. erscheinen sollen* (Hamburg: In Verlegung des Verfassers, 1740), pp. 374–78.
104. Although this production is usually attributed to Matteo Lucchini, it is probable that he simply brought the libretto from Wrocław to Prague and that, thus, the performance in the latter city was based on the Wrocław one; see Freeman, Daniel Evan, 'The Opera Theater of Count Franz Anton von Spork in Prague (1724–35)' (doctoral dissertation, University of Illinois at Urbana-Champaign, 1987).
105. Černá, Zuzana, 'Antonio Bioni and His Compositions Preserved in Kroměříž Archive', *Musicologia Brunensia*, 52 (2017), 217–42.
106. Ricci, Corrado, *I teatri di Bologna, nei secoli XVII e XVIII: storia aneddotica* (Bologna: Successori Monti, 1888).
107. See <https://www.pasticcio-project.eu/database/work/P103BC4> [accessed 26 May 2022].
108. No complete score survives, but, being the libretto of this version very different from the one of 1734's performance in Bologna, we could presume that also the music should not have been the same.

MC | *Alessandro nell'Indie* (1730–1831)

Music sources	[excerpts] *Deh per pietà ben mio* (D-Dl Mus.1-F-49,11 [5])[RISM]; *Mio ben ricordati* (D-Dl Mus.1-F-49,4 [3])[RISM]; *Quell'augelletto*[109] (US-BEm MS 120 [39])[IC,RISM]

1735	mus. by unknown composer(s)
1735 Pisa	Teatro Pubblico (spr.)
Librettos	Pisa: Bindi, 1734
	I-Vgc ROL.0693 [6]

1736	mus. by Hasse, Johann Adolf (2nd version) → see 1731

1736	mus. by Duni, Egidio Romualdo?[C,110]
1736 Prato	Teatro Pubblico (carn., 29/01/1736)
Librettos	Florence: Paperini, [1736]
	I-Fm Mel.2035 [1]

1736	mus. by Händel, Georg Friedrich (3rd version) → see 1731

1736	mus. by Schiassi, Gaetano Maria (2nd version) → see 1734

1737	mus. by Pampani, Antonio Gaetano[111]
1737 Padua	Teatro Obizzi

1738	mus. by Galuppi, Baldassare	
1738 Mantua	Teatro Arciducale (carn., 14/01/1738)	(1)
	1st version	
1752 Stuttgart	Teatro Ducale (30/08/1752)	(2)
	birthday of the Duchess of Württemberg and Teck	
1754 Naples	Teatro di S. Carlo (carn., 20/01/1754)	(3)
1755 Parma	Teatro Ducale (carn.)[112]	(4)
1755 Venice	Teatro Grimani di S. Samuele (Asc., 06/05/1755)	(5)
	2nd version	

---

109. According to an inscription on the preserved source, originally inserted into the composer's *Alessandro Severo* (Alessandria, 1732).
110. Question mark on the author's name in [C]. See also Strohm, 'L'"*Alessandro nell'Indie*"', p. 174. Treated as a pasticcio in <https://www.pasticcio-project.eu/database/work/P102B75> [accessed 25 May 2022].
111. Strohm, 'L'"*Alessandro nell'Indie*"', p. 175.
112. According to the libretto, abridged version with new arias.

1755 Munich	Court theatre (12/10/1755)	(6)
	name day of Maximilian Joseph, elector of Bavaria	
1756 Brescia	Teatro degli Erranti (carn.)	(7)
1756 Lodi	Teatro di Lodi (carn.)	(8)
	pasticcio[113]	
1756 Florence	Teatro della Pergola (aut., 17/09/1756)	(9)
1757 Vicenza	Teatro delle Grazie	(10)
1759 Padua	Teatro Obizzi (carn., 26/12/1758)	(11)
1760 Prague	Teatro Nuovo (aut.)	(12)
1762 Florence[S]	Teatro della Pergola (carn., 06/02/1762)	(13)

Librettos

(1) Mantua: heirs of Pazzoni, [1738]
I-Bc Lo.01828; I-Mb Racc.dramm.4163

(2) Stuttgart: Cotta, 1752 (It./Ger.)[114]
D-Tu Dk III 28 [4]

(3) Naples: Langiano, [1754]
E-Mn T/7974;[115] E-Tp 21958

(4) Parma: Monti, [1755]
I-Bc Lo.01829; I-Fc E.V.0267; I-PAc F. Libretti, sc.013 [205]; I-Vgc ROL.0314 [2]

(5) Venice: Geremia, 1755
I-Bc Lo.01830; I-Mb Racc.dramm.0427; I-Ria MISC. Teatrale 7 [1]; I-Vcg LIBRETTI S.SAMUELE 170; I-Vlevi Dramm. 977; I-Vnm DRAMM.1077 [6]; I-Vnm DRAMM.1275 [1]; US-LAum ML48 .R114 1755 [7]; US-Wc ML48 [S3430]

(6) Munich: Vötter, [1755] (It./Ger.)
D-As A LA 123; D-Mbs 037/4 LA 123; D-Mu 0001/4 P.ital 60; I-Ma ST. G. III. 43; RUS-Mrg 50-8419140; US-Wc ML48 [S3431][116]

(7) Venice: Fenzo, 1756
I-Mb Racc.dramm.2176; I-PAc F. Libretti, sc.013 [206]; I-VIb GONZ 020 010

(8) Milan: Ghislandi, 1756
I-Fc MUS0318246; I-Mb Racc.dramm.3019 [5]

---

113. See <https://www.pasticcio-project.eu/database/work/P103C31> [accessed 26 May 2022].
114. There was a copy in I-Rsc Carv.484, which could not be found among the institution's holdings. We therefore consider it as lost.
115. Microfilm copy: E-Mn R.MICRO/31825.
116. Copy: D-KNmi FH 1185.

MC | *Alessandro nell'Indie* (1730–1831)

(9) Florence: Pieri, [1756]
I-Fc E.V.1499; I-Fc E.V.1500; I-PSrospigliosi [I-PS] BM.257 [8]

(10) Venice: Fenzo, 1757
I-VIb GONZ.020 [10]; I-VIc FCAN I.E 4

(11) Padua: Vidali brothers, [1759]
I-Mb Racc.dramm.4241; I-Pmc^S

(12) [Prague]: Pruscha, [1760][117]
A-Wn 407378-A; CZ-Pnm B 4115; CZ-Pu 65 E 2447; D-Hs A/18921

(13) Florence: Bonajuti,[118] [1762]
D-LEm I.A.100; I-Fc E.V.0268; I-Fc E.V.1484; I-Fn B.17.6.272.1.3; I-PSrospigliosi [I-PS] BM.257 [10]

Music sources

1st version: 1738, Mantua

[complete scores] P-La 44-VI-53/54/55[BA,119]; US-Wc M1500.G2 A4[RISM,120]

[excerpts] *Chi vive amante sai che delira* (D-Dl Mus.2973-F-6 [4][RISM]; D-Dl Mus.2973-F-31 [13][RISM]; GB-Lbl Add. 31632 [3][BL,RISM;R]); *È ver che all'amo intorno* (GB-Lbl Add. 31632 [1][BL,RISM;R]); *Il regno, il consorte* (F-Pn D-4305 [27][BnF,RISM]); *Se mai turbo il tuo riposo* [duet] (B-Bc 3908 [16][RISM]; D-Mbs Mus.ms. 6314 [2][RISM]; F-Pn D-4305 [23][BnF,RISM]; F-Pn D-4305 [26][BnF,RISM]; F-Pn D-4307 [12][BnF,RISM]; I-Bc FF.85 [13][RISM,SBN]; I-CHf [I-CHc] C 7 [10][RISM]; I-FZc A.VI.6 [3][RISM]; I-FZc B.V.39 [12][RISM,SBN]; I-Mc Noseda A.34 [8][SBN]; I-Nc 34.5.29 [22][SBN]; I-Nc 34.5.29 [23][SBN]; I-OS S Mss.Mus.B 3550[SBN]; S-Skma Alströmer saml. 152 [12][RISM]; S-Uu Gimo 106[RISM]; US-BEm MS 96 [16][IC,RISM;R]); *Senza procelle ancora*[121] (D-Dl Mus.2973-F-31 [6][RISM]); *Se viver non poss'io* (A-Wgm VI 15222 [Q 2901][IC]; D-Dl Mus.2973-F-31 [7][RISM,122]); *Sommi dei, se giusti siete* (I-CHf [I-CHc] C 7 [3][RISM]; I-FZc A.VI.6 [2][RISM,SBN]; S-Uu Gimo 109[RISM]); *Vedrai con tuo periglio* (D-Dl Mus.2973-F-6 [2][RISM]; D-Dl Mus.2973-F-31

---

117. According to ^S782, there was a further copy in SK-KRE but, according to the library staff, it can no longer be found. We therefore consider it as lost.
118. 'Si vende da'.
119. A1-S5 missing.
120. Several arias missing. The manuscript's structure, especially in the 2nd act, does not exactly correspond to that of the 1738 libretto, but it cannot be linked to any of the other productions either. Most of the arias are the same as in P-La 44-VI-53/54/55.
121. Missing in US-Wc M1500.G2 A4; therefore, no collation has been possible.
122. In F major instead of E flat major.

[10][RISM]; I-Nc 34.5.29 [14][SBN]); *Voi che adorate il vanto* (GB-Lbl Add. 31632 [2][BL,RISM;R])

[inserts] [Venice, 1754] *Vil trofeo d'un'alma imbelle* (US-BEm MS 25 [2][IC,RISM])

2nd version: 1755, Venice

[complete scores] D-Mbs Mus.ms. 228[RISM]; F-Pn AB O-156[BnF,RISM,123]; US-Wc M1500.A73 A5[RISM,124]

[excerpts] *Chi vive amante sai che delira* (GB-Lbl Add. 31676[BL,RISM]); *Destrier, che all'armi usato* (F-Pn D-4304 [24][BnF,RISM,125]; F-Pn D-4305 [25 bis][BnF,RISM]; I-FZc B.V.39 [9][RISM,SBN]); *Digli che io son fedele* (D-Dl Mus.2973-F-6,6 [1][RISM]; D-Dl Mus.2973-F-31,12 [1][RISM]; F-Pn D-4305 [25][BnF,RISM]; S-Skma T-SE-R[RISM]; US-BEm MS 25 [8][IC,RISM,126]); *Dov'è? Si affretti* (D-W Cod. Guelf. 307 Mus. Hdschr. [7][RISM]); *È ver che all'amo intorno* (GB-Lbl Add. 31632[RISM;R]); *Mio ben ricordati* (D-Dl Mus.2973-F-6 [3][RISM]; D-Dl Mus.2973-F-31 [11][RISM]); *Se è ver che t'accendi* (D-Dl Mus.2973-F-6 [1][RISM]; D-Dl Mus.2973-F-31 [9][RISM]); *Se mai più sarò geloso* (I-FZc A.VI.6 [7][RISM,SBN]); *Se mai turbo il tuo riposo* (F-Pn D-4304 [23][BnF,RISM]; S-Skma T-SE-R[RISM]); *Se mai turbo il tuo riposo* [duet] (GB-Lbl Add.31767[BL,RISM]); *Se troppo crede al ciglio* (F-Pn D-4304 [25][BnF,RISM]); *Son confusa pastorella* (GB-Lbl Add. 31624 [21][RISM]; GB-Lbl Add. 31632 [4][BL,RISM;R]); *Vedrai con tuo periglio* (D-LÜh Mus. Q 176[RISM]; F-Pn D-4304 [22][BnF,RISM]; F-Pn D-4305 [15][BnF,RISM]; F-Pn D-14725 [10][BnF,RISM]; GB-Lam MS 136 [3][RISM]; I-CHf C 7 [I-CHc] [8][RISM]; I-FZc A.VI.6 [6][RISM,SBN]; P-Ln M.M. 1485[IC])

[contrafacta] *Se è ver che t'accendi* ([*Exaudi benigne conditor*] PL-Wu RM 4286 [2][RISM;P]); *Vedrai con tuo periglio* ([*Beata es virgo Maria, quae Dominum portasti*] CZ-Pkřiž XXXV B 310[RISM;P]; CZ-Pkřiž XXXV C 276[RISM;P]; [*Quis dabit capiti meo aquam*] CH-SAf MusSAf.Ms.644[RISM;P])

[undated] [excerpts] *Se mai turbo il tuo riposo* [duet] (F-AIXm F.C. ms. IX [5][BASE])

[unspecified] I-BGc N.C.18.2 [2][RISM;P]

---

123. Although the source has an inscription that attributes the music to F. Alessandri, most of the music is by Galuppi. Only one *Se possono tanto* is by D. Perez, the duet *Se mai turbo il tuo riposo* is by J. Ch. Bach, and *Non sarei sì sventurata* has unknown composer [Galuppi 1754?] → see 1744, mus. by Perez, Davide and → 1780, mus. by Alessandri, Felice. Microfilm copy: CDN-Lu M1500.M57A383 1780a.
124. The source is a copy of F-Pn AB O-156.
125. Microfilm copy: F-Pn VM BOB-21141. It also applies to F-Pn D-4304 [22], F-Pn D-4304 [23], and F-Pn D-4304 [25].
126. The end is missing; Emerson, John A., *Catalog of Pre-1900 Vocal Manuscripts in the Music Library, University of California at Berkeley* (Berkeley: University of California Press, 1988).

MC | *Alessandro nell'Indie* (1730–1831)

[doubtful]	[excerpts][127] *Cara, se le mie pene* (D-Mbs Mus.ms. 182 [19][RISM,128]; F-Pn D-4304 [26][BnF,129]); *Se è ver che t'accendi** (D-MÜs SANT Hs 1580 [3][RISM]); *Se mai turbo il tuo riposo* (F-Pn D-4302 [16][BnF,RISM,130]; F-Pn D-4303 [8][BnF,RISM,131]); *Se possono tanto* (I-FZc A.VI.6 [4][RISM,SBN]); *Son confusa pastorella* (I-Gl A.1.22 [18][SBN]); *Vil trofeo d'un'alma imbelle* (US-BEm MS 25 [2][IC,RISM])
	[contrafacta] *Son confusa pastorella* ([*Salve regina, mater misericordiae vita dulcedo*] D-FUl M 10 [253][RISM;P])
1738	mus. by Hasse, Johann Adolf (3rd version) → see 1731
1738	**mus. by Corselli, Francesco**
1738 Madrid	Court theatre – Teatro del Buen Retiro (09/05/1738) (1)
	wedding of the King of the Two Sicilies and the Princess of Saxony
1738 Madrid	Court theatre – Teatro del Buen Retiro (08/07/1738)[132] (2)
1738 Madrid	Court theatre – Teatro del Buen Retiro (09/12/1738) (3)
	birthday of Felipe V, king of Spain
Librettos	(1) [Madrid: s.n., 1738] (It./Spa.)[133]
	E-Bu 07 B-66/7/2 [2]; E-Mp I/G/295; E-Tp 1-1430; E-Tp 1-1431; E-VALm 4694; GB-Lu;[134] I-PAc PAL 4985
	(2) NA
	(3) Madrid: Sanz, 1738 (It./Spa.)
	E-Mn T/11562; E-Mn T/24184; E-Msi BH FLL 28578
Music sources	[complete scores] E-Mmh Mus 211-1 [I–IV][IC;P,135]

---

127. These arias are different from those in the 1738 and 1755 versions.
128. Included in the 1755 libretto for Parma, but not in those for 1738 (Mantua), 1754 (Naples), and 1755 (Venice). The music is the same as in CH-EN Ms A 690, attributed to Traetta, although in F major instead of E flat major; → see 1762, mus. by Traetta, Tommaso.
129. Microfilm copy: F-Pn VM BOB-21141.
130. Microfilm copy: F-Pn VM BOB-31988.
131. Microfilm copy: F-Pn VM BOB-31989.
132. Llorens, Ana and Álvaro Torrente, 'Constructing *Opera Seria* in the Iberian Courts: Metastasian Repertoire for Spain and Portugal', *Anuario musical*, 76 (2021), 73–110 <https://doi.org/10.3989/anuariomusical.2021.i76>.
133. There was a copy in I-Rsc Carv.481, which we could not find among the institution's holdings. We therefore consider it as lost.
134. Found in [IC], yet call number is illegible.
135. Performed in Madrid on 9 November 1792. It might be by Corselli yet, as no other source has been preserved, we cannot ascertain his authorship.

MC | *Alessandro nell'Indie* (1730–1831)

1738 1738 Rimini	mus. by various unknown composers Teatro Pubblico	
Librettos	Bologna: Stamperia di S. Tommaso d'Aquino, 1738 F-Pn 16-YD-512; I-Mb[C,S]	
1740 1740 Lisbon	mus. by Fabbri, Annibale Pio Teatro de Rua dos Condes (01/1740)	
Librettos	Lisbon: Stamperia Gioaquiniana, 1740 (It./Por.) I-Rsc Carv.482; P-Cug 4-11-11-8	
1740 1740 Florence	mus. by various unknown composers Teatro della Pergola (carn., Feb.?)	
Librettos	Florence: Albizzini, [1740] I-Fc E.V.0266	
1740 1740 Naples or Palermo[136]	mus. by Caballone, Michele	
Music sources	[complete scores] F-Pn MS-2021[BnF,MGG,NG,RISM]	
1741 1741 Modena	mus. by Pulli, Pietro Teatro Molza (carn., 21/01/1741)	
Librettos	Modena: Torri, 1741 GB-Lbl 1507/894	
1741 1741 Erlangen	mus. by unknown composer(s) Court theatre? *birthday of Friedrich II of Brandenburg*	
Librettos	Bayreuth: Schirmers, [1741] (It./Ger.) D-BHu 20/L5026067; D-ERu H61/RAR.A 17; D-HEu G 2811-3 RES [9][137]	
1742 1742 Milan	mus. by Brivio, Giuseppe Ferdinando Teatro Regio Ducale (carn.)	

---

136. Naples according to [NG]; Palermo according to Stieger, Franz, ed., *Opernlexicon* (Tutzing: Schneider, 1977) and Strohm, 'L'"*Alessandro nell'Indie*"', p. 175.
137. Microfilm copies: D-BHu 27/LT 55400 M587 A3.741; D-ERu H05/2015 K 12.

MC | *Alessandro nell'Indie (1730–1831)*

Librettos	Milan: Malatesta, 1742
	I-Bc Lo.00681; I-LDEsormani 297/7/20; I-Ma S. I. H. I. 5 [3]; I-Mb Racc.dramm.1295; I-Mb Racc.dramm.6018 [1]; I-Mb Racc.dramm.6059 [2]; I-Mb Racc.dramm.T.051; I-Mr Libr. 02268; I-Rn 40.9.D.12.8; I-Rvat Stamp.Ferr.V.8119 [2]; US-AUS KL-17 85
Music sources	[excerpts] *Chi vive amante sai che delira* (F-Pn D-1481 [21])[BnF,MGG,NG,RISM]; *Destrier che all'armi usato* (F-Pn D-1481 [1])[BnF,MGG,RISM]; *Digli che io son fedele* (F-Pn D-1481 [14])[BnF,MGG,RISM]; *Dov'è? Si affretti* (F-Pn D-1481 [9])[BnF,MGG,RISM]; *Non sarei sì sventurata* (F-Pn D-1481 [6])[BnF,MGG,RISM]; *Ombra dell'idol mio* (F-Pn D-1481 [15])[BnF,MGG,RISM]; *O sugli estivi ardori* (F-Pn D-1481 [17])[BnF,MGG,RISM]; *Se mai più sarò geloso* (F-Pn D-1481 [20])[BnF,MGG,RISM]; *Se mai turbo il tuo riposo* (F-Pn D-1481 [16])[BnF,MGG]; *Se mai turbo il tuo riposo* [duet] (F-Pn D-1481 [18])[BnF,MGG]; *Se possono tanto* (F-Pn D-1481 [32])[BnF,MGG]; *Serbati a grandi imprese* (F-Pn D-1481 [3])[BnF,MGG,RISM]; *Sommi dei, se giusti siete* (F-Pn D-1481 [30])[BnF,MGG,RISM]; *Son confusa pastorella* (F-Pn D-1481 [13])[BnF,MGG]; *Vedrai con tuo periglio* (F-Pn D-1481 [19])[BnF,MGG,RISM]; *Vil trofeo d'un'alma imbelle* (F-Pn D-1481 [25])[BnF,MGG,RISM]; *Voi che adorate il vanto* (F-Pn D-1481 [24])[BnF,MGG,RISM]
	[doubtful] *Chi vive amante sai che delira* (D-KA Don. Mus. 125 [9])[MGG,RISM;P,138]

1742	mus. by Di Capua, Rinaldo[139]
1742 Città di Castello	NA
Music sources	[excerpts] *Un certo non so che* (B-Bc 4693)[RISM]

1743	mus. by unknown composer(s)
1743 Livorno	Teatro da S. Sebastiano (carn.)
Librettos	Lucca: Marescandoli, 1743
	I-Fc E.V.2512; I-Fm Mel.2265 [1]

1743	mus. by Sarro, Domenico Natale[MGG,NG,140]
1743 Naples	Teatro di S. Carlo (carn., 20/01/1743)
	birthday of Carlo VII, king of Naples?

---

138. The music is different from that in F-Pn D-1481 [21].
139. Strohm, 'L'"*Alessandro nell'Indie*"', p. 175.
140. Strohm, 'L'"*Alessandro nell'Indie*"', p. 175, [NG] 'Alessandro nell'Indie', and Croce, Benedetto, *I teatri di Napoli. Secolo XV-XVIII* (Naples: Pierro, 1891).

MC | *Alessandro nell'Indie* (1730–1831)

Music sources	[excerpts] *Se amore a questo petto* (I-MC 5-E-18 [5][RISM]); *Se mai turbo il tuo riposo* [duet] (I-MC 5-E-18 [6][RISM]); *Se troppo crede al ciglio* (D-B Mus.ms. 30330 [2][RISM])
	[doubtful] *Prendi se mi ami, o caro*[141] (D-B Mus. ms. 30330 [15][RISM]; P-La 47-V-60[BA])
1743	mus. by Uttini, Francesco Antonio Baldassare? or Duni, Egidio Romualdo?[MGG,NG,142]
1743 Genoa	Teatro da S. Agostino
1743	mus. by Araia, Francesco
1743 St Petersburg	Court theatre – Oranienbaum, Summer Palace[143] (1)
1755 St Petersburg	Court theatre – Winter Palace (18/12/1755)[144] (2)
	birthday of the Elizaveta Petrovna Romanova, empress of Russia
1759 St Petersburg	Court theatre – Oranienbaum, Summer Palace[145] (3,4)
Librettos	(1) NA
	(2) St Petersburg: Imperial Academy of the Sciences, 1755 D-Gs 8 P DRAM I, 6785; D-Sl Dr.D.oct 236; RUS-Mrg MK AH - 4° / 55 - M
	(3) St Petersburg: Imperial Academy of the Sciences, 1759 (It./Rus.) I-Bca 8. Y. V. 33
	(4) St Petersburg: Imperial Academy of the Sciences, 1759 (It./Fr.) RUS-Mrg MK KH - 4° / 55 - M [50-7566119]; RUS-Mrg MK AH - 4° / 55 - M [50-15506594]; RUS-SPsc Rossica 13.16.9.17; US-CAt TS 8026.52 1759; US-Wc ML48 [S304]

141. The manuscript in D-B has the pencil inscription, by a later hand, 'aus Alessandro nell Indie' and the source in P-La contains five duets, supposedly from *Alessandro nell'Indie* → see 1780, mus. by Alessandri, Felice. As no libretto for Sarro's setting of *Alessandro* has survived, we cannot ascertain that the duet *Prendi se m'a mio cara* was included in it.
142. [MGG] and [NG] list a 1743 performance of *Alessandro nell'Indie* in Genoa with music by Uttini; diversely, according to Strohm ('L'"*Alessandro nell'Indie*"', p. 175), the music was by Duni. Nevertheless, no libretto survives of this supposed performance. Instead, another one survives testifying the performance in 1743 in Genoa of an *Alessandro Severo* by an unknown composer: most probably, this operatic libretto by Zeno, and not Metastasio's, was the one performed in Genoa that year.
143. Strohm is the only one who speaks of this performance yet, given the dates in which Araia worked for the Russian court and his compositional trajectory in it, it seems plausible; see Strohm, 'L'"*Alessandro nell'Indie*"', p. 175.
144. Although the date on the libretto is clear, Giust gives 18/02/1756 as the date of the premiere; see Giust, Anna, 'Towards Russian Opera: Growing National Consciousness in 18th-Century Operatic Repertoire' (doctoral dissertation, Università degli Studi di Padova, 2012). The music of the Russian version is acknowledged to be lost; see Mooser, Robert-Aloys, *Annales de la musique et des musiciens en Russie au XVIIIe siècle* (Geneva: Mont Blanc, 1948).
145. Giust, 'Towards Russian Opera', pp. 112–13.

MC | *Alessandro nell'Indie* (1730–1831)

1744	mus. by Jommelli, Niccolò	
1744 Ferrara	Teatro Bonacossi da S. Stefano (carn., 26/12/1743) 1st version	(1)
1760 Stuttgart	Teatro Ducale (11/02/1760) *birthday of the Duke of Württemberg and Teck* 2nd version	(2,3)
1776 Lisbon	Court theatre – Palácio da Ajuda (06/06/1776) *birthday of José I, king of Portugal* rev. by J. Cordeiro da Silva	(4)

Librettos

(1) Bologna: Sassi, 1743
I-Bc Lo.02562[146]

(2) Stuttgart: Cotta, 1760 (It./Fr.)
D-Ju 8 MS 24740; D-HR [D-Au] 02/III.10.4.39; D-KNth L 160; D-Sl Fr.D.qt.192[147]

(3) Stuttgart: Cotta, 1760 (It./Ger.)
B-Bc 19036; D-Sl R 18 Met 10;[148] US-Wc ML48 [S4841][149]

(4) [Lisbon]: Stamperia Reale, [1776][150]
BR-Rn V-254,1,5 [11]; I-Rsc Carv.487; US-Wc ML48 [S4899]

Music sources

1st version: 1743, Ferrara

[excerpts] *Chi vive amante sai che delira* (F-Pn D-6267 [11][BnF,NG,151]); *Destrier che all'armi usato* (CDN-Lu GM/AR 726[RISM;P]); *Non ha più pace* (I-Nc 33.2.30 [17][SBN]); *Se mai turbo il tuo riposo* [duet] (I-Nc* 33.2.24 [7][SBN]); *Se troppo crede al ciglio* (I-MC 3-C-10 [21][NG,RISM]; I-Nc 33.2.29 [16][NG,SBN])

2nd version: 1760, Stuttgart

[complete scores] P-La 44-IX-43/44/45[BA,MGG,NG,152]

[excerpts] *Digli che io son fedele* (I-MC 3-C-4 [7][NG,RISM]; I-MC 3-C-7 [5][NG,RISM]; I-Nc 32.2.32 [24][NG,SBN]; I-Nc 32.2.32 [25][NG,SBN]; I-Nc 33.2.28 [8][NG,SBN]; I-Nc 57.2.4 [10][NG,SBN]; S-Skma T-SE-R[RISM]; US-Wc M1505. A1 (vol. 245 B) [4][RISM]); *Dov'è? Si affretti* (D-Mbs Mus.ms. 10515[RISM];

---

146. Photocopy: I-Bc FC.Lo.2562. Microfilm copy: US-CHH 55-ML813 pos.1–10.
147. Microfilm copy: D-Sl R 18 Met 11.
148. Given the format of this call number, the source might be a microfilm reproduction, yet the [IC] treats it as a printed book and offers no information about any other physical source.
149. Copy: D-KNmi FH 1189.
150. [S]816 lists a further source in P-Ln, yet the only potential source does not correspond to this version → see Sources of doubtful identification at the end of this chapter.
151. Microfilm copy: F-Pn VM BOB-25881.
152. For Lisbon 1776.

I-Nc 33.2.32^{NG,SBN}); *Se è ver che t'accendi* (I-Nc 33.2.24 [25]^{SBN}); *Se il ciel mi divide* (D-Mbs Mus.ms. 10516^{RISM}; P-Ln M.M. 123 [15]^{IC}); *Se mai turbo il tuo riposo* (I-Mc Mus. Tr.ms. 583 [1]^{RISM,SBN}; I-Nc 33.2.24 [28]^{SBN}; I-Nc 57.2.5 [14]^{SBN}; I-Nc n/s^{SBN}; US-CAe Mus 503.601 [4]^{RISM}; US-Wc M1505.A1 (vol. 245 B) [3]^{RISM}); *Se mai turbo il tuo riposo* [duet] (I-Nc 33.2.24 [27]^{SBN}); *Se possono tanto* (I-Nc 33.2.24 [18]^{SBN}; US-BEm MS 106 [7]^{IC,RISM}); *Son confusa pastorella* (A-Wn Mus.Hs.17661 [2]^{IC}; D-B Mus.ms. 30408 [2]^{RISM,153}; D-Dl Mus.1-F-28,6 [9]^{NG,RISM,154}; D-MÜs SANT Hs 2270 [16]^{MGG,NG,RISM}; F-Pn D-6269 [13]^{BnF,155}; I-Tf 1 I 1 [6]^{RISM,156}; RUS-Mrg Ф.954 N°139–142 [9]^{RISM;IP})

[undated]	[excerpts] *Dov'è? Si affretti* (F-Pn D-6272 [6]^{BnF}); *Se mai turbo il tuo riposo* (I-Nc 33.2.29 [17]^{SBN}); *Se mai turbo il tuo riposo* [duet] (F-Pn D-6273 [12]^{BnF}); *Son confusa pastorella* (I-Fc D.I.183 [6]^{IC,NG,RISM,SBN})
[doubtful]	[excerpts] *Presagi funesti, che il cor me congete*[157] (I-VEcon MS 136^{RISM,SBN}; S-Skma T-SE-R^{RISM})

1744	**mus. by Perez, Davide**	
1744 Genoa^{NG}	Teatro del Falcone (carn.)	(1)
	1st version	
1749 Naples	Teatro di S. Carlo (04/11/1749)	(2)
	name day of Carlo VII of Bourbon, king of Naples	
1752 Milan	Teatro Regio Ducale (carn., 23/01/1752)	(3)
1755 Lisbon	Royal theatre – Teatro do Tejo (spr., 31/03/1755)[158]	(4)
	birthday of Maria Anna Vittoria, queen of Portugal	
	2nd version	
1756 Pavia	Teatro Omodeo (carn.).	(5)
1764 Cádiz	Teatro Italiano	(6)
	mus. by D. Perez and others[159]	
1805 Lisbon	Teatro de São Carlos (win.)[160]	(7)

---

153. In A major instead of C major.
154. This and the following source are wrongly related to Jommelli's 1st setting in ^{NG}.
155. Microfilm copy: F-Pn VM BOB-33989.
156. Inserted into *Demetrio* (Parma, 1749; Madrid, 1751).
157. The aria was not included in any of the three productions.
158. April 1755 according to Blichmann, Diana, 'Water Symbols in the Stage Design of *Alessandro nell'Indie*: The Portuguese Exploration of India and Political Propaganda at the Lisbon Royal Court', *Music in Art: International Journal of Music Iconography*, 44.1–2 (2019), 139–68.
159. ^SIndex I, p. 429.
160. Moreau, Mário, *O Teatro de S. Carlos: dois séculos de historia* (Lisbon: Hugin, 1999).

MC | *Alessandro nell'Indie* (1730–1831)

Librettos

(1,7) NA

(2) Naples: Langiano, 1749
E-Mn T/7965; E-Tp 25238

(3) Milan: Malatesta, [1752]
CDN-Ttfl Itp Pam 00740; F-Pn LIV IT-3522 [12]; I-Bc Lo.04083; I-LDEsormani 309/1/30; I-Mc Coll.Libr.115; I-Ms MUS. P. XXI. 1; I-Nn SALA FARN. 40. B 51 [4]; I-PAc F. Libretti, sc.013 [203]; I-Vgc ROL.0526 [19]; US-CAt TS 5026.5

(4) Lisbon: Sylviana, 1755
BR-Rn V-309,4,4; GB-Lbl Hirsch IV.1390; I-Rsc Carv.484; P-Cug Misc. 555 [9389]; P-Lcg TC 771; P-Ln 13808; US-Cn ML50.2.A54 P47 1755; US-CAh Typ 735.55.681; US-LAgri 1370-705; US-MAL 363068; US-Wc ML48 [S7882]

(5) Milan: Ghislandi, [1756]
I-Fc E.V.2494

(6) Cádiz: Espinosa, 1764 (It./Spa.)
E-Mn T/22342; I-Bc Lo.4084

Music sources[161]

1st version: 1744, Genoa
1749, Naples

[complete scores] A-Wn Mus.Hs.18035[IC,MGG,NG]; US-BEm MS 4 [a–d][MGG,NG,RISM;IP,162]

[excerpts] *Chi vive amante sai che delira* (D-Dl Mus. 3015-F-1 [7][RISM]); *Digli che io son fedele* (I-Nc 34.6.13 [16][SBN]); *Dov'è? Si affretti* (A-Wn Mus.Hs.942[IC]; D-Dl Mus.3015-F-1 [4][RISM]; D-KA Mus. Hs. 722[RISM]; D-Wa 46 Alt 731[RISM]; GB-Lbl R.M.23.e.9 [5][BL,RISM]; I-Nc 34.6.13 [21][SBN]; I-Nc 57.2.6 [11][SBN]); *Oh dio, la man mi trema* (J-Tk S11-277-4 [6][RISM]); *Se è ver che t'accendi* (B-Bc 4597[RISM]; B-Bc 12442[IC,RISM]; CH-N XB obl. 249[RISM;P]; D-Dl Mus.1-F-21,1 [9][RISM]; D-KA Don Mus.Hs. 116[RISM;P]; F-Pn L-19440[BnF;P]; GB-Lbl Add. 14219 [35][BL,RISM;R,163]; GB-Lbl Add. 31651 [5][BL,RISM,164]; GB-Lcm MS 694 [8][IC,MGG,NG]; I-FZc B.V.39 [7][RISM,SBN];

---

161. As no complete source for Perez's 1st version has been preserved, we cannot ascertain that those excerpts performed the 1749 or 1752 revivals were included in the 1744 version (or even that they are by Perez). Given the significant differences between the music of the 1749 and 1752 performances (only the aria *Son confusa pastorella* is set to the same music) and unlike other cases, we make a distinction between them.
162. Score in three volumes plus Va part. For a description, see Emerson, *Catalog of Pre-1900 Vocal Manuscripts*, p. 77 no. 344.
163. In A major instead of B flat major.
164. Used in Genoa, 1751.

MC | *Alessandro nell'Indie* (1730–1831)

I-Gl A.I.22 [19]^(SBN,165); S-Skma Alströmer saml. 163 [5]^(RISM); US-BEm MS 102 [39]^(IC,RISM;R); US-SFsc *M2.5 v.55 [6]^(RISM;R); *Se il ciel mi divide* (GB-Lbl Lbl Add. 31648 [7]^(BL,RISM)); *Se mai turbo il tuo riposo* (D-LÜh Mus. Q 272^(RISM)); *Se mai turbo il tuo riposo* [duet] (CH-SAf MusSAf. Ms.983^(RISM;P); I-Mc Noseda I.21 [3]^(SBN); US-R n/s [4]^(RISM)); *Son confusa pastorella* (GB-Lbl Add. 31648 [8]^(BL,RISM)); *Vedrai con tuo periglio* (B-Bc 4606^(RISM,166)); *Voi che adorate il vanto* (GB-Lbl R.M.23.e.9 [9]^(BL,RISM))

[contrafacta] *Se è ver che t'accendi* ([*Ad festum volate gentes*] PL-Wu RM 4698^(RISM;P); [*Alma redemptoris mater*] D-KA Don Mus.Hs. 1537^(RISM;P))

1752, Milan

[complete scores] P-La 45-IV-48/49/50^(BA,MGG,NG)

[excerpts] *Compagni nell'amore* (D-Mbs Mus.ms. 180 [3]^(RISM)); *Dov'è? Si affretti* (D-Mbs Mus.ms. 988 [5]^(RISM); I-MAav Cart.16 n.2^(RISM;P)); *Se possono tanto* (F-Pn Mus. AB. O 156^(BnF,RISM,167)); *Vil trofeo d'un'alma imbelle* (I-Gl A.I.18 [13]^(SBN))

2^(nd) version: 1755, Lisbon

[complete scores] D-B Mus.ms. 17103^(RISM); E-LPAu Cop. 849720^(Ic); GB-Lbl Add. 16095/16096/16097^(MGG,NG,RISM); I-Vnm Mss. 9794/9795/9796^(IC,MGG,NG,SBN,168); P-La 45-IV-45/46/47^(BA,MGG,NG); P-La* 54-I-83/84/85^(BA,MGG,NG); P-Ln C.I.C. 96^(NG,RISM); S-Skma T-R^(MGG,NG,RISM,169)

[excerpts] *Chi vive amante sai che delira* (J-Tk S10-612-6 [6]^(RISM); P-Ln C.N. 242 [3a]^(IC)); *Compagni nell'amore* (P-Ln C.N. 242 [1]^(IC)); *Destrier che all'armi usato* (US-BEm MS 64^(IC,RISM); US-BEm MS 100 [4]^(RISM)); *Digli che io son fedele* (E-Mn MP/1988 [3]^(IC)); *Di rendermi la calma* (E-Mn MP/1988 [5]^(IC)); *Dov'è? Si affretti* (GB-Lbl Add. 14224 [11]^(BL,RISM)); *Finché rimango in vita* (B-Bc 4582^(RISM)); *Mio ben ricordati* (I-Gl A.I.18 [22]^(SBN,170)); *Se amore a questo petto* (P-Ln C.N. 242 [3b]^(IC)); *Se è ver che t'accendi* (B-Bc 4596^(RISM); GB-Lbl R.M.23.3.9 [8]^(BL,RISM); I-MC 4-F-2 [13]^(RISM); I-Nc 34.6.13 [27]^(SBN)); *Se viver non poss'io* (US-Wc M1505.A2 P432^(RISM)); *Vedrai*

---

165. In G major instead of B flat major.
166. Not found in ^(IC).
167. Although the source has an inscription that attributes the music to F. Alessandri, most of it is by Galuppi (2^(nd) version). Only one *Se possono tanto* is by D. Perez, the other belongs to Galuppi's 1^(st) version, the duet *Se mai turbo il tuo riposo* is by J. Ch. Bach, and *Non sarei sì sventurata* has unknown composer [Galuppi 1738?] → see 1738, mus. by Galuppi, Baldassare and 1780, mus. by Alessandri, Felice.
168. Wrongly related to Perez's 1^(st) setting in ^(MGG,NG).
169. Wrongly related to Perez's 1^(st) setting in ^(MGG,NG) and Jackson, Paul Joseph, 'The Operas of David Perez' (doctoral dissertation, Stanford University, 1967).
170. For a performance in Lisbon in 1760.

MC | *Alessandro nell'Indie* (1730–1831)

con tuo periglio (D-Mbs Mus.ms. 988 [7]^{RISM,171}; D-SWl Mus.4174$^{RISM;P}$; P-Ln C.N. 242 [2]^{IC}; P-Ln M.M. 217 [16]^{IC,RISM}); *Vil trofeo d'un'alma imbelle* (P-Ln M.M. 217 [12]^{IC,RISM})

1744	mus. by Graun, Carl Heinrich	
1744 Berlin	Court theatre (21/12/1744) *Alessandro e Poro*	(1)
1784 Berlin	Court theatre (26/12/1783)[172]	(2)

Librettos

(1) Berlin: Haude, 1744 (It./Ger.)
D-BFb [D-MÜu] 1 as B-st 110; D-Hs A/34173 [3]; D-Ju 8 MS 24754; D-MHrm Mh 30; D-ROu Ck-1413; D-WRz B 959; US-Wc ML48 [S4087]

(2) Berlin: Haude & Spener, 1784 (It./Ger.)
D-B Mus. T 63 [3]

Music sources

[complete scores] D-B Am.B 191^{RISM}; D-B Mus.ms. 8213^{RISM}; D-B Mus. ms. 8213/1^{IC,RISM}; D-DS Mus.ms 368^{RISM}; D-ROu Mus. Saec. XVI-II:52$^{RISM;IP}$ [Act II]; D-W Cod. Guelf. 83 Mus. Hdschr.^{RISM}; F-Pn D-4997^{BnF,RISM}; US-Eu MSS 527/258$^{IC,RISM;R}$

[excerpts] *Dov'è? Si affretti* (S-Skma T-SE-R^{RISM,173}; S-Skma T-SE-R [11]^{RISM}; S-Uu Vok. mus. i hs. 5:26^{IC,RISM}); *D'un barbaro scortese* (S-Skma T-SE-R [5]^{RISM}); *Finché rimango in vita* (S-Skma T-SE-R [10]^{RISM}); *Il regno, il consorte* (D-SWl Mus.2122$^{RISM;P}$; S-Skma T-SE-R^{RISM,174}); *Se è ver che t'accendi* (S-Skma T-SE-R^{RISM}); *Se mai turbo il tuo riposo* (D-DS Mus. ms 1427m$^{RISM;R}$); *Se mai turbo il tuo riposo* [duet] (S-Skma T-SE-R$^{RISM;P}$; US-WS H B I[.a] [5]^{RISM}); *Serva ad eroe* (D-Bsa [D-B] SA 996$^{RISM;P}$); *Vil trofeo d'un'alma imbelle* (US-WS SCM [325.2] Salem ms$^{RISM;IP}$)

[printed sources] *Se mai turbo il tuo riposo* [duet], in *Duetti, terzetti, quintetti, sestetti ed alcuni chori delle opere del signore Carlo Enrico Graun*, vol. 1 [5] (Berlin: Decker & Hartung, 1773)

[contrafacta] *D'un barbaro scortese* ([*Huc custos advola*] PL-Wu RM 4414/2 [1]$^{RISM;P}$; *Finché rimango in vita* ([*Ach date cordi scintillas amoris*] PL-Wu RM 4399 [1]$^{RISM;P}$; [*Gaudeamus omnes in Domino diem hodie festum*] PL-Wu RM 4414/2 [2]$^{RISM;P}$; [*Splendete o caeli cum luce*] PL-Wu

---

171. According to an inscription on the source, the aria was performed in Naples, presumably in 1749, yet the music corresponds to Perez's 2nd version (Lisbon, 1755).
172. The production ran for five consecutive performances; see Henzel, *Berliner Klassik*, p. 113.
173. In d minor instead of f minor.
174. In g minor instead of c minor.

RM 4424/14 [1]$^{RISM;P}$); *Se mai turbo il tuo riposo* [duet] ([*Divina salve spina perditorum medicina*] PL-Wu RM 5539$^{RISM;P}$; [*Dulce manna mei amoris*] PL-Wu RM 4404$^{RISM;P}$; [*Lauda Sion, salvatorem lauda ducem et pastorem*] PL-Wu RM 5402$^{RISM;P}$)

1745 1745 Turin	mus. by Gluck, Christoph Willibald Teatro Regio (carn., 26/12/1744) *Poro*
Librettos	Turin: Zappata & son, [1745] I-ASs AN.A.LVI.1.30; I-NOVa Biblioteca Teatro Coccia 287 [1]; I-PAc F. Libretti, sc.302 [305]; I-Rig Rar. Libr. Op. 18. Jh. 10; I-Rsc Vol. Carv.145 [5]; I-Tci L.O.0115; I-Tci L.O.2548; I-Tn F VII.356 [1]; I-Tn F XIII.486 [4]; I-Tstrona^S; I-Vgc ROL.0353 [13]; US-BEm ML48 .C65 [7]; US-CAt *2007T-217; US-Wc ML48 [S3933]
Music sources	[excerpts] *Di rendermi la calma* (I-Tf 1 I 1 [4]$^{MGG,RISM;R}$); *Senza procelle ancora* (A-Wn SA.67-H.66^{IC,MGG,RISM}; CH-BEl SLA-Mus-JL MLHs 27/12^{RISM}); *Se mai turbo il tuo riposo* [duet] (I-Tf 1 I 1 [2]$^{MGG,RISM;R}$); *Senza procelle ancora* (A-Wn SA.67.H.66^{IC}; CH-BEl SLA-Mus-JL MLHs 27/12^{RISM}); *Se viver non poss'io* (A-Wn SA.67.H.65^{IC,MGG,RISM}; CH-BEl SLA-Mus-JL MLHs 27/13^{RISM}; CH-BEl SLA-Mus-JL MLHs 33/18^{RISM}; I-Tf Tf 1 I 1 [3]$^{MGG,RISM;R}$); *Son confusa pastorella* (I-Tf 1 I 1 [5]$^{MGG,RISM;R}$)
1745 1745 Verona	mus. by Chiarini, Pietro Teatro Filarmonico (carn.)
Librettos	Verona: Ramanzini, [1745] I-Vc 0100; I-VEc D.379 [6]
1746 1746 Brescia	mus. by Pellegrini, Pietro Teatro degli Erranti (carn.)
Librettos	Brescia: Vendramino, 1746 F-Pn 8-BL-8292; I-Mb Racc.dramm.4164
1746 1746 London	mus. by Lampugnani, Giambattista and others King's Theatre in the Haymarket (15/04/1746)
Librettos	London: [s.n.], 1746 (It./En.) CDN-Lu MZ0.056

MC | *Alessandro nell'Indie (1730–1831)*

Music sources	[excerpts] *Di rendermi la calma* (D-B Mus.ms. 12501/20 [2])[RISM;R]; *Se amore a questo petto* (F-Pn D-11819[BnF]); *Senza procelle ancora* (F-Pn VM4-856[BnF]); *Se viver non poss'io* (F-Pn D-11820[BnF])
	[printed sources] *Cara, di questo core; Di rendermi la calma; Non sarei sì sventurata; Senza procelle ancora; Son confusa pastorella; Vedrai con tuo periglio,* in *The Favourite Songs in the Opera call'd Alexander in India by Sig.r Lampugnani* (London: Walsh, [1746])
	[inserts] [printed sources] *Non ha ragione ingrato* by B. Galuppi, in *Sung by Sigr Monticelli nell'Alessandro nell'Indie del Sigr Hasse,* in *The Favourite Songs in the Opera call'd Antigono* (London: Walsh, [1746])

1746	mus. by unknown composer(s)	
1746 Palermo	NA	
Librettos	Palermo: Amato, 1746	
	I-PLpagano[S,175]	

1747	mus. by Abos, Girolamo	
1747 Ancona	Teatro della Fenice (summ., 07/1747)	(1)
1750 Lucca	Teatro Pubblico (aut.)	(2)
Librettos	(1) Jesi: de' Giuli, 1747	
	I-Bc Lo.00004	
	(2) Lucca: Benedini, 1750	
	I-Bc Lo.00006; I-PAc F. Libretti, sc.013 [204]	
Music sources	[excerpts] *Desta le tue faville* (D-Dl Mus.2987-F-1 [3])[RISM]; *Destrier che all'armi usato* (D-Dl Mus.2987-F-1 [2])[RISM]; D-Hs ND VI 1079 [4][RISM]; F-Pn D-4 [5][BnF,MGG,NG,RISM,176]; F-Pn VM7-130[BnF,MGG,NG,RISM]); *Digli che io son fedele* (D-Dl Mus.2987-F-1 [5])[RISM]; *Ritorna in te stesso* (B-Bc 5211[RISM]; D-Dl Mus.2987-F-1 [1])[RISM]; *Se amore a questo petto* (D-Dl Mus.2987-F-1 [7])[RISM]; D-SWl Mus.114[RISM]; GB-Lbl Add. 14183 [4][BL,NG,RISM]); *Se mai turbo il tuo riposo* [duet] (I-Rdp Ms Musicale 97 [7][SBN]; S-Skma Leuhusens saml.[MGG,RISM]); *Se troppo crede al ciglio* (D-Dl Mus.2987-F-1 [4])[RISM]; I-Nc 22.3.19[NG,SBN]); *Vedrai con tuo periglio* (D-Dl Mus.2987-F-1 [6])[RISM]; D-Hs ND VI 1079 [10][RISM]; US-NYp Mus. Res. *MP (Italian)[RISM]); *Vil trofeo d'un'alma imbelle* (D-Dl Mus.2987-F-1 [8])[RISM])	

---

175. We could not find it among the institution's holdings. We therefore consider it as lost.
176. Microfilm copy: F-Pn VM BOB-21591.

[parodies] *Vedrai con tuo periglio* ([*Vedrà nel suo periglio*] I-Tf 9 VI 30[RISM,177])

[doubtful contrafacta[178]] *Sia pur sdegnato il fato* ([*Benedictus qui venit in nominee Domini*] CH-SAf MusSAf.Ms.1[RISM;P]; [*Huc properate omnes gentes*] PL-Wu RM 4302/2[RISM;P])

[supposed] one aria in I-MAC[179]

1748	mus. by Wagenseil, Georg Christoph
1748 Vienna	Teatro Privilegiato (11/08/1748)[180]
Librettos	[Vienna]: van Ghelen, [1748]
	D-HAu 67 A 4340; CZ-Pn T 440; PL-WRzno XVIII-30308
Music sources	[complete scores] A-Wn Mus.Hs.18018 [13][IC,MGG,181]
	[excerpts] *Ah, se al tuo serto fato* (D-Sla 107[RISM;P]); *Se possono tanto* (D-Dl Mus. 1-F-82,29 [9][RISM]); *Mio ben ricordati* (D-Sla 109[RISM;P]); *Vedrai con tuo periglio* (D-Sla 111[RISM;P])
1749	mus. by Scalabrini, Paolo
1749 Copenhagen	Court theatre – Charlottenborg Palace
Librettos	Copenhagen: Hartvig, 1749 (It./Ger.)
	DK-Kk 56,-368
Music sources	[excerpts] *Destrier che all'armi usato*[182] (DK-Kk* mu7202.1838[RISM])
1750	mus. by Rutini, Giovanni Marco
1750 Prague	Teatro Nuovo (carn.)
Librettos	Prague: Pruscha, 1750 (It./Ger.)
	CZ-Pnm B 4149; CZ-Pu 9 E 3780

---

177. Cantata *L'Arca del testamento* for two vocal parts.
178. Listed in [RISM] as belonging to *Alessandro nell'Indie*, yet the aria was not included in any of the librettos related to Abos' setting.
179. Information found in [NG] but not in [IC].
180. Date in [C]. Klein ('Die Schauplätze', p. 392) gives 17/07/1748.
181. Microfilm copy: US-CAe Mus 3874.032 [1].
182. Although the aria belongs to Metastasio's *Alessandro nell'Indie*, it was not included in the libretto for Scalabrini's setting.

MC | *Alessandro nell'Indie* (1730–1831)

1750	mus. by Scolari, Giuseppe	
1750 Vicenza	Teatro di Piazza (carn.)[183]	(1)
1750 Barcelona	Theatre (04/12/1750)[184]	(2)
	birthday of Maria Barbara of Braganza, queen of Spain	
1753 Puerto de Santa María (04/12/1753)	NA (04/12/1953)	(3)
	birthday of Maria Barbara of Braganza, queen of Spain	
1759 Venice	Teatro Vendramin di S. Salvatore (Asc., c. 23/05/1759)	(4)
1762 Barcelona	Teatre de la Santa Creu (20/09/1762)	(5)
1767 Barcelona	Theatre (04/11/1767)	(6)

Librettos
(1) Vicenza: Berno, 1750
US-CAt TS 8026.428 1750; US-Wc ML48 [S10355]

(2) [Barcelona: s.n., 1750] (It./Spa.)
E-Bbc C400/232; E-Bu 07 XVIII-3226; I-Bc Lo.05182; US-SM 193548

(3) Puerto de Santa María: Rioja y Gamboa, [1753] (It./Spa.)
E-Mn R/39087

(4) Venice: Fenzo, 1759
I-Mb Racc.dramm.0926; I-Pmc^S; I-Ria MISC. Teatrale 6 [10]; I-Vcg LIBRETTI S.SALVATORE 97; I-Vnm DRAMM.1081 [6]; I-Vnm DRAMM.1280 [7]; US-CAh *IC7.A100.B750 [54]; US-LAum ML48 .R114 1759 [6]; US-Wc ML48 [S9786]

(5) Barcelona: Generas, 1762 (It./Spa.)
E-Bu 07 XVIII-3334; E-Mn T/22345; US-CAt TS 8428.26 1762

(6) Barcelona: Gibert, [1767] (It./Spa.)
US-NYpm 077543

Music sources
[excerpts] *Destrier che all'armi usato* (D-MÜs SANT Hs 4006 [4])[RISM,185]; *Digli che io son fedele* (D-MÜs SANT Hs 4006 [3])[RISM]; *Se amore a questo petto* (I-Rdp Ms Musicale 65 [4])[RISM,SBN]; *Vedrai con tuo periglio* (I-Rdp Ms Musicale 65 [5])[RISM,SBN]

[doubtful] *Vo cercando in ogni parte*[186] (D-MÜs SANT Hs 4006 [1])[RISM,187]

---

183. Bellina attributes this performance to A. Tiraboschi and others; see Bellina, 'Metastasio in Venezia', p. 151.
184. For the productions in Barcelona, see Alier y Aixal, Roger, *L'òpera a Barcelona: orígens, desenvolupamenti consolidació de l'òpera com a espectacle teatral a la Barcelona del segle XVIII* (Barcelona: Institut d'Estudis Catalans, 1990).
185. This and the following source: used in the performance in Venice, 1759.
186. Catalogued as belonging to Scolari's *Alessandro nell'Indie*, yet it was not included in the libretto for the premiere in 1750.
187. Used in the performance in Venice 1759.

1752		mus. by unknown composer(s)
	1752 Florence	Teatro del Cocomero (spr., 14/04/1752)
	Librettos	Florence: Stecchi, 1752 US-AUS KL-17 100
1752		mus. by Calderara, Giacinto
	1752 Alessandria[NG]	NA
1752		mus. by Fiorillo, Ignazio
	1752 Brunswick	Teatro Ducale *Alexander in Indien*
	Librettos	Brunswick: [heirs of] Keitel, 1752 (It./Ger.) US-Wc ML48 [S3198]
	Music sources	[complete scores] D-Wa* 46 Alt 9[RISM]; D-W Cod. Guelf. 282 Mus. Hdschr.[RISM;A,P] [excerpts] *Chi vive amante sai che delira* (S-Skma T-SE-R[RISM]); *Digli che io son fedele* (D-W Cod. Guelf. 314 Mus. Hdschr. [47][RISM;R]); *Senza procelle ancora* (D-RH [D-MÜu] Ms 209[RISM;P])
1753		mus. by Latilla, Gaetano and others
	1753 Venice	Teatro Tron di S. Cassiano (carn., *c.* 26/12/1752)
	Librettos	Venice: Fenzo, 1753 F-Pn 8-YTH-51016; F-Pn 8-YTH-52074; I-Mb Racc.dramm.0418; I-Vnm DRAMM.1075 [1]; I-Vnm DRAMM.1272 [2]; US-CAh *IC7.A100.B750 [33]; US-LAum ML48 .R114 1753 [1]; US-Wc ML48 [S5455]
1753		mus. by Scarlatti, Giuseppe
	1753 Reggio Emilia	Teatro Pubblico (Fair, 12/05/1753)
	Librettos	Reggio Emilia: Vedrotti & Davolio, [1753] D-Sl Fr.D.oct.K.236; GB-Lbl 1342.a.37 [5];[188] I-Bc Lo.05149; I-MOe 83.H.30 [3]; I-MOe M.T.Ferr.Mor.30 [2]; I-REm 19.K.102; I-REm 19.K.194; I-REm Racc. Dram. E. Curti 146 [2]; I-Vc 0102; I-Vc 0103; I-Vgc ROL.0608 [1]

---

188. Microfilm copy: GB-Lbl PB.Mic.13959.

MC | *Alessandro nell'Indie* (1730–1831)

Music sources	[complete scores] A-Wgm V 15814 MA G. Scarlatti[IC,MGG,NG,189]
	[excerpts] *Chi vive amante sai che delira* (GB-Lbl R.M.23.e.6 [14])[BL,RISM]; *Destrier che all'armi usato* (CZ-KU Hr 323[RISM]; US-BEm MS 364[RISM]; US-NYp Mus. Res. *MP (Italian)[RISM]); *Digli che io son fedele* (GB-Lbl R.M.23.e.6 [13])[RISM]; *Ma se non vedi* (GB-Lbl R.M.23.e.6 [5])[BL,RISM]; *Quanto mai felici siete* (GB-Lbl Add. 31624[BL,RISM]); *Se viver non poss'io* (A-KR G 29 [85][RISM;P]; F-Pn D-11855 [11][BnF,190]; I-Gl A.I.18 [12][SBN]; I-Nc Cantate 261 [28][RISM]; S-Uu Gimo 284[RISM;IP])
	[printed sources] *Se viver non poss'io*, in *Al signor Giacopo Veroli, che nel nuovo Teatro Dell'illustrissimo pubblico di Reggio rappresenta egregiamente la parte di Gandarte del dramma di Alessandro nell'Indie l'anno 1753* (Modena: Torri, 1753)
1754	mus. by Agricola, Johann Friedrich
1754 Berlin	Court theatre (carn.)
	Cleofide
Librettos	Berlin: Haude & Spener, [1754] (It./Ger.)
	D-B 55 Tb 1144; D-KNth L 1061; I-Rsc Carv.3448; PL-Wu GSD 28.20.4.5877 [1]; US-Wc ML48 [S67]
Music sources	[complete scores] D-B Mus.ms. 383[NG,RISM]; D-B Mus.ms. 383/1[NG,RISM]; D-B Mus.ms. 383/3[NG,RISM;A]; D-Bsa [D-B] SA 940[NG,RISM]; D-Bsa [D-B] SA 941[NG,RISM;R]; D-DS Mus.ms 10[NG,RISM]; D-W Cod. Guelf. 1 Mus. Hdschr.[RISM;A]; D-W Cod. Guelf. 2 Mus. Hdschr.[RISM;A]; S-Skma T-R[RISM]; US-BEm MS 461[IC,RISM]; US-Wc M1500.A64 C4[RISM]
	[excerpts] *Digli che io son fedele* (D-KNh R 490 [1])[RISM;R,191]; *È prezzo leggiero* (D-ROu Mus. Saec. XVIII:1 [1])[RISM;R]; *Saria tormento, affanno* (D-ROu Mus. Saec. XVIII:1 [6])[RISM;R]; *Se amore a questo petto* (D-ROu Mus. Saec. XVIII:1 [7])[RISM;R]; *Se mai più sarò geloso* (D-ROu Mus. Saec. XVIII:1 [4])[RISM;R]; *Se mai turbo il tuo riposo* (D-ROu Mus. Saec. XVIII:1 [5])[RISM;R]; *Se mai turbo il tuo riposo* [duet] (D-ROu Mus. Saec. XVIII:1 [8])[RISM;R]; *Se troppo crede al ciglio* (D-KNh R 490 [2])[RISM;R]; *Vedrai con tuo periglio* (D-ROu Mus. Saec. XVIII:1 [2])[RISM;R]; *Vil trofeo d'un'alma imbelle* (D-ROu Mus. Saec. XVIII:1 [3])[RISM;R]

---

189. Not found in [IC].
190. Used for a performance in Florence, 1757, sung by Giovanni Manzuoli.
191. All the pieces in D-KNh R 490: arrangements for lute, in tablature.

[contrafacta] *Non sarei sì sventurata* ([*Iste confessor Domini*] PL-KŁwnm A-428 [3]^{RISM}); *Se mai turbo il tuo riposo* ([*Iste confessor Domini*] PL-KŁwnm A-428 [2]^{RISM})

| 1754 | mus. by Galuppi, Baldassare (2nd version) → see 1738 |

Alessandro nell'Indie, in *Poesie del signor abate Pietro Metastasio* (Paris: widow of Quillau, 1755), vol. 4, pp. 1–85.

| 1755 | mus. by Perez, Davide (2nd version) → see 1744 |

| 1755 | mus. by Galuppi, Baldassare (3rd version) → see 1738 |

1755	mus. by unknown composer(s)
1755 Amsterdam	Theatre (05/08/1755)
Librettos	[Amsterdam: s.n., 1755] (It./Fr.)
	B-Br II 28.850 A I [3]

1756	mus. by various composers (incl. Corri, Domenico and Giardini, Felice)
1756 London	King's Theatre in the Haymarket (11/12/1756)
Librettos	London: Woodfall, 1756 (It./En.)[192]
	GB-Lbl 163.g.33;[193] GB-Lbl 907.i.10 [7]; US-CAt TS 8026.428 1756
Music sources	[excerpts] *Digli che io son fedele* by F. Giardini (US-BEm MS 105 [5]^{RISM})
	[printed sources] *Ah, che la voce io sento* by unknown composer [1]; *Digli che io son fedele* [3]; *Se mai turbo il tuo riposo* [4]; *Se troppo crede al ciglio* [2] by F. Giardini, in *The Favourite Songs in the Opera call'd Alessandro nell'Indie. Sung by Sig.ra Mingotti* (London: [Oswald., c. 1757])[194]

1756	mus. by Conforto, Nicola
1756 Pisa	Teatro Pubblico?
Music sources	[excerpts] *O sugli estivi ardori* (US-BEm MS 96 [2]$^{IC,RISM;R}$); *Se mai turbo il tuo riposo* (US-BEm MS 96 [4]$^{IC,RISM;R}$); *Vedrai con tuo periglio* (US-

---

192. According to ^{S}775, further copy in the Hicke private collection in London.
193. Microfilm copies: GB-En Mf.134, reel 6563 [4]; GB-Lbl PB.Misc.1504.
194. Burden, Michael, 'Metastasio on the London Stage, 1728 to 1840: A Catalogue', *Royal Musical Association Research Chronicle*, 40 (2007), 1–332.

MC | *Alessandro nell'Indie (1730–1831)*

BEm MS 96 [3]$^{IC,RISM;R}$); *Vil trofeo d'un'alma imbelle* (US-BEm MS 96 [1]$^{IC,RISM;R}$)

[contrafacta] *Se mai turbo il tuo riposo* ([*Giusti dei, se a tanti affanni*] US-SFsc *M2.1 M100$^{RISM;IP}$; US-SFsc *M2.1 M597^{RISM})

Alessandro nell'Indie, in *Poesie del signor abate Pietro Metastasio* (Turin: Stamperia Reale, 1757), vol. 4, pp. 3–84.

1758	mus. by Piccinni, Niccolò	
1758 Rome	Teatro di Torre Argentina (carn., 21/01/1758)[195]	(1)
	1st version	
1762 Palermo	Teatro di Santa Cecilia (summ.)	(2)
1774 Naples	Teatro di S. Carlo (carn., 12/01/1774)	(3)
	birthday of Ferdinando IV, king of Naples	
	2nd version	
1777 Florence	Teatro della Pergola (carn., 26/12/1776)	(4)
1792 Naples	Teatro di S. Carlo (carn., 12/01/1792)	(5)
	birthday of Ferdinando IV, king of Naples	
Librettos	(1) Rome: Amidei,[196] [1758]	
	B-Bc 19034; I-PLcom CXXXVI A 91 4; I-Rb FS3 34.01.23; I-Rsc Libr. n. XVI [7]; I-Rsc Libr. n. XVI [176]; I-Rvat Stamp.Ferr.V.8055 [5]	
	(2) Palermo: Toscano, 1762	
	I-PLn Misc.A.073 [6]	
	(3) Naples: Morelli, [1774]	
	I-Baf FA2.LIB.269; I-Fm Mel.2292 [5]; I-Nc OK.10.15 [9]; I-Nc Rari 10.6.17 [9]; US-NYp *MGTY-Res.; US-NYp Mus. Res. *MZ, A/20/21 [5]	
	(4) Florence: Risaliti,[197] [1777]	
	B-Bc 19038; I-Bc Lo.04229; I-Fc E.V.1502; US-Wc ML48 [S8137]	
	(5) Naples: Flauto, 1792	
	I-Nc Rari 10.5.28 [6]; I-Vgc ROL.0536 [1];[198] US-BEm ML48.I7 [667]; US-NH ML48 L698 [5]	

---

195. Date in ^{NG} 'Piccinni, Niccolò'. Rinaldi, Mario, *Due secoli al Teatro Argentina* (Florence: Olschki, 1978) gives 28/01/1758 instead due to some confusion with the calendar.
196. 'Si vendono da'.
197. 'Si vende da'.
198. Microfilm copy: CDN-Lu ML48.M47P53 1792a.

MC | *Alessandro nell'Indie* (1730–1831)

Music sources

1st version: 1758, Rome

[complete scores] D-ROu[MGG,NG]; GB-Lbl R.M.22.m.8/9/10[MGG,NG,RISM]; GB-Lfm MU.MS.141[IC,MGG,NG]; I-OS Mss.Mus.B 34[SBN]; I-Tf 1 I 5[RISM]; P-La 45-VI-12/13/14[BA,NG]; P-La 54-I-7/8/9[BA,NG,199]

[excerpts] *Cara, se le mie pene* (US-Cn VM2.3.I88a [5][RISM]); *Destrier che all'armi usato* (I-Mc Mus. Tr.ms. 1029[RISM,SBN]; I-Rc Mss. 2765 [18][SBN]; I-Rdp Ms Musicale 80 [4][RISM]; US-SFsc *M2.1 M402[RISM;IP]); *Digli che io son fedele* (US-SFsc *M2.1 M403[RISM;IP]); *Il regno, il consorte* (I-MC 5-A-8 [17][RISM]); *O sugli estivi ardori* (D-B Mus.ms. 17400 [5][RISM]; US-Cn VM2.3.I88a [6][RISM]); *Se mai turbo il tuo riposo* [duet] (US-R n/s [8][IC,RISM]); *Se possono tanto* (I-MC 5-A-9 [1][RISM]; S-Skma Alströmer saml. 163 [27][RISM;R]); *Se troppo crede al ciglio* (US-Cn VM2.3.I88a [4][RISM]); *Vedrai con tuo periglio* (I-Nc Arie 503 [4][SBN]); *Vil trofeo d'un'alma imbelle* (I-MC 5-A-9 [2][RISM])

2nd version: 1774, Naples

[complete scores] I-Nc* 16.5.33/34[IC,MGG,NG,RISM,200]; I-Nc 30.4.30/31/32[IC,MGG,NG,RISM,SBN]; I-Rrai P.S.M. 1145[RISM,SBN,201]; P-La 45-VI-15/16/17[BA,MGG,NG]; S-Skma T-R[RISM]; I-OS Mss.Mus.B 34[RISM] [Acts I&III]

[excerpts] *Chi vive amante sai che delira* (GB-Lcm MS 492 [7][IC]; US-R n/s[IC,RISM]); *Destrier che all'armi usato* (CH-E 129,5[RISM;P]; D-Dl Mus.3264-F-33 [2][RISM]; D-W Cod. Guelf. 196 Mus. Hdschr. [3][RISM]; GB-Lcm MS 492 [5][IC]; I-MC 4-F-25 [2][RISM]; I-MC 5-A-14 [10][RISM]; I-MC 5-A-16 [1][RISM]; I-Nc 57.2.7 [6][SBN]; US-Wc M1505.A1 (vol. 179) [1][RISM]); *Digli che io son fedele* (D-Hs M A/908 [3][RISM]; GB-Lbl R.M.22.m.22 [2][BL,RISM]; I-Nc 57.2.5 [16][SBN]; I-Nc Arie 503 [7][SBN]; I-Vlevi CF.B.78[RISM,SBN]; S-Skma T-SE-R[RISM]; US-Bp M.120.27 [4][RISM]); *Dov'è? Si affretti* (B-Bc 4644[IC,RISM]; D-W Cod. Guelf. 196 Mus. Hdschr. [9][RISM]; GB-Lbl R.M.22.m.22 [7][BL,RISM]; GB-Lcm MS 492 [6][IC]; I-Mc Noseda O.44 [6][SBN]; I-MC 5-A-8 [3][RISM]; I-MC 5-A-12 [17][RISM]; I-MC 5-A-16 [3][RISM]; I-Nc 57.2.7 [2][SBN]; US-CAe Mus 503.603 [13][RISM]; US-Wc M1505.A1 (vol. 180) [4][RISM]); *Mio ben ricordati* (D-B Mus.ms. 30130 [24][RISM]; I-PAc

---

199. The music differs from that in P-La 45-VI-12/13/14 in the overture, the position of the march in act I, the inclusion of a 2nd march in act II; all the closed numbers are exactly the same. Therefore, we hypothesise that this source corresponds to the 1762 revival in Palermo.
200. Partial and incomplete autograph. Despite a wrong inscription on the manuscript which associates it to Piccinni's 1st version, and which is followed in [MGG], the source corresponds to the 1792 revival of his 2nd setting in Venice, according to the singers' names on the manuscript and the correspondences with the libretto. The fact that this source is a partial autograph may indicate that Piccinni supervised this revival.
201. It corresponds to a performance in Naples. As the overture is different from that in I-Nc* 16.5.33/34, we hypothesise that this source was used in the 1792 revival.

Sanv. A.105[RISM,SBN]; I-VEcon MS 312[RISM,SBN;P]); *Non sarei sì sventurata* (D-W Cod. Guelf. 196 Mus. Hdschr. [5][RISM]; US-R n/s[RISM]); *Ombra dell'idol mio* (D-KNu I P 17 [3][RISM]; D-W Cod. Guelf. 196 Mus. Hdschr. [8][IC,RISM]; I-Nc 57.2.5 [17][SBN]); *Se il ciel mi divide* (B-Bc 4644[RISM]; B-Bc 12316[RISM]; CH-Gc Rmo 123 [8][RISM]; D-Hs M A/7896 [9][RISM]; D-MEIr F 557[RISM]; F-Pn D-14683[BnF]; GB-Lbl R.M.22.m.24 [1][RISM]; GB-Lcm MS 492 [2][IC]; I-Baf Fondo antico 2604[SBN]; I-CBp Pepe Ms.227[RISM,SBN]; I-Mc Mus. Tr.ms. 1030[RISM,SBN;P]; I-Mc Noseda O.20 [7][SBN]; I-Mc Noseda O.20 [8][SBN]; I-Mc Noseda O.44 [15][SBN]; I-MC 4-F-25 [9][RISM]; I-MC 5-A-9 [12][RISM]; I-MC 5-A-10 [5][RISM]; I-MC 5-A-11 [6][RISM]; I-MC 5-A-12 [15][RISM]; I-MC 5-A-16 [4][RISM]; I-Nc 6.3.1 [11][SBN]; I-Nc 34.2.1 [5][SBN]; I-Nc 34.4.3 [19][SBN]; I-Nc 34.6.17 [5][SBN]; I-Nc 40.2.29 [4][SBN,202]; I-Nc 40.2.29 [85][SBN,203]; I-Nc 40.2.29 [86][SBN,204]; I-Nc 64.36 [14][SBN]; I-Nc 64.36 [15][SBN]; I-Nc 64.13.3 [1][SBN]; I-Nc 57.2.5 [12][SBN]; I-Nc A 97B [2][SBN;] I-Nc Arie 377 [87-94][SBN;IP,205]; I-PAc Borb.510[SBN]; I-PAc Borb.540[RISM]; I-Rama A.Ms.4 [5][RISM,SBN]; I-Rc MUS.MS 183[IC,SBN]; I-Rsc G.Mss.185 [8][RISM]; IRL-Dtc 3607 [9][RISM]; US-LAuc FA6964M4 [8][RISM]; US-NH Misc. Ms. 36 [1][RISM]; US-R n/s [4][IC,RISM]; US-SFsc *M2.5 v.4 [5][RISM]; S-Skma T-SE-R[RISM]; US-Wc M1505.A1 (vol. 180) [5][RISM]); *Se mai più sarò geloso* (D-KNu I P 17 [6][RISM]; D-W Cod. Guelf. 196 Mus. Hdschr. [4][RISM]; GB-Lbl R.M.22.m.22 [1][RISM]; HR-Dsmb 76/1978[RISM]; I-IBborromeo SM.087[IC]; I-Mc Mus. Tr.ms. 1014[RISM]; I-Mc Noseda O.20 [10][SBN]; I-MC 4-F-25 [9][RISM]; I-MC 5-A-16 [4][RISM]; I-Nc 57.2.4 [14][SBN]; S-Skma T-SE-R[RISM]; S-Skma T-SE-R[RISM;IP]; US-Wc M1505.A1 (vol. 180) [1][RISM]); *Se mai turbo il tuo riposo* (CZ-Pnm XLII A 155[RISM]; D-W Cod. Guelf. 196 Mus. Hdschr. [2][RISM]; GB-Lcm MS 492 [3][IC]; I-MC 4-F-25 [9][RISM]; I-MC 5-B-1 [9][RISM]); *Se mai turbo il tuo riposo* [duet] (CH-Gc O 34 [RISM;R]; D-B Mus.ms. 30123 [1][RISM]; D-Dl Mus.3264-F-5[RISM]; D-Dl Mus.3264-F-33 [3][RISM]; F-Pn L-19498[BnF]; GB-Lcm MS 497 [1][IC]; I-Mc Mus. Tr.ms. 1016[RISM,SBN]; I-Mc Mus. Tr.ms. 1460[SBN]; I-Mc Noseda O.20 [11][SBN]; I-MC 5-A-7 [10][RISM]; I-MC 5-A-14 [6][RISM]; I-MC 5-A-15 [5][RISM]; I-MC 5-A-16 [5][RISM]; I-MC 5-B-1 [9][RISM]; I-Nc 34.6.17 [2][SBN]; I-Nc 34.6.17 [6][SBN]; I-Nc 57.2.16 [12][SBN]; I-Rc Mss. 2243 [3][SBN]; US-BEm MS 104 [2][IC,RISM;R]; US-BEm MS 108 [3][IC,RISM]); *Se possono tanto* (D-Dl Mus.3264-F-33 [1][RISM]; D-KNmi A 4 R [4][RISM]; D-W Cod. Guelf. 196 Mus. Hdschr. [6][RISM]; GB-Lbl R.M.22.m.23

---

202. In d minor instead of f minor.
203. Used for a singing competition in 1860. In e flat minor instead of f minor; for tenor instead of soprano voice.
204. Used for a singing competition in 1860.
205. In d minor instead of f minor.

[6]^(BL,RISM); I-CBp Pepe Ms.224^(RISM,SBN); I-Mc Noseda O.20 12]^(SBN); I-Mc Noseda O.20 [13]^(SBN); I-Mc Noseda O.44 [16]^(SBN); I-Mc Noseda O.44 [17]^(SBN); I-MC 4-F-25 [5]^(RISM); I-MC 5-A-15 [1]^(RISM); I-MC 5-A-16 [2]^(RISM); I-MC 6-A-1 [9]^(RISM); I-Nc 34.6.16 [15]^(SBN); I-Nc 57.2.4 [5]^(SBN); I-Nc 64.133 [4]^(SBN); S-Skma T-SE-R^(RISM); US-BEm MS 104 [1]^(IC,RISM;R); US-BEm MS 108 [4]^(IC,RISM); US-SFsc *M2.1 M404^(RISM); US-SFsc *M2.5 v.4 [3]^(RISM); US-Wc M1505.A1 (vol. 108) [2]^(RISM)); *Se troppo crede al ciglio* (D-W Cod. Guelf. 196 Mus. Hdschr. [7]^(RISM); I-Nc 57.2.6 [9]^(SBN)); *Vedrai con tuo periglio* (B-Bc 4648^(RISM); D-W Cod. Guelf. 196 Mus. Hdschr. [1]^(RISM); GB-Lcm MS 492 [4]^(IC); HR-Dsmb 75/1973^(RISM); I-Mc Noseda O.20 [14]^(SBN); I-Mc Noseda O.20 [15]^(SBN); I-MC 5-A-15 [7]^(RISM); I-Nc 57.2.5 [13]^(SBN)); *Vil trofeo d'un'alma imbelle* (GB-Lcm MS 492 [8]^(IC))

[printed sources] *Se il ciel mi divide*, in *Poro dunque mori? Scena, Journal d'ariettes italiennes*, 34 (Paris: Bailleux, 1780)^(IP); in *Les Délices d'Euterpe. '3e' suite d'airs tirés des opera et opera comique des plus célèbres auteurs, tels que MM. Gluck, Piccini, Sacchini, Paésiello, etc. [A 1 voix] avec accompagnement de clavecin ou de harpe et d'un violon ad libitum, par Mrs Edelmann* (Paris: Bailleux, [c. 1780])

Se mai più sarò geloso, in *Se mai più sarò geloso. Cavatina seria [...] in Napoli [...] il carnovale dell'anno 1774* (Venice: Marescalchi & Canobbio, [1774]); in *Se mai più sarò geloso. Cavatina seria [...] in Napoli [...] il carnovale dell'anno 1774* (Venice: Alessandri & Scataglia, [c. 1775])

Unspecified arias, in *The Favourite Songs in the Opera Alessandro nelle Indie* (London: Napier, [c. 1774])

[arrangements by other composers] *Dov'è? Si affretti* (D-MÜs SANT Hs 1386 [14]^(RISM,206); GB-Lbl R.M.22.m.22 [7]^(RISM))

[undated]	[complete scores] CDN-Lu MZ1409
	[excerpts] *Paventa del mio sdegno* (I-Mc Mus. Tr.ms. 1015^(RISM,SBN)); *Se mai più sarò geloso* (S-Skma T-SE-R^(RISM)); *Se possono tanto* (F-Pn D-14444 [5]^(BnF); F-Pn D-14444 [7]^(BnF))
[doubtful]	[excerpts] *Mio ben ricordati* (I-Nc O.3.7 [6]^(SBN)); *Quel labbro vezzoso* (I-BGi PREIS.248.3656^(SBN,207)); *Se il ciel mi divide* (I-Nc 34.6.17^(SBN,208)); *Se mai più sarò geloso* (I-Mc Mus. Tr.ms. 1014^(SBN,209)); *Se mai turbo il tuo*

---

206. This and the following source: terzetto instead of aria.
207. The aria is not included in the librettos of Piccinni's two original versions.
208. The aria is not included in the libretto of Piccinni's 1st version of *Alessandro*. It is included in the text for his second setting, yet the music is completely different from the aria in the composer's autograph. According to an inscription on the manuscript, it was performed in Naples in 1769.
209. The music is different from that in P-La 45-VI-12/13/14 and I-Nc* 16.5.33/34.

riposo (I-Mc Mus. Tr.ms. 1014bis[RISM,210]; I-MC 5-A-7 [16][RISM]); *Sommi dei, se giusti siete*[211] (I-Rc Mss. 3110 [4][SBN])

1758	mus. by Sciroli, Gregorio?[212]	
1758 Genoa	Teatro da S. Agostino (spr.)	(1)
1764 Bologna	Teatro Pubblico (spr., 31/05/1764)	(2)
1774 Siena	Teatro degli Intronati (carn.)	(3)
Librettos	(1) Genoa: Franchelli, [1758]	
	H-Bn 203.562; I-SAa 3ECC00002183	
	(2) Bologna: Sassi, [1764]	
	I-Bam Ambr.Comunale.002; I-Bc Lo.05176; I-Bu A.V.Tab.IX.Caps. XXI [17]; I-Pmc[S]; I-Vgc ROL.0610 [7]; US-Wc ML48 [S9781]	
	(3) Bologna: Pisarri, [1774]	
	I-Fc E.V.2516	
Music sources	[complete scores] P-La 46-V-42/43[BA,MGG,NG,RISM] [Acts I&II]; S-Skma T-R[RISM]	
	[excerpts] *Non sarei sì sventurata* (I-Gl FONDO ANT. M.(1) 1P[SBN]); *Se mai turbo il tuo riposo* [duet] (F-Pn MS-72 [2][BnF,RISM]; I-MC 6-D-13 [6][RISM]; P-Ln M.M. 521[IC]); *Voi che adorate il vanto* (F-Pn MS-72 [6][BnF,RISM])	
	[doubtful] *Vedrai con tuo periglio*[213] (D-B Mus.ms. 20568[RISM])	

1758	mus. by unknown composer(s)
1758 Madrid	Court theatre – Teatro del Buen Retiro[NP,214]

1759	mus. by Holzbauer, Ignaz
1759 Milan	Teatro Regio Ducale (carn.)

---

210. [SBN] gives I-Mc Mus. Tr.ms. 1016bis.
211. This duet is not included in the librettos for the 1758 and 1774 premieres.
212. According to [C], the author(s) of this version is/are unknown. However, the fact that two sources for Sciroli's setting are dated 1758 —the complete score S-Skma T-R and the duet *Se mai turbo il tuo riposo* in I-MC 6-D-13 [6]— make us hypothesise that they correspond to the Genovese premiere and that, accordingly, Sciroli's setting was latter revived in Bologna (1764) and Siena (1774).
213. The musical setting of this aria is different from that in P-La 46-V-42.
214. The performance of this *Alessandro* was cancelled due to the Queen's (Bárbara of Braganza) passing on 28 August 1758. See Sommer-Mathis, Andrea, 'El tandem Metastasio–Farinelli: producción de óperas y escenografía del *dramma per musica*', *Scherzo*, 384, special dossier: *Metastasio en el Madrid del XVIII* (May 2022), 64–66; Gutiérrez Carou, Javier, 'Nitteti en la correspondencia entre Metastasio y Farinelli', *Scherzo*, 384, special dossier: *Metastasio en el Madrid del XVIII* (May 2002), 67–69.

MC | *Alessandro nell'Indie* (1730–1831)

Librettos	Milan: Malatesta, [1759] F-Pn LIV IT-3525 [12]; I-Bc Lo.02535; I-Fc E.V.2517; I-LDEsormani 309/2/27; I-Ma S. I. H. I. 8 [6]; I-Mb Racc.dramm.6067 [6]; I-Rn 40.9.D.12.3; I-Rsc Vol. 7 [6]
Music sources	[complete scores] I-Nc 28.6.4/5/6[IC,MGG,NG,RISM;A]; P-La 44-IX-21/22/23[BA,MGG,NG] [excerpts] *Parto fra tanti affanni* (D-Dl Mus.3012-F-2 [1][MGG,RISM]) [contrafacta] *È prezzo leggiero* ([En quantos est amor] CH-E 699,4[MGG,RISM;P]); *È ver che all'amo intorno* ([Beatus vir qui timet Dominum] CH-E 498,13[MGG,RISM;P]); *Vil trofeo d'un'alma imbelle* ([Deus tuorum militum sors et corona preaemium] CH-E 699,3[MGG,RISM;P]) [supposed] D-B[MGG]

1760	mus. by Jommelli, Niccolò (2nd version) → see 1744	

1760	mus. by unknown composer(s)	
1760 Bologna	Teatro Formagliari[215]	

1761	mus. by Dal Barba, Daniel	
1761 Verona	Teatro Filarmonico (carn.)	
Librettos	Verona: Ramanzini, 1761 I-VEc D.382 [1]	

1761	mus. by Sarti, Giuseppe	
1761 Copenhagen	Royal Danish Theatre (aut.)	(1)
	1st version	
1766 Padua	Teatro Nuovo (Fair, 12/06/1766)	(2)
1771 Copenhagen	Royal Danish Theatre (aut.)	(3)
1787 Palermo	Teatro di Santa Cecilia (win.)	(4)
	2nd version	
Librettos	(1) Copenhagen: Svare, 1761 (It./Dan.) DK-Kk 56,-368 8° 02299 (2) Padua: Conzatti, [1766] I-Pmc[C,S]; I-Vcg LIBRETTI PADOVA 260	

---

215. Ricci, *I teatri di Bologna*, p. 477.

MC | *Alessandro nell'Indie* (1730–1831)

(3) Copenhagen: [s.n.], 1771 (It./Dan.)
DK-Kk 56,-368 8°

(4) Palermo: Solli, [1787]
I-Bc Lo.07657

Music sources
1st version: 1761, Copenhagen

[complete scores][216] P-La 46-IV-9/10/11[BA,MGG,NG]; P-La 47-V-3/4[BA,MGG,NG]

[excerpts] *Dov'è? Si affretti* (D-SWl Mus.4774[RISM,217]); *Se il ciel mi divide* (P-VV G-Prática 51b[IC,218]); *Se possono tanto* (I-MAav Cart.66 n.44[RISM;IP]; I-MC 5-E-7 [5][RISM]); *Son confusa pastorella* (B-Bc 4844[RISM]; D-Hs NMC: 5 : 2b [3][RISM;R])

[inserts] *Se viver non poss'io*[219] (A-Wn Mus.Hs.1872 [2][IC]; D-Bhm RH 0916 [3][RISM]; D-Bhm RH 0917 [2][RISM]; I-Nc 64.41.14 [SBN])

1761	mus. by Cocchi, Gioacchino and others	
1761 London	King's Theatre in the Haymarket (13/10/1761)[220]	(1)
1764 London	King's Theatre in the Haymarket (13/03/1764)[221]	(2)

Librettos

(1) London: Woodfall, 1761 (It./En.)
GB-Lbl 639.e.27 [4];[222] US-SM La 201

(2) London: Woodfall, 1764 (It./En.)
D-W Textb. 609[223]

Music sources

[printed sources][224]

[1761] Cocchi, Gioacchino, *Digli che io son fedele* [1]; *Se tutti i mali miei* [4]; *Sommi dei, se giusti siete* [2]; *Vedrai con tuo periglio* [3], in *The Favourite Songs in the Opera call'd Alessandro nelle Indie* (London: Walsh, [1761])

[1764] Giardini, Felice, *Ah, che la voce io sento* [1]; *Digli che io son fedele* [3]; *Se mai turbo il tuo riposo* [4]; *Se troppo crede al ciglio* [2], in *The Fa-*

---

216. For Padua 1766.
217. Inserted into Sarti's *Filindo* (Copenhagen, 1760).
218. Used in a pasticcio performed in Rio de Janeiro in the 1780s composed mainly of arias from *Demofoonte*. See relevant entry in the dedicated chapter in this volume.
219. Inserted as *Lungi da te se viver non poss'io* into Piccinni's *Arminda e Rinaldo* (St Petersburg, 1786).
220. The production ran for nine consecutive performances; see Petty, Fred Curtis, 'Italian Opera in London, 1760–1800' (doctoral dissertation, Yale University, 1971).
221. The production ran for nine consecutive performances; see Petty, 'Italian Opera in London', p. 143.
222. Microfilm copies: D-Gs MA 83-57 3112 [13]; GB-En Mf.134, reel 3112 [13].
223. One microfilm copy under the same signature in the same library.
224. Burden, 'Metastasio on the London stage', pp. 38–39.

MC | *Alessandro nell'Indie* (1730–1831)

vourite Songs in the Opera call'd Alessandro nell'Indie. Sung by Sig.ra Mingotti (London: [s.n., 1764])

1762	mus. by Bach, Johann Christian	
1762 Naples	Teatro di S. Carlo (20/01/1762)	(1)
	birthday of Carlos III, king of Spain	
1763 Lodi	Teatro di Lodi (carn.)	(2)
1778 Lodi	Teatro di Lodi (carn.)	(3)

Librettos   (1) Naples: Flauto, 1762
I-Nc Rari 10.5.28 [7]

(2) Lodi: Astorino & Battaglia, [1763]
I-LOcl LODI G 17

(3) Lodi: Stamperia Regia, [1778]
I-LOcl LODI G 18[225]

Music sources   [complete scores] F-Pn D-360/361[BnF,RISM,226]; I-Nc 24.5.19[RISM,SBN;A]; P-La 44-II-31/32/33[BA]; US-Wc M1500.B14 A5[IC,RISM]

[excerpts] *Destrier che all'armi usato* (F-Pn D-636 [4][BnF,RISM,227]; I-Nc 64.1 [5][SBN]; P-La 54-X-37 [66–72][BA;IP]); *Digli che io son fedele* (I-Nc 33.5.1 [12][RISM,SBN]; I-Nc 64.1.9[SBN]); *Mio ben ricordati* (F-Pn D-636 [7][BnF,RISM]); *Non sarei sì sventurata* (F-Pn D-636 [8][BnF,RISM]); *Non so donde viene* (A-Wgm VI 632 [Q 3937][IC]; A-Wgm VI 15329 [Q 3563][IC]; B-Bc 5185 [7][RISM;R]; CH-Bu kr IV 26[RISM;IP]; CH-Gc Rmo 123/12 [4][RISM]; D-Bsa [D-B] SA 1593[RISM;IP]; D-Dl Mus.1-F-82,2 [5][RISM]; D-Hs M A/846 [1/4][RISM]; D-Hs M A/878 [5][RISM]; D-Mbs Mus.ms. 1658[RISM]; F-Pn D-634 [4][BnF,RISM,228]; F-Pn D-636 [9][BnF,RISM]; F-Pn D-637 [3][BnF,RISM,229]; F-Pn D-14372[BnF,RISM]; F-Pn D-14918[BnF,RISM]; F-Pn D-15057[BnF,RISM]; F-Pn L-17132[BnF,RISM;P]; GB-Lbl Add. 31578[RISM]; GB-Lbl Add. 31817[RISM]; GB-Lbl R.M.23.d.5 [11][RISM]; I-Bc DD.100[IC,RISM,SBN]; I-Nc 33.5.1 [24][RISM,SBN]; I-Rama A.Ms.2699[RISM]; I-Rdp Ms Musicale 56 [1][RISM]; S-Uu Gimo 4[RISM]; US-AAu M1505.B12 A44[RISM]); *Oh dio, la man mi trema* (US-BEm MS 107 [1][IC,RISM]); *Ombra del caro sposo* (I-Nc 33.5.1 [12][RISM]); *O sugli estivi ardori* (F-Pn D-636 [10][BnF,RISM]); *Se amore a questo petto* (CH-Zz Mus Ms A 83[SB]; S-Uu Gimo 6[RISM]); *Se è ver che t'accendi* (F-Pn D-636

---

225. The copy could not be found by the library staff. We therefore consider it as lost.
226. Microfilm copy: F-Pn VM BOB-22582.
227. Microfilm copy of all the pieces in F-Pn D-636: F-Pn VM BOB-23846.
228. Microfilm copy of all the pieces in F-Pn D-634: F-Pn VM BOB-23844.
229. Microfilm copy of all the pieces in F-Pn D-637: F-Pn VM BOB-23847.

MC | *Alessandro nell'Indie* (1730–1831)

[15][BnF,RISM]); *Se il ciel mi divide* (B-Bc 5184 [8][RISM]; F-Pn D-634 [8][BnF,RISM]; F-Pn D-636 [11][BnF,RISM]; F-Pn D-637 [2][BnF,RISM]; F-Pn D-14372[BnF,RISM,230]; F-Pn D-14963 [12][BnF,RISM,231]; F-Pn L-17141[BnF,RISM;IP]; GB-Lbl Add. 14183 [13][BL,RISM]; I-MC 1-B-10 [4][RISM]; I-MC 1-B-10 [6][RISM]; I-MC 1-B-11 [10][RISM]; I-MC 5-A-7 [12][RISM]; I-Nc 5.1.4[RISM]; I-Nc 33.5.1 [3][RISM,SBN]; I-Nc 33.5.1 [16][RISM,SBN]; I-Nc O.4.5 [9][SBN]; P-Ln M.M. 9 [1][IC]; S-Uu Gimo 7[RISM]); *Se mai più sarò geloso* (F-Pn D-636 [12][BnF,RISM]; I-MC 1-B-10 [1b][RISM]); *Se mai turbo il tuo riposo* (CH-Gc Rmo 123/12 [5][RISM]; F-Pn D-636 [13][BnF,RISM]; I-Nc Arie 64 [1][SBN]; P-La 54-X-37 [73–79][BA;IP]; S-Skma Alströmer saml. 146 [20][RISM]); *Se mai turbo il tuo riposo* [duet] (B-Bc 3705[RISM]; CH-Zz Mus Ms A 232[SB]; D-Dl Mus.1-F-49,9 [1][RISM]; D-Dl Mus.3374-F-3[RISM]; D-Hs ND VI 2979 [1][RISM]; D-Wa 46 Alt 677[RISM]; DK-Kk mu6309.1735[RISM;P]; F-Pn D-634 [11][BnF,RISM]; F-Pn D-636 [20][BnF,RISM]; F-Pn D-637 [1][BnF,RISM]; F-Pn L-17140[BnF,RISM;P]; GB-Lbl Egerton MS 3686[BL]; I-Bc DD.99a[IC,RISM,SBN]; I-Bc DD.99b[IC]; I-Mc Mus. Tr.ms. 85[RISM,SBN]; I-MC 1-B-10 [14][RISM]; I-MC 1-B-11 [1][RISM]; I-MC 1-B-11 [7][RISM]; I-MC 5-A-8 [14][RISM]; I-MC 5-E-8 [15][RISM]; I-Nc 33.5.1 [6][RISM,SBN]; I-Nc 33.5.1 [27][RISM,SBN]; I-Nc A 205 [11][SBN]; I-PAc Sanv.A.71[RISM,SBN]; S-Uu Gimo 8[RISM]; US-AAu M1505.B12 A47 17--[RISM]); *Se possono tanto* (B-Bc 3706[RISM]; I-MC 1-B-10 [2][RISM]; I-MC 1-B-10/9 [1][RISM]; I-MC 1-B-11 [8][RISM]; I-MC 1-B-11 [11][RISM]; I-Nc 33.5.1 [22][RISM,SBN]; I-Nc 33.5.1 [25][RISM,SBN]; I-Nc 64.1.8[SBN]; I-Nc O.4.5 [5][SBN]; I-Nc Musica Strumentale 170[SBN;IP]; I-Tci Mus.Ms. 14[RISM]; I-Tf 2 IV 5[RISM]); *Se troppo crede al ciglio* (F-Pn D-636 [14][BnF,RISM]; S-Skma Alströmer saml. 146 [21][RISM]); *Son confusa pastorella* (I-MC 5-A-7 [11][RISM]; I-Nc 33.5.1 [13][RISM,SBN]); *Traffigerò quell core* (F-Pn D-636 [16][BnF,RISM]); *Vil trofeo d'un'alma imbelle* (CH-Zz Mus Ms A 85[SB]; F-Pn D-634 [9][BnF,RISM]; F-Pn D-636 [18][BnF,RISM]; F-Pn L-17138[BnF,RISM;P])

[contrafacta] *Non so donde viene* ([*Ah sero te amavi*] CH-A Ms Mus F 1(k) [Ms.6345][RISM;P]); *Se mai turbo il tuo riposo* [duet] ([*Salve regina mater misericordiae*] CH-SAf MusSAf.Ms.455[RISM;P])

---

230. Microfilm copy: F-Pn VM BOB-22003.
231. Microfilm copy: F-Pn VM BOB-25686.

1762	mus. by Traetta, Tommaso	
1762 Reggio Emilia	Teatro Pubblico (Fair, 29/04/1762)	

Librettos   Reggio Emilia: Davolio, [1762]
I-MOe M.T.Ferr.Mor.27 [7]; I-REas Vivi, II 3/1;[232] I-REm 19.K.105; I-REm 19.K.211; I-REm 19.K.216; I-REm 19.K.862; I-REm Racc. Dram. E. Curti 147 [15]; I-Vc 0104; I-Vc 0105; US-NYp *MGTZ-Res.

Music sources   [complete scores] I-MOe Mus. F. 1187[IC;P]; P-La 46-VI-26/27/28[BA,NG]

[excepts] *Cara, se le mie pene* (B-Bc 4908[RISM]; CH-Bu kr IV 357[RISM;P]; F-Pn D-18383[BnF,RISM;P]; I-Vlevi CF.B.84[RISM]); *Chi vive amante sai che delira* (D-B Mus.ms. 22004[RISM,233]; I-PAc Sanv.A.112[RISM,SBN]); *Mio ben ricordati* (D-B Mus.ms. 22004[RISM]); *Se mai turbo il tuo riposo* (A-Wgm VI 15313 [Q 3551][IC]); *Se mai turbo il tuo riposo* [duet] (CH-Gc Rmo 123/13 [3][RISM]; I-Gl FONDO ANT M.(1) 1SS[IC,SBN]; I-Mc Noseda Q.26 [5][SBN]; I-MAav Cart.4 n.13 [17][RISM;P]; I-Nc 33.5.19 [7][SBN]); *Voi che adorate il vanto* (D-B Mus.ms. 22004[RISM])

[doubtful] *Cara, se le mie pene*[234] (CH-EN Ms A 690[RISM;IP,235]; D-Mbs Mus.ms. 182 [19][RISM,236])

1763	mus. by Brunetti, Giovan Gualberto	
1763 Pisa	Teatro Pubblico (carn., 23/01/1763)	

Librettos   Pisa: Carotti, 1763
I-Vgc ROL.0182 [18]

Music sources   [excerpts] *O sugli estivi ardori* (F-Pn VM7-7213[BnF,RISM,237]; I-FZc A.VI.6 [8][SBN])

1763	mus. by Sacchini, Antonio	
1763 Venice	Teatro Vendramin di S. Salvatore (Asc., 12/05/1763)	(1)
	1st version	
1766 Turin	Teatro Regio (carn., 26/12/1765)[238]	(2)

---

232. Pages 33–83 missing.
233. This source and D-B Mus.ms. 22004 belong to Gatti's 1768 setting, yet they contain three arias by Traetta → see 1768, mus. by Gatti, Luigi.
234. The music of these two sources is different from that in the other manuscripts.
235. In E flat major.
236. Attributed to B. Galuppi → see doubtful excerpt in 1738, mus. by Galuppi, Baldassare. In F major.
237. The manuscript dates it in 1756.
238. The production ran for sixteen consecutive performances; see Bouquet, Marie-Thérèse, Valeria Gualerzi, and Alberto Testa, *Storia del Teatro Regio di Torino: cronologie*, ed. by Alberto Basso (Turin: Cassa di Risparmio di Torino, [1988]).

MC | *Alessandro nell'Indie* (1730–1831)

1768 Naples	Teatro di S. Carlo (summ., 29/05/1768)[239]	(3)
	wedding of Ferdinando IV, king of Naples, and Maria Carolina of Austria	
	2nd version	
1771 Livorno	Teatro da S. Sebastiano (carn., 26/12/1770)	(4)
	add. by A. Felici	
1773 Perugia	Teatro del Pavone (carn.)	(5)
1774 Cremona	Teatro Nazari? (carn.)[240]	(6)

Librettos

(1) Venice: Valvasense, 1763
F-Pn 8-YTH-52278; I-Fc E.V.2518; I-Mb Racc.dramm.0426; I-Vcg LIBRETTI S.SALVATORE 97; I-Vnm DRAMM.1086 [7]; I-Vnm DRAMM.1286 [6]; US-LAum ML48 .R114 1763 [6]; US-Wc ML48 [S9243]

(2) Turin: Stamperia Reale, [1766][241]
D-Mbs L.eleg.m. 3912; F-Pn FB-6932; I-MAC 7.8.B.104; I-NOVc CIV 194.F.30; I-Rsc Vol. Carv.149 [1]; I-Tci L.O.0219; I-Tn F VII.365 [3]; I-Tn F XIII.491 [4]; I-Tp P.i.107 [1]; I-TStrona^S; I-Vc 4088 [1]; I-Vgc ROL.0589 [2]; US-BEm ML48 .I7 [391]; US-CAt TS 8000.6 [1]; US-Wc ML48 [S11746]

(3) Naples: Morelli, 1768
I-Nn S.MARTINO 52.7 21 [6]; I-Rsc Libr. n. XVII [4]; P-Ln M. 937 P.

(4) Livorno: Masi & co., 1771
I-LI VM 14458[242]

(5) Perugia: Costantini, 1773
I-PEc ANT Misc. I.C 50 [5]

(6) NA

Music sources

1st version: 1763, Venice

[complete scores] I-Tf 1 V 21/22bis^{MGG,NG,RISM,243}; P-La 46-III-26/27/28^{BA,NG}; P-La 54-II-22/23/24^{BA,NG}

---

239. Date in De Filippis, Felice and Raffaele Arnese, *Cronache del Teatro di S. Carlo (1737–1960)* (Naples: Edizioni Politica Popolare, 1961). Ajello, Rafaele, *Il teatro di San Carlo: la cronologia 1737–1987* (Naples: Guida, 1987) gives 30/05/1767.
240. Liborio, Francesco Maria, *La scena della città: rappresentazioni sceniche nel Teatro di Cremona 1748–1900* (Cremona: Turris, 1994).
241. ^S801 lists a copy in I-FOSc but, as confirmed by the institution's staff, it cannot be found among its holdings.
242. Chiti, Rossana and Federico Marri, *Testi drammatici per musica della Biblioteca Labronica di Livorno* (Livorno: Debatte & figli, 1991). However, the library staff could not find the copy amongst their holdings; lost?
243. This and the following source: used in Turin 1766.

[excerpts] *Deh, se potessi anch'io*[244] (D-B Mus.ms. 30130 [2]^RISM; D-MÜs SANT Hs 3483d [16]^RISM); *Se il ciel mi divide* (US-BEm MS 1168^RISM; US-BEm MS 1308^RISM); *Se mai turbo il tuo riposo* (D-MÜs SANT Hs 3483a [14]^RISM; I-Mc Noseda O.47 [7]^SBN); *Se mai turbo il tuo riposo* [duet] (A-Wn Mus.Hs.10702^IC; I-Mc Noseda O.47 [21]^SBN; US-BEm MS 98 [4]^IC,RISM); *Se possono tanto* (D-SWl Mus.4688^RISM;P); *Vedrai con tuo periglio* (D-RH [D-MÜu] Ms 662^RISM;R,P)

[doubtful] *Cara, se le mie pene*[245] (D-MÜs SANT HS 3483a [13]^RISM)

2nd version: 1768, Naples

[complete scores] F-Pn D-13511^BnF,MGG,NG; I-Nc 31.4.17/18/19^IC,MGG,RISM,SBN; P-La 46-III-29/30/31^BA,MGG,NG; P-La 54-I-68/69/70^BA,MGG,NG

[excerpts] *Chi vive amante sai che delira* (D-MÜs SANT Hs 2456 [9]^RISM,246; GB-Lbl Add. 14135 [22]^BL,RISM; S-Skma T-SE-R^RISM); *Destrier che all'armi usato* (I-MC 5-E-4/1 [5]^RISM; S-Skma T-SE-R^RISM); *Digli che io son fedele* (B-Br Ms II 4042 Mus Fétis 2621 [3]^RISM; GB-Lbl R.M.23.d.5 [1]^RISM,247; I-Rama A.Ms.3805 [13]^RISM,SBN; I-Rvat Chig.Q.VI-II.203 [73]^SBN); *Dov'è! Per me s'affretti* (D-MÜs SANT Hs 3482b [4]^RISM; I-Bc CC.229 [2]^RISM,SBN; I-Mc Noseda O.47 [22]^SBN; I-MC 5-E-4 [3]^RISM; I-Nc 64.41 [20]^SBN; I-Rc Mss. 2552 [2]^SBN; I-Rrostirolla [I-Fn] MS MUS 565 [1]^SBN; S-Skma T-SE-R^RISM; S-SK 48^RISM; US-SFsc *M2.5 v.4 [4]^RISM; US-Wc M1505.A1 (vol. 190B) [1]^IC,MGG,NG,RISM); *Povero cor, tu palpiti* (D-MÜs SANT Hs 3483a [7]^RISM); *Se il ciel mi divide* (S-Skma T-SE-R^RISM); *Se mai più sarò geloso* (B-Bc 4757^RISM; CH-Gc Rmo 123/5 [2]^RISM; CH-Zz III 713 & a–c^RISM;P; F-Pn VM7-7586^BnF; GB-Lbl Add. 14135^BL,RISM; GB-Lbl Add. 14209 [1]^BL,RISM; I-MC 5-E-8 [14]^RISM; I-MC 5-E-17 [1]^RISM; I-Nc 31.8.40 [6]^SBN;IP; I-Nc 33.3.9 [6]^SBN; I-Nc 34.6.26 [17]^SBN; US-R n/s^IC,RISM;P; US-SFsc *M2.5 v.2 [5]^RISM; US-Wc M1505.A1 (vol. 190B) [3]^IC,MGG,NG,RISM; US-Wc M1505.A1 (vol. 249) [13]^IC,MGG,NG,RISM); *Se mai turbo il tuo riposo* (D-Hs M A/821 [11]^RISM,248; F-Pn D-9173^BnF; F-Pn D-14913^BnF; GB-Lbl Add. 14135 [8]^BL,RISM; I-MC 5-E-6 [3]^RISM; I-MC 5-E-17/2 [1]^RISM; I-Nc 6.3.25 [4]^SBN; US-NYp n/s^IC; US-Wc M1505.A1 (vol. 190B) [4]^IC,MGG,NG,RISM; US-Wc M1505.A77 [8]^MGG,NG,RISM); *Se mai turbo il tuo riposo* [duet] (B-Bc 4758 [1]^RISM;

---

244. It is part of Sacchini's setting of Metastasio's *Olimpiade* (Padua, 1763), yet it was first used in A2-S3 of his *Alessandro nell'Indie* in Venice.
245. The aria was included in the 1766 revival in Turin, but not in the Venetian premiere in 1763; therefore, the music may not be by Sacchini.
246. In G major instead of D major.
247. This and the following source: in F major instead of G major.
248. In A major instead of B flat major.

MC | *Alessandro nell'Indie* (1730–1831)

CH-Bu kr IV 278[RISM;P]; CH-Gc O 50[RISM]; CH-Gc Rmo 123/5 [4][RISM]); D-MÜs SANT Hs 3483c [2][RISM]; F-Pn D-14963 [3][RISM]; I-Mc Noseda O.47 [19][SBN]; I-Mc Noseda O.47 [20][SBN]; I-Mc Noseda O.47 [21][SBN]; I-MAav Cart.10 n.17[RISM;P]; I-MC 5-E-6/1 [3][RISM]; I-MC 5-E-17 [6][RISM]; I-MC 5-E-17/2 [1][RISM]; I-MC 5-E-17/4 [3][RISM]; I-Nc 6.3.29 [4][SBN]; I-Nc 22.4.5 [5][SBN]; I-Nc 34.6.26 [10][SBN]; I-Nc 57.2.6 [10][SBN]; I-Nc 64.41.26[SBN]; I-PAc Sanv.A.93[RISM,SBN]; I-Rama A.Ma.3806 [10][IC,RISM,SBN]; I-Rrostirolla [I-Fn] MS MUS 565 [1][SBN]; S-Skma T-SE-R[RISM]; US-Bu BSO Collection, vol. 14 [6][RISM]; US-R n/s[IC,RISM]; US-SFsc *M2.5 v.2 [2][RISM]; US-SFsc *M2.5 v.8 [4][RISM]; US-Wc M1505.A1 (vol. 206) [1][IC,MGG,NG,RISM]; US-Wc M1505.A1 (vol. 249) [2][MGG,NG,RISM;IP]; US-Wc M1505.A77 [8][MGG,NG,RISM]); *Vedrai con tuo periglio* (D-MÜs SANT Hs 3483b [3][RISM]; F-Pn VM7-7467[BnF;IP]; I-MC 5-E-4/6 [3][RISM]; I-Rvat Chig.Q.VIII.203 [75][SBN]; S-Skma T-SE-R[RISM]; S-SK 59[RISM]); *Vil trofeo d'un'alma imbelle* (S-Skma T-SE-R[RISM,249]; US-Wc M1505.A1 (vol. 190B) [2][IC,MGG,NG,RISM]; S-Skma T-SE-R[RISM])

[printed sources] *Se mai più sarò geloso*, in *Cavatina nell'opera Alessandro nell'Indie* (1768) (Moi douter de celle que j'aime) 'Se mai più sarò geloso' (Paris: Heugel & co. [s.d.])

Se mai turbo il tuo riposo [19]; *Se mai turbo il tuo riposo* [duet] [23]; *Se troppo crede al ciglio* [5], in *Journal d'ariettes italiennes*, 125 (Paris: Bailleux, 1784)[IP]

[contrafacta] *Se mai turbo il tuo riposo* ([Ave Jesum summe bonus] PL-OPsm RN 419[RISM;P]; [Paratum cor meum Deus paratum] CH-E 699,13 [Ms.4654][RISM;P])

[undated] [excerpts] *Se mai più sarò geloso* (D-Dl Mus.3372-F-12 [9][RISM,250]); *Se mai turbo il tuo riposo* (A-Wgm VI 647/2 [Q 3875][IC]; A-Wn Mus.Hs.2409 [2][IC]; *Se mai turbo il tuo riposo* [duet] (A-Wgm VI 647/1 [Q 3486][IC]; A-Wn Mus.Hs.10720[IC;IP]; F-AIXm F.C. ms. IX [4][BASE]); *Vedrai con tuo periglio* (A-Wgm VI 648 [Q 3876][IC])

[doubtful][251] [excerpts] *Destrier che all'armi usato* (D-MÜs SANT Hs 173 [22][RISM]); *Se mai più sarò geloso* (I-Nc 34.4.3 [26][SBN]); *Se mai turbo il tuo riposo* [duet] (D-B Mus.ms. 19166 [6][RISM]); *Vil trofeo d'un'alma imbelle* (D-B Mus.ms. 19166 [4][RISM])

---

249. Given as anonymous in [RISM].
250. Not found in [IC].
251. The music is different from the versions in I-Tf 1 V 21/22bis and I-Nc 31.4.17/18/19.

1764	mus. by Fischietti, Domenico	
1764 Prague	Teatro Nuovo (carn.)	
Librettos	[Prague]: Pruscha, [1764] CZ-Pu 65 E 8307	
Music sources	[excerpts] *Chi vive amante sai che delira* (A-Wgm VI 17006 [Q 21084])[IC,252]; *Digli che io son fedele* (D-LÜh Mus Q 223b[MGG,RISM]); *Se il ciel mi divide* (D-LÜh Mus Q 223a[MGG,RISM]); *Voi amanti che vedete* (D-Dl Mus.3269-F-5 [3][MGG,NG,RISM]; D-Dl Mus.1-F-49,12 [18][MGG,NG,RISM])	
1764	mus. by various unknown composers	
1764 Verona	Teatro Filarmonico (carn.)	
Librettos	Verona: Ramanzini, [1764] I-Pmc[C,S]	
1766	mus. by various unknown composers	
1766 Lucca	Teatro Pubblico (23/08/1766)	
Librettos	Lucca: Benedini, 1766 I-Vgc ROL.0676 [12]; US-Cn BLC #444	
1766	mus. by Di Majo, Gianfrancesco lib. rev. by Verazzi, Mattia	
1766 Mannheim	Court theatre (05/11/1766)[253] *name day of the Elector of Saxony*	(1–3)
1767 Mannheim	Court theatre (18/01/1767) *birthday of the Electress of Saxony*	(1–3)
1767 Naples	Teatro di S. Carlo[254]	(4)
Librettos	(1) Mannheim: Academy Press, 1766 D-BFb [D-MÜu] B-St 100; D-Dl XVII 515; D-KA TB 428 RH; D-MHrm Mh 1764;[255] I-Vgc ROL.MUS 2B MET	

252. Used in Naples in 1777.
253. Majo's *Alessandro* was performed on four occasions at the Mannheim court: on 5 November 1766 (premiere, Elector's name day), 20 November 1766 (Electress' name day), 10 December 1766 (Elector's birthday), and 18 January 1767 (Electress' birthday). As the first three ran consecutively within a period of two months and formed part of one single social season, we treat them as a single performance. For the sake of consistency with our treatment of Holzbauer's *Adriano in Siria*, the last performance of Majo's *Alessandro* is listed separately. For a discussion of the dates, see Baker, Nicole Edwina Ivy, 'Italian Opera at the Court of Mannheim, 1758–1770' (doctoral dissertation, University of California, 1994).
254. De Filippis and Arnese, *Cronache del Teatro di S. Carlo*, p. 38.
255. Xerox copy: D-MHu G97.

(2) Mannheim: Academy Press, 1766 (Ger. only)
D-HEu G 5508 RES::3

(3) Mannheim: Academy Press, 1766 (Fr. only)
D-HEu G 5502 RES::4

(4) NA

Music sources [complete scores] D-B Mus.ms. 13400[MGG,NG,RISM;A,256]

[excerpts] *Ah colei che m'arde in seno* (D-KNmi M 250 R [10][RISM]); *Chi vive amante sai che delira* (A-Wn SA.68.D.2 [9][IC;P]; D-KNmi M 250 R [9][RISM]); *Destrier che all'armi usato* (A-Wn SA.68.D.2 [5][IC;P]; D-KNmi M 250 R [4][RISM]); *Digli che io son fedele* (A-Wn SA.68.D.2 [2][IC;P]; D-KNmi M 250 R [6][RISM]); *Di rendermi la calma* (A-Wn SA.68.D.2 [1][IC;P]; D-B Mus.ms. 13400/5[RISM;P]; PL-Wu RM 4660[RISM;P]); *Mio ben ricordati* (F-Pn D-14380[BnF]); *Ombra cara, ombra tradita* (A-Wn SA.68.D.2 [12][IC;P]); *Se il ciel mi divide* (D-Dl Mus.1-F-82,30 [6][RISM]); *Se mai più sarò geloso* (D-KNmi M 250 R [11][RISM]); *Se mai turbo il tuo riposo* [duet] (D-Dl Mus.1-F-82,30 [7][RISM]; DK-Sa R130[RISM]; H-KE 263 Koll.9[RISM]); *Se viver non poss'io* (F-Pn D-7267 [2][BnF,257]; F-Pn L-18950[BnF]); *Son confusa pastorella* (F-Pn D-7267 [3][BnF]; I-Mc Mus. Tr.ms. 610[RISM,SBN,258]; US-SFsc *M2.1 M301[RISM;IP]); *Traffigerò quel core* (D-KNmi M 250 R [5][RISM]); *Vedrai con tuo periglio* (A-Wn SA.68.D.2 [8][IC;P]; D-KNmi M 250 R [7][RISM])

1768	mus. by various unknown composers
1768 Cremona	Teatro Nazari? (carn.)[259]

1768	mus. by Gatti, Luigi
1768 Mantua	Teatro Arciducale (carn., 24/01/1768)
Librettos	Mantua: heirs of Pazzoni, [1768]
	I-Fm Mel.2345 [12]; I-MAc Misc.476/10; I-OS LIBRETTI 29

---

256. Majo's own score was destroyed in 1744; see Baker, 'Italian Opera at the Court of Mannheim', p. 354. There was another manuscript score in D-MHrm, reportedly lost; see Corneilson, Paul Edward, 'Opera at Mannheim, 1770–1778' (doctoral dissertation, The University of North Carolina at Chapel Hill, 1994).
257. Microfilm copy: F-Pn VM BOB-34155. It also applies to F-Pn D-7267 [3].
258. In F major instead of G major.
259. Liborio, *La scena della città*, p. 29.

Music sources	[complete scores] <u>D-B Mus.ms. 22004</u>[RISM,260]; I-MOe Mus. F. 1187[IC;R,261]; P-La 44-VIII-3/4[BA,MGG,NG,262]	
	[excerpts] *Digli che io son fedele* (US-BEm MS 85 [7][RISM]); *Se il ciel mi divide* (B-Bc 14140 [1][RISM]); *Se mai turbo il tuo riposo* (F-Pn D-15342[BnF,RISM,263]; I-MAav Cart.6 n.39[MGG,NG,RISM])	

1768	mus. by Sacchini, Antonio (2nd version) → see 1763	

1768	mus. by Naumann, Johann Gottlieb	
1768 Florence	Teatro del Cocomero	
Librettos	Florence: Stecchi, 1748 [*recte* 1768] F-Pn 8-YTH-50011; I-Bc Lo.05757	
Music sources	[excerpts] *Chi vive amante sai che delira* (B-Bc 645 [1][RISM]); *Se possono tanto* (<u>D-Dl Mus.3480-J-20 [16]</u>[RISM]); *Son confusa pastorella* (D-B* Mus. ms.autogr. Naumann, J. G. 18[RISM]; S-Skma T-SE/Sv.-R[RISM])	

1769	mus. by Bertoni, Ferdinando	
1769 Genoa[NG]	Teatro del Falcone (spr.)	(1)
	1st version	
1771 Venice	Teatro Grimani di S. Benedetto (carn., 26/12/1770)	(2)
	2nd version	
Librettos	(1) NA (2) Venice: Fenzo, [1771] I-Bc Lo.00505; I-Fm Mel.2189 [12]; <u>I-Mb Racc.dramm.4428</u>; I-Vcg LIBRETTI S.BENEDETTO 57 A 14; I-Vcg LIBRETTI S.BENE-DETTO 190; I-Vlevi Dramm. 703; I-Vnm DRAMM.1098 [4]; I-Vnm DRAMM.1306 [3]; I-Vnm DRAMM.4025 [3]	
Music sources	1st version: 1769, Genoa [complete scores] D-B[264]	

---

260. This source contains three arias from Traetta's 1762 setting, written on a different paper and by a different hand → see 1762, mus. by Traetta, Tommaso.
261. Misattributed to Traetta on the source.
262. Not found in [IC].
263. Microfilm copy: F-Pn VM BOB-33863.
264. [MGG] and [NG] list a further source of Act I in D-B, yet we could not find it in [RISM] or [IC]. Lost?

MC | *Alessandro nell'Indie* (1730–1831)

[excerpts] *Destrier che all'armi usato* (D-MÜs SANT Hs 489 [6])[RISM]; *Se possono tanto* (D-MÜs SANT Hs 489 [5])[RISM]

[doubtful] *Se possono tanto* (US-BEm MS 91 [11])[IC,RISM]

2nd version: 1771, Venice[265]

[complete scores] P-La 44-II-47/48[BA,MGG]; P-La 54-I-30/31[BA,MGG]

[excerpts] *Digli che io son fedele* (D-MÜs SANT Hs 478[RISM]); *Se mai turbo il tuo riposo* (D-LÜh Mus. Q 162[RISM]; I-MC 1-B-19/1 [1][RISM]); *Se mai turbo il tuo riposo* [duet] (D-MEIr F 503[RISM]); *Tuona il cielo, scalza il vento* (I-MC 1-B-19/1 [2][RISM])

1769	mus. by Koželuh, Jan Antonín
1769 Prague	Teatro Regio (win.)
Librettos	Prague: Pruscha, [1768] (It./Ger.)
	CZ-Pu 9 K 402; US-CAh *GC7.A100.768m[266]
Music sources	[complete scores] A-Wn Mus.Hs.17792[IC,NG]
	[excerpts] *Se mai turbo il tuo riposo* (CZ-Pnm XLII E 259[NG,RISM;P])
	[contrafacta] *Destrier che all'armi usato* ([Gloria et honore] CZ-TEk[RISM;P]); *Digli che io son fedele* ([Jesu servator mundi] CZ-Pu 59 M 480[RISM]); *Non sarei sì sventurata* ([In hac die tan sacrata] CZ-BRE 499[RISM])
	[doubtful contrafacta][267] *Senza procelle ancora* ([En pulchra et decora – Gaudeas mens redumpta] CZ-Pak 566[RISM])

1771	mus. by Bertoni, Ferdinando (2nd version) → see 1769

1772	mus. by Anfossi, Pasquale	
1772 Rome	Teatro di Torre Argentina (carn., 07/01/1772)	(1)
1772 Florence	Teatro della Pergola (aut., 04/11/1772)	(2)
Librettos	(1) Rome: Casaletti,[268] [1772]	
	B-Bc 19037; F-Pn YD-5398 [4]; I-Fm Mel.2046 [6]; I-MAC 7.14.A.166; I-Rsc Libr. n. XVIII [7]; I-Rvat Stamp.Ferr.V.8061 [4]; I-Vgc ROL.0137 [11]; US-Wc ML48 [S282]	

---

265. As no complete source for Bertoni's 1st setting of *Alessandro* has been preserved, we cannot ascertain that some of the arias were reused in 1771.
266. Microfilm copy: US-MAu Micro Film 6352 Reel 1 [17].
267. Not included in the original libretto.
268. 'Si vendono da Giovanni Bartolomicchio'.

MC | *Alessandro nell'Indie* (1730–1831)

(2) Florence: Risaliti, [1772]
I-Bc Lo.05758; I-Fc E.V.1490; I-FEwalker^S

Music sources

[complete scores] D-Hs ND VII 8 ^RISM; D-MÜs SANT Hs 139 [a–c]^MGG,NG,RISM; F-Pn D-97/98/99^MGG,NG,RISM,269; I-Fc D.I.31/32^IC,NG,RISM,SBN,270; I-Rdp Ms Musicale 143 [A–C]^IC,SBN;P; P-La 44-I-32/33/34^BA,MGG,NG

[excerpts] *Ah, che mancar mi sento* (D-SWl Mus.750^RISM); *Chi vive amante sai che delira* (CH-Gc Rmo 123/10 [6]^RISM; I-VEcon MS 008^SBN); *Destrier che all'armi usato* (CH-Gc Rmo 123/11 [7]^RISM; I-MC 1-A-6/8 [1]^RISM; I-Rc Mss. 2284 [11]^RISM; UA-Knbuv Rozum 120201 [2]^RISM; US-SFsc *M2.5 v.12^RISM); *Dov'è? Si affretti* (CH-Gc Rmo 123/11 [2]^RISM); *Mio ben ricordati* (UA-Knbuv Rozum 120501 [4]^RISM); *Non sarei sì sventurata* (I-Rdp Ms Musicale 142^SBN); *Non trionfa un cor guerriero* (CH-Gc Rmo 123/10 [1]^RISM); *Se il ciel mi divide* (CH-Gc Rmo 123/10 [2]^RISM; D-B Mus.ms. 649^RISM); *Se mai turbo il tuo riposo* (CH-Gc Rmo 123/10 [2]^RISM; D-RH [D-MÜu] Ms 426^RISM;P,271; I-Bsf M.A.IV.14 [2]^SBN); *Se mai turbo il tuo riposo* [duet] (CH-Gc Rmo 123/10 [4]^RISM; D-BFb [D-MÜu] A-nf 38^RISM; I-Mc Noseda A.18 [15]^RISM; I-Rama A.Ms.2551^RISM; US-LAuc FA6964M4 [5]^RISM; US-SFsc *M2.5 v.12 [7]^RISM); *Sperai vicino il lido*[272] (B-Bc 3665^RISM; CH-Gc Rmo123/11 [1]^RISM; CH-BM Mus.Ms. 3 [1]^RISM;P; CZ-BER HU 630^RISM; D-B* Mus.ms. 647 [3]^RISM,273; D-HR [D-Au] III 4 1/2 2° 1084^RISM;P; D-Mbs Mus.ms. 10418^RISM;P; I-Rc Mss. 2284 [9]^RISM; US-LAuc FA6964M4 [19]^RISM; US-SFsc SFsc *M2.5 v.12 [4]^RISM); *Vedrai con tuo periglio* (CH-Gc Rmo 123/10 [5]^RISM; I-Rc Mss. 2284 [8]^RISM,SBN)

[printed sources] *Se il ciel mi divide*, in *Ariette pour chant, violons, alto, hautbois, cors et basse* (Paris: Bailleux, 1779)

[contrafacta] *Sperai vicino il lido* ([*Protector meus Deus*] CH-E 382,6 [Ms.3335]^RISM;P; [*O Deus in te unico spem omnem*] CH-BM Mus.Ms. 3 [2]^RISM;P)

---

269. Microfilm copies: F-Pn VM BOB-25881; US-PRu MICROFILM 1677.
270. Microfilm copy: US-PRu Ru MICROFILM 2141.
271. Wrongly attributed to Jommelli on source.
272. This aria originally belongs to Metastasio's *Demofoonte* (Rome, 1773), but in P. Anfossi's *Alessandro nell'Indie* it is sung by the character of Gandarte in A1-S11.
273. Sketch.

MC | *Alessandro nell'Indie* (1730–1831)

[doubtful] *Porto all'insana greca barbarie* (P-Pca D.II.1482^{SBN,274}); *Se amore a questo petto* (D-MÜs SANT Hs 141 II [8]^{RISM,275})

1773	mus. by various unknown composers
1773 Bologna	Teatro Formagliari (carn.)
Librettos	Bologna: Sassi, [1773]
	I-Bc Lo.05759; I-PAc F. Libretti, sc.013 [207]; I-Vgc ROL.0676 [11]

1774	mus. by Paisiello, Giovanni	
1774 Modena	Teatro Ducale (carn., 26/12/1773)^{MGG,NG}	(1)
1787 Modena	Teatro Rangoni (carn., 27/01/1787)	(2)
	mus. by G. Paisiello?	
1799 St Petersburg	Teatro Hermitage (11/05/1799)^{CA}	(3)

Librettos
(1) Modena: heirs of Soliani, [1774]
US-AM PMC 1371; US-Cn ML50.2.A54 P35 1774

(2) Modena: [heirs of] Soliani, [1787]
I-Vgc ROL.0508 [12];[276] US-Cn ML50.2.A54 M48 1787

(3) NA

Music sources
[complete scores] I-Nc* O.3.19/20/21^{IC,MGG,NG,RISM}

[excerpts] *Di generoso sdegno* (I-Mc Mus. Tr.ms. 927^{RISM,SBN}); *Non mi vedrai dolente* (CZ-Pnm XLII A 224^{RISM;P}; D-Bsa [D-B] SA 1509 [12]^{RISM;P}; D-Mbs Mus.ms. 20869 [4]^{RISM}; D-Tu Mk 14^{RISM;R}; I-MAav Cart.20 n.13 [68]^{RISM;P}; I-MC 4-D-12 [6]^{RISM}; I-Pca D.VI.1821^{SBN;P}; I-Vnm Mss. 1944^{SBN}); *Vedrai con tuo periglio*[277] (D-Dl Mus.3481-F-508^{RISM}; F-Pn D-1884^{BnF,278}; I-Rmassimo n/s^{RISM}; I-Vire 383^{SBN}; J-Tk S10-584^{RISM})

[printed sources] *Non mi vedrai dolente*, in *Journal d'ariettes italiennes* (Paris: Bailleux, [1786]); in *Rondò: Non mi vedrai dolente no. 10 del sig.r*

---

274. Although the source has the inscription 'Nell'Alessandro nell'Indie | Del Sig:r Pasquale Anfossi | In Argentina 1772', the aria was not included in the composer's *Alessandro*. Also, the aria is included in an aria collection for Aurelia Barbaran, who did not participate in that premiere.
275. Dated Rome, Teatro di Torre Argentina, 1774 on source; the aria was not included in the 1772 libretto. Given that there is no surviving libretto of an *Alessandro* by Anfossi in 1774, we hypothesise that the aria was inserted into another opera, perhaps in *Ezio* by P. A. Guglielmi or *Achille in Sciro* by P. Anfossi, which were performed at the Teatro di Torre Argentina that same year.
276. Microfilm copy: CDN-Lu ML48.M47T38 1787a.
277. Inserted into Paisiello's *La Locanda* (London, 1791).
278. Inserted into *La prova di un'accademia*, wrongly attributed to Giovanni Maria Casini. In C major instead of E flat major.

MC | *Alessandro nell'Indie* (1730–1831)

<u>Giovanni Paisiello per la sig.ra Catterina Bonafini nell'Alessandro nell'Indie in Modena nel Teatro Ducale il carnovale dell'anno 1774</u> (Florence: Alessandri & Scataglia, [c. 1775])

[parodies] *Non mi vedrai dolente* ([*Non mi vedrai spergiura*] US-Eu MSS 919[IC,RISM])

[doubtful] *Or che il cielo s me ti rende*[279] (CDN-Lu MZ1245 [4][IC])

1774	mus. by Piccinni, Niccolò (2nd version) → see 1758

1774	mus. by Corri, Domenico
	lib. modif. by Bottarelli, Giovan Gualberto
1774 London	King's Theatre in the Haymarket (03/12/1774)[280]
Librettos	London: Cadell, 1774 (It./En.)
	<u>GB-Lbl 11715.aaa.29</u>;[281] GB-Ob Harding D 2449 [1]
Music sources	[excerpts] *Chi vive amante sai che delira* (D-B Mus.ms. 4160 [6][BL,RISM,282]; F-Pn D-17169 [1][BnF]; GB-Lbl Add. 32178 [6][BL,RISM]); *Digli che io son fedele* (CH-Gc X 5 [3,4][RISM;R]); *Se mai più sarò geloso* (GB-Lbl Add. 32178 [4][BL,RISM]); *Se mai turbo il tuo riposo* (A-Wn Mus.Hs.2409 [2][IC]; GB-Lbl Add. 32178 [5][BL,RISM]); *Se mai turbo il tuo riposo* [duet] (CH-Gc X 5 [33,34][RISM;R]; GB-Lbl Add. 32178 [7][BL,RISM])
	[printed sources] *Chi vive amante sai che delira* [3];[283] *Se mai più sarò geloso* [1]; *Se mai turbo al tuo riposo* [2]; *Se mai turbo a tuo riposo* [duet] [4], in *The Favourite Songs in the Opera Alessandro nell'Indie* (London: Bremner, [1774])

1774	mus. by unknown composer(s)
1774 Valencia	Theatre
Librettos	Valencia: Orga, [1774] (It./Spa.)
	E-VAu BH A-105/058 [3]

---

279. This aria was not included in G. Paisiello original version of *Alessandro*. It may be F. Bianchi's setting instead → see 1785, mus. by Bianchi, Francesco.
280. The production run for four consecutive performances; see Petty, 'Italian Opera in London', p. 183.
281. Microfilm copies: D-Gs MA 93-14:6931 [2]; GB-En Mf.134, reel 6961 [2].
282. The source is dated 1780. In F major.
283. In G major.

MC | *Alessandro nell'Indie* (1730–1831)

1775	mus. by Monza, Carlo Ignazio
1775 Milan	Teatro Regio Ducale (carn., 28/01/1775)[284]
Librettos	Milan: Montani, [1775][285]
	CDN-Ttfl Itp Pam 000506; D-MÜs N Met 1000; F-Pn LIV IT-3531 [18]; H-Bn 160.836; I-Bc Lo.03244; I-LDEsormani 309/5/20; I-Mb Racc.dramm.6072 [6]; I-Mc Coll.Libr.160; I-Ms MUS. M. LIII. 2; I-PAc F. Libretti, sc.013 [208]; I-Rsc Vol. 16 [2]; I-REm 19.I.508; I-Vgc ROL.0468 [16]; US-AUS KL-17 154 [2]
Music sources	[excerpts] *Mio ben ricordati* (US-Wc M1505.A1 (vol. 127) [4][RISM]); *Se mai più sarò geloso* (GB-Lbl Add. 32174 [3][BL,RISM]; I-MAav Cart.6 n.41[MGG,RISM;P]); *Se mai turbo il tuo riposo* (F-Pn D-8277 [2][BnF]); *Se mai turbo il tuo riposo* [duet] (A-Wgm VI 572 [Q 10480][IC]); *Vil trofeo d'un'alma imbelle* (I-MAav Cart.6 n.53[MGG,RISM;P])[286]

1775	mus. by Rust, Giacomo
1775 Venice	Teatro Grimani di S. Samuele (Asc., 25/05/1775)
Librettos	Venice: Casali, [1775]
	I-Bc Lo.04854; I-MOe 83.D.10; I-Rsc Carv.486; I-Vcg LIBRETTI S.SAMUELE 175; I-Vgc ROL.0586 [6]; I-Vnm DRAMM.1314 [6]; S-Uu n/s; US-Wc ML48 [S9175]

1776	mus. by Jommelli, Niccolò (rev. version) → see 1744

1778	mus. by Marescalchi, Luigi
1778 Venice	Teatro Grimani di S. Benedetto (Asc., 27/05/1778)
Librettos	Venice: Fenzo, 1778
	F-Pn LIV IT-1067 [1]; F-Pn 8-YTH-51561;[287] I-PAc F. Libretti, sc.013 [209]; I-Rsc Carv.488; I-Vcg LIBRETTI S.BENEDETTO 193; I-Vivs OP.MINICH 2877; I-Vlevi Dramm. 836; I-Vnm DRAMM.1322 [8–9]; US-Wc ML48 [S5946]

---

284. Monza's *Alessandro* had a total of thirty-one performances; see Hansell, Kathleen Kuzmick, 'Opera and Ballet at the Regio Ducal Teatro of Milan, 1771–1776: A Musical and Social History' (doctoral dissertation, University of California Berkeley, 1980).
285. [C,S] list a further copy in I-Ma. However, as informed by the director of the Biblioteca Ambrosiana in Milan, it was probably destroyed during the bombardment of the city in August 1743; see [S]814. It is not present in the library's card catalogue and we therefore consider it as lost.
286. [MGG] and [NG] indicate that further sources for Monza's *Alessandro* are preserved in I-Gl, yet these have not been found in [RISM] or [IC].
287. Microfilm copy: F-Pn MICROFILM M-2628.

MC | *Alessandro nell'Indie* (1730–1831)

1778	mus. by Mortellari, Michele	
1778 Siena^{NG}	Teatro degli Intronati (22/07/1778)	(1)
1783 Lucca	Teatro Pubblico (aut., 09/08/1783)	(2)

Librettos (1) NA

(2) Lucca: Bonsignori, [1783]
I-BRq 7°.F.fII.16m1; I-Fc E.V.2514; I-Fm Mel.2107 [2]; I-Lg B.ta 285 [10]; I-Vgc ROL.0472 [3]; US-Wc ML48 [S6683]

Music sources [complete scores] I-Mc Part. Tr.ms. 252^{NG,RISM,SBN,288}

[excerpts] *Se mai più sarò geloso* (I-Mc MsCon.6 [3]^{SBN}; I-Vnm Mss. 11266^{SBN}); *Se mai turbo il tuo riposo* [duet] (A-Wgm VI 17207 [Q 3134]^{IC})

1778	mus. by De Vincenti, Melchiorre	
1778 Alessandria	Teatro Nuovo (Oct. Fair)	(1)
1781 Verona	NA^S	(2)

Librettos (1) Alessandria: Vimercati, [1778]
I-Fm Mel.2246 [15]

(2) Verona: [s.n.], 1781
I-VEc^{S,289}

1779	mus. by Calegari, Antonio
1779 Verona	Teatro Filarmonico (carn.)

Librettos Verona: Ramanzini, 1779
I-RVE r-LO 147 (17) [2]; I-VEc D.387 [1]

1779	mus. by various composers[290]
	lib. adap. by Andrei, Antonio
1779 London	King's Theatre in the Haymarket (27/11/1779)[291]

---

288. Microfilm copy: CDN-Lu M1500.M57M6 1778a.
289. The copy reported in ^S could not be found by the library staff. We therefore consider it as lost.
290. The composers included Piccinni, Bertoni, Händel, Alessandri, Anfossi, Sarti, Durán, Mysliveček, Tozzi, and Molza; see Price, Curtis, Judith Milhous, and Robert D. Hume, *Italian Opera in Late Eighteenth-Century London*, vol. 1: *The King's Theatre, Haymarket 1778–1791* (Oxford: Clarendon Press, 1995).
291. The production run for eight consecutive performances; see Petty, 'Italian Opera in London', p. 206 and Price, Milhous, and Hume, *Italian Opera in Late*, p. 220.

MC | *Alessandro nell'Indie* (1730–1831)

Librettos   London: Mackintosh, 1779 (It./En.)
F-Pn RES VS-385;[292] GB-En BH.Lib.7; GB-Lbl 907.i.17 [1];[293] US-CAt TS 8456.143 1787

Music sources   [printed sources] *Affretta i passi o caro* by J. Mysliveček [3]; *Che fa il mio bene* by P. Anfossi [2]; *Se mai più sarò geloso* by N. Piccinni [1], in *The Favourite Songs in the Opera Alessandro nell'Indie* (London: Napier, [1780])[294]; *Mio ben ricordati* by T. Giordani, in *Sig.r Manzoletto's Favorite Song in the Opera Alessandro nell'Indie* (London: Longman & Broderip, [1780])

Alessandro nell'Indie, in *Opere del signor abate Pietro Metastasio* (Paris: widow of Hérissant, 1780), vol. 4, pp. 263–356.

1780   mus. by Alessandri, Felice
1780 Genoa   Teatro da S. Agostino (spr.)

Librettos   Genoa: Gesiniana, [1780]
I-Rsc Carv.489; I-Vnm DRAMM.3259 [5][295]

Music sources   [printed sources] *Se mai più sarò geloso*, in *Se mai più sarò geloso. Cavatina seria [...] in Napoli [...] il carnovale dell'anno 1774* (Venice: Alessandri & Scataglia, [1775?])
[doubtful] [complete scores] F-Pn Mus. O-156[BnF,RISM,296]; US-Wc M1500.A73 A5[RISM,297]
[doubtful] [excerpts] *Se mai turbo il tuo riposo* [duet] (P-La 47-V-60[BA,298])

---

292. Microfilm copy: F-Pn VM BOB-9337.
293. Microfilm copies: D-Gs MA 93-14:6707 [1]; GB-En Mf.134, reel 6707 [1].
294. Burden, 'Metastasio on the London stage', p. 40.
295. Microfilm copy: CDN-Lu ML48.M47A46 1791a.
296. Despite the inscription attributing the music to F. Alessandri, stylistic considerations and collation with other sources indicate that it was composed around 1740. In fact, most of the music belongs to Galuppi's 2nd version. Only one *Se possono tanto* is by Perez, the other is from Galuppi's 1st version, and the duet *Se mai turbo il tuo riposo* is an isolated addition by J. Ch. Bach (1735–1782). The only aria whose composer we do not know is *Non sarei sì sventurata* (A2-S4) [Galuppi 1738?].
297. The source is a copy of F-Pn AB O-156.
298. The manuscript, which is preserved in very bad condition, seems to be wrongly attributed to Alessandri. It contains six duets. One is a *Se mai turbo il tuo riposo*, the compositional style of which aligns with the trends of the 1730s–1740s, and another, *Prendi se mi ami, o caro*, plausibly from Sarro's *Alessandro* (Naples, 1743 → see 1743, mus. by Sarro, Domenico Natale). Furthermore, although the source has the inscription "Alessandro nell'Indie 1° Acto", it contains *Ritorna a questo seno* by Schiassi, which was not included in the composer's *Alessandro*, and *Dimmi una volta addio*, from Vinci's *L'Ernelinda* (Naples, 1726). The origins of the two other duets (*O dio vendetta* and *Consolati non piangere*) are unknown.

MC | *Alessandro nell'Indie* (1730–1831)

1781	mus. by Cimarosa, Domenico
1781 Rome	Teatro di Torre Argentina (carn., 11/02/1781)

Librettos Rome: Puccinelli [brothers], [1781]
B-Bc 19039;[299] F-Pn YD-5431 [2]; I-Rsc Libr. n. XIX [6]; I-Vgc ROL. VINCI AL-AR; US-AUS KL-17 193

Music sources [complete scores] I-Nc* 13.3.11/12[MGG,NG,RISM,SBN]; I-Rmassimo n/s[MGG,NG,RISM]

[excerpts] *Mio ben ricordati* (B-Bc 14137[RISM]; D-Hs M A/831 [1/22][RISM;R]); *Vedrai con tuo periglio* (I-Rmassimo [RISM,300]; PL-ŁA RM 241 [3][RISM])

[doubtful][301] *Dolci moti del cor mio* (D-Mbs Mus.ms. 3478[RISM]); *Per chi perdo, o giusti dei* (A-Wn Mus.Hs.2412[RISM,302])

[doubtful contrafacta] *Se amore a questo petto*[303] ([*Summe Deus bonitatis, fons omnis pietatis*] I-BZf n/s[RISM])

1783	mus. by Méreaux, Nicolas-Jean Le Froid de
1783 Paris	Théâtre de l'Académie Royale de Musique (26/08/1783)
	Alexandre aux Indes (Fr. only)

1784	mus. by Cherubini, Luigi	
1784 Mantua	Teatro Regio Ducale (10/05/1784)	(1)
1786 Cremona	Teatro dell'Associazione (carn.)	(2)
1788 Livorno	Teatro degli Armeni (aut.)	(3)

Librettos (1) Mantua: heirs of Pazzoni, [1784]
I-BRq 5°.P.fl.8m3; I-Mr Libr. 02269; I-MAc 128.F.6/14; I-PAc F. Libretti, sc.013 [214]

(2) Cremona: Manini, [1786]
I-Fc E.V.2511;[304] I-Rrai LIB.MUS 099; I-Rb LIB.MUS 099; I-SORmde LA.007

(3) Livorno: Lami & co., [1788]
D-WRz Tb 63; I-Fm Mel.2101 [2]

---

299. Microfilm copy: CDN-Lu ML48.M7C52 1781a.
300. Inserted into *Le stravaganze del conte*, opera buffa in three acts (Naples, 1772).
301. These duets are not included in I-Nc* 13.3.11/12.
302. Not found in [IC].
303. Not included in I-Nc* 13.3.11/12.
304. Microfilm copy: CDN-Lu ML48.M47V545.

MC | *Alessandro nell'Indie* (1730–1831)

Music sources	[complete scores] PL-Kj[MGG,NG,305]
	[excerpts] *Quanto è fiero il mio tormento* (A-Wgm VI 4040 [Q 4753][IC]; CZ-Pk 3 C 265[RISM]; D-Dl Mus.1-F-82,7 [5][RISM]; F-Pn D-2034 [5][BnF,MGG,RISM,306]; F-Pn D-17319[BnF,MGG,RISM]; GB-Cfm [GB-Cu] MU.MS.218[IC]; GB-Lbl Add. 32038[RISM]; I-Mc Mus. Tr.ms. 42[MGG,RISM,SBN]; I-Mc Mus. Tr.ms. 167[NG,RISM,SBN,307]; I-MAC MSM0040718[IC]; I-OS Mss. Mus.B 1545[RISM,SBN]; I-PAc Borb. 53 [I–XV][MGG,NG,RISM,SBN;P]; I-Tf 2 IV 17 [16][RISM]; I-PEsp M.CXXXI [27][RISM]; I-VEcon MS 045[RISM,SBN]; I-VEcon MS 046[RISM,SBN]); *Se d'amor fra le ritorte* (I-Fc F.P.T.979[RISM;P]); *Se il ciel mi divide* (I-PAc Borb. 54 [I–XV][MGG,NG,RISM,SBN;P]); *Se mai più sarò geloso* (GB-Lbl Add. 49286[BL]; I-Mc Noseda E.24 [45][MGG,SBN]; I-PAc Borb. 543 [I–VIII][MGG,NG,RISM,SBN;P]; I-PAc Sanv.A.78 [2][MGG,RISM,SBN;P])
	[arrangements] *Se viver non poss'io* [canon] (F-Pn* MS-361 [4][BnF,MGG,RISM,308]; F-Pn* VM7-662 [9][BnF,MGG,RISM]; I-MC 1-D-II/3 [5][RISM]; US-CA MS Mus 144 [17][RISM]; US-Wc M1548.C5 [21][RISM]); *Vedrai con tuo periglio* (A-Wgm VI 624 [Q 3715][IC]; B-Bc 3784[NG,RISM]; F-Pn D-14376[BnF,MGG,RISM,309]; I-OS Mss.Mus.B 1546[RISM,SBN])

1785	mus. by Chiavacci, Vincenzo[310]
1785 Genoa	Teatro da S. Agostino (carn., 27/12/1784)
Music sources	[excerpts] *Ombra cara del mio bene* (D-Rtt Chiavacci 5[RISM]); *Voi amanti che vedete* (D-B Mus.ms. 3570[RISM]; D-Rtt Chiavacci 1[RISM])
	[printed sources] *Ombra cara del mio bene*, in *Ombra cara del mio bene. Rondò ricavato dall'opera L'Alessandro nell'Indie* (Vienna: Eder, [c. 1789?])

1785	mus. by Bianchi, Francesco	
1785 Venice	Teatro Grimani di S. Benedetto (carn., 28/01/1785)	(1)
1785 Trieste	Teatro Regio (spr.)	(2)
1787 Verona	Teatro Filarmonico (carn.)	(3)
1787 Bologna	Teatro Zagnoni (08/10/1787)	(4)
1787 Esterháza	Court theatre	(5)
1789 Bergamo	NA (Fair, 26/08/1789)	(6)
1792 Venice	Teatro La Fenice (aut., 17/11/1792)	(7)

305. Microfilm copy: CDN-Lu M1500.M57C444.
306. Microfilm copy: F-Pn VM BOB-12406.
307. In G major instead of F major.
308. Canon a 4.
309. Microfilm copy: F-Pn VM BOB-22003.
310. Frassoni, Edilio, *Due secoli di lirica a Genova* (Genoa: Cassa di Risparmio di Genova e Imperia, 1980).

1792 Warsaw	Teatro Nazionale	(8)
1795 Udine	Teatro Nuovo (Fair, 10/08/1795)	(9)
	opening of the theatre	

Librettos

(1) Venice: Fenzo, 1785
A-Wmi BT-553; B-Br Fétis 4.488 A XIV/4 Mus.; F-Pn 8-YTH-51639; I-Bc Lo.00539;[311] I-Fc E.V.2456; I-Mb Racc.dramm.4700; I-Mr Libr. 02266; I-Mr Libr. 02267; I-Pmc^S; I-Psaggiori^S; I-PAc F. Libretti, sc.013 [213]; I-Vcg LIBRETTI S.BENEDETTO 195; I-Vnm DRAMM.1115 [6]; I-Vnm DRAMM.1306 [3]; US-NYp *MGTY-Res.

(2) Trieste: Stamperia Governiale, [1785]
I-Rn 40.10.F.13.3; I-TSci L.O. 0281

(3) Verona: Ramanzini, 1787
D-LEm PT 630

(4) Bologna: Sassi, [1787]
I-Bc Lo.00540; I-Fc E.V.2515; I-Nc Rari 10.6.17 [10]; I-Nragni L015; I-Vnm MISC.4010 [5]; US-Wc ML50.2.A17B25

(5) Vienna: Kroyss, [1787]
D-WRz Tb 61

(6) Bergamo: [s.n., 1789]
I-BGc Sala 32 D 1.02.21; I-BGi PREIS.268.4058; US-BEm ML48 .I7 [616]

(7) Venice: Fenzo, 1792
I-Bc Lo.00541; I-Fm Mel.2189 [6]; I-Mb Racc.dramm.4427; I-Pmc^S; I-Vcg LIBRETTI MELODRAMMI 5 G 021 [40]; I-Vgc ROL.0809 [2]; I-Vnm DRAMM.1124 [16]; I-Vnm DRAMM.1348 [12]; I-Vt 004; PL-KI^S; US-Wc ML48 [S974]

(8) Warsaw: Bacciagaluppi, 1792
PL-KO B. P. 561 I-2-25; PL-Wu GSD 142421; PL-WRzno XVIII-9632

(9) Venice: Fenzo, 1795
B-Br Fétis 4.488 A X/8 Mus.;[312] I-UDc Misc. Joppi 181 [10]; I-Vcg LIBRETTI UDINE 57 F 75; I-Vnm MISC.3614 [5]

---

311. Microfilm copy: CDN-Lu ML48.M47L442 1783a.
312. Microfilm copy: CDN-Lu ML48.M47L442 1783a.

MC | *Alessandro nell'Indie (1730–1831)*

Music sources	[complete scores][313] F-Pn D-1069/1070[BnF,RISM,314]; H-Bn Ms. Mus. OE-44[IC,MGG,NG]; I-Bc DD.165 [1–3][MGG,NG,SBN,315]
	[excerpts] *Non so frenare il pianto* (D-Dl Mus.3915-F-1 [4][RISM]; HR-Dsmb 16/570[RISM]; I-BGi PREIS.12.107[SBN]; I-Raf 1.A.4 [9][RISM]; US-SFsc *M2.5 v.60[RISM]); *Or che il cielo a me ti rende*[316] (A-Wgm VI 8829 [Q 2723][IC]; GB-Lbl Add. 14207 [10][RISM]); *Se mai più sarò geloso* (GB-Lbl R.M.22.a.25 [5][BL,RISM]); *Se mai turbo il tuo riposo* [duet] (CZ-BER HU 436[RISM]; D-Bhm RH 0924 [9][RISM]; US-BEm MS 1260[RISM]); *Sommi dei, se giusti siete* (D-B Mus.ms. 30004 [6][RISM]; I-Pca D.II.1567[SBN]; J-Tk S10-934-6 [5][RISM]; US-SFsc *M2.5 v.63[RISM]); *Vedrai con tuo periglio* (I-Mc Noseda C.35 [12][SBN])
	[doubtful] *Caro padre, a te vicino*[317] (I-Vc Correr Busta 8.6[SBN]); *Nel lasciarla in questo istante*[318] (US-Eu MSS 940[IC]); *Se mai turbo il tuo riposo* [duet] (D-B Mus.ms. 1752[RISM,319])
	[inserts] [Esterháza, 1787] Haydn, Joseph, *Chi vive amante sai che delira* (A-Wgm VI 41074 [Q 5974][IC])
1786	mus. by various unknown composers [and J. A. Hasse][320]
1786 Florence	Teatro degli Intrepidi (21/05/1786)
Librettos	Florence: Bonducciana, 1786
	US-AUS KL-17 241
1786	mus. by Andreozzi, Gaetano and others?
1786 Siena	Teatro degli Intronati (summ.)
Librettos	Florence: Bonducciana, 1786
	I-Fm Mel.2377 [15]

313. These manuscripts substitute the chorus *Serva ad Eroe*, which figures in the original libretto for Bianchi's premiere, with Poro's aria *Or che il cielo a me ti rende*. This aria appears in the libretto for the 1789 revival in Bergamo. Perhaps Bianchi changed his mind already in 1785 and the aria was written by him.
314. For Venice 1792. Microfilm copies: CDN-Lu M1500.M57B532 1785a; F-Pn VM BOB-25184.
315. Microfilm copy: I-Bc 2574.
316. Included in the libretto for the production in 1789 in Bergamo, but not in that for the Venetian premiere in 1785.
317. This duet was not included in the libretto for Bianchi's premiere.
318. This aria was not included in the libretto for Bianchi's premiere.
319. The music is different from that in I-Bc DD.165 [1–3].
320. Weaver, Robert Lamar and Norma Wright Weaver, *A Chronology of Music in the Florentine Theatre, 1751–1800: Operas, Prologues, Farces, Intermezzos, Concerts, and Plays with Incidental Music* (Warren, MI: Harmonie Park Press, 1993). The authors claim that on p. 4 of the libretto held at the Austin library a manuscript annotation states 'musica di Adolfo Hasse'. This seems to have been the reason why [S]Index I, p. 400 also gives it as Hasse's.

MC | *Alessandro nell'Indie* (1730–1831)

Music sources	[excerpts] *Se mai turbo il tuo riposo* [duet] by G. Andreozzi (I-Rama A.Ms.3719 [2])[RISM]	
1787	mus. by Caruso, Luigi	
1787 Rome	Teatro delle Dame (carn.)	(1)
	1st version	
1791 Venice	Teatro Grimani di S. Samuele (carn.)	(2)
	2nd version	
1792 Madrid	Teatro de los Caños del Peral	(3)
1796 Corfù	Teatro di S. Giacomo	(4)
1800 Lisbon	Teatro de São Carlos (24/06/1800)	(5)
	add. by F. Federici	
	name day of João, prince regent of Portugal	
1800 Lisbon	Teatro de São Carlos (17/12/1800)	(6)
	birthday of Maria I, queen of Portugal	
1801 Lisbon	Teatro de São Carlos (27/01/1801)	(7)
	birthday of João, prince regent of Portugal	

Librettos

(1) Rome: Puccinelli, 1786
B-Bc 19040;[321] D-WRz Ruppert 2598; I-Rsc Carv.491; I-Rsc Libr. n. XIX [7]; I-Rvat Stamp.Ferr.V.8071 [5]; I-Vgc ROL.0204 [3]

(2) Venice: Fenzo, 1791
A-Wmi BT-350; E-Mn T/6014?; F-Pn LIV IT-778; F-Pn 8-YTH-51138; F-Pn 8-YTH-51895; I-Bc Lo.09136; I-Rsc Carv.492;[322] I-Vcg LIBRETTI S.SAMUELE 182; I-Vlevi Dramm. 865; I-Vnm DRAMM.1347 [3]

(3) Madrid: widow of Ibarra, [1792] (It./Spa.)
E-Mn T/21101

(4) Venice: Casali, 1796
I-Vcg LIBRETTI CORFÙ 252-253[323]

(5) Lisbon: Ferreira, 1800 (It./Port.)
I-Rsc;[324] US-Wc ML48 [S1642]

(6,7) NA

---

321. Microfilm copy: CDN-Lu ML48.M47C372 1787a.
322. Microfilm copy: CDN-Lu M1500.M57P287 1800a.
323. Microfilm copies: CDN-Lu ML48.M47B53 1787a; CDN-Lu ML48.M47C37 1796a.
324. The copy seems to be lost but there is a microfilm copy in CDN-Lu ML48.M57P287.

MC | *Alessandro nell'Indie* (1730–1831)

Music sources

1st version: 1787, Rome

[excerpts] *Fra mille cure in seno* (I-Rsc G.Mss.220 [9]^{RISM}; I-SPEbc Î, 1-1 [5]^{RISM}; S-Skma T-SE-R^{RISM}; S-St n/s$^{RISM;P}$); *Se mai turbo il tuo riposo* (I-MC 1-D-6 [3]^{RISM,325}; I-MC 2-D-19 [10]^{RISM,326}; P-Ln M.M. 1506 [1–2]$^{IC;R,P}$); *Vi lascio al primo affetto* (CH-Gc N 60^{RISM}; D-BNu PGB 2° 1148 n^{RISM,327}; D-KA Don Mus.Hs. 244^{RISM}; I-BRc Mus Rari 97^{SBN}; I-MC 1-D-6 [5]^{RISM}; I-PEsp M.CXXXI [15]^{SBN}; I-Rsc G.Mss.209 [4]^{RISM,328}; I-Rcagli 63^{RISM,329}; S-Skma T-SE-R^{RISM}); *Vorrei… ma dove, oh dio* (I-Rsc G.Mss.201 [7]$^{RISM;R}$)

2nd version: 1791, Venice

[complete scores] B-Bc* 2052^{IC,NG,RISM,330}; I-BRs n/s^{SBN} [Act III]

[excerpts] *Al mio ben che m'innamora* (I-Rc Mss. 5791^{IC}); *Se mai turbo il tuo riposo* (I-Mc Mus. Tr.ms. 221^{RISM,SBN}); *Al mio ben che m'innamora* (D-Bsa [D-B] SA 1514^{RISM}; D-BFb [D-MÜu] C-ar 85^{RISM}; D-Hs M A/898 [8]^{RISM}; I-Mc Mus. Tr.ms. 222^{RISM,SBN}; I-OS Mss.Mus.B 4563^{RISM,SBN}; I-Rc Mss. 5791^{RISM,SBN}); *Come! M'inganno! E intanto* (US-SFsc *M2.5 v.63 [14]$^{RISM;R}$); *Or sian pur del cielo irato* (I-Rama A.Ms.2399^{RISM}; I-Rama A.Ms.2462^{RISM}); *Paventa al mio sdegno* (F-Pn MS-47 [10]^{BnF,RISM}; I-Mc Mus. Tr.ms. 225^{RISM,SBN}; I-Rsc G.Mss.209 [1]^{RISM,331}); *Sommi dei, se giusti siete* (RUS-Mk b 1/1488^{RISM}); *Trionfa, o ciel tiranno* (CH-E 128,24 [Ms.2410]^{RISM}; D-B Mus.ms. 3180 [5]^{RISM}; I-Mc MsCon.10 [3]^{SBN}; I-Vire 230^{RISM,SBN}); *Vengo a voi foreste amiche* (I-MFad Peruzzi MS.1.2 [4]^{SBN}; I-Rama A.Ms.2399^{RISM})

2nd rev. version: 1800, Lisbon

[excerpts] *Che giorno di contento* by F. Federici (CH-AR Mus Ms A 14^{RISM}; E-Mp MUS MSS 540^{IC})

1787	mus. by Sarti, Giuseppe (2nd version) → see 1761

---

325. Used in Rome, 1790?
326. Wrongly attributed to Pietro Guglielmi on source.
327. In B flat major instead of E flat major.
328. In D major instead of E flat major.
329. Wrongly attributed to Tarchi on source.
330. Microfilm copy: CDN-Lu M1500.M57C32 1791a.
331. Used in Rome, 1795?

1788	mus. by Tarchi, Angelo	
1788 Milan	Teatro alla Scala (carn.)[332]	(1)
	1st version	
1789 London	King's Theatre in the Haymarket (02/06/1789)[333]	(2)
	libr. rev. by C. F. Badini	
	La generosità d'Alessandro	
1790 London	King's Theatre in the Haymarket (29/04/1790)[334]	(3)
	La generosità d'Alessandro	
1791 Siena	Teatro degli Intronati	(4)
	La generosità d'Alessandro il Grande	
1791 Livorno	Teatro degli Avvalorati (aut.)	(5)
	rev. version	
1798 Turin	Teatro Regio (carn., 20/01/1798)[335]	(6)
	2nd version	
1802 Florence	Teatro della Pergola (carn., 12/1801)	(7,8)

Librettos

(1) Milan: Bianchi, [1788]
CDN-Ttfl Itp Pam 00010; D-KNth L 161; F-Pn LIV IT-1070; F-Pn LIV IT-3543 [5]; I-Fc E.V.2510; I-Fm Mel.2002 [10]; I-LDEsormani 298/4/9; I-Ma S. I. H. I. 29 [1]; I-Mc MISC.-.211.4; I-Mr Libr. 02273; I-Ms MUS. NN. II. 7; I-Nc Rari 10.6.17 [1]; I-PAc F. Libretti, sc.013 [215]; I-PAVbcb ACB/LIBRI_ANTICHI 877B; I-Rsc Carv.490; I-Rsc Libr. n. XIX [8]; I-Rsc Vol. 29 [3]; I-Vc 0106; I-Vnm DRAMM.3262 [1];[336] US-CAh *IC7.A100.B750 [91]

(2) London: Wayland, 1789 (It./En.)
GB-Lbl 1608/3714;[337] US-NH ML48 L698 [18]

(3) London: Hammond & Cane, [1790] (It./En.)[338]
GB-Lbl 907.k.2 [3][339]

(4) Siena: Carli, [1791]
I-Fc E.VI.3669; I-Fn B.17.4.824.25

---

332. Given as by various composers in Cambiasi, Pompeo, *Rappresentazioni date nei Reali Teatri di Milano 1778–1872* (Bologna: Forni, 1969 [1872]).
333. The production ran for eight consecutive performances; see Petty, 'Italian Opera in London', p. 305 and Price, Milhous, and Hume, *Italian opera in Late*, p. 408.
334. The production ran for twelve consecutive performances; see Petty, 'Italian Opera in London', p. 305 and Price, Milhous, and Hume, *Italian opera in Late*, p. 423.
335. The production ran for twenty-eight consecutive performances; see Bouquet, Gualerzi, and Testa, *Storia del Teatro Regio di Torino*, pp. 77, 124 and Price, Milhous, and Hume, *Italian opera in Late*, p. 408.
336. Microfilm copy: CDN-Lu ML48.M47A46 1791a.
337. Microfilm copies: D-Gs MA 93-14:6709 [4]; GB-En Mf.134, reel 6709 [4].
338. Microfilm copies of unspecified copy(s): US-CLp PN1621 .T57X; US-HG ML50.T37G4 1790.
339. Microfilm copies: D-Gs MA 89-24:3837 [4]; GB-En Mf.134, reel 3838 [4].

(5) [Livorno]: Masi & co., [1791]
I-Fc E.V.2493; I-Fm Mel.2040 [3]; I-Rsc Carv.494; US-CAh *IC7.A100.B750 [90]; US-Wc ML48 [S10228]

(6) Turin: Derossi, [1798][340]
CDN-Ttfl Itp Pam 00929; D-Mbs L.eleg.m. 4066; I-NOVc CIV 194.G.23; I-Rsc Carv.495; I-Rsc Vol. 129 [22]; I-Tac Simeom L 135; I-Tci L.O.0493; I-Tn F XIII.500 [2]; I-Tn MSC 174 [3]; I-Tp P.i.107 [9.1]; I-Tt Testa 1101; I-VCc 20 C 567; I-Vgc ROL.0627 [18];[341] RUS-Mrg 50-8419141; US-BEm ML48 .I7 [758]; US-CAt TS 8026.653 1798

(7) Florence: Albizziniana, 1801
I-Bc Lo.05296; I-Vgc ROL.1197 [5]

(8) Florence: Albizziniana, 1802
I-Fc E.V.0269; I-Fc E.V.0270; I-Fc E.V.1504; I-Fm Mel.2075 [13]; I-Fn B.17.6.272.4.14; I-Nragni L118; I-Rsc Carv.496; US-Wc ML48 [S10229]

Music sources
1st version: 1788, Milan

[complete scores] CH-N XB obl. 141[RISM]

[excerpts] *Or che il cielo a me ti rende* (GB-Cfm [GB-Cu] MS.Add.10127 [1][IC]; GB-Lbl Add. 31812[RISM]; I-Mc Noseda L.27 [7][SBN]); *Quel labbro vezzoso* (GB-Cfm [GB-Cu] MS.Add.10127 [3][IC]; I-Mc Mus. Tr.ms. 1260[RISM,SBN]); *Se mai più sarò geloso* (GB-Cfm [GB-Cu] MS.Add.10127 [3][IC]); *Se mai turbo il tuo riposo* [duet] (GB-Lbl Add. 31650 [2][BL,RISM]); *Son prigionier, lo vedo* (B-Bc 4899[RISM]; GB-Lbl Add. 31650 [7][RISM])

[printed sources] *Or che il cielo a me ti rende*, in *Or che il cielo a me ti rende. Rondò Sung by Sigr Marchesi* (London: Longman & Broderip, [1789]); *Quel labbro vezzoso*, in *Quel labbro vezzoso Sung by Sigr Marchesi* (London: Longman & Broderip, [1789]); *Se mai più sarò geloso*, in *Se mai più sarò geloso Sung by Sigr Marchesi* (London: Longman & Broderip, [1789]); *Se mai turbo il tuo riposo* [duet], in *Lodi agli dei. Duett [...] in the Opera Generosità d'Alessandro* (London: Longman & Broderip, [1789]); *Se possono tanto*, in *Se possono tanto Sung by Sigr Marchesi* (London: Longman & Broderip, [1789]); *Son prigionier, lo vedo*, in *Terzetto in the Opera La generosità d'Alessandro* (London: Longman & Broderip, [1789])

---

340. According to ^{S}849, there was a copy of this libretto in I-FPfanan; see note 26 above.
341. Microfilm copy: CDN-Lu ML48.M47T38 1787a.

rev. version: 1791, Livorno[342]

[complete scores] F-Pn D-8960[BnF,MGG,NG]; I-Fc E.V.80/81[MGG,NG,343]

[excerpts] *Chi vive amante sai che delira* (I-Fc D.I.64[IC,344]); *Come? M'inganno*[345] (D-Dl Mus.2-F-537[RISM;R]; I-PAc Sanv.A.127[RISM,SBN]); *Finché rimango in vita* (I-Fc D.I.65[IC,346]); *Io partirò, se vuoi* (I-Fc D.I.65[IC]); *Se mai turbo il tuo riposo* [duet] (I-Mc Noseda L.27 [6][SBN]; I-PAc Sanv.A.118[RISM,SBN]; I-Rsc G.Mss.205[RISM]; S-Skma T-SE-R[RISM,347]); *Son prigionier, lo vedo*[348] (A-Sm* Autogr Var 14[RISM]; B-Bc 4899[RISM]; D-KA Don Mus.Hs. 1906[RISM]; I-Fc D.I.65[IC,349]; I-Mc Mus Tr.ms. 1271[RISM,SBN]; I-Mc Noseda L.27 [4][SBN]; I-Mc Noseda L.27 [5][SBN]); *Tu sei lieta* (I-Fc D.I.6[IC,350]); *Vedrai con tuo periglio* (D-Dl Mus.4061-F-503[RISM])

2rd version: 1798, Turin

[excerpts] *Digli che io son fedele* (CH-Gc M 133[RISM]); *La bella face* (CH-Gc M 134[RISM]); *Nel lasciarti, o bene amato* (A-Wn Mus.Hs.19756[IC]); *Se mai turbo il tuo riposo* [duet] (CH-Gc O 66[RISM]; I-MC 6-A-15 [4][RISM]; I-Tf I II 4 [2][RISM])

[not specified]   [excerpts] D-Dl Mus.4061-F-2[RISM,351]

[undated]   [excerpts] *Vi lascio al primo affetto* (I-Rcagli 63[RISM])

1789	mus. by Guglielmi, Pietro Alessandro
1789 Naples	Teatro di S. Carlo (04/11/1789)
	name day of Maria Luisa of Parma, queen of Naples

Librettos   Naples: Flauto, 1789
D-WRz Tb 62; I-Bc Lo.02377; I-Fc E.V.2495; I-Vgc ROL.0369 [10]; US-AUS KL-17 287; US-BEm ML48.I7 [613]; US-Wc ML48 [S4234][352]

Music sources   [complete scores] B-Bc 2117[MGG,NG,RISM,353] [Act I]; F-Pn D-5085/5086[BnF,MGG,NG,RISM]; I-Nc 27.4.26[IC,MGG,NG,RISM]

---

342. No source for the 1788 premiere has been preserved. Therefore, we consider the 1791 revival in Livorno as a version. We cannot ascertain that the closed numbers included in the 1791 version were not used in 1788.
343. [MGG,NG,RISM] date it 1788, but, based on collation with the librettos, it corresponds to the 1791 revival.
344. Inserted into a pasticcio → see *c.* 1800, music by various unknown composers.
345. Included in the libretto for the 1791 revival in Livorno but not in that for the premiere in 1788.
346. This and the following source: inserted into a pasticcio → see *c.* 1800, music by various unknown composers.
347. Performed in Siena (?) in 1791.
348. Same music as in the London version of 1789. Not included in the 1788 premiere.
349. Inserted into a pasticcio → see *c.* 1800, music by various unknown composers.
350. Inserted into a pasticcio; in C major instead of F major → see *c.* 1800, music by various unknown composers.
351. Not found in institutional catalogue.
352. Microfilm copy: US-PRu MICROFILM 1515.
353. Microfilm copy: US-LAum Microfilm M1500.G939 A43 1768.

MC | *Alessandro nell'Indie* (1730–1831)

[excerpts] *Se mai turbo il tuo riposo* (A-Wgm VI 17055 [Q 2989])[IC]; US-SFsc *M2.1 M158[MGG,NG,RISM]; US-Wc M1505.A1 (vol. 88) [3][MGG,NG,RISM]; *Se mai turbo il tuo riposo* [terzet] (A-Wn Mus.Hs.10404 [8])[IC]; US-Wc M1505.G92 A45 [5][MGG,NG,RISM]); *Vedrai con tuo periglio* (US-Wc M1505.G92 A45 [2][MGG,NG,RISM])

[doubtful] *Quale ardir! oh dio che ascolto*[354] (D-B Mus.ms. 30014 [3][RISM]); *Se mai più sarò geloso*[355] (F-Pn D-5194 [10][BnF,RISM]; F-Pn D-5201 [1][BnF])

[doubtful arrangements] *Senza procelle ancora*[356] (D-MÜs SANT HS 1857[RISM]; I-Bc DD.13[RISM,SBN])

c. 1790	mus. by Zingarelli, Niccolò Antonio[NA]
c. 1790 [s.l.]	lost?
1791	mus. by Caruso, Luigi (2nd version) → see 1787
1791	mus. by Tarchi, Angelo (rev. version?) → see 1788
1798	mus. by Tarchi, Angelo (2nd version) → see 1788
1800	mus. by Gnecco, Pietro
1800 Livorno	Teatro degli Avvalorati (aut.)
Librettos	Livorno: Società Tipografica, [1800]
	I-Fm Mel.2044 [1]; I-LI RM b.258 [1]; I-LI VM 144686; I-PSrospigliosi [I-PS] BM.258 [15]
c. 1800	mus. by various unknown composers

c. 1800 Livorno or Florence[357]

---

354. This terzet is not included in the libretto or the complete score for the 1789 premiere of Guglielmi's setting.
355. Inserted into the dramma giocoso *La sposa fedele* (Venice, 1767), but not in the libretto for Guglielmi's *Alessandro nell'Indie*.
356. Fugue a 5. Text not included in the libretto for Guglielmi's setting of *Alessandro nell'Indie*.
357. It is possible to presume the performance of a pasticcio around 1800 near Livorno or Florence, testified by the score held I-Fc under the signature D.I.65. The manuscript contains one duet by Gnecco (originally from his 1800 version), and a number of arias from Tarchi's 1791 version (one is transposed to a different key). The structure of the first act is the same as the one from a revival of Tarchi's setting performed in Florence in 1802, although that of the second changes. Therefore, it is possible to assume that the pasticcio was performed soon after 1802 in either Florence or Livorno. It is possible to conjecture about the two places because of the relation to the 1802 revival (Florence) and because both Tarchi's 1791 and Gnecco's 1800 versions were premiered in Livorno.

MC | *Alessandro nell'Indie* (1730–1831)

Music sources	[doubtful] *La tromba guerriera* (I-Fc D.I.64[IC]); *Se mai turbo il tuo riposo* (I-Fc D.I.64[IC]); *Se mai turbo il tuo riposo* [duet] (I-Fc D.I.64[IC]); *Tu non mi guardi* (I-Fc D.I.64[IC])

1804	mus. by Neukomm, Sigismund	
1804 St Petersburg	Deutsches Theater (15/09/1804)[358] *Alexander am Indus* (Ger. only)	

1811	mus. by Ritter, Alexander[NG]	
1811 Mannheim	Court theatre (26/12/1811) *Alexander in Indien* (Ger. only)	

1824	mus. by Pacini, Giovanni lib. rev. by Schmidt, Giovanni	
1824 Naples	Teatro di S. Carlo (30/09/1824)	(1)
1827 Milan	Teatro alla Scala (carn., 26/12/1826)	(2)
1827 Lisbon	Teatro de São Carlos (11/06/1827)	(3)
1827 Palermo	Teatro Carolino (19/08/1827) *birthday of Francesco I, king of the Two Sicilies*	(4)
1828 Venice	Teatro La Fenice (carn., 19/01/1828)	(5)
1831 Barcelona	Teatre de la Santa Creu	(6)

Librettos	(1) Naples: Flautina, 1824 B-Bc 19041;[359] I-Bam Ambr.Opere.012 [7]; I-Bam Ambr.Opere.022 [7]; I-Bc Lo.03650; I-Fm Mel.2113 [14]; I-BGi PREIS.237.3281; I-Mc Lib.A.032;[360] I-Nn L.P. Libretti A 0356 [4]; I-Nc De Simone Libretti 059; I-Nc Rari 10.6.17 [8]; I-Ra E.IV.31 [10]; I-Rsc Vol. Carv.25 [3]; I-Rsc Vol. Carv.131 [79]; I-Rsc Carv.497; I-Vgc ROL.0499 [3]; US-AUS KL-18 559; US-CHH IOLC.00551; US-NYp Mus. Res. *MZ, E/1824/25 [7]; US-Wc ML48 [S7384]
	(2) Milan: Fontana, 1826[361] A-Wn 106851-A; CDN-Ttfl Lib 02085; D-Mbs L.eleg.m. 4469; F-Pn LIV IT-146; F-Pn LIV IT-1069 [1]; F-Pn LIV IT-3583 [1]; I-Baf FA2. LIB.237; I-Bc Lo.03651; I-Bc Villa.Lo.084; I-Bca CERVI Opuscoli Cart.86 [17]; I-Bl FS.W.1710; I-Bl FS.W.1713; I-Bl FS.W.1781; I-Fc

---

358. For this and the following setting in German, see Griffel, Margaret Ross, *Operas in Germany: A Dictionary* (Lanham: Rowman & Littlefield, 2018).
359. Microfilm copy: CDN-Lu ML48.M47P283 1824a.
360. Microfilm copy: CDN-Lu M1500.M57S227.
361. Microfilm copy of unidentified copy: CDN-Lu ML48.M47P283 1827a.

MC | *Alessandro nell'Indie* (1730–1831)

E.V.2513; I-Fm Mel.2147 [4]; I-Fm Mel.2191 [3]; I-FEc P 42.31.10; I-FZc RM.N.III.088; I-LDEsormani 311/2/43; I-Mb Racc.dramm.6127 [13]; I-Mb Racc.dramm.6145 [39]; I-Mb Racc.dramm.6145 [40]; I-Mcom MUS.M MUS.1.-234; I-Mr Libr. 02270; I-Mr Libr. 02271; I-Nc Rari 10.6.17 [7]; I-PAc F. Libretti, sc.013 [210]; I-PAc F. Libretti, sc.013 [211]; I-Rn 35. 10.G.12.07; I-Rsc Carv.498; I-Rsc Libr. n. XXIII [42]; I-Rsc Vol. 70 [1]; I-Tci L.O.0951; I-Vc 0108; I-Vgc ROL.1057 [9]; I-Vnm DRAMM.0863 [23]; I-Vnm DRAMM.3312 [19]; I-VAc V.A.R.VI-II.4.10; I-Vqs Opus C. 1177; US-AUS KL-18 645; US-CAt TS 8026.500 1826 [B]; US-CHH IOLC.00583; US-COu PQ4717.A37 1826; US-U Cavagna 19998; US-Wc ML48 [S11897]

(3) Lisbon: Bulhões, 1827 (It./Port.)
I-Rsc Carv.499; P-Cug 5-(4)-1-19-20; P-Ln M. 1099 P.; P-Ln T.S.C. 242 P.; P-Ln T.S.C. 243 P.; P-Ln T.S.C. 244 P.

(4) Palermo: Società Tipografica, 1827
I-Vgc ROL.1057 [10]; I-Vnm DRAMM.3315 [20]; US-BEm ML48 .S5 [S460]

(5) Venice: Casali, 1828
D-Mbs L.eleg.m. 4513; F-Pn 8-YTH-51340; I-Bc Lo.03652; I-Fm Mel.2199 [15]; I-Fm Mel.2291 [2]; I-Mb Racc.dramm.5110;[362] I-Mr Libr. 02272; I-Nc Rari 11.1.3 [3]; I-PAc F. Libretti, sc.013 [212]; I-Rsc Carv.500; I-TSci PRG 108360; I-TSmt LIBRETTI 31 [T 22852]; I-Vcg LIBRETTI LA FENICE 217; I-Vgc ROL.1057 [11]; I-Vnm DRAMM.1384 [2]; I-Vt 258; I-Vqs Opus C. 20; US-AUS KL-18 695[363]

(6) Barcelona: Brusi, 1831
E-Bbc C400/111; E-Bbc C400/405; E-Bu F-8/439/30; E-Mn T/24620

Music sources [complete scores] F-Pn D-12040 [1–2][BnF,364]; GB-Lbl Add. 16067/16068[RISM,365]; I-Nc* 14.1.13/14[MGG,NG,SBN,366]; I-PAc Borb.2972 [I–II][RISM,SBN]

[excerpts] *Bell'ombra adorata* (I-Li FB E12 [3][RISM,SBN]; I-Nc 65.2.76[SBN]); *Che fai! fellon! t'arresta* (I-BRc PORRO.74.b[SBN]); *Mio ben mio tesoro* (P-Ln M.M. 187 [4][IC]); *Nel duol in cui mi vedo* (I-Li FB E12 [1][RISM,SBN]); *Più tollerar non posso* (I-BRc PORRO.53.c[SBN]; I-Li FB E12 [2][RISM,SBN]; I-Mc

---

362. Microfilm copy: CDN-Lu ML48.M47P283 1828a.
363. Microfilm copy of one —unlocated— copy in US-Wc: US-PRu MICROFILM 391.
364. Microfilm copy: F-Pn VM BOB-30515/30516.
365. Microfilm copy: US-PRu MICROFILM 1516.
366. Microfilm copy: CDN-Lu M1500.M57P283 1828a.

Noseda N.29 [9]$^{SBN;R}$); *Risolver non oso* (I-Nc O.8.19 [8]^{SBN}); *Se cangiar potessi in seno* (I-Mc Noseda N.29 [10]^{SBN}); *Se d'amor fra le ritorte* (A-Wgm VI 9987/2 [Q 7832]^{IC}; F-Pn D-8302 [A]^{BnF}; F-Pn D-16750^{BnF}; I-BRc VARI.119$^{SBN;R}$; I-Fc F.P.T.845$^{RISM,SBN;P}$; I-Fc F.P.T.979$^{RISM,SBN;P}$; I-Li FB E12 [4]^{RISM,SBN}; I-Mc Noseda N.29 [11]$^{SBN;R}$; I-MC 6-F-7 [8]$^{RISM;R}$; I-Nc 35.7.147 [2]^{SBN}; P-Ln M.M. 187 [6]^{IC}); *Se fossi a te vicino* (I-Nc 34.3.83^{SBN}); *Senza un'ombra di viltà* (I-Fc D.II.114^{SBN}); further excerpts in I-Mr^{NG}; I-PEA^{MGG,NG}

[printed sources] *Che fai! fellon! t'arresta*, in *Terzetto: Che fai! fellon! t'arresta, Nell'Alessandro nell'Indie del sig.r M.o G. Pacini* (Milan: Ricordi, [1827]); in *Che fai fellon! T'arresta, terzetto nell'opera Alessandro nell'Indie* (Paris: Carli, [c. 1825]); *Se amore soltanto*, in *Se amore soltanto, nell'Alessandro nell'Indie del maestro Pacini eseguita dalla sig.a Lorenzani* (Milan: Ricordi, [1827])^R; *Se d'amor fra le ritorte*, in *Se d'amor fra le ritorte, nell'opera Alessandro nell'Indie del sig.r M.o Pacini ridotta con accompagnamento di piano-forte da Luigi Truzzi* (Milan: Ricordi, [1825])^R; in *Cavatina di Soprano nell'Alessandro nell'Indie, del maestro Pacini* (Paris: Pacini, [c. 1825])^R; various arias, in *2 Airs à 1 et 2 v. tirés de Alessandro nell'Indie*, as part of *Journal d'Euterpe*, 13 (Paris, 1825)

Sources of doubtful identification

Manuscript copy, dated 28/03/1783: (P-Ln COD. 1385//1^{367}). It is not a copy of the librettos performed in Lisbon in 1736, 1740, 1755, or 1766.

Arie sciolte

Adolfati, Andrea, *Destrier che all'armi usato* (US-CHH* VFM3.1.A36 1750z [34]^{RISM}); *Se amore a questo petto* (US-CHH* VFM3.1.A36 1750z [30]^{RISM})

Agnesi, Maria Teresa, *Son confusa pastorella* (D-Dl Mus.3275-J-1 [1]^{RISM}; RUS-Mrg Ф.954 N°131–132 [1]$^{RISM;IP}$)

Aprile, Giuseppe, *Vedrai con tuo periglio* (F-Pn D-11995 [3]^{BnF,RISM,368})

Aurisicchio, Antonio, *Digli che io son fedele* (I-FZc B.V.39 [11]^{RISM,SBN}); *Se il ciel mi divide* (I-FZc B.V.39 [6]^{RISM,SBN}); *Se troppo crede al ciglio* (I-FZc B.V.39 [5]^{RISM})

Babbi, Gregorio, *Vil trofeo [d'un'alma imbelle]* (I-FZc A.VI.6 [1]^{RISM,SBN,369}; I-FZc A.VI.6 [2]^{RISM,SBN,370})

Benda, Georg, *Mio ben ricordati* (DK-Kk mu7408.1332 [6]^{RISM})

---

367. Microfilm copy: P-Ln R.R. 1413.
368. Microfilm copy: F-Pn VM BOB-35132.
369. In C major.
370. In A major.

MC | *Alessandro nell'Indie* (1730–1831)

Bernasconi, Andrea, *Dov'è? Si affretti* (D-ROu Mus. Saec. XVIII:6[16 RISM;P])

Borghi, Giovanni Battista, *Digli che io son fedele* (I-MC 1-C-13/4 [5]^{RISM}); *Senza procelle ancora* (GB-Lbl R.M.23.d.17 [3]^{BL}); *Vedrai con tuo periglio* (GB-Lbl R.M.23.d.17 [2]^{BL}; J-Tk S11-095^{RISM})

Callenberg, Georg Alexander Heinrich Hermann, *Mio ben ricordati* (D-Dl Mus.3496-I-2 [?]^{IC,RISM})

Capuzzi, Antonio, *Mio ben ricordati* (I-Nc 22.3.20 [22]^{SBN})

Celestino, Eligio [?], *D'un barbaro scortese*[371] (US-FAy Quarto 532 MS 9 [1]^{RISM})

Contiero, Giovanni Battista, *Chi vive amante sai che delira* (I-Pca D.II.1526 [2]^{SBN;R})

Duni, Antonio, *Se viver non poss'io* (D-B Mus.ms. 5311 [11]^{RISM;P})

Ferrandini, Giovanni Battista, *Digli che io son fedele* (D-Dl Mus.3037-J-6a [6]^{RISM;IP}); *Se mai turbo il tuo riposo* (<u>D-Dl Mus.3037-J-6a [19]</u>^{RISM;IP}); *Se troppo crede al ciglio* (D-Dl Mus.3037-J-6a [24]^{RISM;IP}); *Voi che adorate il vanto* (US-Wc M1505.A2 F37^{RISM})

Ferrandini, Giovanni Battista [doubtful], *Agitata da più bande*; *Agitato dal furore*; *Di rendermi la calma*; *Dov'è? Si affretti*; *Finché rimango in vita*; *Io non venni*; *Scoglio alpestre*; *Vedrai con tuo periglio*. Inserted into Vinci's *Alessandro* → see 1735, mus. by Vinci, Leonardo.

Fini, Michele, *Se troppo crede al ciglio* (D-B Mus.ms. 30408 [11]^{RISM,372}; D-Hs ND VI 1078 [1]^{RISM}; US-FAy Quarto 532 MS 6 [3]^{RISM})

Fioravanti, Valentino, *Se è ver che t'accendi* [c. 1790] (D-Hs M A/846 [2/2]^{RISM})

Francisconi, Giovanni, *Se mai turbo il tuo riposo* (S-Skma SO-R^{RISM})

Friedrich II the Great, king of Prussia, *Digli che io son fedele* (<u>D-Dl Mus.3018-J-1</u>^{RISM}; S-Skma T-SE-R^{RISM})

Gazzaniga, Giuseppe, *Se mai turbo il tuo riposo* [duet] (I-MC 2-D-5/3 [6]^{RISM})

Häusler, Ernst [c. 1780], *Digli che io son fedele* (<u>D-KA Don Mus.Hs. 638</u>^{RISM}); *Mio ben ricordati* (D-BFb [D-MÜu] H-ae 75^{RISM;IP}); *Se il ciel mi divide* (<u>D-KA Don Mus.Hs. 641</u>^{RISM})

Hertel, Johann Wilhelm, *Se mai turbo il tuo riposo* (B-Bc* 4197^{RISM})

Hurka, Friedrich Franz, *Vil trofeo d'un'alma imbelle* (D-B Mus.ms. 10995 [4]^{RISM})

Imbimbo, Emanuele, *Mio ben ricordati* (I-Rrostirolla [I-Fn] MS MUS 563 [13]^{SBN})

Lanno [?], *Di rendermi la calma* (A-LA 915^{RISM;P}; A-LA 2015^{RISM})

Lemner, Thomas, *Di rendermi la calma* (S-Skma T-SE-R^{RISM;P})

Logroscino, Nicola Bonifazio, *Se mai turbo il tuo riposo* [duet] (I-MC 3-E-16 [3]^{RISM})

Luciani, Domenico, *Dov'è? Si affretti* [1756] (I-FZc B.V.39 [3]^{RISM,SBN})

Lustrini, Bartolomeo, *Se viver non poss'io* (F-Pn L-18670^{BnF;IP})

Mangold, Wilhelm, *Se viver non poss'io* (<u>D-B* Mus.ms.autogr. Mangold, W. 1 M</u>^{RISM;R})

Maraucci, Stefano, *Destrier che all'armi usato* [c. 1780] (<u>I-Nc 34.3.12 [5]</u>^{SBN})

Martínez, Marianna von, *Se viver non poss'io* (<u>I-Nc 33.3.28 [7]</u>^{RISM,SBN})

Martini, Giovanni Battista, *È prezzo leggiero* [1749] (I-Bc HH.40 [11]^{RISM,SBN})

Mayr, Johann Simon, *Cara sposa, amato bene* (I-MC 3-F-12 [3]^{RISM})

Mazzoni, Antonio Maria, *Vil trofeo d'un'alma imbelle* (I-MAav Cart.5 n.11^{RISM})

Merchi, Giacomo, *Se viver non poss'io* [10], in 12 ariette e 4 duetti per cantare o sonare […] (Amsterdam: Hummel, [c. 1760])

Micheli, Benedetto, *Sommi dei, se giusti siete* (B-Bc 4958 [2]^{RISM}; D-Hs M A/894 [25]^{RISM})

Mosel, Ignaz Franz von, *Se mai turbo il tuo riposo* (<u>D-B* Mus.ms.autogr. Mosel, I. F. v. 1 M</u>^{RISM})

Mysliveček, Josef, *In te spero o sposo amato* ([*Se mai turbo il tuo riposo*] I-MC 4-A-16 [2]^{RISM,373})

---

371. Supposedly inserted into a *Catone in Utica*.
372. In F major instead of G major.
373. This aria is an adaptation of *In te spero, o sposo amato*, from the composer's 1st setting of *Demofoonte* (Venice, 1769), transposed from B flat major to A major. It may not be by Mysliveček.

Palma, Silvestro, *Di rendermi la calma* (US-Wc ML96.H83 [1][RISM;R])
Paradies, Pietro Domenico, *Son confusa pastorella* (GB-Cfm [GB-Cu] MU.MS.108[IC])
Persichini, Pietro, *Mio ben ricordati* (I-Rama A.Ms.1758 [2][SBN])
Pircker, Johan, *Digli che io son fedele* (S-SK K 494 [46][RISM])
Quilici, Gaetano, *Destrier che all'armi usato* (D-MGmi HA IV 232[RISM;IP])
Reggio, Antonino, *Digli che io son fedele* [1748] (D-MÜs* SANT Hs 3382 [7][RISM]); *Mio ben ricordati* (D-MÜs* SANT Hs 3386[RISM]); *Se mai turbo il tuo riposo* [quartet] (D-MÜs* SANT Hs 3382 [10][RISM;R]; I-Rrostirolla [I-Fn] MS MUS 338 [10][RISM,SBN])
Reicha, Antoine, *Quanto è fiero il mio tormento* (F-Pn L-13807[BnF])
Santarelli, Giuseppe, *Se possono tanto* (GB-Lbl Add. 31624 [22][BL])
Sellefco, *Mio ben ricordati* (A-LA 791[RISM;P]; A-LA 1941[RISM])
Silverstolpe, Fredik Samuel, *Digli che io son fedele* (S-Skma* Z/Sv.); *Se mai turbo il tuo riposo* (S-Skma* Z/Sv.[RISM])
Skavronsky, count, *Se mai turbo il tuo riposo* (I-Vc Correr Busta 6.18[SBN])
Valente, Saverio, *È prezzo leggiero* (I-Mc Noseda I.88 [2][SBN;R])
Vernier, Girolamo, *Chi vive amante sai che delira* [c. 1745] (I-Vnm Mss. 9995 [10][SBN])
Viani, Francesco, *Finché rimango in vita* (I-Gl B C.3.25 [1][IC,SBN])
Visconti, Giulio, *Se possono tanto* (A-LA 795[RISM;P])
Wetzstein, *Di rendermi la calma* (D-MGmi MGmi HA IV 170[RISM;P]; D-MGmi HA IV 192[RISM;P])

Closed numbers by unknown composer

Chi vive amante sai che delira (CH-Gpu Ms.mus.418[RISM])
Chi vive amante sai che delira (D-Dl Mus.1-F-49,6 [2][RISM])
Chi vive amante sai che delira (D-Hs M A/832 [7a][RISM])
Chi vive amante sai che delira (S-Skma Alströmer saml. 171 [23][IC])
Chi vive amante saic he delira (US-AUS Finney 39[RISM])
Digli che io son fedele (D-SWl Mus.162[RISM])
Digli che io son fedele (I-Vqs MS Cl.VIII.14 [1128][RISM])
Se è ver che t'accendi (US-BEm MS 28 [15][IC,RISM])
Se amore a questo petto (US-BEm MS 96 [13][IC,RISM;R])
Se possono tanto (A-Wn Mus.Hs.17562 [3][IC]; I-Fc D.I.208 [15][IC,RISM,SBN])
Se possono tanto (US-BEm MS 28 [10][IC,RISM])
Se viver non poss'io (US-Cu MS 1267[RISM])
Sommi dei, se giusti siete (US-BEm MS 96 [14][IC,RISM;R])
Vedrai con tuo periglio (D-B Mus.ms. 30408 [12][RISM])
Vedrai con tuo periglio (D-Dl Mus.2477-L-5[RISM])
Vedrai con tuo periglio (D-GOl Mus. 2° 52b [10][RISM])
Vedrai con tuo periglio (I-CHf [I-CHc] C 10 [12][RISM])
Vedrai con tuo periglio (S-Skma T-SE-R[RISM])
Voi che adorate il vanto (GB-Lbl R.M.23.d.9 [7][BL,RISM])

MC | *Alessandro nell'Indie* (1730–1831)

Unspecified contents

Digli che io son fedele (D-BAd EB 606[RISM;P])
Digli che io son fedele (I-Vc Correr Busta 43.33[SBN])
Digli che io son fedele (I-Vc Correr Busta 125.35[SBN])
Di rendermi la calma (F-Pn VM7-125[BnF])
Mio ben ricordati (F-Pn VM7-152 [17][BnF])
Mio ben ricordati (I-Mc Noseda A.50 [23][SBN])
Mio ben ricordati (S-St n/s [2][RISM])
Se troppo crede al ciglio (I-Fc D.I.209 [10][IC,RISM,SBN])
Se viver non poss'io (I-Vc Correr Busta 128.12 [10][SBN])
Se viver non poss'io [canon] (GB-Lbl Add. 32035 [13][BL,RISM]) [Caldara?]
Sommi dei, se giusti siete (I-Vc Correr Busta 119.11 [2][SBN])
Voi che adorate il vanto (I-Mc Noseda A.26 [26][SBN])
Unspecified aria (F-AIXm F.C. ms. VIII [4][BASE])

Artaserse (1730–1850)

Ana Llorens, Lecturer, Department of Musicology, Universidad Complutense de Madrid; scientific director, ERC Didone Project, email: allorens@ucm.es

Gorka Rubiales Zabarte, 'Margarita Salas' postdoctoral researcher, Universidad Complutense de Madrid–Universidad de Salamanca, email: gorka.rubiales@usal.es

Complete operas

1730	mus. by Vinci, Leonardo	
1730 Rome	Teatro delle Dame (carn., 04/02/1730)[1]	(1)
1730 Vienna	Teatro Privilegiato (28/08/1730)[2]	(2)
1730 Florence	Teatro del Cocomero (aut., 19/10/1730) with music by J. A. Hasse[3]	(3)
1731 Fano	Teatro della Fortuna (carn.)[4]	(4)
1731 Livorno	Teatro da S. Sebastiano (carn.)	(5)
1731 Pesaro	Teatro del Sole (carn.)	(6)
1731 Rome	Teatro delle Dame (spr.)[5]	(7)
1731 Ferrara	Teatro Bonacossi da S. Stefano (aut.) pasticcio[6]	(8)

---

1. The performances ended on 21 February due to Pope Benedict VIII's death; see Cametti, Alberto, 'Leonardo Vinci e i suoi drammi in musical al Teatro delle Dame', *Musica d'oggi*, 6 (1924), 297–99, as referred in Sprague, Cheryl Ruth, 'A Comparison of Five Musical Settings of Metastasio's "Artaserse"' (doctoral dissertation, University of California, 1979).
2. Klein, Rudolf, 'Die Schauplätze der Hofoper', *Österreichische Musikzeitschrift*, 24 (1969), 371–422.
3. Schmidt-Hensel, Roland Dieter, *'La musica è del Signor Hasse detto il Sassone…': Johann Adolf Hasses 'Opere serie' der Jahre 1730 bis 1745. Quellen, Fassungen, Aufführungen* (Göttingen: V&R unipress, 2009).
4. A pasticcio according to [C]. It may relate to the music manuscript I-Rama A.Mss.3702, in which one aria by Hasse (*Conservati fedele*) is inserted; see Antolini, Bianca Maria and Annalisa Bini, 'Johann Adolph Hasse nei manoscritti della Biblioteca di S. Cecilia di Roma', *Analecta Musicologica*, 25 (1983), p. 495–511.
5. Sprague, 'A Comparison of Five Musical Settings', p. 49.
6. See <https://www.pasticcio-project.eu/database/work/P102534> [accessed 25 May 2022].

MC | *Artaserse* (1730–1850)

1731 Naples	NA (aut.)[7]	(9)
1732 Perugia	Teatro del Pavone (carn.)	(10)
1733 Naples	NA (carn.)[8]	(11)
1733 Camerino	Teatro di Camerino (carn., 28/01/1733)	(12)
1734 Perugia	Teatro del Pavone (carn.)	(13)
1738 Naples	Teatro di S. Carlo (20/01/1738) *mus. by L. Vinci and others* *birthday of Carlo VII, king of Naples*	(14)
1738 Rome	Teatro delle Dame (spr.)	(15)
1740 Florence	Teatro del Cocomero (carn., 28/12/1739)	(16)
1740 Macerata	Theatro di Macerata (carn.)	(17)
1743 Palermo	Teatro di Santa Cecilia (carn.)	(18)
1743 Naples	Teatro di S. Carlo (04/11/1743) *part of the music by G. Manna* *name day of Carlo VII, king of Naples*	(19)
1745 Ferrara	Teatro Bonacossi da S. Stefano (carn., 06/02/1745) *part of the music by J. A. Hasse*	(20)
1747 Pistoia	Teatro dei Risvegliati (carn.)	(21)
1750 Pisa	Teatro Pubblico (carn.)	(22)
1754 Parma	Teatro Regio Ducale (carn.)	(23)
? Venice	Teatro Grimani di S. Giovanni Grisostomo[9]	(24)

Librettos (1) Rome: Zempel & de Mei,[10] [1730]
B-Bc 19309; CDN-Ttfl Itp Pam 02029; D-ERu H61/RAR.A 23; F-Pn YD-3537;[11] F-Pn YD-5245 [4]; GB-En RB.s.2667 [2]; GB-Lbl 905.k.6 [4]; I-Bc Lo.05524; I-Fc E.V.1547; I-Fm Mel.226 [12]; I-MAC 7.8.B.185; I-Pmc^S; I-Rn 35.10.A.7.1; I-RVE r-Z93 31 [1]; I-Vgc ROL.0650 [8]; US-AUS KL-17 53; US-CAt TS 8056.713 1730; US-DMu ML50.2.A78 V563 1730 [1]; US-Wc ML48 [S10743]; US-NYcu n/s

(2,9,11,24) NA

(3) Florence: Verdi, 1730
I-FEwalker^C

---

7. Piperino, Franco, 'Opera Production to 1780', in *The History of Italian Opera*, ed. by Lorenzo Bianconi and Giorgio Pestelli (Chicago: The University of Chicago Press, 1988), pp. 1–80.
8. Piperino, 'Opera Production'. See also the entries on Faustina Bordoni (no. 63) and Carlo Scalzi (no. 136) in Rostirolla, Giancarlo, ed., *Il 'Mondo novo' musicale di Pier Leone Ghezzi* (Rome and Milan: Academia Nazionale di Santa Cecilia and Skira Editore, 2001).
9. Performance in Venice in an uncertain date. A copy of the opera from the 1780s states: 'Artaserse | Dramma per Musica | Rappresentato nel Teatro di San | Giov. Grisostomo | Del Sig: Leonardo Vinci'.
10. 'Si vendono nella libraria di Pietro Leone'.
11. Microfilm copy of this and the following source: F-Pn MICROFILM M-2404.

(4) Fano: Fanelli, [1731]
I-FAN 7 Q I 31; I-MAC 7.8.B.125; I-MACgiochi Misc.14bis E.VI.2

(5) Lucca: Marescandoli, [1731]
I-Fm Mel.2072 [3]

(6) Pesaro: Gavelli, 1730
I-PESo G-09-B-18

(7) Rome: [s.n.], 1731
F-Pn LIV IT-19

(8) Bologna: Dalla Volpe, [1731]
I-Bc Lo.05525; I-MOe 70.I.32 [2]; US-AUS KL-17 56

(10) Foligno: Campitelli, 1732
I-PEc ANT I.L 3467 [7]; I-PEc ANT I.N 947 [5]

(12) Camerino: Simene, 1733
I-Fm Mel.2211 [1][12]

(13) Perugia: Costantini, [1734]
I-Vgc ROL.1235 [6]

(14) Naples: Ricciardo, 1738
I-Mb Racc.dramm.0658

(15) Rome: De' Rossi, [1738][13]
US-DMu ML50.2.A78 V563 1730 [1]

(16) Florence: [s.n., 1740]
I-Fm Mel.2180 [4][14]

(17) Macerata: Ferri, [1740]
I-MAC 7.5.B.008; I-Rsc Libr. n. XIV [11]; I-Vgc ROL.1235 [7]; US-CAt TS 8056.713 1740

(18) Palermo: Epiro, 1743
I-PLpagano[C,S]

(19) Naples: Ricciardi, [1743]
B-Bc 19312

(20) Ferrara: Barbieri, [1745]
I-Bc Lo.05526

---

12. Microfilm copy at Cambridge, MA: General Microfilm Company, Italian drama, roll 154 [8].
13. Not indexed in Franchi, Saverio, *Le impressioni sceniche: dizionario bio-bibliografico degli editori e stampatori romani e laziali di testi drammatici e libretti per musica dal 1759 al 1800* (Rome: Edizioni di Storia e Letteratura, 1994).
14. Microfilm copy at Cambridge, MA: General Microfilm Company, Italian drama, roll 154 [11].

MC | *Artaserse* (1730–1850)

(21) Pistoia: Gatti, 1747
I-PSrospigliosi [I-PS] BM.255 [6]

(22) Pisa: [s.n.], 1749
I-PAc F. Libretti, sc.037 [619]

(23) Parma: Monti, [1754]
B-Bc 19315

Music sources

(^{L} = re-used in the London pasticcio of 1734 → see 1734, mus. by Händel, Georg Friedrich and others)

[complete scores] A-Wgm IV 11476 [Q 2100]^{IC}; <u>A-Wn Mus. Hs.19120 [1–3]</u>^{IC,MGG,NG}; A-Wn Mus.Hs.19121^{IC}; <u>A-Wn SA.68.C.24 [1–2]</u>^{IC,MGG}; B-Bc 2368^{MGG,NG,RISM}; D-B Am.B 263^{MGG,NG,RISM,15}; D-B Mus.ms. 22375^{MGG,NG,RISM}; D-B Mus.ms. 22375/1^{MGG,NG,RISM} [Acts II&III]; F-Pn D-14258^{BnF,16}; GB-Ge R.d.7/8/9^{RISM}; GB-Lbl Add. 22106$^{BL,MGG,NG,RISM;A}$; GB-Lbl R.M.3.c.2/3/4^{BL,MGG,NG,RISM}; GB-Lbl R.M.23.c.5/6/7^{BL,MGG,NG,RISM}; GB-Lcm MS 629$^{IC,MGG,NG;A}$; GB-Lfom Accession Number 2541 [2–4]$^{RISM;IP}$; GB-Lgc G MUS 387^{IC,MGG,NG}; GB-SMleatham n/s$^{17;}$ HR-Zha LXVII.A^{RISM}; I-FAN Ms. Federici 154^{IC} [Acts I&III]^{18}; I-MC 6-C-7^{MGG,NG,RISM}; <u>I-Nc 3.1.8</u>^{IC,MGG,NG,RISM,SBN}; I-Rama A.Mss.3702^{IC,19}; <u>I-Vnm Mss. 9815/9816/9817</u>^{MGG,NG,SBN}; <u>RUS-Mrg Ф.954 №197/198/199</u>^{RISM}; US-BEm MS 138^{IC,RISM,20}; US-R M1500. V777A^{RISM,21}; US-Wc M1505.V6 A6^{IC,22}

[excerpts] *Amalo e se al tuo sguardo* (D-Hs M A/678 [2]^{RISM}; GB-Cfm [GB-Cu] MU.MS.633^{IC}; GB-Lfom Accession Number 2541 [5]$^{RISM;IP}$); *Ardito ti renda* (D-Hs M A/678 [10]^{RISM}; F-Pm Res F7.29^{BASE}); *Bramar di perdere*^{L,23} (D-Hs M A/678 [14]^{RISM}; F-Pm Res F7.29^{BASE}; F-Pn VM4-960

---

15. It corresponds to the undated performance in Venice.
16. Microfilm copy: F-Pn VM BOB-16129.
17. Meikle, Robert Burns, 'Leonardo Vinci's *Artaserse*: An Edition, with an Editorial and Critical Commentary' (doctoral dissertation, Cornell University, 1970).
18. For Fano 1731.
19. See note 4 above.
20. Roman copy, contemporary to the premiere. For a description, see Emerson, John A., *Catalog of Pre-1900 Vocal Manuscripts in the Music Library, University of California at Berkeley* (Berkeley: University of California Press, 1988).
21. Annotated by Händel in preparation of his pasticcio *Arbace*.
22. This source is a copy of a manuscript, previously preserved in D-Dl, that was reportedly destroyed during the II Word War. A further copy of Vinci's setting may be held in the Oratorio del Filippini in Naples (I-Nf).
23. Inserted into the London pasticcio, yet in a different key; see Sprague, 'A Comparison of Five Musical Settings', pp. 169–70.

[3/3]^(BnF,24); GB-Lbl R.M.23.f.2 [11]^(BL,RISM); S-Skma T-SE-R^(RISM)); *Conservati fedele*^L (CH-Gc R 232 [21]^(RISM); CH-N XB obl. 219^(RISM); D-B Mus.ms. 22375/5 [1]^(RISM); D-Hs M A/681 (Nr. 5–7) [5]^(RISM); F-Pn VM4-960 [1/1]^(BnF); GB-Cfm [GB-Cu] MU.MS.13^(IC); GB-Lbl Add. 31593^(BL,RISM); GB-Lbl R.M.23.f.2 [10]^(BL,RISM); GB-Lfom Accession Number 2541 [12]^(RISM;IP); I-Bc KK.308 [13]^(IC,SBN,25); I-MC 6-B-20/10 [11]^(RISM); I-Rc Mss. 2773 [8]^(SBN); US-BEm MS 870 [3]^(IC,RISM); US-FAy Quarto 532 MS 3 [35]^(RISM); US-NH Misc. Ms. 75 [17]^(RISM;R)); *Così stupisce e cade* (B-Bc 15178 [12]^(RISM); D-B Mus.ms. 22375/5 [6]^(RISM); F-Pn VM4-862^(BnF,RISM,26); I-MC 6-B-20 [5]^(RISM); I-MC 6-B-20/12 [4]^(RISM); I-Nc 34.5.24 [24]^(SBN); I-Rama A.Ms.3702 [7]^(RISM); I-Rc Mss. 2513 [19]^(RISM,SBN); US-BEm MS 870 [7]^(IC,RISM)); *Deh, respirar lasciatemi*^L (B-Bc 5143 [18]^(RISM;R); CH-N XB obl. 218^(RISM); D-B Mus.ms. 22375/5 [3]^(RISM); D-Hs M A/678 [7]^(RISM); F-Pm Res F7.29^(BASE); F-Pn VM4-960 [3/4]^(BnF); GB-Lbl Add. 31603^(BL,RISM); GB-Lbl R.M.23.f.2 [12]^(BL,RISM); GB-Ob Ms. Mus. e.11 [2]^(RISM,27); I-Bc KK.308 [10]^(IC,RISM,SBN); I-Mc Noseda A.2 [10]^(SBN); I-Mc Noseda N.22 [2/1]^(SBN); I-Mc Noseda R.25 [10]^(SBN); I-MC 6-B-20/10 [10]^(RISM); I-Nc 22.2.8 [6]^(SBN); I-Nc 28.2.8 [6]^(SBN); I-Nc 34.5.25 [26]^(SBN); I-Nc 40.2.29^(SBN,28); I-Nc O.4.5 [1]^(SBN); I-Rc Mss. 2773 [6]^(SBN); US-BEm MS 870 [9]^(IC,RISM); US-FAy Quarto 532 MS 3 [11]^(RISM); US-Wc M1505.V64 A6^(MGG,NG,RISM); US-Wc ML96.H83 [13]^(MGG,NG,RISM;R)); *Dimmi che un empio sei* (D-Hs M A/678 [16]^(RISM); D-Hs M A/681 [8]^(RISM); F-Pm Res F7.29^(BASE); F-Pn VM4-960 [2/2]^(BnF); US-BEm MS 870 [4]^(IC,RISM)); *Figlio se più non vivi*^(L,29) (I-MC 6-B-20/12 [8]^(RISM); I-Rama A.Ms.3702 [6]^(RISM); US-BEm MS 869 [13]^(IC,RISM); US-FAy Quarto 532 MS 3 [6]^(RISM)); *Fra cento affanni e cento*^L (B-Bc 4942^(RISM); D-Hs M A /678 [5]^(RISM); F-Pn VM4-960 [1/2]^(BnF); F-Pn VM4-960 [9]^(BnF); GB-Lbl Add. 31592^(BL,RISM); I-Mc Noseda R.7 [6]^(SBN); I-MC 6-B-20/12 [9]^(RISM); I-Rc Mss. 2558 [11]^(SBN); I-Rc Mss. 2773 [13]^(SBN); US-BEm MS 870 [1]^(IC,RISM); US-FAy Quarto 532 MS 3 [12]^(RISM)); *L'onda dal mar divisa*^L (D-Hs M A/681[12]^(RISM); D-SWl Mus.167^(RISM;P,30); F-Pm Res F7.29^(BASE); GB-Lam MS 137 [6]^(RISM); GB-Lbl R.M.23.f.2 [18]^(BL,RISM); GB-Lfom Accession Number 2541 [6]^(RISM;IP); I-Rc Mss. 2558 [15]^(SBN); S-Skma T-SE-R^(RISM); US-BEm MS 870 [5]^(IC,RISM); US-FAy Quarto 532 MS 3 [10]^(RISM)); *Mi credi spietata?*^L (D-Hs M A/678 [18]^(IC,RISM); I-Rc

---

24. Microfilm copy of all the pieces in F-Pn VM4-960: F-Pn VM BOB-9630.
25. Microfilm copy of all the pieces in I-Bc KK.308: I-Bc 5595.
26. Wrongly attributed to Gregorio Lorenzo Babbi on source. Microfilm copy: F-Pn VM BOB-20395.
27. In d minor instead of g minor. This source was probably used in the 1734 London pasticcio.
28. In e minor instead of g minor.
29. Inserted into the London pasticcio, yet in a different key.
30. In G major and C-3 clef instead of D major and C-1 clef.

Mss. 2773 [9]^{SBN}; I-Nc 34.5.23 [12]^{SBN}; US-BEm MS 869 [17]^{IC,RISM}); *Mi scacci sdegnato!*^{L} (D-Hs M A/678 [9]^{RISM}; D-Hs M A/681 (Nr. 5–7) [4]^{RISM}; F-Pm Res F7.29^{BASE}; F-Pn L-5231^{BnF,31}; F-Pn VM4-960 [5]^{BnF}; GB-Ob Ms. Mus. Sch. B.8* [10]$^{RISM;R,IP,32}$; GB-WMl Music Manuscript 10 [10]^{RISM,33}; I-Bc KK.308 [4]^{IC,RISM,SBN}; I-MC 6-B-20/10 [7]^{RISM}; I-Rc Mss. 2772^{IC}; US-BEm MS 870 [2]^{IC,RISM}; US-FAy Quarto 532 MS 3 [13]^{RISM}); *Non conosco in tal momento* (D-Hs M A/678 [12]^{RISM}); *Non temer ch'io mai ti dica*^{L,34} (D-Hs M A/681 (Nr. 5–7) [5]^{RISM}; GB-Cfm [GB-Cu] MU. MS.633^{IC}); *Non ti son padre, non mi sei figlio*^{L} (B-Bc 5147$^{RISM;R}$; D-B Mus. ms. 22375/5 [4]^{RISM}; F-Pm Res F7.29^{BASE}; F-Pn VM4-960 [3/5]^{BnF}; I-Mc Noseda A.25 [27]^{SBN}); *Nuvoletta opposta al sole* (D-Hs M A/678 [15]^{RISM}; D-Hs M A/681 (Nr. 57) [9]^{RISM}; F-Pm Res F7.29^{BASE}); *Perché tarda è mai la morte* (D-Hs M A/678 [11]^{RISM}); *Per pietà bell'idol mio*^{L} (D-Hs M A/678 [6]^{RISM}; D-Hs M A/681 (Nr. 5–7) [2]^{RISM}; F-Pm Res F7.29^{BASE}; F-Pn D-18365 [13]$^{BnF,RISM;R}$; F-Pn VM4-960 [3/1]^{BnF}; GB-Lbl R.M.23.f.2 [13]^{BL,RISM}; GB-Ob Ms. Mus. e.8 [3]^{RISM}; GB-Ob Ms. Mus. e.11 [1]^{RISM}; I-Mc Noseda R.7 [7]^{SBN}; I-MC 6-B-20/10 [8]^{RISM}; I-Nc 22.3.20 [10]^{SBN,35}; S-Skma Alströmer saml. 170 [22]^{RISM}; US-BEm MS 869 [18]^{IC,RISM}; US-Wc ML96.H83 [5]$^{MGG,NG,RISM;R,36}$); *Per quell'affetto che l'incatena*^{L} (D-Hs M A/678 [19]^{RISM}; D-Hs M A/681 (Nr. 5–7) [8]^{RISM}; D-SWl Mus.2479 [12]^{RISM}; F-Pm Res F7.29^{BASE}; F-Pn VM4-960 [7]^{BnF}; GB-Lbl Add. 31601 [1]^{BL,RISM}; GB-Lbl R.M.23.f.2 [17]^{BL,RISM}; GB-Lfom Accession Number 2541 [11]$^{RISM;IP}$; GB-Ob Ms. Mus. e.11 [4]^{RISM,37}; I-MC 6-B-20/10 [12]^{RISM}; I-Nc 34.5.23 [20]^{SBN,38}; I-Rama A.Ms.3702 [4]^{RISM,SBN}; I-Rc Mss. 2558 [13]^{SBN}; I-Rc Mss. 2773 [5]^{SBN}; S-Skma T-SE-R^{RISM}; US-BEm MS 869 [15]^{IC,RISM}); *Per quel paterno amplesso*^{L} (B-Nimep Ms 255$^{RISM;P}$; D-Hs M A/681 (Nr. 5–7) [7]^{RISM}; F-Pm Res F7.29^{BASE}; F-Pn D-6881 [4]^{BnF}; GB-Cfm [GB-Cu] MU.MS.13^{IC}; GB-Cfm [GB-Cu] MU.Ms.167 [19]^{IC}; GB-Lbl Add. 31602 [5]^{BL,RISM}; GB-Lbl R.M.23.e.2 [31]^{BL,RISM}; GB-Lbl R.M.23.f.2 [15]^{BL,RISM}; GB-Ob Ms. Mus. e.11 [26]^{RISM,39}; GB-Ob Ms. Mus. Sch. B.8* [9]$^{RISM;R,IP}$; I-Bc KK.308 [9]^{IC,RISM,SBN}; I-Fc D.I.208 [10]^{IC,RISM,SBN}; I-Mc Noseda R.7 [9]^{SBN}; I-MC 6-B-20/12 [12]^{RISM}; I-PSbsg n/s [16]^{RISM,SBN};

---

31. For Florence 1730.
32. This source was probably used in the 1634 London pasticcio.
33. In G major instead of B flat major.
34. This and the following aria were inserted into the London pasticcio, yet in a different key.
35. Wrongly attributed to A. Bernasconi on source.
36. In F major instead of G major.
37. In F major and C-3 clef instead of B flat major and C-1 clef.
38. In C major instead of B flat major.
39. In D major and C-3 clef instead of G major and C-1 clef.

I-PSbsg n/s [17]^{RISM,SBN}; I-Rama A.Ms.3702 [5]^{RISM}; I-Rc Mss. 2773 [3]^{SBN}; J-Tk S10-891 [5]^{RISM}; US-BEm MS 869 [14]^{IC,RISM}; US-FAy Quarto 532 MS 3 [31]^{RISM}; US-SFsc *M2.1 M519^{RISM}; US-Wc M1497.H13 [8]^{MGG,NG,RISM}); *Rendimi il caro amico*^{L} (D-Hs M A/678 [1]^{RISM}; GB-Lfom Accession Number 2541 [8]$^{RISM;IP}$; I-Rama A.Ms.3702 [16]^{RISM}); *Se del fiume altera l'onda* (D-Hs M A/678 [4]^{RISM}; I-Rama A.Ms.3702 [10]^{RISM}); *Se d'un amor tiranno*^{L} (B-Bc 4949^{RISM}; D-Hs M A/681 (Nr. 5–7) [6]^{RISM}; D-Rtt Prota 4 [15]^{RISM,40}; F-Pm Res F7.29^{BASE}; F-Pn D-6881 [12]^{BnF}; F-Pn D-18365 [14]^{RISM}; F-Pn VM4-960 [6]^{BnF}; GB-Cfm [GB-Cu] MU.MS.13^{IC}; GB-Lbl Add. 31593^{BL,RISM}; GB-Lbl R.M.23.f.2 [14]^{BL,RISM}; GB-Ob Ms. Mus. e.11 [3]^{RISM,41}; I-Bc KK.308 [5]^{IC,RISM,SBN}; I-Nc 34.5.25 [12]^{SBN}; I-Rama A.Ms.3702 [14]^{RISM,SBN}; I-Rc Mss. 2558 [14]^{SBN}; S-Uu Leufsta Mus. ms. 37 [5]$^{RISM;R,IP}$; US-BEm MS 870 [8]^{IC,RISM}); *Sogna il guerrier le schiere* (D-Hs M A/678 [3]^{RISM}; F-Pn VM4-960 [3/2]^{BnF}; GB-Lfom Accession Number 2541 [7]$^{RISM;IP}$; I-MC 6-B-20/10 [3]^{RISM,42}); *Su le sponde del torbido Lete* (D-Hs M A/678 [13]^{RISM}); *Torna innocente e poi* (D-Hs M A/678 [17]^{RISM}; D-Hs M A/681 (Nr. 5–7) [3]^{RISM}; F-Pm Res F7.29^{BASE}; F-Pn VM4-960 [2/1]^{BnF}; US-BEm MS 869 [16]^{IC,RISM}); *Tu vuoi ch'io viva, o cara*^{L} (B-Bc 4953^{RISM}; B-Bc 5093^{RISM,43}; D-B Am.B 274 [2]^{RISM,44}; D-Hs M A/681 [18]^{RISM}; D-KA Don Mus.Hs. 988 [1]^{RISM}; D-RH Ms 584 [1]^{RISM}; F-Pn D-14501 [15]^{BnF}; F-Pn D-14501 [31]^{BnF}; F-Pn VM4-960 [8]$^{BnF;IP}$; GB-Cfm [GB-Cu] MU.MS.13^{IC}; GB-Lbl Add. 31517^{BL,RISM}; GB-Lbl Add. 31596 [2]^{BL,RISM}; GB-Ob Ms. Mus. e.7 [8]^{RISM}; I-Bc KK.308 [7]^{IC,RISM,SBN}; I-Fc D.I.210 [1]^{RISM,SBN}; I-Mc Noseda R.7 [10]^{SBN}; I-MC 6-B-20/10 [6]^{RISM}; I-MC 6-B-20 [11]^{RISM}; I-Nc 34.5.23 [10]^{SBN}; I-Nc 35.4.23 [8]^{SBN}; I-Nc 35.4.23 [9]^{SBN}; I-PSbsg n/s [15]^{RISM,SBN}; I-Rama A.Ms.3702 [11]^{RISM,SBN}; I-Rc Mss. 2773 [14]^{SBN}; RUS-Mrg Ф.954 N°203–205 [9]$^{RISM;IP}$; S-Skma T-SE-R^{IC,RISM}; US-BEm MS 869 [12]^{IC,RISM}; US-FAy Quarto 532 MS 3 [14]^{RISM}; US-SFsc *M2.1 M520^{RISM}; US-Wc ML96.H83 [3]^{MGG,NG,RISM,45}); *Va' tra le selve ircane* (D-Hs M A/678 [8]^{RISM}; GB-Lfom Accession Number 2541 [9]$^{RISM;IP}$; I-Bc FF.244 [16]^{RISM,46}; I-Rama A.Ms.3702 [15]^{RISM,SBN}; I-Rc Mss. 2558 [18]^{SBN}); *Vo solcando un mar crudele* (B-Bc 4956^{RISM,47}; B-Bc

---

40. In F major instead of C major.
41. This and the following source: in G major and C-3 clef instead of C major and C-1 clef.
42. In C-3 instead of C-1 clef.
43. B-Bc 5093 and D-KA Don Mus.Hs. 988 [1]: in A major instead of C major.
44. Wrongly attributed to Leonardo Leo on source.
45. In B flat major instead of C major.
46. Wrongly attributed to Hasse on source. Microfilm copy: I-Bc 3558.
47. For Florence 1730.

12614[RISM]; CH-Gc R 232 [29][RISM]; D-B Mus.ms. 22375/5 [5][RISM]; D-B Mus.ms. 22375/8[RISM;P]; D-B Slg Landsberg 280 [2][RISM]; D-Hs M A/681 [9][RISM]; D-KA Don Mus.Hs. 1028[RISM]; D-SWl Mus.5544 [4][RISM;P]; D-W Cod. Guelf. 301 Mus. Hdschr. [17][RISM]; DK-Kk mu6411.0430[RISM;IP]; F-Pn VM4-960 [2/3][BnF]; F-Pn VM4-960 [4][BnF;IP]; GB-Cfm [GB-Cu] MU. MS.145 [6][IC]; GB-Lbl Add. 14219 [40][BL,RISM]; GB-Lbl Add. 24307 [17][BL,RISM]; GB-Lbl Add. 31592[BL,RISM]; GB-Lbl R.M.23.e.2 [30][BL,RISM]; GB-Lbl R.M.23.f.2 [16][BL,RISM]; GB-Lfom Accession Number 2541 [10][RISM;IP]; I-Bc KK.308 [3][RISM,SBN]; I-Mc Noseda A.50 [15i][SBN;R,P]; I-MC 6-B-20 [4][RISM]; I-MC 6-B-20 [9][RISM]; I-MC 6-B-20/12 [6][RISM]; I-MC 6-E-10 [17][RISM]; I-Nc 34.5.23 [3][SBN]; I-Nc 34.5.23 [5][SBN]; I-Nc 34.5.23 [13][SBN]; I-Nc 34.5.23 [17][SBN]; I-Rc Mss. 2558 [17][SBN]; S-Skma T-SE-R[RISM]; US-BEm MS 27 [1][IC,RISM]; US-BEm MS 120 [31][SBN]; I-Nc 34.5.24 [1][SBN]; US-BEm MS 870 [6][IC,RISM]; US-FAy Quarto 532 MS 3 [9][RISM]; US-Wc ML96.H83 [4][MGG,NG,RISM;R])

[printed sources] → see 1734, mus. by Händel, Georg Friedrich and others

[contrafacta] *Bramar di perdere* ([*Nulla culpa laevi ora*]) CZ-Pu 59 R 4526[RISM;P]); *Conservati fedele* ([*Ad festa convolate*] H-Gk AMC, V. 7/2[RISM;P]); *Deh, respirar lasciatemi* ([*My tears have been my meat*] US-Bp M.140.1 [4][RISM,48]); *L'onda dal mar divisa* ([*Amo te Deus meus*] D-KA Don Mus.Ms. 77[RISM]; [*Laudent te caeli Deus*] CH-SAf Mus-SAf.Ms.1140[RISM;P]); *Mi credi spietata?* ([*Ad laeta faceta cantanda properemus*] PL-Wu RM 4861[RISM;P,49]; [*Lauda Sion, salvatorem lauda ducem et pastorem – Sancti tui Domine*] PL-SA 75/A II 15 [1][RISM;P]); *Per pietà bell'idol mio* ([*Jesu meta fons amoris*] CZ-Pak 1351 [1][RISM]); *Tu vuoi ch'io viva, o cara* ([*O salutaris hostia, quae caeli pandis ostium*] D-FUl M 9 [218/2][RISM;P]; [*Stella caeli exstirpavit, quae lactavit Dominum*] D-FUl M 9 [218/3][RISM;P]); *Vo solcando un mar crudele* ([*Funde terra funde flores*] PL-Wu RM 5509[RISM;P])

[unspecified excerpts] A-Wn Mus.Hs.1583 [7][IC]; A-Wn Mus.Hs.19242/II-GF [142][IC]; A-Wn Mus.Hs.37599 [4][IC]

[doubtful] *Conservati fedele*[50] (I-Bc KK.308 [13][IC,RISM,SBN]; I-Mc Noseda R.7 [5][SBN]; I-Nc 34.5.25 [11][SBN])

---

48. Wrongly attributed to G. B. Pergolesi on source (in pencil).
49. Wrongly attributed to C. Ristori on source.
50. Although these manuscripts attribute the music to Vinci, the aria is different from that in all other sources. Perhaps by L. Leo? One in C major, one in B flat major, and the other in F major, yet all three with the same music.

MC | *Artaserse* (1730–1850)

[inserts by other composers]

[Florence, 1730] Palafati, Domenico, *Non ti son padre, non mi sei figlio* (F-Pn L-5230[BnF])

[Naples, 1738] Leo, Leonardo, *Fra cento affanni e cento* (I-Mc Noseda L.40 [9][SBN]; I-Nc 33.2.27 [17][RISM,SBN]); *Per questo dolce amplesso* (D-B Mus.ms. 30408 [14][RISM,51]; D-F Mus Hs 154 [12][RISM,52]; D-MÜs SANT Hs 2361b [16][RISM]; F-Pn D-6879 [23][BnF]; GB-Lbl Add. 31602 [5][BL]; HR-Dsmb 64/1744[RISM]; I-Fc D.II.80 [9][IC,SBN]; I-Mc Noseda A.26 [5][SBN]; I-Mc Noseda L.39 [31][SBN]; I-Nc 33.2.27 [13][RISM,SBN]; I-Nc 33.4.22 [13][SBN,53]; US-FAy Quarto 532 MS 5 [14][RISM]; *Tu vuoi ch'io viva, o cara* (D-B* Mus.ms.autogr. Leo, L. 5 [2][RISM;R]); *Vo solcando un mar crudele* (GB-Lbl Add. 14307 [17][BL]; I-Mc Noseda A.26 [24][SBN])

[Naples, 1743] Manna, Gennaro, *Bramar di perdere* (GB-Lbl Add. 31624 [9][BL,RISM]; I-MC 3-E-22 [7][RISM]); *Conservati fedele* (I-MC 3-E-22 [5][RISM]); *Non conosco in tal momento* (GB-Lbl R.M.23.e.2 [15][BL,RISM]; I-MC 3-E-22 [8][RISM]); *Non ti son padre, non mi sei figlio* (I-MC 3-E-22 [10][RISM]); *Per pietà bell'idol mio* (I-MC 3-E-22 [6][RISM]; I-MC 3-E-22 [16][RISM]; S-Skma T-SE-R[RISM]); *Se del fiume altera l'onda* (GB-Lbl Add. 31624 [4][BL,RISM]; I-MC 3-E-22 [11][RISM]); *Va' tra le selve ircane* (I-MC 3-E-22 [9][RISM])

1730	mus. by Hasse, Johann Adolph lib. rev. by Lalli, Domenico[54] and Boldini, Giovanni[55]	
1730 Venice	Teatro Grimani di S. Giovanni Grisostomo (carn., 11/02/1730)[56] 1st version	(1,2)
1730 Genoa	Teatro da S. Agostino (spr.)[57]	(3)
1730 Bologna	Teatro Malvezzi (summ., Aug.?) pasticcio[58]	(4)
1730 Turin	Teatro Carignano (aut.)	(5)
1730 Lucca	Teatro Pubblico (aut.)	(6)

51. As *Per questo dolce amplesso*.
52. In G major instead of B flat major.
53. Wrongly attributed to T. Albinoni on source.
54. For a complete discussion of Lalli's potential participation in the reworking of Metastasio's libretto, see Sprague, 'A Comparison of Five Musical Settings', pp. 51–54.
55. Strohm, Reinhard, 'Hasse, Scarlatti, Rolli', *Analecta Musicologica*, 15 (1975), 220–55 and Mellace, Rafaele, *Johann Adolf Hasse* (Palermo: L'Epos, 2004).
56. The production ran for four consecutive performances; Schmidt-Hensel, '*La musica è del Signor Hasse*', vol. 2, p. 23.
57. For this and the two following productions, see Piperino, Franco, 'Opera Production', p. 53 table 1. [NG] contrarily posits P. V. Chiocchetti as possible composer; see [NG] 'Chiocchetti, Pietro Vincenzo'.
58. See <https://www.pasticcio-project.eu/database/work/P102EE5> [accessed 25 May 2022].

		pasticcio[59]	
1731	Milan	Teatro Regio Ducale (carn., 26/12/1730)	(7)
1731	Kremsier	NA	(8,9)
		Artaxerses, performed in German	
		name day of the Cardinal of Schrattenbach	
1733	Verona	Teatro Filarmonico (carn.)	(10)
		pasticcio[60]	
1734	Venice	Teatro Grimani di S. Giovanni Grisostomo (carn., c. 30/01/1734)	(11)
		arias added by B. Galuppi[61]	
1735	La Valletta	Teatro Manoel (carn.)[62]	(12)
1738	Bergamo	Teatro di Bergamo (carn.)	(13)
1738	Klagenfurt	NA (carn., 18/01/1738)[63]	(14)
1738	Treviso	Teatro Dolfin (Fair, 27/04/1738)[64]	(15)
1738	Vicenza	Teatro di Piazza (Fair, 07/08/1738)	(16)
1738	Madrid	Teatro de los Caños del Peral (25/10/1738)[65]	(17)
		pasticcio; mus. by J. A. Hasse and L. Vinci	
1739	Modena	Teatro Molza (carn., 24/01/1739)[66]	(18)
1740	Ljubljana	Palazzo Provinciale (carn.)	(19)
		pasticcio[67]	
1740	Genoa	Teatro del Falcone (spr.)[68]	(20)
1740	Dresden	Court theatre (09/09/1740)[69]	(21)
		2nd version	

59. See <https://www.pasticcio-project.eu/database/work/P102560> [accessed 25 May 2022].
60. See <https://www.pasticcio-project.eu/database/work/P1026E7> [accessed 25 May 2022].
61. Chiarelli, Alessandra and Angelo Pompilio, 'Or vaghi or fieri': cenni di poetica nei libretti veneziani (circa 1760–1740) (Bologna: Coopperativa Libraria Universitaria Editrice Bologna, 2004) and Selfridge-Field, Eleanor, *A New Chronology of Venetian Opera and Related Genres, 1660–1760* (Stanford: Stanford University Press, 2007).
62. Schmidt-Hensel, 'La musica è del Signor Hasse', vol. 2, p. 79.
63. For the attribution of this performance to Hasse, see Kokole, Metoda, 'Two Operatic Seasons of Brothers Mingotti in Ljubljana', *De musica disserenda*, 8.2 (2012), 57–90.
64. For the attribution to Hasse of this, the following, and the Bassano del Grappa performances, see Bellina, Anna Laura, 'Metastasio in Venezia: appunti per una recensio', *Italianistica: Rivista di letteratura italiana*, 13.1–2 (1984), 145–73.
65. Leza, José Máximo, 'Metastasio on the Spanish Stage: Operatic Adaptations in the Public Theatres of Madrid in the 1730s', *Early Music*, 26.4 (1998), 623–31; Llorens, Ana and Álvaro Torrente, 'Constructing *Opera Seria* in the Iberian Courts: Metastasian Repertoire for Spain and Portugal', *Anuario musical*, 76 (2021), 73–110 <https://doi.org/10.3989/anuariomusical.2021.i76>.
66. Schmidt-Hensel, 'La musica è del Signor Hasse', vol. 2, p. 83.
67. For a discussion of the numbers included in this performance, see Kokole, 'Two Operatic Seasons', pp. 69–70.
68. Giazotto, Remo, *La musica a Genova nella vita publica e privata dal XIII. al XVIII. secolo* (Genoa: Società Industrie Grafiche e Lavorazioni Affini, 1951).
69. The production ran for four consecutive performances until 21 September 1740; see Schmidt-Hensel, '*La musica è del Signor Hasse*', vol. 2, p. 37.

MC | *Artaserse* (1730–1850)

1741 Bassano	Teatro Nuovo (carn., 12/1740)	(22)
1742 Parma	Teatro Regio Ducale (carn.)[70]	(23)
1745 Bologna	Teatro Formagliari (spr., 01/05/1745)	(24)
	mus. by J. A. Hasse and G. A. Paganelli?[71]	
1748 Bayreuth	Court theatre (29/09/1748)[72]	(25)
1754 London	King's Theatre in the Haymarket (29/01/1754)	(26)
1755 Lübeck	NA (06/11/1755)[73]	(27)
	mus. by J. A. Hasse and others	
1760 Naples	Teatro di S. Carlo (27/01/1760)[74]	(28)
	birthday of Carlos III, king of Spain	
	3rd version	
1760 Warsaw	Royal Theatre (03/08/1760)[75]	(29)
	name day of Augustus III, king of Poland	
1761 Bratislava	NA	(30)
1762 Naples	Teatro di S. Carlo (25/07/1762)	(31)
1765 Ferrara	Teatro Bonacossi da S. Stefano (carn.)	(32)
1766 London	King's Theatre in the Haymarket (22/02/1766)[76]	(33)

Librettos   (1) Venice: Buonarigo, [1730][77]

I-Bc Lo.02480; I-Mb Racc.dramm.0804; I-Mr Libr. 02789; I-Rig Rar. Libr. Ven. 651/656 [653]; I-Rsc Libr. n. XIV [12];[78] I-Vcg LIBRETTI S.GIO.GRISOSTOMO 151 [5]; I-Vmc Rava H.326; I-Vnm DRAMM.1239 [1]; I-Vnm DRAMMM.3558 [2]; RUS-Mrg H386/224; SI-Lsk AE 49 [1]; US-AUS KL-17 54; US-CAh *IC7 A00 B750 [36];[79] US-LAum ML48 .R114 1730 [9]; US-Wc ML48 [S4576]

---

70. Schmidt-Hensel, 'La musica è del Signor Hasse', vol. 2, p. 85.
71. ⁵Index I, pp. 400, 424.
72. Bauer, Hans-Joachim, *Barockoper in Bayreuth* (Laaber: Laaber, 1982).
73. Schmidt-Hensel, 'La musica è del Signor Hasse', vol. 2, p. 89.
74. Mellace, *Johann Adolf Hasse*, p. 435 and De Filippis, Felice and Raffaele Arnese, *Cronache del Teatro di S. Carlo (1737–1960)* (Naples: Edizioni Politica Popolare, 1961). ᶜ gives 20/01/1760 and Croce speaks of 1759; see Croce, Benedetto, *I teatri di Napoli. Secolo XV-XVIII* (Naples: Pierro, 1891).
75. Hasse may have personally overseen this production; see Żórawska-Witkowska, Alina, 'The Saxon Court of the Kingdom of Poland', in *Music at German Courts, 1715–1760: Changing Artistic Priorities*, ed. by Samantha Owens, Barbara M. Reul, and Janice B. Stockigt (Woodbridge: The Boydell Press, 2011), pp. 51–78.
76. The production ran for four consecutive performances; see Petty, Fred Curtis, 'Italian Opera in London, 1760–1800' (doctoral dissertation, Yale University, 1971).
77. Microfilm copy of unspecified copy: US-I FILM 782.12 H27AR. According to ˢ2932, there used to be a copy in I-Rss yet it can no longer be found. We therefore consider it as lost.
78. Microfilm copy: US-BEm MICROFILM.AA543.ML.
79. Microfilm copy: US-Ccrl MF-3709 r.152.

(2) Venice: Buonarigo, [1730]
I-RVI Silv., op. 656; I-Vcg LIBRETTI S.GIO.GRISOSTOMO 151 [6]; I-Vnm DRAMM.1042 [2]; I-Vnm DRAMM.3558 [3]

(3,20,25) NA

(4) Bologna: Pisarri, [1730]
I-Bc Lo.05938; I-Bu A.V.Tab.IX.Caps.XXI [24]; I-MOe A.58.L.07 [6]; I-MOe 83.H.01 [6]; I-Vgc ROL.0677 [9]; US-CAh *IC7.A100.B750 [96]

(5) Turin: Valetta, [1730]
I-Tn F XIII.464 [2]

(6) Lucca: Ciuffetti, [1730]
I-Vgc ROL.0381 [7]

(7) Milan: Malatesta, 1730
F-Pn LIV IT-3517 [5]; I-Fm Mel.2002 [4];[80] I-LDEsormani 297/6/25; I-Ma S. I. H. I. 4 [2]; US-Cn ML50.2.A78 M48 1730

(8) Brno: Swoboda, [1731]
CZ-Pn langer IV.5.Aa.8

(9) Brno: Swoboda, [1731] (Ger.)
CZ-R R-P.I.d.1/8

(10) Verona: Vallarsi, [1733]
I-Mb Racc.dramm.3487

(11) Venice: Rossetti, 1734
I-Mb Racc.dramm.0811; I-Mb Racc.dramm.0813; I-Pmc[S]; I-RVI Silv., op. 689; I-Vcg LIBRETTI S.GIO.GRISOSTOMO 153; I-Vnm DRAMM.1048 [3]; I-Vnm DRAMM.1246 [7]; I-Vnm DRAMM.3562 [3]; SI-Lsk AE 90 [2]; US-LAum ML48 .R114 1734 [3]

(12) Catania: Bisagni, 1734
M-Vnl[81]

(13) Bergamo: Rossi, 1737
I-Mb Racc.dramm.3709

(14) Venice: Pasinelli, 1738
I-Mb Racc.dramm.1298; SI-Lsk AE 49 [7]

(15) Venice: Lovisa, [1738]
I-Mb Racc.dramm.2817

---

80. Mutilated document.
81. Not found in [IC].

(16) Vicenza: [s.n.], 1738
I-Mb Racc.dramm.3316

(17) Madrid: [s.n.], 1738 (It./Spa.)
E-Mn T/25742; E-MO C*XVII*12o*49

(18) Modena: Soliani, 1739
I-Bc Lo.05939; I-MOe M.T.Ferr.Mor.27 [8]; US-Cn ML50.2.A78 M48 1739

(19) Ljubljana: Reichardt, [1740] (Ger.)
A-Wn 568856-B; SI-Ln 3420; SI-Lsk Z VIII 5/1 SL B X

(21) Dresden: widow of Stössel, [1740] (It./Ger.)
B-Bc 19310; CZ-Pu 9 J 3480; D-B Mus. Ta 1195; D-HAmi Pon IId 1700 [2,4]; D-Mbs Slg.Her 122; I-Vgc ROL.0957 [14]; RUS-Mrg 50-8684647; US-Wc ML48 [S4513]

(22) Bassano del Grappa: [s.n., 1740]
I-Mb Racc.dramm.0686

(23) Bologna: Martelli, [1742]
I-Bca 8-L.ITAL.COMP.MUSIC.05 [15]

(24) Bologna: [Sassi, 1745]
I-Bc Lo.05940; I-Bu A.III.Caps.101 [26]; I-Mb Racc.dramm.2221; I-Rn 40.9.G.16.3

(26) London: Woodfall, 1754 (It./En.)[82]
GB-Lbl 907.i.7 [2];[83] US-CAt 2008TW-772; US-SM La 106

(27) Lübeck: [s.n.], 1755 (It./Ger.)
D-Gs DD91 A 33571 [2]; D-ROu Ck-1610

(28) Naples: Flauto, 1760
D-Dl MT. 2554;[84] I-Bc Lo.02481;[85] I-Nc Rari 15.13.14[86]

(29) Warsaw: [s.n.], 1760
CZ-Pu 9 C 1501;[87] GB-Ob Lib.Polon. B 78; PL-Kj St. Dr. 27577 II; PL-Kj St. Dr. 920173 II; PL-Ptp 23669 II; PL-WRzno XVIII-6747; RUS-Mrg 50-8419142; RUS-Mrg 50-8685648

---

82. Microfilm copy of unspecified copy: US-BL PR1269 .T564 no.M4397.
83. Microfilm copies: D-Gs MA 89-24:3911 [2]; GB-En Mf.134, reel 3911 [2]; GB-Lbl PB.Mic.15787.
84. Unclear relation of this manuscript copy with the rest. The library states it does not contain any information about the editor and dates it around 1760; see <https://katalog.slub-dresden.de/id/0-1759265268> [accessed 20 June 2022].
85. Microfilm copy: US-PRu MICROFILM 198.
86. Pages 33–40 missing.
87. Microfilm copy: CDN-Lu ML48.M47H383 1761a.

MC | Artaserse (1730–1850)

(30) Bratislava: [s.n.], 1761
CZ-Pn T 4706

(31) Naples: Flauto, 1762
I-Nc Rari 10.5.8 [9]

(32) Ferrara: Pomatelli, [1765]
US-Wc ML48 [S4590]

(33) London: Woodfall, 1766 (It./It.)
GB-Lbl 1608/4555 [8]

Music sources

(^{L} = inserted into the London pasticcio in 1734 → see 1734, mus. by Hasse, Johann Adolph, Nicola Porpora; and Riccardo Broschi)

1st version: 1730, Venice

[complete scores] CZ-Pr ARCH 1945^{RISM}; D-Dl Mus.2477-F-2b$^{MGG,NG,RISM;IP}$; D-MÜs SANT Hs 1933^{MGG,NG,RISM}; GB-ABu Mus. MS 12; GB-Cfm MU.MS.25^{IC,MGG,NG}; GB-Cfm [GB-Cu] MU.MS.25^{IC}; GB-CDu Mackworth Collection Vol. 16$^{MGG,RISM;A}$; GB-Lam MS 72^{MGG,NG,RISM}; GB-Lbl Add. 22107^{BL,RISM}; GB-Lbl Add. 22107^{BL,RISM}; GB-Lbl Add. 32582^{BL,MGG,NG,RISM}; GB-Lbl 39568^{BL,MGG,NG,RISM}; I-Vnm Mss. 10005^{MGG,NG,SBN,88}; US-Wc M1500.H35 A68^{MGG,NG,RISM}

[excerpts] *Bramar di perdere** (D-B N.Mus. BP 389^{IC}; D-Dl Mus.2477-F-10 [8]$^{RISM;R}$; D-Dl Mus. 2477-F-112 [4]$^{RISM;IP,89}$; D-Hs ND VI 2918 [23]^{RISM}; D-LEm Becker III.15.47 [21]^{NG,RISM}; D-SWl Mus.2490 [5]$^{RISM;IP}$; D-SWl Mus.2491m$^{MGG,RISM;IP}$; DK-Kk mu6501.1630 [4]^{IC,RISM}; F-Pn VM7-7694^{IC}; I-PLcon Pisani 27 [7]^{IC}); *Che pena al mio core* (D-Dl Mus.2477-F-10 [10]$^{RISM;R}$; D-Hs ND VI 2918 [20]^{RISM}; D-SWl Mus.2479 [35]$^{MGG,RISM\ R}$; D-SWl Mus.2491a [1]$^{MGG,RISM;IP}$; D-SWl Mus.2492^{MGG,RISM}; HR-PORzm ZMP 13702 [6]$^{RISM;R}$); *Conservati fedele* (B-Bc 4103^{NG,RISM}; D-Hs ND VI 2918 [22]^{RISM}; D-KA Don Mus.Hs. 193 [2]$^{RISM;IP}$; D-LEm Becker III.15.47 [21]^{NG,RISM}; D-SWl Mus.2490 [1]$^{MGG,RISM;IP}$; F-Pn D-5465 [8]^{BnF,90}; GB-Lbl Add. 29965 [3]^{BL,RISM}; GB-Lbl R.M.23.f.2 [19]^{BL,RISM}; GB-Lcm MS 629 [2]^{IC}; GB-Lcm MS 690 [16]^{IC}; GB-SA FIN. M.1611 H 19^{IC}; HR-PORzm ZMP 13702 [3]$^{RISM;R}$; I-Nc A.5.2 [73]^{SBN}; I-PLcon Pisani 27 [13]^{IC}; I-PLcon Pisani 29 [10]^{IC}; I-Rama A.Mss.3702 [8]^{IC,RISM}); *Figlio se più non vivi** (D-Dl

---

88. Printed reproduction of a microfilm copy: US-LAum M1500 .H276a 1730a.
89. D-Dl Mus. 2477-F-112 [4] and DK-Kk mu6501.1630 [4]: in G major instead of E flat major.
90. Microfilm copy: F-Pn VM BOB-25743.

Mus.1-F-28,13 [10]^{RISM}; D-Dl Mus.1-F-28,13a [10]$^{RISM;IP}$; GB-Cfm [GB-Cu] MU.MS.633^{IC}); *Fra cento affanni e cento** (D-Dl Mus.2477-F-113 [6]$^{RISM;IP}$; D-Hs ND VI 1081 [2]^{RISM}; D-LEm Becker III.15.47 [22]^{NG,RISM}; D-SWl Mus.2490 [2]$^{MGG,RISM;IP}$; DK-Kk mu7411.0539^{RISM}; F-Pn VM7-7694^{BnF}; HR-PORzm ZMP 13702 [4]$^{RISM;R}$; I-PLcon Pisani 27 [10]^{IC}; US-FAy Quarto 532 MS 1 [3]^{RISM}); *Lascia cadermi in volto*^{L*} (D-Dl Mus.2477-F-113 [1]$^{RISM;IP}$; D-Hs ND VI 2918 [21]^{RISM}; D-MÜs SANT Hs 1982 [28]^{RISM}; D-SWl Mus.2490 [8]^{MGG,RISM}; DK-Kk mu7411.0534^{IC,RISM}; GB-Cfm [GB-Cu] MU.MS.111 [5]^{IC}; GB-Cfm [GB-Cu] MU.MS 111 [8]^{IC}; HR-PORzm ZMP 13702 [8]$^{RISM;R}$; I-MC 2-F-17/17 [4]^{RISM}; I-Nc 33.2.17 [19]^{SBN}; I-PAc Sanv.A.191^{RISM,SBN}; I-Rama A.Ms.3721 [6]^{IC,RISM}; S-Skma T-SE-R^{RISM}); *Mi credi spietata?* (D-Hs ND VI 2918 [26]^{RISM}); *Non è ver che sia contento** (D-Dl Mus.2477-E-532 [2]^{RISM}; D-Dl Mus.2477-F-10 [9]$^{RISM;R}$; D-Dl Mus.2477-F-110 [51]^{RISM}; D-SWl Mus.2490 [11]^{MGG,RISM}; D-W Cod. Guelf. 301 Mus. Hdschr. [31]^{RISM}; GB-Lbl Add. 29965 [4]^{BL,RISM}; I-MC 2-F-15 [9]^{RISM}; S-SK 292 [22]^{RISM}); *Non temer ch'io mai ti dica** (A-Wn Mus.Hs.4051^{IC,NG}; D-Dl Mus.2477-F-113 [7]$^{RISM;IP}$; D-Dl Mus.2477-F-500^{RISM}; D-Hs ND VI 1078 [1]^{RISM}; DK-Kk mu7411.0540^{RISM}); *Non ti son padre, non mi sei figlio* (D-LEm Becker III.15.4 [26]^{NG,RISM}; D-SWl Mus.2490 [9]$^{MGG,RISM;IP}$); *Pallido il sole** (B-Bc 4138^{NG,RISM,91}; B-Bc 5020^{IC,NG,92}; D-B Mus.ms. 9547/20 [2]^{RISM}; D-Dl Mus.2477-F-110 [47]^{RISM}; D-Dl Mus. 2477-F-112 [7]$^{RISM;IP,93}$; D-KA Don Mus.Hs. 193 [1]^{RISM}; D-LEm Becker III.15.46 [2]^{NG,RISM}; D-MÜs SANT Hs 1981 [29]^{RISM}; D-SWl Mus.2479 [25]$^{MGG,RISM;R,94}$; D-SWl Mus.2479 [37]$^{MGG,RISM;R}$; D-SWl Mus.2482^{MGG,RISM}; D-W Cod. Guelf. 301 Mus. Hdschr. [10]^{RISM}; D-W Cod. Guelf. 301 Mus. Hdschr. [45]^{RISM}; DK-Kk mu6501.1630 [7]^{IC,RISM}; F-Pn D-5467 [15]^{IC,95}; GB-Cfm [GB-Cu] MU.MS.633^{IC}; I-Bc FF.244 [20]^{IC,RISM,SBN,96}; I-MC 2-F-17 [16]^{RISM}; I-Rama A.Ms.3459^{IC,RISM,SBN}; S-Skma T-SE-R^{RISM}); *Parto qual pastorello** (B-Bc 5027^{IC}; B-Bc 5498 [22]^{NG,RISM}; D-Dl Mus.1-F-28,13 [7]^{RISM}; D-Dl Mus.1-F-28,13a [7]$^{RISM;IP}$; D-Dl Mus.2477-F-10 [11]$^{RISM;R}$; D-Dl Mus.2477-F-110 [49]^{RISM}; D-Mbs Mus.ms. 141 [12]^{RISM}; D-SWl Mus.2490 [6]$^{MGG,RISM;IP}$; F-Pn VM7-

---

91. In B flat major instead of E flat major. In C-1 instead of C-3 clef.
92. In B flat major instead of E flat major. In C-4 instead of C-3 clef.
93. In G major instead of E flat major.
94. D-SWl Mus.2479 [25]; D-SWl Mus.2479 [37]; and D-W Cod. Guelf. 301 Mus. Hdschr. [10]: in G major instead of E flat major. In C-1 instead of C-3 clef.
95. In B flat major instead of E flat major. In C-1 instead of C-3 clef.
96. In C-1 instead of C-3 clef. Microfilm copy of all the pieces in I-Bc FF.244: I-Bc 3558.

7694[IC]; GB-Lbl Add. 31592[BL,RISM]; GB-Lbl R.M.22.d.25 [5][BL,RISM]; HR-PORzm ZMP 13702 [7][RISM;R]; <u>I-Bc FF.244 [14]</u>[IC,SBN]; I-Mc Noseda O.42 [18][SBN]; I-MC 2-F-15 [19][RISM]; I-Nc 22.3.13 [19][SBN]; I-Rc Mss. 2558 [6][SBN]); *Pensa che l'amor mio** (<u>D-Dl Mus.2477-F-113 [9]</u>[RISM;IP]; DK-Kk mu7411.0632[RISM]); *Per pietà bell'idol mio** (<u>D-Dl Mus. 2477-F-112 [11]</u>[RISM;IP,97]; <u>D-LEm Becker III.15.47 [23]</u>[NG,RISM]; D-SWl Mus.2490 [3][MGG,RISM;IP]; <u>DK-Kk mu6501.1630 [11]</u>[NG,RISM]); *Per questo dolce amplesso*[98] (A-Wn Mus.Hs.4087[IC]; B-Bc 4145[NG,RISM,99]; B-Bc 5498 [4][NG,RISM,100]; <u>D-LEm Becker III.15.47 [7]</u>[NG,RISM,101]; F-Pn D-5466 [12][BnF]; F-Pn VM7-7694[IC]; GB-Cfm [GB-Cu] MU.MS.633[IC]; GB-Lcm MS 690 [14][IC]; HR-PORzm ZMP 13702 [9][RISM;R]; I-Rama A.Ms.3721 [10][IC,RISM]; S-Hä n/s [1][RISM]; S-Skma T-SE-R[RISM]; US-FAy Quarto 532 MS 2 [4][RISM]); *Rendimi il caro amico** (<u>D-Dl Mus.2477-F-110 [58]</u>[RISM]; <u>D-Dl Mus. 2477-F-112 [2]</u>[RISM;IP]; D-SWl Mus.2491e [1][MGG,RISM;IP]; <u>DK-Kk mu6501.1630 [2]</u>[IC,RISM]); *Se al labbro mio non credi** (<u>D-Dl Mus.2477-F-110 [48]</u>[RISM]; <u>D-Dl Mus.2477-F-113 [3]</u>[RISM;IP]; D-Hs ND VI 2918 [25][RISM]; <u>D-LEm Becker III.15.47 [28]</u>[NG,RISM]; D-SWl Mus.2490 [7][MGG,RISM;IP]; DK-Kk mu7411.0536[RISM]; GB-Lam MS 138 [30][RISM]; HR-PORzm ZMP 13702 [5][RISM;R]; I-PLcon Pisani 27 [7][IC]; S-Skma T-SE-R[RISM]); *Se del fiume altera l'onda** (A-Wgm VI 27229 [Q 2916] [17][IC,NG]; <u>D-Dl Mus.2477-E-526 [2]</u>[RISM]; <u>D-Dl Mus.2477-E-526a [2]</u>[RISM;P]; <u>D-Dl Mus. 2477-F-112 [9]</u>[RISM;IP,102]; <u>DK-Kk mu6501.1630 [9]</u>[IC,RISM]; I-PLcon Pisani 29 [15][IC]; US-BEm MS 15 [5][IC,RISM]); *Se d'un amor tiranno* (<u>D-Dl Mus.2477-F-113 [8]</u>[RISM;IP]; D-OB MO 459[RISM;P]; GB-Ob Ms. Mus. e.10 [13][RISM]; HR-PORzm 13702 [2][RISM;R]; S-Skma T-SE-R[RISM]; S-Uu Vok. mus. i hs. 54:23[IC,RISM]); *Sogna il guerrier le schiere** (<u>D-Dl Mus.2477-F-113 [5]</u>[RISM;IP]; <u>D-LEm Becker III.15.47 [24]</u>[NG,RISM]; D-SWl Mus.2490 [4][MGG,RISM;IP]; DK-Kk mu7411.0538[IC,RISM]; F-Pn VM7-7694[IC]; I-PLcon Pisani 27 [20][IC]); *Spiega i lini* (US-FAy Quarto 532 MS 1 [8][RISM]); *Torna innocente e poi* (<u>D-Dl Mus. 2477-F-112 [5]</u>[RISM;IP,103]; <u>D-LEm Becker III.15.47 [27]</u>[NG,RISM]; D-SWl Mus.2490 [10][MGG,RISM]; GB-Lbl Add. 31637[BL,RISM]); *Tu vuoi ch'io viva, o cara** (A-Wn Mus.Hs.4052 [1][IC,NG]; A-Wn Mus.

---

97. D-Dl Mus. 2477-F-112 [11] and DK-Kk mu6501.1630 [11]: in D major instead of C major.
98. Same music as in the 1740 setting but in a different key. 1730: E major; 1740: G major. Inserted into the London pasticcio → see 1734, mus. by Hasse, Johann Adolph; Porpora; Nicola; and Broschi, Riccardo.
99. In A major instead of E major.
100. In F major instead of E major.
101. This source was used in the London pasticcio.
102. D-Dl Mus. 2477-F-112 [9] and US-BEm MS 15 [5]: in C major instead of G major.
103. In g minor instead of c minor.

MC | *Artaserse* (1730–1850)

Hs.4052 [2]^{IC,NG}; B-Bc 4170^{NG,RISM;R}; B-Bc Bc 5083^{NG,RISM}; D-Bsa [D-B] SA 1475^{RISM}; D-Dl Mus.1-F-28,10 [1]^{RISM}; D-Dl Mus.1-F-28 [10a]^{RISM;IP}; D-Dl Mus.1-F-28,13 [8]^{RISM}; D-Dl Mus.1-F-28,13a [8]^{RISM;IP}; D-HVs Kestner No. 146 [27]^{RISM;R}; D-MEIr Ed 129p [15]^{RISM}; D-MGmi HA IV 60^{RISM;R,IP}; D-SWl Mus.2490 [12]^{MGG,RISM}; F-Pn D-5469 [10]^{BnF,104}; F-Pn D-5470 [16]^{BnF}; GB-Lam MS 138 [17]^{RISM,105}; GB-Lbl Add. 31634 [22]^{BL,RISM}; GB-Lbl R.M.23.d.4 [6]^{BL,RISM}; GB-Lbl R.M.23.f.2 [21]^{BL,RISM}; GB-Lcm MS 690 [7]^{IC}; GB-Ob Ms. Mus. d.63 [2]^{RISM;R}; I-Mc Noseda Q.8 [11]^{SBN}; I-Nc 33.3.18 [25]^{SBN}; I-PLcon Pisani 22 [2]^{IC}; I-Rc Mss. 2767 [10]^{SBN}; I-Vqs MS Cl.VIII.14 (1128) [48]^{RISM,SBN;IP,106}; RUS-Mrg Ф.954 N°203–205^{RISM}; S-L Saml.Engelhart 569^{RISM;IP}; S-Skma T-SO-R^{IC,RISM}; S-SK 494 [23]^{RISM}; US-FAy Quarto 532 MS 2 [12]^{RISM}); Va' tra le selve ircane (D-MÜs SANT Hs 1981 [28]^{RISM}; HR-PORzm ZMP 13702 [1]^{RISM;R}; I-MC 2-F-17/17 [6]^{RISM}; S-HÄ [2]^{RISM})

[contrafacta] *Che pena al mio core* ([*Amo te amo o mea vita*] CZ-Pak 450 [2]^{RISM}); *Conservati fedele* ([*Huc gentes properate, hanc fiem celebrate*] CZ-Pnm XL A 191^{RISM}); *Non temer ch'io mai ti dica* ([*Hilf mire in zu deinen Freuden*] D-Dl Mus.2477-E-526a [3]^{RISM;P}); *Pallido il sole* ([*Pallida luna turbitum coaelum*] A-WIL 1318^{RISM;P}); *Parto qual pastorello* ([*Ad arma surge phalanx belli*] CZ-Pu 59 R 2919 [2]^{RISM;P}; [*Age stella lumen nocti*] CZ-Bm A 14559^{RISM;P}); *Sogna il guerrier le schiere* ([*Guds höga kärlek*] S-L Saml.Engelhart 67^{RISM}); *Tu vuoi ch'io viva, o cara* ([*Portertum fratris mai mens pia*] CZ-OSm A 1851 [2]^{RISM;P}; [*Salve o cara mater*] CZ-Pak 465^{RISM;P}; [*Sunt perennes dies*] D-KA Don Mus.Ms. 627^{RISM;P}; [*Venite decantemus adeste celebremus*] PL-Wu RM 5471 [1]^{RISM;P})

[inserts by other composers] *Idolo mio diletto* (D-B Mus.ms. 30330 [14]^{RISM,107}); arias by Galuppi, Baldassare (for Venice 1734) (I-CF[108])

2nd version: 1740, Dresden

[complete scores] A-Wn Mus.Hs.17295 [1–3]^{IC,MGG,NG}; B-Bc 2142^{IC,MGG,RISM}; D-B Mus.ms. 9547^{MGG,NG,RISM}; D-Dl Mus.2477-F-2^{MGG,NG,RISM;109}; D-Dl Mus.2477-F-2a^{MGG,NG,RISM}; D-Dl Mus.2477-F-4^{RISM;A,R}; D-Hhg Hg 200^{MGG,RISM;A}; D-Hs M A/1568^{MGG,NG,RISM;A}; D-LEu N.I.10308^{MGG,NG,RISM}; D-SWl Mus.2471^{MGG,NG,RISM;A,P}; DK-Kk mu6501.1630^{RISM;A,110}

---

104. Microfilm copy of this and the following source: F-Pn VM BOB-26189.
105. Wrongly attributed to Filippo Palma in ^{RISM}.
106. In C major instead of G major.
107. Inserted into the 1733 revival in Verona, as Mandane's aria in A1-S1.
108. Selfridge-Field, *A New Chronology of Venetian Opera*, p. 439 n. 1734/3.
109. Wrongly related to Hasse's 1st setting in ^{MGG}. Microfilm copy: US-AUS FILM 26150.
110. At least some of the arias are transposed to other keys.

[Acts I&II]; F-Pn D-5395[BnF,MGG,NG,RISM,111]; US-NH Misc. Ms. 8[IC,MGG;A]; US-Wc M1500.H35 A682[MGG,NG,RISM]

[excerpts] *Amalo, e se al tuo sguardo* (D-Dl Mus.2477-F-110 [56][RISM]; D-Dl Mus. 2477-F-112 [8][RISM;IP,112]; DK-Kk mu6501.1630 [8][IC,RISM]); *Che pena al mio core* (D-Dl Mus.2477-F-113 [2][RISM;IP]; DK-Kk k mu7411.0535[RISM]); *Conservati fedele* (D-Dl Mus. 2477-F-112 [3][RISM;IP]; D-W Cod. Guelf. 125 Mus. Hdschr. [8][RISM]; DK-Kk mu6501.1630 [3][IC,RISM,113]; F-Pn D-5470 [6][BnF,114]); *Deh, respirar lasciatemi* (D-Dl Mus.2477-F-112 [11][RISM;IP,115]; DK-Kk mu6501.1630 [10][IC,RISM]); *Giusto re la Persia adora* (D-Dl Mus.2477-F-513/513a[RISM;IP]); *Mi credi spietata?*[116] (A-Wgm VI 27229 [Q 2916] [12][IC,NG]; B-Bc 15185 [6][NG,RISM]; D-Dl Mus.2477-E-517 [4][RISM]; D-Dl Mus.1-F-28,13 [9][RISM]; D-Dl Mus.1-F-28,13a [9][RISM;IP]; D-Dl Mus.2477-F-116 [12][RISM;IP]); *Non ti son padre, non mi sei figlio* (D-Dl Mus. 2477-F-112 [6][RISM;IP,117]; DK-Kk mu6501.1630 [6][RISM]); *Pallido il sole* (F-Pn D-5767 [15][BnF]); *Per questo dolce amplesso* (D-B Mus.ms. 9547/20 [1][RISM]; D-Dl Mus.2477-F-110 [45][RISM]; D-Dl Mus.2477-F-113 [4][RISM;IP]; DK-Kk mu7411.0537[RISM]); *Se d'un amor tiranno* (DK-Kk mu7411.0631[IC,RISM]); *Spiega i lini, abbandona la sponda* (A-Wgm VI 27229 [Q 2916] [16][IC,NG]; B-Bc 5387[NG,RISM]; D-Dl Mus.1-F-28,13 [6][RISM]; D-Dl Mus.1-F-28,13a [6][RISM;IP]); *Torna innocente e poi* (DK-Kk mu6501.1630 [5][IC,RISM,118]); *Va' tra le selve ircane* (D-Dl Mus.2477-E-517 [3][RISM]; D-Dl Mus.2477-F-110 [59][RISM]; D-Dl Mus. 2477-F-112 [1][RISM;IP]; DK-Kk mu6501.1630 [1][IC,RISM])

[inserts] [Bologna 1745] *Non è ver che sia contento* (B-Bc 5365[RISM,119])

3rd version: 1760, Naples

[complete scores] A-Wn Mus.Hs.1061[IC]; A-Wgm IV 17317 [Q 20901][IC]; D-Dl Mus.2477-F-3[NG,RISM,120]; D-Dl Mus.2477-F-3a[RISM;IP]; D-Hs ND VI 2927[RISM]; D-LEu N.I.10286 [a–c][NG,RISM]; F-Pn D-2045/2046/2047[BnF];

---

111. Microfilm copy: F-Pn VM BOB-23046.
112. This and the following source: in D major instead of A major.
113. In A major instead of G major.
114. Microfilm copy: F-Pn VM BOB-25125.
115. In f minor instead of g minor.
116. The aria is the same as in the 1760 version yet in a different key. 1740: E flat major; 1760: F major.
117. This and the following source: in G major instead of D major.
118. In g minor instead of c minor.
119. According to an inscription on the source, the aria was inserted into A3-S5 of an *Artaserse* performed in Bologna. In the libretto from 1745 it appears in A3-S6, yet, as the aria has not been found in the librettos for the other performances in the city, we hypothesise that it belongs to this setting.
120. This and the following source: for Warsaw 1760.

MC | *Artaserse* (1730–1850)

F-Pn X-55/56/57[BnF,NG,RISM,121]; I-Mc Noseda G.8[SBN] [Act I]; I-Mc* Part. Tr.ms. 171[NG,RISM,SBN]; I-MC 3-A-13[NG,RISM] [Acts I&II]; I-Nc* 27.2.10/11[NG,RISM,SBN,122]; P-La 46-IV-55[BA]; P-La 46-V-1/2[BA,NG]; P-La 47-I-20/21/22[BA,NG]; P-La 54-III-65[BA]; US-Wc M1500.H35 A684[IC]

[excerpts] *Conservati fedele* (D-B Am.B 488[RISM]; D-MÜs SANT Hs 1977 [22][RISM]; D-W Cod. Guelf. 301 Mus. Hdschr. [29][RISM]; I-MC 1-B-10/8 [2][RISM]; I-Rama A.Ms.3805 [4][IC,RISM,SBN]; J-Tk S11-225[RISM]; P-La 54-II-65 [1–3][BA;P]; S-Skma T-SE-R[RISM]; US-Wc M1500.H35 A684[RISM]); *Così stupisce e cade* (D-MÜs SANT Hs 1977 [26][RISM]); *Deh, respirar lasciatemi* (B-Bc 4106[NG,RISM]; D-MÜs SANT Hs 1953[RISM,123]; D-MÜs SANT Hs 1977 [27][RISM]; I-MC 2-F-17 [4][RISM]; I-Nc 33.3.18 [6][SBN]; I-Nc Arie 658 [26][SBN]); *Figlio se più non vivi* (B-Bc 4117[NG,RISM]); *Fra cento affanni e cento* (D-MÜs SANT Hs 1977 [28][RISM]); *L'onda dal mar divisa* (P-La 54-II-65 [20–22][BA;P]); *Mi credi spietata?* (D-MÜs SANT Hs 1977 [30][RISM]; I-MC 2-F-15 [23][RISM]; I-MC 2-F-16/12 [1][RISM]; I-Nc 33.2.21 [20][SBN]; J-Tk Tk S11-227[RISM]); *Mi scacci sdegnato!* (D-MÜs SANT Hs 1977 [23][RISM]); *Non temer ch'io mai ti dica* (P-La 54-II-65 [12–14][BA;P]); *Per pietà bell'idol mio* (B-Bc 4144[NG,RISM]; D-MÜs SANT Hs 1977 [25][RISM]; I-Nc 22.3.13 [11][SBN]; I-Nc 33.3.18 [16][SBN]); *Per quel paterno amplesso* (D-Dl Mus.2477-F-110 [54][RISM]; D-MÜs SANT Hs 1977 [29][SBN]; I-Mc Noseda Q.8 [14][SBN]; I-MC 2-A-7 [6][RISM]; I-MC 2-F-14/4 [6][RISM]; I-MC 2-F-15 [27][RISM]; J-Tk S11-224[RISM]; S-Skma Alströmer saml. 156 [38][RISM]; P-La 54-II-65 [15–19][BA;P]); *Se al labbro mio non credi* (B-Bc 4152[NG,RISM,124]; I-Mc Noseda I.93 [19][SBN]; P-La 54-II-65 [9–11][BA;IP]); *Se d'un amor tiranno* (D-MÜs SANT Hs 1977 [24][RISM]); *Se vendetta io chiedo* (D-Hs M A/1567 [1][RISM]); *Sogna il guerrier le schiere* (D-MÜs SANT Hs 1977 [31][RISM]; I-MC 2-F-17 [18][RISM]; P-La 54-II-65 [4–8][BA;P]); *Tu vuoi ch'io viva, o cara* (I-Mc Noseda Q.8 [13][SBN]; I-MC 2-F-14/4 [4][RISM]; I-MC 2-F-14 [6][RISM]; PL-MO 986[IC,125]; US-R n/s [3][IC,RISM])

[contrafacta] *Se al labbro mio non credi* ([*Ave cor sacratum*] F-Sgs M 396[RISM;P])

---

121. Microfilm copy: F-Pn VM BOB-29210.
122. For Naples 1762. [NG] wrongly relates it to Hasse's 1st setting.
123. In B flat major instead of E flat major.
124. In E major instead of A major.
125. [S] references a libretto in PL-MO, yet only this musical source has been located in the printed catalogue of the institution's library.

MC | *Artaserse* (1730–1850)

[inserts] *Se penso al tuo periglio* [*Se al ciglio lusinghiero*][126] (I-MC 2-F-17 [1][RISM])

[doubtful] [excerpts] *Conservati fedele* (I-Mc Noseda O.41 [24][SBN]); *Va' tra le selve ircane* [*Vanne pur tra selve ircane*] (<u>I-Bc FF.244 [16]</u>[IC,RISM,SBN,127]); *Veggo il mio fato con alma forte* (D-Dl Mus.2477-F-110 [7][RISM,128])

Artaserse, in *Opere drammatiche del signor abate Pietro Metastasio romano, poeta cesareo* (Venice: Bettinelli, 1733), vol. 1, pp. 1–74.

1733 — mus. by unknown composer (Bioni, Antonio?[129])
1733 Wrocław — Teatro Ballhaus (summ., Jun.)[130]
pasticcio[131]

Librettos — [Wrocław: s.n., 1733] (It./Ger.)
I-Rsc Carv.1300; PL-WRu Yv 986/2

1733 — mus. by Bambini, Eustachio
1733 Holešov — Rottal Theatre (aut., 15/10/1733)[132]

Librettos — Ollomuzio: Hirnle, 1733
CZ-Bu CH-0008 [893]; CZ-KR N/a IX/2 92; CZ-OLu 601.458

1733 — mus. by unknown composer(s)
1733 Siena — Teatro degli Intronati

Librettos — Pistoia: Gatti, 1733
I-Sc IT-SI0046

---

126. From Hasse's *Siroe* (Bologna, 1733), inserted into his *Artaserse* in the 1734 revival in Venice.
127. The music is different from the other sources. Microfilm copy: I-Bc 3558.
128. For London 1754.
129. The dedication on the libretto is by A. Bioni.
130. Spáčilová, Jana, 'Počátky opery ve Slezsku. Současný stav pramenů', *Musicologica Brunensia*, 51.2 (2016), 157–70.
131. Spáčilová, Jana, *Catalogue of the Italian Opera Libretti in Central Europe in the 1st Half of the 18th Century* (Prague: KLP, forthcoming).
132. Spáčilová, Jana, 'Soloists of the Opera Productions in Brno, Holešov, Kroměříž and Vyškov: Italian Opera Singers in Moravian Sources c. 1720–1740', in *Musicians' Mobilities and Music Migrations in Early Modern Europe: Biographical Patterns and Cultural Exchanges*, ed. by Gesa zur Nieden and Berthold Over (Mainz: Transcript, 2016), pp. 255–74 and Jurášková, Kateřina and Jana Spáčilová, *Italská opera na holešovském zámku v době Františka Antonína Rottala* (Holešov: Město Holešov, 2019).

1734	mus. by Händel, Georg Friedrich and others[133]	
1734 London	King's Theatre in the Haymarket (05/01/1734)[134] *Arbace*	
1734 London	King's Theatre in the Haymarket (26/03/1734)[135]	
Librettos	London: Wood, 1733 (It./En.) F-Pn RES VS 388; GB-En Nha-T49 [4]; GB-Lbl 1342.k.21; US-AUS Ak A100 733a	
Music sources	[complete scores] D-Hs* M A/1004[NG,RISM,136]	
	[excerpts] *Son qual nave che agitata*, by D. Alberti (I-Bc CC.158 [4])[IC,RISM]; US-BEm MS 1380 [6][RISM]	
	[printed sources] Vinci, Leonardo. *Fra cento affanni e cento* [5]; *L'onda dal mar divisa* [1]; *Mi credi spietata?* [2]; *Per quel paterno amplesso* [3]; *Se d'un amor tiranno* [4]; *Son qual nave che agitata* [6], in <u>The Favourite Songs in the Opera call'd Arbaces</u> (London: Walsh, 1734)	
	[inserts from previous versions][137] Vinci, Leonardo, *Amalo e se al tuo sguardo*; *Bramar di perdere*;[138] *Conservati fedele*; *Deh, respirar lasciatemi*; *Figlio se più non vivi*;[139] *Fra cento affanni e cento*; *Giusto re la Persia adora*; *L'onda dal mar divisa*; *Mi credi spietata?*; *Mi scacci sdegnato!*; *Non temer ch'io mai ti dica*;[140] *Non ti son padre, non mi sei figlio*;[141] *Per pietà bell'idol mio*; *Per quell'affetto che l'incatena*;[142] *Per quel paterno amplesso*; *Rendimi il caro amico*; *Se d'un amor tiranno*; *Tu vuoi ch'io viva, o cara* → see 1730, mus. by Vinci, Leonardo Porta, Giovanni [from *Lucio Papirio dittatore*], *Caro padre oh forse è questo il funesto* (US-BEm MS 459 [2])[RISM]; *Di te degno non sarei* (GB-Lbl R.M.23.d.8 [15])[BL,RISM]; GB-Ob Ms. Mus. e.7 [2])[RISM]	

---

133. *Arbace (Artaserse)*: A pasticcio with music by Scarlatti, Alessandro; Händel, Georg Friedrich; Hasse, Johann Adolf; Porta, Giovanni; and Vinci, Leonardo. For a list of the contents of this pasticcio, see Strohm, Reinhard, 'Händels Pasticci', *Analecta Musicologica*, 4 (1974), 208–67.
134. Date in Dumigan, Darryl Jacqueline, 'Nicola Porpora's Operas for the "Opera of the Nobility": The Poetry and the Music' (doctoral dissertation, University of Huddersfield, 2014). Schmidt-Hensel (*'La musica è del Signor Hasse'*, vol. 2, p. 76) gives 29/10/1734.
135. Dumigan, 'Nicola Porpora's Operas', p. 344.
136. Possible autograph.
137. Sources for the operas to which these inserts originally belonged are not included in this catalogue. We list only those related to the London performance of this pasticcio.
138. In G major instead of A major.
139. In G major instead of B flat major.
140. In D major instead of F major.
141. In F major instead of G major.
142. In G major instead of B flat major.

MC | *Artaserse* (1730–1850)

	Hasse, Johann Adolph [from *Issipile*], *Impallidisce in campo*[143] (GB-Lbl Add. 31603[BL,RISM]); *Parto se vuoi così*[144] (GB-Lbl Add. 31603[BL,RISM]; GB-Ob Ms. Mus. e.10 [4][RISM,145]; GB-Ob Ms. Mus. e.11 [9][RISM])
[unspecified]	[complete scores] DK-Kk MA ms 9373[IC,146]
[supposed]	I-FAN[NG]

1734	mus. by Giacomelli, Geminiano[CA]	
1734 Pisa	Teatro Pubblico (02/02/1734)	

1734	mus. by unknown composer(s)	
1734 Valencia	Palacio Real (25/10/1734)	
	birthday of Isabel Farnesio, queen of Spain	
Librettos	Valencia: Bordazar, [1734] (It./Spa.)	
	E-Bbc 1-I-84 [1]	

1734	mus. by Hasse, Johann Adolph; Porpora, Nicola; and Broschi, Riccardo lib. rev. by Lalli, Domenico and Boldini, Giovanni	
1734 London	King's Theatre in the Haymarket (29/10/1734)	(1)
1735 London	King's Theatre in the Haymarket (28/12/1734)[147]	
1735 London	King's Theatre in the Haymarket (15/03/1735)[148]	
1735 London	King's Theatre in the Haymarket (17/05/1735)	
1736 London	King's Theatre in the Haymarket (03/01/1736)	(2)
1736 London	King's Theatre in the Haymarket (27/03/1736)	
1736 London	King's Theatre in the Haymarket (01/06/1736)	
Librettos	(1) London: Bennet, 1734 (It./En.)[149]	
	GB-Cfm [GB-Cu] MU.1343.C; GB-Cfm [GB-Cu] MR463.d.70 [29]; GB-Lbl 11714.aa.21.12 [12];[150] GB-Owc XZA.6.28 [6]; <u>I-Fn MAGL.21.8.108</u>	

---

143. In G major instead of F major.
144. In C major instead of B flat major.
145. This and the following source: in F major instead of C major.
146. According to [IC], an *Artaserse* by Alessandro Scarlatti.
147. [C] only mentions Hasse as the composer, but it seems likely that this production is a revival of the pasticcio by Hasse, Porpora, and Broschi premiered in the same theatre two months earlier. See also Dumigan, 'Nicola Porpora's Operas', pp. 44–54.
148. For this and the following dates, see Dumigan, 'Nicola Porpora's Operas', pp. 343–49.
149. [E,S] list a further copy in the Victoria and Albert Theatre Museum, closed since 2007; see [S]2944.
150. Two copies; microfilm reproductions: D-Gs MA 83-57:1530 [42]; GB-En Mf.134, reel 1530 [42]; GB-Ob Fils ESTC (18th C.; reel 1530 [42]).

(2) London: Bennet, 1735 (It./En.)
GB-Bp 782.12 Plays B/42; GB-Lbl 639.d.22 [2];[151] I-NOVc CIV 194.H.24

Music sources [excerpts]
Broschi, Riccardo, *In sen mi tace smarrito il core* (B-Bc 5498 [2][RISM]; D-LEm Becker III.15.47 [5][RISM]; GB-Cfm [GB-Cu] MU.MS.633[IC]; I-Rama A.Ms.3721 [2][IC,RISM]); *Pallido il sole* (D-LEm Becker III.15.47 [6][RISM]; I-MC 3-E-14/4 [3][RISM,152]; I-Nc 33.2.22 [3][SBN]); *Se al labbro mio non credi* (B-Bc 5498 [3][RISM]; D-LEm Becker III.15.47 [4][RISM]; GB-Cfm [GB-Cu] MU.MS.633[IC]; GB-Lam MS 138 [29][RISM]; I-Rama A.Ms.3721 [4][IC,RISM]); *Son qual nave che agitata* (D-B Mus.ms. 5773 [3][RISM]; D-LEm Becker III.15.47 [1][RISM]; F-Pn D-247 [4][BnF,RISM,153]; GB-G MUS 432 [27][RISM]; I-Rama A.Ms.3721 [8][IC,RISM]; S-Skma T-SE-R[RISM]; US-BEm MS 15 [16][RISM]; US-CA 2237.658.12.2[IC])

[printed sources] *Se al labbro mio non credi*, in *Se al labro mio non credi. A Favorite Song* (London: Cahusac, [s.d.])

In sen mi tace smarrito il core [5]; *Pallido il sole* [6]; *Se al labbro mio non credi* [4]; *Son qual nave che agitata* [1], in <u>The Favourite Songs in the Opera call'd Artaxerxes by Sig. Hasse</u> (London: Walsh, [1734])

[doubtful] *Fra cento affanni e cento*[154] (A-LA 781[RISM;IP]; A-LA 1925[RISM;IP]; S-Skma T-SE-R[RISM]; US-BEm MS 27 [6][RISM])

Porpora, Nicola, *Fortunate passate mie pene* (B-Bc 5498 [5][RISM,155]; D-LEm Becker III.15.47 [8][RISM]; GB-ABu POWELL M1529.3.W3[IC,MGG]; GB-Lam MS 138 [30][RISM]; GB-Lbl R.M.23.d.8 [2][BL,RISM]; GB-Ob Harding Mus. G.O.55 [53][IC]; GB-Ob Harding Mus. G.O.56 [49][IC]); *Or la nube procellosa* (B-Bc 5498 [1][RISM]; D-LEm Becker III.15.47 [3][RISM]; D-SWl Mus.2489[RISM;P]; GB-Cfm [GB-Cu] MU.MS.633[IC]); *Quanto affanno bell'aurora* (B-Bc 5498 [6][RISM]; D-LEm Becker III.15.47 [2][RISM]; GB-Lbl Add. 29965 [5][BL,RISM]; I-Rama A.Ms.3721 [7][IC,RISM]; S-Skma T-SE-R[RISM]); *Tu vuoi ch'io viva, o cara* (GB-Lbl R.M.23.f.2 [20][BL,RISM])

[printed sources] *Fortunate passate* [16], in *Gemme d'antichitá, raccolta di pezzi vocali composti dai più celebri maestri antichi*, vol. 1 (London: Lonsdale, [s.d.]); in *A Favourite Minuet Sung by*

---

151. Microfilm copies: D-Gs MA 2004-14:15150 [7]; GB-En Mf.134, reel 15150 [7]; GB-Lbl PB.Mic.4410.
152. This and the following source: wrongly attributed to Hasse on source.
153. Microfilm copy: F-Pn VM BOB-23028.
154. The aria is not included in the libretto for this pasticcio.
155. Wrongly attributed to Ariosti, who set to music Haym's – not Metastasio's – *Artaserse* (London, 1724).

Sigr. Senesino in Artaxerxes: with English Words (London: [s.n., 1734?]); *Or la nube procellosa* [6]; *Quanto affanno bell'aurora* [1], in *Farinelli's Celebrated Songs [...]* (London: Walsh, [1737])[156]
Fortunate passate mie pene [8]; *Or la nube procellosa* [3]; *Quanto affanno bell'aurora* [2], in <u>*The Favourite Songs in the Opera call'd Artaxerxes by Sig. Hasse*</u> (London: Walsh, [1734])

Hasse, Johann Adolph Hasse, *In sen mi tace*; *Lascia cadermi in volto*; *Pallido il sole*; *Per questo dolce amplesso* → see 1730, mus. by Hasse, Johann Adolph

[printed sources] *Per questo dolce amplesso* [17], in *Gemme d'antichitá, raccolta di pezzi vocali composti dai più celebri maestri antichi*, vol. 1 (London: Lonsdale, [s.d.]); [7], in <u>*The Favourite Songs in the Opera call'd Artaxerxes by Sig. Hasse*</u> (London: Walsh, [1734]); *Fortunate passate* [7]; *In sen mi tace* [2]; *Lascia cadermi in volto* [5]; *Per questo dolce amplesso* [4]; *Se al labbro mio non credi* [3], in *Farinelli's Celebrated Songs [...]* (London: Walsh, [1737])

1737	mus. by Poncini Zilioli, Francesco	
1737 Parma	Teatro Ducale (carn., 2nd opera of the season)	
Librettos	Parma: Monti, [1737] I-Bc Lo.04312	
Music sources	[excerpts] *Conservati fedele* (B-Bc 5076^{RISM}); *Nuvoletta opposta al sole* (B-Bc 5077^{RISM})	

1737	mus. by Paganelli, Giuseppe Antonio	
1737 Brunswick	Teatro Ducale (win. Fair) 1st version	(1)
1737 Brunswick	Teatro Ducale (summ. Fair) *Artaxerse*	(2,3)
1742 Venice	Teatro Vendramin di S. Salvatore (Asc., 02/05/1742)[157] mus. by G. A. Paganelli and others[158] 2nd version	(4)

---

156. Reference to this printed source found in Burden, Michael, 'Metastasio on the London Stage, 1728 to 1840: A Catalogue', *Royal Musical Association Research Chronicle*, 40 (2007), 1–332.
157. Date in Selfridge-Field, *A New Chronology of Venetian Opera*, pp. 477–78 n. 1742/5. However, on p. 656 she states that the carnival season of that year in Venice started on 3 May.
158. Given that some arias by Andrea Adolfati have been preserved (see below), [NG] hypothesises about a complete version by him performed in an unspecified city around 1741. However, we follow Selfridge-Field (*A New*

MC | *Artaserse* (1730–1850)

Librettos   (1) Wolfenbüttel: Bartsch, [1737] (It./Ger.)
D-W Textb. 326

(2) Wolfenbüttel: Bartsch, [1737] (It./Ger.)
D-BS Brosch. I 20.585; D-WRz O 8: 32

(3) Wolfenbüttel: Bartsch, [1737] (Ger.)
D-BS Brosch. I 20.558; D-HVl Op.1,162b; D-W Textb. 327; D-WRz O 8: 31

(4) Venice: Rossetti, [1742]
I-Mb Racc.dramm.3728; I-Rsc Carv.1301; I-Vcg LIBRETTI S. SALVATORE 96; I-Vnm DRAMM.1058 [9]; I-Vnm DRAMM.1255 [6]; I-Vnm DRAMM.3570 [6]; US-LAum ML48 .R114 1742 [9]; US-Wc ML48 [S7572]

Music sources

1st version: 1737, Brunswick

    [excerpts] *Se al labbro mio non credi* (D-ROu Mus. Saec. XVIII:6 [1]$^{RISM;IP}$)

2nd version: 1742, Venice

    [excerpts] Adolfati, Andrea, *Conservati fedele* (US-CHH* VFM3.1.A36 1750z [9]^{MGG,RISM,159}); *Vo solcando un mar crudele* (US-CHH* VFM3.1.A36 1750z [31]^{MGG,RISM})

1737	mus. by Schiassi, Gaetano Maria	
1737 Lisbon	Academy on the Trinità Square	

Librettos   Lisbon: da Fonseca, 1737 (It./Port.)
BR-Rn A-XV,A784; P-Cug 4-26-5-21; P-Ln M. 3260//2 V.[160]

1738	mus. by Araia, Francesco	
1738 St Petersburg	Court theatre – Winter Palace (09/02/1738)[161]	(1)
1738 St Petersburg	Court theatre – Winter Palace (01/05/1738)[162]	(2)
	Empress Anna Ioannovna's coronation anniversary	

Chronology of Venetian Opera) and relate them to Paganelli's 2nd setting of *Artaserse*, in which arias by other composers were inserted.
159. This and the following source: possible autographs.
160. Microfilm copy: P-Ln F.6812.
161. Contrarily to ^{C} and ^{CA}, Giust, Anna, 'Towards Russian Opera: Growing National Consciousness in 18th-Century Operatic Repertoire' (doctoral dissertation, Università degli Studi di Padova, 2012) gives 29/01/1738 as the premiere date of Araia's *Artaserse*.
162. Giust, 'Towards Russian Opera', p. 49.

MC | *Artaserse* (1730–1850)

Librettos	(1) St Petersburg: Imperial Academy of the Sciences, [1738] (It./Ger.)	
	D-WRz O 8: 33;[163] RUS-SPtob[S]	
	(2) NA	
Music sources	[excerpts] *Pallido il sole* (S-L Saml.Engelhart 575[RISM;P])	

1738	**mus. by Scalabrini, Paolo and others**	
1738 Graz	Theater am Tummel-Plaz (spr., 04/1738)[164]	(1)
1741 Wrocław	Teatro Ballhaus[165]	(2)
1743 Hamburg	Oper am Gänsemarkt (aut., 13/11/1743)	(3)
1744 Prague	Teatro Nuovo (carn.)	(4)
1746 Dresden	Nuovo Teatro Privilegiato (22/08/1746)[166]	(5)
1746 Hamburg	Oper am Gänsemarkt? (14/10/1746)	(6)
1749 Copenhagen	Court theatre – Charlottenborg Palace (29/01/1749)	(7,8)

Librettos   (1) Graz: heirs of Widmanstadj, [1738] (It./Ger.)
A-Gl [C]688[I]; A-Gu I 57639; A-Wgm 9082/Textbücher

(2) NA

(3) Hamburg: Spiering, [1743] (It./Ger.)
D-B 3 Mus. T 8 [3];[167] D-BÜ[S]; D-Hs A/2620; D-W Textb. 227[168]

(4) Prague: [s.n., 1744] (It./Ger.)
CZ-Pnm B 4136

(5) Dresden: [s.n., 1746] (It./Ger.)
D-Dl MT.1470; D-Dl MT.1936 [2]; D-Mbs P.o.it. 630; RUS-Mrg MK 50-8419143; RUS-Mrg MK 50-8685645; US-CAt TS 8056.713 1740; US-Wc ML48 [S10744][169]

(6) Hamburg: Spiering, 1746 (It./Ger.)
D-DEsa ALW *HB 29989

---

163. Microfilm copies: CDN-Lu ML48.M47A498 1787a; D-WRz M 536; US-CAt Film W 23673.181.20.
164. Although traditionally related to Hasse's setting ([C,S]), Strohm identifies it with the version by Scalabrini that the Mingotti troupe performed in German territories in the late 1730s and the 1740s; see Strohm, Reinhard, 'Metastasio at Hamburg: Newly-Identified Opera Scores of the Mingotti Company, with a Postscript on *Ercole nell'Indie*', in *Il canto di Metastasio. Atti del convegno di studi, Venezia (14–16 dicembre 1999)*, ed. by Maria Giovanna Miggiani (Bologna: Forni, 2004), pp. 541–71.
165. Müller, Erich Hermann, *Angelo und Pietro Mingotti. Ein Beitrag zur Geschichte der Oper im XVIII. Jahrhundert* (Dresden: Bertling, 1917).
166. Strohm, 'Metastasio at Hamburg'.
167. Microfilm reproduction under the same call number.
168. Old call number: Gräflick Schulenburgische Bibñliothel Km 2 [5]; see Thiel, Eberhard, *Kataloge der Herzog August Bibliothek Wolfenbüttel. Libretti. Verzeichnis der bis 1800 erschienenen Textbücher* (Frankfurt am Main: Klostermann, 1970).
169. Microfilm copy: US-I Film 25.

(7) Copenhagen: Berling, [1749] (It./Ger.)
DK-Kk Rom. 16045 4°; US-Wc ML48 [S9515]

(8) Copenhagen: [s.n., 1749] (It./ Dan.)
B-Br Fétis 4.520 A IX,14 Mus.

Music sources [complete scores] I-MOe Mus. F. 1585[IC,170]

[excerpts] *Conservati fedele* (D-Hs ND VI 81 g: 11 [82][RISM]); *Destrier che all'armi usato* (DK-Kk mu7502.1738[IC,RISM]); *Figlio se più non vivi* (DK-KK mu7502.0233[RISM]); *Va' tra le selve ircane* (DK-Kk mu7502.1739[IC,RISM]; D-SWl Mus.188[RISM;IP])

1738	mus. by Brivio, Giuseppe Ferdinando	
1738 Padua	Teatro Obizzi (20/05/1738)	(1)
	visit of Maria Amalia, queen of the Two Sicilies	
	1st version	
1742 London	King's Theatre in the Haymarket (12/12/1742)	(2)
	Mandane (pasticcio)	
	2nd version	

Librettos (1) Padua: Conzatti, 1738
A-Gu 211 H. 15; D-Mbs P.o.it. 629; I-Rsc Carv.1302; I-Vcg LIBRETTI PADOVA 57 E 63; I-Vnm DRAMM.1122. [2]; US-Wc ML48 [S1325]

(2) London: Wood, 1742 (It./En.)
GB-Lbl 907.i.4 [1]

Music sources
1st version: 1738, Padua

[excerpts] *Così stupisce e cade* (F-Pn D-1481 [7][BnF,MGG,RISM]); *Spero in van che questo* (F-Pn D-1481 [8][BnF,MGG,RISM])

1738	mus. by unknown composer and Zamparelli, Dionisio[171]	
1738 Livorno[172]	Teatro da S. Sebastiano (spr.)	(1)
1760 Livorno	Teatro da S. Sebastiano (carn., 26/12/1759)	(2)

Librettos (1) Lucca: Marescandoli, [1738]
I-Bc Lo.05600

---

170. For Hamburg 1746.
171. According to the librettos, D. Zamparelli wrote the recitatives and some of the arias.
172. [NG] lists an *Artaserse* by Zamparelli in 1731, yet no records to support this date have been found; see [NG] 'Metastasio [Trapassi], Pietro (Antonio Domenico Bonaventura) / Artaserse'.

MC | *Artaserse* (1730–1850)

	(2) Livorno: Fantechi & co., 1759	
	NA[173]	

1739	mus. by Ferrandini, Giovanni Battista and others (incl. Porta, Giovanni)	
1739 Munich	Court theatre (22/10/1739)	(1)
	birthday of Maria Amalia, electress of Bavaria	
1752 Forlì	Teatro Pubblico	(2)
1754 Barcelona	Teatre de la Santa Creu (late aut.)	(3)
	Artaxerxes, rey de Persia	

Librettos	(1) Munich: Vötter, [1739]
	D-BHu 73/LQ 43100 F372 A7.739; <u>I-Bc Lo.01611</u>; I-Mb Racc. dramm.3732
	(2) Bologna: Franceschi, [1752]
	<u>I-Bc Lo.01612</u>
	(3) Barcelona: Campins, [1754] (It./Spa.)[174]
Music sources	[complete scores] <u>D-Dl Mus.3037-F-2</u>[MGG,NG,RISM]; <u>D-Dl Mus.3037-F-2a</u>[MGG,NG,RISM;IP]

1739	mus. by unknown composer(s)
1739 Vienna	Teatro Privilegiato

Librettos	Vienna: van Ghelen, [1739] (It./Ger.)
	I-Mb Racc.dramm.1180

1740	mus. by unknown composer(s)
1740 Catania	Teatro dell'Alma Università delli Studi (carn.)
1741 Catania	Teatro dell'Alma Università delli Studi (carn.)

Librettos	Catania: Bisagni, 1742
	I-CATu Ant.D.234.1

---

173. ˢ3042 lists a copy in I-Mc, but it cannot be found in the original card catalogue of the library of the Conservatorio de Milano, handwritten by Sartori. We therefore consider it as lost.
174. Cited by Cotarelo y Mori, Emilio, *Orígenes y establecimiento de la ópera en España hasta 1800* (Madrid: Revista de arch., bibl. y museos, 1917). See also Alier y Aixalà, Roger, *L'òpera a Barcelona: orígens, desenvolupament i consolidació de l'òpera com a espectacle teatral a la Barcelona del segle XVIII* (Barcelona: Institut d'Estudis Catalans, 1990).

1740	mus. by Hasse, Johann Adolph (2nd version) → see 1730

1741	mus. by Chiarini, Pietro	
1741 Verona	Teatro Filarmonico (carn.)	(1)
1742 Genoa	Teatro da S. Agostino (carn.)	(2)
	pasticcio[175]	
1749 Cremona	Private theatre (carn.)	(3)

Librettos
(1) Verona: Ramanzini, [1741]
I-Rsc Vol. Carv.100 [3]; US-Wc ML48 [S1854]

(2) Genoa: Franchelli, [1742]
I-Gc B.S.Misc.A.25.11; I-Rsc Carv.1304

(3) Brescia: Turlino, [1749]
F-Pn 8-YTH-50037; I-LDEsormani 302/7/10; I-PLZc E.IV.I05

Music sources
[excerpts] *Fra cento affanni e cento* (I-Gl A.1.4 [8][IC,MGG,NG,SBN])

1741	mus. by Arena, Giuseppe	
1741 Turin	Teatro Regio (carn., 21/01/1741)[176]	(1,2)

Librettos
(1) Turin: Zappata & son, [1741]
I-Bc Lo.00301; I-Rsc Vol. Carv.142 [4]; I-Tac BCT L.O.106; I-Tci L.O.0106; I-Tn C.SAN 486 [7]; I-Tn F VII.354 [2]; I-Tn F XIII.520 [2]; US-Wc ML48 [S308]

(2) Turin: Zappata & son, 1741 (Fr.)
I-Tac Simeom L 30; US-AUS KL-17 81

Music sources
[excerpts] *Bramar di perdere* (B-Bc 3677[RISM]); *Conservati fedele* (I-Tf 1 I 1 [2][MGG,RISM;R]); *Così stupisce e cade* (B-Bc 3679[RISM]); *Figlio se più non vivi* (B-Bc 3682[RISM]; I-MC 6-D-11 [22][RISM]); *Fra cento affanni e cento* (B-Bc 3683[RISM]); *Per quel paterno amplesso* (I-Tf 1 I 1 [4][MGG,RISM;R]; I-Tf 2 IV 4[MGG,RISM]); *Quel nobile accento* (I-Tf 1 I 1 [3][MGG,RISM;R]); *Se d'un amor tiranno* (D-RH MS 24 [1][RISM;P]; F-Pn VM4-844[BnF,RISM]; I-Mc Noseda Q.40 [7][MGG,SBN]); *Tu vuoi ch'io viva, o cara* (F-Pn D-15425[BnF,RISM]; I-Tf 1 I 1 [5][MGG,RISM;R])

---

175. See <https://www.pasticcio-project.eu/database/work/P103EE9> [accessed 25 May 2022].
176. The production ran for twenty-two consecutive performances; see Bouquet, Marie-Thérèse, Valeria Gualerzi, and Alberto Testa, *Storia del Teatro Regio di Torino: cronologie*, ed. by Alberto Basso (Turin: Cassa di Risparmio di Torino, [1988]).

MC | *Artaserse* (1730–1850)

1742	mus. by Gluck, Christoph Willibald	
1742 Milan	Teatro Regio Ducale (carn., 26/12/1741)	
Librettos	Milan: Malatesta, 1741	
	B-Bc 19311; GB-Lbl Music Collections Tyson P.B.11 [1]; I-Bc Lo.02224; I-LDEsormani 297/7/19; I-Ma S. I. H. I. 5 [2]; I-Mb Racc.dramm.6059 [1]; I-Mr Libr. 02788; I-Ms MUS. G. XXVIII. 1	
Music sources	[excerpts] *Mi scacci sdegnato!* (A-Wgm VI 15148 [Q 21087]^{IC,MGG}; CH-BEl SLA-Mus-JL MLHs 34 [2]^{MGG,NG,RISM}); *Se del fiume altera l'onda* (CH-BEl SLA-Mus-JL MLHs 29 [3]$^{MGG,NG,RISM;P}$; CH-BEl SLA-Mus-JL MLHs 33 [15]^{MGG,NG,RISM}; F-Pn D-4586^{BnF}; GB-Lbl Add. 31632 [9]^{BL,MGG,NG,RISM})	
	[unspecified] B-Bc 12800^{IC,MGG,177}	

1742	mus. by Paganelli, Giuseppe Antonio (2nd version) → see 1737	

1742	mus. by Brivio, Giuseppe Ferdinando (2nd version) → see 1738	

1743	mus. by Graun, Carl Heinrich	
	lib. rev. by Lalli, Domenico	
1743 Berlin	Court theatre (02/12/1743)	(1)
1744 Berlin	Court theatre (21/07/1744)[178]	(2)
	wedding of Princess Ulrike and the Prince of Sweden Adolf Frederik	
1745 Brunswick	Teatro Ducale (win. Fair)	(3)
	Artabanus	
1750 Stuttgart	Teatro Ducale (30/08/1750)	(4)
	birthday of the Duchess of Württemberg and Teck	
1751 Stuttgart	Teatro Ducale (carn.)	(5)
1783 Berlin	Court theatre (27/12/1782)[179]	(6)
Librettos	(1) Berlin: Haude, 1743 (It./Ger.)	
	D-Au 02/III.10.8.292; D-B 169643; D-Hs A/34173 [2]; D-HR [D-Au] 02/III.10.8.292; D-ROu Ck-554; D-W Textb. 183; PL-Wu GSD 28.20.4.5882 [1]	
	(2) NA	

---

177. Scanned copy.
178. Sprague, 'A Comparison of Five Musical Settings', p. 82.
179. The production ran for five consecutive performances; see Henzel, Christoph, *Berliner Klassik* (Beeskow: ortus, 2009).

(3) Wolfenbüttel: Bartsch, [1745] (It./Ger.)
D-BS Brosch. I 20.549; D-HVl Op. 1, 188[180]

(4) Stuttgart: Cotta, [c. 1750]
D-Au 02/III.10.4.37; D-HEu G 2811-3 RES [8]; D-HR [D-Au] 02/III.10.4.37; D-Sl Fr.D.qt.192[181]

(5) Stuttgart: Cotta, [1751] (It./Ger.)
US-Wc ML48 [S4090]

(6) Berlin: Haude & Spener, 1783 (It./Ger.)
D-B Mus. Tg 867

Music sources   [complete scores] D-B Am.B 189[RISM]; D-B* Mus.ms.autogr. Graun, C. H. 9[RISM]; D-B Mus.ms. 8211[RISM]; D-B Mus.ms. 8211/1[IC,RISM]; D-B Mus.ms. 8211/2[IC,RISM]; D-DS Mus.ms 372[RISM]; D-W Cod. Guelf. 81 Mus. Hdschr.[RISM]; GB-En n/s[IC]; S-Skma T-R[RISM]; S-Skma T-R Ej hemlån[IC,RISM] [act I]

[excerpts] *Conservati fedele* (D-DS Mus.ms 1386 [1][RISM;R]; D-Hs ND VI 28 [33][RISM;R]); *Del suo gran padre* (D-Bsa [D-B] SA 999[RISM;R]; D-HER Mus.L 120 [1][RISM;P]; DK-Ch (Christiansfeld No. 6) [3][RISM;P]); *Empio... chi sà... vorrei* (S-Skma T-SE-R[RISM;P]); *Figlio se più non vivi* (D-B Mus.ms. 8211/8[RISM;P]; D-B Mus.ms. 8211/9[RISM;R]; D-KA Don Mus.Ms. 180 [2][RISM;P]); *Fra cento affanni e cento* (D-Dl Mus.1-F-124 [15][RISM;IP]; D-Dl Mus.2953-F-10 [3][RISM]; D-DS Mus.ms 1386 [2][RISM;R]); *Mi credi spietata?* (D-B Mus.ms. 8252/5[RISM;P]); *Non è ver che sia contento* (D-DS Mus.ms 1386 [8][RISM;R]; D-Hs ND VI 28 [28][RISM;R]; D-RH Ms 270 [2][RISM;P]); *Non temer ch'io mai ti dica* (D-Mbs Mus.ms. 5003[RISM;IP]; D-W Cod. Guelf. 314 Mus. Hdschr. [33][RISM;R]); *Pensa che l'amor mio* (D-KA Don Mus.Ms. 180 [1][RISM;P]); *Per pietà bell'idol mio* (D-DS Mus.ms 1386 [4][RISM;R]; S-Skma T-SE-R[RISM;P]); *Per quel paterno amplesso* (D-Dl Mus.1-F-124 [14][RISM;IP]; D-Dl Mus.2953-F-10 [2][RISM]; D-RH Ms 268 [2][RISM;P]; *Rendimi il caro amico* (D-DS Mus.ms 1386 [7][RISM;R]); *Se al labbro mio non credi* (D-B Mus.ms. 8252/3[RISM;P]; S-Skma T-SE-R[RISM;P]); *Se un altro amor m'accende* (D-DS Mus.ms 1386 [5][RISM;P]; D-Hs ND VI 28 [31][RISM;R]; PL-Wu RM 4426/5 [2][RISM;IP]); *Sogna il guerrier le schiere* (D-DS Mus.ms 1386 [6][RISM;R]; D-Hs ND VI 28 [32][RISM;R,P]); *Speravo col mi sdegno* (D-Dl Mus.1-F-124 [18][RISM;IP]; D-Dl Mus.2953-F-10 [6][RISM]; S-Skma T-SE-R[RISM;P]); *Su le sponde del torbido Lete* (D-Dl Mus.1-F-124 [17][RISM;IP]; D-Dl Mus.2953-F-10 [5][RISM];

---

180. Microfilm copies: D-HVl MASTER 494; D-HVl Mifi 2746.
181. Microfilm copy: D-Sl R 18 Met 1.

D-DS Mus.ms 1386 [3]$^{RISM;R}$; D-Hs ND VI 28 [26]$^{RISM;R}$; D-Hs ND VI 28 [34]$^{RISM;R}$; PL-Wu RM 4426/5 [1]$^{RISM;IP}$; S-Skma T-SE-R$^{RISM;P}$); *Tra l'odio d'amore incerto* (D-Dl Mus.1-F-124 [16]$^{RISM;IP}$; D-Dl Mus.2953-F-10 [4]^{RISM}; D-RH Ms 268 [1]$^{RISM;P}$; D-W Cod. Guelf. 314 Mus. Hdschr. [41]$^{RISM;R}$; S-Skma T-SE-R$^{RISM;P}$); *Tu vuoi ch'io viva, o cara* (D-Dl Mus.1-F-28,10a [1]$^{RISM;IP}$; D-RH Ms 269$^{RISM;P}$; D-Sla 115$^{RISM;P}$); *Va' tra le selve ircane* (D-Dl Mus.1-F-124 [13]$^{RISM;IP}$; D-Dl Mus.2953-F-10 [1]^{RISM}; S-Skma T-SE-R$^{RISM;P}$; S-Uu Vok. mus. i hs. 76:6$^{RISM;R,P}$)

[printed sources] *Del suo gran padre* [2], in *Duetti, terzetti, quintetti, sestetti ed alcuni chori delle opere del signore Carlo Enrico Graun*, vol. 4 (Berlin: Decker & Hartung, 1774)

[contrafacta] *Conservati fedele* ([Mit demutsvollen Lippen begrüß ich deine Krippen] D-B Mus.ms. 8290 (3) [2]^{RISM}); *Del suo gran padre* ([Gaudeamus omnes in Domino, diem festum celebrantes sub honore] CZ-Pnm XXXVIII A 392$^{RISM;P}$; [Auf frohe Christen singt freudige Lieder] D-B Mus.ms. 8290 (3) [1]^{RISM}; [Sie werden kommen von Ferne] D-HER Mus.E 29:4 [1]$^{RISM;P}$; PL-Wu RM 6793$^{RISM;P}$); *Figlio se più non vivi* ([Ach liebster Gott – Non lugete mentes humana – Omni die dic Mariae, mea laudes anima] PL-Wu RM 4418 [7]$^{RISM;P}$; [Valete mundi honores] PL-Wu RM 4399 [2]$^{RISM;R,P}$); *Giusto re la Persia adora* ([Lobet Gott, den Herrn der Erden] D-B Mus.ms. 8290 (3) [4]^{RISM}); *Mi credi spietata?* ([Med omsorg och möda] S-Skma Alströmer saml. 155 [2]^{RISM}; S-Skma Ro:85$^{RISM;R}$); *Non è ver che sia contento* ([Alexander ter beate] CZ-Pak 416$^{RISM;P}$; [Salve regina, mater misericordiae vita dulcedo] F-Sgs M 397$^{RISM;IP}$); *Non temer ch'io mai ti dica* ([Clara voce cantabo Deo meo] D-Mbs Mus.ms. 5003 b$^{RISM;P}$); *Parto qual pastorello* ([Caeli ma lacis Olympi gratis] PL-Wu RM 4402$^{RISM;P}$; [Ave maris stella] PL-SA 472/A VIII 112$^{RISM;P}$); *Per pietà bell'idol mio* ([Hjälpen mig mit öde sörja] S-N Finspong 1130$^{RISM;R}$; S-Skma T/Sv.-R [2]^{RISM}; S-Uu Vok. mus. i hs. 54:29 [1]^{RISM}); *Per quel paterno amplesso* ([Martyr paterna manu te pie mens] CZ-OSm A 1923 [1]$^{RISM;P}$; PL-SA 39/A I 39 [1]$^{RISM;P}$; [Regina caeli, laetare alleluia] CZ-Pak 427 [1]$^{RISM;P}$); *Se d'un alto amor m'accende* ([In mari placato jubilant] PL-Wu RM 4416 [1]$^{RISM;P}$); *Tra l'odio d'amore incerto* ([Ach veni mi Jesu noli tardare] D-Mbs Mus.ms. 4993 [2]$^{RISM;P}$; [Mit freudigen Zungen] D-B Mus.ms. 8290 (3) [3]^{RISM}; [Te mi Jesu non cessabo plorare adorare] PL-Wu RM 5376 [2]$^{RISM;P}$); *Tu vuoi ch'io viva, o cara* ([Ave cordis solamen] CZ-Pak 434 [1]$^{RISM;P}$; [Ihr werdet singen wie zur Nacht] D-HER Mus.K 100 [9]$^{RISM;R}$; D-HER Mus.K 215 [4]$^{RISM;P}$; [O Heros invincibilis] PL-Wu RM 4419 [2]$^{RISM;P}$)

[doubtful][182] *Come un amico, oh dio* (DK-Kk mu6410.2031[IC,RISM;P]); *Se del fiume altera l'onda* (S-Skma T-SE-R[RISM;P])

1744	mus. by Duni, Egidio Romualdo
1744 Florence	Teatro della Pergola (carn., 23/01/1744)
Librettos	Florence: Pieri, [1744]
	I-Vgc ROL.0278 [2]
Music sources	[supposed] two arias in D-ROu[MGG,NG]

1744	mus. by Terradellas, Domingo
1744 Venice	Teatro Grimani di S. Giovanni Grisostomo (carn., 06/02/1744)[183]
Librettos	Venice: [s.n., 1744]
	E-Bbc CD 6648; E-Bbc CD 6830; F-Pn 8-YTH-51989; I-Bc Lo.08089; I-Mb Racc.dramm.3787; I-Nc Rari 10.5.26 [4]; I-Pmc[S]; I-Rn 40.9.E.14.9; I-Rsc Carv.1306; I-RVI Silv., op. 789; I-Vcg LIBRETTI S.GIO.GRISOSTOMO 158; I-Vnm DRAMM.1061 [4]; I-Vnm DRAMM.1258 [11]; I-Vnm DRAMM.3572 [4]; US-LAum ML48 .R114 1744 [4]; US-Wc ML48 [S10283]
Music sources	[complete scores] I-Vnm Mss. 10004[IC,MGG,SBN]
	[excerpts] *Bramar di perdere* (D-Dl Mus.1-F-28,5 [5][RISM]; F-Pn D-8940 [2][BnF]; I-Vqs MS Cl.VIII.14 (1128) [56][NG,RISM]; RUS-Mrg Ф.954 N°134–138 [5][RISM;IP]); *Conservati fedele* (CH-E 694,10 [3][RISM]; F-Pn D-8940 [3][BnF]; F-Pn L-20012[BnF;P]; GB-Lbl Add. 31624[RISM]; I-Vqs MS Cl.VIII.14 (1128) [55][NG,RISM,SBN;R]; S-Skma T-SE-R[RISM]); *Deh, respirar lasciatemi* (F-Pn L-20007[BnF;P]; GB-Cfm [GB-Cu] MU.MS.145 [14][IC]; GB-Lbl 31624 [13][BL,RISM]); *Dimmi che un empio sei* (F-Pn D-8940 [7][BnF]); *Io son quel pellegrino* (A-Wn Mus.Hs.17033 [3][IC]; D-KNmi R 613 R [10][RISM]; SI-Mpa SI_PAM/1857[RISM,184]); *L'augellin che in lacci stretto* (F-Pn D-8940 [1][BnF]; F-Pn L-20005[BnF]; I-Vqs MS Cl.VIII.14 (1128) [54][NG,RISM;R]); *L'onda del mar divisa* (GB-AY D/DR/10/6c [1][RISM;P,185]; GB-Lbl Add. 31624 [3][BL,RISM]); *Mi credi spietata?* (CH-Bu kr IV 382 [9][RISM;P]; D-Dl Mus.1-F-28,5 [6][RISM]; F-Pn D-8940 [4][BnF]; I-Vqs MS Cl.VI-

---

182. These arias are not included in the original libretto for the premiere.
183. [CA] dates the premiere of D. Terradellas' *Artaserse* on 26/12/1743, as the first opera of the carnival season. We follow Selfridge-Field, *A New Chronology of Venetian Opera*, p. 487 n. 1744/3.
184. In E flat major instead of F major.
185. Incomplete: the piece breaks off at the foot of fol. [3ᵛ].

II.14 (1128) [57]^{NG,RISM,SBN};^{R}; RUS-Mrg Φ.954 N°134–138 [6]$^{RISM;IP}$); *Per pietà bell'idol mio* (<u>D-Dl Mus.1-F-28,3 [9]</u>^{RISM}; I-Mc Noseda P.34 [2]^{MGG,NG,SBN}); *Per quel paterno amplesso* (<u>D-Dl Mus.1-F-28,5 [8]</u>^{RISM}; F-Pn D-8940 [6]^{BnF}; F-Pn L-20006$^{BnF;IP}$; S-Skma T-SE-R^{RISM}; S-Skma T-SE-R$^{RISM;P}$; RUS-Mrg Φ.954 N°134–138 [8]$^{RISM;IP}$); *Se d'un amor tiranno* (F-Pn D-8940 [5]^{BnF}; F-Pn VM7-7366^{BnF}; GB-Lbl Add. 31624 [16]^{BL,RISM}; I-Vqs MS Cl.VIII.14 (1128) [53]$^{NG,RISM,SBN;R}$); *Se miro quel volto* (F-Pn D-8940 [8]^{BnF}); *Torna innocente e poi* (<u>D-Dl Mus.1-F-28,5 [7]</u>^{RISM}; D-Wa 46 Alt 715^{RISM}; F-Pn D-8940 [9]^{BnF}; GB-AY D/DR/10/6c [8]$^{RISM;P,186}$; I-Vqs MS Cl.VIII.14 (1128) [116]$^{NG,RISM;R}$; RUS-Mrg Φ.954 N°134–138 [7]$^{RISM;IP}$); *Tu vuoi ch'io viva, o cara* (<u>D-Dl Mus.1-F-28,2 [6]</u>^{RISM}; F-Pn D-8940 [11]^{BnF}; S-Skma T-SE-R^{RISM}); *Voi, desolate* (F-Pn D-8940 [10]^{BnF})

[printed sources] five arias and the duet *Tu vuoi ch'io viva, o cara*, in *Dudici arie e due duetti* (London: Walsh, [s.d.])

[contrafacta] *Per quel paterno amplesso* ([*Ad laudes divinas volate*] PL-Wu RM 5031$^{RISM;P}$)

1746	mus. by Abos, Girolamo
1746 Venice	Teatro Grimani di S. Giovanni Grisostomo (carn., c. 28/01/1746)
Librettos	[Venice: s.n., 1746] <u>I-Bc Lo.00002</u>; <u>I-Mb Racc.dramm.0826</u>; I-Pca CSA.MUS.9; I-Pmc^S; <u>I-Rn 40.9.F.04.10</u>; I-Vcg LIBRETTI S.GIO.GRISOSTOMO 159; I-Vnm DRAMM. 1064 [4]; I-Vnm DRAMM.1239 [1]; I-Vnm DRAMM.3574 [5]; US-LAum ML48 .R114 1746 [4]
Music sources	[excerpts] *Bramar di perdere* (<u>D-Dl Mus.1-F-28,2 [7]</u>^{RISM}); *Conservati fedele* (<u>D-Dl Mus.1-F-28,4 [9]</u>^{RISM}); *No, che pietà non senti* (<u>D-Dl Mus.1-F-28,1 [1]</u>^{RISM}; <u>D-Dl Mus.1-F-28,1a [2]</u>$^{RISM;IP}$); *Non conosco in tal momento* (<u>D-Dl Mus.1-F-28,4 [8]</u>^{RISM}); *Non è ver che sia contento* (<u>D-Dl Mus.1-F-28,1 [1]</u>^{RISM}; <u>D-Dl Mus.1-F-28,1a [1]</u>$^{RISM;IP}$); *Per pietà bell'idol mio* (<u>D-Dl Mus.1-F-28,4 [7]</u>^{RISM}); *Per quel paterno amplesso* (<u>D-Dl Mus.1-F-28,4 [11]</u>^{RISM}); *Se al labbro mio non credi* (<u>D-Dl Mus.1-F-28,2 [2]</u>^{RISM}; D-Mbs Mus.ms. 20882 a [8]^{RISM}); *Se d'un amor tiranno* (D-KA Don Mus.Hs. 3^{RISM}); *Va' tra le selve ircane* (<u>D-KA Don Mus.Hs. 1</u>$^{RISM;IP}$); *Vendetta mi chiede* (<u>D-KA Don Mus.Hs. 2</u>^{RISM})

---

186. In D major instead of G major.

[doubtful][187] *Mi credi spietata?* (GB-Lbl Add. 31655[BL,RISM]); *Per quell'affetto che l'incatena* (<u>D-Dl Mus.1-F-28,3 [12]</u>[RISM])

1746	mus. by Bernasconi, Andrea
1746 Vienna	Teatro Privilegiato (08/10/1746) (1)
	name day of the emperor
	1st version
1763 Munich	Court theatre (carn., 10/01/1763) (2)
	2nd version
Librettos	(1) Vienna: van Ghelen, [1746]
	<u>A-Wn 4916-A</u>
	(2) Munich: Thuille, [1763] (It./Ger.)
	<u>CDN-Ttfl Itp Pam 00107</u>; <u>D-Mbs Bavar.4015-15,1 [2]</u>; US-Wc ML48 [S863]

Music sources[188]

2nd version: 1763, Munich

[complete scores] <u>D-Mbs Mus.ms. 151</u>[MGG,NG,RISM]; <u>D-Mbs Mus.ms. 190</u>[MGG,NG,RISM]; <u>F-Pn D-993/994/995</u>[BnF,MGG,RISM,189]

[excerpts] *Conservati fedele* (D-SWl Mus.1220[RISM]); *Fra cento affanni e cento* (D-SWl Mus.1221[RISM]); *Per quel paterno amplesso* (D-SWl Mus.1222[RISM]); *Se del fiume altera l'onda* (D-SWl Mus.1225[RISM;P]); *Vo solcando un mar crudele* (D-SWl Mus.1224[RISM])

1747	mus. by unknown composer(s)
1747 Ravenna	Teatro Pubblico (spr., 20/04/1747)
Librettos	Bologna: Guidotti & Mellini, [1747]
	<u>I-Bc Lo.05941</u>; I-Vgc ROL.0677 [10]

1747	mus. by Maggiore, Francesco	
1747 Trento	Teatro Nuovo (St Virgil Fair, 24/06/1747)	(1,2)
1753 Graz	Theater am Tummel-Platz (carn.)	(3)
	music by F. Maggiore and others	

---

187. These arias are not included in the libretto for Abos' original version.
188. As no source for Bernasconi's 1st setting of *Artaserse* seems to have been preserved, we cannot ascertain that the arias included in the 2nd version were not used in the 1746 premiere.
189. Microfilm copy: F-Pn VM BOB-23861/23832/23863.

MC | *Artaserse* (1730–1850)

Librettos   (1) Trento: Monauri, 1747[190]
I-Mb Racc.dramm.2277; I-RVE r-EO 356 [1]

(2) Venice: Fenzo, 1747
I-Rig Rar. Libr. Op. 18. Jh. 201

(3) Graz: heirs of Widmanstadj, [1753] (It./Ger.)
A-Gl C 10727¹; A-Gu I 57640

1747	mus. by Scarlatti, Giuseppe	
1747 Lucca	Teatro Pubblico (aut., 26/08/1747)	(1)
	1st version	
1763 Vienna	Teatro Privilegiato (carn., 15/02/1763)	(2)
	2nd version	

Librettos   (1) Lucca: Benedini, 1747
I-Bc Lo.05147; I-Lg a. XV. D. 80.

(2) Vienna: van Ghelen, [1763]
A-Gl 207.642; A-Wn 364329-B; CZ-Pnm B 4494; CZ-Pnm B 4450 a; CZ-Pu 9 D 2869; US-CAh *GC7.A100.B750 [18]; US-Wc ML48 [S9541]

Music sources

1st version: 1747, Lucca

[excerpts] *Per quel paterno amplesso* (I-Nc 34.5.11 [6][SBN])

2nd version: 1763, Vienna

[complete scores] A-Wn Mus.Hs.17851 [1–3][IC,MGG,NG]; B-Bc 2354[MGG,NG,RISM]

1747	mus. by Ciampi, Vincenzo Legrenzio
1747 Palermo	Teatro di Santa Cecilia[191]

Music sources   [excerpts] *Figlio se più non vivi* (D-MÜs SANT Hs 184 [25][RISM]); *Torna innocente e poi* (D-MÜs SANT Hs 184 [17][RISM]; GB-Lbl Add. 31655[BL,RISM]); *Tu vuoi ch'io viva, o cara* (D-MÜs SANT Hs 184 [24][RISM])

1748	mus. by Carcani, Giuseppe
1748 Piacenza	Teatro Ducale (carn.)

---

190. According to ˢ2990, there used to be a copy in I-Rss yet it can no longer be found among the institution's holdings. We therefore consider it as lost.
191. Sorge, Giuseppe, *I teatri di Palermo nel secoli XVI-XVII-XVIII* (Palermo: Industrie Riunite Editoriali Siciliane, 1926).

MC | *Artaserse* (1730–1850)

Librettos   Piacenza: Salvoni, [1748]
               I-PAc F. Libretti, sc.037 [620]

Music sources   [excerpts] *Non è ver che sia contento* (D-B Mus.ms. 3040[RISM;P]); *Vo solcando un mar crudele* (S-Skma SO-R[RISM])

1748	mus. by Perez, Davide	
1748 Florence	Teatro della Pergola (29/09/1748) 1st version	(1)
1749 Naples	Teatro di S. Carlo (20/01/1749) birthday of Carlo VII, king of Naples	(2)
1754 Lisbon	Court theatre – Palácio da Ajuda (06/06/1754) birthday of José I, king of Portugal 2nd version[192]	(3)

Librettos   (1) Florence: Pieri, 1748
               S-Uu n/s

               (2) Naples: Langiano, 1749
               I-Fm Mel.2345 [10]

               (3) Lisbon: Sylviana, 1754
               I-Bc Lo.04087; I-Rsc Carv.1307; I-RVE r-Z 93 31 [1]; P-Ln M. 1543 P.; US-CAt TS 8056.512 1754

Music sources

1st version: 1749, Florence

         [complete scores] GB-Lcm MS 474[IC,MGG,NG,193]; I-Nc 30.4.1[IC,MGG,NG,RISM,194]; I-Vnm Mss. 9797/9798/9799[MGG,NG,SBN]; P-La* 47-V-10[BA,MGG,NG]; US-Wc M1500.P41 A66 1750[RISM]

         [excerpts] *Bramar di perdere* (D-Dl Mus.3015-F-1 [8][RISM]); *Conservati fedele* (D-KA Don Mus.Hs. 1031[RISM]; E-Mn MP/1988 [6][IC]; I-MC 6-E-2/3 [2][RISM]); *Deh, respirar lasciatemi* (B-Bc 4578[RISM]; I-Nc 34.6.13 [17][SBN]); *Figlio se più non vivi* (D-W Cod. Guelf. 300 Mus. Hdschr. [2][RISM]); *Mi credi spietata?* (CH-E 150,3 [1][RISM]; GB-Lbl Add. 14208 [12][BL,RISM]; GB-Lbl R.M.23.e.9 [11][BL,RISM,195]; I-MC 4-F-1 [16][RISM]); *Non*

---

192. Although there is no evidence that Perez revised his original score for the Lisbon performance in 1754, his strong connection with the Portuguese court as well as the significant differences between the two musical settings lead us to think of the 1754 performance as forming a version by itself.
193. Related to Perez's 1st *Artaserse* in Jackson, Paul Joseph, 'The Operas of David Perez' (PhD dissertation: Stanford University, 1967); consultation of this manuscript source has not been possible.
194. Wrongly dated 'Lisbona 1752' on source, by a different hand.
195. In F major instead of B flat major.

MC | *Artaserse* (1730–1850)

è ver che sia contento (I-MC 4-F-1 [21]^RISM); *Non conosco in tal momento* (I-MC 4-F-1 [17]^RISM); *Per pietà bell'idol mio* (D-LÜh Mus. Q 278^RISM; GB-Lbl R.M.23.e.9 [7]^BL,RISM; S-Uu Gimo 220^RISM); *Per quel paterno amplesso* (I-MC 4-F-1 [19]^RISM); *Su le sponde del torbido Lete* (I-MC 1-F-13/7 [2]^RISM); *Tu vuoi ch'io viva, o cara** (D-Dl Mus.3015-F-1 [5]^RISM; P-Ln M.M. 217//10^RISM); *Va tra le selve ircane* (I-MC 4-F-1 [18]^RISM)

2nd version: 1754, Lisbon

[complete scores] A-Wn Mus.Hs.20272^IC; D-Hs M A/456^MGG,NG,RISM [Act I]; E-LPAu Cop. 8510430^IC; P-La 45-IV-51/52/53^BA,MGG,NG; P-La 54-I-74/75/76^BA,MGG,NG,RISM; P-Ln C.I.C. 97^IC,MGG,NG,RISM; P-Ln F.C.R. 156 [14]^IC,MGG,NG; US-SFsc *M2.1 M388^RISM; US-Wc M1500.P41 A7^RISM

[excerpts] *Conservati fedele* (J-Tk S10-613 [3]^RISM; P-La 54-III-63 [1–3]^BA;IP); *Così stupisce e cade* (P-Ln M.M. 217 [9]^RISM); *Deh, respirar lasciatemi* (P-La 54-III-63 [9–13]^BA;IP); *Fra cento affanni e cento* (P-La 54-II-63 [4–8]^BA;IP; P-La 54-III-63 [4–8]^BA;IP); *L'onda dal mar divisa* (B-Bc 4586 [1]^RISM; I-FZc A.VI.6 [5]^RISM; I-Nc 34.6.13 [23]^SBN; P-La 54-III-63 [14–18]^BA;IP; S-Skma T-SE-R^IC,MGG,NG; US-BEm MS 100 [1]^IC,MGG,RISM,196; US-CAward [US-CAt] M1505.A148 T5 1756 [20]^RISM; US-Wc M1505.A2 P436^RISM); *Non è ver che sia contento* (US-BEm MS 24 [6]^IC,MGG,NG,RISM; US-SFsc *M2.1 M387 [12]^RISM)

[undated] [excerpts] *Deh, respirar lasciatemi* (I-Nc 8.1.19–22 [7]^SBN)

[doubtful] [excerpts] *Mi credi spietata?* (S-Sm n/s^RISM;R; US-Wc M1505.A2 P436^RISM)

1748	**mus. by various unknown composers**
1748 Prague	Teatro Nuovo (aut.)
Librettos	Prague: Pruscha, [1748] (It./Ger.)
	CZ-Pnm B 4135; I-Mb Racc.dramm.5796

1748	**mus. by Zoppis, Francesco**[197]
1748 Bonn	Poppelsdorf Castle
Librettos	Bonn: heirs of Rommerskirchen, 1748
	F-Pn YD-1435[198]

---

196. In G major instead of F major.
197. Riepe, Juliane, '"Essential to the Reputation and Magnificence of Such a High-Ranking Prince": Ceremonial and Italian Opera at the Court of Clemens August of Cologne and other German Courts', in *Italian Opera in Central Europe*, vol. 1: *Institutions and Ceremonies*, ed. by Melania Bucciarelli, Norbert Dubowy, and Reinhard Strohm (Berlin: Berliner Wissenschafts, 2006), pp. 147–75.
198. Microfilm copies: F-Pn MFICHE YD-1435; F-Pn P94/5182.

MC | *Artaserse* (1730–1850)

Music sources	[complete scores] I-MOe Mus. F. 1586[IC;P]
	[excerpts] *L'onda dal mar divisa* (D-Dl Mus.1-F-82,37 [10])[RISM]; *Per quel paterno amplesso* (D-Dl Mus.1-F-82,37 [6])[RISM]; D-Wa 46 Alt 722[RISM]; *Vo solcando un mar crudele* (D-Dl Mus.1-F-82,37 [7])[RISM])

1749 — mus. by unknown composer(s)

1749 Livorno	Teatro da S. Sebastiano (carn.)	

Librettos	Pisa: Carotti, [1749]
	I-Bc Lo.05942

1749 — mus. by Mele, Giovanni Battista and others

1749 Madrid	Court theatre – Teatro del Buen Retiro (carn., 06/01/1749)[199]	(1)
	L'Artaserse / El Artaxerses	
1749 Madrid	Court theatre – Teatro del Buen Retiro (06/06/1749)[200]	(2)
1750 Madrid	Court theatre – Teatro del Buen Retiro (carn., 31/12/1749)[201]	(3)

Librettos	(1) [Madrid]: Mojados, [1749] (It./Spa.)
	E-Mn T/7992; E-MO C *XIV*8o*35; E-TAu R181-24; F-Pm 4° 11004-14; I-Bu A.VI.B.II [17]; I-Fm Mel.2042 [11]
	(2,3) NA

1749 — mus. by Galuppi, Baldassare

1749 Vienna	Teatro Privilegiato (carn., 27/01/1749)	(1)
	1st version	
1750 Sassuolo	Teatro Pubblico[202]	(2)
1751 Padua	Teatro Nuovo (Fair of St Antonio, 11/06/1751)[203]	(3)
	opening of the theatre[204]	
	2nd version	
1753 Mantua	Teatro Arciducale (carn.)	(4)
1754 Venice	Teatro dei Dilettanti (carn.)	(5)

---

199. Leza, 'Metastasio on the Spanish Stage'; Llorens and Torrente, 'Constructing *Opera Seria*'. For the original source see Broschi, Carlo, *Descripción del estado actual del real teatro de Buen Retiro, de las funciones hechas en él desde el año de 1747 hasta el presente [...]* (1758), E-E II/1412, fol. 46ʳ.
200. Casanova Sánchez de Vega, Teresa, 'El intermezzo en la corte de España, 1738–1758' (doctoral dissertation, Universidad Complutense de Madrid, 2019).
201. Casanova Sánchez de Vega, 'El intermezzo en la corte de España'. Leza ('Metastasio On the Spanish Stage') gives 01/01/1750.
202. Piperino, 'Opera Production', p. 53 table 1.
203. For Galuppi's recomposotions for this production, see Heartz, Daniel, 'Hasse, Galuppi and Metastasio', in *Venezia e il melodramma nel Settecento*, ed. by Maria Teresa Muraro (Florence: Olschki, 1978), pp. 309–79.
204. Brunelli, Bruno, *I teatro di Padova: delle origini alla fine del secolo XIX* (Padua: Draghi, 1921).

MC | *Artaserse* (1730–1850)

last night of the carnival season[205]
mus. by B. Galuppi and others

1755 Treviso	Teatro Dolfin (carn.)	(6)
1756 Brescia	Teatro degli Erranti (carn.)	(7)
1756 Vicenza	Teatro delle Grazie (08/1756)	(8)
1757 Faenza	Teatro dei Remoti (carn.)	(9)
1757 Ferrara	Teatro Bonacossi da S. Stefano (carn.)	(10)
1757 Lucca	Teatro Pubblico (aut.)	(11)
1758 Brescia	Teatro degli Erranti (Aug. Fair)	(12)
1759 Verona	Teatro Filarmonico (carn.)	(13)
1761 Venice	Teatro Grimani di S. Benedetto (carn., 26/12/1760)	(14)

Librettos

(1) [Vienna]: van Ghelen, [1749]
CZ-Pu 9 K 3154; US-Wc ML48 [S3444][206]

(2) Modena: Soliani, [1750]
I-MOe 70.I.24 [1]

(3) Padua: Conzatti, 1751
B-Bc 19314; I-Bl FS.W.1554; I-BGc 16.4.5 [1]; I-Mb Racc.dramm.3699; I-Pmc[C,S]; I-VEc[C,S,207]

(4) Mantua: heirs of Pazzoni, 1753
I-MAc Arm.14.b.258

(5) Venice: Fenzo, 1754
B-Bc 19316; I-Mb Racc.dramm.0800; I-Ria MISC. Teatrale II [15]; I-Rsc Carv.1310; I-Vnm DRAMM.1274 [6]; US-LAum ML48 .R114 1754 [13]

(6) [Treviso: s.n., 1755]
I-Mb Racc.dramm.0689

(7) Brescia: Pasini, 1756
I-Mb Racc.dramm.2184

(8) Venezia: Fenzo, 1756
I-Fc E.V.0346; I-Rsc Carv.1311; US-Cn ML50.2.A78 G35 1756

(9) Faenza, Archi, 1757
I-FZc RM.N.I.34;[208] I-Nragni L055

(10) Venice: Fenzo, 1757
I-Mb Racc.dramm.0768

---

205. Selfridge-Field, *A New Chronology of Venetian Opera*, p. 639.
206. Copy: D-KNmi FH 1185.
207. The copy reported in [S,C] could not be found by the library staff. We therefore consider it as lost.
208. Missing (partial photocopy available).

(11) Lucca: Benedini, 1757
I-Fm Mel.2044 [3]; I-Mb Racc.dramm.3501; I-Ms MUS. G. X. 1

(12) Brescia: Pianta, 1758
I-Mb Racc.dramm.2283

(13) Verona: Ramanzini, [1759]
I-VEc D.381 [5]; US-NYp *MGTY-Res.

(14) Venice: Comino, 1761
A-Wmi BT-562; I-Mb Racc.dramm.3043; I-Ria MISC. Teatrale 8 [1]; I-Vcg LIBRETTI S.BENEDETTO 187; I-Vnm DRAMM.1083 [1]; I-Vnm DRAMM.1282 [1]; US-CAh *IC7 A100 B750 v.44; US-LAum ML48 .R114 1761 [1]

Music sources

1st version: 1749, Vienna

[complete scores] A-Wn Mus.Hs.10878 [1–3][IC,MGG,NG]; D-B* Mus.ms.autogr. Galuppi B. 3[MGG,NG,RISM]; F-Pn D-4266/4267/4268[BnF,MGG,NG,209]

[excerpts] *Così stupisce e cade* (A-Wgm VI 17009 [Q 2914][IC]); *Figlio se più non vivi* (D-SWl Mus.1966[RISM;P]); *Fra cento affanni e cento* (D-Dl Mus.2973-F-34 [15][RISM,210]; F-Pn D-4304 [6][BnF,RISM,211]); *Mi credi spietata?* (D-Dl Mus.2973-F-32 [8][RISM,212]); *Non conosco in tal momento* (D-Mbs Mus.ms. 255 [1][RISM]; *Nuvoletta opposta al sole* (D-Mbs Mus.ms. 255 [9][RISM]); *Per pietà bell'idol mio* (D-Mbs Mus.ms.255 [3][RISM]); *Per quel paterno amplesso* (A-Wgm VI 6746 [Q 3957][IC]; A-Wgm VI 15128 [Q 2907][IC]; A-Wn Mus.Hs.2405 [2][IC,MGG]; D-Dl Mus.2973-F-32 [4][RISM]; D-SWl Mus.1962[RISM;P,213]); *Rendimi il caro amico* (D-Mbs Mus.ms. 255 [4][RISM]; D-SWl Mus.132[RISM]); *Se del fiume altera l'onda* (D-Dl Mus.2973-F-32 [5][RISM]); *Se perdo il caro bene* (CDN-Lu MZ 737[IC,RISM;P]); *Va' tra le selve ircane* (D-Dl Mus.1-F-49,12 [6][RISM]; D-Dl Mus.2953-F-32 [6][RISM])

2nd version: 1751, Padua

[complete scores] F-G H.319[BASE]; I-TLp[MGG,NG,214]; S-St [S-Skma] A 10 [12][MGG,RISM,215]

---

209. Microfilm copy: F-Pn VM BOB-22919.
210. In E flat major instead of D major.
211. Microfilm copy: F-Pn VM BOB-21141.
212. The aria does not appear in Galuppi's autograph for his first *Artaserse* setting, yet in A3-S6 there is an indication 'aria Mand.' supposed to be followed by a *Mi credi spetata?*, which is included in the corresponding libretto.
213. In G major instead of E major.
214. For Lucca 1757.
215. For Vicenza 1756.

[excerpts] *Bramar di perdere* (B-Bc 3868[RISM,216]; F-Pn* MS-1901[BnF,RISM]); *Conservati fedele* (D-Dl Mus.2973-F-32 [3][RISM]); *Così stupisce e cade* (D-B Mus.ms. 6987/9[RISM;P]; US-SFsc *M2.5 v.65 [6][RISM]); *Deh, respirar lasciatemi* (F-Pn* D-4305 [22][BnF,RISM]); *Fra cento affanni e cento* (D-Dl Mus.2973-F-31 [8][RISM]; D-SWl Mus.153a,b [1][RISM]; F-Pn D-4300 [14][BnF,RISM]; F-Pn D-4300 [16][BnF]; US-SFsc *M2.1 M130[RISM;P]); *Mi credi spietata?* (F-Pn* D-4305 [18][BnF,RISM]); *Per pietà bell'idol mio* (F-Pn D-4304 [21][BnF,RISM]); *Per quel paterno amplesso* (D-SWl Mus.153a,b [2][RISM]; I-MAav Cart.9 n.11[RISM;P]; S-Skma T-SE-R[RISM]); *Rendimi il caro amico* (F-Pn* D-4304 [32][BnF,RISM,217]); *Se al labbro mio non credi* (D-Dl Mus.2973-F-32 [7][RISM]; F-Pn D-4302 [3][BnF,RISM,218]; F-Pn D-4304 [33][RISM,219]; S-Skma T-SE-R[IC,RISM]); *Sogna il guerrier le schiere* (F-Pn* MS-1906[BnF,RISM]); *Tu vuoi ch'io viva, o cara* (D-LÜh Mus Q 193[RISM]; I-Vc Correr Busta 71.7[SBN]); *Va' tra le selve ircane* (S-Skma T-SE-R[RISM;IP,220])

[parodies] *Fra cento affanni e cento* ([*Fra cento schiere e cento*] F-Pn D-4300[BnF,RISM,221])

[printed sources] *Se tutti i mali miei* ([*Per quel paterno amplesso*]) [3], in *Four Songs in the Opera call'd Il Demofonte, Sung by Sigra Mingotti* (London: Giardini, 1755)

[inserts] *Non è ver che sia contento* (I-Bc FF.85 [2][RISM,SBN,222])

[doubtful]

[excerpts] *Agitata in alto mare*[223] (D-Dl Mus.2973-F-34 [12][RISM]); *Agitata in tanto affanni*[224] (F-Pn* D-4305 [19][BnF,RISM]); *Bramar di perdere* (D-Dl Mus.2973-F-36 [9][RISM,225]); *Fra cento affanni e cento*[226] (F-Pn* D-4305 [20][BnF,RISM]; S-Skma T-SE-R[RISM]); *Per quel paterno amplesso* (D-B Mus.

---

216. For Venice 1760.
217. Microfilm copy: F-Pn VM BOB-21141.
218. Microfilm copy: F-Pn VM BOB-31988.
219. For Padua 1762. Microfilm copy: F-Pn VM BOB-21141.
220. For Vicenza 1756.
221. Same music as in the doubtful sources for this aria; in F major instead of D major.
222. Wrongly attributed to B. Galuppi, as none of his versions includes this aria; inserted into the revival of Vicenza 1756.
223. Inserted into the librettos for Venice 1754, Treviso 1755, and Brescia 1756.
224. Inserted into the librettos for Lucca 1757, Brescia 1758, and Verona 1759.
225. The music is different from the 1751 sources and the aria was not included in the 1749 libretto.
226. The music of this and the following aria is different from that of the 1749 and 1751 versions.

ms. 6987 [6]$^{RISM;R}$); *Se al labbro mio non credi* (B-Bc 3939^{RISM,227}; I-Pca D.I.1358^{SBN}; S-Uu Gimo 103^{RISM,228}); *Vivrò se vuoi così*^{229} (B-Bc* 3942^{RISM}) [contrafacta] *Vivrò se vuoi così* ([*Geduld in Kreuz und Pein*] D-SDOk 300$^{RISM;P}$)

1749	mus. by Jommelli, Niccolò	
1749 Rome	Teatro di Torre Argentina (carn., 06/02/1749)^{230} 1st version	(1)
1751 Mannheim	Court theatre (carn., 17/01/1751)^{231} rev. version	(2–4)
1756 Stuttgart	Teatro Ducale (30/08/1756) birthday of the Duchess of Württemberg and Teck 2nd version	(5)
1763 Rome	Teatro di Torre Argentina (carn.)	(6)
Librettos	(1) Rome: Salomoni,^{232} 1749 B-Bc 19313; I-Fm Mel.2298 [13]; I-PAc CXXXVI A 92 3; I-PLcom CXXXVI A 92 3; I-Rsc Libr. n. XV [12]; I-Rvat Stamp.Ferr.V.8050 [5]; I-Vgc ROL.0391 [4]; US-CAt TS 8056.343 1749 (2) Mannheim: Pierron, [1751] D-Mbs L.eleg.m. 1554 (3) Mannheim: Pierron, [1751] (It./Ger.) D-HEu G 3062-2 RES; D-MHrm Mh 1760; D-KNth L 392 (4) Mannheim: Pierron, [1751] (It./Fr.) D-RT H 6-R (5) Stuttgart: Cotta, 1756 (It./Ger.) D-Mbs 4 P.o.it. 231; D-Sl Fr.D.qt.192; D-Tu Dk III 28 [4]; US-Wc ML48 [S4843]^{233}	

---

227. Possible autograph according to Wotquenne, Alfred, *Baldassare Galuppi 1706–1785: étude bibliographique sur ses œuvres dramatiques* (Brussels: Schepens & Katto, 1902). The aria was not included in the 1749 version and the music is different from that of the ascertained 1751 sources.
228. The music is different from that of the ascertained 1751 sources; different from the other doubtful sources too. For Lucca 1757.
229. Inserted into the librettos for Vicenza 1756 and Lucca 1757.
230. Date in Rinaldi, Mario, *Due secoli al Teatro Argentina* (Florence: Olschki, 1978). Franchi (*Le impressioni sceniche*, p. 12) gives 07/01/1749, but the date in the *Diario ordinario*, 4923 (08/08/1749) is clear.
231. Corneilson, Paul Edward, 'Opera at Mannheim, 1770–1778' (doctoral dissertation, The University of North Carolina at Chapel Hill, 1994).
232. 'Si vendono da Fausto Amidei'.
233. Copy: D-KNmi FH 1189.

MC | *Artaserse* (1730–1850)

(6) Rome: Puccinelli, [1763]
I-Rvat Stamp.De.Luca.Misc.26 [3]

Music sources

1st version: 1749, Rome

[complete scores] D-Hs M A/145[NG,RISM]; D-Sl* HB XVII 234 [a–c][MGG,NG,RISM]; GB-Lbl Add. 16034/16035/16036[BL,MGG,NG,RISM]; I-Nc 28.6.25[IC,MGG,NG,RISM;A,R]

[excerpts] *Bramar di perdere* (GB-Lbl R.M.23.d.1 [2][BL,RISM;IP]; S-Skma T-SE-R[RISM;R]); *Conservati fedele* (D-B Mus.ms. 11257 [3][RISM]; F-Pn D-6275 [12][BnF,MGG,234]; GB-Lbl R.M.23.f.1 [9][BL,RISM,235]; I-Mc Mus. Tr.ms. 1468[SBN]; US-SFsc *M2.5 v.55 [14][RISM]); *Deh, respirar lasciatemi** (GB-Lbl R.M.22.f.8 [7][BL,RISM]; GB-Lbl R.M.23.f.1 [10][BL,RISM]; I-MC 3-C-9 [4][RISM]; S-Skma T-SE-R[RISM]); *Fra cento affanni e cento* (D-SWl Mus.2982[RISM;P]); *L'onda dal mar divisa* (GB-Lbl Add. 31597 [4][BL,RISM]; S-Skma T-SE-R[RISM;IP]); *Mi scacci sdegnato!* (D-Dl Mus.1-F-21,2 [11][RISM]); *Non è ver che sia contento* (I-Mc Noseda O.36 [11][RISM;P]; I-Nc 33.2.26 [16][SBN]); *Non ti son padre, non mi sei figlio* (GB-Lbl R.M.23.d.1 [5][BL,RISM,236]); *Nuvoletta opposta al sola* (D-KNmi J 255 R [3][RISM]); *Ombre fiere in van fremete* (B-Bc 4279 [4][RISM]; GB-Lbl R.M.23.f.1 [11][RISM]; I-MAav Cart.9 n.23[RISM;P]; I-MC 3-C-12/10 [1][RISM]); *Per pietà bell'idol mio* (GB-Lbl R.M.22.f.9 [5][BL,RISM]); *Per quell'affetto che l'incatena* (B-Bc 4291[RISM]; I-Mc Noseda I.160 [2][SBN]; US-SFsc *M2.5 v.55 [13][RISM;R]); *Per quel paterno amplesso** (B-Bc 4292[RISM]; D-Dl Mus.1-F-21,2 [13][RISM]; GB-Lbl Add. 31597 [3][BL,RISM]; GB-Lbl R.M.22.f.8 [6][BL,RISM]; I-Mc Noseda I.160 [5][SBN]); *Se d'un amor tiranno* (D-Mbs Mus.ms. 181 [4][RISM]; GB-Lbl R.M.22.f.8 [2][BL,RISM]); *Su le sponde del torbido Lete* (I-MC 3-C-9/3 [4][RISM]); *Tu vuoi ch'io viva, o cara** (CDN-Lu MZ 773 [2][IC,RISM]; I-MC 3-C-6 [15][RISM]; I-Nc 33.2.26 [5][SBN]; I-Rc Mss. 2261[IC]); *Va' tra le selve ircane** (GB-Lbl R.M.23.f.1 [12][BL,RISM,237]); *Vo solcando un mar crudele** (CDN-Lu MZ 773 [1][IC,RISM]; D-B Mus.ms. 11245/5[RISM;P]; I-Mc Noseda O.36 [10][SBN]; I-MC 3-C-12/10 [2][RISM])

1st rev. version: 1751, Mannheim

[complete scores] D-B Mus.ms. 11245[MGG,NGG,RISM]; US-Wc M1500.J72 A5[IC,RISM,238]

---

234. Microfilm copy: F-Pn VM BOB-28869.
235. In E flat major instead of F major.
236. For soprano instead of tenor voice.
237. In B flat major instead of D major.
238. Transcript of D-B Mus.ms. 11245.

[excerpts] *Bramar di perdere* (<u>D-KA Don Mus.Ms. 125 [5]</u>[RISM;P]; <u>D-KA Don Mus.Ms. 1867</u>[RISM;IP]; I-MC 3-C-3/21 [2][RISM]; <u>I-Nc 33.2.28 [4]</u>[SBN]); *Mi credi spietata?* (I-MC 3-C-3 [22][RISM]; <u>I-Nc 33.2.32 [1]</u>[SBN]); *Per pietà bell'idol mio* (I-Nc 33.2.30 [7][SBN]); *Se del fiume altera l'onda* (D-BSSp Mus.ms. Jommelli 2[RISM;IP])

2nd version: 1756, Stuttgart

[complete scores] <u>D-Sl HB XVII 730 [a–c]</u>[RISM]; P-La 44-IX-49/50/51[BA]

[excerpts] *Bramar di perdere* (B-Bc 4232 [12][RISM]); *Se d'un amor tiranno* (D-MÜs SANT Hs 2265[RISM])

[undated]   [excerpts] *Mi credi spietata?* (F-Pn D-6273 [3][BnF]; F-Pn D-6276 [21][BnF,239]; I-Nc 33.2.31 [3][SBN]); *Per pietà bell'idol mio* (A-Wgm VI 15174 [Q 3047][IC])

[doubtful]   [excerpts] *Non ti son padre, non mi sei figlio* (D-MGmi HA IV 165[RISM;P,240]); *Per pietà bell'idol mio* (<u>I-Nc 33.2.28 [5]</u>[SBN])

1749	mus. by unknown composer(s)
1749 Alessandria	NA
Librettos	Alessandria: Balbis, 1749 CH-BEms MUE Rar alt 1810 [1]

1749	mus. by Smith, John Christopher[NG]
1749 [s.l.]	NA
Music sources	[excerpts] six arias in J-Tn[NG]

1750	mus. by Lampugnani, Giovanni Battista	
1750 Milan	Teatro Regio Ducale (carn., 26/12/1749)	(1)
1766 Cremona	Teatro Nazari? (carn.)[241]	(2)
Librettos	(1) Milan: Malatesta, 1749 F-Pn LIV IT-3522 [1]; <u>I-Bc Lo.02606</u>; I-LDEsormani 309/1/22; I-Mb Racc.dramm.6044 [3]; I-PAc F. Libretti, sc.037 [621]; <u>I-Rn 40.9.D.12.6</u>; I-Rsc Vol. 5 [6] (2) NA	

---

239. Microfilm copy: F-Pn VM BOB-28501.
240. The music is different from the 1749/1751 version and the aria was not included in the 1756 libretto.
241. Liborio, Francesco Maria, *La scena della città: rappresentazioni sceniche nel Teatro di Cremona 1748–1900* (Cremona: Turris, 1994).

MC | Artaserse (1730–1850)

Music sources [excerpts] *Fra cento affanni e cento* (B-Bc 4324[RISM]; F-Pn D-6556 [14][BnF]); *Mi scacci sdegnato!* (F-Pn D-6556 [12][BnF]); *Per quel paterno amplesso* (B-Bc 5086[RISM]; F-Pn D-6556 [13][BnF]; I-VEcon MS 139[RISM;SBN]); *Vo solcando un mar crudele* (F-Pn D-6556 [11][BnF])

[contrafacta] *Per quel paterno amplesso* ([*Vos caelitum favores amores*] CZ-Pak 1458 [2][RISM;P])

1750	mus. by Pampani, Antonio Gaetano
1750 Venice	Teatro Grimani di S. Giovanni Grisostomo (carn., 24/01/1750) (1)
	1st version
1756 Venice	Teatro Grimani di S. Benedetto (carn., 24/01/1756) (2)
	2nd version

Librettos (1) Venice: Insegna della Scienza, [1750][242]
I-Pmc[S]; I-Rsc Carv.1308; I-Vcg LIBRETTI S.GIO.GRISOSTOMO 160; I-Vnm DRAMM.1072 [4]; I-Vnm DRAMM.1268 [5]; I-Vnm DRAMM.3578 [5]; US-LAum ML48 .R114 1750 [4]; US-Wc ML48 [S7754]

(2) Venice: Geremia, [1756]
D-B Mus. T 52; I-Mb Racc.dramm.3804; I-Rsc Carv.1309; I-Vcg LIBRETTI S.BENEDETTO 187; I-Vgc ROL.0515 [6]; I-Vnm DRAMM.1078 [3]; I-Vnm DRAMM.1276 [3]; US-CAh *IC7 B750 [56]; US-LAum ML48 .R114 1756 [3]

Music sources
1st version: 1750, Venice

[complete scores] I-MOe Mus. F. 1586[IC]

[excerpts] *Bramar di perdere* (I-Nc 34.4.3 [16][SBN]); *Conservati fedele* (GB-Lbl Add. 34597 [18][BL,NG,RISM]); *Deh, respirar lasciatemi* (GB-Lbl Add. 34597 [17][BL,NG]); *Fra cento affanni e cento* (D-KA Don Mus.Hs. 717[RISM]); *Mi scacci sdegnato!* (D-KA Don Mus.Hs. 719[RISM]); *Per quel paterno amplesso* (D-KA Don Mus.Hs. 715[RISM]; GB-Lbl Add. 34597 [15][BL,NG,RISM]; I-Vc Correr Busta 43.16[SBN]; US-BEm MS 30 [5][RISM]); *Se al labbro mio non credi* (D-Dl Mus.1-F-49,6 [14a][RISM]; D-Dl Mus.1-F-49,6 [14b][RISM;IP]; D-KA Don Mus.Hs. 718[RISM]; D-Mbs Mus.ms. 253 [6][RISM]; D-SWl Mus.1978[RISM;P]; D-SWl Mus.4135[RISM;P]; F-Pn L-19421[BnF]; GB-Lbl Add. 34597 [16][BL,NG,RISM]; US-BEm MS 95 [16][RISM,243]); *Viverò, se tu lo vuoi* (D-

---

242. Microfilm copy of unspecified copy: US-AAu FILM M1596.
243. In D major instead of C major.

MC | *Artaserse* (1730–1850)

Dl Mus.1-F-82,21 [1]^{RISM}; D-KA Don Mus.Hs. 716^{RISM}; D-Mbs Mus.ms. 253 [1]^{RISM}; GB-Lam MS 143 [6]^{RISM;R}; GB-Lbl Add. 34597 [14]^{BL,NG,RISM}; I-MAav Cart.16 n.10^{NG,RISM;P}; I-Vc Correr Busta 43.21^{NG,SBN})

[contrafacta] *Viverò, se tu lo vuoi* ([*Maria caeli et mundi gaudium*] CZ-Bm A 14690^{RISM;P})

2nd version: 1756, Venice

[excerpts] *Per quel paterno amplesso* (D-Mbs Mus.ms. 253 [9]^{RISM})

1750	mus. by unknown composer(s) (Bollano, G.?^{NG})
1750 Cagliari	Teatro di Cagliari (31/05/1750)
	wedding of Vittorio Amadeo, duke of Savoy, and Maria Antonia of Spain
Librettos	Cagliari: Bonaria, 1750
	US-Wc ML48 [S11310]

1750	mus. by unknown composer(s)
1750 Strasbourg	NA
Librettos	Strasbourg: Heitz, 1750 (It./Fr?)
	F-CO A 20472

1751	mus. by Dal Barba, Daniel and others
1751 Verona	Teatro dietro alla Reina (carn., 01/1751)
Librettos	Verona: Ramanzini, [1751]
	I-Vcg LIBRETTI VERONA 57 F 71
Music sources	[complete scores] I-VEc^{NG,244}

1751	mus. by Jommelli, Niccolò (1st rev. version) → see 1749

1751	mus. by Galuppi, Baldassare (2nd version) → see 1749

1751	mus. by Fiorillo, Ignazio[245]	
1751 Brunswick	Teatro Ducale (summ. Fair)	(1)
1765 Kassel	Theatre	(2)

---

244. The score reported in ^{NG} could not be found by the library staff or in ^{IC}. We therefore consider it as lost.
245. The composer of this setting is unknown, but, following ^{NG}, we hypothesise that it is by Fiorillo. ^SIndex I, p. 400 and Schmidt-Hensel ('*La musica è del Signor Hasse*', vol. 2, pp. 88–89) give it as Hasse's. Henzel treats it as a possible pasticcio; see Henzel, Christoph, '"Dichter der Regenten und der Hofleute": Metastasio and deutschen Fürstenhöfen', in *Metastasio im Deutschland der Aufklärung*, ed. by Laurenz Lütteken and Gerhard Splitt (Tübingen: Niemeyer, 2002), pp. 59–72.

MC | *Artaserse* (1730–1850)

rev. version

Librettos	(1) Brunswick: Keitel, [1751] (It./Ger.)	
	D-W Textb. 605[246]	
	(2) [Kassel]: Estienne, 1765 (It./Ger.)	
	D-Ju 8 MS 23293	
Music sources	[complete scores] D-Kl Israël-Anhang 9[IC,MGG,NG] [Acts II&III][247]	
	[excerpts] *Fra cento affanni e cento* (D-Wa 46 Alt 708[RISM]); *Vo solcando un mar crudele* (D-Wa 46 Alt 765[RISM])	
	[contrafacta] *Vo solcando un mar crudele* ([*Flammae amoris ad Jesum volate*] D-Mbs Mus.ms. 5005 [2][RISM;P]; [*Quot terra profert germina*] PL-Wu RM 4443[RISM;P])	
	[doubtful] *Lascia cadermi in volto*[248] (I-Mc Noseda O.31 [4][SBN])	

1752	**mus. by Pescetti, Giovanni Battista**	
1752 Milan	Teatro Regio Ducale (carn., 26/12/1751)	(1)
1755 Bergamo	Teatro di Bergamo (carn.)	(2)
1779 Lodi	Teatro di Lodi (carn.)	(3)
Librettos	(1) Milan: Malatesta, 1751	
	F-Pn LIV IT-3522 [11]; I-Bc Lo.04147; I-LDEsormani 309/1/31; I-Rn 40.9.E.7.2	
	(2) Bergamo: Santini, [1755]	
	I-Mb Racc.dramm.3495	
	(3) Lodi: Pallavicini, [1779]	
	I-LDEsormani 302/8/18; I-PAc F. Libretti, sc.038 [623]	
Music sources	[excerpts][249] *Per quel paterno amplesso* (D-Mbs Mus.ms. 179 [6][RISM]); *Se del fiume altera l'onda* (D-TRb 104/165 00[RISM;IP])	

1753	**mus. by unknown composer(s)**
1753 Livorno	Teatro da S. Sebastiano (aut., 06/11/1753)

---

246. Although there is no such indication on the libretto, the library considers this is a revival of Hasse's *Artaserse*.
247. For Kassel 1765.
248. The aria is not included in the libretto for Fiorillo's original setting. According to an inscription on the source, it was performed in Venice in 1742, but it does not feature in Paganelli's 2nd setting either → see 1737, mus. by Paganelli, Giuseppe Antonio.
249. [MGG,NG] list other musical sources in I-Fc, but the library staff confirmed that this information is not correct.

MC | *Artaserse* (1730–1850)

Librettos	Livorno: Santini & co., [1753]
	I-Bc Lo.05943; I-Mb Racc.dramm.2332

1754	mus. by unknown composer(s)
1754 Bologna	Teatro Formagliari (spr., 14/05/1754)²⁵⁰
Librettos	Bologna: Sassi, [1754]
	I-Baf FA2.LIB.174; I-Bc Lo.05944; I-Bca 17-ARTISTICA Gb, 024; I-BRq 9°.E.IV.3m5; I-Vgc ROL.0698 [10]

1754	mus. by Perez, Davide (2ⁿᵈ version) → see 1749

Artaserse, in *Poesie del signor abate Pietro Metastasio* (Paris: widow of Quillau, 1755), vol. I, pp. 3–110.

1755	mus. by Cocchi, Gioacchino
1755 Reggio Emilia	Teatro Pubblico (Fair, 29/04/1755)
Librettos	Reggio Emilia: Davolio, [1755]
	D-Mbs L.eleg.m. 3884; I-REas Vivi, II 3/9; I-REm 19.K.115; I-REm Racc. Dram. E. Curti 145 [11]; I-REm Racc. Dram. E. Curti 147 [4]; I-Vc 0298
Music sources	[excerpts] *Bramar di perdere* (CH-E 694,9^(RISM;P); CH-EN Ms A 256^(RISM;P)); *Per pietà bell'idol mio* (D-Wa 46 Alt 678^(RISM)); *Se del fiume altera l'onda* (US-BEm MS 30 [10]^(RISM)); *Torna innocente e poi* (I-MC 1-F-11/9 [9]^(RISM;R)); I-PLcon^(MGG,NG)
	[printed sources] *Bramar di perdere*, in *Bramar di perdere per troppo affetto* ([Reggio Emilia]: Manfredi, [c. 1755]); *Conservati fedele*, in *Conservati fedele* ([Reggio Emilia]: Manfredi, [c. 1755]); *Così stupisce e cade*, in *Così stupisce e cade* ([Reggio Emilia]: Manfredi, [c. 1755]); *Per pietà bell'idol mio*, in *Per pietà bell'idol mio* ([Reggio Emilia]: Manfredi, [c. 1755])
	[contrafacta] *Così stupisce e cade* ([*Jesu salvator meus*] CH-EN Ms A 257^(RISM;P)); *Per pietà bell'idol mio* ([*Ad hoc festum properate*] CZ-Pak 1424^(RISM;P))

---

250. It was postponed from 7 to 14 May due to a musician's illness; see Ricci, Corrado, *I teatri di Bologna, nei secoli XVII e XVIII: storia aneddotica* (Bologna: successori Monti, 1888).

MC | *Artaserse* (1730–1850)

1755	mus. by unknown composer(s) (O. Mei or N. Peretti?)	
1755 Dresden	Nuovo Teatro Privilegiato	
Librettos	Dresden: widow of Stössel & Krause, [1755]	
	F-Pn TH B-2572; RUS-Mrg MK 50-8419145; RUS-Mrg MK 50-8685646	

1756	mus. by Pampani, Antonio Gaetano (2nd version) → see 1750

1756	mus. by Jommelli, Niccolò (2nd version) → see 1749

1757	mus. by Gasparini, Quirino
1757 Milan	Teatro Regio Ducale (carn., 26/12/1756)
Librettos	Milan: Malatesta, 1756
	CDN-Ttfl Itp Pam 00264; F-Pn LIV IT-3525 [1]; I-Baf FA2.LIB.377; I-Bc Lo.02013; I-CRg CIV.A.DD.3.11.02; I-LDEsormani 309/2/20; I-Ma S. I. H. I. 8 [3]; I-Mb Racc.dramm.6067 [2]; I-Mc Coll.Libr.124; I-Nc Rari 10.5.8 [8]; I-Rn 40.9.D.12.2; US-Cn ML50.2.A5708 S33 1755
Music sources	[complete scores] S-St [S-Skma] It. Part. A 11$^{RISM;A}$; S-St [S-Skma] It. A 11$^{RISM;P}$

1757	mus. by various unknown composers (incl. Quagliattini, G.?)^{NG}
1757 Florence	Teatro della Pergola (carn., 26/12/1756)
Librettos	Florence: Stamperia dirimpetto all'Oratorio di S. Filippo Neri, [1757]
	I-Fc E.V.1582; I-Fc E.V.1583

> *Artaserse*, in *Poesie del signor abate Pietro Metastasio* (Turin: Stamperia Reale, 1757), vol. 1, pp. 3–107.

1757	mus. by Scolari, Giuseppe	
1757 Pavia	Teatro Omodeo?	(1)
1758 Venice	Teatro Vendramin di S. Salvatore (Asc., *c.* 04/05/1758)	(2)
1768 Lisbon	Teatro de Rua dos Condes (carn.)	(3)
Librettos	(1) NA	
	(2) Venice: Fenzo, 1758	

MC | *Artaserse* (1730–1850)

	F-Pn 8-YTH-52284; <u>I-Mb Racc.dramm.0812</u>; I-Ria MISC. Teatrale 5 [14]; I-Rsc Carv.1313; I-Vcg LIBRETTI S.SALVATORE 97; I-Vnm DRAMM.1080 [8]; I-Vnm DRAMM.1279 [2]; US-BEm ML48 .I7 [366]; US-CAh *IC7 A100 B750 [33]; US-LAum ML48 .R114 1758 [7]; <u>US-Wc ML48 [S9787]</u>
	(3) Lisbon: Ferreira, [1768]
	P-Cug Mis. 568 [9830]; P-Cug Misc. 573 [9592]; P-Cug Misc. 603 [9722]
Music sources	[excerpts] *Conservati fedele* (I-Nc Arie 21(8) [1][NG,SBN;R]); *Deh, respirar lasciatemi* (I-MC 6-A-3 [2][RISM]); *Se non vive il figlio* (I-Nc Arie 21(9) [2][NG,SBN;R]); *Su le sponde del torbido Lete* (I-Rdp Ms Musicale 65 [3][RISM]); *NA* (I-Nc 22.2.22[NG,SBN;R,251]); I-CMbc[NG]

1758	mus. by various unknown composers
1758 Pisa	Teatro Pubblico (spr.)
Librettos	Pisa: Carotti, 1758
	US-Wc ML50.2 .A84

1778	mus. by Uttini, Francesco Antonio Baldassare
1758 Stockholm	Royal Theatre – Drottningholm Palace (24/06/1758)[CA]
Music sources	[excerpts] *Non ti son padre, non mi sei figlio* (S-Skma Alströmer saml. 170 [6][RISM]); *Deh, respirar lasciatemi* (S-Skma Alströmer saml. 170 [4][RISM]; S-Skma Alströmer saml. 170 [5][RISM;P])

1759	mus. by unknown composer(s)
1759 Cartagena	Teatro de Cartagena (30/05/1759?)[252]
	name day of Fernando VI, king of Spain
Librettos	Murcia: Teruel, 1769 [recte 1759?] (It./Spa.)
	E-Mn T I/324 [5]

---

251. The manuscript contains two arias, but not title is given in the catalogue.
252. Both [C] and Cotarelo y Mori refer to this performance as a revival of A. Sacchini's version that took place in Cartagena in 1769; see Cotarelo y Mori, *Orígenes y establecimiento de la ópera en España*, p. 288 and → 1768, mus. by Sacchini, Antonio. However, the libretto states that the performance was celebrated the name day of the King of Spain Fernando. In 1769 the throne was occupied by his successor Carlos III, whose name day was on 4 November. Therefore, we hypothesise that the correct date for the performance is 1759 and that, therefore, it took place three months prior to Fernando VI's death in August that same year.

1760	mus. by Sarti, Giuseppe
1760 Copenhagen	Royal Danish Theatre (carn., 01/1760)[253]
Librettos	Copenhagen: [s.n., 1760] (It./Dan.) DK-Kk Rom. 12300 8°, vol. 2; DK-Kk 56,-369 8°
Music sources	[excerpts][254] *Cara, deh prendi in pace* (I-Tn Giordano 56[IC,MGG,NG]); *Vo solcando un mar crudele* (D-SWl Mus.4771[MGG,RISM;P]); I-Gl[MGG,NG]; I-Nc[MGG,NG]

1760	mus. by Hasse, Johann Adolph (3rd version) → see 1730

1761	mus. by Bach, Johann Christian lib. rev. by Cigna-Santi, Vittorio Amedeo
1761 Turin	Teatro Regio (carn., 27/12/1760)[255]
Librettos	Turin: Avondo, [1760] CDN-Ttfl Lib 00425; F-Pn FB-6922; I-CHRc C.3120; I-NOVc CIV 194.F.32; I-Rsc Lib. Carv.147 [4]; I-Tci L.O.0193; I-Tn F XIII.490 [1]; I-Tstrona[S]; I-Vgc ROL.0148 [16]; US-Wc ML48 [S532][256]
Music sources	[complete scores] GB-Lbl* R.M.22.a.18/19/20[BL,RISM,257]; I-Tf VIII 1/2/3[RISM]; P-La 44-II-34/35/36[BA]; P-La 54-II-73/74/75[BA] [excerpts] *Dimmi che un empio sei* (I-Tf 2 IV 17 [3][RISM]); *Fortunate passate mie pene* (US-AAu M1505.B12 D4[RISM,258]); *Mi scacci sdegnato!* (CH-Zz Mus Ms A 84[SB]); *Nuvoletta opposta al sole* (I-Tf Tf 2 IV 18[RISM]); *Per quel paterno amplesso* (F-Pn D-14371[BnF,RISM,259]; F-Pn MS-17[BnF,RISM]; I-Bc DD.102[IC,RISM,S-BN]; I-VEcon MS 022[RISM,SBN]); *Su le sponde del torbido Lete* (I-Nc 27.4.5 [7][RISM]); *Va' tra le selve ircane* (I-Tf 2 IV 17[RISM]); *Vivrò se vuoi così* (GB-Lbl Egerton MS 3685 [1][BL]); *Vo solcando un mar crudele* (I-Nc 64.1 [1][SBN])

253. Jensen, Niels Martin, 'Giuseppe Sarti: attività danese e manoscritti sopravvissuti', in *Giuseppe Sarti musicista faentino: Atti del convegno internazionale*, ed. by Mario Baroni and Maria Gioia Tavoni (Modena: Mucchi, 1986), pp. 159–65.
254. [MGG,NG] list other musical sources in I-Fc, but the *Deh s'affretti astri tiranni: cavatina* that is classified on the institution's card catalogue as belonging to Sarti's *Artaserse* is from his *Medonte* (Florence, 1777).
255. The production ran for seven consecutive performances; see Bouquet, Gualerzi, and Testa, *Storia del Teatro Regio di Torino*, p. 133.
256. Copy: D-KNmi FH 1183.
257. Some arias are missing. Microfilm reproduction: US-CAe n/s.
258. Dated 1765 on source.
259. Microfilm copy: F-Pn VM BOB-22003.

MC | *Artaserse* (1730–1850)

1761	mus. by unknown composer(s)
1761 Prague	Teatro Nuovo (aut., 03/10/1761)
Librettos	[Prague: s.n., 1761] (It./Ger.)
	CZ-Pdobrovského 57 E 00022

1762	mus. by Zannetti, Francesco and unknown composer
1762 Genoa	Teatro da S. Agostino (carn.)
Librettos	Genoa: Franchelli, [1762]
	NA[260]

1762	mus. by Di Majo, Gianfrancesco
1762 Venice	Teatro Grimani di S. Benedetto (carn., 30/01/1762)
Librettos	Venice: Colombani, 1762
	F-Pm 8° 42675 [7]; F-Pn 8-YTH-51530; I-Bc Lo.02783; I-Mb Racc. dramm.3006; I-Rn 40.9.E.10.4; I-Rsc Carv.1315; I-Rsc Libr. n. XVII [20]; I-Vnm DRAMM.1084 [5]; I-Vnm DRAMM.1285 [3]; US-CAh *IC7 A100 B750 v.44; US-LAum ML48 .R114 1762 [3]; US-Wc ML48 [S5861][261]
Music sources	[complete scores] D-B Mus.ms. 13395[MGG,NG,RISM]; P-La 47-III-6/7[BA,MGG,NG]; US-Wc M1500.M237 A6[MGG,NG,RISM,262]
	[excerpts] *Agitata in van m'affanno* (D-Dl Mus.1-F-49,9 [9][RISM]); *Mi credi spietata?* (D-B Mus.ms. 30131 [2][RISM]; S-Uu Gimo 187[RISM])

1762	mus. by Arne, Thomas Augustine
	lib. probably adap. by Arne himself and rev. by Rolt, Richard
1762 London	Covent Garden (02/02/1762)
	Artaxerxes (En. only)

1762	mus. by Piccinni, Niccolò	
1762 Rome	Teatro di Torre Argentina (carn., 03/02/1762)	(1)
	1st version	
1763 Foligno	Teatro dell'Aquila (carn.)	(2)
1763 Barcelona	Teatre de la Santa Creu (15/01/1763)	(3)

---

260. According to [C.S], there was a copy of this libretto in I-FPfanan (previously in Turin), yet the items of the collection were sold independently and can no longer be traced; see [S]3048a and <http://corago.unibo.it/libretto/V5APP00018> [accessed 17 June 2022].
261. Microfilm copy: US-BEm ML50.2.A7062 M3.
262. Copied from D-B Mus.ms. 13395 in 1909. Microfilm copy: US-BEm MICROFILM A559 M.

		birthday of Carlos III, king of Spain	
1768 Naples		mus. by N. Piccinni and others	(4)
		Teatro di S. Carlo (04/11/1768)	
		name day of Carlos III, king of Spain	
		2nd version	

Librettos (1) Rome: [s.n.],[263] 1762
I-Rsc Libr. n. XVII [17]; I-Rvat Stamp.Ferr.V.8057 [8]

(2) Foligno: Campana, [1763]
I-FOLc MISC HL 8-6

(3) Barcelona: Generas, [1763] (It./Spa.)
E-Bbc 2-II-83; E-Bbc 10-I-26; US-Cn ML50.2.A78 P53 1763; US-Wc ML48 .A4

(4) Naples: Morelli, 1768
I-Bc Lo.04210; I-Nc Rari 10.5.8 [6]; P-Ln M. 938 P.; US-Eu 782.5 P588aZ

Music sources
1st version: 1762, Rome

[complete scores] D-Mbs^{MGG}; D-MÜs SANT Hs 3185 [I–III]$^{RISM;A}$; F-Pn D-12660^{BnF,NG}; I-Fc D.I.543/544/545^{IC,MGG,NG,SBN}; I-Nc* 16.4.5/6^{MGG,NG,RISM,SBN}; I-Rc Mss. 2783/2784/2785^{IC,S}; P-La 45-VI-23/24/25^{BA,MGG,NG}; P-La 54-III-64^{BA,MGG,NG} [Act I][264]; US-NH Misc. Ms. 13^{RISM}

[excerpts] *Conservati fedele* (F-Pn D-9006 [2]^{BnF,265}; P-La 54-III-64 [2–4]$^{BA;IP}$; S-Skma Alströmer saml. 163 [29]^{RISM}); *Deh, respirar lasciatemi* (P-La 54-III-64 [12–14]$^{BA;IP}$; S-Skma Alströmer saml. 163 [30]^{RISM}); *Dimmi che un empio sei* (I-PEsp M.CXXVIII [2]^{SBN}; P-La 54-III-64 [15–17]$^{BA;IP}$); *Fra cento affanni e cento* (HR-Sk LX-738$^{RISM;P}$; I-PEsp M.CXXVIII [13]^{SBN}; I-Rdp Ms Musicale 58 [2]^{RISM}; P-La 54-III-64 [5–11]$^{BA;IP}$); *Mi credi spietata?* (P-La 54-III-64 [27–29]$^{BA;IP}$); *Non è ver che sia contento* (P-La 54-III-64 [30–34]$^{BA;IP}$); *Per quell'affetto che l'incatena* (D-MÜs SANT Hs 1580 [12]^{RISM}; D-SWl Mus.4235$^{RISM;P}$; F-Pn D-9006 [3]$^{BnF;MGG}$; I-Nc 34.6.20 [21]^{SBN}; S-Skma Alströmer saml. 163 [31]^{RISM}; S-Uu Gimo 233$^{RISM;R,P}$); *Per quel paterno amplesso* (D-Hs M A/878 [18]^{MGG,NG,RISM}; P-La 48-III-17 [6–23]$^{BA;IP}$; P-La 48-III-47 [6–12]$^{BA;IP}$; S-Skma Alströmer saml. 164 [1]^{RISM}); *Rendimi il caro amico* (D-KA Don Mus.Ms. 2142^{RISM,266}); *Su le sponde del torbido Lete* (D-MÜs SANT Hs 1580 [13]^{RISM}; S-Skma Alströmer saml.

---

263. 'Si vendono da Giovanni Giuliani'.
264. Incomplete copy of the first act. It starts in the 9th scene.
265. Wrongly attributed to T. Traetta.
266. In G major instead of D major.

MC | *Artaserse* (1730–1850)

164 [3]^(RISM); US-BEm MS 104 [3]^(IC,RISM); *Vo solcando un mar crudele* (I-PEsp M.CXXVIII [3]^(RISM,SBN); I-Rvat Chigi Q VIII 195^(SBN); P-La 54-III-64 [18–26]^(BA;IP))

2nd version: 1768, Naples

[complete scores] I-Nc* 15.1.7/8^(MGG,SBN,267); I-Nc 30.4.33/34/35^(MGG,RISM,SBN); I-Nc 30.4.36/37^(MGG,RISM,SBN); P-La 45-VI-26/27/28^(BA); US-Wc M1500.P58 A68 1768^(IC,MGG,NG,RISM)

[excerpts] *Conservati fedele* (US-Bu H. C. Robbins Landon Collection, Scores ˟781A, Box 5, Folder 2^(RISM;P); US-BEm MS 93 [4]^(IC,RISM,268)); *Fra cento affanni e cento* (I-MC 5-A-14 [17]^(IC,RISM); I-PEsp M.CXXVIII [13]^(RISM,SBN); I-Rdp Ms Musicale 91 [4]^(SBN); US-BEm MS 93 [5]^(IC,RISM)); *Mi credi spietata?* (A-Wgm VI 8737 [Q 3377]^(IC); D-SWl Mus.4233^(RISM); CH-Gc Rmo 123/8 [5]^(RISM); DK-Sa R162^(RISM); I-Mc Noseda O.44 [10]^(SBN); I-MC 5-A-11 [8]^(RISM); I-Nc 33.3.7 [27]^(SBN); I-Nc 34.4.3 [18]^(SBN); I-Nc 34.6.16 [16]^(SBN); US-BEm MS 93 [2]^(IC,RISM)); *Perché tarda è mai la morte* (US-BEm MS 93 [1]^(IC,RISM)); *Per quel paterno amplesso* (B-Bc 4641^(RISM); I-MC 5-A-11 [1]^(RISM); I-MC 5-A-14 [5]^(RISM); I-MC 5-A-15 [8]^(RISM); US-BEm MS 93 [7]^(IC,RISM)); *Se al labbro mio non credi* (CH-Gc Rmo 123/7 [5]^(RISM)); *Se vendetta io chiedo, oh dio* (F-Pn D-12658^(BnF,MGG); I-MC 5-A-8 [6]^(RISM); I-MC 5-A-12 [10]^(RISM); I-MC 5-A-14 [18]^(RISM)); *Sogna il guerrier le schiere* (I-MC 5-A-12 [1]^(RISM)); *Tu vuoi ch'io viva, o cara* (I-MC 5-A-12 [15]^(RISM); US-Bu H. C. Robbins Landon Collection, Scores ˟781A, Box 5, Folder 2^(RISM)); *Va' tra le selve ircane* (DK-Kc R317^(RISM); I-Nc 34.6.20 [8]^(SBN); US-BEm MS 93 [3]^(IC,RISM))

[undated] [excerpts] *Conservati fedele* (A-Wgm VI 15343 [Q 3387]^(IC); GB-Lbl Add. 31652 [10/1]^(RISM)); *Mi credi spietata?* (GB-Lbl Add. 31652 [10/2]^(RISM)); *Nuvoletta opposta al sole* (I-Tf 2 IV 18^(RISM))

[unspecified] [excerpts] one aria (P-La 48-III-47 [13–23]^(BA;IP))

[doubtful] [excerpts] *Conservati fedele* (I-MC 5-A-15 [27]^(RISM,269)); *Vacilla, o padre*[270] (P-La 48-III-47 [6–12]^(BA;IP))

1762	mus. by various unknown composers
1762 Montepulciano	Teatro Nuovo (spr.)

---

267. Possible autograph.
268. Despite the inscription on the manuscript, the arias on the source are wrongly dated 1762 in Emerson, John A., *Catalog of Pre-1900 Vocal Manuscripts in the Music Library, University of California at Berkeley* (Berkeley: University of California Press, 1988).
269. The music is different from Piccinni's two authorised versions of the aria.
270. No such aria is included in any of Piccinni's settings.

MC | *Artaserse* (1730–1850)

Librettos	Florence: Albizzi, 1762
	I-Rsc Libr. n. XVII [18]; I-Vc 4091 [6]
1763	mus. by Bernasconi, Andrea (2nd version) → see 1746
1763	mus. by Scarlatti, Antonio (2nd version) → see 1747
1765	mus. by Sartori, Girolamo
1765 Lodi	Teatro di Lodi (carn.)[271]
Librettos	Lodi: heirs of Trabatti, [1765]
	I-Mr Libr. 02792
1765	mus. by various unknown composers (incl. Colla, Giuseppe?)[272]
1765 Genoa	Teatro da S. Agostino (summ.)
Librettos	Genoa: Casamara, [1765]
	D-Tu k III 86 aa
1765	mus. by Fiorillo, Ignazio (rev. version) → see 1751
1766	mus. by Ponzo, Giuseppe
1766 Venice	Teatro Grimani di S. Benedetto (carn., 03/01/1766)
Librettos	Venice: Fossati, [1766]
	I-Mb Racc.dramm.4399; I-Vcg LIBRETTI S.BENEDETTO 188; I-Vnm DRAMM.1090 [6]; I-Vnm DRAMM.1302 [4]; US-LAum ML48 .R114 1766 [8]; <u>US-Wc ML48 [S8355]</u>
Music sources	[complete scores] P-La 46-II-12/13/14[BA]
	[excerpts] *Conservati fedele* (I-Vc Correr Busta 71.43 [8][SBN]); *Nuvoletta opposta al sole* (I-Vc Correr Busta 71.43 [3][SBN]); *Per quel paterno amplesso* (I-Vc Correr Busta 71.43 [9][SBN])
1767	mus. by unknown composer(s)
1767 Palma de Mallorca	Teatro de Palma (07/1767)

---

271. Schmidt-Hensel ('*La musica è del Signor Hasse*', vol. 2, p. 93) hypothesises that this setting may have had music by Hasse.
272. [CA] lists an *Artaserse* on 26/12/1764 in the Teatro da Sant'Agostino by Giuseppe Colla. No further evidence on the composer's setting has been found. Furthermore, [CA] does not include the performance in the summer of that year.

MC | *Artaserse* (1730–1850)

Librettos	Barcelona: [s.n.], 1767 (It./Spa?)[273]	
	NA	

1767 — mus. by Boroni, Antonio

1767 Prague	Teatro Nuovo	(1)
1770 Verona	Teatro Filarmonico (carn.)	(2)

Librettos (1) NA

(2) Verona: Ramanzini, [1770]
I-VEc D.383 [7]; US-NYp *MGTY-Res.; US-Wc ML48 [S1250]

Music sources [complete scores] D-Dl Mus.3406-F-8[IC,274]

[excerpts] *Conservati fedele* (CZ-Pkřiž XXXV E 184[RISM;P,275]); *Disperata invan m'affanno* (D-Dl Mus.1-F-49,9 [11][MGG,NG,RISM]); *Fra cento affanni e cento* (CZ-Pnm VI C 87[IC;P]; US-Wc M1505.B73[RISM]); *Su le sponde del torbido Lete* (HR-Zha LXXXI.P[RISM]); *Tu vuoi ch'io viva, o cara* (D-KA Don Mus.Ms. 217[IC,RISM])

[contrafacta] *Disperata invan m'affanno* ([*Moesta semper lacrymabo*] CZ-Pnm XXXVIII A 186[RISM])

1768 — mus. by Sacchini, Antonio

1768 Rome	Teatro di Torre Argentina (carn., 02/01/1768)[276]	(1)
1769 Valencia	Palace of the Dukes of Gandía (carn., 20/01/1769)	(2)

Librettos (1) Rome: Puccinelli,[277] [1768]
B-Bc 19317; I-Bc Lo.04926; I-Rsc Libr. n. XVII [19]; US-Wc ML50.2.A8S2

(2) Valencia: Burguete, [1769] (It./Spa.)
E-Mn T/22274; F-Pn 8-YG-1349[278]

Music sources [complete scores] GB-G MUS 395/396/397[IC,MGG]; I-MC 5-E-12[MGG,RISM] [Acts I&II]; I-Rc* Mss. 2810/2811/2812[MGG,NG,RISM,279]; I-Rdp Ms Musicale 11[MGG,NG,RISM]; I-Rsc G.Mss.314[SBN]

---

273. Cited in Cotarelo y Mori, *Orígenes y establecimiento de la ópera en España*, p. 282.
274. Microfilm copy: US-PRu MICROFILM 1687.
275. For a performance on 20/05/1781.
276. 09/01/1768 according to [MGG], yet the date given in the *Diario ordinario*, 7884 (09/02/1768) is clear: 'Sabato 2 gennaio nel Teatro a Torre Argentina si è dato principio al dramma in music ache ha per titolo l'*Artaserse*'; as cited in Rinaldi, *Due secoli al Teatro Argentina*, p. 171.
277. 'Si vendono nella sudetta stamperia, e da Lorenzo Corradi'.
278. Microfilm copy: F-Pn MICROFILM M-4215.
279. Possible autograph.

[excerpts] *Bramar di perdere* (US-Wc M1505.A1 (vol. 191) [3]^(RISM)); *Conservati fedele* (D-MÜs SANT Hs 3483b [11]^(RISM); I-Mc Noseda O.47 [8]^(SBN); I-Nc 51.2.51 [6]^(SBN); I-PAc Sanv.A.91^(RISM,SBN); US-BEm MS 87 [10]^(IC,RISM); US-BEm MS 1159 [3]^(RISM); US-Wc M1505.A1 (vol. 205) [2]^(RISM)); *Deh, respirar lasciatemi* (B-Br Ms II 4042 Mus Fétis 2621 [2]^(RISM); US-Wc M1505.A1 (vol. 191) [2]^(RISM)); *Fra cento affanni e cento* (US-BEm MS 87 [3]^(IC,RISM); US-Wc M1505.A1 (vol. 205) [2]^(RISM)); *Mentre il cor con meste voci* (D-LEm Becker III.15.71^(RISM); DK-Sa R149^(RISM); S-Skma T-SE-R^(RISM)); *Mi credi spietata?* (US-Wc M1505.A1 (vol. 205) [1]^(RISM)); *Non è ver che sia contento* (US-Wc M1505.A1 (vol. 191) [1]^(RISM)); *Per quel paterno amplesso* (D-KNmi P 294 R [4]^(RISM); D-MÜs SANT Hs 3483d [6]^(RISM,280); GB-Lbl Add. 31649 [14]^(BL); I-Mc Mus. Tr.ms. 1550^(SBN); I-Gl FONDO ANT. NN.350^(IC,SBN;IP,281); I-Nc 51.2.51 [10]^(SBN); I-Rama A.Ms.3805 [9]^(RISM,SBN); I-Tf 2 IV 4^(RISM,282); US-BEm MS 122 [1]^(IC,RISM); US-CAe Mus 503.603 [9]^(RISM); US-SFsc *M2.1 M445^(RISM)); *Se al labbro mio non credi* (D-Tl G 7^(RISM;R,P,283); I-Rc Mss. 2765 [20]^(SBN); US-BEm MS 87 [2]^(IC,RISM); US-BEm MS 1169 [4]^(RISM); US-CAt 2010YW-694^(IC); US-Wc M1505.A1 (vol. 205) [3]^(RISM)); *Sento che l'alma è oppressa* (US-Wc M1505.A1 (vol. 191) [4]^(RISM)); *Su le sponde del torbido Lete* (D-Mbs Mus.ms. 5418 [6]^(RISM); US-Wc M1505.A1 (vol. 191) [5]^(RISM)); *Tu vuoi ch'io viva, o cara* (HR-Dsmb 26/803^(RISM); US-BEm MS 106 [9]^(IC,RISM); US-Wc M1505.A1 (vol. 203) [2]^(RISM)); *Va' tra le selve ircane* (D-Sla 96 [4]^(RISM;R); US-BEm MS 87 [9]^(IC,RISM))

[unspecified] various arias in I-Rvat Chigi Q VII 156–164^(IC,MGG,NG)

[parodies] *Se al labbro mio non credi*[284] ([*Oh dio, mancar mi sento*] D-WRl HMA 3922^(RISM;IP))

1768	mus. by various unknown composers
1768 Mantua	Teatro Arciducale (carn.)
Librettos	Mantua: heirs of Pazzoni, 1768
	I-MAc Misc.476/9
1768	mus. by Piccinni, Niccolò (2^(nd) version) → see 1762

---

280. En E flat major instead of D major.
281. Vn I part only.
282. In e minor instead of D major.
283. In G major instead of F major.
284. The aria belongs to Metastasio's *Adriano in Siria*, yet the music of this version does not correspond to Sacchini's setting (Venice, 1771), but rather to the aria *Se al labbro mio non credi* from his *Artaserse*.

1770	mus. by various unknown composers	
1770 Florence	Teatro della Pergola (carn., 26/12/1769)	
Librettos	Florence: Risaliti,[285] 1770 I-Fc E.V.1565; I-Mt Triv.L.3629.3	
1770	mus. by various unknown composers	
1770 Pisa	Teatro Pubblico (spr.)	
Librettos	Pisa: Polloni & co., 1770 US-Wc ML48.A5 [30]	
1770	mus. by various unknown composers	
1770 Siena	Teatro degli Intronati (summ.)	
Librettos	Siena: Rossi, [1770] I-Fc E.V.0342; I-Fc E.V.2656	
1770	mus. by various unknown composers	
1770 Lucca	Teatro Pubblico (aut.)	
Librettos	Lucca: Benedini, 1770 US-CAt TS 8056.428 1770	
1771	mus. by Vento, Mattia	
1771 London	Harmonical Meeting, Soho Square (24/01/1771)	
Music sources	[printed sources] *Bramar di perdere* [3]; *Conservati fedele* [2]; *Deh, respirar lasciatemi* [4]; *Mi credi spietata?* [7]; *Se al labbro mio non credi* [5]; *Se d'un amor tiranno* [6], in *The Ouverture and Favourite Songs in the Opera of Artaxerxes Composed for the Harmonical Meeting in Soho Square* ([London: s.n., 1771])[286]	
1772	mus. by Paisiello, Giovanni	
1772 Modena	Teatro Ducale (carn., 26/12/1771)	(1)
1773 Prague	Teatro Regio (carn.)	(2)
1778 Verona	Teatro Filarmonico (carn.)	(3)
Librettos	(1) Modena: heirs of Soliani, [1772] I-Bc Lo.03778	

---

285. 'Si vende da'.
286. Burden, 'Metastasio on the London Stage', p. 78.

MC | *Artaserse* (1730–1850)

	(2) Prague: Pruscha, [1773]
	CZ-Pu Mus Li 0210; <u>CZ-Pu 65 E 2726</u>
	(3) Verona: Moroni, 1778
	I-Ms MUS. G. XXVIII. 13; I-VEc D.386 [7]
Music sources	[complete scores] <u>I-Nc* 16.8.18/19</u>^{IC,MGG,NG,RISM,SBN}
	[excerpts] *Conservati fedele* (D-B Mus.ms. 16608/5^{RISM}); *Per quel paterno amplesso* (US-Wc M1505.A1 (vol. 185) [2]^{RISM}); *Se vendetta io chiedo* (I-Vnm Mss. 11323^{SBN}); *Tu vuoi ch'io viva, o cara* (I-Vnm Mss. 11319^{SBN})
	[doubtful] *Per pietà bell'idol mio*[287] (US-Bu H. C. Robbins Landon Collection, Scores ^X781A, Box 6 [26]^{RISM;R})
1772	mus. by Manfredini, Vincenzo
1772 Venice	Teatro Grimani di S. Benedetto (carn., 03/01/1772)
Librettos	Venice: Fenzo, [1772]
	A-Wmi BT-732; <u>I-Mb Racc.dramm.4400</u>; I-Vcg LIBRETTI S.BENEDETTO 190; I-Vnm DRAMM.1099 [7]; I-Vnm DRAMM.1308 [5]; US-BEm ML48 .I7 [430]; <u>US-Wc ML48 [S5892]</u>
Music sources	[complete scores] <u>F-Pn D-7280/7281</u>^{BnF,MGG,NG,288}; P-La 44-XI-68/69/70^{BA,NG}
	[excerpts] *Bramar di perdere* (CH-Zz Mus Ms A 141 [1]^{SB}); *Conservati fedele* (J-Tk S10-891 [6]^{RISM}); *Fra cento affanni e cento* (DK-Kk mu7501.1538^{RISM}); *Tu vuoi ch'io viva, o cara* (<u>D-B Mus.ms. 13434</u>^{RISM;P})
1772	mus. by Giordani, Tommaso; Vento, Mattia; and Hasse, Johann Adolph lib. rev. by Lalli, Domenico; poetry rev. by Bottarelli, Gualberto Giovan; trans. into English by Carara, Antonio
1772 London	King's Theatre in the Haymarket (25/04/1772)[289] (1)
1773 London	King's Theatre in the Haymarket (01/12/1772)[290] (2)
1774 London	NA (17/05/1774)[291] (3)

---

287. The aria ins not included in Paisiello's original setting.
288. Microfilm copies: F-Pn VM BOB-25637; US-PRu MICROFILM 2267.
289. The production ran for thirteen consecutive performances; see Petty, 'Italian Opera in London', p. 173.
290. The production ran for fourteen consecutive performances; see Petty, 'Italian Opera in London', p. 177.
291. The production ran for two consecutive performances; see Petty, 'Italian Opera in London', p. 181 and Burden, 'Metastasio on the London Stage', p. 80. ^SIndex I, p. 395 lists another revival in London in 1782, yet no corresponding libretto is included in the main catalogue; we therefore consider it as an indexing mistake.

MC | *Artaserse* (1730–1850)

Librettos	(1) London: Griffin, 1772 (It./En.)[292]
	CH-Gpu Ng 430/2 [9]; D-Au 02/III.10.8.296; D-HR [D-Au] 02/III.10.8.296; F-Pm 8° 46764 [5]; F-Pn RES VS-642; GB-Lbl 907.i.15 [1];[293] GB-Ob Harding D 2443 [1]; US-I ML48 .E342 [7]; US-NH ML48 L698 [10]
	(2) London: Griffin, 1773 (It./En.)
	GB-Ob Harding D 2443 [1][294]
	(3) NA
Music sources	[excerpts] Giordani, Tommaso, *Infelice! Ah dove io vado* (CH-Gc X 5 [2][RISM;R]; GB-NOr DD7P/6/15/76[RISM]; GB-WWro CR1291/474 [36][RISM]; I-Bc CC.229 [9][IC,RISM,SBN]); *Non è ver che sia contento* (I-Rama A.Ms.3753 [2][RISM,SBN]); *Se al labbro mio non credi* (CH-Gc X 5 [1][RISM;R]; GB-NOr DD/P/6/15/80[RISM]); *Tu vuoi ch'io viva, o cara* (CH-Gc X 5 [3][RISM;R]; S-STr n/s[RISM])
	[printed sources] Giordani, Tommaso, *Conservati fedele* [1]; *Infelice ah dov'io vado* [4]; *Se al labbro mio non credi* [3]; *Tu vuoi ch'io viva, o cara* [6], in <u>The Favourite Songs in the Opera Artaserse by Sig.r Giordani</u> (London: Bremner, [1772])
	The Overture and Favourite Songs in the Opera of Artaxerxes, Composed for the Harmonical Meeting in Soho Square, to which is Added two Songs Sung by Sigra. Grassi in the Present Opera of the same Name (London: Welcker, [c. 1772])
1774	**mus. by various unknown composers**
1774 Pavia	Teatro dei Quattro Cavalieri Associati (carn., 26/12/1773[CA])
Librettos	Pavia: Bianchi & co., [1774]
	I-Vnm DRAMM.3258 [4]
1774	**mus. by Mysliveček, Josef**
1774 Naples	Teatro di S. Carlo (13/08/1774)
	birthday of Maria Carolina, queen of Austria
Librettos	Naples: Morelli, 1774
	<u>I-Bc Lo.03186</u>; I-Nn S.MARTNO 52.7 23 [1]; I-Pmc[S]; US-NYp Mus. Res. *MZ, A/20/21 [7]

---

292. According to [S]3067, further copy in the Hicke private collection in London.
293. Microfilm copy: GB-En Mf.134, reel 5684 [23].
294. Microfilm copies: D-Gs MA 2001-46:13147 [9]; GB-En Mf.134, reel 13147 [9].

Music sources	[complete scores] I-Fc D.I.370/371/372[IC,MGG,NG,SBN]; I-Nc 29.4.32/33/34[IC,MGG,NG,RISM,SBN,295]	
	[excerpts] *Cara, oh dio nel volto espresso* (CZ-Pu 59 R 31 [4][RISM]; F-Pn D-8205 [5][BnF,296]); *Conservati fedele* (CZ-Pnm XLII E 216[RISM]; F-Pn D-8206 [5][BnF]; F-Pn D-8208 [1][BnF]; I-Mc Noseda O.25 [2][SBN]; I-MC 4-A-12 [4][RISM]; I-MC 4-A-13 [2][RISM]; I-MC 6-A-1 [10][RISM]; I-Nc 34.6.5 [10][SBN]; US-Wc M1505.A1 (vol. 129) [5][RISM]); *Pace e calma in questo seno* (CH-Bu kr IV 185[RISM;P]; CZ-LIT 699[RISM;P]; CZ-Pu 59 R 31 [5][RISM]; F-Pn D-8205 [9][BnF]; I-BGc E.1.3 [7][RISM]; I-MC 4-A-15 [4][RISM]; I-MC 4-A-16 [3][RISM]; I-Nc 34.6.5 [9][SBN]); *Per pietà bell'idol mio* (CZ-Pu 59 R 31 [1][RISM]); *Per quel paterno amplesso* (CZ-Pu 59 R 31 [2][RISM]; D-MÜs SANT Hs 2697[RISM]; I-Bsf M.M.II.7[SBN;P]; I-Mc Noseda O.25 [3][SBN]; I-MC 4-A-11 [5][RISM]; I-MC 4-A-13 [1][RISM]; I-MC 4-A-15 [9][RISM]; I-Nc 34.6.4 [1][SBN]; I-Raf 1.E.6 [5][RISM]); *Tu vuoi ch'io viva, o cara* (CZ-Pu 59 R 31 [6][RISM]); *Va' tra le selve ircane* (CZ-Pu 59 R 31 [3][RISM])	

1774	mus. by Caruso, Luigi	
1774 London[MGG,NG]	King's Theatre in the Haymarket?	(1)
1780 Florence	Teatro degli Intrepidi (04/04/1780) *rev. version*	(2)
Librettos	(1) NA	
	(2) [Florence]: Pagani, [1780] I-Fc E.V.0343; I-Fc E.V.1581; I-Fc E.V.2657; US-Cn ML50.2.A78 C37 1780; US-CAh *IC7 A100 B750 [112]; US-Wc ML48 [S1656]	
Music sources	[complete scores] I-Bc EE.28[IC,NG,297]	
	[excerpts] *Tu vuoi, ch'io viva, o cara* (GB-Cfm [GB-Cu] MU.MS.777[IC])	

1776	mus. by Borghi, Giovanni Battista	
1776 Venice	Teatro Grimani di S. Benedetto (carn., 26/12/1775)	
Librettos	Venice: Fenzo, 1776 F-Pn 8-YTH-51547; I-Bc Lo.00641;[298] I-Mb Racc.dramm.3998; I-Rsc Carv.1316; I-Vcg LIBRETTI S.BENEDETTO 192; I-Vnm DRAMM.1316 [5]; US-Wc ML48 [S1227]	

---

295. Microfilm copy: US-PRu MICROFILM 2359.
296. Microfilm copy of all the pieces in F-Pn D-8205: F-Pn VM BOB-24019.
297. For Florence 1780. Microfilm copies: CDN-Lu M1500.M57C33 1780a; I-Bc 0130.
298. Mutilated on pp. 24–38, 55–68.

MC | *Artaserse* (1730–1850)

Music sources   [complete scores] P-La 44-III-59[BA,MGG,NG]

1776	**mus. by Bertoni, Ferdinando**	
1776 Forlì	Teatro Pubblico	(1)
	1st version	
1777 Milan	Teatro Interinale (carn., 26/12/1776[299])	(2)
1777 Macerata	Teatro dei Nobili (carn.)	(3)
1777 Genoa	Teatro da S. Agostino (spr.)	(4)
1777 Lucca	Teatro Pubblico (aut.)	(5)
1779 London	King's Theatre in the Haymarket (23/01/1779)[300]	(6)
	English trans. by Ms. Rigaud	
1785 Brescia	Teatro degli Erranti (Fair, 15/02/1785?)	(7)
1785 Treviso	Teatro Onigo (aut.)	(8)
1785 Verona	Teatro Filarmonico (aut.)	(9)
1787 Pavia	Teatro dei Quattro Cavalieri Associati (carn., 26/12/1787[CA])	(10)
1788 Cremona	Teatro dell'Associazione (spr.)	(11)
1788 Genoa	Teatro da S. Agostino (18/11/1788)	(12)
	rev. version[NG]	
1790 Ancona	Teatro della Fenice (spr.)[301]	(13)
1792 Imola	Teatro dei Cavalieri (summ.)	(13,14)

Librettos (1,13) NA

(2) Milan: Bianchi, [1777][302]
F-Pn LIV IT-3673 [4]; I-Bc Lo.00513; I-FEu[S]; I-LDEsormani 309/6/12; I-Mb Racc.dramm.0185; I-Mc Coll.Libr.167; I-Mr Libr. 02787; I-Rsc Vol. 18 [9]; US-HA ML50.B477 A7; US-Wc ML48 [S905]

(3) Macerata: Capitani, [1777]
I-Vgc Rol.[C,PM]

(4) Genoa: Gesiniana, [1777]
F-Pn YD-5447 [4][303]

(5) Lucca: Bonsignori, [1777]
I-La Dono Pellegrini – Libretti d'opera, 35

---

299. Date in [C, CA] gives 01/01/1777.
300. The production ran for five consecutive performances; see Petty, 'Italian Opera in London', p. 202.
301. Salvarani, Marco, *Il teatro La Fenice di Ancona: cenni storici e cronologia dei drammi in musica e balli (1712–1818)* (Rome: Fratelli Palombi, 1999).
302. [S]3078 lists a further copy in I-Ma. However, it is not present in its card and online catalogues. As informed by the director of the Biblioteca Ambrosiana in Milan, it was probably destroyed during the bombardment of the city in August 1743.
303. Microfilm copy: F-Pn MICROFILM M-2650.

(6) London: Bigg, 1779 (It./En.)[304]
GB-Ob Harding D 2446 [1]; US-NHs Hd45 528h; US-Wc ML48 [S906]

(7) Brescia: Pasini, 1785
I-Vcg LIBRETTI BRESCIA 250[305]

(8) Venice: Fenzo, 1785
I-Vcg LIBRETTI TREVISO 272;[306] I-Vgc ROL.0808 [6]

(9) Verona: Ramanzini, 1785
B-Br Fétis 4.488 A XIV/5 Mus.;[307] I-VEc D.388 [2]; US-BEm ML48 .I7 [560]

(10) Pavia: Galeazzi, [1787]
I-BRq Misc.E.774[308]

(11) Cremona: Manini, [1788]
I-CRg CIV.A.PP.23.10[309]

(12) Genoa: Gesiniana, [1788]
B-Bc 19320; I-Fm Mel.2269 [5]; I-Gl^{C,S}; I-Rsc Carv.1317; I-SML 29 FC 2186 7; US-Wc ML48 [S907]

(14) Bologna: Sassi, [1792]
I-Bc Lo.00514

(15) Imola: Monte, [1792]
I-Bl FS.W.1099

Music sources   [complete scores] I-Mc Part. Tr.ms. 25[NG,RISM,SBN,310]; I-Rc Mss. 5810[IC,RISM;IP,311]; I-Rrostirolla [I-Fn] MS MUS 228[RISM,SBN;IP,312]; P-La 47-II-17/18[BA,NG] [Act II]

[excerpts] *Ah, che parlar non posso* (CH-E 694,16[RISM;IP]; F-Pn D-1061 [10][BnF,RISM,313]; GB-Lbl Add. 32170[BL,RISM]; I-Gl 1 FONDO ANT. NN.594[IC]; I-SPEbc Î, 1-1 [4][RISM]); *Conservati fedele* (I-PAc Sanv.A.44[RISM,SBN]); *Figlio se più non vivi* (I-FZc A.VI.18 [4][RISM,SBN]; US-Wc M1505.A1 (vol. 5) [3][RISM]); *Fra cento affanni e cento* (I-Gl FON-

---

304. Microfilm copies of unspecified copy(s): D-Gs MA 2001-46:13147 [10]; GB-En Mf.134, reel 13147 [10].
305. Microfilm copy: CDN-Lu ML48.M47B53 1787a; photocopy: CDN-Lu ML48.M47B48 1785a.
306. Photocopy: CDN-Lu ML48.M47B482 1785a.
307. Microfilm copy: CDN-Lu ML48.M47L442 1783a.
308. Photocopy: CDN-Lu ML48.M47A498 1787a.
309. Photocopy: CDN-Lu ML48.M47B4812 1788a.
310. For Genoa 1788; additions by Generali and Andreozzi.
311. Vn II part only.
312. Vn II and Ob. parts only.
313. Microfilm copy of all the pieces in F-Pn D-1061: F-Pn VM BOB-25761.

DO ANT. M.[4].28.41[IC,SBN]); *Non ho pace mille pene* (F-Pn D-1059 [7][BnF,RISM,314]; F-Pn D-1061 [5][BnF,RISM]; F-Pn L-17262[BnF,RISM;IP]; I-FZc A.VI.18 [5][RISM]; US-Wc M1505.A1 (vol. 5) [2][RISM]); *Per pietà bell'idol mio* (I-Gl FONDO ANT. M.(1) 1WW[SBN]); *Per quel paterno amplesso* (A-LA 1965[RISM;P]; CZ-Pnm XLII A 318[RISM]; F-Pn D-1060 [6][BnF,RISM,315]; I-Bl FS AP 10[IC,SBN,316]; I-FZc A.VI.18 [2][RISM,SBN]; I-Mc Noseda C.31 [3][SBN]; US-Wc M1505.A2 A79[RISM]); *Se al labbro mio non credi* (D-LÜh Mus. Q 164[RISM]; F-Pn D-1061 [6][BnF,RISM]; I-FZc A.VI.18 [3][RISM,SBN]; I-OS Mss.Mus.B 4929[RISM,SBN]; I-Rama A.Ms.2750[RISM]); *Tu vuoi ch'io viva, o cara* (I-FZc A.VI.18 [1][RISM,SBN])

[printed sources] *Deh ti fermi, deh m'aspetta* [1]; *Figlio se più non vivi* [3]; *Non ho pace mille pene* [2], in *The Favourite Songs in the Opera Artaserse by Sig.r Bertoni* (London: Napier, [c. 1779])

[inserts] *A tanto duol resistere gli affetti miei* by Gaetano Andreozzi[317] (I-Gl SCAT. 63.1[IC,SBN]); *Perché tarda la morte* by Raimondo Mei (B-Bc 4417[RISM,318])

[doubtful] *Cara, deh prendi in pace*[319] (I-OS Mss.Mus.B 1540 [2][RISM,SBN]); *Caro mio ben, credimi almen* (I-VEcon MS 034[RISM,SBN,320]); *Deh! Si affretti*[321] (I-OS Mss.Mus.B 1540 [4][RISM,SBN]); *Deh signor, s'è ver che m'ami dal tuo amor*[322] (D-BFb [D-MÜu] B-er 83[RISM,R]; D-Dl Mus.1-F-82,34 [6][RISM]; D-MÜs SANT Hs 491[RISM]; F-Pn D-111[BnF,RISM,323]; F-Pn D-1060 [4][BnF,RISM]; HR-Dsmb 16/562[RISM]; I-Gl FONDO ANT. NN.622[IC,SBN;R]; I-Gl B M.1.23 [24][IC,SBN]; I-Mc Mus. Tr.ms. 119[RISM]; I-VEcon MS 033[RISM]); *In così fatal momento*[324] (F-Pn D-111[BnF,RISM,325]; I-FZc A.VI.17[RISM]); *Padre, un addio*[326] (I-OS Mss.Mus.B 3067[RISM,SBN]; I-VEcon MS 032[RISM,SBN]);

---

314. Microfilm copy: F-Pn VM BOB-24071.
315. Microfilm copy of all the pieces in F-Pn D-1060: F-Pn VM BOB-24072.
316. For Imola 1792.
317. From Andreozzi's *Catone in Utica* (Livorno, 1787).
318. For Pavia 1787.
319. This aria is not included in any of Bertoni's authorial settings.
320. This aria is not included in any of Bertoni's authorial settings; inserted into the 1785 Veronese revival.
321. This aria is not included in any of Bertoni's authorial settings; inserted into the 1785 revival in Brescia.
322. This aria is not included in any of Bertoni's authorial settings. In F-Pn D-110/111 (→ see 1788 Venice, mus. by various unknown composers), Bertoni's name is crossed out in favour of Mattia Vento's, yet the text does not feature in the latter's setting either. According to the inscriptions on several sources, the theatre and the singer correspond to the Veronese revival of Bertoni's in 1785.
323. → see 1788 Venice, mus. by various unknown composers
324. This duet was not included in Bertoni's original setting; inserted into the 1785 Veronese revival.
325. → see 1788 Venice, mus. by various unknown composers.
326. This duet was not included in Bertoni's original setting; inserted into the 1785 Veronese revival.

Parto ma il cor mi trema[327] (I-OS Mss.Mus.B 1540 [3]^{RISM,SBN}); *Per quel paterno amplesso* (I-Vlevi CF.B.97^{RISM,SBN}); *Sciogli o cara un dolce riso* (I-OS Mss.Mus.B 1540 [1]^{RISM,SBN}); *Tu vuoi ch'io viva, o cara* (A-LA 802^{RISM,328})

1777	mus. by Guglielmi, Pietro Alessandro	
1777 Rome	Teatro di Torre Argentina (carn., 29/01/1777)[329]	(1)
1789 Bologna	Teatro Zagnoni (carn.)	(2)
Librettos	(1) Rome: Settari, 1777	
	F-Pn YD-5413 [1];[330] I-Rsc Libr. n. XVIII [33]; I-Rvat Stamp.Ferr.V.8064 [3]; PL-Wu GSD 142409	
	(2) Bologna: Sassi, [1789]	
	I-Bam Op.X.Hd.014.FG; <u>I-Bc Lo.02361</u>; I-Bca 17-ARTISTICA Gb, 055; <u>I-Rn 40.10.C.21.8</u>; I-Rsc Carv.1318; I-Vgc ROL.0369 [3]; PL-KO B.P. 495 V-2-393; <u>US-Wc ML48 [S4298]</u>	
Music sources	[complete scores] P-La 47-III-24/25^{BA,MGG,NG} [Acts II&III]	
	[excerpts] *Deh, respirar lasciatemi* (S-Skma T-SE-R^{MGG,RISM}); *Se al labbro mio non credi* (HR-Zha XLVI.2C^{RISM;IP}; I-MC 2-E-8 [10]^{RISM}); *Tu vuoi ch'io viva, o cara* (I-Mc Mus. Tr.ms. 560^{MGG,RISM,SBN;P})	
1777	mus. by Re, Giuseppe Abate	
1777 Alessandria	Teatro Nuovo (Oct. Fair)	
Librettos	Alessandria: Vimercati, [1777]	
	US-CAh *IC7.A100.B750 [96]	
Music sources	[excerpts] *Per quel paterno amplesso* (US-BEm MS 1163 [7]^{RISM})	
1777?[331]	mus. by Schacht, Theodor von	
1777 Regensburg	Theatre	(1)
1781 Regensburg	Theatre	(1)
	Artaxerxes	

---

327. This aria is not included in any of Bertoni's authorial settings.
328. Dated 1777 on the score, but the music is different from that in the other sources.
329. Rinaldi (*Due secoli al Teatro Argentina*, p. 1472) and Franchi (*Le impressioni sceniche*, p. 719) give 28/02/1777, yet the press announcement is clear (*Diario ordinario*, 218 (01/02/1777)): 'Mercoledì sera nel Teatro di Torre Argentina andò in scena il secondo dramma intitolato *Artaserse*'; as quoted in Rinaldi, *Due secoli al Teatro Argentina*, p. 214.
330. Microfilm copy: F-Pn MICROFILM M-2651.
331. 1781 according to ^{C,NG}; 1777 according to ^{MGG} and inscriptions on some musical sources. The libretto is undated and the copy in GB-En has the inscription '1785?' written in pencil by a later hand.

MC | *Artaserse* (1730–1850)

Librettos	Regensburg: Breitfeld, [1777?] (It./Ger.)
	D-Mbs P.o.it. 628; GB-En DC.m.64 [4]; US-Wc ML48 [S9562]
Music sources	[complete scores] D-Rtt* Schacht 146 [I–II][RISM]
	[excerpts] *Conservati fedele* (D-Rtt* Schacht 138 [I][RISM]); *Deh, respirar lasciatemi* (D-Rtt Schacht 146 [III][RISM;P]); *Perché tarda è mai la morte* (D-Rtt Sammelband 3/5[RISM;R]); *Per quel paterno amplesso* (D-Rtt* Schacht 138 [IIa][RISM]; D-Rtt* Schacht 138 [IIb][RISM]); *Vo solcando un mar crudele* (F-Pn L-4580 [1][BnF])

1777–1781	mus. by Ullinger, Augustin[NG]

1778	mus. by unknown composer(s)
1778 Valencia	Theatre
Librettos	Valencia: Orga, [1778] (It./Spa.)
	E-VAu BH A-105/058 [5]

Artaserse, in *Opere del signor abate Pietro Metastasio* (Paris: widow of Hérissant, 1780), vol. I, pp. 1–112.

1780	mus. by Caruso, Luigi (rev. version) → see 1774

1780s	mus. by Parenti, Paolo Francesco[NG]
1780s [s.l.]	NA
Music sources	[excerpts] F-Pn[NG]

1781	mus. by Rust, Giacomo	
1781 Perugia	Teatro Civico del Verzaro (aut.)	(1)
1782 Livorno	Teatro degli Armeni (spr.)	(2)
1783 Florence	Teatro della Pergola (carn., 27/12/1782)	(3)
1783 Rome	Teatro di Torre Argentina (carn., 15/02/1783)	(4)
Librettos	(1) Perugia: Riginaldi, [1781]	
	I-PEcANT Misc.I.C 53 [7]; I-Vgc ROL.0586 [7]; US-Wc ML50.2.A8R8	
	(2) Livorno: Falorni, [1782]	
	B-Bc 19318[332]	

---

332. Photocopy: CDN-Lu ML48.M47R83 1782a.

(3) Florence: Risaliti,[333] 1783
I-Fc E.V.0344; I-Fc E.V.1495; I-Fn B.17.6.272.2.10; I-Rsc Carv.1319; US-Wc ML48 [S9165]

(4) Rome: Cannetti, 1783
I-Rsc Libr. n. XIX [23]; I-Rsc Libr. n. XIX [187]; I-Rvat Stamp. Ferr.V.8068 [13]; I-Vgc ROL.1171 [8]; US-PRV MSC Thurston Library Libretti 1 [29]

Music sources — [excerpts] *Ah, che mi sento, oh dio* (B-Bc 5166[NG,RISM;R]; D-B Mus.ms. 19143/3[NG,RISM;IP]; D-KA Don Mus.Ms. 1698[NG,RISM;P]; I-Gl FONDO ANT. NN.623[IC,SBN;R]; I-PEsp M.CXXX [5][NG,RISM]); *Deh, respirar lasciatemi* (I-PEsp M.CXXX [6][NG,RISM,SBN]); *Io ti lascio o mio tesoro* (I-Rsc G.Mss.200 [3][RISM]); *L'onda dal mar divisa* (D-B Mus.ms. 19143/1[NG,RISM;IP]); *Mia speranza, amato bene* (D-Dl Mus.1-F-82,26 [8][NG,RISM]; D-Mbs Mus. ms. 3958 [5][RISM]); *Non sa dir che sia tormento* (I-Rsc G.Mss.222 [5][RISM]); *Rendimi il caro amico* (I-PEsp M.CXXVIII [35][NG,RISM,SBN]); *Se tu sapessi, o cara* (HR-Dsmb 45/1263[NG,RISM])

[printed sources] *Per quel paterno amplesso*, in *Journal d'ariettes italiennes* (Paris: Bailleux, 1785)[P]

1782	mus. by Zannetti, Francesco
1782 Treviso	Teatro Onigo (aut.)
Librettos	Venice: Fenzo, 1782 I-Vcg LIBRETTI TREVISO 57 E 61[334]

1782	mus. by unknown composer(s)
1782 Lviv	NA
Librettos	Lviv: Pillera, [1782] PL-Kj St. Dr. 26786 I; PL-Wn SD XVIII.2.2407; PL-WRzno XVI-II-6391; PL-WRzno XVIII-7239

1783	mus. by Alessandri, Felice
1783 Naples	Teatro di S. Carlo (04/11/1783) *name day of Carlos III, king of Spain*

---

333. 'Si vende da'.
334. Microfilm copy: CDN-Lu ML48.M47B53 1787a; photocopy: CDN-Lu ML48.M47Z34 1782a.

MC | *Artaserse* (1730–1850)

Librettos	Naples: Flauto, 1783
	I-Bc Lo.00120; I-Fc E.V.2653;[335] I-Fm Mel.2198 [1]; I-Nc Rari 10.6.10 [1]; I-Vgc ROL.0133 [14]
Music sources	[complete scores] I-Nc* 24.6.3/4[MGG,NG,RISM,SBN]
	[doubtful] *Deh! Si affretti*[336] (I-OS Mss.Mus.B 45 [1/6][RISM,SBN])

1785	**mus. by Cimarosa, Domenico**	
1785 Turin	Teatro Regio (carn., 26/12/1784)[337]	(1)
1786 Cremona	Teatro dell'Associazione (carn.)	(2)
1801 Lisbon	Teatro de São Carlos (01/02/1801)	(3)
	performance in the benefit of G. Crescentini	

Librettos	(1) Turin: Derossi, [1785]
	I-ASs AN.A.LVI.1.28; I-Nragni L091; I-NOVc CIV 194.G.20; I-FPfanan[S,338]; I-Rsc Libr. n. XIX [24]; I-Rsc Vol. Carv.157 [4]; I-Tac Simeom L 116; I-Tci L.O.0368; I-Tmnr MUSIMA.40; I-Tn F XIII.497 [5]; I-Tp P.i.107 [6.5]; US-CAt TS 8000.6 [6]; US-Wc ML48 [S1905]
	(2) Cremona: Manini, [1786]
	I-PAc F. Libretti, sc.038 [624]
	(3) Lisbon: Ferreira, 1801
	I-Rsc Carv.1321; P-Ln T.S.C. 282 P.; P-Lt[S]
Music sources	[complete scores] I-Nc* 13.3.16/17[IC,MGG,NG,RISM,SBN,339]; I-Rmassimo n/s[MGG,NG,RISM,SBN]; P-La 47-II-45[BA,MGG,NG] [Act I]; RUS-SPsc[MGG,NG,340]
	[excerpts] *Conservati fedele* (I-Raf 1.A.3 [4][RISM,341]; I-Rsc G.Mss.199 [2][RISM]; US-Wc M1505.A1 (vol. 33) [1][RISM]); *Per quel paterno amplesso* (D-F Mus Hs 2211[RISM]; D-MÜs SANT Hs 1120[RISM]; D-MÜs SANT Hs 1243 [5][RISM]; F-Pn D-2169 [6][BnF,RISM,342]; F-Pn D-2173 [5][BnF,RISM,343]; I-Mc Mus. Tr.ms. 286[RISM,SBN]; I-Rama A.Ms.2454[RISM]; I-Tci Mus.Ms.31[RISM]; I-Raf 1.A.4 [2][RISM]); *Quanto è grave il mio tormento* (D-Bhm RH 0916

257

---

335. Microfilm copy: CDN-Lu ML48.M47A364 1783a.
336. This aria is not included in I-Nc* 24.6.3/4.
337. The production ran for fourteen consecutive performances; see Bouquet, Gualerzi, and Testa, *Storia del Teatro Regio di Torino*, pp. 77, 133.
338. The copy was previously a part of the Legger private collection in Turin and was subsequently transferred to I-FPfanan; see note 261 above.
339. Possible autograph.
340. It does not appear in the library's [IC] and the library staff have not been able to locate it either.
341. In G major instead of A major.
342. Microfilm copy: F-Pn VM BOB-31540.
343. Microfilm copy of all the pieces in F-Pn D-2173: F-Pn VM BOB-31813.

[21]^{RISM}; D-Bhm RH 0917 [10]^{RISM}; F-Pn D-2173 [2]$^{BnF,RISM.}$; I-BRc MS vari 71^{IC,RISM,SBN}; I-Gl B D.3.45 [3]^{IC,SBN}; I-Mc Noseda E.15 [9]^{SBN}; I-Mc Noseda E.15 [16]^{SBN}; I-OS Mss.Mus.B 438^{RISM,SBN}); *Su le sponde del torbido Lete* (D-HVs Kestner No. 157 II^{RISM})

1785	mus. by various composers (incl. Gassmann, Florian Leopold and Paisiello, Giovanni)
	dir. and arr. by Cherubini, Luigi
1785 London	King's Theatre in the Haymarket (16/04/1785)[344]
Librettos	London: Garland, 1785 (It./En.)
	D-Hs MS 600/3 [5]; F-Pn RES VS-725[345]
Music sources	[excerpts]
	Gassmann, Florian Leopold, *Figlia ascolta di padre* (US-CAward [US-CAt] M1497 .C813 1765 [2]^{IC,RISM})
	Paisiello, Giovanni, *Nel cor più non sento*[346] ([*Ah, che nel petto io sento*], in *Ah che nel petto io sento. Aria* […] *in the Opera of Artaxerxes* (London: Andrews, [s.d.]))

1787	mus. by Bianchi, Francesco	
1787 Padua	Teatro Nuovo (11/06/1787)	(1)
1787 Siena	Teatro degli Intronati	(2)
1789 Padua?	NA [Teatro Nuovo?]	(3)
Librettos	(1) Padua: Conzatti, [1787]	
	F-Pn LIV IT-1205 [1]; I-Vcg LIBRETTI PADOVA 262;[347] I-Vnm DRAMM.1122 [1]	
	(2) Siena: Carli, [1787?]	
	I-Rvat Stamp.De.Luca.Misc.357 [7]	
	(3) NA	
Music sources	[complete scores] I-Pl ATVa 17 [I–II]^{NG,RISM,SBN}; P-La 44-III-21/22^{BA,NG}	

---

344. The production ran for six consecutive performances; see Petty, 'Italian Opera in London', p. 261 and Price, Curtis, Judith Milhous, and Robert D. Hume, *Italian Opera in Late Eighteenth-Century London*, vol. 1: *The King's Theatre, Haymarket 1778–1791* (Oxford: Clarendon Press, 1995).
345. Microfilm copy: CDN-Lu ML48.M47A57 1785a.
346. This aria is not included in Paisiello's original setting. It might have been inserted into a pasticcio performed in London, plausible this one of 1785.
347. Microfilm copy: CDN-Lu ML48.M47B53 1787a; photocopy: CDN-Lu ML48.M47B533 1787a.

MC | *Artaserse* (1730–1850)

[excerpts] *Su le sponde del torbido Lete* (I-MC 1-B-21 [1]^{RISM})
[doubtful] *Dal braccio mio trafitto*[348] (I-Mc Noseda D.16 [11]^{SBN})

1788	mus. by Anfossi, Pasquale
1788 Rome	Teatro delle Dame (carn.)
Librettos	Rome: Puccinelli, [1788]
	B-Bc 19319;[349] D-WRz Ruppert 2599; I-Bc Lo.00280; I-Nc Rari 10.5.8 [7]; I-Rvat Stamp.Ferr.V.8073 [5]; I-Vgc ROL.0137 [5]; US-CAt *2004T-104
Music sources	
	[excerpts] *Fra cento affanni e cento* (I-Rsc G.Mss.216 [4]^{RISM}); *La ragion d'un infedele* (D-KA Don Mus.Ms. 14$^{RISM;P}$; I-Rsc G.Mss.185 [5]^{RISM}; *Per quel paterno amplesso* (D-LÜh Mus. Q 139^{RISM})
	[contrafacta] *La ragion d'un infedele* ([*Felices caeli, incolae accurrite*] A-HALn n/s [5]$^{RISM;P}$; D-B Mus.ms. 642/22$^{RISM;P}$; B-D Sulp 128 [8]$^{RISM;P}$; CH-SGd ArchDom 1/125 [1]^{RISM,350}; D-MT Mus.ms.218 [18]^{RISM}; D-TEGha Ms 74 [5]^{RISM}; PL-OPsm 522 [2]^{RISM})
	[doubtful] *Per quel paterno amplesso* (I-MC 1-A-8/1 [2]^{RISM,351})

1788	mus. by Tarchi, Angelo	
1788 Mantua	Teatro Regio Ducale (11/05/1788?)	(1)
1790 Modena	Teatro Rangoni (spr.)	(2)
1790 Reggio Emilia	Teatro Pubblico (Fair, 25/06/1790)	(3)
Librettos	(1) Mantua: heirs of Pazzoni, [1788]	
	CZ-Pu 65 E 005667; D-Mbs L.eleg.m. 4007; US-AUS KL-17 275[352]	
	(2) Reggio Emilia: Davolio & son, [1790]	
	I-MOe M.T.Ferr.Mor.10 [4]	
	(3) Reggio Emilia: Davolio & son, [1790]	
	I-Mr Libr. 02793; I-REm 19.J.48; I-REm 19.K.143; I-REm 19.K.909; I-REm Racc. Dram. E. Curti 152 [9]	

---

348. This duet was not included in Bianchi's original setting; according to an inscription on the source, inserted into a later revival (Padua, 1789).
349. Photocopy: ML48.M47A477 1788a.
350. This and the following two sources: in E flat major instead of C major.
351. The music is different from D-LÜh Mus. Q 139 and the recitativo that precedes the aria does not correspond to Anfossi's libretto.
352. Microfilm copy: CDN-Lu ML48.M47T37 1788a.

MC | *Artaserse* (1730–1850)

Music sources	[complete scores] <u>D-Mbs Mus.ms. 547</u>[MGG,NG,RISM]; F-Pn D-8952 [1–2][BnF,MGG,NG,353]	
1788	mus. by Bertoni, Ferdinando (rev. version) → see 1776	
1788	mus. by various unknown composers (incl. Bertoni, Ferdinando)	
1788 Venice	Teatro Grimani di S. Samuele (aut., 18/11/1788)[354]	
Librettos	Venice: Fenzo, 1788 A-Wmi BT-346; F-Pn 8-YTH-51889; <u>I-Mb Racc.dramm.3997</u>; I-Pmc[S]; I-Rsc Libr. n. XIX [25]; I-Vcg LIBRETTI S.SALVATORE 181;[355] I-Vnm DRAMM.1117 [1]; I-Vnm DRAMM.1343 [5]	
Music sources	[complete scores] <u>F-Pn D-100</u>/<u>101</u>[BnF,RISM,356] [excerpts] Cherubini, Luigi, *Tu vuoi, ch'io viva, o cara*[357] (CDN-Lu GM/AR 776[RISM]; CZ-BER HU 710[RISM]; D-B Mus.ms. 3500[RISM;P]; I-Rsc G.Mss.223 [8][RISM]; I-Rama A.Ms.2439[RISM])	
1789	mus. by Zingarelli, Niccolò Antonio	
1789 Trieste	Teatro Regio (19/03/1789) 1st version	(1)
1794 Milan	Teatro alla Scala (carn., 26/12/1793) 2nd version	(2)
1804 Pavia	Teatro dei Quattro Cavalieri Associati (carn.)	(3)
Librettos	(1) Trieste: Stamperia Governiale, [1789] CZ-Pnm B 4531; I-Vnm DRAMM.3263 [2][358]	
	(2) Milan: Bianchi, [1793][359] B-Bc 19322; <u>CDN-Ttfl Itp Pam 00993</u>; <u>D-Mbs L.eleg.m. 4048</u>; <u>GB-Lbl 906.e.7 [1]</u>; F-Pn LIV IT-1204 [1]; F-Pn LIV IT-3549 [1]; I-Bc Lo.05659;	

353. Microfilm copies: CDN-Lu M1500.M57T373 1788a; F-Pn VM BOB-25097.
354. [C,S] list this performance as a revival of Bertoni's 1st *Artaserse*, yet it is a pasticcio with music by several composers. See description of F-Pn D-110/111.
355. Microfilm copy: CDN-Lu ML48.M47B53 1787a; photocopy: CDN-Lu ML48.M47B482 1788a.
356. The source is ascribed to Anfossi, yet none of the closed numbers correspond to the composer's setting. The manuscript includes one aria (*Se al labbro mio non credi*, A1-S14) and duet (*In così fatal momento*, A2-S2) by Bertoni, one aria by Rauzzini (*Rendimi il caro amico*, A2-S1), and a terzet by Vento (*Deh signor s'è ver che m'ami*, A3-S7). Microfilm copies: CDN-Lu M1500.M57B42 1788a; F-Pn VM BOB-25197.
357. Interestingly, the music for this duet is notably similar to *Mille volte mio tesoro* from Tarchi's *Demetrio* (Milan, 1787) and, in fact, in I-Rsc G.Mss.223 [8] it appears under that title and lyrics.
358. Microfilm copy: CDN-Lu ML48.M47A46 1791a.
359. Microfilm copy of unspecified copy at Cambridge, MA: General Microfilm Company, Italian drama, roll 154 [3].

I-Fc E.V.2621; I-Fm Mel.2004 [1]; I-LDEsormani 298/7/12; I-Ma S.I.H.I. 36 [1]; I-Mc Coll.Libr.212; I-Mcom MUS.M MUS.I.-257; I-Mfil I.VII 60; I-Mr Libr. 02795; I-Ms MUS. Z. VII. 3; I-Nragni L019; I-PAc F. Libretti, sc.038 [625]; <u>I-Rn 40.9.H.7.2</u>; I-Rsc Carv.1322; I-Rsc Libr. n. XX [15]; I-Rsc Vol. 36 [1]; I-Vc 0300; I-Vgc ROL.0673 [5]; I-Vnm DRAMM.3266 [1]; US-AUS KL-17 329; US-CAt 2007TW-255; US-CAt YTS 8056.774 1794; US-CHH IOLC.00310[360]; <u>US-Wc ML48 [S11240]</u>

(3) Pavia: Bolzani, [1804]

I-Mr Libr. 02796; I-BRq Misc.E.855; I-PAc F. Libretti, sc.038 [626]

Music sources

1st version: 1789, Trieste

[excerpts] *Conservati fedele* (CZ-Pk 7725 [3][RISM]); *Per quel paterno amplesso* (S-Skma n/s[RISM])

2nd version: 1794, Milan

[excerpts] *Come vivere potrei* (I-BGc E.1.2 [8][RISM]; I-Mc Mus. Tr.ms. 1366[RISM,SBN;P]; I-Mc Mus. Tr.ms. 1340 [9][RISM]; I-Mc Mus. Tr.ms. 1340 [10][SBN]; <u>I-PAc Sanv.A.203</u>[RISM,SBN]); *Conservati fedele* (CH-E 147,12[RISM]); *Fra cento affanni e cento* (D-MÜs SANT Hs 4402 [3][RISM]; I-Rama A.Ms.475 [11][RISM]); *M'accusa l'aspetto* (HR-OSm M-3/81[RISM]; I-Mc Noseda Q.29 [4][SBN]; I-MC 6-C-19 [1][RISM]; I-OS Mss.Mus.B 2970[RISM,SBN]; I-Tf 9 II 12 [3][RISM]; I-Tf 10 III 10 [1][RISM]); *Mi scacci sdegnato!* (D-B Mus.ms. 30012 [6][RISM]; I-Mc Mus. Tr.ms. 1342 [1][RISM,SBN]; I-Rama A.Ms.3054[SBN]); *Per quel paterno amplesso* (D-KIl Ws 898[RISM]; I-Mc Noseda I.164[SBN]; I-Mc Noseda Q.29 [3][SBN]; I-Mc Noseda Q.29 [5][SBN]); *Se tu sapessi, oh dio* (I-Gl G.1.2.5[SBN]; I-Mc Mus. Tr.ms. 1343 [3][RISM,SBN]; I-Mc Noseda R.24 [3][SBN])

[printed sources] *Se tu sapessi, oh dio*, in *Se tu sapessi oh Dio!: duetto nell'Artaserse / musica del sig. Nicola Zingarelli* (Venice: Minatelli & co., [c. 1794])

[undated] [complete scores] F-Pn AB O-147 [1–3][BnF,MGG,361]

[doubtful] [excerpts] *Bella fiamma e solo oggetto*[362] (CH-N XB obl. 220[RISM]; I-Mc Mus. Tr.ms. 1364[RISM,SBN]); *Perché mai la ingrata sorte* (I-Mc Noseda R.24

---

360. Microfilm copy: US-Ccrl 24644174.
361. Microfilm copy: F-Pn VM BOB-30947. [MGG] lists a further source in US-Wc, yet it has not been found in [LC].
362. This and the following two pieces were not included in any of Zingarelli's settings.

MC | *Artaserse* (1730–1850)

[1]^{SBN}); *Tu vuoi ch'io viva, o cara*[363] (D-MÜs* SANT Hs 4406^{RISM}; I-Rama* A.Ms.880^{SBN}); *Vo solcando un mar crudele* (I-Nc Arie 691 [a–c] 1^{SBN;P})

1789	mus. by Andreozzi, Gaetano^{NG}
1789 Livorno	Teatro degli Armeni (aut.)

1792	mus. by various unknown composers
1792 Florence	Teatro della Pergola (08/09/1792)
Librettos	Florence: Albizziana, 1792
	B-Bc 19321; I-Bc Lo.05945; I-Fc E.V.1494;[364] I-Fc E.V.2622; I-Fn 403 [9]; I-Nragni L095; I-PSrospigliosi [I-PS] BM.257 [19]

1794	mus. by Zingarelli, Niccolò Antonio (2nd version) → see 1789

1794	mus. by unknown composer(s)
1794 Genoa	Teatro da S. Agostino (carn.)
Librettos	Genoa: Gesiniana, [1794]
	I-Gc B.S.Misc.A.26.3; I-Vc 0299; I-Vnm DRAMM.3265 [18];[365] US-CAt 2007TW-255
Music sources	[complete scores] I-Gl FONDO ANT. NN.321^{IC,SBN;R}
	[excerpts] *Giacchè morir degg'io dimmi* by Gaetano Isola (I-Gl FONDO ANT. NN.593^{IC;R}; I-Rsc G.Mss.195 [2]^{RISM}); *Se piango, se peno, non piango per me* by Marcos António Portugal (I-Gl FONDO ANT. Gl NN.621^{IC,SBN}); *Se al labbro mio non credi* (I-Gl FONDO ANT. NN.110^{IC,SBN})

1794	mus. by Isouard, Nicolas
1794 Livorno	Teatro degli Avvalorati (30/08/1794)
	Artaserse, re di Persia
Librettos	[Livorno]: Masi & co., [1794]
	I-Baf FA2.LIB.296; I-Fc E.V.2529; I-Fm Mel.2017 [9]; I-Rsc Carv.1323
Music sources	[excerpts] *Per quel paterno amplesso* (I-PAc Sanv.A.140^{MGG,RISM,SBN}); *Senza mirarmi in volto* (I-Rama A.Ms.3035^{SBN})

363. If the sources are indeed autograph manuscripts and Zingarelli is the composer, it may be a closed number composed before his first complete version.
364. Microfilm copy: CDN-Lu ML48.M47Z54 1786a.
365. Microfilm copy: CDN-Lu ML48.M47A46 1791a.

MC | *Artaserse* (1730–1850)

1795	mus. by Nicolini, Giuseppe	
1795 Venice	Teatro la Fenice (aut., 14/11/1795)	

Librettos Venice: Valvasense, [1795]
B-Br Fétis 4.488 A X/9 Mus.; F-Pn 8-YTH-51205; I-Mr Libr. 02790; I-Rsc Carv.1324; I-Vt 042; I-Vnm DRAMM.1353 [3]; US-BEm ML48 .I7 [712]; US-CAh *IC7 M5648A5 1795c; US-Wc ML48 [S7140]

Music sources [excerpts] *Cara, gli sdegni tuoi* (US-Eu MSS 990[IC,RISM])

1795	mus. by Ceracchini, Francesco[NG]	
1795 [s.l.]	NA	

Music sources [excerpts] *Coll'innocenza in seno* (I-PAc Borb.2777[SBN])

1806	mus. by Portugal, Marcos António (?)	
	lib. rev. by Caravita, Giuseppe	
1806 Lisbon	Teatro de São Carlos (aut.)	(1)
	Eufemia Eckart-Neri's benefit evening	
1810 Florence	Teatro della Pergola (Lent)	(2)
1812 Rio de Janeiro	Court theatre (17/12/1812)[366]	(3)
	birthday of Maria I, queen of Portugal	
1817 Parma	Teatro Ducale (carn.)	(4)

Librettos (1) Lisbon: Ferreira, 1806 (It./Port.)
I-PAc F. Libretti, sc.038 [627]; I-Rsc Carv.1325; I-Rsc Carv.1326; I-Rsc Libr. n. XXII [26]; P-Ln M. 1108 P.; P-Ln T.S.C. 283 P.; US-Wc ML48 [S8444]

(2) Florence: Fantosini, 1810
CDN-Ttfl Itp Pam 00773; I-Bc Lo.04401; I-Fc E.V.0345; I-Fc E.V.1567; I-Fc E.V.2655; I-Fm Mel.2394 [17]; I-LI [Toro 30];[367] I-Rsc Carv.1327; I-Vgc ROL.0553 [2]; S-Uu n/s; US-AUS KL-18 149; US-AUS KL-18 308; US-AUS KL-18 2136; US-CAh *IC7.A100.B750 [73]; US-Wc ML48 [S8398]

(3) Rio de Janeiro: Royal print, 1812
I-Rsc Carv.1328

---

366. [C] establishes that Portugal's *Artaserse* was performed in the Royal Theatre of Sao João yet, according to the theatre's website, it was inaugurated on 13 October 1813. The libretto only refers to the 'Theatre of the court of Rio de Janeiro' and clearly establishes the date of the performance on 17 December 1812. Therefore, either the printed date is incorrect or the revival took place in a different theatre.
367. Chiti, Rossana and Federico Marri, *Testi drammatici per musica della Biblioteca Labronica di Livorno* (Livorno: Debatte & figli, 1991). However, the library staff could not find the copy amongst their holdings; lost?

MC | *Artaserse* (1730–1850)

(4) Parma: Rossi–Ubaldi, [1817]
CDN-Tfl Itp Pam 00945; I-Mr Libr. 02791; I-PAc F. Libretti, sc.038 [628bis]; I-PAt REG.Libretti.010; I-Rsc Carv.1329; I-REas Vivi, II 3/7; I-Vnm DRAMM.3293 [19]; I-Vnm DRAMM.3294 [17]

Music sources [complete scores] GB-Lcm MS 512[IC,MGG,NG]

[excerpts] *Condanni a morte un figlio* (D-Dl Mus.4092-F-2 [7][RISM]); *Non ti son padre, non mi sei figlio* (I-OS Mss.Mus.B 189 [6][SBN]); *Oh, come volano* (D-Dl Mus.4092-F-2 [6][RISM]); *Per quel paterno amplesso* (B-Bc 12425[RISM]; I-Mc Mus. Tr.ms. 1063[RISM,SBN;P]); *Quanto affetti in un momento* (D-Dl Mus.4092-F-2 [9][RISM]); *Se la mia morte vuoi* (D-Dl Mus.4092-F-2 [1][RISM]); *Sospirando afflitta e sola* (I-Nc Arie 113B [10][SBN]; Us-Wc M1505.P855[RISM])

[doubtful] [excerpts] *Sono desta oppur traveggo*[368] (F-Pn D-17630[BnF;P,369]; F-Pn L-19605[BnF,370]; I-Nc Arie 518 [3][SBN]; I-Nc Arie 518 [4][SBN]; I-Nc Arie 518 [5][SBN]; I-OS S Mss.Mus.B 1273[SBN]; I-Rama A.Ms.3960[SBN])

1813	mus. by Bishop, Henry Rowley[371]
1813 London	Covent Garden (23/09/1813) (En. only)
1840	mus. by Lucas, Charles
1840 London[372]	NA (En. only: *The Regicide*)
1850	mus. by Dorn, Heinrich Ludwig Egmont
1850 Berlin	NA (Ger. only)

Arie sciolte

Armeni, Gioacchino, *Sogna il guerrier le schiere* (US-R n/s[IC,RISM])
Astarita, Gennaro, *Su le sponde del torbido Lete* (F-Pn D-62 [9][BnF,RISM,373]; I-Pca D.I.1325[SBN])
Azzopardi, Francesco, *Conservati fedele* (US-SFsc *M2.1 M25[RISM]); *Per quel paterno amplesso* (US-SFsc *M2.1 M27[RISM]); *Vo solcando un mar crudele* (US-SFsc *M2.1 M28[RISM])
Bajamonti, Julije, *Per quel paterno amplesso* (HR-Zha XLVI.B,D[RISM;P])

---

368. This quintet is not included in any of Portugal's original settings.
369. Microfilm copy: F-Pn VM BOB-23513.
370. Microfilm copy: F-Pn VM BOB-23527.
371. Based on the Thomas Augustine Arne's *Artaxerxes*. Sung in English.
372. Burden, 'Metastasio on the London Stage', p. 82.
373. Microfilm copy: F-Pn VM BOB-21638.

MC | *Artaserse* (1730–1850)

Barthélemon, François-Hippolyte, *Conservati fedele* (GB-Lbl MS Mus. 1588 [1])[BL]; *L'onda dal mar divisa* (GB-Lbl MS Mus. 1588 [6])[BL]; *Per pietà bell'idol mio* (GB-Lbl MS Mus. 1588 [3])[BL]; *Vo solcando un mar crudele* (GB-Lbl MS Mus. 1588 [2])[BL])

Beltramo, Agostino, *Tu vuoi ch'io viva, o cara* (I-MC 1-B-18/3 [1])[RISM]

Benda, Georg, *Vo solcando un mar crudele* (DK-KK mu7408.1335)[RISM]

Bernetti, *Deh, respirar lasciatemi* [1758] (A-LA 779)[RISM]

Boccherini, Luigi, *Deh, respirar lasciatemi* (F-Pn* RES-506 [3])[BnF,RISM]; *Per quel paterno amplesso* (F-Pn RES-506 [11])[BnF,RISM]; *Se d'un amor tiranno* (I-Gl H.2.22.4)[SBN]

Brunetti, Giovan Gualberto, *Per pietà bell'idol mio* (D-MÜs SANT Hs 181 [10])[RISM]

Callenberg, Georg Alexander Heinrich Hermann, *Non ti son padre, non mi sei figlio* (D-Dl Mus.3496-I-2 [?])[IC,RISM]

Campanile, Giuseppe, *Tu vuoi ch'io viva, o cara* (I-Mc Noseda D.46 [13])[SBN]

Campobasso, Alessandro Vincenzo, *Conservati fedele* (<u>I-Nc 34.3.15 [5]</u>)[SBN]

Capuzzi, Antonio, *Per pietà bell'idol mio*[374] (F-Pn VM7-7260[RISM;P]; P-Ln C.I.C. 15 [21])[RISM]

Ceccoli, Tommaso Maria, *Conservati fedele* [1780] (D-W Cod. Guelf. 307 Mus. Hdschr. [4])[RISM]

Cerro, Antonio, *Per quel paterno amplesso* (D-KNmi P 294 R [3])[RISM]

Cimarosa, Domenico, *Per pietà bell'idol mio*[375] [1797] (F-Pn D-2066[BnF,RISM]; F-Pn D-10320[BnF,RISM]; GB-Lbl Add. 30169 [7][BL]; I-Mc Noseda E.15 [16][SBN]; <u>I-Nc 13.3.19/20</u>[RISM,SBN]; <u>I-Nc 25.4.36/37</u>[RISM,SBN]; I-Rmassimo n/s[RISM])

Conforto, Nicola, *Per pietà bell'idol mio*[376] (I-Mc Noseda E.59 [2][RISM]; <u>I-Nc 34.3.13 [4]</u>[SBN])

Cornet, Alessandro, *Conservati fedele* (D-B Mus.ms. 4140)[RISM]

Curcio, Giuseppe Maria, *Non ti son padre, non mi sei figlio* (I-MC 1-F-19 [4])[RISM]

D'Astorga, Emmanuele, *Conservati fedele* (I-Mc Noseda B.23 [18][SBN]); *Per pietà bell'idol mio* [1754] (D-MÜs SANT Hs 208 [2])[RISM]

De Ficis, Giulio, *Conservati fedele* (I-Mc Noseda G.65.3 [1])[SBN]

Ebell, Heinrich Carl, *Bramar di perdere* (D-Dl Mus.4318-F-9[IC,RISM]); *Deh, respirar lasciatemi* (D-Dl Mus.4318-F-7[IC,RISM]); *Per pietà, bell'idol mio* (D-Dl Mus.4318-F-5[IC,RISM]); *Per quel paterno amplesso* (D-Dl Mus.4318-F-3[IC,RISM]); *Torna innocente, e poi* (D-Dl Mus.4318-F-6[IC,RISM])

Ettore, Guglielmo, *Tu vuoi ch'io viva, o cara* (<u>D-Dl Mus.1-F-82,9 [4]</u>)[RISM]

Feldmayr, Georg, *Conservati fedele* [1785] (D-HR [D-Au] III 4 1/2 4|o 155[RISM;P]); *Vo solcando un mar crudele* [1785] (D-HR* [D-Au] III 4 1/2 4º 153[RISM;P])

Fenaroli, Fedele, *Nuvoletta opposta al sole* (I-MC 2-C-1 [3])[RISM]

Fortunati, Gian Francesco, *Conservati fedele* (I-PAc Borb.274 [5][SBN]); *Se d'un amor tiranno* (<u>F-Pn D-14725 [8]</u>)[RISM]

Francone, Michele, *Va' tra le selve ircane* (I-Nc 22.3.15 [2])[SBN]

Gherardeschi, Filippo Maria, *Nel lasciarti amato bene* [1798] (US-NH Misc. Ms. 66 [6])[RISM,377]

Gherardi, Gerardo, *Per quel paterno amplesso* D-B Mus.ms. 7450/1[RISM]

---

374. It may be related to the tragic ball entitled *Artaserse Mnemone, re di Persia*, with music by Capuzzi, that was inserted into Paisiello's *Pirro* (Naples, 1787), performed in the Teatro di S. Samuele of Venice in 1787 (librettos in I-Vgc LIB 8; I-Vnm DRAMM.1341 [4]).

375. This aria was included not in Cimarosa's *Alessandro* but in his *Artemisia, regina di Caria* (Naples, 1797).

376. Inserted into Conforto's *Adriano in Siria* (Naples, 1754); complete scores of the latter in <u>I-Nc 25.2.32</u> and P-La 44-V-36/37/38.

377. According to an inscription on the source, the aria was performed in Pisa in 1798 by Andrea Martini as part of Gherardeschi's *Artaserse*. However, we have not found any other reference to such performance. That year, Martini sang the role of Oreste in Giuseppe Moneta's homonymous opera (in Pisa).

Giardini, Felice, *Per quel paterno amplesso* (<u>D-Dl Mus.1-F-21,3 [7]</u>^{RISM}; F-Pn D-15397^{BnF,RISM})
Gresnick, Antoine Frédéric, *Per pietà bell'idol mio* (<u>F-Pn D-15402</u>^{BnF,RISM})
Höpken, Arvid Niclas von, *Fra cento affanni e cento* (S-Skma* T-SE-R^{RISM}); *Su le sponde del torbido Lete* (S-Skma* T-SE-R^{RISM})
Insanguine, Giacomo, *Fra cento affanni e cento* (D-SDOk 307^{RISM;P}; GB-Lbl Add. 14192 [5]^{BL,RISM})
Klein, Bernhard, *Deh, respirar lasciatemi* (D-B* Mus.ms.autogr. Klein, B. 70 N^{RISM}; D-B Mus.ms. 11683/15^{RISM})
Kraus, Joseph Martin, *Conservati fedele* (S-Uu Vok. mus. i hs. 57:3a [49]^{IC,RISM}; S-Uu Vok. mus. i hs. 57:3° [42]^{RISM}); *In te spero o sposa amata* [1801] (S-Uu Vok. mus. i hs. 57:3a [40]^{IC,RISM})
La Barbiera, Baldassare, *Mi credi spietata?* (I-MC 3-D-3/5 [1]^{RISM}); *Vo solcando un mar crudele* (I-MC 3-D-3 [14]^{RISM})
Levis, Giovanni Battista, *Conservati fedele* (CZ-Pkříž XXXV E 162^{RISM})
Martínez, Marianna von, *Conservati fedele* [1767] (<u>I-Nc 33.3.27 [10]</u>^{RISM,SBN}); *L'onda dal mar divisa* (<u>I-Nc 33.2.28 [11]</u>^{RISM,SBN}); *Per pietà bell'idol mio* [1769] (<u>D-Dl Mus.1-F-82,16 [7]</u>^{RISM}); *Se del fiume altera l'onda* (I-Nc 33.2.27 [8]^{RISM,SBN}); *Vo solcando un mar crudele* [1767] (<u>I-Nc 33.3.27 [2]</u>^{RISM,SBN})
Mazzoni, Antonio Maria, *L'onda dal mar divisa* [c. 1748] (GB-Lbl Add. 34655^{RISM}); *Se al labbro mio non credi* (I-Gl A.1.18.F.6^{SBN})
Millico, Giuseppe, *Per quel paterno amplesso* (F-Pn D-8178 [9]^{BnF})
Moroni, Filippo, *Dimmi che un empio sei* [1815] (I-PAc Borb.2883^{RISM,SBN}); *Per pietà bell'idol mio* (I-PAc n/s [5]^{RISM,SBN}; I-Rama A.Ms.233 [13]^{SBN})
Mozart, Wolfgang Amadeus, *Conservati fedele* [1765] (<u>D-Mbs Mus.ms. 1277</u>^{RISM}; <u>F-Pn VMA MS-498</u>^{BnF,378}; F-Pn VM7-7452^{BnF}; US-Cn* MS 6A 48^{RISM}); *Fra cento affanni e cento* [1770] (<u>D-Mbs Mus.ms. 1276</u>^{RISM}); *Per pietà bell'idol mio* [1766]; *Per quel paterno amplesso* [1766] (<u>F-Pn MS-242 [1]</u>^{RISM,379}); *Se al labbro mio non credi* [1778] (<u>D-B* Mus.ms.autogr. Mozart, W. A. 295</u>^{RISM}; D-F Mus Hs 626^{RISM;P})
Naumann, Johann Gottlieb, *Conservati fedele* (B-Bc* 15458^{RISM}; D-B Mus.ms. 15971 [3]^{RISM})
Notte, Girolamo, *Per quel paterno amplesso* (I-Pca D.II.1398^{SBN;P})
Orgitano, Vincenzo, *Vo solcando un mar crudele* (GB-Lbl R.M.23.4 [8]^{BL})
Pazzaglia, Salvatore, *Così stupisce e cade*, in *Così stupisce e cade: aria con accomp. Di violini, oboi, corni e bassi / Paccaglia* ([s.l.: s.n., s.d.])
Pellizzari, Benedetto, *Tu vuoi ch'io viva, o cara* [1769] (HR-Sm* VI/81^{RISM;P,380})
Pepe, Francesco Cherubino, *Per quel paterno amplesso* (<u>I-CBp* Pepe Ms.308</u>^{RISM,SBN})
Pergolesi, Giovanni Battista, *Non ti son padre, non mi sei figlio* (GB-Lbl Add. 31598 [2]^{BL,RISM}); *Se al labbro mio non credi* (US-FAy Quarto 532 MS 8 [6]^{RISM}; US-FAy Quarto 532 MS 10 [12]^{RISM})
Platone, Luigi, *Tu vuoi ch'io viva, o cara* (I-Nc 34.3.18^{SBN})
Pompili, Marcello, *Conservati fedele* (I-Rsc G.Mss.207^{SBN})
Predieri, Luca Antonio, *Su le sponde del torbido Lete* (A-LA 798^{RISM;P}; B-Bc 5388^{RISM}); *Tu vuoi ch'io viva, o cara* (A-LA 797^{RISM;P}; A-LA 2014^{RISM})
Reggio, Antonino, *Non temer ch'io mai ti dica* [1748] (D-MÜs* SANT Hs 3382 [6]^{RISM}); *Se del fiume altera l'onda* [1764] (D-MÜs* SANT Hs 3385 [4]^{RISM}; *Tu vuoi ch'io viva, o cara* (D-MÜs) SANT Hs 3383 [2]^{RISM;R}; I-Rrostirolla [I-Fn] MS MUS 338 [2]^{RISM,SBN})
Reichardt, Johann Friedrich, *Conservati fedele* (<u>I-Nc 34.3.2</u>^{SBN}; S-Skma SO-R^{RISM}; S-Skma T-SE-R^{RISM}; S-SK 494 [50]^{RISM}; US-NH Misc. Ms. 92^{RISM})

---

378. Microfilm copy: F-Pn VM BOB-7848 (SL).
379. Microfilm copy: F-Pn VM BOB-3278 (SL).
380. This and the following source: possible autographs.

MC | *Artaserse* (1730–1850)

Robuschi, Ferdinando, *Sogna il guerrier le schiere* (I-Bc II.278 [6][IC,RISM,SBN])
Savoja, Paolo, *Vo solcando un mar crudele* (D-MÜs SANT Hs 180 [15][RISM])
Sciroli, Gregorio, *Va' tra le selve ircane* [c. 1770] (I-Gl A.1.18.X[IC])
Sellitto, Giacomo, *Conservati fedele* (I-MC 6-A-4/8 [6][RISM]); *Vo solcando un mar crudele* (I-MC 6-A-4/1 [1][RISM])
Seydelmann, Franz, *Se del fiume altera l'onda* (DK-Kk mu7502.1139[RISM])
Silva, José Gomes da, *Vo solcando un mar crudele* (US-NYp *Mus. Res. MN 79[RISM]; US-NYp *Mus. Res. MN 179[RISM])
Skavronsky, count, *Per pietà bell'idol mio* (I-Vc Correr Busta 4.6[SBN])
Stuntz, Joseph Hartmann, *Conservati fedele* [1831] (D-B* Mus.ms.autogr. Stuntz, J. H. 2 N[RISM]; D-Mbs* Mus.ms. 4441 [34][RISM]); *Per quel paterno amplesso* [1824] (D-Mbs* Mus.ms. 4059 [4][RISM])
Süssmayr, Franz Xaver, *Figlio se più non vivi* (H-Bn* Ms.mus IV 5[RISM])
Traetta, Tommaso, *Per pietà bell'idol mio* (I-Nc 34.5.21 [5][RISM]); *Va' tra le selve ircane* (I-Nc 34.2.32 [11][SBN]); *Vo solcando un mar crudele*[381] (F-Pn D-9007 [1/20][BnF]; F-Pn L-20003[BnF;P])
Tulli, Pietro, *Nacqui all'affanni in seno* (I-Rrostirolla [I-Fn]* MS MUS 300[RISM;R])
Vernier, Girolamo, *Conservati fedele* [1745] (I-Vnm Mss. 9995 [3][SBN]); *Per quell'affetto che l'incatena* (I-Vnm Mss. 9995 [11][SBN])
Wagenseil, Georg Christoph, *Se del fiume altera l'onda* (GB-Lbl Zweig Ms 98[BL]); *Se d'un amor tiranno* (D-RH Ms 423 [1][RISM])
Wiseman, Charles, *Non temer ch'io mai ti dica* (B-Bc 4966[RISM])
Wranitzky, Paul, *Vo solcando un mar crudele* (D-Dl Mus.3978-F-6[RISM;P])

Unknown composer

Ah, che non sono le parole[382] (F-Pn D-15153[BnF,RISM,383]; S-Skma T-SE-R[RISM])
Bramar di perdere (I-Gl FONDO ANT. NN.172[IC])
Bramar di perdere (S-Uu Vok. mus. i hs. 76:10 [3][RISM;R])
Conservati fedele (I-Gl FONDO ANT. NN.388[IC,SBN])
Conservati fedele (I-Tf 9 III 17 [2][RISM])
Conservati fedele (US-BEm MS 120 [22][IC,RISM,384])
Dimmi che un empio sei (I-MC 6-E-10 [7][RISM])
Io mi trovo nel cimento (I-Vc Correr Busta 42.48[SBN])
Non è ver che sia contento (I-Tf 2 IV 19 [15][RISM])
Non temer ch'io mai ti dica (I-Gl FONDO ANT. NN. 619[IC])
Non temer ch'io mai ti dica (S-Skma Alströmer saml. 171 [39][RISM])
Non ti son padre, non mi sei figlio (DK-Kk mu7502.0140[RISM])

---

381. This aria is an adaptation of *Se fedele mi brama el regnante*, from Traetta's *Ezio* (Rome, 1757).
382. This aria was supposedly sung by Carlo Broschi, Farinelli, but is has not been found in any of the performances in which he took part → see 1730 Venice, 1730 Lucca, 1734 Venice in 1730, mus. by Hasse, Johann Adolph; 1731 Ferrara in 1730, mus. by Vinci, Leonardo; and → 1734 mus. by Hasse, Johann Adolph; Porpora, Nicola; and Broschi, Riccardo.
383. Microfilm copy: F-Pn VM BOB-24633.
384. Aria by an unknown composer, whose second opera is, according to an inscription on the manuscript, an *Artaserse* performed in the Teatro Grimani di S. Giovanni Grisostomo in Venice.

Padre, un addio (I-Gl FONDO ANT. NN.618[IC,385])
Per pietà bell'idol mio (CH-AR Mus Ms A 19 [10][RISM])
Per pietà bell'idol mio (GB-Cfm [GB-Cu] MU.MS .III [AD][IC])
Per pietà bell'idol mio (S-Skma T-SE-R[RISM])
Per quel paterno amplesso (US-BEm MS 29 [9][RISM])
Per quel paterno amplesso (US-BEm MS 95 [9][IC,RISM;R,386])
Quel sospir, quel pianto amaro tergi o bella (I-Gl Gl FONDO ANT. NN.620[IC;R])
Rendimi il caro amico (I-Gl FONDO ANT. NN.624[IC;R])
Su le sponde del torbido Lete (I-Gl FONDO ANT. NN.673[IC;R])
Su le sponde del torbido Lete (I-PAc Borb.474[RISM,SBN])
Su le sponde del torbido Lete (I-Tf 2 IV 19 [1][RISM])
Torna innocente e poi (I-Gl Gl FONDO ANT. NN.644[IC,SBN;R])
Tu vuoi ch'io viva, o cara (D-B Mus.ms. 30235 [91][RISM;R])
Tu vuoi ch'io viva, o cara [1811] (US-SFsc *M2.5 [59][RISM])
Vo solcando un mar crudele (B-Bc 5396[RISM])
Vo solcando un mar crudele (I-Nc 642 [23–26][SBN;P])

Contrafacta and parodies

Bach, Carl Philip Emanuel, *Vo solcando un mar crudele* ([*Exaltabo te Deus meus*] A-Vpk 201/4[RISM;P])
Rust, Friedrich Wilhelm, *Vo solcando un mar crudele*[387] ([*Edle großmutsvolle Herze*] D-B Mus.ms. 19107[RISM])
Vinci, Leonardo, *Vengo a voi funesti orrori*[388] [*Non temer ch'io mai ti dica*] (I-Bc DD.46 [4][RISM,SBN,389])
Per pietà bell'idol mio ([*Jesu mi dilecte amabo te perfecte*] CH-EN Ms A 258[RISM,390])
Torna innocente e poi ([*Ljuvaste min herdinna*] S-Skma T/Sv.-R[RISM])

Unspecified contents

Conservati fedele (I-Fc D.I.208 [6][IC,RISM,SBN])
Conservati fedele (I-Vc Correr Busta 43.18 [5][SBN])
Deh, respirar lasciatemi (F-Pn VM7-105[BnF])
L'onda dal mar divisa (I-Fc D.I.209 [13][IC,SBN])
Mi credi spietata? (Gb-Lbl Add. 31633 [19][BL])
Per quel paterno amplesso (I-Gl FONDO ANT. NN.90[SBN;R,IP])
Per quel paterno amplesso (GB-Lbl Add. 31649 [11][BL])

---

385. Two particellas.
386. Reduction for soprano, fl., and bc.
387. Although Rust wrote a complete version of *Artaserse* (Perugia, 1781), this aria was not included in it. Also, according to an inscription on the manuscript, this contrafactum was performed in Wörlitz in 1773. Therefore, we do not relate it to the complete setting.
388. From Vinci's *Medo* (Parma, 1728).
389. Microfilm copy: I-Bc 2629.
390. Wrongly attributed to Gioacchino Cocchi; the music does not correspond to the other located sources.

MC | *Artaserse* (1730–1850)

Per quel paterno amplesso[391] (I-MAav Cart.18/1 [5]^{RISM;P}; I-MC 6-F-10 [2]^{RISM})
Rendimi il caro amico (I-Gl FONDO ANT. NN.465^{SBN;R})
Tu vuoi ch'io viva, o cara (CH-Zz Mus Ms A 243^{SB})
Vo solcando un mar crudele (I-Fc D.I.209 [5]^{IC,SBN})
Unspecified aria (I-Gl FONDO ANT. NN.452bis^{IC,SBN;R})

Unspecified librettos

E-VAu BH T/0998 [3] (It./Spa.)
F-Pn 8-BL-8297 [1746] → see (probably) 1744, mus. by Graun, Carl Heinrich

---

391. Although the inscription on I-MAav Cart.18/1 [5] relates it to Guglielmi's setting (1777), the music is different from that in P-La 47-III-24. Furthermore, I-MC 6-F-10 [2] indicates that the aria was inserted into A2-S11, whereas in Guglielmi's *Artaserse* it is located in A2-S10. That position does not coincide with the libretto for the 1789 revival either.

Adriano in Siria (1732–1828)

Ana Llorens, Lecturer, Department of Musicology, Universidad Complutense de Madrid; scientific director, ERC Didone Project, email: allorens@ucm.es

Tatiana Aráez Santiago, Lecturer, Department of Musicology, Universidad Complutense de Madrid, ERC Didone Project, Instituto Complutense de Ciencias Musiales, email: tarez.santiago@ucm.es

Complete operas

1732	mus. by Caldara, Antonio	
1732 Vienna	Court theatre (09/11/1732)	(1,2)
	name day of Emperor Charles VI	
1737 Brunswick	Teatro Ducale	(3)
	Der grossmuethige Hadrianus in Syrien	
1739 Rome	Teatro di Torre Argentina (carn.)[1]	(4)
1764 Salzburg	Court theatre[2]	(5)

Librettos

(1) Vienna: van Ghelen, [1732]
A-Wn 4656-A; A-Wst A.15064; CZ-Pnm B 4087; I-Vnm DRAMM.0849 [4];[3] US-Wc ML48 [S1478]

(2) Vienna/Rome: [van Ghelen/P. Leone],[4] [1732]
A-Wgm Op. Car.8°, VI 6; I-Fm Mel.2258 [9]; I-Rsc Libr. n. XIV [4]; I-Rvat Stamp.Ferr.V.7764 [7]; I-RVE r-Z93 31 [5]; I-Vc 4089 [1]; US-AUS KL-17 62; US-Cn BLC #146b; US-CHH IOLC.00162

(3) Brunswick: Bartsch, [1737] (It./Ger.)
D-BS Brosch. I 20.534; D-HVl Op.I, 164; D-W Textb. 671

---

1. Rinaldi, Mario, *Due secoli al Teatro Argentina* (Florence: Olschki, 1978).
2. See ˢ421.
3. Mutilated on p. 8.
4. 'Si vendono a Pasquino all'Insegna di San Giovanni di Dio'.

MC | *Adriano in Siria* (1732–1828)

(4) NA

(5) Salzburg: Stamperia di Corte, 1764
A-MB Per. 119; A-Su I 5594; D-AM 999/L. ext. 75 [7,1/3]; D-Mth 001/8 18291 [1]

Music sources

[complete scores] A-Wgm* A 388^(MGG,NG); A-Wn Mus.Hs.17162 [1–3]^(IC,MGG,NG); A-Wn Mus.Hs.17163 [1–4]^(IC,MGG,NG); D-B Mus.ms. 2770^(MGG,RISM); D-B Mus.ms. 2770/1^(MGG,RISM); F-Pn L-3398^(BnF,RISM)

Adriano in Siria, in *Opere drammatiche del signor abate Pietro Metastasio romano, poeta cesareo* (Venice: Bettinelli, 1733), vol. 1, pp. 75–147.

1733	mus. by Giacomelli, Geminiano
1733 Venice	Teatro Grimani di S. Giovanni Grisostomo (carn., 30/01/1733)
Librettos	Venice: Buonarigo, 1733[5] D-Bfb; I-Bc Lo.02157; I-Mb Racc.dramm.2815; I-Mb Racc.dramm.2835; I-MOe 83.D.25 [10]; I-Nragni L107 [7]; I-Rig Rar. Libr. Ven. 661; I-Rn 40.9.E.14.3; I-Rsc Libr. n. XIV [5]; I-RVI Silv., op. 687; I-RVI Conc., Pubbl. Var. Gr. 25 [1–12]; I-TSmt^(S,6); I-Vcg LIBRETTI S.GIO.GRISOSTOMO 153; I-Vgc ROL.0341 [4]; I-Vnm DRAMM.1047 [3]; I-Vnm DRAMM.1245 [2]; I-Vnm DRAMM.3561 [4]; SI-Lsk AE 57 [6]; US-Cn ML50.2.A33 G53 1733; US-LAum ML48 .R114 1733 [3]; US-Wc ML48 [S3805]
Music sources	[complete scores] D-B Mus.ms. 7470^(MGG,NG,RISM,7) [excerpts] *Amor, dover, rispetto* (A-Wn Mus.Hs.17566/2 [17]^(IC); GB-Lbl R.M.23.e.2 [26]^(BnF,RISM); US-BEm MS 120 [15]^(IC,MGG,RISM)); *Digli ch'è un infedele* (A-Wn Mus.Hs.17566/2 [18]^(IC)); *Disperato agricoltore* (A-Wn Mus.Hs.17566/2 [13]^(IC); US-BEm MS 120 [20]^(IC,MGG,RISM)); *Già, presso al termine* (A-Wn Mus.Hs.17566/2 [9]^(IC); F-Pn D-4630 [10]^(BnF,RISM,8); US-BEm MS 120 [34]^(IC,MGG,RISM)); *Infelice invan mi lagno* (US-BEm MS 120 [17]^(IC,MGG,RISM)); *Leon piagato a morte* (A-Wn Mus.Hs.17566/2 [16]^(IC)); *Non ho nel sen costanza* (A-Wn Mus.Hs.17566/2 [20]^(IC)); *Numi, se giusti siete* (A-Wn Mus.Hs.17566/2 [11]^(IC)); *Passaggier che incerto errando* (A-Wn Mus.Hs.17566/2 [15]^(IC); D-B Mus.ms. 7474 [1]^(RISM;P); US-BEm MS 120 [40]^(IC,MGG,RISM)); *Prigioniera abbandonata* (A-Wn Mus.Hs.17566/2

5. According to ^S367, there used to be a copy in I-Rss yet it can no longer be found. We therefore consider it as lost.
6. Cataloguing in process.
7. The manuscript presents some differences in act II with respect to the libretto.
8. Microfilm copy: F-Pn VM BOB-17398.

[10]^{IC}); *Quanto e misero il mio amore* (A-Wn Mus.Hs.17566/2 [14]^{IC}); *Se non ti moro allato* (US-BEm MS 120 [13]^{IC,MGG,RISM})

[parodies] *Passaggier che incerto errando* ([*Al dolor che vò sfogando*[9]] D-Dl Mus.2413-J-1 [11]^{RISM})

[doubtful] *Mancar oh Dio, mi sento*[10] (A-Wn Mus.Hs.17566/2 [19]^{IC}; D-Dl Mus.1-F-82,14 [3]^{RISM})

1734		mus. by unknown composer(s)
1734 Florence		Teatro della Pergola (carn., 26?/12/1733)
Librettos		Florence: Verdi, [1734]
		I-Fc E.V.0251
1734		mus. by Sandoni, Pietro Giuseppe
1734 Genoa		Teatro da S. Agostino (carn.)
Librettos		Genoa: Franchelli, [1734]
		CDN-Ttfl Itp Pam 01113; I-Mb Racc.dramm.1451
1734		mus. by Pergolesi, Giovanni Battista
1734 Naples		Teatro di S. Bartolomeo (25/10/1734)
		birthday of Isabel Farnesio, queen of Spain
Librettos		Naples: [s.n.], 1734
		D-F n/s; I-GRA FINIA B 2-42 [2]; I-Nc Rari 10.5.10 [3]; US-NYp Mus. Res. *MZ, A/11 [2]
Music sources		[complete scores] A-Wgm IV 15995 [Q 1825]^{IC}; GB-Lbl Add. 16102$^{BL,NG,RISM;A}$; I-Nc 30.4.10/11^{IC,RISM,SBN,11}; US-Wc M1500.P42 A3^{RISM,12}
		[excerpts] *Ah ingrato, m'inganni* (I-Mc Noseda Q.40 [7]^{SBN}; S-Skma T-SE-R^{RISM}; US-Wc M1505.A1 (vol. 182) [3]^{RISM}); *Chi soffre senza pianto* (B-Bc 5045^{RISM}; D-MÜs SANT Hs 3078 [1]^{RISM}; D-MÜs SANT Hs 3089 [26]^{RISM}; D-MÜs SANT Hs 3091 [1]^{RISM}; GB-Lbl Add. 31620 [4]^{BL}; I-BGi PREIS 8415 [2]^{RISM}; I-MC 4-F-7/4 [1]^{RISM}; I-MC 4-F-7/7 [2]^{RISM}; I-Nc 34.6.20 [30]^{SBN}; I-Nc 34.6.22 [29]^{SBN,13}); *Contento forse vivere* (I-MC 3-C-8/2 [3]^{RISM}; I-Rama A.Ms.3787 [6]^{RISM}; I-Rama A.Mss.18 [5]$^{IC;SBN}$; S-Skma T-SE-R^{RISM}; US-CAt TS 513.139 [38]$^{RISM;R}$; US-Wc M1505.

9. Inserted into the pasticcio *Sabrina* (London, 1737); in B flat major instead of C major, also sung by Farinelli.
10. The aria is not included in the libretto for Giacomelli's setting.
11. Microfilm copy: US-BEm MICROFILM A790 M.
12. Transcription of GB-Lbl Add. 16102.
13. In A major instead of C major.

A1 (vol. 183) [1]^{RISM}); *Dal labro che t'accende* (B B-Bc 4609^{RISM}; B-Bc 5046^{RISM}; D-MÜs SANT Hs 3089 [18]^{RISM}; GB-Lbl Add. 31620 [1]^{BL}; S-Skma T-SE-R^{IC,RISM}); *Digli ch'è un infedele* (US-Wc M1505.A1 (vol. 182) [2]^{RISM}); *Leon piagato a morte* (D-MÜs SANT Hs 3089 [16]^{RISM}; GB-Lbl Add. 31620 [8]^{BL}); *L'estremo pegno almeno* (D-B Mus.ms. 30010 [7]^{RISM}; D-Dl Mus.1-F-49,12 [7]^{RISM}; D-MÜs SANT Hs 3089 [19]^{RISM}; D-SWl Mus.4183$^{RISM;P}$; GB-Lbl Add. 29274 [4]^{BL,RISM}; GB-Lbl Add. 31620 [9]^{BL}; GB-Ob Ms. Mus. c.106 [8]^{RISM}; I-Fc D.I.210 [5]^{RISM,SBN}; I-MC 4-F-8/10 [1]^{RISM}; I-Nc 34.6.22 [9]^{SBN}; I-Nc 34.6.22 [38]^{SBN}; RUS-Mrg Ф.954 N°203–205 [2]$^{RISM;IP}$; US-Wc M1505.A1 (vol. 240) [5]^{RISM}); *Lieto così tavolta* (B-Bc 15176 [7]^{RISM}; D-MÜs SANT Hs 3089 [22]^{RISM}; GB-Lbl Add. 31620 [5]^{BL}; S-Skma Alströmer saml. 160 [10]$^{RISM;P}$); *Prigioniera abbandonata* (D-MÜs SANT Hs 3090 [4]^{RISM}; F-Pn VM7-7243^{BnF}; I-Bsf M.P.IV.13^{SBN}; I-Nc 34.5.23 [4]^{SBN}; US-Cu MS 1267 [8]^{RISM}); *Quell'amplesso, e quel perdono* (D-MÜs SANT Hs 3089 [25]^{RISM}); *Saggio guerrier antico* (D-B Mus.ms. 30110 [5]^{RISM}; D-MÜs SANT Hs 3089 [21]^{RISM}; I-MC 3-C-8/2 [4]^{RISM}); *Sola mi lasci a piangere* (B-Bc 5051^{RISM}; D-MÜs SANT Hs 3090 [16]^{RISM}; I-MC 4-F-7/4 [2]^{RISM}; S-Skma SO-R^{RISM}); *Splenda per voi sereno* (B-Bc 15176 [8]^{RISM}; D-MÜs SANT Hs 2089 [20]^{RISM}; GB-Lbl Add. 14227 [2]^{RISM}; GB-Lbl Add. 31620 [6]^{BL}; I-Mc Noseda B.23 [14]^{SBN}; I-Nc 34.6.22 [13]^{SBN}; S-L Saml.Kraus 120$^{RISM;P}$); *Sprezza il furor del vento* (GB-Lbl Add. 31620 [2]^{BL}; US-Wc M1505.A1 (vol. 182) [4]^{RISM}); *Su 'l mio cor so ben qual sia* (GB-Lbl Add. 31602 [12]^{BL}; GB-Lbl Add. 31620 [3]^{BL}; D-MÜs SANT Hs 3089 [24]^{RISM}); *Torbido in volto, e nero* (D-MGmi HA IV 59$^{RISM;IP}$; I-BGi PREIS 8414 [6]^{RISM}; I-Mc Noseda L.4 [4]^{SBN}; I-Mc L.4 [11]^{SBN}; US-BEm MS 27 [17]$^{RISM;R}$; US-FAy Quarto 532 MS 7 [7]^{RISM}; US-Wc M1505.A1 (vol. 183) [8]^{RISM}); *Tutti nemici e rei* (B-Bc 15176 [9]^{RISM}; GB-Lbl Add. 31620 [7]^{BL}); *Vuoi punir l'ingrato amante?* (B-Bc 4623^{RISM}; D-MÜs SANT Hs 3089 [23]^{RISM}; HR-Dha I/12^{RISM}; I-Mc Noseda L.4 [9]^{SBN}; I-MC 4-F-7/7 [3]^{RISM}; S-Sk S 170$^{RISM;R}$; S-Skma T-SE-R^{IC,RISM}; S-Skma T-SE-R$^{RISM;P}$; US-Wc M1505.A1 (vol. 182) [1]^{RISM})

[contrafacta] *Torbido il volto, è nero* ([*Conturbat mentem meam*] PL-Wu RM 2017$^{RISM;P}$); *Vuoi punir l'ingrato amante?* ([*Ave regina, caelorum ave domina angelorum*] B-D Sulp 090$^{RISM;P}$)

[parodies] *Leon piagato a morte* ([*Son qual per mare ignoto*] CH-Gc Rmo 123/1 [3]^{RISM})

[doubtful] *La ragion, gli affetti*[14] (GB-Lbl Add. 29274 [3]^{BL})

14. The aria is not included in the libretto for Pergolesi's setting.

MC | *Adriano in Siria* (1732–1828)

1735	mus. by Veracini, Francesco Maria
	lib. rev. by Cori, Angelo Maria
1735 London	King's Theatre in the Haymarket (25/11/1735)[15]
1736 London	King's Theatre in the Haymarket (03/02/1736)
1736 London	King's Theatre in the Haymarket (18/05/1736)

Librettos   London: Bennet, 1735 (It./En.)[16]
F-Pn RES VS-712;[17] GB-Cu MR463.d.70 [22]; GB-Lbl Lbl 163.g.31;[18] GB-Lbl 11714.aa.12 [2]; GB-Lbl 11714.aa.23 [3]; US-BEm ML48 .C62.; US-LAum ML50.2.A36 V47 1735

Music sources   [complete scores] D-Mbs Mus.ms.143[IC,RISM]; GB-Lbl Add. 32460[BL,RISM;A]; GB-Mp F520 Vl6[MGG,NG,RISM]

[excerpts] *Amor, dover, rispetto* (S-Skma Alströmer saml. 170 [16][RISM]; S-Skma T-SE-R[RISM]); *Ascolta, idolo mio* (US-SFsc *M2.1 M517[RISM;R]); *Dal labro che t'accende* (GB-Lbl R.M.23.d.8 [4][BL,RISM]); *È vero che oppresso la sorte* (GB-Lbl R.M.23.d.8 [13][BL,RISM]); *La ragion gli affetti ascolta* (GB-Lbl R.M.23.d.8 [5][BL,RISM]; S-Skma T-SE-R[RISM]; US-R M1500.V474As [10][RISM]); *Mi parla al core amore* (US-NH Misc. Ms. 78 [25][RISM]); *Non ritrova un'alma forte* (GB-Lam MS 140 [25][RISM]; S-Skma T-SE-R[RISM]; US-R M1500.V474As [6][RISM]); *Numi, se giusti siete* (US-R M1500.V474As [3][RISM]); *Per punir l'ingrato amante* (D-HVs Kestner No. 146 [28][RISM]); *Più bella al tempo usato* (US-R M1500.V474As [4][RISM]); *Prendi o cara in quest'amplesso* (I-PSbsg n/s [23][RISM,SBN]; S-Skma T-SE-R[RISM]); *Prigioniera abbandonata* (US-R R M1500.V474As [1][RISM]); *Quel cor che mi donasti* (GB-Mp MS. 130Hd4v.314 [85][RISM;R]; S-Skma T-SE-R[RISM]; US-R M1500.V474As [7][RISM]); *Son sventurato* (GB-Lgc G MUS 432 [38][RISM]; I-Rama A.Ms.3721 [11][RISM]; S-Skma T-SE-R[RISM]; US-R M1500.V474As [8][RISM]); *Tutti nemici e rei* (GB-Lbl R.M.23.d.8 [19][BL,RISM]); *Va superbo e del tuo fato* (GB-Lbl R.M.23.d.8 [20][BL,RISM]; US-R M1500.V474As [5][RISM])

[supposed] [complete scores] I-Rsc[NG,19]

---

15. The opera was postponed from 22 to 25 November because Farinelli was feeling unwell; see Dumigan, Darryl Jacqueline, 'Nicola Porpora's Operas for the "Opera of the Nobility": The Poetry and the Music' (doctoral dissertation, University of Huddersfield, 2014). For a complete schedule of the performances, see pp. 348–49. This version is treated as a pasticcio in <https://www.pasticcio-project.eu/database/work/P1002C0> [accessed 26 May 2022]. See also Hill, John Walter, 'The Life and Works of Francesco Maria Veracini' (doctoral dissertation, Harvard University, 1972).
16. ^{S}371 lists a further copy in the Victoria and Albert Museum, yet it is closed at the edition time of this volume.
17. Microfilm copy: F-Pn VM BOB-13265.
18. Microfilm copy: GB-Lbl PB.Mic.12022.
19. The manuscript cannot be found in the library; we therefore consider it as lost.

MC | *Adriano in Siria* (1732–1828)

[printed sources] *Amor, dover, rispetto* [5]; *La ragion gli affetti ascolta* [3]; *Non ritrova un'alma forte* [2]; *Quel cor che mi donasti* [4]; *Son sventurato* [1], in *The Favourite Songs in the Opera call'd Adriano by Sig.r Francesco Maria Veracini* (London: Walsh, 1736); *Quel cor che mi donasti*, in *Arie by Sigr. Veracini in Adriano in Farinelli's Celebrated Songs* (London: Walsh, [1739])[20]

1735	mus. by unknown composer(s)	
1735 Venice?	NA	
Librettos	Venice: [s.n.], 1735	
	I-MOe 83.D.09	

1736	mus. by Bernasconi, Andrea?[21]	
1736 Milan	Teatro Regio Ducale (carn., 26/12/1735)	(1)
	1st version	
1737 Stuttgart	Teatro Ducale (carn.)[22]	(2)
1755 Munich	Court theatre (carn., 05/01/1755)	(3)
	2nd version	

Librettos

(1) Milan: Malatesta, 1735
CDN-Ttfl Itp Pam 00002; F-Pn LIV IT-3518 [5]; I-Bc Lo.05725; I-LDEsormani 297/7/7; I-Mb Racc.dramm.6048 [3]; I-Mc Coll. Libr.099; I-Mr Libr. 02188; I-Ms MUS. G. X. 7

(2) [Stuttgart?: s.n.], 1737 (It./Ger.)
D-ERu H00/R.L 109; D-Ju 8 MS 27137; D-ROu Ck-380; D-Sl Fr.D.oct.5061; I-Mb Racc.dramm.3540; US-Wc ML48 [S1338]

---

20. Reference to this printed source found in Burden, Michael, 'Metastasio on the London Stage, 1728 to 1840: A Catalogue', *Royal Musical Association Research Chronicle*, 40 (2007), 1–332.
21. ᶜ attributes the 1736 setting to Riccardo Broschi. We follow Kokole in hypothesising that it was Bernasconi's 1st *Adriano*. The fact that so many arias attributed to Bernasconi —and different from those of the Munich version— have been preserved attests to the composer's setting the libretto twice. See Kokole, Metoda, 'Andrea Bernasconi's Earliest Operatic Music on its Way North of the Alps', *Musicologica Brunensia*, 53 (2018), 207–26; 'Did Andrea Bernasconi Compose 'Adriano in Siria' Twice?', in *Music Migration in the Early Modern Age: Centres and Peripheries – People, Works, Styles, Paths of Dissemination and Influence*, ed. by Jolanta Guzy-Pasiak and Aneta Markuszewska (Warsaw: Liber Pro Arte, 2016), pp. 237–62.
22. Krauß, Rudolf, *Das Stuttgarter Hoftheater von den ältesten Zeiten bis zur Gegenwart* (Stuttgart: Metzler, 1908).

(3) Munich: Vötter, [1755] (It./Ger.)[23]
D-HR [D-Au] 02/III.7.4.55.14; D-Mbs Res/4 Bavar.2165,8 [11]; D-Mth 0014/W 4 P.ital 89 [1]; D-Pu 266/G128; D-Sl Fr.D.oct.5060; I-Mb Racc.dramm.5656 [2]; US-Wc ML48 [S854]

Music sources

1st version: 1736, Milan

[excerpts] *Ah ingrato, m'inganni* (D-ROu Mus. Saec. XVIII:6 [15][RISM;P]); *Dal labro che t'accende* (B-Bc 3720[RISM]; D-ROu Mus. Saec. XVIII:6 [7][RISM;P]; F-Pn VM7-13 [3][BnF,RISM]; I-Nc 22.310 [9][SBN]); *Digli ch'è un infedele* (D-ROu Mus. Saec. XVIII:6 [12][RISM;P]; GB-Cfm [GB-Cu] MU.MS.137[IC]; I-Mc Noseda A.25 [9][SBN]; SI-Mpa SI_PAM/1857/010 [55][RISM;R]); *Dopo un tuo sguardo, ingrata* (B-Bc 5094[RISM]; D-ROu Mus. Saec. XVIII:6 [8][RISM;P]); *È ingrato io veggio* (B-Bc 3721[IC,RISM]); *È vero che oppresso la sorte* (GB-Cfm [GB-Cu] MU.MS.137[IC]; I-Mc Mus. Tr.ms. 175[RISM,SBN]; SI-Mpa SI_PAM/1857/010 [30][RISM;R]); *La ragion gli affetti ascolta* (B-Bc 5095[RISM]; D-Dl Mus.3017-F-1 [5][RISM]; D-ROu Mus. Saec. XVIII:6 [11][RISM;IP]; GB-Lbl Add. 29274[RISM,24]; I-Mc Mus. Tr.ms. 173[RISM,SBN]; I-Nc 57.2.5 [11][SBN]; SI-Mpa SI_PAM/1857/010 [52][RISM;R]); *Numi, se giusti siete* (A-Wn Mus.Hs.18294[IC,25]; B-Bc 5096[RISM]; D-B Mus.ms. 30110 [2][RISM,26]; D-ROu Mus. Saec. XVIII:6 [10][RISM;P]; GB-Lbl Add. 31674[BL,RISM]; SI-Mpa SI_PAM/1857/010 [28][RISM]); *Oh dio, mancar mi sento* (B-Bc 3726[RISM]; D-ROu Mus. Saec. XVIII:6 [14][RISM]); *Prigioniera abbandonata* (D-ROu Mus. Saec. XVIII:6 [13][RISM;P]); *Quell'amplesso e quel perdono* (B-Bc 3727[IC,RISM]); *Se non ti moro allato* (D-MÜs SANT Hs 1813 [12][RISM]; F-Pn VM7-9 [7][BnF,RISM]; GB-Cfm [GB-Cu] MU.MS.111 [1][IC]; I-MC 3-E-13/5 [3][RISM]; I-Nc 22.3.10 [7][SBN]; SI-Mpa SI_PAM/1857/010 [222][RISM;R]; US-Cu MS 1267 [7][RISM]; US-FAy Quarto 532 MS 9 [30][RISM])

[contrafacta] *È vero che oppresso la sorte* ([*Odorem spirate, vos elegantes flores*] F-Sgs M 361[RISM;P])

2nd version: 1755, Munich

[complete scores] D-Mbs Mus.ms. 148[MGG,NG,RISM]; D-Mbs Mus.ms. 185 [MGG,NG,RISM]; F-Pn D-990/991/992[BnF,MGG,NG,RISM,27]; US-Wc M1500.B536 A2[RISM]

23. [S]403 lists a further copy in D-MHrm, yet it cannot be found in the Museum's card catalogue; we therefore consider it as lost.
24. Wrongly attributed to Pergolesi.
25. Inserted into Bernasconi's *Flavio Anicio Olibrio* (Vienna, 1737); see Kokole, 'Andrea Bernasconi's Earliest Operatic Music', p. 223.
26. Wrongly attributed to Finacci on source.
27. Source originally from Munich; same music as in D-Mbs Mus.ms.148 and D-Mbs Mus.ms.185. Microfilm copy: F-Pn VM BOB-23858/23859/23860.

MC | *Adriano in Siria* (1732–1828)

[excerpts] *Dopo un tuo sguardo, ingrata* (D-SWl Mus.1217[RISM]); *Infelice invan mi lagno* (<u>D-Dl Mus.1-F-49,12 [1]</u>[RISM]); *Vuoi punir l'ingrato amante?* (<u>D-Dl Mus.1-F-46,12 [2]</u>[RISM])

1736	mus. by Duni, Egidio Romualdo
1736 Rome	Teatro di Tordinona (carn., 27/12/1735)[28]
Librettos	Rome: de' Rossi, [1735]
	B-Bc 18988; <u>I-Bc Lo.01462</u>; <u>I-Mb Racc.dramm.3616</u>; I-MATts Luc. O.B.02068; I-Rn 34.2.E.7; I-Rn 34.2.E.45.1; S-Uu n/s; <u>US-CHH IOLC.00185</u>
Music sources	[excerpts] *Dopo un tuo sguardo, ingrata* (DK-Kk mu6403.0530[RISM;P]); *Sprezza il furor del vento* (F-Pn VM7-7218 (BIS)[BnF,RISM,29])
1736	mus. by unknown composer(s)
1736 Caltagirone	Teatro di S. Francesco (aut.)
1737	mus. by Ferrandini, Giovanni Battista
1737 Munich	Court theatre (carn.)
Librettos	Munich: Vötter, [1737]
	A-Wgm 5769/Textbücher; D-BHu 73/LQ 43100 F372 A2.2006; D-KNth L 74; I-Mb Racc.dramm.3730
Music sources	[complete scores] <u>D-Dl Mus.3037-F-1</u>[NG,RISM]
	[excerpts] *Volga il ciel felici amanti* (<u>D-Mbs Mus.ms. 141 [13]</u>[RISM,30])
	[doubtful] *Se non ti moro allato* (F-Pn D-15155[BnF,RISM,31])
1737	mus. by Porta, Giovanni
1737 Mantua	Teatro Arciducale (carn.) (1)
1737 Treviso	Teatro Dolfin (Fair, 27/04/1737) (2)
Librettos	(1) Mantua: Pazzoni, 1737
	<u>I-Mb Racc.dramm.4236</u>; I-MAc MISC.-.115 [13]

28. Date in Franchi, Saverio, *Drammaturgia romana II (1701–1750)* (Rome: Edizione di Storia e Letteratura, 1997). In his previous work (*Le impressioni sceniche: dizionario bio-bibliografico degli editori e stampatori romani e laziali di testi drammatici e libretti per musica dal 1759 al 1800* (Rome: Edizioni di Storia e Letteratura, 1994) he gives 21/12/1725.
29. Microfilm copy: F-Pn VM BOB-19888.
30. In G major instead of D major.
31. The music is different from D-Dl Mus.3037-F-1; incomplete. Microfilm copy: F-Pn VM BOB-24634.

MC | *Adriano in Siria* (1732–1828)

(2) Venice: Rossetti, 1737
I-Mb Racc.dramm.2276

1737	mus. by Hasse, Johann Adolph	
1737 Vyškov	Theatre (31/10/1737) *festivity of St Wolfgang* 1st version[32]	(1)
1752 Dresden	Court theatre (17/01/1752) 2nd version[33]	(2,3)
1755 Naples	Teatro di S. Carlo (04/11/1755)[34]	(4)
1777 Kassel	Theatre	(5)

Librettos

(1) Brno: Swobodiana, [1737]
A-Sca 14245

(2) Dresden: widow of Stössel, [1752]
D-Dl MT.1942; D-HAu Pon IId 1700 (3,1/5) [2]; PL-Kj St. Dr. 588152 I; RUS-Mrg L 22/30; RUS-Mrg 50-8419137; RUS-Mrg 50-8419138; RUS-Mrg 50-8685639; US-Wc ML48 [S4503]

(3) Dresden: widow of Stössel, [1752] (It./Ger.)
A-Wn 4155-B; CZ-Pu 9 E 7436; D-Dl MT.1552; D-KNth L 73; F-Pn 8-TH B-23; F-Pn TH B-55; PL-Wu GSD 17.1.3.37 [1];[35] US-Wc ML48 [S4504]

(4) NA

(5) Kassel: Estienne, 1777 (It./Fr.)
D-Ju 8 MS 23548; D-Mth 001/8 01406 [1]; D-Mgu 095 XVI C 713

Music sources

1st version: 1737, Wischau

[excerpts] *La ragion gli affetti ascolta* (D-LB [D-NEhz] La 170 Bü 323[RISM;P])

[contrafacta] *La ragion gli affetti ascolta* ([*Alleluia*] CZ-Pkřiž XXXVI B 70 [1][RISM;R,P])

---

32. Treated as a pasticcio in Spáčilová, Jana, *Catalogue of the Italian Opera Libretti in Central Europe in the 1st Half of the 18th Century* (Prague: KLP, forthcoming).
33. According to [MGG,NG], and Mellace, Hasse only wrote one setting of *Adriano*, dated 1752; see Mellace, Raffaele, *Johann Adolf Hasse* (Palermo: L'Epos, 2004). However, the title page of the 1737 libretto clearly states his authorship.
34. De Filippis, Felice and Raffaele Arnese, *Cronache del Teatro di S. Carlo (1737–1960)* (Naples: Edizioni Politica Popolare, 1961).
35. Wrongly attributed to C. H. Graun in the institution's card catalogue.

[doubtful] *Già presso al termine*[36] (SI-Mpa SI_PAM/1857/010 [40][RISM;R,IP])

2nd version: 1752, Dresden[37]

[complete scores] A-Wn Mus.Hs.1803[IC,MGG,RISM]; B-Bc 2158[IC,MGG,NG,RISM]; B-Bc 2159[IC,MGG,NG,RISM]; B-Bc 3265[MGG,NG,RISM;R]; CDN-Lu MZ1257[IC,MGG,RISM;R]; D-B Mus.ms. 9563[MGG,NG,RISM]; D-Bsa [D-B] SA 1066[MGG,RISM]; D-BDk 49a[MGG,NG,RISM;A,R]; D-Dl Mus.2477-F-65[MGG,NG,RISM]; D-Dl Mus.2477-F-66[MGG,RISM;A]; D-Dl Mus.2477-F-67[MGG,NG,RISM;P]; D-Dl Mus.2477-F-527[MGG,RISM;A]; D-Hs ND VI 2921[MGG,RISM]; D-LEu N.I.10290 [a–c][MGG,RISM]; D-Mbs Mus.ms. 4462[MGG,RISM;A,R]; I-Mc* Part. Tr.ms. 176[MGG,NG,RISM,SBN,38]; I-MOe Mus. F. 548[IC,39]; S-Skma T-SE-R[MGG,NG,RISM;A]; S-Uu Vok. mus. i hs. 56:5[IC,NG,RISM;P]; US-Wc M1500.H35 A3[MGG,NG,RISM]

[excerpts] *Digli ch'è un infedele* (D-Bsa [D-B] SA 1573 [2][RISM]); *Numi, se giusti siete* (I-MC 2-F-14/4 [9][RISM]; I-Nc 33.38 [9][SBN]); *Saggio guerriero antico* (D-Bsa [D-B] SA 1573 [1][RISM]); *Se non ti moro allato* (D-Hs M A/1567 [5][RISM,40]; GB-Lbl Add. 31634 [20][BL,MGG,RISM]; S-L Saml.fallén 9[RISM;R]); *Vivi a noi, vivi all'impero* (S-Skma T-SO-R[IC,RISM])

[arrangements] *Prigioniera abbandonata* (F-Pn D-5403 [4][BnF,41]; F-Pn VM BOB-26159 [4][BnF])

[contrafacta] *Ah! Che mancar mi sento* ([*Caro mea vere, est cibus et sanguis*] PL-Wu RM 5594 [2][RISM;P]); *Dopo un tuo sguardo, ingrata* ([*Fideles properate applausus decantae*] PL-Wu RM 4462[RISM;P]); *Numi, se giusti siete* ([*Benedictus qui venit in nomine Domini*] PL-Wu RM 5574 [1][RISM;P]; [*Maria gustim sentio, quando tui fit*] PL-Wu RM 4457 [14][RISM;P]); *Per te novella speme* ([*Applausus parate et lilia captate*] PL-Wu RM 4452 [7][RISM;P]; [*Ich glaub' ein ewig's Leben*] D-Tl [D-Tmi] S 31[RISM;P]; D-SDO k 281[RISM;P]); *Prigioniera abbandonata* ([*Lauda Sion savatorem*] PL-Wu RM 5574 [2][RISM;P]; [*Pauvre Annette*] F-Pn D-18350[BnF,RISM]); *Saggio guerriero antico* ([*Caelorum plaudite dulce carite*] PL-Wu RM 4452 [8][RISM;R]); *Se non ti moro allato* ([*Fideles properate applausus decantae*] PL-Wu RM 4457 [1][RISM;P]); *Son per deserte selve* ([*Astra caelorum plaudite*] PL-Wu RM 4453 [1][RISM;P]); *Sprezza il furor del vento* ([*Surrexit Heros fortis*] CZ-TEk n/s[RISM;P]); *Vivi a*

36. We could not doublecheck if this aria was included in Hasse's 1737 setting; it was not so in the 1752 and 1777 productions.
37. As no complete source for Hasse's 1st version has been preserved, we cannot ascertain that the arias used in 1752 were not originally from 1737.
38. Possible autograph.
39. Wrongly dated 1762 on source.
40. In F major instead of E major.
41. This and the following source: arrangement for two flutes.

noi, vivi all'impero ([*Caeli cives accurrite*] CZ-TEk n/s [1]$^{\text{RISM;P}}$; [*Jauchzet, jauchzt ihr Frommen*] D-Dl Mus.2477-E-515$^{\text{RISM;P}}$); *Vuoi punir l'ingrato amante?* ([*Estote fortes in bello*] PL-Wu RM 4455 [1]$^{\text{RISM;P}}$; [*Veni electa mea, et ponam in te thronum meum*] PL-Wu RM 5594 [1]$^{\text{RISM;P}}$)

1739	mus. by Ristori, Giovanni Alberto	
1739 Naples	Teatro di S. Carlo (19/12/1739)[42]	
	birthday of Felipe V, king of Spain	
Music sources	[complete scores] D-Dl* Mus.2455-F-9$^{\text{MGG,NG,RISM,43}}$; I-Nc 31.6.23$^{\text{IC,MGG,NG,SBN}}$	
	[excerpts] *Dopo un tuo sguardo, ingrata* (D-Dl Mus.2455-F-16 [1]^{RISM}); *Oh dio, mancar mi sento* (I-Nc Arie 29 [12]^{SBN}; S-Skma T-SE-R$^{\text{IC,RISM}}$)	
1740	mus. unknown composer(s)	
1740 Siena	Teatro Grande (carn.)	
Librettos	Florence: Viviani, [1740]	
	I-Fc E.V.2565	
1740	mus. by Galuppi, Baldassare	
1740 Turin	Teatro Regio (carn., 01?/1740,)	(1)
	1st *version*	
1750 Naples	Teatro di S. Carlo[44]	(2)
1758 Livorno	Teatro da S. Sebastiano (spr.)	(3)
	2nd *version*	
1759 Naples	Teatro di S. Carlo (10/07/1759)[45]	(4)
	Name day of the Queen and the King of Naples	
1760 Venice	Teatro Vendramin di S. Salvatore (Asc., 14/05/1760)	(5)
	3rd *version?*[46]	
1761 Palermo	Teatro di Santa Cecilia (aut.)	(6)

42. ^{C} gives 26/12/1739; we follow ^{NG} and De Filippis and Arnese, *Cronache del Teatro di S. Carlo*, p. 28.
43. This source differs from I-Nc 31.6.23 in the aria *Numi, se giusti siete* (A1-S11), which presents a different musical setting.
44. Wotquenne, Alfred, *Baldassare Galuppi 1706-1785: étude bibliographique sur ses œuvres dramatiques* (Brussels: Schepens & Katto, 1902).
45. Contrarily to ^{MGG} and ^{NG}, ^{C} lists this and the following performance as proper versions, yet most of the arias from 1758 were used in the later revivals. Therefore, we do not consider the 1759 and 1760 settings as versions and treat the authorship of numbers modified with respect to Galuppi's 2nd version as doubtful.
46. The libretto indicates that the music was 'tutta nueva del signore Baldassare Galuppi'; yet, contrarily to ^{C}, $^{\text{MGG,NG}}$ do not consider this as a proper version. For his part, Wotquenne (*Baldassare Galuppi*, p. 42) considers this as the composer's 2nd version, not acknowledging as such the 1758 setting.

1763 Udine   Teatro della Racchetta (carn.)   (7)

Librettos

(1) Turin: Zappata & son, [1740]
D-Mbs L.eleg.m. 3854; I-Ms MUS. G. X. 6; I-MOe 7.T.13.19 [5]; I-Rsc Vol. Carv.142 [2]; I-Tac Simeom L 27; I-Tci L.O.0100; I-Tn C.SAN 434 [1]; I-Tn C.SAN 486 [4]; I-Tn F VII.353 [3]; I-Tn F XIII.519 [6]; I-Tstrona[S]

(2) NA

(3) Livorno: Santini & co., 1758
I-Vgc ROL.0314 [12]

(4) Naples: Flauto, 1759
I-Bc Lo.01884; I-Rsc Libr. n. XVI [8]

(5) Venice: Fenzo, 1760[47]
I-Mb Racc.dramm.0438; I-Ria MISC. Teatrale 6 [9]; I-Vcg LIBRETTI S.SALVATORE 97; I-Vmc Rava H.158; I-Vmc Rava H.253; I-Vnm DRAMM.1082 [6]; I-Vnm DRAMM.1281 [5]; US-LAum ML48 .R114 1760 [7]; US-Wc ML48 [S3473][48]

(6) Palermo: Toscano, 1761
I-PLn Misc.A.073 [8]

(7) Udine: Gallici alla fontana, 1763
I-UDc Misc. Joppi 231 [10]

Music sources

1st version: 1740, Turin

[complete scores] B-Bc 2093[IC,MGG,NG,RISM,49]

[excerpts] *Ah ingrato, m'inganni* (B-Bc 2094 [1][IC,RISM]); *Digli ch'è un infedele* (B-Bc 2094 [4][IC,RISM]); *Dopo un tuo sguardo, ingrata* (GB-Lbl Add. 31647[RISM]); *È ingrato io veggio* (B-Bc 2094 [3][RISM]; US-FAy Quarto 532 MS 9 [10][RISM]); *Infelice invan mi lagno* (GB-Lbl Add. 31647[RISM]; S-Skma T-SE-R[RISM]); *Leon piagato a morte* (I-Bc CC.158 [3][IC,RISM,SBN]); *Numi, se giusti siete* (D-B Mus.ms. 6987 [2][RISM]); *Prigioniera abbandonata* (GB-Lbl Add. 31647[RISM]; US-FAy Quarto 532 MS 9 [11][RISM]); *Se non ti moro allato* (GB-Lbl Add. 31647[RISM]); *Sprezza il furor del vento* (A-LA 787[RISM;P]; A-LA 1919[RISM]); *Volga il ciel felici amanti* (B-Bc 2094 [2][IC,RISM])

---

47. There used to be a copy in I-Rsc Libr. n. XVI [4], but it could not be found. We therefore consider it as lost.
48. Microfilm copy: D-KNmi FH 1187. According to [S], there used to be a further copy in I-Rss yet it could not be found. We therefore consider it as lost.
49. Act I: arias only; singers correspond to those of the premiere of Galuppi's 1st setting (Turin, 1740); Acts II & III date from later productions.

MC | *Adriano in Siria* (1732–1828)

[contrafacta] *Digli ch'è un infedele* ([*Justus ut palma florebit sicut cedrus*] CH-SAf MusSAf.Ms.643[RISM;P]; [*Nil est in hoc mundo*] CH-E 200,5[RISM;P])

2nd version: 1758, Livorno

[complete scores] D-Dl Mus.2973-F-7[MGG,NG,RISM,50]; P-La 44-VI-39/40/41[BA,MGG,NG]; P-La 44-VI-42/43/44[BA,MGG,NG,51]; P-La 44-VI-45/46/47[BA,MGG,NG]; P-La 54-I-24/25/26[BA,MGG,NG]; S-Skma T-R[MGG,NG,RISM]; US-SFsc *M2.1 M123[RISM] [Act I]; US-Wc M1500.G2 A3[MGG,RISM]

[excerpts] *Barbaro non comprendo* (US-BEm MS 24 [13][IC,RISM]); *Dopo un tuo sguardo, ingrata* (D-Dl Mus.2973-F-31 [1][RISM,52]; D-MÜs SANT Hs 1580 [1][RISM]; F-Pn D-4300 [11][BnF,RISM]; GB-Lbl Add. 14208 [10][BL,RISM]; GB-Lbl R.M.22.c.9 [3][RISM]; I-LEpastore MS.A. 9[RISM]; I-MC 2-C-16/8 [1][RISM]; I-MC 2-C-16/9 [2][RISM]); *Figlia… oh Dio… l'orror… l'affanno…* (F-Pn D-18169[BnF,RISM]; F-Pn* MS-18233[BnF,RISM,53]); *In quel paterno amplesso* (D-LEm Becker III.15.39[RISM]; S-Skma T-SE-R[RISM]); *Non so bell'idol mio* (D-WRgs 32/363[RISM]); *Numi, se giusti siete* (S-Skma T-SE-R[IC,RISM]; S-Skma T-SE-R[RISM;IP]); *Per quel paterno amplesso* (I-Tf 10 V 19[RISM]); *Prigioniera abbandonata* (B-Bc 3904[RISM]; F-Pn D-4301 [19][BnF,RISM,54]; F-Pn L-17952[BnF,RISM;IP]; I-MC 2-C-16 [7][RISM]; US-BEm MS 24 [14][IC,RISM]; US-BEm MS 1073 [13][IC,RISM]); *Se non ti moro allato* (US-SFsc *M2.1 M125[RISM;R,IP]); *Son sventurato* (D-LÜh Mus. Q 175[RISM]; I-Rama A.Ms.2691[RISM]; D-SWl Mus.158[RISM]); *Sprezza il furor del vento* (I-Rc Mss. 5864[RISM,SBN;IP,55])

[contrafacta] *Dal labro che t'accende* ([*Salve regina, mater misericordiae vita dulcedo*] A-ST Mus.ms. 360[RISM;P]); *Son sventurato* ([*Tremar non sento*] F-Pn VMB MS-87 [15–20][BnF,RISM])

[doubtful] [excerpts] *Ah ingrato, m'inganni* (I-MC 2-D-1 [10][RISM])

[Naples, 1759] [excerpts] *Dopo un tuo sguardo, ingrata* (F-Pn D-15187 [1][BnF,RISM])

[Venice, 1760] [excerpts] *Barbaro non comprendo* (D-GOl Mus. 4° 46b [3][RISM;P]); *Dopo un tuo sguardo ingrata* (CH-N XB obl. 170[RISM])

---

50. D-Dl Mus.2973-F-7; P-La 44-VI-45/46/47; and US-Wc M1500.G2 A3: for Venice 1760.
51. For Naples 1759.
52. D-Dl Mus.2973-F-31 [1]; F-Pn D-4300 [11]; I-MC 2-C-16/8 [1]; and I-MC 2-C-16 [7]: for Naples 1759.
53. Possible autograph.
54. Microfilm copy: F-Pn VM BOB-31987.
55. [SBN] gives Mss. 254818 as the call number for this manuscript, but a four-digit numbering is more frequent for the catalogue of I-Rc; therefore, we follow the numbering given by [RISM].

[undated]	[excerpts] *Dopo un tuo sguardo, ingrata* (A-Wgm VI 15134 [Q 2913]^{IC}); *Digli che io son fedele* (I-Nc M.S.app.8.1 [19–22]$^{SBN;IP,56}$); *Oh dio, mancar mi sento* (US-SFsc *M2.1 M124$^{RISM;P}$)
1740	mus. by Giai, Giovanni Antonio
1740 Venice	Teatro Grimani di S. Giovanni Grisostomo (carn., 06/02/1740)
Librettos	Venice: Rossetti, 1740 I-Bc Lo.02165; I-Rsc Carv.213; I-RVI Silv., op. 754; I-Vcg LIBRETTI S.GIO.GRISOSTOMO 156; I-Vnm DRAMM.1055 [7]; I-Vnm DRAMM.1252 [5]; I-Vnm DRAMM.3568 [4]; US-LAum ML48 .R114 1740 [6]; US-Wc ML48 [S3819]
Music sources	[excerpts] *Ah ingrato, m'inganni* (D-Dl Mus.1-F-82,14 [11]^{MGG,NG,RISM}); *Barbaro non comprendo* (D-Dl Mus.1-F-82,14 [8]^{MGG,NG,RISM}); *Digli ch'è un infedele* (D-Dl Mus.1-F-82,14 [9]^{MGG,NG,RISM}); *Infelice invan mi lagno* (I-Fc D.I.209 [8]^{RISM}; S-Sk 494 [19]$^{RISM;P}$); *Numi, se giusti siete* (D-Dl Mus.1-F-82,14 [7]^{MGG,NG,RISM}); *Oh dio, mancar mi sento* (D-KA Mus. Hs. 170$^{RISM;IP}$; I-Fc D.I.209 [2]^{IC,SBN}; S-Sk 494 [20]$^{RISM;P}$); *Son sventurato* (A-LA 2027$^{RISM;P}$; D-MÜs SANT Hs 2384 [26]^{RISM,57}; I-Vnm Mss. 10002 [23]$^{IC,SBN;R}$; S-Sk 494 [67]^{RISM,58}); *Volga il ciel felici amanti* (D-Dl Mus.1-F-82,14 [10]^{MGG,NG,RISM})
1740	mus. by Lampugnani, Giovanni Battista
1740 Vicenza	Teatro delle Grazie (Fair, 07/08/1740?)
Librettos	Padua: Conzatti, [1740] I-Mb Racc.dramm.4575; I-Vcg LIBRETTI VICENZA 277; I-VIb RN 31 b 08 [4]
Music sources	[excerpts] *Passaggier che incerto errando* (D-Dl Mus.1-F-82,15 [1]^{RISM}); *Se non ti moro allato* (I-Mc Noseda L.17 [1]^{SBN}; I-Rc MUS.MS 198^{IC}); *Son sventurato* (F-Pn D-11954 [7]^{BnF}); *Sprezza il furor del vento* (US-BEm MS 834 [3]^{RISM}) [doubtful] *Se non ti moro allato* (I-Rsc Mus.Ms. 198^{IC,SBN,59})

56. Vn I part only.
57. Attributed to G. B. Lampugnani on source. In F major instead of G major.
58. In A major instead of G major.
59. The music is different from I-Mc Noseda L.17 [1] and, moreover, it is a duet, whereas in Lampugnani's setting it is an aria.

1740	mus. by Caballone, Michele?[NG]
1740 Naples	NA[60]
Music sources	[complete scores] F-Pn MS-2022 [1–3][BnF,NG,RISM]

1741	mus. by Giaino, Pietro
1741 Brescia	Teatro degli Erranti (carn.)
Librettos	Brescia: Pasini, [1741]
	I-Mb Racc.dramm.4225; I-Rn 40.10.F.3.3; I-Vcg LIBRETTI BRESCIA 249

1741	mus. by various unknown composers
1741 Ferrara	Teatro Bonacossi da S. Stefano (20/01/1741)
Librettos	Ferrara: Barbieri, [1741]
	I-Mb Racc.dramm.2142; I-Rvat Stamp.Ferr.V.8149 [1]

1742?	mus. by Logroscino, Nicola Bonifacio?
1742? [s.l.]	NA

1743	mus. by unknown composer(s)
1743 Vienna	Teatro Privilegiato
Librettos	[Vienna]: van Ghelen, [1743]
	I-Mb Racc.dramm.2336

1745	mus. by unknown composer(s)
1745 Gorizia	NA (carn., 20/01/1745)
Librettos	Udine: Murero, [1745]
	I-GOs St.Pt. u 86 Vi Civ; I-Mb Racc.dramm.3617

1745	mus. by Verocai, Giovanni
	lb. rev. and music add. by Schürmannn, Georg Gaspar
1745 Brunswick	Teatro Ducale (Candlemass, 02/02/1745)
	Die getreue Emirena Parthische Prinzessin
Librettos	Wolfenbüttel: Bartsch, [1745] (Ger. only)
	D-BS Brosch. I 20.527; D-HVl Op. 1, 189; D-W Textb. 575

---

60. Either 1740[NG] or 1754; see Stieger, Franz, ed., *Opernlexicon* (Tutzing: Schneider, 1977). As Caballone died in 1740, the latter date is not plausible.

MC | *Adriano in Siria* (1732–1828)

1746	mus. by Abos, Girolamo
1746 Florence	Teatro della Pergola (carn., 26/12/1745)
Librettos	Florence: Pieri, [1746]
	F-Pn 8-BL-8291; I-Fc E.V.1571; I-Fc E.V.2562; I-Fc E.V.2715

1746	mus. by Graun, Carl Heinrich
1746 Berlin	Court theatre (07/01/1746)[61]
Librettos	Berlin: Haude, 1745 (It./Ger.)
	A-Wn 621610-A; D-ERu Hoo/R.L 133; D-Hs A/34173 [4]; D-MHrm T 6; D-KNth L 72; D-ROmi Ck-380.a; D-W Textb. 186; PL-Wu GSD 17.1.3.37 [1]; PL-Wu GSD 28.20.4.3316 [1]
Music sources	[complete scores] B-Bc 26269[RISM;A]; D-B Am.B 193[RISM]; D-B Mus.ms. 8215[IC,RISM]; D-DS Mus.ms 367[RISM;P]; D-KNh R 67[RISM;A]; D-ROu Mus. Saec. XVIII:27[RISM;IP,62]; D-W Cod. Guelf. 85 Mus. Hdschr[RISM]; F-Dc In fol.402[BASE,IC;R]; F-Pn D-5006[BnF,RISM;A,63]; F-Sim P 28[IC,RISM;R]; S-Uu Leufsta Mus. ms. 37[RISM;A,R,IP]
	[excerpts] *Ah ingrato, m'inganni* (D-RH [D-MÜu] Ms 261 [2][RISM;P]; S-Skma T-SE-R[RISM]); *Barbaro non comprendo* (D-RH [D-MÜu] Ms 265 [1][RISM;P]; S-Skma T-SE-R[RISM]); *Dal labro che t'accende* (B-Bc 7317[RISM;R,IP]; D-W Cod. Guelf. 315 Mus. Hdschr. [5][RISM;R]); *Già presso al termine* (D-FUl M 9 [224][RISM;P]); *La ragion gli affetti ascolta* (D-RH [D-MÜu] Ms 262 [1][RISM;P]); *Non ritrova un'alma forte* (D-RH [D-MÜu] Ms 265 [2][RISM;P]); *Numi, se giusti siete* (D-RH [D-MÜu] Ms 260 [3][RISM;P]); *Ov'è il mio bene?* (D-RH [D-MÜu] Ms 263 [2][RISM;P]; S-Skma T-SE-R[RISM]); *Partirò bella tiranna* (S-Skma T-SE-R[RISM]); *Passi da me, ben mio* (D-Bsa [D-B] SA 3926[RISM;P]; S-Skma T-SE-R[RISM]); *Per te d'eterni allori* (D-RH [D-MÜu] Ms 261 [1][RISM;P]); *Sprezza il furor del vento* (D-Bsa [D-B] SA 1522 [8][RISM]); *Prigioniera abbandonata* (D-RH [D-MÜu] Ms 260 [2][RISM;P]; S-L Saml.Engelhart 568 [1][RISM;P]; S-Skma T-SE-R[RISM]; *Quell'amplesso e quel perdono* (D-RH [D-MÜu] Ms 263 [4][RISM;P]; D-W Cod. Guelf. 314 Mus. Hdschr. [60][RISM;R]; S-Skma T-SE-

---

61. The production ran for three consecutive performances between 7 and 14 January 1746; see Schmidt-Hensel, Roland Dieter, 'Carl Heinrich Grauns *Demofoonte*-Vertonung (Berlin 1746)', in *Demofoonte come soggetto per il dramma per musica: Johann Adolf Hasse ed altri compositori del Settecento*, ed. by Milada Jonášová and Tomislav Volek (Prague: Academia, 2020), pp. 189–212. Contrarily, Schneider gives 29/12/1745 as the date of premiere; see Schneider, Louis, *Geschichte der Opern und des königlichen Opernhauses in Berlin* (Berlin: Dunker & Humbolt, 1852).
62. Act I incompletely copied.
63. Microfilm copy: F-Pn VM BOB-34193.

MC | *Adriano in Siria* (1732–1828)

R[RISM]); *Saggio guerriero antico* (D-RH [D-MÜu] Ms 262 [2][RISM;P]; D-W Cod. Guelf. 314 Mus. Hdschr. [59][RISM;R]; D-WRha Mus.ms. B 36 [13][RISM;R,IP]); *Se mai piagato a morte* (CZ-Pnm XXXVIII A 267[RISM;P]); *Se pur non moro allato* (B-Bc 5331[RISM;R]; D-B* Mus.ms.autogr. Graun, C. H. 6 [8][RISM;R,64]; D-RH [D-MÜu] Ms 264[RISM;IR,IP]); *Sprezza il furor del vento* (D-RH [D-MÜu] Ms 260 [1][RISM;P]); *Tutti nemice e rei* (D-RH [D-MÜu] Ms 263 [3][RISM;P]); *Vivi a noi, vivi all'impero* (D-Hs ND VI 81 g: II [79][RISM]; S-L Saml.Kraus 69[RISM;IP]); *Volga il ciel felici amanti* (B-Bc 5291b[RISM;R]; D-RH [D-MÜu] Ms 263 [1][RISM;P])

[printed sources] *Passi da me, ben mio* [7], in *Duetti, terzetti, quinteti, sestetti ed alcuni chori delle opere del signore Carlo Enrico Graun* (Berlin: Decker & Hartung, 1773)

[contrafacta] *Barbaro non comprendo* ([Ack låt oss vara glada] S-L Saml. Engelhart 342[RISM;P]; [Ave virgo singularis] PL-Wu RM 5708 [2][RISM;P]; [Beata Salomea] PL-SA 134/A III 34 [1][RISM;P]); *Dal labro che t'accende* ([O lux beata trinitas, et principalis unitas] PL-Wu RM 4424 [6][RISM;P]; [Redempta gens accende amoris] PL-Wu RM 4424 [5][RISM;P]); *Non ritrova un'alma forte* ([Ecce tempus est salutis] PL-Wu RM 4405 [1][RISM;P]); *Partirò bella tiranna* ([Salve regina misericordiae vita dulcedo] PL-Wu RM 5466[RISM;P]); *Per te d'eterni allori* ([A solis ortus cardine] PL-Wu RM 4401 [4][RISM;P]; [Numinis mater amata] PL-Wu RM 5708 [1][RISM;P]); *Quell'amplesso e quel perdono* ([Omni die dic Mariar, mea laudes anima] PL-Wu RM 4420 [2][RISM;P]; [Sulle sponde al pigro Lete] D-Hs ND VI 28 [26][RISM;R,P]; D-Hs ND VI 81 g: II [76][RISM;R]); *Saggio guerriero antico* ([O sole virgo pulchrior] PL-Wu RM 5429[RISM;P]; [Sancte pater Francisce] PL-SA 134/A III 34 [3][RISM;P]); *Se pur non moro allato* ([O virgo gloriosa super omnes speciosa] PL-Wu RM 4422 [1][RISM;P]); *Sprezza il furor del vento* ([Omnes de Saba, venient aurum] PL-Wu RM 4420 [1][RISM;P]; [Salve regina] PL-Wu RM 5463[RISM;P]); *Vivi a noi, vivi all'impero* ([Alites pennis veloces] CZ-LIT 445[RISM;P]; [Huc gentes convolate, matrem clientis salutate] CZ-Pnm XXXVIII A 391[RISM;P]; [Laetentur caeli exsultet terra] PL-Wu RM 4417[RISM;P]; [Omnes laetantes Deum amantes] PL-Wu RM 5534 [2][RISM;P]); *Volga il ciel felici amanti* ([Adoro te devote, latens deitas] CZ-OSm A 1924[RISM;P]; [Mundanos sperno favores] CZ-Pnm XL A 48[RISM;P]; [O Jesus mi ad te suspiro, tu me o Jesu] CZ-Pak 424[RISM;P])

---

64. In F major instead of G major.

1746	mus. by various unknown composers[65]
1746 Livorno	Teatro da S. Sebastiano (carn.)
Librettos	Lucca: Marescandoli, 1746
	D-Sl Fr.D.oct.5060

1746	mus. by unknown composer(s)
1746 Perugia	Teatro del Pavone (carn.)
Librettos	Perugia: Costantini & Maurizi, 1746
	I-Vgc ROL.0692 [8]

1747	mus. by Latilla, Gaetano
1747 Naples	Teatro di S. Carlo (19/12/1747)[66]
	name day of Maria Maddalena of Portugal
Librettos	Naples: Langiano, 1747
	E-Mn T/10791; E-Tp 22571; I-Mb Racc.dramm.3619
Music sources	[excerpts] *Prigioniera abbandonata* (GB-Cfm [GB-Cu] MU.MS.224[IC]); *Se non ti moro allato* (GB-Cfm [GB-Cu] MU.MS.224[IC]); *Tutti nemici e rei* (GB-Cfm [GB-Cu] MU.MS.224[IC]; I-MC 3-D-8/8 [6][RISM])

1748	mus. by Ciampi, Vincenzo Legrenzio	
1748 Venice	Teatro Tron di S. Cassiano (carn., *c.* 16/01/1748)[67]	(1,2)
1750 London	King's Theatre in the Haymarket (26/02/1750)[68]	(3)
	rev. version	
Librettos	(1) [Venice: s.n., 1748]	
	B-Bc 18989; I-Bc Lo.08067; I-Rsc Libr. n. XV [2]; I-Rsc Carv.211; I-Vcg LIBRETTI S.CASSIANO 19; I-Vnm DRAMM.1264 [1]; US-LAum ML48 .R114 1748 [1]; US-Wc ML48 [S1875]	
	(2) Venice: [s.n., 1748][69]	
	I-Bc Lo.08068; I-Mb Racc.dramm.2991; I-Vnm DRAMM.1068 [1]	
	(3) London: Woodfall, 1750 (It./En.)	
	GB-Lbl 11714.b.39 [3]	

---

65. See <https://www.pasticcio-project.eu/database/work/P103695> [accessed 26 May 2022].
66. Date in De Filippis and Arnese, *Cronache del Teatro di S. Carlo*, p. 30. [C] gives 18/12/1747.
67. New arias for Teresa Castellini of Milan, who performed the role of Sabina.
68. Burden ('Metastasio on the London Stage', p. 31) gives 20/02/1750 as the date of the London premiere.
69. This libretto includes an appendix with some 'Arie nuove'.

MC | *Adriano in Siria* (1732–1828)

Music sources	[excerpts] *Infelice invan mi lagno* (F-Pn D-14924[BnF,RISM]); *Mi vuoi tradir lo so* (D-Dl Mus.1-F-82,8 [3][RISM]); *Numi, se giusti siete* (D-Dl Mus.1-F-82,8 [6][RISM]); *Rendimi il mio ben, Nume* (D-Dl Mus.1-F-82,8 [2][RISM]; I-MOe Mus. F. 890[IC,NG]); *Sento pietade anch'io* (D-Dl Mus.1-F-82,8 [5][RISM]); *Tanto rigore, oh dio* (D-Dl Mus.1-F-82,8 [4][RISM]); *Vicino ad antro, o speco* (D-Dl Mus.1-F-82,8 [7][RISM])
	[printed sources][70] *Dal labro che t'accende* [2]; *Infelice invan mi lagno* [3]; *Oh dio, mancar mi sento* [6]; *Parto da te be mio* [5]; *Prigioniera abbandonata* [1]; *Rendimi il mio ben, Nume* [4], in <u>The Favourite Songs in the Opera call'd Adriano in Siria</u> (London: Walsh, [1750])

1749	mus. by Scalabrini, Paolo[71]
1749 Copenhagen	Court theatre – Charlottenborg
Librettos	Copenhagen: Hartvig, 1749 (It./Ger.)
	DK-Kk 56,-368 4°; US-Cn BLC #540a
Music sources	[excerpts] *Dal labro che t'accende* (S-Sk 494 [66][RISM,72])

1750	mus. by Ciampi, Vincenzo Legrenzio (rev. version) → see 1748

1750	mus. by Pescetti, Giovanni Battista
1750 Reggio Emilia	Teatro Pubblico (Fair, 17/05/1750) (1)
	Il Farnaspe
1750 Siena	Teatro degli Intronati (01/07/1750) (2)
Librettos	(1) Reggio Emilia: Vedrotti, 1750[73]
	D-Mbs L.eleg.m. 3871; I-Mb Racc.dramm.6082 [1]; I-REm 19.K.118; I-Vgc ROL.0531 [2]
	(2) Siena: Bonetti, 1750
	CDN-Ttfl Itp Pam 01544; US-CHH IOLC.00240
Music sources	[complete scores] B-Bc 12508[IC,RISM] [Acts I&II][74]

---

70. The following arias were performed in the 1750 revival in London; in fact, pieces nos 1, 5, and 6 did not appear in the libretto for the 1748 setting.
71. Treated as a pasticcio in <https://www.pasticcio-project.eu/database/work/P102162> [accessed 25 May 2022].
72. Given as anonymous in [RISM].
73. The copy in I-Rn listed in S9782 cannot be found; lost?
74. Although the manuscript does not indicate the composer of the music, the structure of the *dramma* corresponds to Pescetti's setting. Coincidences with some excerpts further support this attribution. The overture is the same as in Pescetti's *Ezio* (Venice, 1747).

[excerpts] *Cara, ti lascio, addio*[75] (D-HR III 4 1/2 4° 239[RISM]; S-Skma T-SE-R Alströmer saml. n/s[RISM]; US-BEm MS 29 [6][IC,RISM]); *Nel caro amabil volto* (A-Wgm VI 6746 [Q 3857][IC]; US-BEm MS 103 [4][RISM]; US-Wc M1613.A2 M2[RISM;P,76]); *Nocchier che in mar* (A-LA 473[RISM;P]); *Pupille care* (D-Dl Mus.1-F-49,12 [5a][RISM]; F-Pn D-14963 [20][BnF,RISM,77]; J-Tk S10-891-9 [9][RISM]); *Serba l'intata fede* (D-SWl Mus.4185[RISM;P,78])

[contrafacta] *Pupille care* ([*Dans nos prairies*] F-Pn D-18350 [15][BnF,RISM])

[parodies] *Ricordati che sola sei* ([*Non ingannar ben mio*] D-Sla 84[RISM;P,79])

[doubtful] *Se non ti moro allato*[80] (CH-N XB obl. 209[RISM;P]; I-MAav Cart.1 n.5[RISM])

1750	mus. by Fiorillo, Ignazio[MGG]	
1750 Brunswick	Teatro Ducale?	
1751	mus. by Pampani, Antonio Gaetano	
1751 Milan	Teatro Regio Ducale (carn., 26/12/1750)	(1)
1754 Pavia	Teatro Omodeo	(2)
Librettos	(1) Milan: Malatesta, 1750	
	CDN-Ttfl Itp Pam 00715; F-Pn LIV IT-3522 [6]; I-Bc Lo.03977; I-Fc E.V.2561; I-FEwalker[S]; I-LDEsormani 309/1/28; I-Ms MUS. P. XII. 2; I-Rn 40.9.C.8.4	
	(2) Pavia: Bolzani, 1754	
	I-Vgc ROL.0515 [10]	
Music sources	[excerpts] *Parto, ti lascio, o cara* (D-Mbs Mus.ms. 181 [10][RISM])	
	[doubtful] *Nel caro amabil volto* (D-Dl Mus.1-F-82,21 [6][RISM,81])	
1751	mus. by Adolfati, Andrea	
1751 Genoa	Teatro del Falcone (carn.)	

---

75. The aria first appeared in Pescetti's *Ezio* (Venice, 1747).
76. Wrongly attributed to F. Maggiore on source.
77. Wrongly attributed to B. Galuppi on source.
78. Wrongly attributed to G. M. Pergolesi on source.
79. In B flat major instead of C major.
80. This text was not included in the librettos corresponding to Pescetti's setting or in the musical source B-Bc 12508.
81. According to [IC] and [RISM], this aria was inserted into A2-S2 of Pampani's setting, yet the aria that appears in that position in the libretto of the premiere is *Del caro bene accanto*; it does not appear in the rest of the text either.

MC | *Adriano in Siria* (1732–1828)

Librettos	Genoa: Franchelli, [1751]
	CDN-Ttfl Itp Pam 00001; I-PAp BB XI.25664
Music sources	[complete scores] F-Pn AB O-161/162[BnF,MGG,RISM,82]
	[excerpts] *Cara, ti lascio, addio?* (I-Gl FONDO ANT. M.2.9.1[IC,S-BN]; I-Gl FONDO ANT. M.2.9.2[IC]); *Numi, se giusti siete* (US-CHH* VFM3.1.A36 1750z [15][MGG,RISM,83]); *Prigioniera abbandonata* (US-CHH* VFM3.1.A36 1750z [14][MGG,RISM]); *Quell'amplesso e quel perdono* (US-CHH* VFM3.1.A36 1750z [33][MGG,RISM]); *Sotto ciel turbato, oscuro* (US-CHH* VFM3.1.A36 1750z [13][MGG,RISM])

1752	mus. by unknown composer(s)
1752 Cremona	Teatro Nazari (carn.)
Librettos	Milan: Ghislandi, 1751
	I-Rsc Vol. Carv.100 [1]; I-SORmde LA.005

1752	mus. by Hasse, Johann Adolph (2nd version) → see 1737

1752	mus. by Scarlatti, Giuseppe	
1752 Venice	Teatro Tron di S. Cassiano (carn., c. 26/01/1752)	(1)
1752 Lucca	Teatro Pubblico (27/08/1752)	(2)
1754 Livorno	Teatro da S. Sebastiano (carn., 19/01/1754)	(3)
1760 Prague	Teatro Nuovo	(4)
1767 Livorno	Teatro da S. Sebastiano[84]	(5)
Librettos	(1) [Venice: s.n., 1752]
	B-Bc 18990; I-Mb Racc.dramm.2837; I-Pmc[S]; I-Ria MISC. Teatrale 3 [5]; I-Vcg LIBRETTI S.CASSIANO 21; I-Vnm DRAMM.1074 [4]; I-Vnm DRAMM.1271 [4]; US-LAum ML48 .R114 1752 [4]; US-Wc ML48 [S9540]
	(2) Lucca: Benedini, 1752
	GB-Lbl 1342.a.37 [4];[85] I-PAc F. Libretti, sc.007 [99]
	(3) Livorno: Santini & co., [1754]
	I-Bc Lo.05150

---

82. Microfilm copy: F-Pn VM BOB-18158.
83. This and the following sources are possibly the composer's autographs.
84. Mazzoni, Stefano, 'Teatri e opera nell Settecento: Livorno', in *Theatre Spaces for Music in 18th-century Europe*, ed. by Iskrena Yordanova, Giuseppina Raggi, and Maria Ida Biggi (Vienna: Hollitzer, 2020), pp. 321–86.
85. Microfilm copy: GB-Lbl PB.Mic.13959.

(4) [Prague]: Pruscha, 1760
CZ-Bu ST1-0161 [49]; CZ-Pnm 003081695; CZ-Pu 65 E 2449

(5) NA

Music sources [complete scores] S-St n/s[RISM;P]

[excerpts] *Dal labro che t'accende* (GB-Lbl Add. 31516[BL,RISM]); *Non ritrova un'alma forte* (D-KA Don Mus.Ms. 1728[RISM;P]); *Numi, se giusti siete* (GB-Lbl Add. 31512[BL,RISM]); *Prigioniera abbandonata* (US-BEm MS 96 [13][IC,RISM]); *Quell'amplesso e quel perdono* (D-Dl Mus.2804-F-2 [5][RISM]; D-Dl Mus.2804-F-2 [10][RISM]; D-SWl Mus.4830[RISM;P]; D-SWl Mus.48460[RISM;IP]; US-BEm MS 96 [12][IC,RISM]; US-NYp Mus. Res. *MNZ (General) [13][RISM]); *Sotto ciel turbato, oscuro* (D-Dl Mus.2804-F-2 [6][RISM]; D-Dl Mus.2804-F-2 [11][RISM]; D-Mbs Mus.ms. 179 [11][RISM])

[doubtful] *Caro l'affanno mio*[86] (I-Mc Noseda L.24 [15][SBN])

1752 mus. by Jommelli, Niccolò
1752 Rome Teatro delle Dame

Music sources [excerpts] *Sprezza il furor del vento* (B-Bc 4315[IC,RISM])

1753 mus. by Valentini, Michelangelo
1753 Bologna Teatro Formagliari (spr.)

Librettos Bologna: successors of Benacci, [1753]
I-Bc Lo.05467; I-Bu A.V.Tab.IX.Caps.XXI [19]; I-FZc RM.N.II.110; I-Rn 40.10.E.7.2

Music sources [excerpts] *Ah ingrato, m'inganni* (GB-Lbl I R.M.23.e.6 [8][BL,NG,RISM]); *Dal labro che t'accende* (GB-Lbl R.M.23.e.6 [11][BL,NG,RISM]); *È falso il dir che uccida* (GB-Lbl R.M.23.e.6 [2][BL,NG,RISM]); *Prigioniera abbandonata* (GB-Lbl R.M.23.e.6 [3][BL,NG,RISM]); *Se non ti moro allato* (GB-Lbl R.M.23.e.6 [7][BL,NG,RISM]); US-NYp Mus. Res. *MP (Italian) [31][RISM]); *Quell'amplesso e quel perdono* (GB-Lbl R.M.23.e.6 [1][BL,NG,RISM]); *Son le lusinghe, credimi* (GB-Lbl R.M.23.e.6 [10][BL,NG,RISM])

[contrafacta] *Oh dio, mancar mi sento* ([*Ah virgo ad te suspiro*] PL-Wu RM 5038[RISM;P])

---

86. This aria does not appear in the libretto for the premiere of Scarlatti's setting nor in those for its later revivals.

MC | *Adriano in Siria* (1732–1828)

1753	mus. by Cocchi, Gioacchino
1753 Crema	Teatro di Crema (aut.)
Librettos	Venice: [s.n., 1753] F-Pn LIS IT-3705 [4]
Music sources	[excerpts] *È vero che oppresso la sorte* (US-NYp Mus. Res. *MNZ (General) [2]^{RISM}); *Prigioniera abbandonata* (F-Pn D-15262^{BnF,RISM}); *Quell'amplesso e quel perdono* (F-Pn D-15264^{BnF,RISM})
1754	mus. by Perez, Davide
1754 Lisbon	Court theatre – Palácio de Salvaterra de Magos (carn.)
Librettos	Lisbon: Sylviana, 1753 I-Rsc Carv.215
Music sources	[complete scores] A-Wgm IV 27701 [Q 1823]^{IC}; GB-Lbl Add. 16100/16101^{BL,MGG,NG,RISM} [Acts II&III]; GB-Lcm MS 473^{IC,MGG,NG}; I-MC 4-F-4^{RISM}; I-Vnm Mss. 9791/9792/9793^{IC,MGG,NG,SBN}; P-La 45-IV-39/40/41^{BA,MGG,NG}; P-La 54-I-86/87/88^{BA,MGG,NG}; P-Ln C.I.C. 95^{IC,MGG,NG,RISM}; S-Skma T-R^{MGG,NG,RISM}; US-BEm MS 6 [a–c]$^{IC,MGG,NG,RISM;A,87}$ [excerpts] *Ah ingrato, m'inganni* (D-Mbs Mus.ms. 988 [10]^{RISM}); *Dal labro che t'accende* (I-Nc 34.6.13 [6]^{SBN}; US-BEm MS 100 [3]^{IC,RISM}); *Digli ch'è un infedele* (D-Hs M A/453 [5]^{MGG,RISM}; US-Wc M1505.A2 P43^{RISM}); *Dopo un tuo sguardo, ingrata* (D-Hs M A/453 [2]^{MGG,RISM}); *Infelice invan mi lagno* (D-Mbs Mus.ms. 988 [9]^{RISM}; US-BEm MS 100 [5]^{IC,RISM}); *Leon piagato a morte* (F-Pn L-19438$^{BnF;IP}$); *Non ritrova un'alma forte* (D-Hs M A/453 [6]^{MGG,RISM}); *Numi, se giusti siete* (D-Hs M A/453 [3]^{MGG,RISM}; GB-Lbl Add. 31605^{BL,RISM}; I-Gl B A.1.22 [19]^{IC,MGG,NG}; P-Ln M.M. 217 [15/1]$^{IC,RISM;R,P}$; US-BEm MS 95 [4]^{IC,RISM}); *Prigioniera abbandonata* (I-Mc Noseda I.21 [8]^{SBN}; US-BEm *M2.1 M387 [2]^{RISM}); *Se non ti moro allato* (GB-Lbl Lbl Add. 32169 [20]^{BL,RISM}; I-Gl A.1.22 [12]^{IC,SBN}); *Son sventurato* (B-Bc 4576 [5]^{RISM}; CH-N XB obl. 232$^{RISM;P}$; D-Hs M A/453 [7]^{MGG,RISM}; D-Mbs Mus.ms. 988 [12]^{RISM}; GB-Lbl Add. 31651 [3]^{BL,RISM}; I-Mc Noseda I.21 [2]^{SBN}; I-MC 4-F-1 [14]^{RISM}; I-MC 5-A-12 [12]^{RISM}; I-Nc 34.6.13 [4]^{SBN}; I-Nc 34.6.13 [28]^{SBN}; I-Nc 34.6.13 [38]^{SBN}; I-Pca D.IV.1592^{SBN}; J-Tk S10-613-2 [2]^{RISM}; S-Skma T-SE-R^{RISM}; US-BEm MS 1073 [3]^{IC,RISM}; US-BEm *M2.1 M387 [7]^{RISM,88}); *Sprezza il furor del vento* (D-Hs M A/453 [1]^{MGG,RISM})

87. Only arias and two recitatives.
88. According to an inscription on the source, used for a performance in Rome in 1757, by Gioacchino Conti, who also sung the role of Farnaspe in the premiere of Perez's setting in 1754.

MC | *Adriano in Siria* (1732–1828)

1754	mus. by Scolari, Giuseppe	
1754 Venice	Teatro Grimani di S. Samuele (carn., 02/02/1754)	

Librettos Venice: Geremia, [1754]
I-Bc Lo.05184; I-BDG REC 97.B.32 [1]; I-Mb Racc.dramm.3851; I-Pmc^S; I-Vcg LIBRETTI S.SAMUELE 170; I-Vnm DRAMM.0176 [5]; I-Vnm DRAMM.1273 [5]; US-LAum ML48 .R114 1754 [5]; US-Wc ML48 [S9802]

Music sources [excerpts] *Se non ti moro allato* (US-SFsc *M2.1 M481[RISM;IP])

1754	mus. by Conforto, Nicola	
1754 Naples	Teatro di S. Carlo (04/11/1754)	(1)
1757 Madrid	Court theatre – Teatro del Buen Retiro (23/09/1757)	(2)
	birthday of Fernando VI, king of Spain	
	lib. rev. by Metastasio[89]	
	rev. version	
1758 Madrid	Court theatre – Teatro del Buen Retiro (28/03/1758)[90]	(3)

Librettos (1) Naples: Langiano, 1754
E-Mn T/7986

(2) Madrid: Escrivano, [1757] (It./Spa.)
E-Msi BH FLL 29004; E-Tp 1-1426; US-E PQ 4717 A24 1757; US-Wc ML48 [S2121][91]

(3) NA

Music sources
1st version: 1754, Naples

[complete scores] I-Nc 25.2.32[IC,NG,RISM,SBN;A]; P-La 44-V-36/37/38[BA,MGG,NG]

[excerpts] *Dal labro che t'accende* (I-Nc 34.3.5[SBN]); *Per pietà bell'idol mio*[92] (I-Mc Noseda E.59 [2][RISM]; I-Nc 34.3.13 [4][SBN]); *Prigioniera abbandonata** (I-Nc 34.3.5[SBN]); *Se non ti moro allato* (D-LÜh Mus. Q 202[RISM]; D-WRz Mus VIIb:151[RISM;IP]; I-Nc 34.3.5[SBN]); *Son sventurato* (D-Dl Mus.3069-F-2 [5][RISM])

---

89. Sommer-Mathis, Andrea, 'El tandem Metastasio–Farinelli: producción de óperas y escenografía del *dramma per musica*', *Scherzo*, 384, special dossier: *Metastasio en el Madrid del XVIII* (May 2022), 64–66.
90. Casanova Sánchez de Vega, Teresa, 'El intermezzo en la corte de España, 1738–1758' (doctoral dissertation, Universidad Complutense de Madrid, 2019).
91. Microfilm copy: US-Ccrl 6126B.
92. Text from Metastasio's *Artaserse*.

MC | *Adriano in Siria* (1732–1828)

[contrafacta] *Prigioniera abbandonata* ([*Amor sancte in me cresce*] CH-SAf MusSAf.Ms.141^(RISM;P))

rev. version: 1757, Madrid

[complete scores] E-Mp MUS MSS 303/304/305^(IC,MGG); E-Mp* MUS MSS 422^(IC,MGG,93) [Acts I&III]; P-La 44-V-39^(BA,MGG,NG)

[excerpts] *Non ritrova un'alma forte* (D-WWW K 8 Nr. 41 [3]^(RISM)); *Oh dio, mancar mi sento* (GB-Lbl Add. 31649 [15]^(BL,RISM))

[undated] [excerpts] *Leon piagato a morte* (GB-Lbl Add. 31651^(RISM))

Adriano in Siria, in *Poesie del signor abate Pietro Metastasio* (Paris: widow of Quillau, 1755), vol. 1, pp. 111–204.

1757	mus. by Brusa, Giovanni Francesco
1757 Venice	Teatro Grimani di S. Benedetto (carn., 29/01/1757)
Librettos	Venice: Fenzo, 1757
	D-B Mus. T55; I-Mb Racc.dramm.0439; I-Mr Libr. 02187; I-Pmc^S; I-PAc F. Libretti, sc.007 [100]; I-Rsc Carv.216; I-Rsc Libr. n. XVI [1]; I-Vcg LIBRETTI S.BENEDETTO 187; I-Vnm DRAMM.1079 [6]; I-Vnm DRAMM.1277 [6]; US-CAt *Ic7.A100.B750 [16]; US-LAum ML48 .R114 1757 [6]; US-Wc ML48 [S1376]
Music sources	[complete scores] S-St A 7^(MGG,RISM); S-St n/s^(MGG,RISM;P)
1757	mus. by Uttini, Francesco Antonio Baldassare[94]
1757 Stockholm	Royal theatre – Drottningholm Palace (25/08/1757)
	name day of Luisa Ulrica, queen of Sweden
Librettos	Stockholm: Stamperia di corte, 1757 (It./Fr.)
	CDN-Ttfl Volt .V65 O763 1755f; S-Sk 1700-1829 37 E; S-Skma 55: 68/11

Adriano in Siria, in *Poesie del signor abate Pietro Metastasio* (Turin: Stamperia Reale, 1757), vol. 1, pp. 109–96.

---

93. Under this call number E-Mp holds the composer's autograph for acts I&III and a set of complete parts for Vn I, Vn II, and Va.
94. For a discussion of Uttini's stay in Sweden, see Burden, Michel, '"Twittering and Thrilling": Swedish Reaction to Metastasio', *Early Music*, 26.4 (1998), 608–21.

MC | *Adriano in Siria* (1732–1828)

1757	mus. by Conforto, Nicola (rev. version) → see 1754

1758 1758 Rome	mus. by Di Capua, Rinaldo Teatro di Torre Argentina (carn., 02/01/1758)

Librettos Rome: Amidei,⁹⁵ [1758]
B-Bc Bc 18991; I-Rb FS3 34.04.14]; I-Rsc Libr. n. XVI [2]; I-Rsc Libr. n. XVI [175]; I-Rvat Stamp.Ferr.V.8055 [6]; I-Vgc ROL.0574 [14]; US-Wc ML50.2.A36 R4⁹⁶

Music sources [complete scores] P-La 44-IV-40/41/42^(BA,MGG,NG)

[excerpts] *Infelice invan mi lagno* (US-SFsc *M2.1 M432^(MGG,RISM;IP)); *Oh dio, mancar mi sento* (US-SFsc *M2.1 M433^(MGG,RISM;IP)); *Se non ti moro allato* (F-Pn L-19771^(BnF); GB-Lbl Add. 31653 [11]^(BL,RISM))

1758	mus. by Galuppi, Baldassare (2ⁿᵈ version) → see 1740

1759 1759 Turin	mus. by Borghi, Giovanni Battista Teatro Regio (carn., 26/12/1758)⁹⁷

Librettos Turin: Avondo, [1759]⁹⁸
CDN-Ttfl Liv Pam 00425; F-Pn FB-6918; I-NOVa Biblioteca Teatro Coccia 286 [1]; I-NOVc CIV 194.I.25; <u>I-Rn 40.8.A.4.0</u>;⁹⁹ I-Rsc Vol. Carv.144 [6]; I-Tci L.O.0175; I-Tn F VII.362 [1]; I-Tn F XIII.521 [3]; US-BEm ML48 .C65

Music sources [complete scores] I-Tf 1 T 3^(RISM;A,R); I-Tf 10 V 19^(IC,RISM;A,100); P-La 46-III-69/70/71^(BA,MGG,NG)

[excerpts] *Minaccia altero il fiume* (GB-Lbl R.M.24.f.3 [1/5]^(BL,RISM)); *Non ritrova un'alma forte* (GB-Lbl Lbl R.M.24.f.3 [1/2]^(BL,RISM)); *Numi, se giusti siete* (GB-Lbl R.M.24.f.3 [1/6]^(BL,RISM)); *Quell'amplesso e quel perdono* (GB-

---

95. 'Si vendono da'. ˢ407 further lists a copy in I-PLcom, yet it cannot be found in the Biblioteca Communale of Palermo; we therefore consider it as lost.
96. Microfilm reproduction: US-CHH 55-ML513.
97. The production ran for nineteen consecutive performances; see Bouquet, Marie Thérèse, Valeria Gualerzi, and Alberto Testa, *Storia del Teatro Regio di Torino: cronologie*, ed. by Alberto Basso (Turin: Cassa di Risparmio di Torino, [1988]).
98. According to ˢ409, there was a copy of this libretto in I-FPfanan (previously in Turin), yet the items of the collection were sold independently and can no longer be traced. There was also one in I-Rsc Libr. n. XVI [3], but we could not find it among the institution's holdings. We therefore consider it as lost.
99. Pages 11–13, 35–76 are handwritten.
100. It includes a terzet by Baldassare Galuppi (fols 1–20) —*In quel paterno amplesso*— and an aria attributed to Giovanni Battista Borghi (fols 1–6) —*Che fa il mio bene?*— not included in the composer's setting of *Adriano*. The folios are unordered. Microfilm reproduction in CDN-Lu M1500.M57B675 1759a.

MC | *Adriano in Siria* (1732–1828)

Lbl R.M.24.f.3 [1/4]^{BL,RISM}); *Se non ti moro allato* (GB-Lbl R.M.24.f.3 [1/7]^{BL,RISM}); *Sprezza il furor del vento* (GB-Lbl R.M.24.f.3 [1/3]^{BL,RISM}) [doubtful] *Che fa il mio bene?* (GB-Lbl R.M.24.f.3 [1/1]^{BL,RISM}); *Si smarrisce in tanto affanno*[101] (A-Wgm VI 15495 [Q 2748]^{IC})

1759	mus. by Brunetti, Giovan Gualberto
1759 Pisa	Teatro Pubblico (carn., 31/12/1758)
Librettos	Pisa: Carotti, 1759
	CDN-Ttfl Itp Pam 00150
1760	mus. by various unknown composers
1760 Verona	Teatro Filarmonico (carn.)
Librettos	Brescia: Pianta, 1760
	I-LDEsormani 314/4-5/25; I-Mb Racc.dramm.6066 [3]
1760	mus. by various unknown composers
1760 Pavia	Teatro Omodeo (carn., 18/01/1760)
Librettos	Pavia: heirs of Ghidini, [1760]
	I-Mb Racc.dramm.6066 [2]
1760	mus. by Mazzoni, Antonio Maria
1760 Venice	Teatro Grimani di S. Samuele (Asc., 14/05/1760)
Librettos	Venice: Fenzo, 1760
	A-Wmi BT-563; I-Mb Racc.dramm.0541; I-Ria MISC. Teatrale 4 [3]; I-Rsc Libr. n. XVI [4]; I-Vcg LIBRETTI S.SAMUELE 172; I-Vnm DRAMM.1082 [5]; I-Vnm DRAMM.1281 [6]; US-LAum ML48 .R114 1760 [8]; US-Wc ML48 [S6225]
Music sources	[excerpts] *Dopo un tuo sguardo, ingrata* (A-KR F 37 [118]^{RISM;P})
1760	mus. by Galuppi, Baldassare (3rd version) → see 1740
1761	mus. by unknown composer(s)
1761 Florence	Teatro della Pergola (carn., 26/12/1760)

---

101. Although the manuscript relates the aria to Borghi's *Adriano*, the aria does not appear in the libretto for his setting.

MC | *Adriano in Siria* (1732–1828)

Librettos	Florence: Stamperia dirimpetto all'Oratorio di S. Filippo Neri, [1761]	
	I-Fc E.V.0252; I-Fc E.V.1570	
1762	**mus. by Schwanenberger, Johann Gottfried**	
1762 Brunswick	Teatro Ducale (08/1762)	(1)
1762 Brunswick	Teatro Ducale (win. Fair)	(2)
Librettos	(1) NA	
	(2) [Brunswick: s.n., 1762] (It./Ger.)	
	A-Wn 28539-A; D-KNth L 71	
Music sources	[complete scores] D-LEm Becker III.15.26[MGG,RISM]	
	[excerpts] *Dal labro che t'accende* (D-WRgs 32/252 [1][RISM;P]); *È ver che oppresso* (D-WRgs 32/252 [2][RISM;P]); *Se non ti mor allato* (D-SWl Mus.5013[RISM]); *Sprezza il furor del vento* (CZ-BER HU 490 [2][RISM]); *Tutti nemici e rei* (I-OS Mss.Mus.B 4540[RISM])	
	[contrafacta] *Prigioniera abbandonata* ([*Terrena tantum petere*] PL-Wu RM 4179 [2][RISM;P])	
	[doubtful] *Numi, se giusti siete*[102] (D-B Mus.ms. 20504/8 [2][RISM])	
1763	**mus. by Colla, Giuseppe**	
1763 Milan	Teatro Regio Ducale (carn., 31/12/1762)	
Librettos	Milan: Malatesta, 1762	
	CDN-Ttfl Itp Pam 00178; F-Pn LIV IT-3527 [1]; I-Bc Lo.01245; I-LDEsormani 309/3/17; I-Ma S. I. H. I. 9 [7]; I-Mc Coll.Libr.132; I-Ms MUS. G. XLIV. 1; I-Rsc Vol. 9 [7]	
Music sources	[complete scores] I-Nc 25.2.27/28/29[MGG,NG,RISM,SBN;A,103]; P-La 44-V-18/19/20[BA,MGG,NG]; P-La 48-I-10/11/12[BA,MGG,NG]	
	[excerpts] *Se non ti moro allato* (A-Wgm VI 448 [Q 2823][IC]; GB-Lbl Add. 29966[BL,RISM])	
1763	**mus. by unknown composer(s)**	
1763 Ferrara	Teatro Bonacossi da S. Stefano (carn.)	
Librettos	Ferrara: Fornari, [1763]	
	US-PHu 782.5 G135A	

102. The music is different from that in D-LEm Becker III.15.26. Furthermore, in the libretto for Schwanenberger's setting this text is set as an aria, whereas in D-B Mus.ms. 20504/8 [2] it is arranged as a duet.
103. Microfilm Copy: US-PRu MICROFILM 2391 [1–2].

1763	mus. by Sciroli, Gregorio
1763 Barcelona	Teatre de la Santa Creu (06/05/1763)
Librettos	Barcelona: Generas, [1763] (It./Spa.)
	E-Bbc 16-I-12; E-Mn T/17139 [3]
Music sources	[excerpts] *Son sventurato* (D-Dl Mus.1-F-49,12 [11]^{RISM})
1764	mus. by Concialini, Carlo Giovanni and others
1764 Lucca	Teatro Pubblico (25/08/1764)
Librettos	Lucca: Benedini, 1764
	I-Fm Mel.2044 [4]; I-PAc F. Libretti, sc.007 [101]; I-PS BM 256 [26]; I-Vgc ROL.0676 [10]
Music sources	[excerpts] *La ragion gli affetti ascolta* (CZ-Pnm XXXII D 233^{IC})
1764	mus. by Wimmer, Marian^{NG}
1764 [s.l.]	NA
1765	mus. by Bach, Johann Christian
1765 London	King's Theatre in the Haymarket (26/12/1764)[104]
Librettos	London: Woodfall, 1765 (It./En.)
	D-HAmi ulb.55173115X; F-Pn RES VS-605; GB-Lbl 1608/4555 [9];[105] US-Cu PQ4717.A5 1765; US-I ML50.B11 A2; US-NH ML48 L698 [17]
Music sources	[complete scores] B-Bc 2037^{IC,RISM} [Acts II&III]; P-La 44-II-28/29/30^{BA}
	[excerpts] *Cara la dolce fiamma* (D-Mbs Mus.ms. 20695^{RISM}); *Se non ti moro allato* (D-W Cod. Guelf. 13 Mus. Hdschr.^{RISM}; I-Nc 64.1 [16A]^{SBN}; S-Skma T-SE-R^{RISM})
	[printed sources] *Cara la dolce fiamma* [9]; *Chi mai d'iniqua stella* [3]; *Dal labro che t'accende* [10]; *Deh lascia, oh ciel pietoso* [12]; *Disperato in mar turbato* [5]; *Dopo un tuo sguardo, ingrata* [1]; *Leon piagato a morte* [11]; *Oh dio, mancar mi sento* [6]; *Quanto grato nell'amare* [8]; *Se non ti moro allato* [2]; *Son sventurato* [7]; *Vuoi punir l'ingrato amante?* [4], in <u>The Favourite</u>

---

104. Burden, 'Metastasio on the London Stage', p. 32 and Petty, Fred Curtis, 'Italian Opera in London, 1760–1800' (doctoral dissertation, Yale University, 1971) give 26/01/1765 as the date for this production. It ran for seven consecutive performances.
105. Microfilm copy: GB-En Mf.134, reel 6564 [14]. Reproduction in US-NYp.

MC | *Adriano in Siria* (1732–1828)

<u>Songs in the Opera Adriano in Siria / Composed by Sig.r Bach</u> (London: Welcker, [1765])

[doubtful] *Infelice invan mi lagno* (US-LAuc FA6964M4 [11]^{RISM})

1765	mus. by Di Majo, Gianfrancesco	
1765 Naples	Teatro di S. Carlo (20/01/1765?)^{106} *birthday of Carlos III, king of Spain?*	(1)
1769 Rome	Teatro delle Dame (carn.)	(2)

Librettos

(1) NA

(2) Rome: Corradi, [1769]
F-Pn YD-5391; <u>I-Bc Lo.02787</u>; I-Fm Mel.2046 [7]; I-MAC 7.II.A.120; I-Nc Rari 10.5.16 [2]; I-Pmc^S; I-Rsc Libr. n. XVII [1]; I-Rvat Stamp. Ferr.V.7764 [1]; I-Rvat Stamp.Ferr.V.8058 [3]; I-Tci L.O.2472; I-Vc 0051

Music sources

[complete scores] B-Bc 2198^{IC,NG,RISM}; P-La 44-XI-33/34/35^{BA,NG}; US-Wc M1500.M237 A3^{NG,RISM,107}

[excerpts] *Leon piagato a morte* (F-Pn D-14500 [3/1]^{BnF}; I-MC 6-C-17 [5]^{RISM}; I-Rc Mss. 2549 [7]^{SBN}; S-Skma T-SE-R^{RISM}; US-SFsc *M2.1 M300$^{RISM;IP}$); *Numi, se giusti siete* (US-BEm MS 91 [10]^{IC,RISM}); *Prigioniera abbandonata* (S-Skma T-SE-R^{RISM}); *Se non ti moro allato* (US-CAe Mus 503.603 [11]^{RISM})

[doubtful] *Leon piagato a morte*^{108} (D-MÜs SANT HS 2453^{RISM})

1766	mus. by Guglielmi, Pietro Alessandro	
1766 Venice	Teatro Grimani di S. Benedetto (carn., 26/12/1765)	

Librettos

Venice: Fossati, [1766]
I-Fm Mel.2123 [3]; I-Rsc Carv.218; I-Vcg LIBRETTI S.BENEDETTO 188; I-Vmc Rava G.403; I-Vnm DRAMM.1090 [1]; I-Vnm DRAMM.1302 [6]; US-LAum ML48 .R114 1766 [1]; <u>US-Wc ML48 [S4232]</u>

Music sources

[complete scores] P-La 44-VIII-31/32/33^{BA,MGG,NG,109}; P-La 47-V-69/70/71^{BA,MGG,NG}

---

106. The performance is referenced in De Filippis and Arnese, *Cronache del Teatro di S. Carlo*, p. 37 with no specific date. ^{CA} infers it took place coinciding with the king's birthday on 20 January.
107. Copy of B-Bc 2198.
108. The music is different from the other sources for this aria and is written for a tenor voice, whereas the singer who premiered Majo's setting in the role of Osroa, Ercole Ciprandi, was a soprano.
109. The manuscript presents some discrepancies with respect to the libretto for Guglielmi's *Adriano*, especially in Act III.

MC | *Adriano in Siria* (1732–1828)

[excerpts] *Figlia… oh dio… l'amor… l'affanno* (D-B Mus.ms. 8813/35[RISM]); *Prigioniera abbandonata* (D-B Mus.ms. 30136 [16][RISM]; I-VEcon MS 124[RISM,SBN]); *Se non ti moro allato* (I-Raf I.E.5 [8][RISM])

1768	mus. by Mango, Hieronymus	
1768 Eichstätt	Court theatre (01/1768) *celebration of the New Year 1768*	

Librettos Eichstätt: Straussin, [1768] (It./Ger.)
D-Mbs Slg.Her 2749

1768	mus. by Holzbauer, Ignaz	
1768 Mannheim	Court theatre (05/11/1768) *Hadrian in Syrien* *name day of the Elector of Saxony*	(1–3)
1769 Mannheim	Court theatre (11/01/1769) *wedding of the Elector of Saxony and the Countess Palatine*	(4–6)
1769 Mannheim	Court theatre (05/11/1769)[110]	(7)

Librettos

(1) Mannheim: Academy Press, [1768]
D-BFb [D-MÜu] I an B-St 105

(2) Mannheim: Academy Press, 1768 (Ger. only)
D-B Mus. Th 944; D-BFb [D-MÜu] B-St 107; D-Mbs Slg.Her 699; US-Wc ML48 [S4779]

(3) Mannheim: Academy Press, 1768 (Fr. only)
D-GZbk F: IV: MET: 1769: 8°; D-KA TB 431 RH; D-Sl Fr.D.oct 5062

(4) Mannheim: Academy Press, [1769]
B-Br Fétis 4.489 A V,29 Mus.; D-BAs 22/Bip.L.it.o.31; D-Eu 14/LP 40200 H762; D-KA TB 430 RH; D-Mbs P.o.it 656 n-1; D-Mbs Slg. Her 2698; D-Rtt 769/6; D-MHrm Mh 1747; US-Wc ML48 [S4778]

(5) Mannheim: Academy Press, 1769 (Ger. only)
D-MHrm Mh 1748; D-W Textb. 263; D-TRp KASTOR 688d

(6) Mannheim: Academy Press, 1769 (Fr. only)
D-ASh 4500/X-1654; D-HEu G 3077 X RES; D-KA TB 431 RH; D-MHrm Mh 1749; F-Sn CD.117.746; US-NYp Orexel 3743

(7) NA

---

110. Corneilson, Paul Edward, 'Opera at Mannheim, 1770–1778' (doctoral dissertation, The University of North Carolina at Chapel Hill, 1994).

MC | *Adriano in Siria* (1732–1828)

Music sources	[excerpts] *Che fa il mio bene?* (A-Wgm VI 19091[IC,MGG]); *Numi, se giusti siete* (CH-Bu kr IV 382 [7][RISM;P]; D-B Mus.ms. 10779[MGG,RISM;P]; D-MT Mus.ms. 258[RISM;R,P,111]); *Se non ti moro allato* (GB-Lcm MS 715 [6][IC]); *Son sventurato* (CH-Bu kr IV 164[MGG,RISM;P])

1769	mus. by various unknown composers
1769 Genoa	Teatro del Falcone (spr.)
Librettos	Genoa: Tarigo, 1769
	I-Nragni L007

1769	mus. by De Vincenti, Melchiorre
1769 Alessandria	Teatro Solerio (Oct. Fair)
Librettos	Alessandria: Vimercati, [1769]
	NA[112]

1769	mus. by Monza, Carlo Ignazio
1769 Naples	Teatro di S. Carlo (04/11/1769)
	name day of Carlos III, king of Spain
Librettos	Naples: Morelli, 1769
	B-Bc 18992; F-Pn YD-5446; <u>GB-Lbl 11714.aaa.8</u>; I-Pmc[S]; <u>I-Ra E.I.14 [3]</u>
Music sources	[complete scores] <u>I-Nc 29.5.12/13/14</u>[IC,MGG,NG,RISM,SBN]; P-La 45-II-38/39/40[BA,MGG,NG]
	[excerpts] *Deh frena il pianto* (B-Bc 4423[RISM]; CH-Gc Rmo 123/9 [5][RISM]; I-MC 4-A-19/1 [2][RISM]; I-MC 4-A-19/1 [3][RISM]; <u>I-Nc 34.4.3 [6]</u>[SBN]; US-CAe Mus 503.301 [3][RISM]); *Dopo un tuo sguardo, ingrata* (I-MC 4-A-19/1 [7][RISM]; I-MC 4-A-19/3 [4][RISM]; <u>I-Nc n/s</u>[RISM]; I-Rdp Ms Musicale 93 [5][SBN]); *Non ti affannar ben mio* (CH-Gc Rmo 123/9 [6][RISM]; I-Rdp Ms Musicale 93 [7][SBN]); *Numi, se giusti siete* (I-MC 4-A-19 [2][RISM]; I-MC 4-A-19/3 [2][RISM]); *Oh dio, mancar mi sento* (I-Rdp Ms Musicale 93 [1][SBN]); *Pallide larve e meste* (I-Rdp Ms Musicale 93 [6][SBN]); *Prigioniera abbandonata* (B-Bc 4426[RSM]; CH-Gc Rmo 123/9 [1][RISM]; D-RH [D-MÜu] Ms 512[RISM;P]; I-MC 4-A-19/3 [1][RISM]; I-Rama A.Ms.3806 [13][IC,RISM,SBN]; <u>I-Nc 34.4.3 [7]</u>[SBN]; I-Rdp Ms Musicale 93 [3][SBN]); *Quel labbro adorato* (B B-Bc 4427[RISM]; I-Rdp Ms Musicale 93 [2][SBN]); *Se non ti moro allato* (B-Br Ms II 4047 Mus Fétis 2626 [2][RISM]; CH-Gc Rmo 123/9 [7][RISM]; I-MC 4-A-19/1 [6][RISM]; I-Rdp Ms Musicale 93

---

111. Wrongly attributed to J. Mysliveček on source.
112. According to [S]425, there was a copy of this libretto in I-FPfanan; see note 98 above.

[4]^{SBN}; US-SFsc *M2.5 v.9 [3]^{RISM}); *Si smarrisce in tanto affanno* (I-MC 4-A-19/1 [5]^{RISM}; I-MC 4-A-19/3 [3]^{RISM}; I-Rdp Ms Musicale 93 [8]^{SBN})

[contrafacta] *Leon piagato a morte* ([*Clamat ferali morte*] I-MC 1-A-1971 [4]^{RISM})

1770	mus. by Tozzi, Antonio
1770 Modena	Teatro Ducale (carn., 17/01/1770)
Librettos	Modena: heirs of Soliani, [1770]
	I-MOe M.T.Ferr.Mor.16 [11]

1771	mus. by Sacchini, Antonio	
1771 Venice	Teatro Grimani di S. Benedetto (Asc., 09/05/1771)	(1)
1771 Prague	Teatro Regio (aut.)[113]	(2)
	Adrianus in Sirien	

Librettos

(1) Venice: Fenzo, 1771

A-Wmi BT-728; F-Pn RES VS-697; F-Pn 8-YTH-51537; I-Bc Lo.04927; I-BDG REC 97.B.20 [8]; I-BRq 4°.F.XI.7m8; I-Fm Mel.2217 [9]; I-Mb Racc.dramm.4007; I-Nc Rari 10.5.22 [5]; I-PAc F. Libretti, sc.007 [102]; I-Vcg LIBRETTI S.BENEDETTO 190; I-Vnm DRAMM.1098 [5]; I-Vnm DRAMM.1108 [8]; I-Vnm DRAMM.1307 [1]; US-BEm ML48 .I7 [424]; US-Wc ML48 [S9204]

(2) Prague: Pruscha, [1771] (It./Ger.)

A-Wn 641432-A.24,1; CZ-Pdobrovského 57 F 00048

Music sources

[excerpts] *Che fa il mio bene?* (D-MÜs SANT Hs 3483c [13]^{RISM}); *Dopo un tuo sguardo, ingrata* (CZ-Pnm XLII B 284^{RISM}; D-LB [D-NEhz] La 170 Bü 411^{RISM}; D-Mbs Mus.ms. 5418 [11]^{RISM}; D-MÜs SANT Hs 3483c [9]^{RISM}; I-BGc N.C.19.2 [8]^{RISM,SBN}; I-Raf 1.E.9 [3]^{RISM}); *Leon piagato a morte* (B-Bc 4733^{IC,RISM}; CH-SO n/s$^{RISM;P}$; D-MÜs SANT Hs 3483d [18]^{RISM}; D-MÜs SANT Hs 3485^{RISM}; DK-Kk mu7502.1433^{RISM}; GB-Lbl Add. 31667^{BL,RISM}; I-Gl B G.1.17 [8]$^{IC,MGG,NG,SBN;P}$; I-Tf 2 IV 15 [4]^{RISM}; I-Vnm Mss. 11410^{IC,SBN}); *Lieta per te felice* (CZ-Pnm XLII A 268^{RISM}; I-MC 5-E-5/3 [14]^{SBN}); *Numi e giusti siete* (CZ-Pnm XLII A 48$^{RISM;P}$); *Oh dio, mancar mi sento* ([*Mancar oh Dio mi sento*] CZ-Pkřiž

---

113. The production ran for eleven performances at the most; see Niubo, Marc, 'The Italian Opera between Prague and Dresden in the Second Half of the Eighteenth Century', in *Musiker-Migration und Musik-Transfer zwischen Böhmen und Sachsen im 18. Jahrhundert*, ed. by Hans-Günter Ottenberg and Reiner Zimmermann (Dresden: Technische Universität, 2012), pp. 58–73.

XXXVI B 128[RISM;P]; CZ-Pnm XLII B 285[RISM]; D-BAd EB 511[RISM;IP]; I-MAav Cart.20 n.16 [71][RISM;P]); *Prigioniera abbandonata* (CH-Bu kr IV 280[RISM;P]; CZ-LIT 690[RISM;P]; D-MÜs SANT Hs 3483d [17][RISM]; I-Mc Noseda O.47 [3][IC,SBN]; I-MAav Cart.20 n.3 [58][RISM;R,P]; I-Vc Correr Busta 71.14[SBN]); *Son sventurato* (I-MC 5-A-8 [15][RISM])

[contrafacta] *Dopo un tuo sguardo, ingrata* ([*Amor divini amoris*] CZ-Pnm XXXVIII A 309 [2][RISM;P]); *Leon piagato a morte* ([*Deo in vita et morte*] H-VEs Grad.412[RISM;P]); *Lieta per te felice* ([*Gaude o gens devota*] CZ-Pnm XXXVIII A 308[RISM;P]); *Prigioniera abbandonata* ([*Aurora surgit*] A-SCH 428[RISM;P]; [*O Domine Deus meus*] CZ-Pu 59 R 2928[RISM;R,P])

[doubtful] *Se non ti moro allato*[114] (I-Vnm Mss. 11073 [18][IC,SBN])

1771	mus. by Anfossi, Pasquale	
1771 Padua	Teatro Nuovo (06/1771)	(1)
1777 Padua	Teatro Nuovo (Fair, c. 13/06/1777)[115]	(2)
1780 Treviso	Teatro Onigo (aut.)	(3)
Librettos[116]	(1) NA	
	(2) Venice: [s.n.], 1777	
	I-Pci BP.2582.III; I-Vcg LIBRETTI PADOVA 57 E 64; I-Vgc ROL.0137 [6]	
	(3) Venice: [s.n., 1780]	
	<u>CDN-Ttfl Itp Pam 00039</u>	
Music sources	[complete scores] F-Po[MGG,NG]; I-Pl ATVa 7 [I–II][MGG,RISM,SBN,117]; P-La 44-I-38[BA,MGG,NG]	
	[excerpts] *Che fa il mio bene?* (GB-Ob Ms. North Mus. d.1[RISM]; I-Mc Mus. Tr.ms. 107[RISM,SBN]); *Prigioniera abbandonata* (US-Eu MSS 928[IC,RISM;R,118]); *Son sventurato* (CZ-Pnm XLII A 228; I-Bas IV 86/746d[IC,RISM,SBN]; I-Pca D.I.1350[SBN;P]; I-VEcon MS 009[RISM,SBN])	
1773	**mus. by various unknown composers**	
1773 Palermo	Teatro di Santa Cecilia (carn.)	

---

114. This aria was not included in the libretto for Sacchini's premiere or in that for its later revival in Prague.
115. [CA] gives 12/06/1777.
116. Further unspecified libretto: D-F n/s.
117. For Padua 1777.
118. This and the following source: for Padua 1777.

MC | *Adriano in Siria* (1732–1828)

Librettos   Palermo: Ferrer, 1773
I-PLn Misc.A.145 [8]

1773	mus. by Mysliveček, Josef	
1773 Naples	Teatro di S. Carlo[119]	(1)
1776 Florence	Teatro del Cocomero (aut., 08/09/1776)	(2)
1777 Perugia	Teatro del Pavone (carn.)	(3)
1777 Pavia	Teatro dei Quattro Cavalieri Associati (spr.)	(4)

Librettos   (1) NA

(2) Florence: Pagani, 1776[120]
I-Bc Lo.03188; I-Fc E.V.1552; S-Uu n/s

(2) Perugia: Riginaldi & Tantini, 1777
NA[121]

(3) Pavia: Porro & Bianchi, [1777]
I-LDEsormani 314/3/17; I-PAc F. Libretti, sc.007 [103]; I-Vgc ROL.0480 [2]; US-Wc ML48 [S6533]

Music sources   [complete scores] I-Fc D.I.385/386/387[IC,MGG,NG,SBN,122]

[excerpts] *A ritrovar mi chiama* (D-Mbs Mus.ms. 4326[RISM;P]; D-MÜs SANT Hs 2703[RISM]); *Barbaro non comprendo* (I-MC 4-A-11 [11][RISM]; I-MC 4-A-13 [16][RISM]); *Chi della sorte infida* (D-B Mus.ms. 30119 [2][RISM]); *Dopo un tuo sguardo, ingrata* (D-MÜs SANT Hs 2702[RISM]); *Leon piagato a morte* (D-B Mus.ms. 30119 [1][RISM]); *Parto? Resto? Figlia? Amico?* (D-MÜs SANT Hs 2723[RISM]); *Prigioniera abbandonata* (D-MÜs SANT Hs 2704[RISM])

[doubtful] *Padre ti lascio, addio*[123] (DK-Sa R165[RISM])

1773	mus. by Insanguine, Giacomo
1773 Naples	Teatro di S. Carlo (04/11/1773)
	name day of Carlos III, king of Spain

---

119. De Filippis and Arnese, *Cronache del Teatro di S. Carlo*, p. 40.
120. According to ^{S}436, there was a copy of this libretto in I-FPfanan; see note 98 above.
121. ^{C,S} list a copy in US-SY, yet, as confirmed by the Syracuse University Music Library staff, it can no longer be found; see ^{S}441 and <http://corago.unibo.it/libretto/DRT0000805> [accessed 18 June 2022]. Therefore, it should be considered as lost.
122. Without sinfonia and final chorus. All the closed numbers except *Infelice invan mi lagno*, which presents an oboe staff, are orchestrated for Vn I and Bs only.
123. The aria was inserted into the libretto for the 1777 revival of Mysliveček's setting in Pavia (A2-S11), yet it is not present in the text for the 1776 premiere.

MC | *Adriano in Siria* (1732–1828)

Librettos	Naples: Morelli, 1773
	I-Fm Mel.2292 [7];[124] US-NYp Mus. Res. *MZ, A/20/21 [4]
Music sources	[complete scores] I-Nc 28.6.7/8/9[IC,MGG,NG,RISM]; P-La 45-II-12/13/14[BA,MGG,NG]
	[excerpts] *Dopo un tuo sguardo, ingrata* (I-MC 3-B-5 [7][RISM]; I-MC 3-B-5 [10][RISM]; I-MC 3-B-6 [10][RISM]; I-MC 3-B-7 [10][RISM]; I-Nc 34.3.15 [10][MGG,SBN]; US-Wc M1505.A1 (vol. 245 B) [12][RISM]); *Leon piagato a morte* (I-MC 3-B-6 [8][RISM]; I-MC 4-A-16 [9][RISM]); *Pallide larve e meste* (I-MC 3-B-5 [5][RISM]); *Prigioniera abbandonata* (F-Pn D-6172 [6][BnF,125]; I-MC 3-B-6 [11][RISM]; I-Nc 34.3.15 [11][MGG,SBN]; US-Wc M1505.A1 (vol. 245 B) [11][RISM]); *Se non ti moro allato* (GB-Lcm MS 710 [6][IC])
1774	**mus. by various unknown composers**
1774 Verona	Teatro Filarmonico (carn.)
Librettos	Verona: Ramanzini, [1774]
	I-Vcg LIBRETTI VERONA 57 F 7[126]
Music sources	[excerpts] Lucchesi?, *Dal labro che t'accende* (I-VEcon MS 149[SBN])
1775	**mus. by Monti, Gaetano**
1775 Modena	Teatro Ducale (carn., 31/01/1775)
Librettos	Modena: heirs of Soliani, [1775][127]
	I-MOe M.T.Ferr.Mor.14 [7]; I-Rn 40.10.H.8.3; US-BEm ML48 .I7 [457]; US-Wc ML48 [S6605]
1776	**mus. by unknown composer(s)**
1776 Genoa	Teatro da S. Agostino (carn.)
Librettos	Genoa: Gesiniana, [1776]
	NA[128]

---

124. The digitised reproduction is incomplete; act I and first scenes of acts II&III.
125. Microfilm copy: F-Pn VM BOB-28468.
126. There used to be a copy in I-VEc D 384 [9], yet, as confirmed by the library staff, it can no longer be found. We therefore consider it as lost.
127. According to [C,S], there was a copy of this libretto in I-FPfanan (previously in Turin); see note 98 above. [S]445 also lists a further copy in I-Rn, yet it has not been located in the [IC].
128. According to [C], there used to be a copy in I-SML but it can no longer be found. We therefore consider it as lost.

MC | *Adriano in Siria* (1732–1828)

1777	mus. by various unknown composers
1777 Livorno	Teatro da S. Sebastiano (carn.)
Librettos	Livorno: Masi & co., 1777
	I-Fc E.V.2564

1779	mus. by Sarti, Giuseppe
1779 Rome	Teatro di Torre Argentina (carn., 28/12/1778)
Librettos	Rome: Bendio,[129] 1779
	B-Bc 18993; F-Pn YD-5424; I-FEwalker; I-Rsc Libr. n. XVIII [3]; I-Vc 0052; I-Vgc ROL.0600 [2]; US-AUS KL-17 177; US-Wc ML48 [S9470]
Music sources	[complete scores] I-Rc Mss. 2553[IC,SBN;R]; F-Pn D-13724[BnF,MGG,NG] [Act I]; RUS-SPit[MGG]; RUS-SPtob[MGG,NG]
	[excerpts] *Dal labro che t'accende* (D-Eu Esl VIII 598h[RISM]); *Dopo un tuo sguardo, ingrata* (S-Skma T-SE-R[RISM]); *Leon piagato a morte* (A-Wgm VI 21625 [Q 3511][IC]; B-Bc 4822[MGG,RISM]; D-B Mus.ms. 19508 [9][RISM]; F-Pn L-19964[BnF]; GB-Lbl R.M.23.b.26 [3][BL,RISM]; I-Mc Noseda Q.12 [15][SBN]); *Non ritrova un'alma forte* (I-Mc Noseda Q.12 [14][SBN]); *Padre... oh Dio* (A-Wgm VI 748 [Q 3903][IC]); *Prendi un estremo amplesso* (CH-E 150,4 [5][RISM]; D-Hs M A/271 [3][RISM]; D-LEm Becker III.15.73[RISM]; D-MÜs SANT Hs 3852[RISM]; I-Mc Mus. Tr.ms. 1224[RISM,SBN;P]; I-Mc Noseda Q.12 [13][SBN]; I-PAc Sanv.A.125[RISM,SBN]); *Prigioniera abbandonata* (D-LÜh Mus. Q 295[RISM,130]); *Saggio guerrier antico* (S-Skma T-SE-R[IC]); *Sprezza il furor del vento* (I-PEsp M.CXXVIII [11][RISM,SBN]; US-Bu BSO Collection, vol. 14 [5][RISM])
	[printed sources] *Leon piagato a morte* [13], in *Journal d'ariettes italiennes* (Paris: Bailleux, 1785)
	[doubtful][131] *Idol mio, serena i rai* (D-Dl Mus.3273-F-14 [3][RISM]; D-Mbs Mus.ms. 1031[RISM]; D-MÜs SANT Hs 3849[RISM]); *Saggio guerriero antico* (S-Skma T-SE-R[RISM])

Adriano in Siria, in *Opere del signor abate Pietro Metastasio* (Paris: widow of Hérissant, 1780), vol. 1, pp. 113–212.

---

129. 'Si vendono da'.
130. In G major instead of A major.
131. These numbers are included in neither the libretto for Sarti's setting or the musical source I-Rc Mss. 2553.

MC | *Adriano in Siria* (1732–1828)

1780	mus. by Alessandri, Felice
1780 Venice	Teatro Grimani di S. Benedetto (carn., 26/12/1779)
Librettos	Venice: Fenzo, 1780
	F-Pn LIV IT-1041 [1]; <u>I-Mb Racc.dramm.4016</u>; I-Vcg LIBRETTI S.BENEDETTO 194; I-Vmc Rava H.188; I-Vnm DRAMM.1323 [1–2]; <u>US-Wc ML48 [S153]</u>
Music sources	[complete scores] <u>D-Mbs Mus.ms. 521</u>^{MGG,NG,RISM}; GB-Lbl^{NG,132}; P-La 44-I-21^{BA,NG}
	[excerpts] *Dopo un tuo sguardo, ingrata* (I-Pca D.I.1313^{SBN}); *Gelosi affetti miei* (I-BRmd GRAZ.125.2 [14])^{IC,SBN}; *Nel lasciare il ben che adoro* (I-BRmd GRAZ.125.27 [13])^{IC,SBN}
1780	mus. by unknown composer(s)
1780 Palermo	Teatro di Santa Cecilia (*c.* 25/12/1780)
Librettos	Palermo: Picciotto, 1780
	US-BEm ML48 .S5 [S117]
1782	mus. by Rust, Giacomo
1782 Turin	Teatro Regio (carn., 26/12/1781)[133]
Librettos	Turin: Derossi, [1782]
	B-Bc 18994; <u>D-Mbs L.eleg.m. 3980</u>; I-Fm Mel.2003 [13]; I-NOVc CIV 194.F.31; I-Rsc Vol. Carv.156 [3]; I-Tac Simeom L 105; I-Tci L.O.0344; <u>I-Tn F XIII.496 [3]</u>; I-Tp P.i.107 [5.1]; I-Vgc ROL.0586 [5]; US-BEm ML48 .I7 [529]; US-CAt TS 8012.591 1782; <u>US-Wc ML48 [S9166]</u>
Music sources	[complete scores] I-Tf 1 VI 16/17/18^{IC,NG,RISM}; P-La 46-III-2/3^{BA,NG}
	[excerpts] *Dopo un tuo sguardo, ingrata* (I-Tf 2 IV 17 [6])^{RISM}; *Prigioniera abbandonata* (D-Dl Mus.1-F-82,24 [6])^{NG,RISM}
1782	mus. by Cherubini, Luigi
1782 Livorno	Teatro degli Armeni (spr., 16/04/1782)
Librettos	Livorno: Falorni, [1782]
	I-Bc Lo.00980

---

132. The manuscript could not be found in ^{BL}; lost?
133. The production ran for seventeen consecutive performances; see Bouquet, Gualerzi, and Testa, *Storia del Teatro Regio di Torino*, p. 76.

MC | *Adriano in Siria* (1732–1828)

Music sources	[complete scores] CDN-Lu M1500.M57C443 1782a[IC,134] [Acts I&II] [excerpts] *Saprò scordarmi, ingrata* (D-B* [PL-Kj])[MGG,NG]; *Vorrei da lacci sciogliere quest'alma* (F-Pn D-17321[BnF,RISM,135]; F-Pn D-17322[BnF,RISM])
1788 1788 Stuttgart	mus. by Gauss, Jakob Friedrich NA (Ger. only: *Hadrian in Syrien*)[136]
1790 1790 Milan	mus. by Nasolini, Sebastiano Teatro alla Scala (carn., 26/12/1789)
Librettos	Milan: Bianchi, [1789] B-Bc 18995; CDN-Ttfl Itp Pam 00575; F-Pn LIV IT-1044 [1]; F-Pn LIV IT-3545 [1]; F-Pn RES VS-654; I-Bc Lo.03369; I-Fc E.V.2563; I-Fm Mel.2003 [10]; I-LDEsormani 298/5/9; I-Ma S. I. H. I. 32 [1]; I-Mc Coll. Libr.200; I-Mcom MUS.M MUS.1.-231; I-Mr Libr. 02193; I-PAc F. Libretti, sc.007 [104]; I-Rn 40.9.H.22.3; I-Rsc Carv.220; I-Rsc Vol. 32 [1]; I-Rvat Stamp.Ferr.V.8125 [5]; I-REm 19.J.240; I-Vnm DRAMM.3263 [11]; I-VCc 20 C 546; US-NYp *MGTY-Res.; US-Wc ML48 [S6998]
Music sources	[complete scores] I-Mr MS PART.02876[IC,MGG,RISM,SBN] [excerpts] *Nel lasciarti in tal momento* (US-SFsc *M2.1 M331[RISM]) [printed sources] *Adriano in Siria* [...] [s.l.: s.n., 1790]
***c*. 1790** *c*. 1790 [s.l.]	mus. by Zingarelli, Niccolò Antonio[NG] NA
Music sources	[excerpts] *Che fa il mio bene?* (I-Mc Noseda R.32 [10][SBN]); *Se non ti moro allato* (I-Rsc G.Mss.857[SBN])
1798 1798 Venice	mus. by Mayr, Johann Simon Teatro Vernier in S. Benedetto (Asc., 23/04/1798)[137]
Librettos	Venice: Fenzo, 1798 E-Mn T/7986;[138] F-Pn 8-YTH-51684; I-Bc Lo.02914; I-Mb Racc. dramm.5326; I-Mb Racc.dramm.5640; I-Mr Libr. 02192; I-Pmc[S]; I-Vcg LIBRETTI S.BENEDETTO 57 A 15; I-Vnm DRAMM.1358 [15]

---

134. Microfilm reproduction of the composer's holograph, supposedly in Poland.
135. Microfilm copy of this and the following source: F-Pn VM BOB-25029.
136. Griffel, Margaret Ross, *Operas in Germany: A Dictionary* (Lanham: Rowman & Littlefield, 2018).
137. Date in [C, CA] gives 23/05/1798.
138. Microfilm reproduction: E-Mn R.MICRO/20680.

MC | *Adriano in Siria* (1732–1828)

Music sources	[complete scores] I-BGc* Mayr 311.8[IC,SBN]
	[excerpts] *Dal labro che t'accende* (I-BGc* Mayr 311.51[MGG,RISM]); *Dopo un tuo sguardo, ingrata* (I-BGc* Mayr 311.22[MGG,RISM]); *Leon piagato a morte* (I-BGc* Mayr 311.49[MGG,RISM]); *Numi, se giusti siete* (I-BGc* Mayr 311.48[MGG,RISM]); *Quell'amplesso e quel perdono* (I-BGc* Mayr 311.46[MGG,RISM]); *Se non ti moro allato* (I-BGc* Mayr 311.38[MGG,RISM]; I-BGc* Mayr 324.18[MGG,SBN]); *T'aspetta* (I-BGc* Mayr 302.12[MGG,RISM]); *Tutti nemici e rei* (I-BGc* Mayr 311.40[MGG,RISM]; I-BGc* Mayr 311.47[MGG,RISM])

1799	mus. by Méhul, Étienne-Nicolas
1799 Paris	NP (04/06/1799)
	Adrien, empereur de Rome (Fr. only)

c. 1800	mus. by Bernardini, Carlo
c. 1800 [s.l.]	NA
Music sources	[complete scores] D-Mbs Mus.ms. 12657[RISM]

1807	mus. by Weigl, Joseph
1807 Vienna	Court theatre (21/05/1807)[139]
	Kaiser Hadrian (Ger. only)

1809	mus. by unknown composer(s)
1809 Forlì	Teatro Comunale (spr.)
Librettos	Forlì: Roveri & Casali, 1809
	I-Nragni L023

1809	mus. by Portugal, Marcos António	
1809 Padua	Teatro Nuovo (06/1809)	(1)
1813 Como	Nuovo Teatro (summ.)	(2)
	opening of the theatre	
1814 Verona	Teatro Filarmonico	(3)
1815 Milan	Teatro Re in Salvatore (carn.)	(4)
Librettos	(1) NA	
	(2) Milan: Dova, [1813]	
	F-Pn LIV IT-1043; I-Ma S. I. H. II. 34 [2]; I-PAc F. Libretti, sc.007 [105]; I-Rsc Carv.221; I-Mr Libr. 02195	

---

139. Griffel, *Operas in Germany*, p. 252.

MC | *Adriano in Siria* (1732–1828)

(3) Verona: Bisesti, 1813
D-Hs MS 784/3; I-Rsc Libr. n. XXII [4]; I-Vgc ROL.0553 [1]; US-Wc ML48 [S8441]

(4) Milan: Dova, [1815]
A-Wn 106842-A; CDN-Ttfl Itp Pam 00774; F-Pn LIV IT-1040; F-Pn LIV IT-3652 [3]; I-Bc Lo.04403; I-Mr Libr. 02194; I-Ms MUS. P. LXII. 1; I-PAc F. Libretti, sc.007 [106]; I-Rsc Carv.222; I-Vgc ROL.1116 [1]; I-Vnm DRAMM.3291 [7]; US-BEm ML48 .I7 [1116]

Music sources	[excerpts] *Non più sdegni* (D-Dl Mus.4092-F-2 [2][RISM]); *Se non ti moro allato* (P-Ln* C.N. 198 [2])[IC,NG]
1811	mus. by Migliorucci, Vincenzo?[NG]
1811 Naples	NA
1821	mus. by Airoldi, Pietro
1821 Palermo	Teatro Carolino
	Giovanni David's benefit evening, first absolute tenor
Librettos	Palermo: Crisanti, 1821
	I-Bc Lo.07529; I-Mr Libr. 02185;[140] I-Mr Libr. 02186; I-PLcom CXXXVI A 31 1; I-Vgc ROL.0131 [15]; US-BEm ML48 .S5 [S382]
1826	mus. by Mirecki, Franciszek
1826 [s.l.]	NA (Fr. only: *Adrian en Syrie*)
1828	mus. by Mercadante, Saverio
	lib. rev. by Profumo, Antonio
1828 Lisbon	Teatro de São Carlos (24/02/1828) (1)
1828 Lisbon	Teatro de São Carlos (22/09/1828) (1)
	Giuseppina Tuvo's benefit evening
Librettos	Lisbon: Bulhões, 1828 (It./Port.)
	I-Nn L.P. Libretti A 0069 [1]; I-Vgc ROL.0455 [3]; P-La 151-VII-11 [4]; P-Ln C.N.64 P.; P-Ln M.1095 P.; P-Ln T.S.C.222 P.; P-Ln T.S.C.223 P.; P-Ln T.S.C.224 P.; US-Wc ML48 [S6377]
Music sources	[complete scores] I-Nc 28.2.29/30[SBN]
	[excerpts] *Parti al nostro ardir felice* (P-Ln F.C.R. 133 [4])[IC]; *Quando la notte avvolge* (P-Ln F.C.R. 835//32 A.)[IC]

140. Manuscript copy, dated 1818.

MC | *Adriano in Siria* (1732–1828)

Poetic sources of doubtful identification

I-OS LIBRETTI 73

Arie sciolte

Asioli, Bonifacio, *Oh dio, mancar mi sento* (CZ-Pk 3 C 5[RISM]; I-PAc Borb.73.5 [5][RISM,SBN]; US-Cn MS VM4.A833c [4][RISM]); *Se non ti moro allato* (I-MC 1-B-4 [9][RISM]; I-Nc 46.1.11[SBN]; I-Pca E.I.1950[SBN]; I-PAc Borb.73.5.g [5][RISM])

Astarita, Gennaro, *Già presso al termine*, in *Aria 'Già presso al termine' für Canto, Violini, Corni in Es, Viole, Basso* (Venice: Zatta, [s.d.]); in *Aria 'Già presso al termine' für Canto, Violini, Corni in Es, Viole, Violonc.* (Leipzig: Schwivkerstschen, 1789)

Bachschmid, Johann Anton Adam, *Saggio guerriero antico* (D-B Mus.ms. 995 [18][RISM;P])

Balduino, Domenico, *Numi, se giusti siete* (I-Gsl MS. B/19 [7][RISM;R])

Barthélemon, Hippolyte, *Son sventurato* (GB-Lbl MS Mus. 1588 [4][BL])

Beecke, Ignaz von, *Numi, se giusti siete* (D-HR [D-Au] III 4 1/2 4° 134[RISM])

Bioni, Antonio, *Se non ti moro allato* (CZ-KRa A 4103[141])

Boccherini, Luigi, *Infelice invan mi lagno* (F-Pn* RES-506 [7][BnF,RISM]); *Numi, se giusti siete* (F-Pn* RES-506 [8][BnF,RISM]); *Se non ti moro allato* (F-Pn* RES-506 [2][BnF,RISM])

Bonno, Giuseppe, *Infelice invan mi lagno* (CZ-Pnm XLII B 142[RISM;P])

Bononcini, Giovanni, *Oh dio, mancar mi sento*[142] (B-Bc 3726[IC,RISM,143]; D-ROu Mus. Saec. XVIII:6 [14][RISM;P]; F-Pn VM4-855[BnF,RISM,144]; SI-Mpa SI_PAM/1857/010 [16][RISM;R])

Callenberg, Georg Alexander Heinrich Hermann, *Digli ch'è un infedele* (D-Dl Mus.3496-I-2 [?][IC,RISM])

Celestino, Eligio, *Se non ti moro allato* (D-SWl Mus.1460[RISM;P])

Danzi, Franz Ignaz, *Leon piagato a morte* (D-B Mus.ms. 30127 [6][RISM]; S-Skma T-SE-R[RISM])

De Luca, Giambattista, *Che fa il mio bene?* (I-Mc Noseda G.61 [3][SBN])

Fago, Pasquale, *Son sventurato* (I-MC 6-D-6/6 [2][RISM])

Feldmayr, Georg, *Saggio guerriero antico* (D-HR* [D-Au] III 4 1/2 4° 143[RISM]; D-HR [D-Au] III 4 1/2 4° 144[RISM;P])

Fighera, Salvatore, *Volga il ciel felici amanti* (I-MC 2-C-4 [2][RISM])

Gassmann, Florian Leopold, *Saggio guerriero antico* (A-Wn Mus.Hs.3972[IC])

Giordani, Giuseppe, *Oh dio, mancar mi sento* (D-WO Mus.ant. 24 [3][RISM;R]); *Son sventurato* (D-WO Mus.ant. 24 [4][RISM;R])

Haydn, Michael, *Ah ingrato, m'inganni* [1764] (F-Pn* MS-17672[BnF,RISM])

Hertel, Johann Wilhelm, *Saggio guerriero antico* (B-Bc 4214[RISM])

Isola, Gaetano, *Numi, se giusti siete* (D-Mbs Mus.ms. 3991[RISM;R,P])

Koželuh, Jan Antonín, *Infelice invan mi lagno* (CZ-BER HU 324[RISM])
[contrafacta] *Infelice invan mi lagno* ([*Infelicem quis se sentit*] CZ-Pak 556[RISM;P])

---

141. Černá, Zuzana, 'Antonio Bioni and his Compositions Preserved in Kroměříž Archive', *Musicologia Brunensia*, 52 (2017), 217–42.
142. Wrongly attributed to A. Bernasconi on some of the sources. The aria is not included in the libretto for Bernasconi's setting or in the corresponding complete musical manuscripts.
143. In C major instead of D major.
144. Microfilm copy: F-Pn VM BOB-13909.

MC | *Adriano in Siria* (1732–1828)

Kraus, Joseph Martin, *Se non ti moro allato* (I-Mc MsCon.10 [12]^{IC,SBN}; S-Skma Engsö saml.^{RISM}; S-Skma 2 SO/Sv.-R^{RISM}; S-Sn Sjögrens arkiv^{RISM}; S-Uu Vok. Mus. i hs. 57:3a [34]^{IC,RISM}; S-Uu Vok. Mus. i hs. 92:3^{IC,RISM;R,IP})
  [contrafacta] *Se non ti moro allato* ([Om ej mig döden] S-Skma 2 SP/Sv.-R^{RISM;R})
Kunzen, Adolph Carl, *Numi, se giusti siete* (D-SWl Mus.3265^{RISM;P})
La Barbiera, Baldassare, *Che fa il mio bene?* (I-MC 3-D-3/8 [2]^{RISM}); *Numi, se giusti siete* (I-MC 3-D-3 [10]^{RISM})
Leo, Leonardo, *Già presso al termine* (I-Fc D.II.101–102 [32]^{SBN})
López Jiménez, Melchor, *Infelice in van mi lagno* (E-SC 1407 [4]^{RISM})
Maraucci, Giacomo, *È vero che oppresso la sorte* (I-Nc 22.3.23 [33]^{SBN})
Marziani, Mauro Maria, *Prigioniera abbandonata* (I-MC 6-D-10 [7]^{RISM})
Maziotti, Michele, *Dal labro che t'accende* (I-CBp Pepe Ms. 302^{RISM,SBN}); *Se non ti moro allato* (CH-N XB obl. 197^{RISM;P})
Milani, Matteo, *Se non ti moro allato* (I-Bc HH.167 [19]^{RISM,SBN})
Naselli, Diego, *Per te d'eterni allori* (I-Nc 34.3.14 [4]^{SBN})
Naumann, Johann Gottlieb, *Ah ingrato, m'inganni* (D-Dl Mus.3480-L-5 [3]^{RISM;R}); *Oh dio, mancar mi sento* (D-Dl Mus.3480-F-48 [4]^{RISM}; I-Nc 34.4.3 [8]^{SBN})
Ottani, Bernardo, *Numi, se giusti siete* [1765] (I-MAav Cart.7 n.29^{RISM;P})
Paradies, Pietro Domenico, *Volga il ciel felici amanti* (US-Wc ML96.P25 [2]^{RISM})
Rauzzini, Venanzio, *Che fa il mio bene?*[145] (I-Rama A.Ms.3753 [16]^{RISM,SBN})
Reichardt, Johann Friedrich, *Numi, se giusti siete* (US-NH Misc. Ms. 94^{RISM}; US-Wc M1502.A2 R35^{RISM;R,IP})
Rocco, Benett, *Numi, se giusti siete* (D-BFb [D-MÜu] R-oc 20 [1]^{RISM})
Sala, Nicola, *Digli ch'è un infedele* (I-Nc 22.3.4 [25]^{SBN})
Selvaggi, Gaspari, *Che fa il mio bene?* (I-Mc Noseda Q.15 [34]^{SBN}; I-Nc* 32.1.12 [6]^{SBN})
Silva, José Gomes da, *Numi, se giusti siete* (J-Tk S10-933-4 [3]^{RISM})
Spalletta, Raffaele, *Se non ti moro allato* (US-BEm MS 1065 [a–c]^{IC,RISM;IP})
Uhde, Johann Otto, *Numi, se giusti siete* (US-CAh MS Mus 242 [24]^{RISM,146})
Zamparelli, Dionisio, *Numi, se giusti siete* (D-MÜs SANT Hs 181 [24]^{RISM}); *Prigioniera abbandonata* (GB-Lbl Add. 31742 [13]^{BL,RISM})
Zonca, Giuseppe, *Fra tanti pensieri* (D-Dl Mus.1-F-82,30 [10]^{RISM}); *Oh dio, mancar mi sento* (D-Dl Mus.1-F-82,30 [9]^{RISM}); *Quell'amplesso e quel perdono* (D-Dl Mus.1-F-82,30 [11]^{RISM})

Closed numbers by unknown composer

Digli ch'è un infedele (B-Bc FRW 12200 [11]^{RISM})
La ragion gli affetti ascolta (I-Rsc G.Mss.658 [11]^{SBN})
Numi, se giusti siete (CH-Bu kr IV 382 [6]^{RISM;P})
Oh dio, mancar mi sento (D-Hs M A/832 [1/14b]^{RISM;R})
Oh dio, mancar mi sento (D-LB [D-NEhz] La 170 Bü 477^{RISM;P})
Prigioniera abbandonata (B-Bc 5375^{RISM})
Prigioniera abbandonata (US-BEm MS 95 [15]^{IC,RISM;R})

---

145. Inserted into a revival of P. Guglielmi's *La sposa fedele* (Venice, 1767) in London in 1775.
146. Incomplete sketch.

Se non ti moro allato (A-LA 1892[RISM;P])
Se non ti moro allato (I-Rsc G.Mss.17 [8][RISM])
Son sventurato (GB-Lbl Add. 24307 [14][BL])
Son sventurato (SI-Mpa SI_PAM/1857/010 [29][RISM;R,147])
Sprezza il furor del vento (D-ZL n/s[RISM;P])
Tutti nemici e rei (I-MAav Cart.18/1 n.3[RISM;P])
Volga il ciel felici amanti (I-MC 3-C-12/4 [2][RISM])

Unspecified contents

Che fa il mio bene? (GB-Lbl Add. 32079 [8][BL])
Dopo un tuo sguardo, ingrata (CZ-BER HU 490 [2][RISM])
Numi, se giusti siete (I-Fc D.I.183 [21][SBN])
Prigioniera abbandonata (F-Pn D-15993[BnF])
Son sventurato (I-Bas IV 86/746f[SBN])

147. Reduction for S, fl., and bc.

Demofoonte (1733–1836)[1]

Ana Llorens, Lecturer, Department of Musicology, Universidad Complutense de Madrid; scientific director, ERC Didone Project, email: allorens@ucm.es

Gorka Rubiales Zabarte, 'Margarita Salas' postdoctoral researcher, Universidad Complutense de Madrid–Universidad de Salamanca, email: gorka.rubiales@usal.es

Nicola Usula, senior postdoctoral researcher, Faculté des Lettres, Université de Fribourg, email: nicola.usula@unifr.ch

Complete operas

1733	mus. by Caldara, Antonio	
1733 Vienna	Court theatre (04/11/1733) *name day of Emperor Charles VI*	(1–3)
Librettos	(1) Vienna: van Ghelen, [1733] A-Wgm 21/5; A-Wn SA.3.J.8; D-DI Mag/XVII 1023; D-W Textb. 85; F-Pn LIV IT-3694 [1]; I-Rsc Carv.4231; I-Rsc Libr. n. XIV [25]; I-Vnm DRAMM.849 [6]; SI-Lsk AE 58 [4]	
	(2) Vienna: van Ghelen, 1733 (Ger.) A-Wn 4929-A; D-RT F.177-R; H-Bn 327.840	
	(3) Vienna/Rome: [van Ghelen/Leone],[2] [1733] I-CDGbm FA.IX.F.22; I-Fm Mel.2251 [14]; I-Vc 4089 [4]; US-AUS KL-17 69; US-CAt ML50.2.D45 C34 17	

---

1. This chapter presents an updated version of Llorens, Ana, Gorka Rubiales, and Nicola Usula, 'Operatic Sources for *Demofoonte*: Librettos and Scores after Metastasio's "figliuolo"', in *Demofoonte come soggetto per il dramma per musica: Johann Adolf Hasse ed altri compositori del Settecento*, ed. by Milada Jonášová and Tomislav Volek (Prague: Academia, 2020), pp. 271–317.
2. 'Si vendono a Pasquino all'Insegna di San Giovanni di Dio'.

MC | *Demofoonte* (1733–1836)

Music sources	[complete scores] A-Wgm* A 389[MGG,NG]; A-Wn Mus.Hs.17107 [1–3][IC,MGG,NG]; A-Wn Mus.Hs.17168 [1–3][IC,MGG,NG]; A-Wn Mus.Hs.17169 [1–3][IC,MGG,NG]; I-MOe Mus. F. 1313[IC]

Demofoonte, in *Opere drammatiche del signor abate Pietro Metastasio romano, poeta cesareo* (Venice: Bettinelli, 1733), vol. 2, pp. 323–92.

1735	mus. by Schiassi, Gaetano Maria	
1735 Venice	Teatro Grimani di S. Giovanni Grisostomo (carn., 26/12/1734)	(1)
1735 Vyškov	[Theatre]	(2)
1737 Lisbon	Academy on the Trinità Square (05/1737)[3]	(3)
1738 Madrid	Teatro de los Caños del Peral	(4)
	mus. by G. M. Schiassi and others	
Librettos	(1) Venice: Rossetti, [1735]	
	I-Bc Lo.5164; I-Mb Racc.dramm.0806; I-Rsc Libr. n. XIV [26]; I-RVI Silv., op. 702; I-Vcg LIBRETTI S.GIO.GRISOSTOMO 154; I-Vnm DRAMM.1049 [5]; I-Vnm DRAMM.1247 [1]; I-Vnm DRAMM.3563 [1]; LI-Lsk AE 58 [4]; US-LAum ML48 .R114 1735 [1]; US-Wc ML48 [S9600]	
	(2) Brno: Swoboda, 1735 (It./Ger.)	
	H-Ba Hf1245	
	(3) Lisbon: da Fonseca, 1737 (It./Port.)	
	BR-Rn A-XV,D383; D-Rp 9995/SWS Cl.m. 100; GB-Cu 7740.d.1; I-Rsc Carv.4232; P-Ln F. 6812	
	(4) Madrid: [s.n.], 1738 (It./Spa.)	
	E-Mn T/7313; E-Mp IX/5544; E-MO C*XVII*12º*49; E-Tp Res.725	
Music sources	[complete scores] B-Bc 2355[IC,MGG,NG,RISM]	
	[excerpts] *L'empia mia stella irata* (D-Wa 46 Alt 700[RISM]); *Son qual legno* (D-Dl Mus.1-F-82,36 [1][RISM])	
1735	mus. by Sarro, Domenico Natale; Mancini, Francesco; Leo, Leonardo mus. of the recit. by Sellitto, Giuseppe	
1735 Naples	Teatro di S. Bartolomeo (20/01/1735) birthday of Carlo VII, king of Naples	

---

3. Brito, Manuel Carlos de, *Opera in Portugal in the Eighteenth Century* (Cambridge: Cambridge University Press, 1989). Treated as a pasticcio in <https://www.pasticcio-project.eu/database/work/P100212> [accessed 26 May 2022].

MC | *Demofoonte* (1733–1836)

Librettos   Naples: [s.n.], 1735
I-Mb Racc.dramm.0653; I-Nc n/s; US-NYp Mus. Res. *MZ, A II [4]

Music sources   [complete scores] I-MC 3-D-17[RISM]; I-Nc 28.4.20[IC,RISM,SBN]; I-Nc 28.5.3[SBN] [Act III]

[excerpts][4]

Leo, Leonardo, *Il suo leggiadro viso* (D-B Mus.ms. 12832 [26][RISM]; I-Nc 33.3.26 [14][SBN]); *La destra ti chiedo*[5] (D-B B Am.B 274 [4][RISM]; D-B Mus.ms. 12832 [25][RISM]; D-F Mus Hs 154 [15][RISM]; F-Pn D-6880 [19][BnF]; GB-Lbl Add. 31625[BL,RISM]; GB-Ob Ms. Mus. c.106 [9][RISM]; I-MC 3-E-10 [32][RISM]; I-MC 3-E-13 [1][RISM]; I-Nc 22.2.8 [20][SBN]; I-Nc 33.3.35 [8][SBN]; I-Nc 34.6.1 [25][SBN,6]); *Misero pargoletto* (B-Bc 5120[RISM]; D-F Mus Hs 154 [4][RISM]; D-Hs M A/1560[RISM]; D-MÜs SANT Hs 2361b [30][RISM]; F-Pn D-14665[BnF]; F-Pn L-18661[BnF]; GB-Cfm [GB-Cu] MU.MS.167 [9][IC]; GB-Lbl R.M.23.e.1 [8][BL,RISM]; I-Bc GG.101 [8][IC,RISM,SBN,7]; I-Mc Mus. Tr.ms. 596[RISM,SBN]; I-Mc Noseda L.39 [15][SBN]; I-Mc Noseda L.39 [50][SBN]; I-MC 3-E-10 [17][RISM]; I-MC 6-A-4/3 [3][RISM]; I-Nc A 205 [8][SBN]; I-Nc M.S.app.8.1 [19–22][SBN;IP]; I-Nc 6.3.2 [4][SBN]; I-Nc 33.3.35 [9][SBN]; I-Nc 33.3.36 [16][SBN]; US-NH Misc. Ms. 33 [1][RISM]; US-Wc M1505.A1 (vol. 237) [3][RISM]); *O più tremar non voglio* (I-MC 3-D-17[RISM]); *Se tutti i mali miei* (F-Pn D-6879[BnF]; F-Pn D-6880 [3][BnF]; F-Pn D-6880 [12][BnF]; F-Ps Res F7 [29][GVK]; I-MC 3-E-10 [11][RISM]; I-Nc 33.3.23 [7][SBN])

Sarro, Domenico Natale, *Che mai risponderti* (I-Bc GG.101 [13][IC,NG,RISM,SBN,8]); *Se ardire e speranza* (I-Nc 34.4.3 [28][SBN,9])

[doubtful] Sarro, Domenico Natale, *Pensa che tua son io* (I-Bc DD.52 [11][IC,RISM,SBN,10])

---

4. Attributions have been contrasted with those in the libretto and Romagnoli, Angela, 'Una gara per il compleano del re Carlo: il "Demofoonte" di Leo, Mancini, Sarro e Sellitto (Napoli 1735) e i suoi rapporti con la partitura di Leonardo Leo del 1741', in *Responsabilità d'autore e collaborazione nell'opera dell'Età barocca. Il Pasticcio*, ed. by Gaetano Pitarresi (Reggio Calabria: Laruffa, 2011), pp. 221–56. See also Pastore, Giuseppe A., *Don Lionardo: vita e opere di Leonardo Leo* (Cuneo: Bertola & Locatelli, 1994).
5. Both the duet *La destra ti chiedo* and the aria *Misero pargoletto* by Leo remained almost unchanged in the composer's 1741 revision (→ see 1741, mus. by Leo, Leonardo). Therefore, and although small differences may appear on the various sources, we cannot attribute the sources to one performance or the other.
6. In F major instead of G major.
7. Microfilm copy: I-Bc 4470.
8. Following the authorial ascriptions on the libretto, wrongly attributed to L. Leo on source; microfilm copy: I-Bc 4470.
9. In A major instead of D major.
10. Microfilm copy: I-Bc 3462.

MC | *Demofoonte* (1733–1836)

1735	mus. by Ciampi, Francesco
1735 Rome	Teatro di Tordinona (carn., 05/02/1735)
Librettos	Rome: [Leone],[11] 1735
	B-Bc 19883; GB-Lbl 905.l.3 [5]; I-Bc Lo.8039; I-PESo B-22-11-08 [3]; I-REm 19.K.230; US-Cn ML50.2.I87 M48 1732; US-CHH IOLC.00179
Music sources	[excerpts] *Perfidi, già che in vita* (I-Mc Noseda E.25 [23])[SBN]
1735	mus. by Chiocchetti, Pietro Vincenzo
1735 Genoa	Teatro del Falcone
Librettos	Genoa: Franchelli, 1735[12]
	CDN-Ttfl Itp Pam 00275; I-PAp BB XI.256664
1737	mus. by various unknown composers
1737 Livorno	Teatro da S. Sebastiano (carn.)
Librettos	Lucca: Marescandoli, 1737
	I-Fn MAGL.21.8.165
1737	mus. by Duni, Egidio Romualdo
1737 London	King's Theatre in the Haymarket (24/05/1737)
	Demophontes King of Thrace
Librettos	London: Chrichley, 1737 (It./En.)
	D-Hs M A/401; US-Cum PQ4688.D9D4 1737; US-Wc ML48 [S2837]
Music sources	[printed sources] *Al tuo volto lunsinghier* [6]; *La dolce compagna* [1]; *Misero pargoletto* [5]; *Non v'è più barbaro* [4]; *Prudente mi chiedi?* [3]; *Sperai vicino il lido* [2], in *Arie per Farinelli* (London: [s.n.], 1737)
1737	mus. by Ferrandini, Giovanni Battista
1737 Munich	Court theatre (22/10/1737) (1,2)
Librettos	(1) [Munich]: Vötter, 1737
	SI-Lsk AE 83 [5]; US-DMu ML50.2.A78 V563 1730 [1]

---

11. 'Si vendono a Pasquino'.
12. Hortschansky claims having consulted a copy in I-Vgc, but it cannot be found in [IC]; lost? See Hortschansky, Klaus, 'Die Wiener Dramen Metastasios in Italien', in *Venezia e il melodramma nel Settecento*, ed. by Maria Teresa Muraro (Florence: Olschki, 1978), pp. 407–23.

MC | *Demofoonte* (1733–1836)

	(2) [Munich]: Vötter, 1737 (It./Ger.) D-As LA 5569; D-Mbs Bavar.4015-35 [2]; D-Mbs Slg.Her 2081; D-Mms 0001/8 Don. 10-1017
Music sources	[excerpts] *L'empia mia stella irata* (CH-N XB obl.230[RISM;P])
1738	**mus. by Latilla, Gaetano**
1738 Venice	Teatro Grimani di S. Giovanni Grisostomo (carn., 26/12/1737)
Librettos	Venice: Rossetti, 1738[13] I-Bc Lo.2623; I-Mb Racc.dramm.0808; I-RVI Silv., op. 730; I-Vcg LIBRETTI S.GIO.GRISOSTOMO 155; I-Vnm DRAMM.1053 [1]; I-Vnm DRAMM.1250 [1]; I-Vnm DRAMM.2566 [1]; SI-Lsk AE 88 [6]; US-LAum ML48 .R114 1738 [1]; US-Wc ML48 [S5458]
Music sources	[excerpts] *In te spero, o sposo amato* (D-MÜs SANT Hs 183 [4])[RISM]; *Padre, perdona… oh pene* (D-MÜs SANT Hs 183 [3])[RISM]
1738	**lib. mus. by Lampugnani, Giovanni Battista** **lib. rev. by Vitturi, Bartolomeo**
1738 Piacenza	Teatro Ducale (01/1738)
Librettos	Piacenza: Bazacchi, [1738] I-Bc Lo.2599; I-Mb Racc.dramm.3878; I-OS LIBRETTI 141
Music sources	[excerpts] *Fra cento affanni e cento*[14] (B-Bc 5085[IC,RISM]); *Misero pargoletto* (J-Tk S10-591 [5])[RISM]; *Sentirsi il petto accendere* (B-Bc 5087[RISM]; GB-Lbl Add. 31667 [1])[RISM]; *Sperai vicino il lido* (B-Bc 5192[RISM;R])
1738	**mus. by Brivio, Giuseppe Ferdinando**
1738 Turin	Teatro Regio (carn., 18/01/1738)[15] (1)

---

13. [C,S] list a further libretto, allegedly linked to this production, as held in I-Vmc; see [S]7474. Based on this, Chiarelli and Pompilio speak of an unperformed production; see Chiarelli, Alessandra and Angelo Pompilio, 'Or vaghi or fieri': cenni di poetica nei libretti veneziani (circa 1760–1740) (Bologna: Cooperativa Libraria Universitaria Editrice Bologna, 2004). However, as confirmed by the staff of the Biblioteca Nazionale Marciana, no such libretto can be found among their holdings.
14. Although this aria originally belongs to Metastasio's *Artaserse*, it appears in A2-S2 in Lampugnani's *Demofoonte*.
15. The production ran for twenty-seven consecutive performances until 18 February 1738; see Bouquet, Marie-Thérese, Valeria Gualerzi, and Alberto Testa, *Storia del Teatro Regio di Torino: cronologie*, ed. by Alberto Basso (Turin: Cassa di Risparmio di Torino, [1988]).

MC | *Demofoonte* (1733–1836)

1738 Jaroměřice	Count's Adam of Questenberg's castle (28/12/1738)[16] *wedding of the count's daughter* various unknown composers, after G. F. Brivio?	(2,3)
1747 Pavia	Teatro Omodeo (carn., 19/01/1747)	(4)
1752 Cremona	Private theatre (carn., 19/01/1752)	(5)

Librettos

(1) Turin: Scotto, 1738
I-Rsc Vol. Carv.141 [5]; I-Tac Simeom L 25; I-Tci L.O.0092; I-Tn F VII.352 [4]; I-Tstrona^S

(2) Vienna: van Ghelen, [1738]
A-Wgm 5593; CZ-NH 1431; I-Mb Racc.Dramm.3461; US-DMu ML50.2.C35 H377 1737 [1]

(3) Vienna: van Ghelen, [1738] (Ger.)
A-Wgm 6220; CZ-Bu ST1-0572.267; CZ-Pn 10 F 30

(4) Milan: Ghislandi, 1747
I-LDEsormani 314/3/7

(5) Cremona: Ricchini, 1752
I-Rsc Carv.4234

Music sources

[complete scores] A-Wgm IV 27698 [Q 20883][IC,MGG,NG]

[excerpts] *Fra mille pensieri* (B-Bc 5180[RISM]); *In te spero, o sposo amato* (D-OB MO 571a[RISM;R]; F-Pn D-1481 [33][BnF,MGG,NG]); *Non curo l'affetto* (F-Pn D-1481 [29][BnF,MGG,NG]); *Prudente mi chiedi?* (F-Pn D-1481 [31][BnF,MGG,NG]); *Se sperar così pietoso* (B-Bc 4334[RISM]); *Sperai vicino il lido* (F-Pn D-1481 [28][BnF,MGG,NG]); *Tu sai chi son; tu sai* (F-Pn D-1481 [26 BIS][BnF,MGG,NG])

1739	mus. by various unknown composers
1739 Graz	Theater am Tummel-Platz (carn.)

Librettos

Graz: heirs of Widmanstadj, [1739] (It./Ger.)
A-Gl C 10710¹; A-Gu I 57365^S; <u>A-Wn 28530-B</u>; I-Rsc Carv.4235

1739	mus. by Reina, Giuseppe
1739 Alessandria	Teatro Solerio (10/1739)

Librettos

Alessandria: Vimercati, [1739]
<u>I-Tn F XII.145</u>

---

16. Perutková, Jana, *Der glorreiche Nahmen Adami: Johann Adam Graf von Questenberg (1678–1752) als Förderer der italienischen Oper in Mähren* (Vienna: Hollitzer, 2016).

MC | *Demofoonte* (1733–1836)

1741	mus. by Vinci, Leonardo	
1741 Lucca	Teatro Pubblico (carn.)	(1)
1781 Siena	Teatro degli Intronati (summ.)[17]	(2)

Librettos (1) Lucca: Marescandoli, [1741]
US-Wc ML48 [S10745]

(2) Siena: Rossi, 1781
I-Fc E.V.2076[18]

Music sources [excerpts] *Padre, perdona… oh pene* (US-FAy Quarto 532 MS 3 [25]^{IC,RISM})

1741	mus. by Bernasconi, Andrea	
1741 Rome	Teatro delle Dame (carn., 02/01/1741)	(1)
	1st version	
1766 Munich	Court theatre (carn., 26/01/1766)	(2)
	rev. version	
1770 Cádiz	Teatro Italiano (carn.)[19]	(3)

Librettos (1) Rome: heirs of Ferri,[20] 1741
H-Bu KNY.18.00702; I-Nn L.P. Libretti A 0028; US-Cn BLC #638a; US-CHH IOLC.00215

(2) Munich: Thuille, [1766] (It./Ger.)
D-Mbs Bavar.4015,32 [4]; D-Rs 999/Bav.2638 [22]; US-Wc ML48 [S864]

(3) NA (It./Spa?)

Music sources
1st version: 1741, Rome

[excerpts] *Benché innocente sia* (D-Dl Mus.1-F-49,12 [3]^{RISM}; GB-Lbl Add. 31623 [2]^{BL,RISM}; GB-Lbl R.M.23.e.1 [7]^{BL,RISM}; US-BEm MS 868 [12]^{IC,RISM}); *Felice età dell'oro* (D-MÜs SANT Hs 183 [22]^{RISM}); *In te spero, o sposo amato* (D-MÜs SANT Hs 183 [18]^{RISM}; US-Cu MS 1267 [1]^{IC,RISM}); *La destra ti chiedo* (GB-Lbl Add. 31623 [14]^{BL,RISM}); *Misero pargoletto* (D-MÜs SANT Hs 183 [23]^{RISM}; S-SK 494 [2]^{RISM;P}); *Non curo l'affetto* (DK-Kk mu6310.0230^{IC,RISM}); *O più tremar non voglio* (D-HR [D-Au] III 4 1/2 4° 626^{RISM}); *Padre, perdona… oh pene* (D-MÜs SANT Hs 183 [26]^{RISM}; GB-

---

17. ^SIndex I, p. 464.
18. Attribution to L. Vinci [?] added on this copy. Microfilm copy: CDN-Lu ML48.M47V545 1781a.
19. Díez Rodríguez, Cristina, 'Cádiz, centro operístico peninsular en la España de los siglos XVIII y XIX (1761–1830)' (doctoral dissertation, Universidad Complutense de Madrid, 2015).
20. 'Si vendono da Fausto Amidei'.

MC | *Demofoonte* (1733–1836)

Lbl R.M.23.d.16 [3]^{RISM,21}; US-BEm MS 868 [11]^{IC,RISM}); *Parto. La sorte irata* (A-LA 777$^{RISM;P}$; A-LA 2011^{RISM}; GB-Lbl Add. 31623 [5]^{BL,RISM}); *Perfidi, già che in vita*[22] (GB-Lbl Add. 31623 [13]^{BL,RISM}); *Per lei fra l'armi dorme il guerriero* (GB-Lbl Add. 31623 [6]^{BL}); *Se tutti i mali miei* (D-MÜs SANT Hs 183 [19]^{RISM}; GB-Lbl Add. 14207 [13]^{BL,RISM}; GB-Lbl Add. 31623 [15]^{BL,RISM})

rev. version: 1766, Munich

[complete scores] D-Mbs Mus.ms.152^{MGG,NG,RISM}; D-Mbs Mus.ms.184^{MGG,NG,RISM}

[excerpts] *Odo il suono de' queruli accenti* (D-KNmi H 211 R [19]^{RISM}; D-MÜs SANT Hs 183 [21]^{RISM}; F-Pn VM7-9 [6]^{BnF,RISM})

1741	**mus. by Verocai, Giovanni**	
1741 Florence	Teatro del Cocomero (09/06/1741)	(1)
1741 Brunswick	Teatro Ducale (summ. Fair)	(2)
1742 Brunswick	Teatro Ducale (win. Fair)	(3)

Librettos (1) Florence: Albizzini, [1741]
I-Fn^{S,23}; US-Cn BLC #638b; US-CAt TS 8146.707 1741

(2) Wolfenbüttel: Bartsch, [1741] (It./Ger)
D-BS Brosch. I 21.020

(3) Wolfenbüttel: Bartsch, [1742] (It./Ger.)
D-HVs Op. 1, 178; US-Wc ML48 [S10719]

1741	**mus. by Leo, Leonardo**
1741 Naples	Teatro di S. Carlo (19/12/1741)[24]
1742 Rome	Teatro di Torre Argentina (carn.)[25]

Music sources [complete scores] GB-Lbl Add. 16043/16044^{BL,RISM,26}; US-Wc M1500.L57 D4^{IC,RISM}

---

21. Given as anonymous in ^{BL} and ^{RISM}.
22. As no incipit for this and the following aria in Bernasconi's 1741 setting is available, we cannot ascertain that they were not reused in 1766.
23. Destroyed.
24. Date in Pastore, *Don Lionardo*, p. 185 n. 50 and Mellace, Raffaele, '*Demofoonte* all'ombra del Vesuvio (1735–1775)', in *Demofoonte come soggetto per il dramma per musica: Johann Adolf Hasse ed altri compositori del Settecento*, ed. by Milada Jonášová and Tomislav Volek (Prague: Academia, 2020), pp. 143–66. De Filippis, Felice and Raffaele Arnese, *Cronache del Teatro di S. Carlo (1737–1960)* (Naples: Edizioni Politica Popolare, 1961) give 19/11/1741.
25. See the entry (no. 238) on Gregorio Babbi in Rostirolla, Giancarlo, ed., *Il 'Mondo novo' musicale di Pier Leone Ghezzi* (Rome and Milan: Academia Nazionale di Santa Cecilia and Skira Editore, 2001).
26. Microfilm copy: US-PRu MICROFILM 2073 [3].

MC | *Demofoonte* (1733–1836)

[excerpts] *È soccorso d'incognita mano* (GB-Lbl R.M.23.d.1 [7]^{BL,RISM}; I-Nc M.S. app. 8.1 [15–18]$^{MGG,NG,SBN;P}$); *Felice età dell'oro* (I-Fc D.II.101–102 [25]^{SBN,27}; I-Nc 33.3.35 [14]^{SBN}); *In te spero, o sposo amato* (I-MC 3-E-11 [11]^{RISM}); *No, non chiedo, amate stelle* (I-MC 3-E-11 [6]^{MGG,RISM}); *Non curo l'affetto* (I-Nc 33.3.35 [25]^{MGG,SBN}); *Odo il suono de' queruli accenti* (GB-Mp BRm411Cr72 [2]^{RISM}; I-Fc D.II.101–102 [41]^{SBN}); *O più tremar non voglio* (I-Fc D.II.101–102 [29]^{SBN}); *Padre, perdona… oh pene* (GB-Lbl R.M.23.d.1 [11]^{BL,RISM}; I-Fc D.II.101–102 [26]^{SBN}); *Per lei fra l'armi dorme il guerriero* (I-Fc D.II.101–102 [18]^{SBN}; US-SFsc *M2.1 M285$^{RISM;IP}$); *Se tutti i mali miei* (B-Bc 4373^{RISM}; D-F Mus Hs 154 [11]^{RISM}; I-Fc D.II.101–102 [34]^{SBN}; I-MC 3-E-10 [16]^{RISM}; I-MC 3-E-11/5 [1]^{RISM}); *Sperai vicino il lido* (I-MC 3-E-11/5 [2]^{RISM})

1742	mus. by unknown composer(s)
1742 Milan	Teatro Regio Ducale (13/05/1742)
	birthday of Maria Theresa, queen of Austria
Librettos	Milan: Malatesta, 1742[28]
	B-Bc 19884; I-Ma S. I. H. I. 5 [4]

1743	mus. by Gluck, Christoph Willibald	
1743 Milan	Teatro Regio Ducale (carn., 06/01/1743)	(1)
1743 Reggio Emilia	Teatro Pubblico (Fair, 04/05/1743)	(2,3)
	mus. by C. W. Gluck with add. by F. Maggiore	
1744 Bologna	Teatro Marsigli Rossi (carn.)	(4)
	mus. by C. W. Gluck and others	
1744 Vienna	Burgtheater (06/10/1744)[29]	(5)
1745 Ferrara	Teatro Bonacossi da S. Stefano (carn., 26/12/1744)	(6)
1747 Milan	Teatro Regio Ducale (13/05/1747)	(7)
	birthday of Maria Theresa, queen of Austria	
Librettos	(1) Milan: Malatesta, 1742	
	GB-Lbl Tyson P.B.11. [2]; I-Bc Lo.02225; I-LDEsormani 297/7/22; I-Ma S.I.H.I.5 [4]; I-Mb Racc.dramm.0654; I-Mb Racc.dramm.6058 [1]; I-Ms MUS. G. XXVIII. 4; US-Cn ML50.2.D4 G68 1744	

---

27. We have not been able to collate the materials in this source. If the arias are indeed by Leo, as the inscription on the manuscript claims, they must belong to the 1741 production, as they were composed by either Sarro or Mancini in the 1735 setting → see 1735, mus. by Sarro, Domenico Natale; Mancini, Francesco; Leo, Leonardo.
28. There was a copy in I-Rsc, but we could not find it. We therefore consider it as lost.
29. Klein, Rudolf, 'Die Schauplätze der Hofoper', *Österreichische Musikzeitschrift*, 24 (1969), 371–422.

MC | *Demofoonte* (1733–1836)

(2) Bologna: Pisarri, 1743[30]
I-Bc Lo.02226; I-MOe 83.D.17 [4]; I-Rsc Carv.4236; I-REm 19.K.22; I-REm Pop. 18516; I-REm Racc. Dram. E. Curti 146 [7]

(3) Reggio Emilia: Vedrotti, 1743
I-Rc Misc.300 [4]; US-CAt TS 740 10

(4) Bologna: [Pisarri, 1743][31]
I-Bc Lo.02227; I-Bu A.V.Caps.214 [22]

(5) NA

(6) Ferrara: Barbieri, 1745
I-Fm Mel.2164 [2]

(7) Milan: Malatesta, 1747
B-Bc 19885; F-Pn 16-YD-174; I-LDEsormani 309/1/17; I-Mb Racc. dramm.6057 [3]; I-Rsc Vol. 5 [4][32]

Music sources   [complete scores] B-Bc 12801[IC,NG]; CH-BEl SLA-Mus-JL MLHs 1[RISM;A]

[excerpts] *Ah, che né mal verace* (CH-BEl SLA-Mus-JL MLHs 32 [38][NG,RISM]; F-Pn D-4713 [7][BnF,RISM]); *Che mai risponderti* (CH-BEl SLA-Mus-JL MLHs 32 [37][NG,RISM]; CH-BEl SLA-Mus-JL MLHs 33 [3][NG,RISM]; F-Pn D-4713 [6][BnF,RISM]; I-Bc GG.85 [5][IC,NG]); *È soccorso d'incognita mano* (CH-BEl SLA-Mus-JL MLHs 32a [5][NG,RISM]; F-Pn D-4714 [5][BnF,RISM]); *Felice età dell'oro* (CH-BEl SLA-Mus-JL MLHs 32 [33][NG,RISM]; F-Pn D-4713 [2][BnF,RISM]); *Gemo in un punto e fremo*[33] (A-Wn Mus.Hs.4013[IC,NG]; CH-BEl SLA-Mus-JL MLHs 32 [46][NG,RISM]; F-Pn D-4713 [15][BnF,RISM]); *Il suo leggiadro viso* (CH-BEl SLA-Mus-JL MLHs 32 [48][NG,RISM]; F-Pn D-4713 [17][BnF,RISM]); *In te spero, o sposo amato* (CH-BEl SLA-Mus-JL MLHs 32a [2][NG,RISM]; F-Pn D-4713 [2][BnF,RISM]); *La destra ti chiedo* (CH-BEl SLA-Mus-JL MLHs 32 [34][NG,RISM]; F-Pn D-4713 [3][BnF,RISM]; I-Mc Mus. Tr.ms. 532[NG,RISM,SBN]; I-Nc 34.3.1 [4][SBN]); *Misero pargoletto* (CH-BEl SLA-Mus-JL MLHs 32 [40][NG,RISM]; CH-BEl SLA-Mus-JL MLHs 33 [2][NG,RISM]; D-Dl Mus.3030-F-88 [1][RISM]; D-Dl Mus.3030-F-110 [1][RISM]; F-Pn D-4713 [9][BnF,RISM]; I-Bc GG.85 [4][IC,NG]); *Nel tuo dono io veggo assai* (CH-BEl SLA-Mus-JL MLHs 32 [41][NG,RISM]; F-Pn D-4713 [10][BnF,RISM]); *Non curo l'affetto*

---

30. According to [C,S], there was a copy of this libretto in I-FPfanan (previously in Turin); see [S]7487, 7492. However, the items of the collection were sold independently and can no longer be traced. Another supposed copy in I-Rn could be found either.
31. [S,C] separate the two copies into two different performances; see [S]7487, 7492. This seems to be due to [S]'s wrong reading of the performance date of the libretto in I-Bc as 1743 [*recte* 1744]. However, both correspond to a performance in 1744 and are, indeed, copies of the same text.
32. With handwritten annotations.
33. The aria originally belonged to Metastasio's *Olimpiade* (1733).

(CH-BEl SLA-Mus-JL MLHs 32 [49][NG,RISM]; F-Pn D-4713 [18][BnF,RISM]); *Non dura una sventura* (CH-BEl SLA-Mus-JL MLHs 32 [36][NG,RISM]; F-Pn D-4713 [7][BnF,RISM]); *Non è ver che l'ira insegni* (CH-BEl SLA-Mus-JL MLHs 32a [3][NG,RISM]; F-Pn D-4713 [3][BnF,RISM]); *Non odi consiglio?* (CH-BEl SLA-Mus-JL MLHs 32 [39][NG,RISM]; F-Pn D-4713 [8][BnF,RISM]); *No, non chiedo, amate stelle* (CH-BEl SLA-Mus-JL MLHs 32 [43][NG,RISM]; F-Pn D-4713 [12][BnF,RISM]); *Odo il suono de' queruli accenti* (CH-BEl SLA-Mus-JL MLHs 32 [42][NG,RISM]; F-Pn D-4713 [11][BnF,RISM]); *O più tremar non voglio* (CH-BEl SLA-Mus-JL MLHs 32a [4][NG,RISM]; F-Pn D-4714 [4][BnF,RISM]); *Padre, perdona… oh pene* (CH-BEl SLA-Mus-JL MLHs 32 [47][NG,RISM]; F-Pn D-4713 [16][BnF,RISM]); *Par maggiore ogni diletto* (CH-BEl SLA-Mus-JL MLHs 32 [35][RISM]; F-Pn D-4713 [4][BnF,RISM]); *Perfidi, già che in vita* (CH-BEl SLA-Mus-JL MLHs 32a [6][RISM]; F-Pn D-4714 [6][BnF,RISM]); *Per lei fra l'armi dorme il guerriero* (CH-BEl SLA-Mus-JL MLHs 32a [1][RISM]; F-Pn D-4714 [1][BnF,RISM]); *Prudente mi chiedi?* (CH-BEl SLA-Mus-JL LHs 32a [9][NG,RISM]; F-Pn D-4714 [9][BnF,RISM]); *Se tronca un ramo, un fiore* (CH-BEl SLA-Mus-JL MLHs 32a [8][NG,RISM]; F-Pn D-4714 [8][BnF,RISM]); *Se tutti i mali miei* (CH-BEl SLA-Mus-JL MLHs 32 [44][NG,RISM]; CH-BEl SLA-Mus-JL MLHs 33 [1][NG,RISM]; F-Pn D-4713 [13][BnF,RISM]; I-Bc GG.85 [2][IC,NG]); *Sperai vicino il lido* (CH-BEl SLA-Mus-JL MLHs 32 [51][NG,RISM]; F-Pn D-4713 [20][BnF]); *T'intendo, ingrata* (CH-BEl SLA-Mus-JL MLHs 32 [50][NG,RISM]; F-Pn D-4713 [19][BnF,RISM]); *Tu sai chi son; tu sai* (CH-BEl SLA-Mus-JL MLHs 32a [7][NG,RISM]; F-Pn D-4714 [7][BnF,RISM])

[printed sources] *La destra ti chiedo* [3], in <u>The Favourite Songs in the Opera call'd il Demofoonte</u> (London: Walsh, 1755) → see 1755, mus. by various unknown composers

[inserts] [Reggio Emilia, 1743] Maggiore, Francesco, *Nel fiero periglio* (US-BEm MS 1380 [8][RISM])

1743	mus. by various unknown composers recit. by Chinzer, Giovanni
1743 Rimini	Teatro Pubblico (spr.)
Librettos	Rimini: Albertini, 1743 F-Pn 16-YD-169; I-Mb Racc.dramm.3470

1743	mus. by Jommelli, Niccolò	
1743 Padua	Teatro Obizzi (Fair, 13/06/1743) 1st version	(1)

MC | *Demofoonte* (1733–1836)

1753 Milan	Teatro Regio Ducale (carn., 03/02/1753)[34]	(2)
	mus. by N. Jommelli, with G. Sammartini?	
	2nd version	
1754 Lodi	Teatro di Lodi (carn.)	(3)
1764 Stuttgart	Teatro Ducale (11/02/1764)	(4,5)
	birthday of the Duke of Württemberg and Teck	
	3rd version	
1765 Ludwigsburg	Teatro Ducale (11/02/1765)	(6)
	birthday of the Duke of Württemberg and Teck	
1770 Naples	Teatro di S. Carlo (04/11/1770)	(7)
	name day of Carlos III, king of Spain	
	4th version	
1775 Lisbon	Court theatre – Palácio da Ajuda (06/06/1775)	(8)
	birthday of José I, king of Portugal	
	revision of 3rd version by J. Cordeiro da Silva[MGG,NG]	
1778 Stuttgart	Teatro Ducale (10/01/1778)	(9)

Librettos

(1) Padua: Conzatti, 1743
I-Mb Racc.dramm.4493; I-Rn 40.10.H.5.8; I-Vcg LIBRETTI PADOVA 259; US-Cn BLC #844; US-Wc ML50.2.D39 J5

(2) Milan: Malatesta, 1753
F-Pn LIV IT-3523 [2]; I-Bc Lo.02580; I-LDEsormani 309/2/2; I-Ma S. I. H. I. 7; I-Mb Racc.dramm.6076 [2]; I-Mc Coll.Libr.116; I-Mr Libr. 04248; I-Rn 40.9.D.19.2; I-Rsc Carv.4237; US-Cn ML50.2.D4 J66 1743; US-U Cavagna 20275; US-Wc ML50.2.D39 J6

(3) Milan: Ghislandi, 1753
I-Rsc Carv.4238

(4) Stuttgart: Cotta, 1764 (It./Ger.)[35]
D-Bu 38/79/9779 [2]; D-HEu G 3077-10 RES

(5) Stuttgart: Cotta, 1764 (It./Fr.)[36]
B-Br II 28.849 A 17/172; D-Hs A/6036; D-HEu G 3077 U RES; D-KNth L 1268; D-Tu Dk III 30 [4]; I-Nragni L107 [4]; US-Wc ML48 [S4852][37]

---

34. Contrarily to [C], Balbo and [CA] give 27/07/1753 as the premiere date for Jommelli's 2nd setting of *Demofoonte*; cf. Balbo, Tarcisio, 'Quando il poeta tace (o parla sottovoce): rimandi e sottintesi in un'aria del *Demofoonte* metastasiano, nel quattro intonazioni di Niccolò Jommelli', in *Il canto di Metastasio. Atti del convegno di studi, Venezia (14–16 dicembre 1999)*, ed. by Maria Giovanna Miggiani (Bologna: Forni, 2004), pp. 231–43. [CA] lists the February performance as a 'replica' of the premiere.
35. Microfilm reproduction of unspecified copy: D-WRz M 2517 (two copies).
36. Microfilm reproduction of unspecified copy: US-NYp *ZBD-90.
37. Copy: D-KNmi FH 1189.

MC | *Demofoonte* (1733–1836)

(6) Stuttgart: Cotta, 1765 (It./Fr.)
D-Mbs s/n; D-Sl Fr.D.qt.K.67[38]

(7) Naples: Morelli, 1770
I-Bc Lo.02581; I-Nc Rari 10.3.1 [11]; I-Rig Rar. Libr. Op. 18. Jh. 247; I-Rss Libr. n. XVII [50]

(8) Lisbon: Stamperia Reale, [1775]
B-Bc 19891; BR-Rn V-251,1,10 [2]; I-Rsc Carv.4239; I-Vgc ROL.0392 [1]; P-Ln M. 992 P.; P-Ln M. 1443 P.; P-Ln T.S.C. 54 P.; P-Lt^S; US-PRu HC392 .M57 [4]; US-Wc ML48 [S4853][39]

(9) Stuttgart: Cotta, 1778 (It./Fr.)
D-Sl W.G.qt.K.1069[40]

Music sources

1st version: 1743, Padua

[complete scores] D-Sl* HB XVII 239 [a–c][IC,MGG,NG]; D-Sl HB XVII 241 [a–b][IC,MGG,NG,RISM]; F-Pn X-778[BnF,MGG,NG,41]; US-CHH 55-M1236[IC]

[excerpts] *Che mai risponderti* (CH-E 128,34[RISM;P]; F-Pn D-6275 [9][BnF,42]; GB-Cfm [GB-Cu] MU.MS.150 [9][IC]; S-Skma T-SE-R[RISM]); *La destra ti chiedo* (D-Mbs Mus.ms. 180 [10][RISM]); *Misero pargoletto* (US-SFsc *M2.5 v.15[RISM]); *Non curo l'affetto* (F-Pn D-6280 [9][BnF,43]; US-NH Misc. Ms. 62 [21][RISM]); *Se ardire e speranza* (F-Pn D-6278 [7][BnF]); *Se tutti i mali miei* (D-B Mus.ms. 11247 [6][RISM;P])

2nd version: 1753, Milan

[complete scores] I-Nc 28.5.4[MGG,NG,RISM,SBN]; I-Nc* 15.4.11[MGG,NG,RISM,SBN,44]

[excerpts] *Che mai risponderti* (F-Pn D-6274 [8][BnF,45]); *Di pena sì forte* (F-Pn D-6274 [5][BnF]); *È soccorso d'incognita mano* (F-Pn D-6274 [9][BnF]); *In te spero, o sposo amato* (F-Pn D-6274 [7][BnF]; GB-Lbl R.M.23.e.3 [1][BL,RISM]; I-Nc 33.2.32 [19][SBN]; US-NYp Mus. Res. *MP (Italian) [41][RISM]); *Misero pargoletto* (F-Pn D-6274 [6][BnF]; US-NYp Mus. Res. *MP (Italian) [38][RISM]); *Odo il suono de' queruli accenti* (D-SWl Mus.2993[RISM;P]; D-SWl Mus.2993a [1][RISM;R]; F-Pn D-6274 [1][BnF]; I-MAav Cart.1 n.18[RISM]; US-NYp Mus. Res. *MP (Italian) [43][RISM]); *Padre, perdona… oh pene*

---

38. Microfilm copy: D-Sl MC R 18 Met 12.
39. Copy: D-KNmi FH 1189.
40. Microfilm copy: D-Sl R 18 Met 13.
41. Microfilm copy: F-Pn VM BOB-439.
42. Microfilm copy: F-Pn VM BOB-28869.
43. Microfilm copy of all the pieces in F-Pn D-6280: F-Pn VM BOB-28497.
44. Microfilm copy: US-Eu Film 20181.
45. Microfilm copy of all the pieces in F-Pn D-6274: F-Pn VM BOB-28500.

MC | *Demofoonte* (1733–1836)

(CH-E 128,35[RISM;P]; CH-Gc R 253/2 [1][RISM]; D-SWl Mus.2986[RISM;P]; D-SWl Mus.2986a [1][RISM;R]; F-Pn D-6268 [22][BnF,46]; F-Pn D-6273 [2][BnF]; F-Pn D-6280 [11][BnF;] F-Pn L-18422[BnF]; GB-Lbl R.M.23.e.3 [5][BL,RISM]; GB-Lbl R.M.23.e.11 [12][BL,RISM]; I-Bc GG.70 [9][IC,RISM,SBN]; I-MC 3-C-8/1 [1][RISM]; I-MC 6-E-9/7 [3][RISM]; I-Nc 33.2.30 [10][SBN]; US-NH Misc. Ms. 62 [22][RISM]; US-NYp Mus. Res. *MP (Italian) [39][RISM]); *Perfidi, già che in vita* (GB-Lbl R.M.23.e.11 [13][BL,RISM]); *Per lei fra l'armi dorme il guerriero* (D-SWl Mus.2987[RISM;P]; D-SWl Mus.2991a [2][RISM;R]; F-Pn D-6276 [22][BnF,47]; GB-Lb Add. 31653 [9][BL,RISM]); *Prudente mi chiedi?* (F-Pn D-6274 [4][BnF]); *Sperai vicino il lido* (F-Pn D-6274 [3][BnF])

[printed sources] *No, non chiedo, amate stelle* [5], in <u>The Favourite Songs in the Opera call'd il Demofoonte</u> (London: Walsh, 1755) → see 1755, mus. by various unknown composers

3rd version: 1764, Stuttgart

[complete scores] B-Bc 2186[MGG,NG,RISM]; <u>D-Sl* HB XVII 240 [a–c]</u>[IC,MGG,NG,RISM]; P-La 44-IX-93[BA,MGG,NG,48]; P-La 44-X-1/2[BA,MGG,NG]

[excerpts] *Che mai risponderti* (B-Bc 4238[RISM]); *Il suo leggiadro viso* (B-Bc 4257[RISM]; <u>D-BAR [D-NEhz] Ba 120 Bü 119</u>[IC]; <u>I-Nc 33.2.32 [16]</u>[SBN]); *In te spero, o sposo amato* (I-MC 3-C-3 [13][RISM]; <u>I-Nc 33.2.32 [20]</u>[SBN]); *La destra ti chiedo* (I-Nc 33.2.32 [6][SBN]; US-BEm MS 555[IC,RISM,49]); *Non curo l'affetto* (F-Pn D-6268 [14][BnF]); *Non dura una sventura* (D-Bsa [D-B] SA 1509 [11][RISM;P]); *Odo il suono de' queruli accenti* (B-Bc 4275[RISM]; D-HR [D-Au] III 4 1/2 4° 192[RISM]; D-SWl Mus.2992[RISM]; I-Mc Noseda O.36 [12][SBN]); *O più tremar non voglio* (B-Bc 4280[RISM]; D-KNmi J 101[RISM]); *Se tutti i mali miei* (B-Bc 4310[RISM]; <u>I-Nc 33.2.24 [12]</u>[SBN]; US-CAe Mus 503.601 [5][IC,RISM]); *Sperai vicino il lido* (F-Pn D-6269 [15][BnF,50]; US-NH Misc. Ms. 62 [14][IC,RISM])

4th version: 1770, Naples[51]

[complete scores] D-B Mus.ms. 11247[MGG,NG,RISM]; F-Pn D-6231/6232/6233[MGG,NG,52]; I-Mc Noseda H.26 [1–2][MGG,NG,SBN]; I-Mc Noseda H.54 [1–3][IC,MGG,NG,SBN]; I-Mc* Noseda F.99 [1–2][MGG,NG,SBN,53];

---

46. Microfilm copy of all the pieces in F-Pn D-6268: F-Pn VM BOB-13296.
47. Microfilm copy of all the pieces in F-Pn D-6276: F-Pn VM BOB-28501.
48. This and the following source: for Lisbon 1775.
49. Wrongly dated 1764 in Emerson, John A., *Catalog of Pre-1900 Vocal Manuscripts in the Music Library, University of California at Berkeley* (Berkeley: University of California Press, 1988). Although the accompaniment is not exactly the same as in D-Sl* HB XVII 239 [a–c], the vocal line corresponds to Jommelli's 1st setting of *Demofoonte*.
50. Microfilm copy: F-Pn VM BOB-33989.
51. For a discussion of this musical setting, see McClymonds, Marita, 'Niccolò Jommelli: The Last Years' (doctoral dissertation, University of California, 1978).
52. Microfilm copy: US-PRu MICROFILM 1767 [1–3].
53. Microfilm copies: US-PRu MICROFILM 1766; US-PRu MICROFILM 2349 [1–2].

MC | *Demofoonte* (1733–1836)

I-MC 3-C-15[RISM]; I-Nc 28.6.38/39/40[IC,MGG,NG,RISM,SBN]; I-Nc 28.5.1/2/3[MGG,NG,RISM,SBN]; I-Nc 28.5.5[MGG,NG,RISM,SBN]; I-Nn MS S.Mart. 764 [1–5][NG,RISM;IP,54]; P-La 44-X-3/4/5[BA,MGG,NG]

[excerpts] *Che mai risponderti* (I-MC 3-C-6 [6][RISM]; I-MC 3-C-10/13 [2][RISM]; US-NYp Mus. Res. *MP (Italian) [45][RISM]); *È soccorso d'incognita mano* (I-MC 3-C-10 [12][RISM]); *Il suo leggiadro viso* (I-MC 3-C-7 [14][RISM]; I-MC 3-C-10 [4][RISM]; US-BEm MS 1081 [14][RISM]); *In te spero, o sposo amato* (CH-Gc R 213/4 [4][RISM]; D-KA Don Mus.Ms. 812[RISM]; D-MÜs SANT Hs 2283[RISM]; DK-Kk mu6505.2135[IC,RISM]; GB-Lbl R.M.22.f.8 [5][BL,RISM]; GB-Lbl R.M.23.d.5 [5][BL,RISM]; I-MC 3-C-12/4 [1][RISM]; I-Nc 57.2.3 [11][SBN]; I-Nc 22.2.3 [5][SBN]; I-Nc 33.2.29 [18][SBN]; I-Rrostirolla [I-Fn] MS MUS 563 [42][SBN]; US-Wc M1505.A77[RISM]); *La destra ti chiedo* (CH-Gc R 213/4 [7][RISM]; I-MC 3-C-6 [1][RISM]; I-MC 3-C-6 [13][RISM]; I-Nc 33.2.26 [4][SBN]; I-Nc 33.2.28 [14][SBN]); *Misero pargoletto* (CH-Gc R 213/4 [5][RISM]); *No, non chiedo, amate stelle* (I-MC 3-C-10/13 [1][RISM]); *O più tremar non voglio* (I-MC 3-C-10 [15][RISM]); *Padre, perdona… oh pene* (CH-Gc R 213/4 [3][RISM]; D-MÜs SANT Hs 2249[RISM]; F-Pn D-6271 [10][BnF,55]; F-Pn D-6278 [1][BnF,56]; F-Pn D-14814[BnF]; I-BGi PREIS.O.9262a [4][RISM,SBN]; I-Mc Noseda O.36 [4][IC,SBN]; I-MC 3-C-11 [9][RISM]; I-Nc 33.2.26 [1][SBN]; I-Rama A.Ms.453[SBN]; S-Skma T-SE-R[RISM]); *Perfidi, già che in vita* (I-MC 3-C-10 [11][RISM]); *Per lei fra l'armi dorme il guerriero* (F-Pn D-6214 [9][BnF,57]; I-Nc 57.2.3 [17][SBN]; US-Bp M.120.25 [2][RISM]); *Prudente mi chiedi?* (CH-Gc R 213/4 [8][RISM]; I-MC 3-C-6 [7][RISM]; I-MC 3-C-10 [10][RISM]; I-Nc 33.2.29 [8][SBN]); *Se tronca un ramo, un fiore* (I-MC 3-C-10 [14][RISM]); *Se tutti i mali miei* (CH-Gc R 213/4 [2][RISM]; I-Mc Noseda O.36 [9][SBN]; I-MC 3-C-10 [5][RISM]; I-MC 3-C-11 [8][RISM]; I-Nc 33.2.26 [10][SBN]; I-Rc Mss. 2549 [1][SBN]); *Sperai vicino il lido* (CH-Gc R 213/4 [9][RISM]; D-LEm Becker III.15.50 [4][RISM]; I-Mc Noseda I.160 [13][SBN]; I-MC 3-C-4 [3][RISM]; I-Nc 33.2.28 [13][SBN]; I-Nc 57.2.3 [12][SBN]; I-PAc Sanv.A.194[RISM,SBN]; S-Skma T-SE-R[RISM]; US-NH Misc. Ms. 63 [3][IC,RISM]); *Tu sai chi son; tu sai* (I-MC 3-C-6 [5][RISM]; I-MC 3-C-10 [3][RISM])

[undated] [excerpts] *La destra ti chiedo* (F-Pn D-6274 [2][BnF]); *Misero pargoletto* (F-Pn D-6280 [8][BnF,RISM]); *Nel tuo dono io veggo assai* (F-Pn D-6274 [11][BnF]); *Non curo l'affetto* (F-Pn D-6274 [10][BnF]); *Non dura una sventura* (I-Nc 33.2.30 [12][SBN]); *Padre, perdona… oh pene* (I-Nc 33.2.31 [2][SBN]); *Perfidi, già che in*

---

54. Score in three volumes plus Vn parts.
55. Microfilm copy of all the pieces in F-Pn D-6271: F-Pn VM BOB-28494.
56. Microfilm copy: F-Pn VM BOB-28495.
57. Microfilm copy: F-Pn VM BOB-28477.

MC | *Demofoonte* (1733–1836)

		vita (F-Pn D-6276 [20][BnF]); *Se tutti i mali miei* (F-Pn D-14817[BnF]); *Sperai vicino il lido* (F-Pn D-6271 [5][BnF]; F-Pn D-12605 [7][BnF,58]; F-Pn L-18389[BnF])	
	[doubtful]	[excerpts] *Aspri rimorsi atroci*[59] (CH-Gc R 213/4 [1][RISM]); *Da questo speco* (CH-Gc R 213/4 [6][RISM]); *Misero pargoletto*[60] (B-Bc 4266[RISM]; US-Bp M.416 [46][RISM]); *Se tutti i mali miei* (B-Bc 623[RISM,61]); *Tu ch'il mio cor conosci*[62] (D-Dl Mus.1-F-28 [2][RISM])	
1746		mus. by Graun, Carl Heinrich	
	1746 Berlin	Court theatre (17/01/1746)[63] *Demofoonte, re di Tracia*	(1)
	1774 Berlin	Court theatre (carn., 10/01/1774)[64] with arias by Frederick II, king of Prussia	(2)
	Librettos	(1) Berlin: Haude, 1745 (It./Ger.)[65] D-ERu H58/EZ-II 178; D-Hs A/34173 [4]; D-KNth L 1269; D-ROu Ck-951; I-Vgc ROL.0362 [2]; US-Wc ML48 [S4113]	
		(2) Berlin: Haude & Spener, 1774 (It./Ger.) D-B Mus. T 67 [5]; D-Bga A I k 217; D-Kl 39 RE 2659; I-Rsc Carv.4240; I-Vgc ROL.0944 [8]; PL-Wu GSD 28.20.4.5896 [1]; US-Wc ML48 [S4094]	
	Music sources	[complete scores] D-B Am.B 194[IC,NG,RISM]; D-B Mus.ms. 8216[IC,NG,RISM]; D-B Mus.ms. 8216/1[IC,NG,RISM]; D-Bsa [D-B] SA 1040[RISM;R]; D-Bsa [D-B] SA 1043[RISM]; D-BDk 35[RISM] [Act II]; D-DS Mus.ms 380/381[RISM;P]; D-LEm PM 1636[RISM;A,R]; D-ROu Mus. Saec .XVIII:22[RISM]; D-W Cod. Guelf. 86 Mus. Hdschr.[RISM,66]; US-Wc M1500.G76 D3[IC,RISM]	

---

58. Microfilm copy: F-Pn VM BOB-25059.
59. Although the sources for this and the following two arias bear the inscription 'Napoli 1770', they are not found in the other manuscripts for Jommelli's 1770 version or in its libretto.
60. Similar to the 1753 setting.
61. The music corresponds with none of Jommelli's four ascertained versions.
62. Although attributed to Jommelli on the source, the aria was included in none of his four settings of *Demofoonte*.
63. The production ran for seven consecutive performances between 17 January and 7 February 1746; see Schmidt-Hensel, Roland Dieter, 'Carl Heinrich Grauns *Demofoonte*-Vertonung (Berlin 1746)', in *Demofoonte come soggetto per il dramma per musica: Johann Adolf Hasse ed altri compositori del Settecento*, ed. by Milada Jonášová and Tomislav Volek (Prague: Academia, 2020), pp. 189–212. [C,NG] give 07/02/1746 as the date of the premiere. Ledebur, Carl Friedrich, *Tonkünstler-Lexicon Berlin's von den ältesten Zeiten bis auf die Gegenwart* (Berlin: Rauh, 1861) gives 07/01/1746, yet that date coincides with the premiere of Graun's *Adriano in Siria* in the same theatre.
64. The production ran for four consecutive performances between 10 and 21 January 1774; see Henzel, Christoph, *Berliner Klassik* (Beeskow: ortus, 2009) and Schmidt-Hensel, 'Carl Heinrich Grauns *Demofoonte*', p. 207.
65. [S] lists a copy of this libretto in I-Fc, but the library staff confirmed that the information is not correct; see [S]7594.
66. For Berlin 1774; it includes three arias by King Friedrich II: *Non odi consiglio?*, *Prudente mi chiedi*, and *Tu sai chi son; tu sai*.

MC | *Demofoonte* (1733–1836)

[excerpts] *La destra ti chiedo* (D-B Mus.ms. 8216 [8]^(RISM;P); S-Skma T-SE-R^(RISM)); *La dolce compagna* (B-Bc 5319^(RISM); D-B Mus.ms. 8216 [6]^(RISM); D-Bsa [D-B] SA 1358^(RISM;P); D-Bsa [D-B] SA 1522 [15]^(RISM;R); D-DS Mus.ms 1427e [1]^(RISM;R); S-L Saml.Engelhart 568 [2]^(RISM;R)); *Misero pargoletto* (D-B Mus.ms. 8216 [5]^(RISM); D-BHm RH 0430 [3]^(RISM); D-W Cod. Guelf. 300 Mus. Hdschr. [4]^(RISM); GB-Lbl Add. 32314 [1]^(BL)); *Padre, perdona... oh pene* (D-DS Mus.ms 1427e [2]^(RISM;R); D-SWl Mus.2485^(RISM;P,67)); *Par maggiore ogni diletto* (D-Bsa [D-B] SA 1540^(RISM;R,P); D-DS Mus.ms 1427e [6]^(RISM;R)); *Tu sai chi son; tu sai* (D-DS Mus.ms 1427e [8]^(RISM;R))

[printed sources] *La destra ti chiedo* [8], in *Duetti, terzetti, quintetti, sestetti, ed alcuni cori delle opere del Signore Carlo Enrico Graun*, vol. 1 (Berlin: Decker & Hartung, 1773)

[contrafacta] *Che mai risponderti* ([*Ach allergrößter Gott*] PL-Wu n/s^(RISM;P); [*Salve regina*] PL-Wu RM 5458^(RISM;P)); *Felice età dell'oro* ([*Salve regina*] PL-Wu RM 5466^(RISM;P)); *In te spero, o sposo amato* ([*In te credo sponse*] PL-SA 129/A III 29^(RISM;P); [*O quam suavis est*] PL-Wu RM 4457 [22]^(RISM;P)); *La destra ti chiedo* ([*Poena cantate fidelium chori*] PL-Wu RM 5592^(RISM;P)); *La dolce compagna* ([*Veni creator spiritus*] PL-KŁwnm A-427 [1]^(RISM;P)); *Misero pargoletto* ([*Salve regina*] PL-Wu RM 5461 [1]^(RISM;P)); *Nel tuo dono io veggo assai* ([*Salve regina*] PL-Wu RM 5459^(RISM;P)); *No, non chiedo, amate stelle* ([*Salve regina*] PL-Wu RM 5461 [2]^(RISM;P); [*Ubi moraris Jesu*] PL-Wu RM 5593 [1]^(RISM;P)); *Perfidi, già che in vita* ([*Israel gaude plaude laetare Sion hodie*] PL-Wu RM 4416 [3]^(RISM;P); [*Plaudite, exultate*] PL-Wu RM 5593 [2]^(RISM;P)); *Se tutti i mali miei* ([*Antoni splendor*] PL-SA 134/A III 34^(RISM;P); [*Salve regina*] PL-Wu RM 5460^(RISM;P)); *Sperai vicino il lido* ([*Adeste devote*] PL-Wu RM 4452 [1]^(RISM;P); [*Ad plausus properate*] CZ-Pnm XI A 144^(RISM;P))

[inserts] King Friedrich II, *Non odi consiglio?* (D-Bsa [D-B] SA 1044 [2]^(RISM); US-Wc* ML30 4c [2775])[68]

1746	mus. by unknown composer(s)
1746 Florence	Teatro della Pergola (03/09/1746)
Librettos	Florence: Pieri, 1746
	I-Bc Lo.06195; I-Fc E.V.0523; I-Fc E.V.1422

---

67. Wrongly attributed to J. A. Hasse on source.
68. Henzel, Christoph, 'Berliner Komponisten im Notenarchiv der Sing-Akademie zu Berlin', in *Jahrbuch des Staatlichen Instituts für Musikforschung Preußischer Kulturbesitz*, ed. by Günther Wagner (Stuttgart: Metzler, 2003), pp. 31–98.

MC | *Demofoonte* (1733–1836)

1747–1748	mus. by Smith, John Christopher[NG]	
1747–1748 [s.l.]	NA	
Music sources	[excerpts] four arias in J-Tn[NG]	
1748	by Hasse, Johann Adolf	
1748 Dresden	Court theatre (carn., 09/02/1748)[69]	(1,2)
	1st version	
1749 Venice	Teatro Grimani di S. Giovanni Grisostomo (carn., 26/12/1748)[70]	(3)
	uncertain authorship[71]	
	2nd version	
1750 Mannheim	Court theatre (17/01/1750)[72]	(4,5)
	birthday of the Electoral Princess	
1750 Naples	Teatro di S. Carlo (20/01/1750)	(6?)
	birthday of Carlo VII, king of Naples?	
	mus. by J. A. Hasse and G. Latilla[73]	
1754 Vicenza	Teatro delle Grazie (carn.)	(7)
1758 Naples	Teatro di S. Carlo (04/11/1758)	(8?)
	name day of Carlo VII, king of Naples?	
	3rd version	
1759 Warsaw	Royal Theatre (07/10/1759)[74]	(9,10)
	birthday of August III, king of Poland	
1760 Catania	NA	(11)
1765 La Valletta	[Teatro Manoel] (aut.)	(12)
1776 Warsaw	Theatre (26/07/1776)	(13)
	name day of Stanislaw II, king of Poland	

69. The production had two further performances on 12 and 14 February; see Hochstein, Wolfgang, 'Metastasios Libretto *Demofoonte* in den Vertonungen von Johann Adolph Hasse', in *Demofoonte come soggetto per il dramma per musica: Johann Adolf Hasse ed altri compositori del Settecento*, ed. by Milada Jonášová and Tomislav Volek (Prague: Academia, 2020), pp. 19–56.
70. Contrarily to [C] and Selfridge-Field, Mellace gives 29/12/1748 as the date for the premiere of Hasse's 2nd setting of *Demofoonte*; see Mellace, Raffaele, *Johann Adolf Hasse* (Palermo: L'Epos, 2004) and Selfridge-Field, Eleanor, *A New Chronology of Venetian Opera and Related Genres, 1660–1760* (Stanford: Stanford University Press, 2007).
71. For an account of Hasse's possible stay in Venice, see Hochstein, 'Metastasios Libretto *Demofoonte*', p. 31.
72. Corneilson, Paul Edward, 'Opera at Mannheim, 1770–1778' (doctoral dissertation, The University of North Carolina at Chapel Hill, 1994).
73. According to the libretto, the arias *Che mai risponderti, Il suo leggiadro viso, Non curo l'affetto, Prudente mi chiedi*, and *Sperai vicino il lido* were newly composed by G. Latilla.
74. Hasse may have personally overseen this production; see Żórawska-Witkowska, Alina, 'The Saxon Court of the Kingdom of Poland', in *Music at German Courts, 1715–1760: Changing Artistic Priorities*, ed. by Samantha Owens, Barbara M. Reul, and Janice B. Stockigt (Woodbridge: The Boydell Press, 2011), pp. 51–78.

MC | *Demofoonte* (1733–1836)

Librettos

(1) [Dresden: s.n., 1748]
D-B Mus. Th 250

(2) [Dresden: s.n., 1748] (It./Ger.)
A-Wn 627648-A; D-Sl HBF 3334; D-WRz Tb 82; F-Pn TH B-2488; PL-Wu GSD 17.4.II.76.[1]; PL-Wu GSD 142779; RUS-Mrg Нем 281/38; RUS-Mrg 50-8419154; RUS-Mrg 50-8419155; RUS-Mrg 50-868566; US-Wc ML48 [S4534]

(3) Venice: [s.n.],[75] 1749
CDN-Ttfl Itp Pam 00389; F-Pn 8-YTH-51994; I-Bc Lo.02505; I-Mb Racc.dramm.3785; I-Rsc Libr. n. XV [24]; I-Vcg LIBRETTI S.GIO. GRISOSTOMO 159; I-Vnm DRAMM.1070 [1]; I-Vnm DRAMM.1266 [1]; I-Vnm DRAMM.3577 [6]; US-LAum ML48 .R114 1749 [1]; US-Wc ML48 [S4582]

(4) Mannheim: Pierron, 1750 (It./Ger.)
D-Dl Mag / XVII 517; D-HEu G 3062-2 RES; D-HEu G 3077 V RES; D-KNu K16ᵃ 1985; D-MHrm Mh 1720; D-MHrm Mh 1721; F-Pn YD-5469 [4]; GB-LEbc German G-20 MET

(5) Mannheim: Pierron, 1750 (Ger. only)
D-HEu G 5502 RES

(6?, 8?) [Naples: s.n., 1750? 1758?]
I-Nc 5.1.11 [9][76]

(7) Venice: Fenzo, 1753
F-Pn 8-YTH-52275; I-Bc Lo.02506; I-Rsc Carv.4241

(9) Warsaw: [s.n.], 1759
PL-Kj BJ St. Dr. 26613 I; PL-Kj BJ St. Dr. 391229 II

(10) Warsaw: [s.n.], 1759 (It./Fr.)
F-Pn 4-BL-2793; PL-Kc XVIII.2.1508; PL-Kj 26613 I; PL-Kj 391119 II; PL-Kj BJ St. Dr. 391119 II; PL-Ptu Echo 1882 [285]; PL-Wn XVI-II.3.2665;[77] PL-Wu 13.47.1.25 [2]; PL-Wu GSD 142779; PL-WRzno XVIII-1708; RUS-Mrg 50-8419153; RUS-Mrg 50-8685663

(11) Catania: Bisagni, 1760
I-CATu^(C,S,)[78]

---

75. 'In Merceria all'insegna della Scienza'.
76. Title page missing.
77. Microfilm copies: CDN-Lu ML48.M47H383 1761a; PL-Wn 0068006.
78. The copy reported in [S,C] could not be found by the library staff. We therefore consider it as lost.

MC | *Demofoonte* (1733–1836)

(12) Valletta: Capaci, [1765]
US-CHH ML48 .T442 v.6 [12]; US-Wc ML48 [S4574]

(13) Warsaw: Dufour, 1776 (It./Fr.)
PL-Kj St. Dr. 26309 I; PL-Kj St. Dr. 586338 I; PL-Kp PAU St.Dr. 2962; PL-ŁZu 1002432; PL-Ptu 10481 II; PL-Wn SD XVIII.2.2509[79]

Music sources

1st version: 1748, Dresden

[complete scores][80] B-Bc 2152[RISM]; B-Bc 2153[RISM]; B-Bc 14988[RISM]; B-Br Ms II 3989 Mus Fétis 2554[IC,NG,RISM]; D-B Mus.ms. 9575[RISM]; D-B Mus.ms. 9575/1[IC,RISM]; D-Bsa [D-B] SA 1085[RISM]; D-Bsa [D-B] SA 1086[RISM;A]; D-Bsommer Mus.ms. Hasse 4[RISM;A]; D-Dl Mus.2477-F-53[NG,RISM]; D-Dl Mus.2477-F-53a[NG,RISM;IP]; D-Dl Mus.2477-F-54[RISM;A]; D-Dl Mus.2477-F-55[RISM;A,IP]; D-HAmi MS 63[RISM]; D-LEm Becker III.15.12[RISM;A]; D-LEm PM 1222[NG,RISM]; D-WRz Mus IIa:48[RISM]; F-Pn D-5426/5427/5428[BnF]; F-Pn L-3202[BnF;A]; F-Pn X-43/44/45[BnF,NG,81]; GB-Lbl Add. 32025[BL,NG,RISM]; GB-Lcm MS 269[IC]; I-Mc* Part. Tr.ms. 156[IC,RISM,SBN]; I-Nc n/s[IC,SBN]; US-Wc M1500.H35 D3[RISM]

[excerpts] *Ah, che né mal verace** (D-Hs ND VI 2937 a [6][RISM]); *Che mai risponderti** (F-Pn D-5469 [15][BnF,82]); *È soccorso d'incognita mano** (DK-Kk mu6502.1031[IC,RISM]); *Felice età dell'oro** (DK-Kk mu7410.1232[IC,RISM]; F-Pn D-5469 [22][BnF]); *Il suo leggiadro viso** (F-Pn D-5468 [3][BnF,83]; I-Tf 2 IV 4 [8][RISM]); *In te spero, o sposo amato** (D-F Mus Hs 1665[RISM;P]; D-Hs ND VI 2937 a [2][RISM]; D-MGmi HA IV 64[RISM;P]; F-Pn D-5468 [39][BnF]; I-Rama A.Ms.3805 [6][IC,RISM,SBN]; PL-Wu RM 4457 [9][RISM;P]; US-BEm MS 1167 [5][RISM]); *La destra ti chiedo** (D-Bsa [D-B] SA 1473[RISM;P]; D-LÜh Mus. Q 147[RISM]; DK-Kk mu7410.1233[RISM]; F-Pn D-5467 [18][BnF,84]; F-Pn D-5468 [30][BnF]; F-Pn D-5468 [31][BnF]); *Misero pargoletto** (F-Pn D-5469 [2][BnF]); *Nel tuo dono io veggo assai* (D-Hs ND VI 2937 a [5][RISM]; F-Pn D-5468 [5][BnF]); *No, non chiedo, amate stelle* (D-Bhm RH 0426[RISM]); *Non curo l'affetto** (F-Pn D-5468 [40][BnF]); *Non odi consiglio?** (D-Hs ND VI 2937 a [4][RISM]); *Odo il suono de' queruli accenti* (F-Pn D-5468 [1][BnF]); *O più tremar non voglio* (F-Pn D-5469 [20][BnF]); *Padre, perdona... oh pene**

---

79. Microfilm copy: PL-Wn Mf. 68006.
80. Discrepancies with the information given in [NG] are based on our scrutiny of the sources. D-Hs ND VI 2937 is dated 1748 in [NG], yet it corresponds to the 1758 setting; the three copies in B-Bc, the two in D-B, as well as those in D-HAmi, D-LEm, D-WRz, and I-Mc* contain music related to the 1748 premiere.
81. Microfilm copy: F-Pn VM BOB-29209.
82. Microfilm copy of all the pieces in F-Pn D-5469: F-Pn VM BOB-26190.
83. Microfilm copy of all the pieces in F-Pn D-5468: F-Pn VM BOB-11717.
84. Microfilm copy: F-Pn VM BOB-23048.

MC | *Demofoonte* (1733–1836)

(D-Bsommer Mus.ms. Hasse 4a[RISM]; D-Bsommer Mus.ms. Hasse 4b[RISM,85]; D-WRz Mus VIIb:62 [2][GVK,RISM;P]; F-Pn D-5469 [12][BnF]; F-Pn D-17380[BnF]); *Per lei fra l'armi dorme il guerriero** (D-BAd EB 505[RISM;P,86]; F-Pn D-5469 [3][BnF,87]); *Perfidi, già che in vita* (S-Skma T-SE-R[RISM]); *Prudente mi chiedi?** (D-Dl Mus.2477-F-110 [26][RISM]; D-Hs ND VI 2937 a [3][RISM]; F-Pn D-5469 [18][BnF]); *Se tronca un ramo, un fiore** (F-Pn D-5469 [14][BnF]); *Se tutti i mali miei* (D-WRz Mus VIIb:62 [1][GVK,RISM;P]; DK-Kk mu7410.1231[IC,RISM]; GB-Lcm MS 691 [9][IC]; I-Mc Mus. Tr.ms. 496 [2][RISM,SBN]; I-Nc 33.2.17 [13][SBN]); *T'intendo, ingrata* (F-Pn D-5468 [4][BnF,88]); *Tu sai chi son; tu sai* (F-Pn D-5469 [1][BnF]; F-Pn D-5469 [13][BnF])

[contrafacta] *Il suo leggiadro viso** ([*In hoc die omnes gentes exultate*] CZ-Pu 59 R 4521[RISM;P]); *In te spero, o sposo amato* ([*In te spero sponso meo*] SK-J H-674[RISM;P]; [*Schmeckedt und sheet wie freundlich der Herr ist*] D-HER Mus.E 35:106[RISM;P]; D-HER Mus.J 120:10 [2][RISM;R]; D-HER Mus.B 214:13 [2][RISM;P]; D-HER Mus.K 100:10 [26][RISM;R]; D-HER Mus.K 200:74[RISM;R]; D-HER Mus.K 226:20 [3][RISM;P]; PL-Wu RM 6734 [3][RISM;P]); *O più tremar non voglio* ([*Ad festa convolute fideles properate*] CZ-TEk n/s[RISM;P]; [*Erfreute Stunden eilet*] D-MÜG Mus.ant.146 [1][RISM;P]); *Par maggiore ogni diletto** ([*So kommt ihr Bürger dieser Erden*] D-Dl Mus.2477-E-521[RISM]); *Prudente mi chiedi?** ([*Fideles, devoti convolate*] PL-Wu RM 5563 [2][RISM;P]; [*Iacebo ar loquar pro tuo*] D-Mbs Mus.ms. 4996 [1][RISM]); *Se ardire e speranza* ([*O flora mundi*] PL-Wu RM 5563 [1][RISM;P])

[printed sources] *Padre, perdona... oh pene* [1], in *Four Songs in the Opera call'd Il Demofoonte Sung by Signora Mingotti* (London: Giardini, 1755) → see 1755, mus. by various unknown composers

[arrangements] *In te spero, o sposo amato*, for lute (D-LEm Becker III.11.46a [1][RISM]); *Padre, perdona... oh pene*, for voice and pianoforte (I-Nc 22.2.8 [16][SBN])

2nd version: 1749, Venice

[complete scores] I-Vc*;[89] I-Vnm Mss. 9818[IC,NG,SBN]

---

85. Used in 1750 in Mannheim.
86. Wrongly attributed to J. Mysliveček on source.
87. Microfilm copy: F-Pn VM BOB-26189.
88. Microfilm copy: F-Pn VM BOB-11717.
89. Incomplete; Selfridge-Field, *A New Chronology of Venetian Opera*, pp. 515–516 n. 1748/10.

MC | *Demofoonte* (1733–1836)

[excerpts] *Giacchè vivendo, o perfide* (S-Skma T-R[RISM]); *Per lei mi nacque amore* (D-Mbs Mus.ms. 141 [16][RISM,90]); *Se sapessi i mali miei* (B-Bc 4159[RISM]; F-Pn D-5469 [16][BnF])

[inserts] [Venice, 1750] Galuppi, Baldassare, *A questa bianca mano*[91] ([*Misero pargoletto*] D-KA Mus. Hs. 204[RISM]; I-Nc 33.2.17 [12][SBN]; I-Nc 33.2.21 [23][SBN])[92]

3rd version: 1758, Naples

[complete scores] D-Dl Mus.2477-F-57[NG,RISM]; D-Dl Mus.2477-F-57a[NG,RISM;IP]; D-Hs ND VI 2937[RISM]; F-Pn X-116 [A–C][BnF,NG]; F-Pn X-1032 [1–3][BnF,NG,93]; I-Mc Noseda H.9[NG,SBN]; I-Nc 27.2.16[NG,RISM,SBN,94]; I-Vire 325[SBN]; P-La 46-IV-40/41/42[BA]; US-Wc M1500.H35 D4[RISM]

[excerpts] *Che mai risponderti* (D-MÜs SANT Hs 1977 [5][RISM]); *Felice età dell'oro* B-Bc 4116[RISM]; I-Rama A.Ms.3806 [5][IC,RISM,SBN]); *Il suo leggiadro viso* (B-Bc 4124[RISM]); *In te spero, o sposo amato* (I-Nc 22.3.13 [12][SBN]; I-Nc 33.2.21 [2][SBN]; I-Nc 33.2.29 [18][SBN]; I-Nc 33.3.18 [8][SBN]; I-Nc 33.3.18 [9][SBN]); *La destra ti chiedo* (CH-Gc R 253/1 [9][RISM]; D-MÜs SANT Hs 1977 [9][RISM]; GB-Lam MS 136 [1][IC,RISM]; I-CBp Pepe Ms.255[RISM,SBN]; I-Mc Noseda Q.8 [15][SBN]; I-MC 2-F-14/4 [1][RISM]; I-MC 6-E-9 [3][RISM]; I-Nc 22.2.8 [23–25][SBN;IP,95]; I-Nc 33.2.21 [16][SBN]; I-Nc 33.2.21 [17][SBN]; I-Nc 33.3.18 [26][SBN]; I-Rama A.Ms.3806 [7][IC,RISM,SBN]; P-Ln F.C.R. 95[IC]; S-Skma T-SE-R[RISM]; US-R n/s [2][IC,RISM]); *Misero pargoletto* (D-B Mus.ms. 9550 [8][RISM]; D-MÜs SANT Hs 1977 [2][RISM]; D-WRz Mus VIIb:17[RISM]; GB-Lbl Add. 14180 [3][BL,RISM]; GB-Lcm MS 691[IC]; I-Mc Noseda I.93 [1][SBN]; I-Mc Noseda Q.8 [20][SBN]; I-MC 2-F-17 [3][RISM]; I-MC 2-F-14/4 [8][RISM]; I-MC 2-F-14 [5][RISM]; I-Nc 33.2.22 [1][SBN]; I-Nc 33.3.18 [10][SBN]; S-Skma Alströmer saml. 171 [36][RISM]; US-AAu M1505. H35 D45 17--[RISM,96]); *Nel tuo dono io veggo assai* (B-Bc 4131[RISM]); *Non curo l'affetto* (I-MC 2-F-15/25 [2][RISM]); *Odo il suono de' queruli accenti* (D-MÜs SANT Hs 1977 [10][RISM]; I-Nc 33.2.21 [22][SBN]; I-Rama A.Ms.3806 [3][IC,RISM,SBN]); *Padre, perdona… oh pene* (D-MÜs SANT

---

90. In B flat major instead of E flat major.
91. According to an inscription on D-KA Mus. Hs. 204, an adaptation of B. Galuppi's aria *A questa bianca mano*, originally from his *Penelope* (London, 1741), was inserted into Hasse's setting of *Demofoonte* in Naples in 1750.
92. For a conjectural insertion → see Arie sciolte / contrafacta at the end of this chapter.
93. Microfilm copy: F-Pn VM BOB-29377.
94. The position and number of arias in the manuscript I-Nc 27.2.16 correspond to the libretto for Hasse's 1758 version. An inscription on the front page states it is from 1748, and therefore [RISM] wrongly attributes to Latilla four arias that did not appear in Hasse's 1748 version (but are present in the 1758 version): *Che mai risponderti*, *Non curo l'affetto*, *Prudente mi chiedi?*, and *Sperai vicino il lido*; see note 73 above.
95. All the pieces in I-Nc 22.2.8: parts of Vn I and II only.
96. In A major instead of B flat major.

Hs 1977 [7]^{RISM}; I-Nc 33.3.18 [12]^{SBN}; I-Nc 22.2.8 [13–14]$^{SBN;IP}$); *Perfidi, già che in vita* (S-Skma T-SE-R^{RISM}); *Per lei fra l'armi dorme il guerriero* (D-MÜs SANT Hs 1977 [6]^{RISM}); *Per lei mi nacque amore* (I-MC 2-F-15/25 [1]^{RISM}); *Prudente mi chiedi?* (D-MÜs SANT Hs 1977 [3]^{RISM}; I-Nc 33.2.29 [8]^{SBN}); *Se tutti i mali miei* (CH-Gc R 253/1 [10]^{RISM}; D-Hs M A/1567 [3]^{RISM}; D-MÜs SANT Hs 1977 [4]^{RISM}; F-Pn D-17653^{BnF}; F-Pn D-17662^{BnF,97}; F-Pn D-17663^{BnF}; I-Nc 22.2.8 [19–22]$^{SBN;IP,98}$; I-Nc 33.2.21 [1]^{SBN}; I-Nc 33.2.21 [18]^{SBN}; I-Nc 34.3.15^{SBN}; I-Rama A.Ms.3458^{IC,RISM,SBN}; I-Rc Mss. 2767 [4]^{SBN}; I-Tf 2 IV 11 [4]^{RISM,99}; US-NH Misc. Ms. 275^{RISM}); *Sperai vicino il lido* (D-Hs M A/1567 [2]^{RISM}; I-Nc 33.3.18 [19]^{SBN}); *Tu sai chi son; tu sai* (D-MÜs SANT Hs 1977 [1]^{RISM})

[undated]	[excerpts] *La destra ti chiedo* (A-Wn Mus.Hs.1074 [2]^{IC}; I-Nc M.S. app. 8.1.15 [1]$^{SBN;IP,100}$); *Misero pargoletto* (F-Pn D-14412^{BnF,101}; US-CAt M1507 .O6 1760 vol. 1 [5]^{IC}); *Padre, perdona... oh pene* (DK-Kk Rung No 1547 1954-55.661^{IC}); *Par maggiore ogni diletto* (D-Bsa [D-B] SA 1540$^{RISM;R,P}$); *Se tutti i mali miei* (F-Pm Res F7.29^{BASE}; F-Pn D-5466 [16]^{BnF,102}; I-Mc Noseda I.93 [5]^{SBN}); one unspecified aria (CZ-Pnm XXXIII E 44$^{IC;P}$)
1748	mus. by unknown composer(s)
1748 Palermo	Teatro de' Valguarneri marchesi di S. Lucia
Librettos	Palermo: Valenza, 1748
	I-PLn ANTIQUA Y.7.II.31
1749	mus. by Hasse, Johann Adolph (2nd version) → see 1748
1749	mus. by various unknown composers
1749 Copenhagen	Court theatre – Charlottenborg Palace
Librettos	Copenhagen: Godiche, 1749 (It./Ger.)
	DK-Kk 56-368
1750	mus. by Galuppi, Baldassare
1750 Madrid	Court theatre – Teatro del Buen Retiro (carn., 18/12/1749) (1)

---

97. This and the following source: in b minor instead of c minor.
98. Fl. and Vn parts only.
99. Given as anonymous in ^{RISM}.
100. In A major instead of E major (1748/1749) or G major (1758).
101. Microfilm copy: F-Pn VM BOB-22876.
102. Microfilm copy: F-Pn VM BOB-25807.

MC | *Demofoonte* (1733–1836)

mus. by B. Galuppi and G. B. Mele[103]
1st version

1750 Madrid	Court theatre – Teatro del Buen Retiro (21/02/1750)	(2)
1751 Madrid	Court theatre – Teatro del Buen Retiro (14/02/1751)	(3)
1751 Barcelona	Teatre de la Santa Creu (30/05/1751)	(4)
	name day of Fernando VI, king of Spain	
1752 Madrid	Court theatre – Teatro del Buen Retiro (20/01/1752)	(5)
1752 Madrid	Court theatre – Teatro del Buen Retiro (11/04/1752)	(6)
1755 Madrid	Court theatre – Teatro del Buen Retiro (23/09/1755)	(7–9)
	birthday of Fernando VI, king of Spain	
1755 Madrid	Court theatre – Teatro del Buen Retiro (18/12/1755)[104]	(10)
1756 Bologna	Teatro Formagliari (spr., 18/05/1756)[105]	(11)
1758 Padua	Teatro Nuovo (Jun. Fair, c. 13/06/1758)	(12)

2nd version[106]

1760 Prague	Teatro Nuovo	(13)
1763 Barcelona	Teatre de la Santa Creu (after 22/08/1763)[107]	(14)
1764 Cádiz	Teatro Italiano (26/05/1764)	(15)
1767 Palma de Mallorca	Teatro de Palma (after 03/08/1767)	(16)
1768 Palermo	Teatro di Santa Cecilia (win.)	(17)

Librettos

(1) Madrid: [Mojados, 1750] (It./Spa.)
F-Pn 8-RE-4709; E-Mlg Inv. 12145 [7]; E-Mtnt RES/6350; E-Tp 17750; I-Bc Lo.01845; I-Tbnb A*Patetta 60 H 39 06; US-NO PQ4718.A7 D46 1750

(2,5,6,10) NA

(3) Madrid: Mojados, [1751] (It./Spa.)
E-Bim RES/6350

---

103. For this and subsequent performances of Galuppi (and Mele's) setting in Madrid, see Leza, José Máximo, 'Metastasio on the Spanish Stage: Operatic Adaptations in the Public Theatres of Madrid in the 1730s', *Early Music*, 26.4 (1998), 623–31; and Llorens, Ana and Álvaro Torrente, 'Constructing *Opera Seria* in the Iberian Courts: Metastasian Repertoire for Spain and Portugal', *Anuario musical*, 76 (2021), 73–110 <https://doi.org/10.3989/anuariomusical.2021.i76>. For the original source, see Broschi, Carlo, *Description del estado actual del real teatro de Buen Retiro, de las funciones hechas en él desde el año de 1747 hasta el presente [...]* (1758), E-E II/1412, fol. 47ʳ.
104. Carreras, Juan José, 'Farinelli's Dream: Theatrical Space, Audience and Political Function of Italian Court Opera', in *Musiktheatre im höfischen Raum des frühneuzeitlichen Europa*, ed. by Margret Scharrer, Heiko Laß, and Matthias Müller (Heidelberg: Heidelberg University, 2020), pp. 357–93.
105. Ricci, Corrado, *I teatri di Bologna, nei secoli XVII e XVIII: storia aneddotica* (Bologna: Successori Monti, 1888).
106. A pasticcio according to Selfridge-Field, *A New Chronology of Venetian Opera*, p. 557.
107. May 1763 according to Kleinertz, Reiner, *Grundzüge des spanischen Musiktheatres im 18. Jahrhundert* (Kassel: Reichenberger, 2003). We follow Alier y Aixalà, Roger, *L'òpera a Barcelona: orígens, desenvolupament i consolidació de l'òpera com a espectacle teatral a la Barcelona del segle XVIII* (Barcelona: Institut d'Estudis Catalans, 1990).

MC | *Demofoonte* (1733–1836)

(4) Barcelona: Campins, 1751 (It./Spa.)
E-Bbc C400/232 (lost); E-Bu 07 B-68/8/9

(7) Madrid: heirs of Mojados, 1755 (It./Spa.)
D-LEm PT 1036; E-Bbc C400/2777; E-Mn T/21869; E-Mresad 0719 D; E-Tp 1-1447 bis; F-Nm 30215; I-Rsc Carv.4243; P-Cug Misc. 546 [9295];[108] P-Ln T.S.C. 53 P.; P-Lt[C.S]; US-BEm ML50.G23 D3

(8) Madrid: heirs of Mojados, 1755 (It./Spa.)
E-Mn T/6126; E-Mba B-1455; E-ME Biblioteca 9883;[109] E-Tp 1-1429; P-Ln T.S.C. 53 P.

(9) Madrid: [s.n.], 1755 (It./Spa.)
E-Mn T/35181

(11) Bologna: Sassi, 1756
I-Bca 17-ARTISTICA Gb, 26; I-Bca 8-L.ITAL.COMP.MUSIC.05 [6]; I-MOe 83.I.19 [4]; I-Rn 40.10.E.15.2; US-AUS KL-17 108; US-Wc ML31.H43g [1]

(12) Padua: Conzatti, 1758
I-Pmc; I-Rsc Carv.4242; US-Wc ML48 [S3484][110]

(13) [Prague]: Pruscha, [1759–1760][111]
CZ-Pu 65 E 2983

(14) Barcelona: Generas, 1763 (It./Spa.)
US-CAt TS 8428.146 1763

(15) Cádiz: Espinosa, 1764 (It./Spa.)
E-Mn T/22344; US-CAt TS 8146.250 1764

(16) Palma de Mallorca: Bausa, 1767 (It./Spa.)
E-PAp Mall. 366; US-CAt TS 8146.250 1767

(17) Palermo: Ferrer, 1768[112]
I-PLn Misc.A.073.13

Music sources
1st version: 1749, Madrid

[excerpts] *Che mai risponderti* (D-Dl Mus.2973-F-31 [19][RISM]); *Il suo leggiadro viso* (F-Pn* MS-1905[BnF,RISM]); *La destra ti chiedo* (D-Dl

---

108. First eight pages missing; translation into Portuguese: P-Cug Misc. 582 [9631].
109. Last pages missing.
110. Copy: D-KNmi FH 1187.
111. According to [C,S], there was a further copy in SK-KRE but it can no longer be found according to the library staff; cf. [S]7465. We therefore consider it as lost.
112. [S]7545 dates the libretto in 1767.

Mus.2973-F-36 [12]^RISM; DK-Kk mu6409.1535^IC,RISM); *Misero pargoletto* (I-MC 2-C-16 [3]^RISM); *Se tutti i mali miei* (D-Dl Mus.2973-F-10 [3]^RISM); *Sperai vicino il lido* (D-Dl Mus.2973-F-10 [1]^RISM); *Tu sai chi son; tu sai* (D-Dl Mus.2973-F-10 [2]^RISM;P)

2nd version: 1758, Padua

[complete scores] B-Bc 2091^IC,NG,RISM; D-Dl Mus.2973-F-8^NG,RISM; I-MOe Mus. F. 1313^IC,NG,113; P-La 44-VII-12/13/14^BA; P-La 44-VII-15/13/17^BA

[excerpts] *Che mai risponderti* (D-Dl Mus.2973-F-31 [16]^RISM; F-Pn D-4304 [31]^BnF,RISM,114; I-Nc 27.6.15 [19]^IC,RISM,SBN,115; S-Skma T-SE-R^RISM; US-SFsc *M2.1 M133^RISM); *In te spero, o sposo amato* (CZ-Pnm XXX-VIII A 255^RISM;P; D-Dl Mus.2973-F-31 [15]^RISM; D-LÜh Mus. Q 185^RISM; F-Pn D-4300 [19]^BnF,RISM; PL-CZ III-773^RISM;P); *La destra ti chiedo* (D-Dl Mus.2973-F-31 [18]^RISM; F-AIXm F.C. ms. VI [2]^IC); *Misero pargoletto* (D-Dl Mus.2973-F-31 [20]^RISM); *Odo il suono de' queruli accenti* (GB-Lbl R.M.22.c.10 [6]^BL,RISM; S-Uu Gimo 102^RISM; US-SFsc *M2.1 M134^RISM;P); *Padre, perdona… oh pene* (D-Dl Mus.2973-F-31 [14]^RISM; D-LÜh Mus. Q 171^RISM; I-Nc 27.6.15 [7]^IC,MGG,NG,RISM,SBN; S-Skma T-SE-R^RISM); *Perfidi, già che in vita* (I-Bc MS.MART.2.44 [12]^RISM,SBN; S-Skma T-SE-R^RISM); *Per lei gfra l'armi dorme il guerriero* (S-Skma T-SE-R^RISM); *Se tutti i mali miei* (D-Dl Mus.2973-F-31 [17]^RISM; S-Skma T-SE-R^RISM); *Sperai vicino il lido* (I-Rdp Ms Musicale 98 [40]^SBN; S-Skma T-SE-R^RISM); *T'intendo, ingrata* (I-Rama A.Ms.2678 [2]^RISM,SBN; US-CAe Mus 503.603 [7]^RISM;R)

[undated] [excerpts] *In te spero, o sposo amato* (F-Pn D-4307 [5]^BnF); *Misero pargoletto* (A-Wn SA.67.F.68^IC)

[doubtful] [excerpts] *Misero pargoletto*[116] (CH-E 694,10 [1]^RISM; J-Tk S10-612 [4]^RISM)

1750	mus. by Fiorillo, Ignazio	
1750 Brunswick	Teatro Ducale (summ. Fair)	(1)
1751 Brunswick	Teatro Ducale (win. Fair)	(2)

113. Wrongly attributed to Caldara on the manuscript by a posthumous hand. It corresponds to Galuppi's 1758 setting.
114. Microfilm copy: F-Pn VM BOB-21141.
115. The source I-Nc 7.6.15 presents the name "Galuppi" on the front page. It contains, besides an overture —which is different from the one in the scores for Galuppi's 2nd version—, two arias that coincide with the ones we find in Galuppi's 1758 setting: *Che mai risponderti* [20] and *Padre, perdona… oh pene* [8]. The rest, however, belong to A. Ferrandini's setting → see 1758, mus. by Ferradini, Antonio.
116. The music in this manuscript does not coincide with any of the other versions allegedly by Galuppi: we question the attribution to Galuppi.

MC | *Demofoonte* (1733–1836)

Librettos	(1) Brunswick: Keitel, 1750 (It./Ger.) D-W Textb. Sammelbd 5 [5] (2) Brunswick: Keitel, [1751] (It./Ger.) D-B Mus. T 81 [5]; D-HVs Op. 1, 209
Music sources	[excerpts]: *La destra ti chiedo* (D-MGmi HA IV 37[RISM;IP]; D-MGmi HA IV 37a[RISM;R]; D-W Cod. Guelf. 314 Mus. Hdschr. [10][RISM;R]); *Misero pargoletto* (D-W Cod. Guelf. 314 Mus. Hdschr. [24][RISM;R]); *Non odi consiglio?* (D-Wa* 46 Alt 690[MGG,NG,RISM]); *Padre, perdona… oh pene* (D-W Cod. Guelf. 314 Mus. Hdschr. [23][RISM;R])

1750	mus. by Uttini, Francesco Antonio Baldassare[NG]
1750 Ferrara	NA [Teatro Bonacossi da S. Stefano?]
1759 Stockholm	Royal theatre – Drottningholm Palace (24/07/1759)[CA]
Music sources	[excerpts] *Se tutti i mali miei* (B-Bc 4934[IC,MGG,NG,RISM])

1751	mus. by Santini, Leopoldo
1751 Palermo	Teatro di Santa Cecilia (01/1751)

1752	mus. by unknown composer(s)
1752 Livorno	Teatro da S. Sebastiano (aut.)
Librettos	Livorno: Fantechi & co., 1752 I-Mb Racc.dramm.0924

1752	mus. by Perez, Davide	
1752 Lisbon	Court theatre – Palácio da Ajuda (17/12/1752)	(1)
1772 Porto	Theatre (06/06/1772) *birthday of João I, king of Portugal*	(2)
Librettos	(1) Lisbon: Sylviana, 1752 P-Ln M. 1559 P. (2) Porto: Durand, Grouteau, & co., 1772 (It./Port.) I-Rsc Carv.4244	
Music sources	[complete scores] I-Vnm Mss. 9803/9804/9805[IC,MGG,NG,SBN]; P-La 45-V-5/6/7[BA]; P-La* 54-I-80/81/82[BA,MGG,NG]; P-Ln C.I.C. 98[IC,MGG,NG,RISM]; S-Skma T-R[MGG,NG,RISM]; US-NH Misc. Ms. 23[RISM] [Act II] [excerpts] *Che mai risponderti* (I-MC 4-F-2 [9][RISM]); *In te spero, o sposo amato* (P-La 54-III-71[BA]); *Misero pargoletto* (I-MC 4-F-1 [1][RISM]; P-La	

MC | *Demofoonte* (1733–1836)

54-III-71 [99]^{BA;IP,117}; US-BEm MS 100 [6]^{IC,RISM}); *Padre, perdona... oh pene* (F-Pn L-19440^{BnF}; I-MC 4-F-1 [10]^{RISM}; P-La 54-III-71 [98]^{BA;IP,118}; US-BEm MS 1302^{RISM}; US-SFsc *M2.1 M387 [12]^{RISM}); *Per lei fra l'armi dorme il guerriero* (D-Hs M A/454^{MGG,NG,RISM}); *Perfidi, già che in vita* (D-KNmi P 81 R^{RISM;P}; D-Mbs Mus.ms. 988 [6]^{IC,RISM}); *Se ardire e speranza* (D-Dl Mus.3015-F-1 [2]^{RISM}; I-Nc 34.6.13 [9]^{SBN}; I-Nc 65.2.90 [1]^{SBN}; S-Skma T-SE-R^{RISM}; US-Wc M1505.A2 P439^{IC,RISM}); *Se tronca un ramo, un fiore* (US-BEm MS 100 [2]^{IC,RISM}); *Sperai vicino il lido* (P-La 54-III-71^{BA}); *Se tutti i mali miei* (I-MC 4-F-2 [8]^{RISM})

[printed sources] unidentified arias [1, 2], in *The Favourite Songs in the Opera Demofoonte* (London: [s.n., c. 1760])

[contrafacta] *Misero pargoletto* ([*Mizero amado filho*] P-VV G-Prática 51b^{IC})

1753	mus. by Jommelli, Niccolò (2nd version) → see 1743
1753 1753 Lisbon	mus. by unknown composer(s) Nossa Senhora do Cabo *Mais vale amor do que hum reyno* (Port. only)
1754 1754 Parma	mus. by Mazzoni, Antonio Teatro Ducale (carn., after 24/01/1754)
Librettos	Parma: Monti, [1754] I-Bc Lo.03033; I-PAc F. Libretti, sc.109 [70]
Music sources	[excerpts] *Misero pargoletto* (US-SFsc *M2.1 M322^{RISM;R,IP}); *Non temer, bell'idol mio* (US-BEm MS 28 [2]^{IC,RISM}); *Se ardire e speranza* (CZ-Pkřiž XXXV D 68^{RISM;P}); *T'intendo, ingrata* (F-Pn D-14973^{BnF;IP,119}); *Vado... ma dove?... oh dio!*[120] (I-MAav Cart.7 n.34^{RISM;IP})
1754 1754 Turin	mus. by Manna, Gennaro Teatro Regio (carn., 26/01/1754)

---

117. Va part only.
118. Vn II part only.
119. Microfilm copy: F-Pn VM BOB-13149.
120. Text originally from Metastasio's *Didone abbandonata* and, in fact, it appears in A3-S21 of A. Mazzoni's setting of that libretto (Bologna, 1753). As no complete source has been preserved for either *Didone* or *Demofoonte* by him, we cannot determine to which of them the setting in I-MAav Cart.7 n.34 belongs, or if the composer reused the earlier version of the aria in his *Demofoonte*.

MC | *Demofoonte* (1733–1836)

Librettos   Turin: Zappata & Avondo, 1754
D-ERu H00/R.L 78; F-Pn FB-6908; I-Ms MUS. M. XII. 1; I-NOVa Biblioteca Teatro Coccia 283 [2]; I-Rsc Libr. n. XVI [47]; I-Rsc Vol. Carv. 140 [1]; I-Tci L.O.0152; I-Tn F VII.359 [4]; I-Tn F XIII.488 [2]; I-Tstrona[C,S]; US-Wc ML48 [S5903]

Music sources   [complete scores] I-Nf* Inv.N°.347[MGG,NG,SBN] [Acts II&III]

[excerpts] *Doverti perdere* (I-Rsc G.Mss.15 [2][RISM,SBN]); *La destra ti chiedo* (I-Rsc G.Mss.15 [7][RISM,SBN]); *Misero pargoletto* (I-Rsc G.Mss.15 [9][RISM,SBN]); *Nel tuo dono io veggo assai* (I-Rsc G.Mss.15 [8][RISM,SBN]); *No, non chiedo, amate stelle* (I-Rsc G.Mss.15 [6][RISM,SBN]); *Odo il suono de' queruli accenti* (I-Rsc G.Mss.15 [10][RISM,SBN]); *Padre, perdona… oh pene* (I-MC 3-E-22 [4][RISM]; I-Rsc G.Mss.15 [3][SBN]; US-SFsc *M2.1 M316[RISM;IP]); *Passaggier, che in folta selva* (I-Rsc G.Mss.15 [4][RISM,SBN]); *Per lei fra l'armi dorme il guerriero* (D-Dl Mus.1-F-82,16 [4][RISM]; S-Skma T-SE-R[RISM,121]); *Prudente mi chiedi?* (I-Tf 2 IV 4 [6][RISM]); *Se tutti i mali miei* (I-Rsc G.Mss.15 [5][RISM,SBN]); *Sperai vicino il lido* (I-Rsc G.Mss.15 [1][RISM,SBN])

[unidentified arias] A-KR[MGG]

1754 Venice	mus. by Cocchi, Gioacchino	
1754 Venice	Teatro Vendramin di S. Salvatore (Asc., 23/05/1754)	(1)
1754 Lucca	Teatro Pubblico (aut., 10/1754)	(2)
1757 Pistoia	Teatro dei Risvegliati (24/07/1757)[122]	(3)

Librettos   (1) Venice: Fenzo, 1754
F-Pn 8-YTH-52275; I-Bc Lo.01187; I-Mb Racc.dramm.0773; I-Rsc Carv.4246; I-Vnm DRAMM.1761 [9]; I-Vnm DRAMM.1274 [2]; US-LAum ML48 .R114 1754 [9]; US-Wc ML48 [S2042]

(2) Lucca: Benedini, 1754
B-Bc 19886; CZ-Bu CH-0008 [65]

(3) Pistoia: Bracali, 1757[123]
US-CAt *2004T-172; US-BEm ML48 .I7 [365]

Music sources   [complete scores] S-St [S-Skma] D 2 [31][RISM;P, 124]

[excerpts] *Se tutti i mali miei* (Gb-Lbl Add. 31633 [2][BL,RISM])

---

121. Given as anonymous in [RISM].
122. [S]Index I, p. 427 lists it as G. Pampani's setting.
123. Hortschansky claims having consulted a copy in I-Vgc, but it cannot be found in [IC]; lost? Cf. Hortschanksy, 'Die Wiener Dramen Metastasios', p. 423.
124. For Lucca 1754.

MC | *Demofoonte* (1733–1836)

> *Demofoonte*, in *Poesie del signor abate Pietro Metastasio* (Paris: widow of Quillau, 1755), vol. 3, pp. 357–463.

1755	mus. by unknown composer(s)	
1755 Florence	Teatro della Pergola (carn., 26/12/1754)	

Librettos   Florence: Pieri, [1755]
I-Bc Lo.06196; I-Fc E.V.1420; I-Fm Mel.2181 [7]

1755	mus. by Sarti, Giuseppe	
1755 Copenhagen	Royal Danish Theatre (carn.)	(1)
	pasticcio?[MGG,125]	
	1st version	
1771 Copenhagen	Royal Danish Theatre (30/01/1771)[126]	(2)
	2nd version	
1782 Rome	Teatro di Torre Argentina (carn., 26/01/1782)	(3)
	3rd version	
1787 Perugia	Teatro Civico del Verzaro (carn.)	(4)

Librettos   (1) Copenhagen: Godiche, 1755 (It./Ger.)
DK-Kk 56-369; I-Rsc Carv.4247

(2) Copenhagen: Svare, [1771] (It./Dan.)
I-Bc Lo.05037; D-KIl Xn 208; DK-Kk Rom. 12300 8°, vol. 7; S-Uu n/s

(3) Rome: Puccinelli brothers, 1782
F-Pn YD-5433 [4]; I-Rsc Libr. n. XIX [39];[127] I-Rsc Libr. n. XIX [191]; I-Rvat Stamp.Ferr.V.6818 [3]

(4) Perugia: Costantini, 1787
I-PEc ANT Misc. I.C 52 [9][128]

Music sources

1st version: 1755, Copenhagen

[excerpts] *Misero pargoletto* (D-B Mus.ms. 19496/5[RISM]); *Prudente mi chiedi?* (US-Bu H. C. Robbins Landon Collection, scores |x781A Box

---

125. A pasticcio according to [MGG]. Venturi does not treat it as such; cf. Venturi, Simonetta, 'Il periodo danese di Giuseppe Sarti e la "Didone abbandonata"', *Studi e Documentazioni-Rivista umbra di Musicologia*, 15.1 (2007), 23–38.
126. Venturi treats this performance as a revival ('replica') of Sarti's 1755 setting, yet the structure of the libretto and the extant musical sources indicate that at least part of the music was newly composed. Cf. Venturi, 'Il periodo danese di Giuseppe Sarti', p. 28.
127. Microfilm copy: CDN-Lu M1500.M57P287 1800a.
128. Microfilm copy: CDN-Lu ML48.M47P76 1784a.

MC | *Demofoonte* (1733–1836)

7[RISM]); *Se tutti i mali miei* (D-BFb [D-MÜu] S-ar 67 [2][RISM]; D-SWl Mus.4772[RISM;P]; D-SWl Mus.4795[RISM])

2nd version: 1771, Copenhagen

[complete scores] DK-Kk* mu7502.0838[IC,MGG,NG,RISM,129]

[excerpts] *Che parlar! Che dir potrei?* (DK-Sa R321[RISM;R]); *L'affanno, oh dio, mi lacera* [i.e., *L'affanno in sen mi lacera*] (DK-Kk mu7502.0731[IC,RISM]); *Son qual nave in mezzo all'onda* (S-Skma T-SE-R[RISM])

3rd version: 1782, Rome

[complete scores] I-Rmassimo n/s[MGG,NG,RISM,SBN,130]; RUS-SPtob[MGG]

[excerpts] *In te spero, o sposo amato* (D-B Mus.ms. 19508 [8][MGG,RISM]; D-Hs M A/831 [1/26][RISM;R]; D-Mbs Mus.ms. 20868 [5][IC,RISM]); *La dolce compagna* (CH-Gc X 5 [30][RISM;R,131]; D-B Mus.ms. 19508 [6][MGG,RISM]; D-Dl Mus.3276-F-14 [6][RISM]; D-Hs M A/831 [1/27][RISM]; D-Mbs Mus.ms. 20868 [3][IC,RISM]; D-MÜs SANT Hs 3850[RISM]; I-FZc RM cart.48 [3][RISM]; I-Mc Mus.Tr.ms.1498[SBN]; I-MC 5-F-1 [10][RISM]; I-Nc 34.6.30 [4][SBN]; I-Nc 34.6.30 [5][SBN]; I-Pl rari 1/II/29[RISM,SBN]; I-PEsp M CXXXI [18][RISM,SBN;R]; I-Rsc G.Mss.217 [5][RISM]; I-Rsc G.Mss.838[SBN;P]; S-Skma T-SE-R[RISM]; US-R M1613.3 S249 [2][RISM]); *Misero pargoletto* (D-MÜs SANT Hs 3851[RISM]); *Per lei fra l'armi dorme il guerriero* (D-Mbs Mus. 20868 [7][IC,RISM]); *Sperai vicino il lido* (D-Mbs Mus.ms. 20868 [8][IC,RISM]; I-Rsg ms. mus. C.55[RISM])

[printed sources] *La dolce compagna*, in *Numi possenti...* (Paris: Bailleux, [1783])

[doubtful] *Sperai vicino il lido* (I-PAc Sanv.A.131[SBN,132])

1755	mus. by various composers (incl. Galuppi, Baldassare; Gluck, Christoph Willibald; Hasse, Johann Adolph; and Jommelli, Niccolò)
1755 London	King's Theatre in the Haymarket (09/12/1755) *pasticcio*

129. [NG] lists two sources for Sarti's *Demofoonte* at DK-Kk, one for the 1st setting from 1755 and another for the 2nd version from 1771. For his part, Jensen refers to only one setting with music purportedly preserved in DK-Kk; cf. Jensen, Niels Martin, 'Giuseppe Sarti: attività danese e manoscritti sopravvissuti', in *Giuseppe Sarti musicista faentino: Atti del convegno internazionale*, ed. by Mario Baroni and Maria Gioia Tavoni (Modena: Mucchi, 1986), pp. 159–65. However, DK-Kk holds only one (mu 7502.0838), which presents the composer's 2nd musicalisation. No further score is preserved. Microfilm copy: US-PRu MICROFILM 2245.
130. Wrongly related to Sarti's 1st version in [S].
131. In C major instead of D major.
132. The aria was not included in the 1755 premiere and, since the musical incipit does not correspond with Sarti's versions from 1771 or 1782, it may not be by Sarti. In fact, the singer indicated on the manuscript, Luigi Marchesi, participated in none of Sarti's performances. Based on our examination of the extant sources, we conclude that this aria may have belonged to F. Bianchi's *Demofoonte* (Genoa, 1781) or to a setting of unknown authorship (Pisa, 1780; Lucca, 1782; Livorno, 1791; Venice, 1795).

MC | *Demofoonte* (1733–1836)

Librettos	London: Woodfall, 1755 (It./En.)[133]
	GB-Lbl 1342.c.16 [5];[134] GB-Lbl 11714.b.39 [3]; GB-Ob Harding D 2444 [1]; US-CAt TS 8653.272 1724; US-LAum ML50.2.P325 G2 1754
Music sources	[printed sources]
	In te spero, o sposo amato by unknown composer [2]; *Or ch'è salvo l'idol mio* by J. A. Hasse [4];[135] *Padre, perdona... oh pene* by J. A. Hasse [1],[136] *Se tutti i mali miei* by B. Galuppi [3],[137] in <u>Four Songs in the Opera call'd Il Demofonte, sung by Sigra Mingotti</u> (London: Giardini, 1755)
	La destra ti chiedo by C. W. Gluck [3];[138] *No, non chiedo, amate stelle* by N. Jommelli [5];[139] *Ogni amante puo dirsi guerriero* by C. W. Gluck [1];[140] *Padre, sposa, io vado* by N. Jommelli [4];[141] *Tu sai chi son; tu sai* by unknown composer [2], in <u>The Favourite Songs in the Opera call'd il Demofoonte</u> (London: Walsh, 1755)

Demofoonte, in *Poesie del signor abate Pietro Metastasio* (Turin: Stamperia Reale, 1757), vol. 3, pp. 335–438.

1757	mus. by unknown composer(s)	
1757 Verona	Teatro Filarmonico (carn.)	
Librettos	Verona: Ramanzini, 1757	
	I-Vmc Rava G.370	

1757	mus. by Pampani, Antonio Gaetano	
1757 Rome	Teatro delle Dame (carn., 06/02/1757)[142]	(1)
1764 Venice	Teatro Tron di S. Cassiano (carn.)	(2)
Librettos	(1) Rome: Amidei, [1757]	
	B-Bc 19887; I-Bc Lo.03981; I-Mgentili[C,S]; I-Rsc Libr. n. XVI [48]; I-Rvat Stamp.Ferr.V.8055 [2]; US-CAh *GC7 A100 B750 [14]	

---

133. There was a further copy in the Theatre Museum, London, closed since 2007[C,E,S]. As the future of the collections is not clear, no [RISM] siglum can be used.
134. Microfilm copies: D-Gs MA 83-57:1341 [5]; GB-En Mf.134, reel 1341 [5].
135. From Hasse's 3rd setting of *Arminio* (Dresden, 1751).
136. → see 1748, mus. by Hasse, Johann Adolph.
137. The aria is an adaptation of *Per quel paterno amplesso* from B. Galuppi's 2nd *Artaserse* (Padua, 1751).
138. → see 1743, mus. by Gluck, Christoph Willibald.
139. → see 1743, mus. by Jommelli, Niccolò.
140. This aria is an adaptation of *Se all'impero amici dei* from Gluck's *La clemenza di Tito* (Naples, 1752).
141. Adapted from Jommelli's *Caio Mario* (Foligno, 1749).
142. Franchi, Saverio, *Le impressioni sceniche: dizionario bio-bibliografico degli editori e stampatori romani e laziali di testi drammatici e libretti per musica dal 1759 al 1800* (Rome: Edizioni di Storia e Letteratura, 1994).

MC | *Demofoonte* (1733–1836)

(2) Venice: Colombani, 1764
F-LM BL 8° 2747; F-Pn 8-YTH-52055; I-Bc Lo.03982; I-Mb Racc.dramm.3938; I-Vcg LIBRETTI S.CASSIANO 22; I-Vnm DRAMM.1017 [6]; I-Vnm DRAMM.1300 [2]; US-LAum ML48 .R114 1764 [14]; US-Wc ML48 [S7752]

Music sources [complete scores] P-La 45-IV-28/29/30[BA,NG]; P-La 45-IV-31/32/33[BA,NG]

[excerpts] *La destra ti chiedo* (US-NYp Mus. Res. *MNI 79 [11][RISM]; US-NYp Mus. Res. *MNI 179 [11][RISM]); *Misero pargoletto* (I-Rc Mss. 2765 [17][NG,SBN]); *Padre, perdona… oh pene* (D-RH Ms 576[NG,RISM;P]); *Sperai vicino il lido* (GB-Lbl R.M.23.d.17 [17][BL,NG,RISM]; I-MC 6-D-11 [31][RISM])

1758	mus. by Vinci, Pasquale	
1758 Siena	Teatro degli Intronati (carn.)	(1)
1759 Rimini	Teatro Pubblico (carn., 30/01/1759)	(2)

Librettos (1) Siena: Stamperia del Pubblico, 1757
I-Fc E.VI.4241

(2) Rimini Albertini, [1759]
I-Bc Lo.05527

1758	mus. by Traetta, Tommaso	
1758 Mantua	Teatro Arciducale (carn., 14/01/1758)	(1)
1759 Pesaro	Teatro del Sole (carn., 05/01/1759)	(2)
1770 Mantua	Teatro Arciducale (carn., 03/02/1770)	(3)

Librettos (1) Mantua: heirs of Pazzoni, [1758]
I-Bc Lo.05350; I-OS LIBRETTI 36

(2) Pesaro: Gavelliana, 1759
I-PESo[C,S,143]

(3) Mantua: heirs of Pazzoni, [1770]
I-Bc Lo.04647; I-Ms MUS. T. XI. 1; I-PAc F. Libretti, sc.110 [71]; US-Wc ML48 [S10408]

Music sources [complete scores] I-MAav Cart.34[NG,RISM;IP]

[excerpts] *Già mi sembra oscuro il giorno* (B-Bc 4255[RISM]; I-MAav Cart.36 n.2[RISM;P]); *In te spero, o sposo amato* (D-B Mus.ms. 22015 [4][IC,RISM]); *La destra ti chiedo* (I-MAav Cart.10 n.18[RISM;P]); *Misero pargoletto* (I-MAav

---

143. The library staff could not find it. Hortschansky claims having consulted it, presumably around 1977–1978; cf. Hortschanksy, 'Die Wiener Dramen Metastasios', p. 423. We therefore consider it as lost.

MC | *Demofoonte* (1733–1836)

Cart.16 n.14[RISM;P]; I-OS Mss.Mus.B 2831[RISM,SBN]); *Nell'affanno, oh dio, nel pianto* (D-MÜs SANT Hs 4181 I [5][RISM]; F-Pn D-9007 [1,9][BnF]; F-Pn MS-9806[BnF]; I-MAav Cart.8 n.3[RISM;P]); *Nel tuo dono io veggo assai* (I-MAav Cart.36 n.5[RISM;R]); *Non curo l'affetto* (D-B Mus.ms. 22015 [5][IC,RISM]; *Non dura una sventura* (I-MAav Cart.7 n.4[RISM;R,P]); *O più tremar non voglio* (I-MAav Cart.36 n.3[RISM;R,P]); *Perfidi, già che in vita* (I-MAav Cart.36 n.4[RISM;R,P]); *Per lei fra l'armi dorme il guerriero* (I-MAav Cart.36 n.1[RISM;R,P]); *Se ardire e speranza* (I-MAav Cart.8 n.1[RISM;P]; I-MC 6-A-20 [12][RISM]); *Se tronca un ramo, un fiore* (I-MAav Cart.7 n.9[RISM;R,P]); *Sperai vicino il lido* (I-MAav Cart.8 n.21[RISM;R,P]; I-MC 6-A-20 [10][RISM])

1758	mus. by Galuppi, Baldassare (2nd version) → see 1750
1758	mus. by Hasse, Johann Adolph (3rd version) → see 1748
1759 1759 Milan	mus. by Ferradini, Antonio (one aria by J. Ch. Bach) Teatro Regio Ducale (carn., 26/12/1758)
Librettos	Milan: Malatesta, 1758 F-Pn LIV IT-3525 [11]; I-Bc Lo.01619;[144] I-LDEsormani 309/2/31; I-Mb Racc.dramm.6066 [1]; I-Rn 40.9.E.2.1; I-Rsc Vol. 7 [8]; US-Wc ML48 [S3063]
Music sources	[complete scores] I-Nc 27.6.15[SBN;A,145]; P-La 44-VI-12/13/14[BA,MGG,146]; P-La 54-II-58/59/60[BA,MGG] [excerpts] *Felice età dell'oro* (P-La 54-III-71 [42–46][BA;IP]); *Misero pargoletto* by J. C. Bach (F-Pn VM4-861 [2][BnF,147]; P-La 54-III-71 [47–51][BA;IP]); *Non cimentar gli affetti* (P-La 54-III-71 [36–38][BA;IP]); *Se tutti i mali miei* (P-La 54-III-71 [39–41][BA;IP])
1759 1759 Venice	mus. by various unknown composers Teatro Grimani di S. Benedetto (carn.)

---

144. Pages 33–40 missing.
145. The source I-Nc 6.5.17 is attributed to Galuppi in [NG] and [MGG], yet, except for the overture and two arias from Galuppi's 2nd setting of *Demofoonte*, also from 1758 – *Che mai risponderti* [20] and *Padre, perdona... oh pene* [8] –, it contains A. Ferrandini's version. See discussion in → 1749, mus. by Galuppi, Baldassare.
146. The printed catalogue of the Ajuda library ([BA]) incorrectly lists this and the following complete score, as well as the excerpts below, under the name 'Ferrandini'. Similarly, [S]7525 lists the corresponding libretto under that surname.
147. Microfilm copy: F-Pn VM BOB-9629.

MC | *Demofoonte* (1733–1836)

Librettos	Venice: Fenzo, 1759
	A-Wmi BT-506; I-Mb Racc.dramm.0775; I-Ria MISC. Teatrale 6 [11]; I-Vcg LIBRETTI S.BENEDETTO 187; I-Vnm DRAMM.1081 [4]; I-Vnm DRAMM.1280 [4]; US-CAt *IC7.A100.B750 [74]; US-LAum ML48 .R114 1759 [4]

1759	mus. by Eberlin, Johann Ernst
1759 Salzburg	Court theatre (26/09/1759)
	anniversary of the consecration of the Prince of Salzburg
Librettos	Salzburg: Stamperia di Corte, 1759
	A-MB Per. 108; A-Sfr 58/75; A-Ssp SPS-19574; A-Su I 5576; D-AM 999/L. ext. 75 [6,1/3]; D-Rp 9995/Mus.tx. 70; US-BEm ML50 .E2 D4[148]
Music sources	[excerpts] *Misero pargoletto* (A-LA 827[RISM;P])

1760	mus. by Brunetti, Giuseppe[NG]
1760 [s.l.]	NA

1761	mus. by Piccinni, Niccolò
1761 Reggio Emilia	Teatro Pubblico (Fair, 10/05/1761) (1)
1762 Naples?	Teatro di S. Carlo (2)
Librettos	(1) Reggio Emilia: Davolio, [1761]
	D-Mbs L.eleg.m. 3901; I-MOe M.T.Ferr.Mor.27 [2]; I-REm 19.K.104; I-REm 19.K.837; I-REm Racc. Dram. E. Curti 147 [13]; I-Vc 1026; I-Vgc ROL.0537 [1]; US-AUS KL-17 115; US-CAt TS 8146.519 1761
	(2) NA
Music sources	[complete scores] I-Nc* 15.I.9/10[IC,MGG,NG,RISM,SBN,149]; P-La 46-I-4/5/6[BA,MGG,NG]
	[excerpts] *Di quel ciglio il dolce impero* (D-Eu Esl VIII 744[IC,RISM]; D-MÜs SANT Hs 3193[RISM]; I-BGi PREIS.BIS.9690.101a[IC,SBN]; I-Rdp Ms Musicale 64 [5][RISM,SBN]); *Misero pargoletto* (CH-Gc R 123/7 [6][RISM]; D-MÜs SANT Hs 3191[RISM]; I-MAav Cart.16 n.22[RISM;P]; I-MC 1-B-11/6 [9][RISM]; I-MC 5-A-11 [9][RISM]; I-Nc 34.6.16 [13][SBN]; I-Rdp Ms Musicale 64 [3][RISM,SBN]); *No, non chiedo, amate stelle* (I-MC 5-A-9 [8][RISM]); *Padre, perdona... oh pene* (D-MÜs SANT Hs 1580 [10][RISM]; D-MÜs

---

148. Microfilm copy: US-BEm MICROFILM C2.
149. Possible autograph; for Naples 1762.

MC | *Demofoonte* (1733–1836)

SANT Hs 3190[RISM]; I-MC 4-F-24 [11][RISM]; I-Rdp Ms Musicale 64 [4][RISM,SBN]); *Parto, crudel, se vuoi* (D-MÜs SANT Hs 3192[RISM]; I-CBp Pepe Ms.225[SBN]); *Prudente mi chiedi?* (D-MÜs SANT Hs 3194[RISM]); *Se ardire e speranza* (D-Mbs Mus.ms. 182 [4][RISM]; D-MÜs SANT Hs 1580 [14][RISM]; I-MC 5-A-11 [3][RISM]); *Se potesse il core oppresso* (CH-BEb Mss.h.h.IV.182 [10][RISM;R]; I-MAav Cart.8 n.13[RISM;P]); *Sperai vicino il lido* (I-Rdp Ms Musicale 64 [6][RISM,SBN])

1761	mus. by Boroni, Antonio and others	
1761 Senigallia	Teatro di Senigallia (Fair, 22/06/1761)	(1)
1761 Treviso	Teatro Dolfin (17/10/1761)[CA]	(2)
1762 Vicenza	Teatro [delle Grazie?] (carn.)	(3)

Librettos
(1) Venice: Fenzo, 1761
I-Pci H.49432; I-Pmc[C,S]

(2) NA

(3) Venice: Fenzo, 1762
I-VIb GONZ.019 [23]

Music sources [excerpts] *L'idea di quel sembiante* (F-Pn D-15311[BnF,RISM])

1762	mus. by various unknown composers
1762 Florence	Teatro della Pergola (aut., 15/08/1762)

Librettos
Florence: Bonajuti,[150] 1762
B-Bc 19889; I-Fc E.V.1421; I-Fc E.V.1741

1763	mus. by Di Majo, Gianfrancesco
1763 Rome	Teatro di Torre Argentina (carn., 03/02/1763)

Librettos
Rome: Cartolaro a Monte Citorio,[151] [1763]
F-Pn LIV IT-3740 [2]; I-Bc Lo.02784

Music sources [complete scores] B-Bc 2197[MGG,NG,RISM] [Acts II&III]; F-Pn D-7257[BnF,NG,152]; D-B Mus.ms. 13394[MGG,NG,RISM] [Acts I&III]; P-La 44-XI-49/50/51[BA,MGG,NG]; US-BEm MS 132[IC,RISM;A,R]

[excerpts] *Che mai risponderti* (D-B Mus.ms. 13394/11[RISM;IP]; F-Pn D-7266 [8][BnF,MGG]; US-BEm MS 1218[RISM]; US-SFsc *M2.1 M307[RISM;IP]);

---

150. 'Si vende da'.
151. 'Si vende dal'.
152. Microfilm copies: F-Pn D-7257; US-PRu MICROFILM 1783.

MC | *Demofoonte* (1733–1836)

Già si desta la tempesta (UA-Knbuv Rozum 120501 [20]^{RISM}); *In te spero, o sposo amato* (D-Mbs Mus.ms. 182 [3]^{IC,RISM}; D-MÜs SANT Hs 2451 [2]^{RISM}); *La destra ti chiedo* (D-B Mus.ms. 13394/6^{RISM}); *La dolce compagna* (D-KNmi M 250 R [8]^{RISM}; D-MÜs SANT Hs 2451 [6]^{RISM}; GB-Lbl Add. 31652 [3]^{BL,RISM}; I-Rama A.Ms.1541^{SBN}; I-Rdp Ms Musicale 80 [1]^{RISM,SBN}; US-SFsc M2.1 M312^{RISM}); *Misero pargoletto* (D-B Mus.ms. 13394/8^{RISM}; D-Mbs Mus.ms. 182 [5]^{IC,RISM}; D-RH Ms 494^{RISM;P}; Gb-Lbl Add. 31652 [5]^{BL,RISM}; I-Fc D.I.203 [1]^{IC,SBN}; I-Mc Mus. Tr.ms. 611^{RISM,SBN}; US-BEm MS 1163 [46]^{RISM}); *Non curo l'affetto* (D-MÜs SANT Hs 2451 [4]^{RISM}); *O più tremar non voglio* (D-B Mus.ms. 13394/9^{RISM}; D-Mbs Mus.ms. 182 [6]^{IC,RISM}; D-MÜs SANT Hs 2451 [1]^{RISM}; I-Mc Mus. Tr.ms. 606^{RISM,SBN}); *Padre, perdona… oh pene* (D-B Mus.ms. 13394/12^{RISM;IP}; D-Hs M A/896 [12]^{RISM}; D-MÜs SANT Hs 2451 [5]^{RISM}; F-Pn D-7266 [17]^{BnF,MGG}; I-MC 2-A-6/7 [2]^{RISM}); *Per lei fra l'armi dorme il guerriero* (D-B Mus.ms. 13394/10^{RISM}; D-MÜs SANT Hs 2451 [3]^{RISM}; D-MÜs SANT Hs 2456 [2]^{RISM}; F-Pn D-7266 [16]^{BnF,MGG,153}; GB-Lbl Add. 31652 [4]^{BL,RISM}; I-Fc D.I.203 [3]^{IC,SBN}; I-Mc Mus. Tr.ms. 612^{RISM,SBN}; I-Rdp Ms Musicale 80 [3]^{RISM,SBN}; S-Skma T-SE-R^{RISM}; US-SFsc *M2.1 M308^{RISM;IP}); *Se tutti i mali miei* (D-B Mus.ms. 13394/4^{RISM;IP}; D-MÜs SANT Hs 2456 [1]^{RISM}; D-SWl Mus.3507^{RISM;IP}; DK-Kk 1929-30.859^{IC}; GB-Lbl Add. 31652 [2]^{BL,RISM}; I-Fc D.I.203 [2]^{SBN}; I-Tf 2 IV 11 [3]^{RISM}; I-PEsp M.CXXXI [13]^{SBN}; I-Rdp Ms Musicale 80 [2]^{RISM}; I-Rrostirolla [I-Fn] MS MUS 978^{SBN}; J-Tk S10-591 [10]^{RISM}; P-Ln M.M. 142 [2]^{IC}); *Sono in mar, non veggo sponde* (B-Bc 4387^{RISM}; D-KNmi M 250 R [3]^{RISM}; D-MÜs SANT Hs 2452^{RISM}; D-MÜs SANT Hs 2456 [4]^{RISM}; D-RH Ms 492^{RISM;P}; D-RH Ms 493^{RISM;R}; D-SWl Mus.3506^{RISM;P}; F-Pn D-7267 [4]^{BnF}; P-Pn D-7267 [13]^{BnF}; F-Pn D-7268 [10]^{BnF}; F-Pn D-14932^{BnF}; F-Pn L-18948^{BnF}; GB-Lbl Add. 31652 [1]^{BL,RISM}; I-Mc Mus. Tr.ms. 617^{SBN}; I-MC 2-A-6/7 [3]^{RISM}; <u>I-Nc 51.2.51</u> [4]^{SBN}; I-Rdp Ms Musicale 80 [5]^{SBN}; J-Tk S10-591 [11]^{RISM}; P-VV G-Prática 51b^{IC}; S-Skma T-SE-R^{RISM}; US-BEm MS 97 [2]^{IC,RISM}; US-SFsc *M2.1 M314^{RISM})

[printed sources] *Sono in mar, non veggo sponde* [10], in *Journal d'ariettes italiennes* (Paris: Bailleux, 1779)

[parodies] *Sono in mar, non veggo sponde* ([*Quand la mer frémit de rage*] F-Lm M 5642^{RISM;R,IP})

---

153. Microfilm copy: F-Pn VM BOB-34147.

MC | *Demofoonte* (1733–1836)

1763	mus. by various unknown composers (incl. Caldara, Antonio)	
1763 Prague	Teatro Nuovo (aut.)	

Librettos [Prague: s.n., 1763]
A-Gu I 132618; CZ-Pu 65 E 2981

1764   mus. by Jommelli, Niccolò (3rd version) → see 1743

1765	mus. by Vento, Mattia	
1765 London	King's Theatre in the Haymarket (02/03/1765)[154]	(1)
1766 London	King's Theatre in the Haymarket (22/03/1766)[155]	(2)
1776 London	King's Theatre in the Haymarket	(3)

Librettos (1) London: Woodfall, 1765 (It./En.)
GB-Lbl RB.23.a.6324;[156] GB-WMl^E; US-U X 782.1 V566D1765

(2) London: Woodfall, 1766 (It./En.)
US-I ML48 .E342 [8]

(3) London: Woodfall, 1776 (It./En.)
US-I ML48 .E342 [8]; US-U X 782.1 V566D1765

Music sources [excerpts] *La destra ti chiedo* (I-OS Mss.Mus.B 4405^RISM,SBN); *Non è ver che l'ira insegni*[157] (I-Rama A.Ms.3753 [1]^RISM,SBN; US-Wc M1505.A2 B2 [1]^IC,RISM); *Prudente mi chiedi?* (I-Nc 34.4.6 [9]^SBN; US-SFsc *M2.5 v.45 [30]^RISM;R); *Se tutti i mali miei* (US-Wc M1505.A2 B2 [2]^IC,RISM)

[printed sources] *Che mai risponderti* [5]; *La destra ti chiedo* [4]; *Misero pargoletto* [3]; *Non è ver che l'ira insegni* [2]; *No, non chiedo, amate stelle* [6]; *Prudente mi chiedi?* [1]; *Se ardire e speranza* [7]; *Se tutti i mali miei* [8], in *The Favorite Songs in the Opera Demofoonte* (London: Bremner, 1765)

[doubtful] *Non dura una sventura*[158] (US-AAu M1505.B12 D4^RISM)

---

154. The production ran for fourteen consecutive performances; see Petty, Fred Curtis, 'Italian Opera in London, 1760–1800' (doctoral dissertation, Yale University, 1971).
155. Burden, Michael, 'Metastasio on the London Stage, 1728 to 1840: A Catalogue', *Royal Musical Association Research Chronicle*, 40 (2007), 1–332. The production ran for six consecutive performances; see Petty, 'Italian Opera in London', p. 155.
156. Microfilm copies: D-Gs MA 2001-46:12523 [5]; GB-En Mf.134, reel 12523 [5].
157. On the source in US-Wc appears an attribution to 'Bach', but its music coincides with the one in the aria collection printed in London (*The Favorite Songs in the Opera Demofoonte*), where it is attributed to Vento.
158. On the source in US-AAu appears an attribution to 'Bach', yet ^NG,RISM call this attribution into question and give Vento as the most plausible author.

MC | *Demofoonte* (1733–1836)

1765	music by various composers (incl. Petrucci, Brizio)	
1765 Lucca	Teatro Pubblico (aut.)	(1)
1766 Ferrara	Teatro Bonacossi da S. Stefano (26/12/1765)[159]	(2)
Librettos	(1) Lucca: Benedini, 1765[160]	
	I-La Dono Pellegrini – Libretti d'opera, 24	
	(2) NA	
Music sources	[excerpts] Petrucci, Brizio, *Che mai risponderti* (I-PAc Sanv.A.251[SBN]); *Padre, perdona… oh pene* (I-Gl FONDO ANT. M.(1) 1U[SBN])	
1766	mus. by Bernasconi, Andrea (2nd version) → see 1741	
1766	mus. by Guglielmi, Pietro Alessandro	
1766 Treviso	Teatro Onigo (aut., 08/10/1766)	
	opening of the theatre	
Librettos	Treviso: Trento, [1766]	
	I-Vcg LIBRETTI TREVISO 271; I-FPfanan[S,161]	
Music sources	[complete scores] P-La 44-VIII-41/42[BA,MGG,NG]	
	[excerpts] *Che mai risponderti* (GB-Lbl Add. 31667[BL,RISM]; I-Raf 1.E.5 [12][RISM]); *In te spero, o sposo amato* (A-LA 805[RISM;P]); *La destra ti chiedo* (P-VV G-Prática 51b[IC]); *No, non chiedo, amate stelle* (DK-Kk* mu6410.1732[IC,MGG,RISM]); *Padre, perdona… oh pene* (I-Raf 1.E.5 [15][RISM]); *Per lei fra l'armi dorme il guerriero* (DK-Kk* mu6410.1932[IC,RISM]); *Sposa, oh dio, perché* (I-Raf 1.E.5 [13][RISM])	
1769	mus. by Mysliveček, Josef	
1769 Venice	Teatro Grimani di S. Benedetto (carn., 17/01/1769)	(1)
	1st version	
1775 Naples	Teatro di S. Carlo (20/01/1775)	(2)
	birthday of Carlos III, king of Spain	
	2nd version	

---

159. *Laberinto degli amanti fabbricato in 43. teatri dell'Europa disposto per ordine d'alfabeto a comodo de' grandi, de' mezzani, e de' piccioli a piacere de' nobili, de' cittadini, e de' plebei per il carnovale dell'anno 1765* (Florence: Bassanese, 1765).
160. According to [C,S], there was a copy of this libretto in I-FPfanan; see [S]7541 and note 29 above.
161. The copy was previously a part of the Legger private collection in Turin and was subsequently transferred to I-FPfanan; see note 30 above.

MC | *Demofoonte* (1733–1836)

Librettos

(1) Venice: Fenzo, 1769
A-Wmi BT-258; CZ-Pu V 100820; F-Pn 8-YTH-51535; I-Mb Racc. dramm.3957; I-Vcg LIBRETTI S.BENEDETTO 189; I-Vnm DRAMM.1108 [5]; I-Vnm DRAMM.1296 [4]; I-Vnm DRAMM.1304 [5]; US-LAum ML48 .R114 1769 [2]; US-Wc ML48 [S6529]

(2) Naples: Morelli, 1775
I-Fm Mel.2338 [14]; I-Nc Rari 10.3.9 [3]; I-Ra E.I.15 [5]; US-NYp Mus. Res. *MZ, A/20/21 [12]

Music sources

1st version: 1769, Venice

[complete scores] I-Vnm Mss. 9831^{IC,NG,S,SBN}; P-La 45-I-41/42^{BA,MGG,NG}; P-La 54-I-42/43/44^{BA,MGG,NG}

[excerpts] *Che mai risponderti* (I-MC 4-A-16 [1]^{RISM}); *In te spero, o sposo amato* (I-MC 4-A-16 [19]^{RISM}; US-BEm MS 89 [5]^{IC,RISM}); *La destra ti chiedo* (CH-Gc R 253/12 [7]^{RISM}; US-BEm MS 89 [6]^{IC,RISM}); *Misero pargoletto* (CH-Zz Mus Ms A 145^{SB}; I-OS Mss.Mus.B 2402^{RISM,SBN}; US-BEm MS 86 [3]^{IC,RISM}); *Padre, perdona… oh pene* (I-MC 4-A-16 [7]^{RISM}; US-BEm MS 89 [3]^{IC,RISM}); *Prudente mi chiedi?* (US-BEm MS 89 [4]^{RISM}); *Se tutti i mali miei* (US-BEm MS 89 [7]^{IC,RISM}); *Sperai vicino il lido* (D-BAd EB 537$^{RISM;P}$; D-LÜh Mus. Q 259^{RISM}; I-Bsf M.M.II.8 [1]^{SBN}; I-Tci Mus.Ms. 94^{RISM}; US-BEm MS 90 [1]^{IC,RISM})

[contrafacta] *In te spero, o sposo amato* ([*Grata lucente aurora, aura suavis*] CZ-LIT 701$^{RISM;P}$; CZ-Pak 906$^{RISM;P}$; *Misero pargoletto* ([*Quaeso amati quaeso montes*] CZ-LIT 717$^{RISM;P}$); *Sperai vicino il lido* ([*Ah sponse mi dilecte*] D-Tl B 301$^{RISM;P}$; [*Cantemus preconia*] CZ-NYd DÚ 276$^{RISM;P}$; CZ-Pak 904$^{RISM;P}$)

[parodies] *In te spero, o sposo amato* ([*Se mai turbo il tuo riposo*] I-MC 4-A-16 [2]^{RISM,162})

2nd version: 1775, Naples

[complete scores] A-Wn* Mus.Hs.16421 [1–2]^{IC,NG,163}; I-Fc D.I.394/395/396^{IC,NG,SBN}; I-Nc 29.3.7/8/9^{IC,NG,RISM,SBN,164}; P-La 45-I-38/39/40^{BA,NG}; US-Wc M1500.M658 D3^{IC,NG,RISM}

---

162. In A major instead of B flat major.
163. Microfilm copies: CZ-Bu Skř.17-0577.916; US-PRu MICROFILM 2368.
164. Microfilm copy: US-PRu MICROFILM 2361 [1–2].

MC | *Demofoonte* (1733–1836)

[excerpts] *Che mai risponderti* (US-BEm MS 453 [8])[IC,RISM,165]; *In te spero, o sposo amato* (A-Wn Mus.Hs.10542[IC]; US-BEm MS 453 [1])[IC,RISM]; *La destra ti chiedo* (US-BEm MS 453 [6])[IC,RISM]; *Misero pargoletto* (US-BEm MS 453 [7])[IC,RISM]; *Padre, perdona... oh pene* (I-MC 4-A-12 [10])[RISM]; I-MC 4-A-14 [2])[RISM]; I-MC 4-A-15 [8])[RISM]; I-MC 4-A-16 [7])[RISM]; I-Nc 57.2.3 [1])[SBN]; US-BEm MS 453 [3])[IC,RISM]); *Per lei fra l'armi dorme il guerriero* (CZ-Pu 59 R 140[RISM]; F-Pn D-8208 [7])[BnF]); *Se ti bramassi estinto* (US-BEm MS 453 [9])[RISM]); *Se tutti i mali miei* (US-BEm MS 453 [4])[IC,RISM]); *Sperai vicino il lido* (US-BEm MS 453 [2])[IC,RISM])

[printed sources] *In te spero, o sposo amato* [2]; *Padre, perdona... oh pene* [7], in <u>The Favourite Songs in the Opera Demofoonte</u> (London: Napier, [1778?]) → see 1778, mus. mainly by Bertoni, Ferdinando Gasparo

[contrafacta] *In te spero, sposo amato* ([*Ave maris stella*] F-Susc M 422[RISM;P])

[undated]	[excerpts] *Misero pargoletto* (F-Pn D-8206 [8])[BnF]); *Se tutti i mali miei* (F-Pn MS-8 [3])[BnF])
1769	**mus. by unknown composer(s)**
1769 Valencia	Palace of the Dukes of Gandía (04/11/1769)
	name day of Carlos III, king of Spain
Librettos	Valencia: widow of Orga, 1769
	E-Bbc 1-I-84 [4]; E-Mn T/22285; E-VAu A-105/057 [5]
1770	**mus. by Jommelli, Niccolò (4th version) → see 1743**
1770	**mus. by Vanhal, Johann Baptist**[NG]
1770 Rome	NA, *lost*
1771	**mus. by various unknown composers**
1771 Pavia	Teatro Omodeo (carn.)
Librettos	Pavia: Bolzani, [1771]
	I-Vgc ROL.0680 [9]
Music sources	[excerpts] *Non curo l'affetto*, by W. A. Mozart (CZ-Pu M II 11e [5])[RISM])
	→ see Arie sciolte

---

165. Although the inscription on the source is clear, the manuscript is wrongly dated 1769 in Emerson, *Catalog of Pre-1900 Vocal Manuscripts*, p. 67 no. 299.

MC | *Demofoonte* (1733–1836)

1771	mus. by Sarti, Giuseppe (2nd version) → see 1755	

1771 1771 Bologna	mus. by various unknown composers Teatro Formagliari (08/04/1771)	
Librettos	Bologna: Sassi, [1771] I-Bc Lo.06197; I-Mb Racc.dramm.6240; I-Mr Libr. 04250; I-Rn 40.9.E.6.2; I-Vgc ROL.0680 [7]; I-Vgc ROL.0680 [8]	

1772 1772 Prague	mus. by Koželuh, Jan Antonín Teatro Regio[166] (carn., 27/12/1771)[167]	
Librettos	Prague: Pruscha, [1771] (It./Ger.) CZ-Bu ST1-0121 [782]; CZ-Pu 65 E 2982	
Music sources	[complete scores] CZ-Pnm* IV C 77[MGG,NG,RISM] [excerpts] *Che mai risponderti* (CZ-Pnm XLII E 258[RISM;P]); *In te spero, o sposo amato* (CH-Zz Mus Ms A 1259[SB]); *Padre, perdona… oh pene* (D-HR [D-Au] III 4 1/2 4|o 201[RISM;P]); *Se ardire e speranza* (DK-Sa R94[RISM]); *Sperai vicino il lido* (CZ-Pak 1703[RISM]) [contrafacta] *Il suo leggiadro viso* ([*Beatus vir qui timet Dominum*] CZ-TEk n/s[RISM;P])	

1772 1772 Barcelona	mus. by unknown composer(s) Teatre de la Santa Creu (04/11/1772)[168] *name day of Carlos III, king of Spain*	

1773	mus. by Anfossi, Pasquale	
1773 Rome	Teatro di Torre Argentina (carn., 06/02/1773)	(1)
1773 Florence	Teatro del Cocomero (aut.)	(2)
1774 Macerata	Teatro dei Nobili (carn.)	(3)
1774 Modena	Teatro Ducale (carn.)	(4)
1774 Genoa	Teatro da S. Agostino (spr.) *mus. by P. Anfossi and others*	(5)

---

166. Although the Italian text of the libretto may induce error by naming the theatre as the 'Teatro Nuovo', the German translation is clear: 'Konigl. Prater Teatro'.
167. The libretto dates the performance in the carnival season of 1771, yet there are no accounts thereof until December of that year, i.e., the carnival season of 1772. The 1771 date may be a typographic error; see Hálova, Kamila, 'Il Demofoonte di Jan Evangelista Antonín Koželuh', in *Demofoonte come soggetto per il dramma per musica: Johann Adolf Hasse ed altri compositori del Settecento*, ed. by Milada Jonášová and Tomislav Volek (Prague: Academia, 2020), pp. 213–27.
168. Alier y Aixalà, *L'òpera a Barcelona*.

MC | *Demofoonte* (1733–1836)

Librettos

(1) Rome: Capponi & Bartolomicchi, [1773]
B-Bc 19890; F-Pn YD-5403 [2]; I-Bc Lo.00186;[169] I-Fm Mel.2046 [5]; I-Rsc Libr. n. XVIII [69]

(2) Florence: Pagani, 1773
I-Bc Lo.00187; I-Fc E.V.1742; I-Vgc ROL.0137 [16]

(3) Osimo: Quercetti, 1774
I-MAC 7.5.B.015

(4) Modena: heirs of Soliani, 1774
NA[170]

(5) Genoa: Gesiniana, [1774]
US-CAt TS 8146.30 1774; US-PRV n/s; US-Wc ML48 [S274]

Music sources

[complete scores] D-MÜs SANT Hs 140 [a–c][MGG,NG,RISM,171]; D-B Mus. ms. 19496[RISM,172] [Act III]

[excerpts] *Dall'affanno ho il core oppresso* (F-Pn D-215 [5][BnF,RISM,173]; I-Fc D.I.207 [4][IC,RISM]; I-MC 1-A-8/2 [10][RISM]; US-R n/s[IC,RISM]); *In te spero, o sposo amato* (I-Fc D.I.207 [2][IC,RISM]; I-MC 1-A-7/2 [2][RISM]; I-Rc Mss. 2284 [10][RISM,SBN]); *La destra ti chiedo* (A-SF XII 2[RISM;P]; B-Bc 3654[RISM]; D-Hs M A/831 [2/2][RISM]; D-Mbs Mus.ms. 3953 [2][IC,RISM]; F-BO 646/4 [2][BASE]; F-Pn D-216 [5][BnF,RISM,174]; F-Pn D-220 [5][BnF,RISM,175]; F-Pn D-220 [6][BnF,RISM]; F-Pn D-16000[BnF]; I-Bc CC.214[IC,RISM,SBN]; I-Fc D.I.207 [7][IC,RISM]; I-Mc Mus. Tr.ms. 23[RISM,SBN;P]; I-Mc Noseda A.18 [22][SBN]; I-Mc Noseda A.18 [22a][SBN]; I-MC 1-A-6/8 [6][RISM]; I-MTc A172c[IC,RISM,SBN;IP]; I-Nc 33.4.23 [7][SBN]; I-PAc Sanv.A.32[RISM,SBN]; J-Tk S10-930 [2][RISM]; UA-Knbuv 120501 [11][RISM]; US-Bp M.120.17 [1][IC]; US-BEm MS 109 [7][IC,RISM]; US-R n/s[IC,RISM]); *Misero pargoletto* (B-Br Ms II 4043 Mus Fétis 2622 [4][IC,RISM]; D-B* Mus.ms. 647 [2][RISM,176]; D-Hs M A/831 [1/2][RISM;R]; D-KNmi A 68[RISM]; D-RH Ms 21[RISM;P]; F-Pn D-215 [8][BnF,RISM]; F-Pn D-220 [12][BnF,RISM]; I-Fc D.I.207 [1][IC,RISM]; I-Mc Noseda A.18 [7][SBN]; I-MC 1-A-6/8 [3][RISM]; I-MC 1-A-8/1 [1][RISM]; I-MC 1-A-8/2 [10][RISM]; US-BEm MS 105 [2][IC,RISM]; US-BEm MS 109 [1][IC,RISM]; US-R n/s[IC,RISM]; US-SFsc *M2.1 M13[RISM]); *Odo il suono de' queruli accenti* (I-Fc

---

169. Mutilated on pp. 49–60.
170. According to [C], there was a copy of this libretto in I-FPfanan (previously in Turin); see note 30 above.
171. Microfilm copy: US-CA 6833346.
172. Wrongly attributed to G. Sarti on the source and, consequently, in [MGG,NG].
173. Microfilm copy of all the pieces in F-Pn D-215: F-Pn VM BOB-10089.
174. Microfilm copy: F-Pn VM BOB-18160.
175. Microfilm copy of all the pieces in F-Pn D-220: F-Pn VM BOB-22043.
176. Sketch.

D.I.207 [3]^{IC,RISM}; UA-Knbuv Rozum 120501 [5]^{RISM}); *Padre, perdona… oh pene* (B-Bc 3659^{RISM}; I-Mc Noseda A.18 [3]^{SBN}); *Perfidi, gia ché in vita* (F-BO 646/4 [1]^{BnF}; I-Fc D.I.207 [6]^{IC,RISM}); *Per lei fra l'armi dorme il guerriero* (I-Fc D.I.207 [5]^{IC,RISM}; I-MAav Cart.5 n.21$^{RISM;P}$; UA-Knbuv Rozum 120501 [7]^{RISM}; S-Sm n/s$^{RISM;IP,177}$); *Se tutti i mali miei* (UA-Knbuv Rozum 120501 [8]^{RISM}); *Son fra l'onde, in mar turbato* (I-Rc Mss. 5667$^{IC,RISM,SBN;IP}$)

[contrafacta] *La destra ti chiedo* ([*Ich sterbe Geliebte*] D-Mbs Mus.ms. 3103 [2]$^{RISM;R}$; [*O anima, veni*] D-KA Don Mus.Ms. 16^{RISM}); *Sperai vicino il lido* ([*Protector meus Deus*] CH-E 382,6$^{RISM;P}$; [*O Deus in te unico spem omnem*] CH-BM Mus.Ms. 3 [2]$^{RISM;P}$)

[inserts] [Florence, 1773] *A morir se mi condanna* (US-R n/s^{IC,RISM}); *Sperai vicino il lido*[178] by Pasquale Anfossi (B-Bc 3665^{RISM}; CH-Gc Rmo 123/11 [1]^{RISM}; CH-BM Mus.Ms. 3 [1]$^{RISM;P}$; CZ-BER HU 630$^{RISM;P}$; D-B* Mus.ms. 647 [3]^{RISM,179}; D-HR [D-Au] III 4 1/2 2° 1084$^{RISM;P}$; D-Mbs Mus.ms. 10418$^{RISM;P}$; I-Rc Mss. 2284 [9]^{RISM}; US-LAuc FA6964M4 [19]^{RISM}; US-SFsc *M2.5 v.12 [4]^{RISM})

[Genoa, 1774] *Se tutti i mali miei*, by Giusto Ferdinando Tenducci (I-Rama A.Ms.2605 [4]^{RISM}; I-Rama A.Ms.2711 [1]^{RISM}; US-R n/s^{IC,RISM})

1773	mus. by Berezovskij, Maksim Sozontovič^{NG}
1773 Livorno	NA [Teatro da S. Sebastiano?]
Music sources	[excerpts][180] *Mentre il cor con meste voci* (I-Fc D.I.207 [12]^{IC,RISM,SBN}); *Misero pargoletto* (I-Fc D.I.207 [10]^{IC,RISM,SBN}); *Per lei fra l'armi dorme il guerriero* (I-Fc D.I.207 [11]^{IC,RISM,SBN}); *Prudente mi chiedi?* (I-Fc D.I.207 [13]^{IC,RISM,SBN})
1775	mus. by Mysliveček, Josef (2nd version) → see 1769
1775 Venice	mus. by Paisiello, Giovanni
1775 Venice	Teatro Grimani di S. Benedetto (carn.) (1)
1776 Cremona	Teatro Nazari (carn.) (2)

177. Given as anonymous in ^{RISM}.
178. This aria, originally for the character of Timante in *Demofoonte*, was inserted into P. Anfossi's setting of *Alessandro nell'Indie* (Rome, 1772), sung by the character of Gandarte in A1-S11. It was later used in the revival of his *Demofoonte* in Venice in 1773.
179. Sketch.
180. Photocopies of the following excerpts: CH-Gpu Ib 3436.

MC | *Demofoonte* (1733–1836)

1776 Perugia	Teatro del Pavone (carn., 17/01/1776)	(3)

Librettos
(1) Venice: Fenzo, 1775
D-Bs Mus. Tp 124; D-Sl Fr.D.oct 5066; F-Pn 8-YTH-51113; F-Pn 8-YTH-51548; I-Bc Lo.03809; I-BDG REC 97.A.12 [9]; I-Mb Racc. dramm.4001; I-Vcg LIBRETTI S.BENEDETTO 191; I-Vnm DRAMM.1102 [3]; I-Vnm DRAMM.1315 [7]; US-BEm ML48 .I7 [458]; US-Wc ML48 [S7698]

(2) Cremona: Manini, [1776]
I-CRg CIV.A.30.E.147; I-Fc E.VI.3926; I-SORmde LA.038

(3) Perugia: Costantini, 1776
I-PEc ANT Misc. I.C 50 [8]; I-Vgc ROL.0509 [12]

Music sources
[complete scores] F-Pn D-10150[BnF,MGG,181]; I-Mc* Part. Tr.ms. 305[IC,182]; P-La 45-III-34[BA,MGG,NG]

[excerpts] *Che mai risponderti* (GB-Cfm [GB-Cu] MU.MS.222[IC]); *Da qual vezzosi rai* (GB-Cfm [GB-Cu] MU.MS.222[IC]); *In te spero, o sposo amato* (H-KE 189 Koll.9[RISM]; I-Vnm Mss. 11337[SBN]); *La destra ti chiedo* (D-B Mus.ms. 16644 [3][RISM]); *Misero pargoletto* (B-Bc 5362[RISM]; D-B Mus.ms. 16607 [5][RISM]; D-B Mus.ms. 16607 [20][RISM]; F-Pn D-14465 [3][BnF,183]; GB-Cfm [GB-Cu] MU.MS.222[IC]; GB-Lbl R.M.22.k.5 [3][BL,RISM;P]; I-Fn MUS 207 [1][RISM]; I-Pca D.VI.1812[SBN;P]; I-Rrostirolla [I-Fn] MS MUS 207 [1][RISM,SBN;IP,184]; I-Vnm Mss. 11323[IC,SBN]; US-BEm MS 1284[RISM]; US-BEm MS 1285[RISM]); *Non temer, bell'idol mio* (B-Bc 4530[RISM]; CH-Gc X 5 [20][RISM;R]; CH-Zz Mus Ms A 147[SB]; CZ-Pnm XLII A 34[RISM;IP]; CZ-Pnm XLII B 163[RISM;P]; CZ-Pnm XLII C 101[RISM;P]; D-B Mus.ms. 647 [15][RISM]; D-B Mus.ms. 16607/5 [4][RISM]; D-Dl Mus.1-F-82,20 [9][RISM]; D-Hs M A/830 [2][RISM]; D-KA Don Mus.Ms. 1514[RISM]; D-Mbs Mus.ms. 8738 [18][RISM]; F-Pn A-35232[BnF]; F-Pn D-9643 [8][BnF]; F-Pn D-12026 [1][BnF]; F-Pn D-12028 [16][BnF]; F-Pn D-14453 [8][BnF]; F-Pn D-14465 [2][BnF]; F-Pn L-19245[BnF]; GB-Lbl R.M.22.k.5 [2][BL,RISM;P]; I-Baf Fondo antico 2597[SBN;P]; I-FZc A.VI.4 [2][RISM,SBN]; I-Gl B C.3.20 [5][IC,SBN]; I-MAav Cart.20 n.75[RISM;P]; I-Mc Noseda O.5 [8][MGG,NG,SBN]; I-Nc 32.3.14 [13][MGG,SBN]; I-Pca D. VI.1820[SBN]; I-Rsc G.Mss.515[SBN]; I-Vc Correr Busta 4.20[SBN]; I-Vc Correr Busta 4.21[SBN]; I-Vlevi CF.B.65[RISM] [*Che sarà dell'idol mio*];

---
181. Microfilm copies: F-Pn VM BOB-25622; US-PRu MICROFILM 1822.
182. Microfilm copy: US-PRu MICROFILM 1821.
183. Microfilm copy of all the pieces in F-Pn D-14465: F-Pn VM BOB-31588.
184. All the pieces in I-Rrostirolla [I-Fn] MS MUS 207: Vn parts only.

I-VEcon MS 299[RISM,SBN;P]; PL-ŁA RM 222 [4][RISM]; S-Skma T-SE-R[RISM]; S-Skma Alströmer saml. 162 [27][RISM;R]; US-CAe Mus 503.603 [6][IC,RISM]; US-LOu Profana 1418[RISM]); *Perfidi, già che in vita* (GB-Cfm [GB-Cu] MU.MS.222[IC]); *Risorgera più bella* (GB-Cfm [GB-Cu] MU.MS.222[IC]); *Se tutti i mali miei* (D-B Mus.ms. 16607/5 [2][RISM]; GB-Cfm [GB-Cu] MU.MS.222[IC]; I-OS Mss.Mus.B 2582[RISM,SBN]; I-Vnm Mss. 11323[SBN]; US-Bu H. C. Robbins Landon Collection, Scores |x781A, Box 6 [25][RISM;R]; US-SFsc *M2.5 v.14 [5][RISM]); *Sperai vicino il lido* (D-B Mus.ms. 16607/5 [1][RISM]; F-Pn D-14465 [1][BnF]; GB-Lbl R.M.22.k.5 [1][BL,RISM;IP]; I-Rdp Ms Musicale 98 [59][SBN]; I-Rrostirolla [I-Fn] MS MUS 207 [2][RISM,RISM;IP]; I-Vnm Mss. 11319 [9][SBN]); *Tu sai chi son; tu sai* (GB-Cfm [GB-Cu] MU.MS.222[IC])

[printed sources] *Misero pargoletto* [2]; *Non temer, bell'idol mio* [3]; *Sperai vicino il lido* [1], in *Due arie e un rondò nel Demofoonte* (Venice: Zatta & sons, [s.d.]); *Non temer, bell'idol mio* [14], in *Journal d'ariettes italiennes* (Paris: Bailleux, 1779)

[contrafacta] *Non temer, bell'idol mio* ([Hallelujah singt ihm Lieder] D-B Mus.ms. 20560 [5][RISM;P]; [Ganz umsonst sind meine Tränen] CH-Bu kr IV 414[RISM;R])

1775	mus. by Jommelli, Niccolò (3rd rev. version) → see 1743	
1776	mus. by Schuster, Joseph Anton	
1776 Forlì	Teatro Pubblico (spr.)	(1)
1777 Pavia	Teatro dei Quattro Cavalieri Associati (carn.)	(2)
Librettos	(1) Forlì: Barbiani, [1776]	
	I-FZc RM.N.3.219	
	(2) Pavia: Bolzani, [1777][185]	
	I-LDEsormani 314/3/16; <u>US-Wc ML48 [S9760]</u>	
Music sources	[complete scores] D-Dl* Mus.3549-F-5[MGG,NG,RISM]; D-Dl Mus.3549-F-6[MGG,NG,RISM]; F-Pn D-13963 [1–2][BnF,MGG,NG]; I-Tf 1 IV 16/17[RISM] [Acts II&III]; P-La 46-V-24/25/26[BA]	
	[excerpts] *La destra ti chiedo* (D-Dl Mus.3549-F-510[RISM]; I-FZc B.V.2 [3][RISM,SBN]; I-Nc 64.41[SBN]); *Misero pargoletto* (D-Dl Mus.3549-F-7 [1][RISM]); *Non temer, bell'idol mio* (B-Bc 4882[RISM]; CZ-Pk 3186[RISM]; <u>D-Dl Mus.3549-F-35 [3]</u>[RISM]; <u>D-Dl Mus.3549-F-35 [9]</u>[RISM]; <u>D-Dl Mus.3549-</u>	

185. According to [C], there was a copy of this libretto in I-FPfanan; see note 30 above.

F-38[RISM;IP]; D-Eu Esl VIII 598d[RISM]; I-FZc B.V.2 [1][RISM,SBN]; I-FZc B.V.3 [3][RISM,SBN]; I-MC 5-F-24 [7][RISM]; I-Nc 6.3.26 [11][SBN]; I-Nc 34.3.18[SBN]); *Per lei fra l'armi dorme il guerriero* (D-Dl Mus.3549-F-35 [11][RISM]; D-Dl Mus.3796-F-502[RISM]); *Se non mostrano gli dèi* (B-Bc 4886[RISM]; D-Dl Mus.1-F-49,4 [23][RISM]; D-Dl Mus.3549-F-49,4 [23][RISM]; D-MGmi HA IV 147[RISM;P]; D-RH Ms 924 [1][RISM;P]; S-Skma SO-R[RISM]); *Sperai vicino il lido* (D-Dl Mus.3549-F-8[RISM]; I-FZc B.V.3 [2][RISM,SBN]); *Tu sai chi son; tu sai* (D-Dl Mus.3549-F-511[RISM]); *Vanne da questo istante* (D-Dl Mus.3549-F-509[RISM])

[contrafacta] *In te spero, o sposo amato* ([*Jesu dulcis momoria, dans vera cordis gaudia*] D-NEZkpn 2/40[RISM;P]); *Per lei fra l'armi dorme il guerriero* ([*Per lei nel foco vado contento*] D-Dl Mus.3549-F-36 [1][RISM]; D-Dl Mus.3796-F-502 [2][RISM]); *Sperai vicino il lido* ([*Huc mente devota*] PL-Wu RM 4970[RISM;P])

[doubtful] *Padre, perdona... oh pene* (I-FZc B.V.3 [1][RISM,SBN,186]); *Se ardire e sperare*[187] (I-FZc B.V.2 [2][RISM,SBN]; I-FZc B.V.3 [4][RISM,SBN])

1776	mus. by Monza, Carlo Ignazio
1776 Alessandria	Teatro Nuovo (Oct. Fair)
Librettos	Alessandria: Vimercati, 1776 I-Tci L.O.0289
Music sources	[excerpts] *Misero pargoletto* (CZ-Pnm XLII A 320[RISM]; D-B Mus.ms. 30119 [8][IC,RISM]; D-KA Don Mus.Ms. 1345[RISM]; S-Skma Engsö saml. [RISM]); *Non temer, bell'idol mio* (D-B Mus.ms. 30136 [18][IC,RISM]; I-MAav Cart.20 n.6 [61][MGG,NG,RISM;P]) [printed sources] *Misero pargoletto* [5], in *The Favourite Songs in the Opera Demofoonte* (London: Napier, [1778?]) → see 1778, mus. mainly by Bertoni, Ferdinando
1778	mus. mainly by Bertoni, Ferdinando Gasparo; with arias by Mysliveček, Josef; Monza, Carlo; and Sarti, Giuseppe lib. adap. by Andrei, Antonio or Badini, Carlo Francesco
1778 London	King's Theatre in the Haymarket (28/11/1778)[188] (1)

---

186. The setting is different from that in P-La 46-V-24/25/26.
187. This aria was not included in Schuster's premiere or in the later revival in Pavia.
188. The production ran for fourteen consecutive performances; see Petty, 'Italian opera in London', p. 202 and Price, Curtis, Judith Milhous, and Robert D. Hume, *Italian Opera in Late Eighteenth-Century London*, vol. 1:

MC | *Demofoonte* (1733–1836)

1784 London	King's Theatre in the Haymarket (04/03/1784)[189]	(2)

Librettos
(1) London: Bigg, 1778 (It./En.)
B-Bc 19892; F-Pn RES VS-601; GB-DRu SC 07776/3; GB-Lbl 907.i.16 [8];[190] GB-Ob Vet.A5 e.7094; US-CAt TS 8149.73 1778; US-Wc ML48 [S911][191]

(2) London: Reynell, 1784 (It./En.)
CH-Lz V.1077.8 [K2]; CDN-Mlr PR1269 H63 [72]

Music sources
[excerpts] *Non temer, bell'idol mio* by Bertoni (D-KNh R 738[RISM]; F-Pn D-15324[BnF]; J-Tk S10-934 [5][RISM]; US-LAum MS 22[RISM]); *Per lei fra l'armi dorme il guerriero* (US-LAuc FA6964M4 [2][RISM]); *Teco resti, anima mia* by Sarti (F-MOa MS34[BASE]; F-MOc Ms 34[BASE]; S-Skma T-SE-R[RISM]; US-Eu MSS 938[IC])

[printed sources] *In te spero, o sposo amato* [2] by Mysliveček; *Misero pargoletto* [5] by Monza; *Non temer, bell'idol mio* [1] by Bertoni; *Padre, perdona... oh pene* [7] by Mysliveček; *Se i detti miei comprendi* [4] by Bertoni; *Sperai vicino il lido* [3] by Bertoni; *Teco resti, anima mia* [6] by Sarti, in <u>The Favourite Songs in the Opera Demofoonte</u> (London: Napier, [1778?]); *Dall'affanno ho il core oppresso* by Anfossi, in *Dall' affanno ho il core* (London: Houston & Hyde, [1784?]); in *Dall' affanno ho il core* (London: Bland, [1784?]); *Non temer, bell'idol mio* by Bertoni, in <u>Non temer [...] Demofoonte [...], Sung by sigr Pacchierotti</u> (London: Dale, [c. 1788])

Demofoonte, in *Opere del signor abate Pietro Metastasio* (Paris: widow of Hérissant, 1780), vol. 4, pp. 151–262.

1780	mus. by unknown composer(s)
1780 Pisa	Teatro Prini (27/03/1780)

Librettos
Pisa: Pieraccini, 1780
I-PIu Franceschi Busta 1. 23; I-PSrospigliosi [I-PS] BM.258 [3]; I-Vgc ROL.0709 [8][192]

The King's Theatre, Haymarket 1778–1791 (Oxford: Clarendon Press, 1995). It coincided with Pacchierotti's London debut.
189. The production ran for seven consecutive performances; see Petty, 'Italian opera in London', p. 249 and Price, Milhous, and Hume, *Italian Opera in Late*, p. 297.
190. Microfilm copies: D-Gs MA 2001-46:13777 [24]; GB-En Mf.134, reel 13777 [24].
191. Copy: D-KNmi FH 1186.
192. Microfilm copy: CDN-Lu ML48.M47T38 1787a.

MC | *Demofoonte* (1733–1836)

1780	mus. by Rust, Giacomo
1780 Florence	Teatro della Pergola (26/10/1780)[193]
Librettos	Florence: Risaliti, 1780
	I-Fc E.V.1739;[194] I-PSrospigliosi [I-PS] BM.257 [15]
Music sources	[excerpts] *Sperai vicino il lido* (D-B Mus.ms. 19143 [5][RISM]; D-B Mus. ms. 19143 [6][RISM]); *Non temer, bell'idol mio* (I-Gl FONDO ANT. NN.256[IC,MGG,SBN]; I-Rrostirolla [I-Fn] MS MUS 1023[RISM;IP]); *Flebil suon di mesti accenti* (D-Dl Mus.1-F-82,24 [7][RISM])

1780–1790	mus. by various unknown composers
1780–1790 Rio de Janeiro	
Music sources	[complete scores] P-VV G-Prática 51b[IC,195]

1781	mus. by Bianchi, Francesco and Anfossi, Pasquale[S,196]
1781 Genoa	Teatro da S. Agostino (spr.)
Librettos	Genoa: Gesiniana, 1781
	I-Fc E.VI.4529; I-Mr Libr. 04249; S-Uu n/s
Music sources	[excerpts] *Luci amate, se volete* (CZ-Pnm XLII C 72[RISM]; <u>D-Dl Mus.1-J-12 [10]</u>[RISM]; GB-Lbl R.M.22.a.23 [1][BL,RISM]); *Misero pargoletto* (CH-Gmu BMU RA 343[IC]; I-MC 1-C-1 [8][RISM]); *Prudente mi chiedi?* (GB-Lbl R.M.22.a.25 [1][BL,RISM])
	[doubtful] *Sperai vicino il lido* (I-Rsc G.Mss.221 [7][RISM,197])
	[printed sources] *Misero pargoletto*, in *Cahier d'ariettes italiennes* ([s.l.: s.n., c. 1780])

1781	mus. by unknown composer(s)
1781 Pavia	Teatro dei Quattro Cavalieri Associati (spr.)
Librettos	Pavia: [s.n.], 1781
	<u>I-Mb Racc.dramm.6082 [7]</u>; I-PAc F. Libretti, sc.110 [72]; I-Vc 1027

---

193. [CA] gives 25/10/1780.
194. Microfilm copy: CDN-Lu ML48.M47V545 1781a.
195. Among the *Demofoonte* arias, it contains a *Padre, perdona... oh pene* by an unknown composer; *Sono in mar, non veggo sponde* by G. di Majo; *La destra ti chiedo* by P. A. Guglielmi; and *Misero pargoletto* by D. Perez. Information found in Budasz, Rogério, 'Demofonte: A Luso-Brazilian pastiche?', *Diagonal*, 1.2 (2016), 52–81.
196. [S]Index I, p. 343.
197. → see 1783, mus. by Alessandri, Felice.

MC | *Demofoonte* (1733–1836)

1782 1782 Palermo	mus. by Gazzaniga, Giuseppe Teatro di Santa Cecilia (carn.)
Librettos	Palermo: Picciotto, 1782 US-BEm ML48 .S5 [120]

1782	mus. by Sarti, Giuseppe (3rd version) → see 1755

1782 1782 Lucca	mus. by various composers (incl. Bianchi, Francesco) Teatro Pubblico (aut., 27/07/1782)
Librettos	Lucca: Bonsignori, 1782[198] I-Rc Misc.Dramm.A.23 [3];[199] I-Rig Rar. Libr. Op. 18. Jh. 275; I-Vgc ROL.0680 [10];[200] US-CAt TS 8146.428 1782
Music sources	[excerpts] *Ah perché, se mia tu sei* by F. Bianchi[201] (D-B Mus.ms. 1758 [10][RISM]; D-Hs M A/830 [12][RISM]; D-MÜs SANT Hs 3843[RISM]; D-W Cod. Guelf. 303 Mus. Hdschr. [2][RISM]; F-Pn D-1098 [7][BnF,RISM]; F-Pn D-1101 [6][BnF,RISM]; F-Pn D-1101 [11][BnF,RISM]; GB-WMl Music Manuscript 17 [1][RISM]; I-FZc B.V.1 [3][RISM,SBN]; I-Rsc G.Mss.216 [6][RISM])

1783 1783 Modena	mus. by Pio, Antonio Teatro Rangoni (carn.)
Librettos	Modena: heirs of Soliani, [1783] I-MOe M.T.Ferr.Mor.27 [19]; US-Wc ML48.A5 vol. 30 [1]
Music sources	[excerpts] *La destra ti chiedo* (S-Skma Alströmer saml. 164 [8][RISM])

1783 1783 Padua	mus. by Alessandri, Felice Teatro Nuovo (Fair, 12/06/1783)
Librettos	Padua: Conzatti, [1783] B-Br Fétis 4.488 A XIII/5 Mus.;[202] I-Pmc[C,S]; I-Psaggiori[C,S]; I-Vcg LIBRETTI PADOVA 57 E 64
Music sources	[complete scores] I-Pl ATVa 13 [I–II][NG,RISM,SBN;P]; P-La 47-II-11/12[BA,NG] [Acts II&III]

198. According to [S], there was a copy of this libretto in I-FPfanan; see note 30 above.
199. Wrongly dated 1728 in the library's card catalogue.
200. Microfilm copy: CDN-Lu ML48.M47T38 1787a.
201. This aria was taken from F. Bianchi's *Il trionfo della pace* (Turin, 1782).
202. Microfilm copy: CDN-Lu ML48.M47L442 1783a.

[excerpts] *La destra ti chiedo* (D-BFb [D-MÜu] A-le 80[RISM;P]; D-HR [D-Au] III 4 1/2 4° 125[RISM]; F-Pn D-61 [6][BnF,MGG,RISM]); *Misero pargoletto* (CZ-Pn Kinsky Ms 102 [2][RISM]; I-OS Mss.Mus.B 276[RISM,SBN]); *Nel partir da te, ben mio* (US-Eu MSS 1028[IC,MGG,RISM]); *Prudente mi chiedi?* (HR-Dsmb 1/15[RISM]; I-Raf 1.E.1.II[RISM]; I-Tf 9 III 19 [12][RISM;P]; I-Rc Mss. 2540 [2][SBN]); *Sperai vicino il lido* (GB-Lbl R.M.23.c.19 [3][BL,RISM]; I-Rsc G.Mss.221 [7][RISM,SBN,203]; US-Eu MSS 924[IC,MGG,RISM])

[parodies] *Sperai vicino il lido* ([*Non temo il fasto insano*] I-MC 5-F-2 [5][RISM,204])

1786	mus. by Tarchi, Angelo	
1786 Crema	Teatro di Crema (24/09/1786) *opening of the theatre*	(1)
1787 Reggio Emilia	Teatro Pubblico (Fair, 25/06/1787)	(2)
1791 Pavia	Teatro dei Quattro Cavalieri Associati (carn., 20/01/1791)	(3)
1791 Livorno	Teatro degli Avvalorati (aut.) *with mus. by Vittorio Trento*[NG]	(4)
1793 Modena	Teatro Rangoni (carn., after 21/01/1793)	(5)
Librettos	(1) Milan: Bianchi, [1786]	

D-Mbs L.eleg.m. 3997; I-BRq 7a.F.fII.16m6; I-Ma S. I. H. II. 52 [3]; I-Mr Libr. 04252; I-PAc F. Libretti, sc.110 [73]; I-Rb LIB.MUS 085; I-Vgc ROL.0109 [1]; I-Vnm DRAMM.1123 [8]; US-CAt TS 8146.653 1786; US-Wc ML48 [S10218]

(2) Reggio Emilia: Davolio, [1787]
I-Bl FS.W.1884; I-Bl FS.W.1890; I-PAc F. Libretti, sc.110 [74]; I-Rb LIB.MUS 030; I-Rsc Libr. n. XIX [41]; I-REm 19.K.57; I-REm Racc. Dram. E. Curti 151 [17]; I-Vc 1028; I-Vc 1029; I-Vgc ROL.0709 [9];[205] US-Cn ML50.2.D4 M47 1787

(3) Pavia: Galeazzi, [1791]
I-Bc Lo.07659; I-BRq Misc.E.824; I-Mr Libr. 04253; I-TRsf ffb-A 369; I-Vgc ROL.1197 [6][206]

---

203. Wrongly attributed to F. Bianchi on source. Although no comparison with a complete source for Alessandri's setting has been possible, the inscriptions on the two other sources point towards him as the composer of this aria.
204. Wrongly attributed to G. Sarti on source.
205. Microfilm copy: CDN-Lu ML48.M47T38 1787a.
206. Microfilm copy: CDN-Lu ML48.M47P53 1792a.

MC | *Demofoonte* (1733–1836)

(4) [Livorno]: Masi & co., 1791

I-Fc E.VI.5623;[207] I-Fm Mel.2073 [4]; I-Gl P.4.20.3; I-LI RM b.259 [17]; I-Rsc Carv.4248

(5) Modena: heirs of Soliani, [1793]

I-FPfanan;[208] I-MOe M.T.Ferr.Mor.12 [15]; I-MOe MD.K.2 [9]

Music sources   [complete scores] F-Pn D-2093/2094/2095[BnF,209]

[excerpts] *Non temer, bell'idol mio* (I-MC 6-A-15 [6][RISM]; I-Vnm Mss. 11339[SBN]); *La destra ti chiedo* (I-Mc Mus. Tr.ms. 1265[MGG,NG,RISM,SBN]; I-PAc Sanv.A.110[RISM,SBN]); *Sperai vicino il lido* (US-Wc M1505.A1 (vol. 217) [3][RISM])

1787 mus. by Prati, Alessio
1787 Venice Teatro Grimani di S. Benedetto (carn., 26/12/1786)

Librettos   Venice: Fenzo, 1787

B-Br Fétis 4.488 A XV/8 Mus; F-Pn LIV IT-37; F-Pn LIV IT-1620; F-Pn 8-YTH-51121; F-Pn 8-YTH-51646; I-Fc E.V.1369; I-Mb Racc. dramm.4432; I-Rsc Carv.4249; I-Vcg LIBRETTI S.BENEDETTO 196;[210] I-Vlevi Dramm. 757; I-Vnm DRAMM.1116 [8]; I-Vnm DRAMM.1339 [8]; US-Wc ML48 [S8454]

Music sources   [complete scores] P-La 46-II-25/26/27[BA,NG]

[excerpts] *Non temer, bell'idol mio* (I-BEc Miari AM.ms104[RISM,SBN;P]); *Padre, perdona... oh pene* (D-Hs ND VI 2688 a[RISM;R,P])

1787 mus. by Gatti, Luigi
1787 Mantua Teatro Regio Ducale (spr., 12/05/1787)

Librettos   Mantua: heirs of Pazzoni, [1787]

I-MAc Misc.358/12;[211] US-AUS KL-17 256

---

207. Microfilm copy: CDN-Lu ML48.M47V545 1781a.
208. According to [S], there was a copy of this libretto in I-FPfanan; see note 30 above.
209. Doubtfully attributed to D. Cimarosa, as there are no records that he composed a *Demofoonte*. The manuscript has the inscription 'Livorno 1791' and also mentions Luigi Montanari, who sung the role of Cherinto in Venice that same year but not in Livorno → see 1788, mus. by Pugnani, Gaetano; microfilm copy: F-Pn VM BOB-31323.
210. Microfilm copies: CDN-Lu ML48.M4G287 1762aa; CDN-Lu ML48.M47P664 1786a.
211. Microfilm copy: CDN-Lu ML48.M47G378 1787a.

MC | *Demofoonte* (1733–1836)

Music sources	[excerpts] *Quest'amplesso e quest'addio* (I-Rsc G.Mss.216 [9][MGG,NG,RISM]; S-Skma T-SE-R[MGG,NG,RISM]); *La destra ti chiedo* (I-MAav Cart.4 n.1[MGG,NG,RISM;P]); *Padre, perdona… oh pene* (S-Skma T-SE-R[MGG,NG,RISM])

1787	mus. by unknown composer(s)
1787 Modena	Teatro Rangoni (spr.)
Librettos	Modena: Zerbini, [1787] US-Cn BLC #276a

1787	mus. by various unknown composers
1787 Livorno	Teatro degli Armeni (aut.)
Librettos	Livorno: Falorni, [1787] I-Fm n/s

1788	mus. by Pugnani, Gaetano	
1788 Turin	Teatro Regio (carn., 26/12/1787)[212]	(1)
1791 Venice	Teatro Grimani di S. Benedetto (carn.) mus. by G. Pugnani and others?[213]	(2)
Librettos	(1) Turin: Derossi, [1787] B-Bc 19893; D-Mbs L.eleg.m. 4011; F-Pn 8-BL-7238; F-Pn 8-BL-7239; F-Pn 8-BL-7240; F-Pn 8-BL-7241; I-Bc Lo.08933; I-NOVc CIV 194.G.25; I-PAc F. Libretti, sc.110 [75]; I-Rsc Vol. Carv.158 [3]; I-Rsc Libr. n. XIX [40]; I-Tac Simeom L 123 (?); I-Tci L.O.0404; I-Tn F XIII.498 [3]; I-Tbgg P.i.107/7.5; I-Tstrona^S; I-Vgc ROL.0558 [3]; I-Vnm DRAMM.3262 [5]; US-BEm ML48 .I7 [590]; US-NYp *MGTY-Res.; US-Wc ML48 [S8504] (2) Venice: Fenzo, 1791 A-Wmi BT-560; F-Pn 8-YTH-51136; F-Pn 8-YTH-51660; I-Bc Lo.06199; I-Rsc Carv.4251; I-Vcg LIBRETTI S.BENEDETTO 198; I-Vnm DRAMM.1118 [8]; I-Vnm DRAMM.1347 [9]	
Music sources	[complete scores] F-Pn D-12808[BnF,MGG,NG] [Act I]; P-La 46-II-40[BA,MGG,NG] [excerpts] *Del trono Augusto* (D-Dl Mus.3350-F-1 [8][RISM]); *In te spero, o sposo amato* (D-Dl Mus.3350-F-1 [1][RISM]); *La destra ti chiedo* (D-Dl Mus.3350-F-1 [6][RISM]); *Misero pargoletto* (D-B Mus.ms. 30135	

---

212. The production ran for eleven consecutive performances; see Bouquet, Gualerzi, and Testa, *Storia del Teatro Regio di Torino*, pp. 77, 158.
213. → see the description of the music source in 1791, mus. by unknown composer(s).

[21]^(IC,NG,RISM); D-Mbs Mus.ms. 6798^(IC,RISM); I-BGc 236.41^(RISM,SBN,214); I-Mc Mus. Tr.ms. 1075^(RISM,SBN); J-Tk S10-931 [4]^(RISM)); *Perfidi già che in vita* (D-Dl Mus.3350-F-1 [7]^(RISM)); *Prudente mi chiedi?* (CH-Gc M 102^(RISM); D-Rtt Pugnani 9^(RISM,215); I-Mc Mus. Tr.ms. 1078^(RISM,SBN); I-VEcon MS 321^(RISM,SBN); J-Tk S10-931 [5]^(RISM); US-SFsc *M2.5 v.60^(RISM)); *Sperai vicino* (D-Dl Mus.3350-F-1 [2]^(RISM))

1788	mus. by various unknown composers
1788 Florence	Teatro della Pergola (17/10/1788)
Librettos	Florence: Albizziniana, [1788] F-Pn LIV IT-1621; <u>I-Bc Lo.06198</u>; I-Fc E.V.0524; I-Fc E.V.0525; I-Fc E.VI.3270; I-Vnm DRAMM.3262 [4][216]
1788	mus. by Cherubini, Luigi
1788 Paris	Opéra (02/12/1788) *Démophon* (Fr. only)
1789	mus. by Vogel, Johann Christoph lib. adap. by Desriaux, Philippe
1789 Paris	Opéra (22/09/1789) *Démophon* (Fr. only)
1789	mus. by Zingarelli, Niccolò Antonio?[217]
1789 Trieste	Teatro Regio (1)
1795 Venice	Teatro La Fenice (aut., 25/11/1795) (2) *pasticcio*[218]
Librettos	(1) NA (2) Venice: Valvasense, [1795] F-Pn 8-YTH-51206; I-Bc Lo.06200; I-Fm Mel.2190 [13]; <u>I-Mb Racc. dramm.4702</u>; I-Pmc^S; I-Vcg LIBRETTI LA FENICE 203; I-Vmc RAV 103729; I-Vmc Rava H.175; I-Vnm DRAMM.1352 [10]; <u>I-Vt 030</u>

214. This and the following two sources: for Venice 1791.
215. D-Rtt Pugnani 9; I-Mc Mus. Tr.ms. 1078; J-Tk S10-931 [5]; and US-SFsc *M2.5 v.60: in F major instead of G major; for Venice 1791.
216. Microfilm copy: CDN-Lu ML48.M47A46 1791a.
217. The attribution to Zingarelli appears in the online archive of the Teatro La Fenice, where it is stated that the Venetian version of the opera was premiered in 1789 in Trieste. We have found no information about the production in Trieste, or about Zingarelli's authorship for the Venetian revival.
218. Bellina, Anna Laura, 'Metastasio in Venezia: appunti per una recensio', *Italianistica: Rivista di letteratura italiana*, 13.1–2 (1984), 145–73.

1790	mus. by Federici, Vincenzo
1790 London	King's Theatre in the Haymarket (06/04/1790)[219]
	L'usurpator innocente
Librettos	London: Hammond & Cane, 1790 (It./En.)
	CDN-Ttfl Itp Pam 01932; F-Pn YD-5528 [5]; GB-Lbl 162.g.31;[220] I-Bc Lo.01580; US-Cn V 4609 .038[221]
Music sources	[excerpts] *Misero pargoletto* (GB-Lbl Add. 31817[BL,RISM;R]); *Prudente mi chiedi?* (D-B Mus.ms. 6094[RISM]; GB-Lbl Add. 31812[RISM;R]); *Sperai vicino il lido* (J-Tk S10-931 [3][RISM])
	[printed sources] *Che mai felici dei*, in *Che mai felici dei. Cavatina, Sung by Madam Mara in the Opera L'Usurpator innocente* (London: Longman & Broderip, [1790]); *La destra ti chiedo*, in *La destra ti chiedo, a Favorite Duett; Sung by Madame Mara, and Signor Marchesi, etc.* ([London]: Holland, [1790]); *Misero pargoletto*, in *Misero, misero pargoletto: A Favorite Song, Sung by Sigr Marchesi, in the New Serious Opera of L'usurpator innocente* ([London]: Holland, [1790]); *Prudente mi chiedi?*, in *Prudente mi chiedi: Sung by Signor Marchesi in the Opera of L'Usurpator innocente* ([London]: Holland, [1790]); *Se ti perdo, o caro bene*, in *Se ti perdo, o caro bene. Rondo, sung by Madam Mara in the Opera L'Usurpator innocente* (London: Longman & Broderip, [1790]); *Sposa amata a questo addio*, in *Sposa amata a questo addio, a favorite Rondo, Sung by Sigr Marchesi* ([London]: Holland, [1790])

1790	mus. by various composers (incl. Federici, Vincenzo?)
1790 Madrid?	NA
	El Demofoonte: Inocente usurpador
Librettos	Madrid: [s.n.], 1791 (It.?/Spa.)
	E-Mn T/12223; US-Eu Spanish Plays no.7590

1791	mus. by various composers? (incl. Nicolini, Giuseppe)
1791 Rome	Teatro delle Dame (carn.)
Music sources	[excerpts] Nicolini, Giuseppe, *Questo mio cor ti lascio* (US-SFsc *M2.5 v.64[RISM])

---

219. The production ran for fifteen consecutive performances; Petty, 'Italian Opera in London', p. 314 and Price, Milhous, and Hume, *Italian opera in Late*, p. 423.
220. Microfilm copies: D-Gs MA 2004-14:15151 [23]; GB-En Mf.134, reel 15151 [23].
221. Microfilm copy: NZ-Wt REng ANDR Quin 1780.

MC | *Demofoonte* (1733–1836)

1792	mus. by unknown composer(s)	
1792 Genoa	Teatro da S. Agostino (carn.)	
Librettos	Genoa: Gesiniana, [1792]	
	I-Gc B.S.Misc.A.26.10	

1794	mus. by Portugal, Marcos António	
1794 Milan	Teatro alla Scala (08/02/1794)	(1)
	1ˢᵗ version	
1808 Lisbon	Teatro de São Carlos (15/08/1808)	(2)
	birthday of Napoleon Bonaparte	
	2ⁿᵈ version	
1819 Lisbon	Teatro de São Carlos (25/04/1819)	(3)
	birthday of Carlota Joaquina, queen of Portugal	

Librettos (1) Milan: Bianchi, [1794]
B-Bc 19894;[222] B-Br Fétis 4.488 A XX,3 Mus; CDN-Ttfl Itp Pam 00778; F-Pn LIV IT-1622; F-Pn LIV IT-3549 [4]; GB-Ob Vet. F5 f.83; I-Bc Lo.04371; I-Fc E.VI.3610; I-Fm Mel.2008 [10]; I-LDEsormani 298/7/13; I-Ma S. I. H. I. 36 [2]; I-Mafb I.VII 63; I-Mc Coll. Libr.213; I-Mcom MUS.M MUS.1.-447; I-Mfil I.VII 63; I-Mr Libr. 04251; I-Ms MUS. P. LXII. 2; I-Nragni L051; I-PAc F. Libretti, sc.110 [76]; I-Rn 40.9.K.8.3; I-Rsc Carv.4252; I-Rsc Libr. n. XX [39]; I-Rsc Vol. 36 [3]; I-Vc 1030; I-Vgc ROL.0553 [4]; I-Vnm DRAMM.3266 [5]; I-Vverardo^S; US-AUS KL-17 330; US-BEm ML48.I7 [699]; US-Wc ML48 [S8403]

(2) Lisbon: Ferreira, 1808
I-Rsc Carv.4253; P-Ln T.S.C. 512 P.

(3) Lisbon: Bulhões, 1819 (It./Port.)
I-Rsc Carv.4254; P-Ln T.S.C. 513 P.

Music sources
1ˢᵗ version: 1794, Milan

[complete scores] B-Bc 2303[MGG,NG,RISM]; I-Mr* MS PART.03368[IC,MGG,NG,RISM,SBN]

[excerpts] *La destra ti chiedo* (A-Wn Mus.Hs.10680[IC]; D-B Mus.ms. 30135 [18][IC,RISM]; D-Mbs Mus.ms. 2476[RISM]; H-PH Mus.sacr.ant. P 8[RISM;P]; I-Mc Mus. Tr.ms. 1065[RISM,SBN]; I-Rama A.Ms.3032[SBN]; I-Rsc

---

222. Microfilm copy: CDN-Lu M1500.M57P674 1794a.

MC | *Demofoonte* (1733–1836)

G.Mss.19 [4]^(RISM); I-Rsc G.Mss.834 [2]^(SBN)); *Misero pargoletto* (I-Rc Mss. 2540 [4]^(SBN)); *Prudente mi chiedi?* (I-BGi 17809^(RISM,SBN); I-Mc Noseda P.1 [12]^(SBN;P); I-Nc 34.3.2 [5]^(SBN)); *Sperai vicino il lido* (CH-Gc M 97^(RISM); HR-Zha XLVI.2A^(RISM); S-Skma T-SE-R^(RISM))

[contrafacta] *La destra ti chiedo* ([*O Jesu te invocamus*] H-PH Mus.sacr. ant. P 7^(RISM;P); [*Venite filii, audite me timorem Domini*] CZ-Pnm XLIX F 71^(RISM;P); SK-BRnm MUS VII 148^(RISM;P))

2nd version: 1808, Lisbon

[complete scores] P-Laa^(MGG) [Act II]; P-Ln* M.M. 231^(IC,MGG,NG,223) [Act I]; US-Wc ML96.P81^(MGG,NG,RISM) [Act I]

[excerpts] *Misero pargoletto* (B-Bc 11000^(RISM)); *Sperai vicino il lido* (I-MC 5-B-20 [7]^(RISM))

[unspecified] unspecified aria (P-Ln F.C.R. 168 [69]^(IC;R))

1808	mus. by Portugal, Marcos António (2nd version) → see 1794
1811 1811 Munich	mus. by Lindpaintner, Peter Joseph von[224] Court theatre (29/01/1811) *Demophoon* (Ger. only)
1821 1821 London	mus. by Horn, Charles Edward Theatre Royal, Drury Lane (02/06/1821) *Dirce, or The Fatal Urn* (En. only)
1836 1836 Florence	mus. by Sborgi, Giuseppe Maria Teatro Pagliano

Dramatic texts of doubtful identification

Demofoonte (Milan: Barrois son, 1820)
F-Pn 8-YTH-50188

---

223. P-Ln also holds a microfilm reproduction of the source.
224. Lib. by Ignaz Franz Castelli, after P. Desriaux's French version of Vogel's *Démophoon* → see 1789, mus. by Vogel, Johann Christoph.

MC | *Demofoonte* (1733–1836)

Arie sciolte

Abati, Carlo, *Se tutti i mali miei* (D-Mbs Mus.ms. 670[IC,RISM])
Adolfati, Andrea, *La destra ti chiedo* (US-CHH* VFM3.1.A36 1750z [35][RISM])
Bach, Johann Christian, *Per lei fra l'armi dorme il guerriero* (CH-N XL obl. 156[RISM;P])
Bachschmid, Johann Anton Adam, *Tu sai chi son; tu sai* (D-B Mus.ms. 995 [17][RISM;P])
Boccherini, Luigi, *La destra ti chiedo* (F-Pn RES-506 [12][BnF])
Bonno, Giuseppe, *Il suo leggiadro viso* (CZ-Pnm XLII A 36[RISM;R])
Brandl, Johann Evangelist, *La destra ti chiedo* (D-Mbs Mus.ms. 10429[RISM;P])
Brunetti, Giovan Gualberto, *Se tronca un ramo, un fiore* (S-Uu Gimo 32[IC,RISM])
Buonanni, *La destra ti chiedo* (I-Mc Noseda C.73 [13][SBN])
Busecchi, Ignazio, *Sperai vicino il lido* (I-COLbarcella* 120[RISM,SBN])
Caffi, Francesco, *La destra ti chiedo* (I-Vnm* Mss. 10802[SBN,225])
Cherubini, Luigi, *Misero pargoletto* (I-Gl FONDO ANT. M.(4) 26.1[SIC,SBN,226]); *Sperai vicino il lido* (D-B* Mus.ms.autogr. Cherubini, L. 329[RISM]; S-Skma* SO-R[RISM,227])
Colla, Giuseppe, *Che mai risponderti* (D-B Mus.ms. 3922[RISM]; S-Skma T-SE-R[RISM,228])
Conforto, Nicola, *Il suo leggiadro viso* (F-Pn D-15286[BnF,RISM,229])
Coppola, Luigi, *La destra ti chiedo* (I-MC 1-F-14 [1][RISM])
Dalfiume, Pellegrino, *Se tutti i mali miei* (I-Bl FS AP 68[IC,SBN])
Danzi, Franz Ignaz, *La destra ti chiedo* (D-Mbs* Mus.ms. 1944[IC,RISM])
Dittersdorf, Carl Ditters von, *Sperai vicino il lido* (US-Wc M1505.A2 S75[RISM;P,230])
Errichelli, Pasquale, *Misero pargoletto* (D-F Mus Hs 154 [21][RISM])
Fighera, Salvatore, *Se tutti i mali miei* (I-Nc 22.1.6 [6][RISM])
Fillembaum, *O più tremar non voglio* (I-Gl FONDO ANT. SCAT.141.3[IC,SBN])
Hamal, Henri, *Sperai vicino il lido* (B-Br * Ms II 778 Mus [13][RISM])
Hertel, Johann Wilhelm, *No, non chiedo, amate stelle* (D-ROu Mus. Saec. XVIII:42 [12][RISM;P]); *O più tremar non voglio* (B-Bc 4192[RISM]); *Padre, perdona... oh pene* (D-ROu Mus. Saec. XVIII:42 [7][RISM;P]); *Se tutti i mali miei* (D-ROu Mus .Saec. XVIII:42 [8][RISM;P]; D-ROu Mus. Saec. XVIII:42 [13][RISM;P]); *Sperai vicino il lido* (B-Bc* 4201[RISM])
Kraus, Joseph Martin, *In te spero, o sposo amato* (S-Skma* Z/Sv.[RISM]; S-Uu Vok. mus. i hs. 57:3a [40][RISM]); *Misero pargoletto* (S-Skma SO/Sv.-R[RISM]; S-Uu Vok. mus. i hs. 57:3a [36][IC,RISM]); *Se tutti i mali miei* (S-Uu Vok. mus. i hs. 57:3a [37][IC,RISM])
Lapis, Santo, *No, non chiedo, amate stelle* (CH-N XB obl. 178[RISM])
Lenzi, Carlo, *In te spero, o sposo amato* (I-Nc 34.4.3 [2][SBN])
Leonardi, Silvestro, *Non temer, bell'idol mio* [1810] (US-Eu MSS 1109[RISM])
Maraucci, Giacomo, *No, non chiedo, amate stelle* [1755] (I-Nc 22.3.23 [29][SBN])
Mercadante, Saverio, *La destra ti chiedo* (I-Nc 22.3.24[SBN])

---

225. Possible autograph.
226. According to an inscription on this source, this aria was sung by Luigi Marchesi as part of a *Demofoonte* performed in Genoa in 1784; no further reference to such production have been found.
227. Possible autograph.
228. Given as anonymous in [RISM].
229. Microfilm copy: F-Pn VM BOB-25304.
230. The composer of this aria has been determined through comparison with the source PL-Wu RM 7867, which contains an *Iste confessor*, allegedly by C. D. von Dittersdorf. We cannot ascertain that the Latin piece is a contrafactum of the Metastasian aria.

MC | *Demofoonte* (1733–1836)

Mortellari, Michele, *Misero pargoletto* (I-OS Mss.Mus.B 2382[RISM,SBN])

Mozart, Wolfgang Amadeus, *In te spero, o sposo amato* (KV 440) (<u>US-Wc* ML30.8b .M8 K.383h</u>[RISM;R,231]); *Misero pargoletto* (KV 73e); *Non curo l'affetto* (KV 74b) (<u>CZ-Pu M II 11e [5]</u>[RISM,232]); *Se ardire e speranza* (KV 730) (<u>F-Pn* MS-237</u>[BnF,RISM]; I-Bda M.LEIB. 649bis [1][IC,RISM,SBN]); *Se tutti i mali miei* (KV 73p); *Sperai vicino il lido* (KV 368) (D-Dl Mus.3972-J-509 [2][RISM;P]; D-FUl M12 [307][RISM]; D-FUl M12 [308][RISM;IP]; S-Skma T-SE-R[RISM])

Naumann, Johann Gottlieb, *Che mai risponderti* (<u>D-Dl Mus.3480-J-10 [8]</u>[RISM]; I-MC 4-B-20 [3][RISM])

Niola, Gennaro, *Sperai vicino il lido* (I-Mc Noseda L.17 [11][SBN])

Panerai, Vincenzo, *Felice età dell'oro* [1792] (I-Rama A.Ms.2483 [5][RISM;R])

Paradies, Pietro Domenico, *O più tremar non voglio* (GB-Cfm [GB-Cu] MU.MS.108[IC])

Parolini, Pietro Giovanni, *La destra ti chiedo* [1816] (I-Fc F.P.T.906[SBN])

Pergolesi, Giovanni Battista, *Che mai risponderti?* (I-Bsf M.P.IV.12[SBN])

Perotti, Giovanni Domenico, *Se tutti i mali miei* (D-SWl Mus.4166[RISM])

Pignatelli, Giuseppe, *Perfidi, già che in vita* [1824] (US-Bu BSO Collection, vol. 123 [53][RISM;R])

Ponzo, Giuseppe, *In te spero, o sposo amato* (<u>D-Dl Mus.1-F-21,3 [6]</u>[RISM]); *Se tutti i mali miei* (<u>D-Dl Mus.1-F-21,3 [5]</u>[RISM])

Quantz, Johann Joachim, *Che mai risponderti* (D-Bsa [D-B] SA 1863[RISM;P]; D-Bsa [D-B] SA 1864[RISM]); *Padre, perdona… oh pene* (D-Dl Mus.2470-J-1[RISM;P])

Reichardt, Johann Friedrich, *La destra ti chiedo* (D-B* Mus.ms.autogr. Reichardt, J. F. 34[RISM]; S-Skma T-SE-R[RISM]); *Se ardire e speranza* [1773] (D-B* Mus.ms.autogr. Reichardt, J. F. 39[RISM]); *Sperai vicino il lido* (GB-Lbl Add. MS 32079 [3][BL,RISM])

Reno, Carlo, *Il suo leggiadro viso* (D-Dl Mus.1-F-82,23 [1][RISM]); *T'intendo, ingrata* (<u>D-Dl Mus.1-F-82,23 [2]</u>[RISM])

Rutini, Giovanni Marco, *No, non chiedo, amate stelle* (US-SFsc *M2.1 M438[RISM;P])

Sacchini, Antonio, *Se tutti i mali miei* (I-Vlevi CF.B.132[IC,SBN])

Schubert, Franz, *Misero pargoletto* D.42 (for voice and piano; see in addition a doubtful orchestral version with a similar incipit, although not completely coincident, in D-BFb [D-MÜu] S-chu 16[RISM])

Sellitto, Giuseppe, *Se tutti i mali miei* (I-MC 6-A-4/8 [2][RISM])

Sickingen, Karl von, *Tu sai chi son; tu sai* (D-KNmi S 703[RISM])

Valentini, Michelangelo, *Non temer, bell'idol mio* (US-SFsc *M2.5 v.65 [2][RISM])

Vernier, Girolamo, *Felice età dell'oro* (I-Vnm Mss. 9995 [13][SBN])

Zonca, Giuseppe, *No, non chiedo, amate stelle* (<u>D-KA Don Mus.Ms. 2083</u>[RISM;P])

Zoppis, Francesco, *Odo il suono de' queruli accenti* (D-B Mus.ms. 23651 [5][RISM;P])

Arias by unknown composer

Che mai risponderti (B-Bc FRW 12200 [12][RISM])
Felice età dell'oro (B-Bc FRW 12220 [7][IC,RISM])
In te spero, o sposo amato (B-Bc FRW 12220 [8][IC,RISM])
In te spero, o sposo amato (I-MC 6-D-9/6 [4][RISM])
In te spero, o sposo amato (GB-Lbl Add. 31713 [2/4][BL])

---

231. Possible autograph. Microfilm copy: US-NYp *ZBT-109 [124].
232. According to an inscription on this source, the aria *Non curo l'affetto* by Mozart was used in the pasticcio performed in Pavia in 1771 → see 1771, mus. by various unknown composers.

MC | *Demofoonte* (1733–1836)

La destra ti chiedo (CH-SAf MusSAf.Ms.152[RISM;P])
La destra ti chiedo (CZ-Pak 1701[RISM;R])
Misero pargoletto (I-BGc 245.9[RISM])
Non odi consiglio? (US-BEm MS 834 [7][RISM])
No, non chiedo, amate stelle (D-Wa 46 Alt 633[IC,RISM])
Padre, perdona… oh pene (B-Bc FRW 12200 [4][IC,RISM])
Padre, perdona… oh pene (P-VV G-Prática 51b[IC]) → see 1780–1790, mus. by various unknown composers
Se tutti i mali miei (B-Bc FRW 12200 [9][IC,RISM])
Se tutti i mali miei (I-OS Mss.Mus.B 540[RISM,SBN])
Se tutti i mali miei [1744] (US-BEm MS 1166 [5][RISM])
Tu sai chi son; tu sai (B-Bc FRW 12200 [6][IC,RISM])
Tu sai chi son; tu sai (I-Mc MsCon.9 [14][IC,SBN])

Unidentified contents

In te spero, o sposo amato (I-Nc pacco 2632[SBN,233])
Se ardire e speranza (I-MTa A265[IC,SBN])
unspecified aria (F-Pn VM7-7520[BnF])

Contrafacta

Galuppi, Baldassare, *Voi che sciolto il piede avete*[234] ([*In te spero o sposo amato*] CDN-Lu GM/AR 741[RISM])

---

233. Vn part only.
234. The original aria belongs to B. Galuppi's *Enrico* (London, 1743) and was later adapted, presumably by a different composer, to the Metastasian text *In te spero, o sposo amato*. Given that an aria from another opera by Galuppi was also adapted to a *Demofoonte* poem and then inserted into the Venetian revival of J. A. Hasse's *Demofoonte* in 1750, this aria might have shared the same destiny → see 1748, mus. by Hasse, Johann Adolph.

Bibliography

Ajello, Rafaele, ed., *Il teatro di San Carlo: la cronologia 1737–1987* (Naples: Guida, 1987).
Alier y Aixalà, Roger, *L'òpera a Barcelona: orígens, desenvolupament i consolidació de l'òpera com a espectacle teatral a la Barcelona del segle XVIII* (Barcelona: Institut d'Estudis Catalans, 1990).
Allacci, Leone, *Drammaturgia di Leone Allacci accresciuta e continuata fino all'anno MDCCLV* (Venice: Pasquali, 1755).
___ *Il Teatro Alibert o delle Dame (1717–1863) nella Roma papale* (Tivoli: Chicca, 1951).
Antolini, Bianca Maria and Annalisa Bini, 'Johann Adolph Hasse nei manoscritti della Biblioteca di S. Cecilia di Roma', *Analecta Musicologica*, 25 (1983), 495–511.
Antolini, Bianca Maria and Teresa Maria Gialdroni, 'L'opera nei teatri pubblici a Roma nella prima metà del Settecento', *Roma moderna e contemporanea. Rivista interdisciplinare di storia*, 4 (1996), 113–42.
Baker, Nicole Edwina Ivy, 'Italian Opera at the Court of Mannheim, 1718–1770' (doctoral dissertation, University of California, 1994).
Balbo, Tarcisio. 'I quatro Demofoonte di Niccolò Jommelli: uno sgurdo d'assieme', in *Demofoonte come soggetto per il dramma per musica: Johann Adolf Hasse ed altri compositori del Settecento*, ed. by Milada Jonášová and Tomislav Volek (Prague, Academia, 2020), pp. 167–88.
___ 'Quando il poeta tace (o parla sottovoce): rimandi e sottintesi in un'aria del *Demofoonte* metastasiano, nel quattro intonazioni di Niccolò Jommelli', in *Il canto di Metastasio. Atti del convegno di studi, Venezia (14–16 dicembre 1999)*, ed. by Maria Giovanna Miggiani (Bologna: Forni, 2004), pp. 231–46.
Bärwald, Manuel, *Italienische Open in Leipzig (1744–1756)* (Beeskow: ortus, 2016).
Bauer, Hans-Joachim, *Barockoper in Bayreuth* (Laaber: Laaber, 1982).
Bellina, Anna Laura, 'Appunti sul repertorio padovano (1738–1797)', in *Mozart, Padova e la Betulia liberata: Committenza, interpretazione e fortune delle azioni sacre metastasiane nel '700. Atti del Convegno internazionale di studi, 28–30 settembre 1989* (Florence: Olschki, 1991), pp. 173–90.
___ 'Metastasio in Venezia: appunti per una recensio', *Italianistica: Rivista di letteratura italiana*, 13.1–2 (1984), 145–73.
Bianconi, Lorenzo and Giorgio Pestelli, eds, *Storia dell'opera italiana* (Turin: Edizione di Torino, 1987).
___ *The History of Italian Opera* (Chicago: The University of Chicago Press, 1988). Original edition: *Storia dell'opera italiana* (Turin: Edizione di Torino, 1987).
Blichmann, Diana, 'Water Symbols in the Stage Design of *Alessandro nell'Indie*: The Portuguese Exploration of India and Political Propaganda at the Lisbon Royal Court', *Music in Art: International Journal of Music Iconography*, 44.1–2 (2019), 139–68.
Bouquet, Marie-Thérèse, Valeria Gualerzi, and Alberto Testa, *Storia del Teatro Regio di Torino: cronologie*, ed. by Alberto Basso (Turin: Cassa di Risparmio di Torino, [1988]).
Brito, Manuel Carlos de, *Opera in Portugal in the Eighteenth Century* (Cambridge: Cambridge University Press, 1989).
Broschi, Carlo, *Descripción del estado actual del real teatro de Buen Retiro, de las funciones hechas en él desde el año de 1747 hasta el presente [...]* (1758), E-E II/1412.

Brunelli, Bruno, *I teatro di Padova: delle origini alla fine del secolo XIX* (Padua: Draghi, 1921).

___ *Tutte le opere di Pietro Metastasio* (Milan, Mondadori, 1943).

Budasz, Rogério, 'Demofonte: A Luso-Brazilian pastiche?', *Diagonal*, 12 (2016), 52–81.

Burden, Michael, 'Metastasio on the London Stage, 1728 to 1840: A Catalogue', *Royal Musical Association Research Chronicle*, 40 (2007), 1–332.

___ 'Metastasio's "London Pasties": Curate Egg or Pudding's Proof?', in *Pietro Metastasio – uomo universale (1698–1782): Festgabe der Österreichischen Akademie der Wissenschaften zum 300. Geburtstag von Pietro Metastasio*, ed. by Andrea Sommer-Mathis and Elisabeth Theresia Hilscher (Vienna: Österreichische Akademie der Wissenschaften, 2000), pp. 290–390.

___ 'The King's Theatre in London, 1705–1820', in *The Oxford Handbook of the Operatic Canon*, ed. by Cormac Newark and William Weber (New York: Oxford University Press, 2020), pp. 115–30.

___ '"Twittering and Thrilling": Swedish Reaction to Metastasio', *Early Music*, 26.4 (1998), 608–21.

Calella, Michele, 'Zwischen Autorwillen und Produktionssystem. Zur Frage des "Werkcharakters" in der Oper des 18. Jahrhunderts', in *Bearbeitungspraxis in der Oper des späten 18. Jahrhunderts. Bericht über die internationale wissenschaftliche Tagung von 18. bis 20. Februar in Würzburg*, ed. by Ulrich Konrad and others (Tutzing: Schneider, 2007), pp. 15–32.

Cambiasi, Pompeo, *Rappresentazioni date nei Reali Teatri di Milano 1778–1872* (Bologna: Forni, 1969 [1872]).

Cametti, Alberto, 'Leonardo Vinci e i suoi drammi in musica al Teatro delle Dame', *Musica d'oggi*, 6 (1924), 297–99.

Carreras, Juan José, 'Farinelli's Dream: Theatrical Space, Audience and Political Function of Italian Court Opera', in *Musiktheater im höfischen Raum des frühneuzeitlichen Europa*, ed. by Margret Scharrer, Heiko Laß, and Matthias Müller (Heidelberg: Heidelberg University, 2020), pp. 357–93.

Casaglia, Gherardo, *L'Almanacco di Gherardo Casaglia* <https://almanac-gherardo-casaglia.com> [accessed 7 May 2022].

Casanova Sánchez de Vega, Teresa, 'El intermezzo en la corte de España, 1738–1758' (doctoral dissertation, Universidad Complutense de Madrid, 2019).

Černá, Zuzana, 'Antonio Bioni and his Compositions Preserved in Kroměříž Archive', *Musicologia Brunensia*, 52 (2017), 217–42.

Charteris, Richard, 'The Music Collection of the Staats- und Universitätsbibliothek, Hamburg: A Survey of its British Holdings prior to the Second World War', *Royal Musical Association Research Chronicle*, 30 (1997), pp. 1–138 <https://doi.org/10.1080/14723808.1997.10540978>.

Chiarelli, Alessandra and Angelo Pompilio, *'Or vaghi or fieri': cenni di poetica nei libretti veneziani (circa 1740–1740)* (Bologna: Cooperativa Libraria Universitaria Editrice Bologna, 2004).

Clement, Felix and Pierre Larousse, *Dictionnaire lyrique ou Histoire des operas* ([s.l.]: Keissinger, 1869).

Corago. Repertorio e archivio di libretti del melodramma italiano dal 1600 al 1900, ed. by Angelo Pompilio (Bologna, Università di Bologna) <http://corago.unibo.it> [accessed 24 June 2022].

Corneilson, Paul Edward, 'Opera at Mannheim, 1770–1778' (doctoral dissertation, The University of North Carolina at Chapell Hill, 1994).

Chiti, Rossana and Federico Marri, *Testi drammatici per musica della Biblioteca Labronica di Livorno* (Livorno: Debatte & figli, 1991).

Cotarelo y Mori, Emilio, *Orígenes y establecimiento de la ópera en España hasta 1800* (Madrid: Revista de arch., bibl. y museos, 1917).

Cotticelli, Francesco and Paologiovanni Maione, *Le istituzioni musicali a Napoli durante il Viceregno austriaco (1707–1734): materiali inediti sulla Real Cappella ed il Teatro di San Bartolomeo* (Naples: Luciani, 1993).

SC | Bibliography

Croce, Benedetto, *I teatri di Napoli. Secolo XV-XVIII* (Naples: Pierro, 1891).
Cummings, Graham, 'Reminiscence and Recall in Three Early Settings of Metastasio's *Alessandro nell'Indie*', *Proceedings of the Royal Musical Association*, 109 (1982–1983), 80–104.
Dean, Winton, *Handel's Operas 1726–1741* (Woodbridge: The Boydell Press, 2006).
Díez Rodríguez, Cristina, 'Cádiz, centro operístico peninsular en la España de los siglos XVIII y XIX (1761–1830)' (doctoral dissertation, Universidad Complutense de Madrid, 2015).
De Angelis, Alberto, 'I drammi di Pietro Metastasio rappresentati al Teatro Alibert o "Delle Dame"', *Rivista italiana del teatro*, 2.6 (1943), 211–24.
De Filippis, Felice and Raffaele Arnese, *Cronache del Teatro di S. Carlo (1737–1960)* (Naples: Edizioni Politica Popolare, 1961).
D'Ovidio, Antonella, 'Da Roma a Vienna: scelte drammaturgiche e compositive nelle prime due intonazioni della "Didone abbandonata" (1747, 1749) di Niccolò Jommelli', in *Niccolò Jommelli: L'esperienza europea di un musicista 'filosofo'. Atti del Convegno internazionale di studi (Reggio Calabria, 7–8 ottobre 2011)*, ed. by Gaetano Pitarresi (Reggio Calabria: Conservatorio di Musica 'F. Cilea', 2014), pp. 189–221.
Dumigan, Darryl Jacqueline, 'Nicola Porpora's Operas for the "Opera of the Nobility": The Poetry and the Music' (doctoral dissertation, University of Huddersfield, 2014).
Emerson, John A., *Catalog of Pre-1900 Vocal Manuscripts in the Music Library, University of California at Berkeley* (Berkeley: University of California Press, 1988).
Fassini, Sesto, *Il melodramma italiano a Londra nella prima metà del Settecento* (Turin: Bocca, 1914).
Franchi, Saverio, *Drammaturgia romana II (1701–1750)* (Rome: Edizione di Storia e Letteratura, 1997).
____ *Le impressioni sceniche: dizionario bio-bibliografico degli editori e stampatori romani e laziali di testi drammatici e libretti per musica dal 1759 al 1800* (Rome: Edizioni di Storia e Letteratura, 1994).
Frassoni, Edilio, *Due secoli di lirica a Genova* (Genoa: Cassa di Risparmio di Genova e Imperia, 1980).
Fürstenau, Moritz, *Zur Geschichte der Musik und des Theaters am Hofe der Kurfürsten von Sachsen und Könige von Polen: Friedrich August I. (August II.) und Friedrich August II. (August III.)* (Dresden: Kunze, 1862).
Freeman, Daniel Evan, 'The Opera Theater of Count Franz Anton von Spork in Prague (1724–35)' (doctoral dissertation, University of Illinois at Urbana-Champaign, 1987).
Gallico, Claudio, 'Vivaldi dagli archivi di Mantova', in *Vivaldi veneziano europeo*, ed. by Francesco Degrada (Florence: Olschki, 1980), pp. 77–88.
Gialdroni, Teresa Maria, 'I primi dieci anni della *Didone abbandonata* di Metastasio: il caso di Domenico Sarro', *Analecta Musicologica*, 30 (1998), 437–500.
Giazotto, Remo, *La musica a Genova nella vita publica e privata dal XIII. al XVIII. secolo* (Genoa: Società Industrie Grafiche e Lavorazioni Affini, 1951).
Giovine, Alfredo and Ulisse Prota-Giurleo, *Giacomo Insanguine detto Monopoli: musicista monopolitano* (Bari: Archivio delle tradizioni popolari baresi, 1969).
Giust, Anna, 'Towards Russian Opera: Growing National Consciousness in 18th-Century Operatic Repertoire' (doctoral dissertation, Università degli Studi di Padova, 2012).
Gluxam, Dagmar, 'Verzeichnis der Sänger in der Wiener Opern- und Oratorienpartituren 1705–1711', in *Studien zur Musikwissenschaft. Beihefte der Denkmäler der Tonkunst in Österreich*, ed. by Theophil Antonicek and Elisabeth T. Hilscher (Tutzing: Schneider, 2002), pp. 269–320.
Griffel, Margaret Ross, *Operas in Germany: A Dictionary* (Lanham: Rowman & Littlefield, 2018).
Gutiérrez Carou, Javier, 'Nitteti en la correspondencia entre Metastasio y Farinelli', *Scherzo*, 384, special dossier: *Metastasio en el Madrid del XVIII* (May 2022), 67–69.
Hálova, Kamila, 'Il Demofoonte di Jan Evangelista Antonín Koželuh', in *Demofoonte come soggetto per il*

dramma per musica: Johann Adolf Hasse ed altri compositori del Settecento, ed. by Milada Jonášová and Tomislav Volek (Prague: Academia, 2020), pp. 213–27.

Hansell, Kathleen Kuzmick, 'Opera and Ballet at the Regio Ducal Teatro of Milan, 1771–1776: A Musical and Social History' (doctoral dissertation, University of California Berkeley, 1980).

Hartmann, Carl and Carl Schäffer, eds, *Die königlichen Theater in Berlin: Statischer Rückblick auf die Kunstlerische Thätigkeit und die Personal-Verhältnisse während des Zeitraums vom 5. December 1786 bis 31. December 1885* (Berlin: Berliner Verlag-Comtoir, 1886).

Hartmann, Johann Georg August von, 'Kurze fragmentarische geschichte der wirtembergiscgen Hof-Theaters (1750–1799)', in *Musik und Musiker am Stuttgarter Hoftheater (1750–1918): Quellen und Studien*, ed. by Reiner Nägele (Stuttgart: Württembergische Landesbibliothek, 2000), pp. 85–109.

Heartz, Daniel, 'Hasse, Galuppi and Metastasio', in *Venezia e il melodramma nel Settecento*, ed. by Maria Teresa Muraro (Florence: Olschki, 1978), pp. 309–79.

Henzel, Christoph, *Berliner Klassik* (Berlin: ortus, 2009).

____ 'Berliner Komponisten im Notenarchiv der Sing-Akademie zu Berlin', in *Jahrbuch des Staatlichen Instituts für Musikforschung Preußischer Kulturbesitz*, ed. by Günther Wagner (Stuttgart: Metzler, 2003), pp. 31–98.

____ '"Dichter der Regenten und der Hofleute": Metastasio and deutschen Fürstenhöfen', in *Metastasio im Deutschland der Aufklärung*, ed. by Laurenz Lütteken and Gerhard Splitt (Tübingen: Niemeyer, 2002), pp. 59–72.

____ 'Johann Friedrich Agricola und die friderizianische Oper nach dem Siebenjährigen Krieg', *Jahrbuch 2013 des Staatlichen Instituts für Musikforschung Preußischer Kulturbesitz*, 1 (2013), 253–75.

Hill, John Walter, 'The Life and Works of Francesco Maria Veracini' (doctoral dissertation, Harvard University, 1972).

Hochmuth, Michael, 'Oper in del kursächsischen Landschlössern', in *Musiktheater im höfischen Raum des frühneuzeitlichen Europa*, ed. by Margret Scharrer, Heiko Laß, and Matthias Müller (Heidelberg: Heidelberg University, 2019), pp. 161–73.

Hochstein, Wolfgang, '*Didone abbandonata* in der Vertonung von Johann Adolph Hasse', in *Didone come soggetto nel dramma per musica*, ed. Milada Jonášová and Tomislav Volek (Prague: Academia, 2018), pp. 185–212.

____ 'Metastasios Libretto *Demofoonte* in den Vertonungen von Johann Adolph Hasse', in *Demofoonte come soggetto per il dramma per musica: Johann Adolph Hasse ed altri compositori del Settecento*, ed. by Milada Jonášová and Tomislav Volek (Prague: Academia, 2020), pp. 19–56.

Holmes, William C., *Opera Observed: Views of a Florentine Impresario in the Early Eighteenth Century* (Chicago: University of Chicago Press, 1993).

____ 'Vivaldi e il Teatro la Pergola a Firenze: nuove fonti', in *Nuovi Studi Vivaldiani: edizione e cronologia critica delle opere*, ed. by Antonio Fanna and Giovanni Morelli (Florence: Olschki, 1988), pp. 117–30.

Hortschansky, Klaus, 'Die Wiener Dramen Metastasios in Italien', in *Venezia e il melodramma nel Settecento*, ed. by Maria Teresa Muraro (Florence: Olschki, 1978), pp. 407–23.

Hucke, Helmut, 'Die beide Fassungen der Oper "Didone abbandonata" von Domenico Sarri', in *Gesellschaft für Musikforschung Kongreßbericht* (Hamburg: [s.n.], 1956), pp. 113–17.

Hughes-Hughes, August, *Catalogue of Manuscript Music in the British Museum* (London: Clowes, 1906–1909).

Huss, Fran, *Der Wiener Kaiserhof: Eine Kulturgeschichte von Leopold I. bis Leopold II.* (Vienna: Katz, 2008).

____ 'Die Oper am Wiener Kaiserhof unter den Kaisern Josef I. und Karl VI. Mit einem Spielplan von 1706 bis 1740' (doctoral dissertation, Universität Wien, 2003).

Informazioni e Studi Vivaldiani: Bollettino dell'Istituto Italiano Antonio Vivaldi (Venice: Fondazione Giorgio Cini–Ricordi, 1984).

Jackson, Paul Joseph, 'The Operas of David Perez' (doctoral dissertation, Stanford University, 1967).

Jeanneret, Christine, 'Costumes and Cosmopolitanism: Italian Opera in the North', *Cambridge Opera Journal*, 21.1 (2020), 27–51.

___ 'Made in Italy, Tailored for Danes: Giuseppe Sarti and Italian Opera in Copenhagen', *Music & Letters*, 102.2 (2021), 271–93.

Jensen, Niels Martin, 'Giuseppe Sarti: attività danese e manoscritti sopravvissuti', in *Giuseppe Sarti musicista faentino: Atti del convegno internazionale*, ed. by Mario Baroni and Maria Gioia Tavoni (Modena: Mucchi, 1986), pp. 159–65.

Jurášková, Kateřina and Jana Spáčilová, *Italská opera na holešovském zámku v době Františka Antonína Rottala* (Holešov: Město Holešov, 2019).

Kade, Otto, *Die Musikalien-Sammlung des Großherzoglichen Mecklenburg-Schweriner Fürstenhauses aus den letzten zwei Jahrhunderten* (Schwerin: Sandmeyerschen Hofbuchdruckerei, 1893).

Kirkpatrick, Ralph, *Domenico Scarlatti* (Princeton: Princeton University Press, 1983).

Klein, Rudolf, 'Die Schauplätze der Hofoper', *Österreichische Musikzeitschrift*, 24 (1969), 371–422.

Kleinertz, Reiner, *Grundzüge des spanischen Musiktheaters im 18. Jahrhundert* (Kassel: Reichenberger, 2003).

Kobuch, Agatha, 'Ferdinando Paer in Dresden', in *Die italienische Oper in Dresden von Johann Adolf Hasse bis Francesco Morlacchi*, ed. by Günther Stephan and Hans John (Dresden: Hochschule für Musik 'Carl Maria von Weber', 1987), pp. 482–94.

Kokole, Metoda, 'Andrea Bernasconi's Earliest Operatic Music on its Way North of the Alps', *Musicologica Brunensia*, 53 (2018), 207–26.

___ 'Did Andrea Bernasconi Compose 'Adriano in Siria' Twice?', in *Music Migration in the Early Modern Age: Centres and Peripheries – People, Works, Styles, Paths of Dissemination and Influence*, ed. by Jolanta Guzy-Pasiak and Aneta Markuszewska (Warsaw: Liber Pro Arte, 2016), pp. 237–62.

___ 'Two Operatic Seasons of Brothers Mingotti in Ljubljana', *De musica disserenda*, 8.2 (2012), 57–90.

Laberinto degli amanti fabbricato in 43. teatri dell'Europa disposto per ordine d'alfabeto a comodo de' grandi, de' mezzani, e de' piccioli a piacere de' nobili, de' cittadini, e de' plebei per il carnovale dell'anno 1765 (Florence: Bassanese, 1765).

Krauß, Rudolf, *Das Stuttgarter Hoftheater von den ältesten Zeiten bis zur Gegenwart* (Stuttgart: Metzler, 1908).

Labruna, Serena, 'La Didone abbandonata al Teatro Riccardi di Bergamo nel 1791: nascita di un teatro stabile ai margini della Repubblica di Venezia', in *Theatre Spaces for Music in 18th-Century Europe*, ed. by Iskrena Yordanovam Giuseppina Raggi, and Maria Ida Biggi (Vienna: Hollitzer, 2020), pp. 387–408.

Landmann, Ortum, *Die Dresdner italienische Oper zwischen Hasse und Weber. Ein Daten und Quellenverzeichnis für die Jahre 1765–1817* (Dresden: Sächsische Landesbibliothek, 1976).

___ 'Die italienische Oper in Dresden nach Johann Adolph Hasse. Entwicklungszüge, 1765–1832', in *Die italienische Oper in Dresden von Johann Adolf Hasse bis Francesco Morlacchi*, ed. by Günther Stephan and Hans John (Dresden: Hochschule für Musik 'Carl Maria von Weber', 1987), pp. 394–416.

Ledebur, Carl Friedrich, *Tonkünstler-Lexicon Berlin's von den ältesten Zeiten bis auf die Gegenwart* (Berlin: Rauh, 1861).

Leza, José Máximo, 'Metastasio on the Spanish Stage: Operatic Adaptations in the Public Theatres of Madrid in the 1730s', *Early Music*, 2.4 (1998), 623–31.

Lianovosani, Luigi, *La Fenice, Gran teatro di Venezia: serie degli spettacoli dalla primavera 1792 a tutto il carnovale 1876* (Milan: Ricordi, 1876).

Liborio, Francesco Maria, *La scena della città: rappresentazioni sceniche nel Teatro di Cremona 1748–1900* (Cremona: Turris, 1994).

Liggett, Margaret McGuiness, 'A Biography of Piccinni and a Critical Study of his "La Didone" and "Didon"' (doctoral dissertation, Washington University, 1977).

Llorens, Ana, Gorka Rubiales, and Nicola Usula, 'Operatic Sources for *Demofoonte*: Librettos and Scores after Metastasio's "figliuolo"', in *Demofoonte come soggetto per il dramma per musica: Johann Adolf Hasse ed altri compositori del Settecento*, ed. by Milada Jonášová and Tomislav Volek (Prague: Academia, 2020), pp. 271–317.

Llorens, Ana and Álvaro Torrente, 'Constructing *Opera Seria* in the Iberian Courts: Metastasian Repertoire for Spain and Portugal', *Anuario musical*, 76 (2021), 73–110 <https://doi.org/10.3989/anuariomusical.2021.i76>.

Loewenberg, Alfred, *Annals of Opera, 1597–1940* (Cambridge: Heffer & Sons, 1943).

Mangum, John, 'The Repertory of the Italian Court Opera in Berlin, 1740–1786', in *The Oxford Handbook of the Operatic Canon*, ed. by Cormac Newark and William Weber (New York: Oxford University Press, 2020), pp. 75–92.

Markstrom, Kurt S., *The Operas of Leonardo Vinci, Napoletano* (Hillsdale, NY: Pendragon, 2007).

Mattheson, Johann, 'Verzeichnis aller welschen Opern, welche von 1725 bis 1734 auf dem breslauischen Schauplatz vorgestellt worden sind', in *Grundlage einer Ehrenpforte, woran der Tüchtigsten Capellmeister, Componisten, Musikgelehrten, Tonkünstler etc. Leben, Werke, Verdienste etc. erscheinen sollen* (Hamburg: In Verlegung des Verfassers, 1740), pp. 374–78.

Mazzoni, Stefano, 'Teatri e opera nell Settecento: Livorno', in *Theatre Spaces for Music in 18th-century Europe*, ed. by Iskrena Yordanova, Giuseppina Raggi, and Maria Ida Biggi (Vienna: Hollitzer, 2020), pp. 321–86.

McClymonds, Marita, 'Niccolò Jommelli: The Last Years' (doctoral dissertation, University of California, 1978).

Meikle, Robert Burns, 'Leonardo Vinci's *Artaserse*: An Edition, with an Editorial and Critical Commentary' (doctoral dissertation, Cornell University, 1970).

Mellace, Raffaele, 'Demofoonte all'ombra del Vesuvio (1735–1775)', in *Demofoonte come soggetto per il dramma per musica: Johann Adolf Hasse ed altri compositori del Settecento*, ed. by Milada Jonášová and Tomislav Volek (Prague: Academia, 2020), pp. 143–66.

___ *Johann Adolf Hasse* (Palermo: L'Epos, 2004).

___. *'L'autunno del Metastasio.' Gli ultimi drammi per musica di Johann Adolf Hasse* (Florence: Olschki, 2007).

Mooser, Robert-Aloys, *Annales de la musique et des musiciens en Russie au XVIIIe siècle* (Geneva: Mont Blanc, 1948).

Moreau, Mário, *O Teatro de S. Carlos: dois séculos de historia* (Lisbon: Hugin, 1999).

Müller, Erich Hermann, *Angelo und Pietro Mingotti. Ein Beitrag zur Geschichte der Oper im XVIII. Jahrhundert* (Dresden: Bertling, 1917).

Niubo, Marc, 'The Italian Opera Between Prague and Dresden in the Second Half of the Eighteenth Century', in *Musiker-Migration und Musik-Transfer zwischen Böhmen und Sachsen im 18. Jahrhundert*, ed. by Hans-Günter Ottenberg and Reiner Zimmermann (Dresden: Technische Universität, 2012), pp. 58–73.

Opere del signor abate Pietro Metastasio (Paris: widow of Hérissant, 1780).

Opere del Signor Ab. Pietro Metastasio, poeta cesareo, Giusta le Correzione e Aggiunte dell'Autore nell'Edizione di Parigi del MDCCLXXX (Venice: Zatta, 1781–1783).

Opere drammatiche del signor abate Pietro Metastasio romano, poeta cesareo (Venice: Bettinelli, 1733).

Over, Berthold, 'Dido Abandoned? Shifts of Focus and Artistic Choices in *Didone* Pasticcios of the Mingotti Opera Troupe', in *Operatic Pasticcios in 18th-Century Europe: Contexts, Materials and Aesthetics*, ed. by Berthold Over and Gesa zur Nieden (Bielefeld: Verlag, 2021), pp. 285–328.

Pagano, Roberto, *Scarlatti Alessandro e Domenico: due vite in una* (Milan: Mondadori, 1985).

Pastore, Giuseppe A., *Don Lionardo: vita e opere di Leonardo Leo* (Cuneo: Bertola & Locatelli, 1994).

Pečman, Rudolf, 'Schloß Jaroměřice und seine Musikkultur im 18. Jahrhundert', *Musicologica Brunensia*, 45 (1996), 5–11.

Pegah, Rashid-S., 'The Court of Brandenburg-Culmbach-Bayreuth', in *Music at German Courts, 1715–1760: Changing Artistic Priorities*, ed. by Samantha Owens, Barbara M. Reul, and Janice B. Stockigt (Woodbridge: The Boydell Press, 2011), pp. 389–412.

Perutková, Jana, *Der glorreiche Nahmen Adami: Johann Adam Graf von Questenberg (1678–1752) als Förderer der italienischen Oper in Mähren* (Vienna: Hollitzer, 2016).

Petty, Fred Curtis, 'Italian Opera in London, 1760–1800' (doctoral dissertation, Yale University, 1971).

Piperino, Franco, 'Opera Production to 1780', in *The History of Italian Opera*, ed. by Lorenzo Bianconi and Giorgio Pestelli (Chicago: The University of Chicago Press, 1988), pp. 1–80.

Pitarresi, Gaetano, ed., *Leonardo Vinci e il suo tempo* (Reggio Calabria, Iiriti, 2005).

Poesie del signor abate Pietro Metastasio (Paris: widow of Quillau, 1755).

Poesie del signor abate Pietro Metastasio (Turin: Stamperia Reale, 1757).

Price, Curtis, Judith Milhous, and Robert D. Hume, *Italian Opera in Late Eighteenth-Century London*, vol. I: *The King's Theatre, Haymarket 1778–1791* (Oxford: Clarendon Press, 1995).

Ricci, Corrado, *I teatri di Bologna, nei secoli XVII e XVIII: storia aneddotica* (Bologna: Successori Monti, 1888).

Riemann, Hugo, *Opern-Handbuch* (Hildesheim: Olms, 1887).

Riepe, Juliane, '"Essential to the Reputation and Magnificence of Such a High-Ranking Prince": Ceremonial and Italian Opera at the Court of Clemens August of Cologne and other German Courts', in *Italian Opera in Central Europe*, vol. I: *Institutions and Ceremonies*, ed. by Melania Bucciarelli, Norbert Dubowy, and Reinhard Strohm (Berlin: Berliner Wissenschafts, 2006), pp. 147–75.

Rinaldi, Mario, *Due secoli al Teatro Argentina* (Florence: Olschki, 1978).

Roberts, John H., 'Handel and Vinci's "Didone Abbandonata": Revisions and Borrowings', *Music & Letters*, 68.2 (1987), 141–50.

Romagnoli, Angela, 'Una gara per il compleano del re Carlo: il "Demofoonte" di Leo, Mancini, Sarro e Sellitto (Napoli 1735) e i suoi rapporti con la partitura di Leonardo Leo del 1741', in *Responsabilità d'autore e collaborazione nell'opera dell'Età barocca. Il Pasticcio*, ed. by Gaetano Pitarresi (Reggio Calabria: Laruffa, 2011), pp. 221–56.

Rostirolla, Giancarlo, ed., *Il 'Mondo novo' musicale di Pier Leone Ghezzi* (Rome and Milan: Academia Nazionale di Santa Cecilia and Skira Editore, 2001).

Sala di Felice, Elena, *Sogni e favole in sen del vero. Metastasio ritrovato* (Rome: Aracne, 2008).

Salvarani, Marco, *Il teatro La Fenice di Ancona: cenni storici e cronologia dei drammi in musica e balli (1712–1818)* (Rome: Fratelli Palombi, 1999).

Salvioli, Giovanni and Carlo Salvioli, *Bibliografia universale del teatro drammatico italiano* (Venice: Ferrari, 1903).

Sartori, Claudio, *Dizionario degli editori musicali italiani (tipografi, incisori, librai, editori)* (Florence: Olschki, 1958).

___ *I libretti italiani a stampa dalle origini al 1800. Catalogo analitico con 16 indici*, 7 vols (Cuneo: Bertola & Locatelli, 1990–1994).

Schmidt-Hensel, Roland Dieter, 'Carl Heinrich Grauns *Demofoonte*-Vertonung (Berlin 1746)', in *Demo-*

foonte come soggetto per il dramma per musica: Johann Adolf Hasse ed altri compositori del Settecento, ed. by Milada Jonášová and Tomislav Volek (Prague: Academia, 2020), pp. 189–212.

―― 'Hasses Opern auf Friedrichs Bühne. Zur Rezeption der seria-Opern Johann Adolf Hasses im Berlin des 18. Jahrhunderts', in *Johann Adolf Hasse. Tradizion, Rezeption, Gegenwart (Kongressbericht Hamburg 2010)*, ed. by Wolfgang Hochstein (Stuttgart: Carus, 2013), pp. 49–68.

―― '*La musica è del Signor Hasse detto il Sassone…*': *Johann Adolf Hasses 'Opere serie' der Jahre 1730 bis 1745. Quellen, Fassungen, Aufführungen* (Göttingen: V&R unipress, 2009).

Schneider, Louis, *Geschichte der Opern und des königlichen Opernhauses in Berlin* (Berlin: Dunker & Humbolt, 1852).

Selfridge-Field, Eleanor, *A New Chronology of Venetian Opera and Related Genres, 1660–1760* (Stanford: Stanford University Press, 2007).

Seller, Francesca, 'La *Didone abbandonata* di Saverio Mercadante (1825)', in *Pietro Metastasio: il testo e il contesto*, ed. by Marta Columbro and Paologiovanni Maione (San Marcellino: Altrastampa, 2000), pp. 165–70.

Sommer-Mathis, Andrea, '*Didone abbandonata*–Aufführungen am Wiener Kärntnertortheater in der ersten Hälfte des 18. Jahrhunderts', in *Didone come soggetto nel dramma per musica*, ed. by Milada Jonášová and Tomislav Volek (Prague: Academia, 2018), pp. 213–34.

―― 'El tandem Metastasio–Farinelli: producción de óperas y escenografía del *dramma per musica*', *Scherzo*, 384, special dossier: *Metastasio en el Madrid del XVIII* (May 2022), 64–66.

Sommer-Mathis, Andrea and Elisabeth Theresia Hilscher, eds, *Pietro Metastasio – uomo universale (1698–1782): Festgabe der Österreichischen Akademie der Wissenschaften zum 300. Geburtstag von Pietro Metastasio* (Vienna: Österreichische Akademie der Wissenschaften, 2000).

Sonneck, Oscar George Theodore, *Catalogue of Opera Librettos Printed before 1800* (Washington: Library of Congress, 1914).

Sorge, Giuseppe, *I teatri di Palermo nel secoli XVI-XVII-XVIII* (Palermo: Industrie Riunite Editoriali Siciliane, 1926).

Spáčilová, Jana, *Catalogue of the Italian Opera Libretti in Central Europe in the 1st Half of the 18th Century* (Prague: KLP, forthcoming).

―― 'Počátky opery ve Slezsku. Současný stav pramenů', *Musicologica Brunensia*, 51.2 (2016), 157–70.

―― 'Soloists of the Opera Productions in Brno, Holešov, Kroměříž and Vyškov: Italian Opera Singers in Moravian Sources c. 1720–1740, in *Musicians' Mobilities and Music Migrations in Early Modern Europe: Biographical Patterns and Cultural Exchanges*, ed. by Gesa zur Nieden and Berthold Over (Mainz: Transcript, 2016), pp. 255–74.

Sprague, Cheryl Ruth, 'A Comparison of Five Musical Settings of Metastasio's "Artaserse"' (doctoral dissertation, University of California, 1979).

Stieger, Franz, ed., *Opernlexicon* (Tutzing: Schneider, 1977).

Strohm, Reinhardt, 'Händels Pasticci', *Analecta Musicologica*, 4 (1974), 208–67.

―― 'Hasse, Scarlatti, Rolli', *Analecta Musicologica*, 15 (1975), 220–55.

―― 'Italian Pasticcio Opera, 1700–1750: Practices and Repertoires', in *Operatic Pasticcios in 18th-Century Europe. Context, Materials and Aesthetics*, ed. by Berthold Over and Geza Zur Nieden (Bielefeld: Transcript, 2021), pp. 45–67.

―― 'Italienische Opernarien des frühen Settecento', *Analecta Musicologica*, 16.1–2 (1976).

―― 'L'"*Alessandro nell'Indie*" del Metastasio e le sue prime versioni musicali', in *La drammaturgia musicale*, ed. by Lorenzo Bianconi (Bologna: il Mulino, 1986), pp. 157–76.

―― 'Metastasio at Hamburg: Newly-Identified Opera Scores of the Mingotti Company, with a Postscript on *Ercole nell'Indie*', in *Il canto di Metastasio. Atti del convegno di studi, Venezia (14–16 dicembre 1999)*, ed. by Maria Giovanna Miggiani (Bologna: Forni, 2004), pp. 541–71.

___ *The Operas of Antonio Vivaldi* (Florence: Olschki, 2008).

___ 'Wer entscheidet? Möglichkeiten der Zusammenarbeit an Pasticcio-Opern', in *'Per ben vestir la virtuosa'. Die Oper des 18. und frühen 19. Jahrhunderts im Spannungsfeld zwischen Komponisten und Sängern*, ed. by Daniel Brandenburg and Thomas Seedorf (Schliengen: Argus, 2011), pp. 62–79.

The London Stage 1660–1800: A calendar of Plays, Entertainments & Afterpieces together with Casts, Box-receipts and Contemporary Comments: Compiled from the Playbills, Newspapers and Theatrical Diaries of the Period (Carbondale, IL: Southern Illinois University Press, 1961–1968).

Thiel, Eberhard, *Kataloge der Herzog August Bibliothek Wolfenbüttel. Libretti. Verzeichnis der bis 1800 erschienenen Textbücher* (Frankfurt am Main: Klostermann, 1970).

Tintori, Giampiero and M. Maddalena Schito, eds, *Il Regio Ducal Teatro di Milano (1717–1778): cronologia delle opere e dei balli con 10 indici* (Cuneo: Bertola & Locatelli, 1998).

Tribuzio, Giovanni, 'Pasquale Anfossi: operista alla moda', in *Il secolo d'oro della musica a Napoli. Per un canone della Scuola musicale napoletana del '700*, ed. by Lorenzo Fiorito (Frattamaggiore: Diana Edizioni, 2019), vol. 2, pp. 133–48.

Veneziano, Giulia Anna Romana, 'Da Napoli a Roma: il Teatro Alibert come spazio performativo dinamico attraverso la produzione di Leonardo Vinci (1724–1730)', *Mélanges de l'École Française de Rome*, 131.1 (2019), 169–175.

Venturi, Simonetta, 'Il periodo danese di Giuseppe Sarti e la "Didone abbandonata"', *Studi e documentazioni: Rivista umbra di musicologia*, 15.1 (2007), 23–38.

Verti, Paolo and Roberto Fabbri, *Due secoli di teatro per musica a Reggio Emilia: repertorio cronologico delle opere e dei balli 1645–1857* (Reggio Emilia: Teatro Municipale Valli, 1987).

Voss, Steffen, 'Musica di Nicola Porpora al teatro d'opera di Amburgo: *Siface*, *Didone abbandonata*, *Gli orti esperidi* ad alcuni pasticci', in *Nicola Porpora musicista europeo: le corte, i teatri, i cantanti, i librettisti. Atti del Convegno Internazionale di Studi / Reggio Calabria, 3–4 ottobre 2008*, ed. by Niccolò Maccavino (Reggio Calabria: Laruffa, 2001), pp. 95–120.

Weaver, Robert Lamar and Norma Wright Weaver, *A Chronology of Music in the Florentine Theater, 1751–1800: Operas, Prologues, Farces, Intermezzos, Concerts, and Plays with Incidental Music* (Warren, MI: Harmonie Park Press, 1993).

Wiel, Taddeo, *I teatri musicali veneziani del Settecento: Catalogo delle opera in musica rappresentate nel secolo XVIII in Venezia (1701–1808) con prefazione dell'autore* (Venice: Visenti, 1897).

Wolff, Hellmuth Christian, 'Johann Adolph Hasse und Venedig', in *Venezia e il melodramma nel Settecento*, ed. by Maria Teresa Muraro (Florence: Olschki, 1978), pp. 295–308.

Wotquenne, Alfred, *Baldassare Galuppi 1706–1785: étude bibliographique sur ses œuvres dramatiques* (Brussels: Schepens & Katto, 1902).

___ *Catalogue thématique des oeuvres de Cgr. W. v. Gluck (1714–1797)* (Leipzig: Breitkopf & Härtel, 1904).

___ *Table alphabétique dex morceaux contenús dans les oeuvres dramatiques de Zeno, Metastasio et Goldoni* (Leipzig: Breitkopf & Härtel, 1905).

Żórawska-Witkowska, Alina, 'The Music Library of the Warsaw Theatre in the Years 1788 and 1797: An Expression of the Migration of European Repertoire', *Arti musices: hrvatski muzikološki zborni*, 47.1–2 (2016), 103–16.

___ 'The Saxon Court of the Kingdom of Poland', in *Music at German Courts, 1715–1760: Changing Artistic Priorities*, ed. by Samantha Owens, Barbara M. Reul, and Janice B. Stockigt (Woodbridge: The Boydell Press, 2011), pp. 51–78.

Reference works

Die Musik in Geschichte und Gegenwart. MGG online, ed. Ludwig Finscher, 1994–2007 <https://www.mgg-online.com> [accessed 17 May 2022].

The New Grove Dictionary of Music and Musicians. Oxford Music Online, ed. by Stanley Sadie, 2001 <https://www.oxfordmusiconline.com> [accessed 29 May 2022].

Bibliographic Tools

Printed catalogues

Allacci, Leone, *Drammaturgia accresciuta e continuata fino all'anno MDCCLV* (Venice: Pasquali, 1755).

A-Wn. *Tabulae codicum manu scriptorium praeter grecos et orientales in Bibliotheca Palatina Vindobonensi asservatorum* (Vienna: Geroldi, 1897).

___ Eybl, Martin, 'Die Opern- und Ariensammlung der Erzherzogin Elisabeth von Österreich (1742–1808): Musizierpraxis in Kontext feudaler Bildungs- und Repräsentationskonzepte', *Die Musikforschung*, 68 (2015), 255–79.

Bärwald, Manuel, *Italienische Open in Leipzig (1744–1756)*, vol. 2: *Katalogteil* (Beeskow: ortus, 2016).

B-Bc. van Lamperen, M, *Catalogue de la Bibliothèque du Conservatoire royal de Musique de Bruxelles, dressé par ordre de matières, alphabétique et chronologique* (Brussels: Poot & co., 1870).

Bonlini, Giovanni Carlo, *Le Glorie della poesia, e della musica contenute nell'esatta Notitia de' teatri della città di Venezia, e nel Catalogo purgatissimo de drami musicali quivi sin'hora rapresentati* (Venice: Buonarigo, 1730, 1742).

Bouquet, Marie-Thérèse, Valeria Gualerzi, and Alberto Testa, *Storia del Teatro Regio di Torino: cronologie*, ed. by Alberto Basso (Turin: Cassa di Risparmio di Torino, [1988]).

Burden, Michael, 'Metastasio on the London Stage, 1728 to 1840: A Catalogue', *Royal Musical Association Research Chronicle*, 40 (2007), 1–332.

Chiarelli, Alessandra and Angelo Pompilio, *'Or vaghi or fieri'*: *Cenni di poetica nei libretti veneziani (circa 1760–1740)* (Bologna: Cooperativa Libraria Universitaria Editrice Bologna, 2004).

Chiti, Rossana and Federico Marri, *Testi drammatici per musica della Biblioteca Labronica di Livorno* (Livorno: Debatte & figli, 1991).

D-B. Henzel, Christoph, 'Auf dem Weg zur Werküberlieferung: Die Partituren der Berliner Opernbibliothek', in *Berliner Klassik* (Berlin: ortus, 2009), pp. 63–117.

De Filippis, Felice and Raffaele Arnese, *Cronache del Teatro di S. Carlo (1737–1960)* (Naples: Edizioni Politica Popolare, 1961).

D-Hs. Charteris, Richard, 'The Music Collection of the Staats- und Universitätsbibliothek, Hamburg: A Survey of its British Holdings Prior to the Second World War', *Royal Musical Association Research Chronicle*, 30 (1997), 1–138.

D-Kdma. *Deutsches Musikgeschichtliches Archiv Kassel: Mitteilungen und Katalog del Filmsammlung*, 27 vols (Kassel: Bärenreiter, 1955).

D-W. Thiel, Eberhard, *Kataloge der Herzog August Bibliothek Wolfenbüttel. Libretti. Verzeichnis der bis 1800 erschienenen Textbücher* (Frankfurt am Main: Klostermann, 1970).

DK-Kk. Marx, Hans Joachim and Dorothea Schröder, *Die Hamburger Gänsemarkt-Oper. Katalog der Textbücher (1678–1748)* (Bremen: Laaber, 1995.)

DK-Kk; DK-Ku. *Bibliotheca danica. Systematisk fortegnelse over den danske literatur fra 1482 til 1830 efter samlingerne i det Store kongelige bibliothek i København. Med supplementer fra Universitetsbiblioteket i København og Karen Brahes bibliothek i Odense* ([Copenhagen]: Gyldendal, 1877).

Franchi, Saverio, *Le impressioni sceniche: dizionario bio-bibliografico degli editori e stampatori romani e laziali di testi drammatici e libretti per musica dal 1759 al 1800* (Rome: Edizioni di Storia e Letteratura, 1994).

Freeman, Daniel Evan, 'The Opera Theater of Count Franz Anton von Spork in Prague (1724–35)' (doctoral dissertation, University of Illinois at Urbana-Champaign, 1987).

GB-Bp. Timms, Colin, 'Handelian and other Librettos in Birmingham Central Library', *Music & Letters*, 65.2 (1984), 141–67.

GB-Lbl. Hughes-Hughes, August, *Catalogue of Manuscript Music in the British Museum* (London: Clowes, 1906–1909).

Girardi, Michele and Franco Rossi, *Il Teatro La Fenice: cronologia degli spettacoli 1792–1936* ([Venice]: Albrizzi, [1989]).

Groppo, Antonio, *Catalogo di tutti i drammi per musica recitati ne' teatri di Venezia dall'anno 1637. in cui ebbero principio le pubbliche rappresentazioni de' medesimi fin all'anno presente 1745* (Venice: Groppo, 1745).

I-Bas. Vitali, Carlo, 'Un fondo di musiche operistiche settecentesche presso l'Archivio di Stato di Bologna', *Nuova Rivista Musicale Italiana*, 2 (1979), 1–16.

I-IBborromeo. Boggio, Enrico, *Il fondo musiche dell'Archivio Borromeo dell'Isola Bella* (Lucca: Libreria Musicale Italiana, 2004).

I-MOe

    Chiarelli, Alessandra, *I codici di musica della raccolta estense: ricostruzione dall'inventario settecentesco* (Florence: Olschki, 1987).

    Lodi, Pio, *Catalogo delle Opere Musicali teoriche e pratiche di autori vissuti suno ai primi decenni del seccolo XIX, esistenti nelle biblioteche e necli archivi pubblici e privati d'Italia – Città di Modena: R. Biblioteca estense* (Parma: Fresching, 1916–1923).

I-Nc

    Ajello, Rafaele, ed., *Il teatro di San Carlo: la cronologia 1737–1987* (Naples: Guida, 1987).

    Melisi, Francesco, *Conservatorio di musica 'S. Pietro a Majella' di Napoli. Biblioteca. Catalogo dei libretti d'opera in musica dei secoli XVII e XVIII* (Naples: Buonaiuti, 1985).

    Catalogo delle Opere Musicali teoriche e pratiche di autori vissuti suno ai primi decenni del seccolo XIX, esistenti nelle biblioteche e necli archivi pubblici e privati d'Italia – Città di Napoli: Biblioteca del R. Conservatorio di S. Pietro a Majella, ed. by Guido Gasperini and Franca Gallo (Parma: Fresching, 1934).

I-OS. OSTIGLIA, *Biblioteca dell'Opera Pia Greggiati: catalogo del Fondo Musicale*, ed. by Claudio Sartori, vol. 1 (Milan: Nuovo Istituto Editoriale Italiano, 1983).

I-PSrospigliosi. *Catalogo del Fondo Musicale Rospigliosi*, ed. by Teresa Dolfi and Luciano Vannucci (Lucca: Libreria Musicale Italiana, 2011).

I-Rama. Antolini, Bianca Maria and Annalisa Bini, 'Johann Adolph Hasse nei manoscritti della Biblioteca di S. Cecilia di Roma', *Analecta Musicologica*, 25 (1983), 495–511.

I-Rvat. Gialdroni, Giuliana and Teresa Maria Gialdroni, *Libretti per musica del Fondo Ferrajoli della Biblioteca Apostolica Vaticana* (Lucca and Rome: LIM and Biblioteca Apostolica Vaticana, 1993).

I-Vqs. Rossi, Franco, *Le opere musicali della Fondazione 'Querini-Stampalia' di Venezia* (Turin: Società Italiana di Musicologia, 1984).

Llorens, Ana, Gorka Rubiales, and Nicola Usula, 'Operatic Sources for *Demofoonte*: Librettos and Scores after Metastasio's "figliuolo"', in *Demofoonte come soggetto per il dramma per musica: Johann Adolf*

Hasse ed altri compositori del Settecento, ed. by Milada Jonášová and Tomislav Volek (Prague: Academia, 2020), pp. 271–317.

Passadore, Francesco and Franco Rossi, *Il Teatro San Benedetto di Venezia: cronologia degli spettacoli 1755–1810* (Venice: Fondazione Levi, 2003).

P-Cu. Pinto de Castro, Aníbal, *Catálogo da Colecção de Miscelâneas. Teatro* (Coimbra: Biblioteca Geral da Universidade, 1974).

P-La. Machado Santos, Marianna Amélia, ed., *Biblioteca da Ajuda: Catálogo de Música Manuscrita* (Lisbon: Biblioteca da Ajuda, 1958).

PL. Streicher, Karol, *Bibliografia polska* (Krakow: Druckarno Uniwersytetu Jagiellońskieg, 1891).

PL-MO. Kaczmarczyk, Krazimierz, ed., *Katalog Archiwum Opactwa Cystersów w Mogile* (Mogile: Z ZasIłkiem oo. Cystersów w mogile, 1919).

Rinaldi, Mario, *Due secoli al Teatro Argentina* (Florence: Olschki, 1978).

Sartori, Claudio, *I libretti italiani a stampa dalle origini al 1800. Catalogo analitico con 16 indici*, 7 vols (Cuneo: Bertola & Locatelli Editori, 1990–1994).

Schmidt-Hensel, Roland Dieter, 'La musica è del Signor Hasse detto il Sassone…': *Johann Adolf Hasses 'Opere serie' der Jahre 1730 bis 1745. Quellen, Fassungen, Aufführungen*, vol. 2: *Werk-, Quellen- und Aufführungsverzeichnis* (Göttingen: V&R unipress, 2009).

Selfridge-Field, Eleanor, *A New Chronology of Venetian Opera and Related Genres, 1660–1760* (Stanford: Stanford University Press, 2007).

Spáčilová, Jana, *Catalogue of the Italian Opera Libretti in Central Europe in the 1st Half of the 18th Century* (Prague: KLP, forthcoming).

____ 'Současný stav libret italské opery na Moravě v 1. polovině 18. století', *Acta* musicologica.cz*. Revue pro hudební vědu*, 2 (2006) <http://acta.musicologica.cz/06-02/0602s06.html> [accessed 19 May 2022].

The London Stage 1660–1800: A Calendar of plays, Entertainments & Afterpieces together with Casts, Box-Receipts and Contemporary Comments: Compiled from the Playbills, Newspapers and Theatrical Diaries of the Period (Carbondale, IL: Southern Illinois University Press, 1961–1968).

US-BEm. Emerson, John A, *Catalog of Pre-1900 Vocal Manuscripts in the Music Library, University of California at Berkeley* (Berkeley: University of California Press, 1988).

US-LAum. Alm, Irene, *Catalog of Venetian Librettos at the University of California, Los Angeles* (Berkeley: University of California Press, 1993).

US-Wc.
> *Library of Congress – Dramatic Music* (Class M 1500, 1510, 1520). *Catalogue of Full Scores* (Washington: Government Printing Office, 1908).
>
> Sonneck, Oscar George Theodore, *Catalogue of Opera Librettos printed before 1800* (Washington: Library of Congress, 1914).

Wiel, Taddeo, *I teatri musicali veneziani del Settecento: catalogo delle opera in musica rappresentate nel secolo XVIII in Venezia (1701–1808) con prefazione dell'autore* (Venice: Visenti, 1897).

Institutional catalogues online

A-Gl. ATMK. Landesbibliothek: Allgemeiner Systematischer Katalog <https://literatur.stmk.gv.at> [accessed 5 April 2022]. Digitised card catalogue <https://literatur.stmk.gv.at/katzoom/cgi-katzoom/katzoom.cgi?katalog=1&faktor=8> [accessed 6 April 2022].

A-Gu. UB Nominalkatalog 1501–1982, digitised card catalogue <https://webapp.uibk.ac.at/alo/cat/collection.jsp?id=1004> [accessed 6 April 2022].

SC | Bibliographic Tools

A-Scu. UBSearch, online catalogue of the Paris Lodron Universität Salzburg <https://ubsearch.sbg.ac.at> [accessed 6 April 2022].

A-Wgm. Online catalogue of the Gesellschaft der Musikfreunde in Wien <https://www.katalog.a-wgm.at> [accessed 27 April 2022].

A-Wmi. PDF catalogue of libretti for the Musikwissenschaftliches Institut der Universität Wien <https://bibliothek.univie.ac.at/fb-musikwissenschaft/files/libretti.pdf> [accessed 3 April 2022].

A-Wn. Online catalogue of the Österreichische Nationalbibliothek <https://search.onb.ac.at> [accessed 8 May 2022].

B-Bc. Online catalogue of the Bibliothèque du Conservatoire royal de Bruxelles <https://catalog.b-bc.org> [accessed 18 May 2022].

CDN-HNu. Online catalogue of the McMaster University <https://library.mcmaster.ca> [accessed 14 April 2022].

CDN-Lu. Western Libraries online catalogue <https://www.lib.uwo.ca/> [accessed 16 April 2022].

CDN-Ttfl. LibrarySearch, online catalogue of the University of Toronto Libraries <https://librarysearch.library.utoronto.ca> [accessed 16 April 2022].

CZ-Bu. Online catalogue of The Moravian Library in Brno <https://www.mzk.cz> [accessed 7 May 2022].

CZ-Pnm. Online catalogue of the Czech Museum of Music <https://cmh.opac.nm.cz> [accessed 7 May 2022].

CZ-Pu. Electronic catalogue of the National Library of the Czech Republic <https://aleph.nkp.cz> [accessed 7 May 2022].

D-Au. Katalog OPAC der Universitätsbibliothek Augsburg <https://opac.bibliothek.uni-augsburg.de> [accessed 17 April 2022].

D-AHs. Hofbibliothek Aschaffenbug, Online-Katalog <https://recherche.bibkatalog.de> [accessed 9 April 2022].

D-B. stabikat+, online catalogue of the Staatsbibliothek zu Berlin, Preußischer Kulturbesitz <http://stabikat.de> [accessed 22 May 2022].

D-B. Imagekataloge (IPAC), digitised card catalogues of the music collections at the Staatsbibliothek zu Berlin <https://staatsbibliothek-berlin.de/die-staatsbibliothek/abteilungen/musik/recherche-und-ressourcen/imagekataloge> [accessed 21 May 2022].

D-BFb [D-MÜu]. Digitised card catalogue of the Fürst zu Bentheimische Musiksammlung <https://miami.uni-muenster.de/Record/d22d066a-149e-453f-8e8b-8d133fe7fb89> [accessed 10 April 2022].

D-BS. Online catalogue of the Stadtbibliothek Braunschweig <https://www.braunschweig.de/kultur/bibliotheken_archive/stadtbibliothek/katalog_konto.php> [accessed 10 April 2022].

D-Dl. SLUB, Online catalogue of the Sächsische Landesbibliothek – Staats- und Universitätsbibliothek Dresden <https://www.slub-dresden.de> [accessed 11 May 2022].

D-Eu. OPAF of the Katholische Universität Eischstätt-Ingolstadt <https://opac.ku.de> [accessed 10 April 2022].

D-F. Katalog der Universität Frankfurt <https://lbsopac.rz.uni-frankfurt.de> [accessed 10 April 2022].

D-FUl. Online catalogue of the Hochschul- und Landesbibliothek Fulda <https://www.hs-fulda.de> [accessed 10 April 2022].

D-Gu. GöDiscovery, the Discovery Service of the Göttingen State and University Library <https://discovery.sub.uni-goettingen.de> [accessed 20 April 2022].

D-Hs. Online catalogue of the Staats- und Universitätsbibliothek Carl von Ossietzky <https://www.sub.uni-hamburg.de> [accessed 20 April 2022].

D-HVl. Online catalogue of the Gottfried Wilhelm Leibniz Library, State Library of Lower Saxony [Niedersächsische Landesbibliothek] <https://opac.tib.eu/DB=3/LNG=DU/> [accessed 10 April 2022].

D-KNth. Online librettos catalogue, A-L, M-Z [accessed 5 April 2022].

D-KNu. Online catalogue of the Universitäts- und Stadtbibliothek Köln <https://www.ub.uni-koeln.de> [accessed 20 April 2022].

D-Ju. Online-Katalog Thüringer Universitäts- und Landesbibliothek <https://www.thulb.uni-jena.de/Online_Katalog.html> [accessed 12 April 2022].

D-KA. Katalog plus, online catalogue of the Badische Landesbibliothek <https://rds-blb.ibs-bw.de/opac> [accessed 22 April 2022].

D-LEm. Online catalogue of the Leipziger Städische Bibliotheken <https://stadtbibliothek.leipzig.de> [accessed 23 April 2022].

D-LEu. Online catalogue of the Universitätsbibliothek Leipzig <https://katalog.ub.uni-leipzig.de> [accessed 10 April 2022].

D-Mbs. Katalog OPACplus <https://www.bsb-muenchen.de> [accessed 25 April 2022].

D-MÜu. Online catalogue of the Universitäts- und Landesbibliothek Münster <https://katalogix.uni-muenster.de> [accessed 10 April 2022].

D-Pu. Passauer Suchportal, online catalogue of the Universität Passau <https://literatursuche.ub.uni-passau.de> [accessed 10 April 2022].

D-Sl. Online catalogue of the Badische Landesbibliothek <https://www.blb-karlsruhe.de> [accessed 19 April 2022].

D-TRp. Onlinekatalog der Bibliothek des Priesterseminars Trier <https://katalog.dombibliothek-koeln.de> [accessed 10 April 2022].

DK-Kk. Online catalogue of Det Kongelige Bibliotek på Slotsholmen <https://www.kb.dk/en/find-materials> [accessed 29 April 2022].

DK-Ku. Online catalogue of Copenhagen University Library <https://kub.ku.dk> [accessed 3 May 2022].

F-Pn. Catalogue général de la Bibliothèque nationale de France <https://catalogue.bnf.fr> [accessed 10 June 2022].

E-Bbc. Explora la BC, online catalogue of the Biblioteca de Catalunya <https://explora.bnc.cat> [accessed 19 May 2022].

E-Bcapdevilla. Online catalogue of the Universitat Ramon Llull <https://discovery.url.edu> [accessed 19 May 2022].

E-Bu. Cercabib, online catalogue of the Universitat de Barcelona <https://cercabib.ub.edu> [accessed 19 May 2022].

E-Mmh. Online catalogue of the Biblioteca Histórica Municipal de Madrid <https://catalogos.madrid.es/cgi-bin/historica> [accessed 19 May 2022].

E-Mn. Catálogo BNE, online catalogue of the Biblioteca Nacional de España <http://catalogo.bne.es> [accessed 22 May 2022].

E-Mp. IBIS, online catalogue of the Real Biblioteca <https://realbiblioteca.patrimonionacional.es> [accessed 26 May 2022].

E-MO. Online catalogue of the Biblioteca de Montserrat <https://bibliotecademontserrat.cat/es/index.php/catalogo> [accessed 10 April 2022].

GB-Bp. Online catalogue of Birmingham City Council <https://birmingham.spydus.co.uk> [accessed 15 April 2022].

SC | Bibliographic Tools

GB-Cu. iDiscover, online catalogue of the Cambridge Libraries Collection (including the Fitzwilliam Museum) <https://idiscover.lib.cam.ac.uk> [accessed 5 June 2022].

GB-DRu. Discover Durham Collections <https://discover.durham.ac.uk> [accessed 15 April 2022].

GB-En. Library Search, online catalogue of the National Library of Scotland <https://search.nls.uk> [accessed 16 April 2022].

GB-Lbl. Explore the British Library, main catalogue of the British Library <http://explore.bl.uk> [accessed 3 Ma 2022].

GB-Lbl. Explore Archives and Manuscripts, online catalogue for unique collection items at the British Library <https://searcharchives.bl.uk> [accessed 3 May 2022].

GB-Lcm. Online catalogue of the Royal College of Music <https://rcm.koha-ptfs.co.uk> [accessed 18 April 2022].

GB-Ob. SOLO, Search Oxford Libraries Online, online catalogue for the Bodleian Library <https://solo.bodleian.ox.ac.uk> [accessed 20 April 2022].

GB-SA. Library catalogue of the University of Andrews <https://www.st-andrews.ac.uk/library> [accessed 18 April 2022].

H-Bn. NEKTÁR, online catalogue of the Országos Széchényi Könyvtár <https://nektar2.oszk.hu> [accessed 4 April 2022].

H-Bu. Online catalogue of the Eötvös Loránd Tudományegyetem Egyetemi Könyvtár <http://aleph.elte.hu> [accessed 4 April 2022].

I-Bc. Gaspari online, online catalogue of the Museo Internazionale e biblioteca della musica di Bologna <http://www.bibliotecamusica.it> [accessed 22 May 2022].

I-BRq. Online catalogue of the Biblioteca Queriniana in Brescia <https://queriniana.comune.brescia.it> [accessed 18 May 2022].

I-Fc. Online catalogue of the Biblioteca Nazionale Centrale di Firenze <https://opac.bncf.firenze.sbn.it> [accessed 19 May 2022].

I-Lg. Digitised card catalogue of the Biblioteca statale di Lucca – Catalogo di musica <http://cataloghistorici.bdi.sbn.it/dett_catalogo.php?IDCAT=39> [accessed 15 May 2022].

I-Mb. Online catalogue of the Biblioteca Nazionale Braidense <http://opac.braidense.it> [accessed 16 May 2022].

I-MAc. Biblioteca Digitale Teresiana, catalogo bibliografico storico <http://digilib.bibliotecateresiana.it>.

I-OS. OSTIGLIA Biblioteca dell'Opera Pia Greggiati. Catalogo del Fondo Musicale <http://web.tiscali.it/ostiglia/html/index.htm>.

I-PIu. Online catalogue of the Biblioteca Universitaria di Pisa <https://opac.bibliotecauniversitaria.pi.it/opacpisa/opac/pisa/free.jsp> [accessed 8 May 2022].

I-Rc. Online catalogue of the Biblioteca Casanatense <https://casanatense.on.worldcat.org> [accessed 12 April 2022]. Digitised alphabetical card catalogue <http://cataloghistorici.bdi.sbn.it/dett_catalogo.php?IDCAT=106> [accessed 12 April 2022]. Index Re di Musica, digitized card catalogue <http://cataloghistorici.bdi.sbn.it/dett_catalogo.php?IDCAT=198> [accessed 13 April 2022].

I-Rn. OnlinePublicAccessCatalogue, online catalogue of the Biblioteca Nazionale Centrale di Roma <http://bve.opac.almavivaitalia.it> [accessed 14 April 2022].

I-Rvat. General Catalogue of the Biblioteca Apostolica Vaticana <https://opac.vatlib.it> [accessed 7 May 2022].

I-REm. Catalogo storico a schede <https://openapps.comune.re.it/cataloghispecialibiblio/catalogo-storico-e-schede/index.jsp> [accessed 6 May 2022].

I-Tn. Online catalogue of the Biblioteca Nazionale Universitaria di Torino <https://bnto.comperio.it> [accessed 6 May 2022].

LI-Ln. COBISS+. Online catalogue of the National and University Library of Ljubljana <https://plus.cobiss.net> [accessed 10 May 2022].
M-Vnl. Online Catalogue of the National Library of Malta <https://maltalibraries.gov.mt/iguana> [accessed 3 April 2022].
NZ-Wt. National Library of New Zealand Catalogue <https://natlib.govt.nz/> [accessed 16 April 2022].
P-Cug. OPAC of the Biblioteca Geral Digital <https://web.bg.uc.pt/cmisc> [accessed 30 April 2022].
P-Lcg. Online catalogue of the Biblioteca de Arte of the Caloste Gulbenkian Foundation <https://www.biblartepac.gulbenkian.pt> [accessed 30 April 2022].
P-Ln. Online catalogue of the Biblioteca Nacional de Portugal <https://catalogo.bnportugal.gov.pt> [accessed 25 May 2022].
PL-Kj. Jagiellonian Library. The Old Catalogue (printed items since the beginning of the print era through 1949), digitised card catalogue <http://pka.bj.uj.edu.pl/PKA/index_en.php> [accessed 3 June 2022].
PL-Ptu. Digitised card catalogue <http://katalogkartkowy.ptpn.poznan.pl/ptpn> [accessed 28 April 2022].
PL-Wn. Catalogue of the Biblioteka Narodowna <https://katalogi.bn.org.pl> [accessed 28 April 2022].
PL-Wu. Online catalogue of the Biblioteka Uniwersytecka <https://buuam.digital-center.pl> [accessed 29 April 2022]. Digitised card catalogue of the Early Printed Books Department <https://stare-druki.ckk.buw.uw.edu.pl> [accessed 29 April 2022].
Progetto Metastasio, dir. by Anna Laura Bellina <http://www.librettodopera.it> [accessed 7 May 2022].
RUS-Mrg. Online catalogue of the Rossijskaja Gosudarstvennaja biblioteka <http://aleph.rsl.ru>. RSL Catalog, digitised card catalogue <http://aleph.rsl.ru> [accessed 4 May 2022].
RUS-SPsc. Electronic catalogue of the Rossijskaja nacional'naja biblioteka <https://primo.nlr.ru> [accessed 4 April 2022]. Electronic catalogue of the Department of Manuscripts <http://nlr.ru/manuscripts/RA3124/online-catalogues> [accessed 4 April 2022].
S-Sk. Online catalogue of Stockholms stadsbibliothek <https://biblioteket.stockholm.se> [accessed 24 March 2022].
S-Skma. Online catalogue of the Musik- och teaterbiblioteket <https://discover.musikverket.se> [accessed 24 March 2022].
S-Uu. Digitised card catalogue of books and magazines until 1962 <https://www.ub.uu.se/library-catalogues-a-z/catalogue-1962> [accessed 24 March 2022]; digitised catalogue of vocal music manuscripts in Uppsala University Library <http://files.webb.uu.se/uploader/798> [accessed 24 March 2022].
US-AUS. Online catalogue of University of Texas Libraries <https://www.lib.utexas.edu> [accessed 24 April 2022]; online catalogue for the Kraus libretti collection <https://www.hrc.utexas.edu/search/kraus/libretti#>.
US-BEm. UC Library Search, University of California's discovery and borrowing system <https://search.library.berkeley.edu> [accessed 30 April 2022].
US-Cn. Primoe, online catalogue for The Newberry Library <https://i-share-nby.primo.exlibrisgroup.com/discovery/search?vid=01CARLI_NBY:CARLI_NBY&lang=en> [accessed 25 April 2022].
US-Cu. The University of Chicago Library Catalog <https://catalog.lib.uchicago.edu> [accessed 26 April 2022].
US-CA. HOLLIS, Harvard Library's catalog <https://hollis.harvard.edu> [accessed 4 May 2022].
US-Eu. Online catalogue of Northwestern Libraries <https://www.library.northwestern.edu> [accessed 5 May 2022].

US-FAy. Quicksearch, Online catalogue of Yale University <https://search.library.yale.edu> [accessed 29 April 2022].
US-BL; US-I. IUCAT, Indiana University Library Catalog <https://iucat.iu.edu> [accessed 28 April 2022].
US-NH. Yale Library, online catalogue of Yale University Library <https://library.yale.edu> [accessed 28 April 2022].
US-NYp. Online catalogue of New York Public Library <https://www.nypl.org> [accessed 6 May 2022].
US-PRu. Online catalogue of Princeton University Library <https://library.princeton.edu> [accessed 27 April 2022].
US-SY. Summon, Online catalogue of the Syracuse University Libraries <https://library.syr.edu> [accessed 28 April 2022].
US-U. Online catalogue of Illinois University Library <https://i-share-uiu.primo.exlibrisgroup.com/discovery/search?vid=01CARLI_UIU:CARLI_UIU&lang=en> [accessed 28 April 2022].
US-Wc. Online catalogue of the Library of Congress <https://www.loc.gov> [accessed 30 April 2022].

Meta-catalogues

BASE, Catalogue collectif de France <https://ccfr.bnf.fr> [accessed 14 May 2022].
BiblioMarcheNORD, Catalogo unificato delle province di Ancona e Pesaro-Urbino <https://bibliomarchenord.it> [accessed 28 May 2022].
Biblioteca Digitale Italiana. Catalogui Storici Digitalizzati <https://www.iccu.sbn.it> [accessed 20 May 2022].
BSZ. Online catalogue of the Bibliotheksservice-Zentrum Baden-Württemberg <https://www.bsz-bw.de/index.html> [accessed 25 April 2022].
CBL. Catalogo delle Biblioteche Liguri <https://www.catalogobibliotecheliguri.it> [accessed 7 May 2022].
Centre for Research Libraries, Global Resources Network <https://www.crl.edu> [accessed 8 April 2022].
English Short Title Catalogue <http://estc.bl.uk> [accessed 13 May 2022].
EROMM, European Register of Microform and Digital Masters <https://www.eromm.org> [accessed 8 May 2022].
Casaglia, Gherardo, *L'Almanacco di Gherardo Casaglia* <https://almanac-gherardo-casaglia.com> [accessed 7 May 2022].
Corago. Repertorio e archivio di libretti del melodramma italiano dal 1600 al 1900 <http://corago.unibo.it> [accessed 24 June 2022].
GVK. Online Gemeinsamer Verbundkatalog <https://kxp.k10plus.de/DB2.1> [accessed 28 April 2022].
Internet Culturale <https://www.internetculturale.it> [accessed 7 June 2022].
Leggere Piace, Polo bibliotecario piacentino <https://leggerepiace.it/SebinaOpac/.do> [accessed 14 May 2022].
MAL. MetaOPC delle biblioteche pubbliche lombarde <https://www.biblioteche.regione.lombardia.it> [accessed 17 May 2022].
Neville, Don. Eighteenth-Century Studies. Handbook for Metastasio Research <https://publish.uwo.ca/%7Emetastas/index.html> [accessed 11 May 2022].

SC | Bibliographic Tools

Pasticcio. Ways of arranging attractive operas <https://www.pasticcio-project.eu> [accessed 13 May 2022].
Polo regionale di Sicilia <http://opac.sicilia.metavista.it/opac_sicilia/opac/sicilia/free.jsp> [accessed 12 May 2022].
PORBASE. Base Nacional de Dados Bibliográficos <http://porbase.bnportugal.pt> [accessed 21 April 2022].
RISM. Répertoire International des Sources Musicales, Catalog of Musical Sources <https://rism.info> [accessed 21 June 2022].
SB Swissbib, Online Catalogue of Switzerland's institutional libraries <https://www.swissbib.ch> [accessed 24 April 2022].
SBN, Catalogo del Servizio Bibliotecario Nazionale <https://opac.sbn.it> [accessed 20 June 2022].
Sistema Bibliotecario di Milano <https://milano.biblioteche.it> [accessed 28 May 2022].
Sistema Documentatio Territoriale Livornese <https://opacsol.comune.livorno.it> [accessed 24 May 2022].
Souborný Katalog. Unified digital catalogue for the National Museum in Prague (including CZ-Pdobrovského, CZ-Pn, and CZ-Pnm) <https://nmcentral.kpsys.cz> [accessed 7 May 2022].
Online catalogue of the Public Libraries in Jefferson County <https://jeffa.na.iiivega.com> [accessed 16 April 2022].
Polo SBN Napoli. Catalogo collettivo delle biblioteche del Polo Napoli del Servizio Bibliotecario Nazionale <https://opac.bnnonline.it/SebinaOpac/.do> [accessed 10 May 2022].
Polo SBN Venezia. Online catalogue of the libraries in the region of Venice <https://polovea.sebina.it> [accessed 23 May 2022].
Regional Katalog Rostock <http://opac.lbs-rostock.gbv.de> [accessed 25 April 2022].
Rete Bibliotecaria Bresciana e Cremonense <https://opac.provincia.brescia.it> [accessed 13 May 2022].
Sistema Bibliotecario Parmense <https://biblioteche.parma.it> [accessed 12 May 2022].
Sistema Bibliotecario Reggiano <https://opac.provincia.re.it/opac/.do> [accessed 12 May 2022].
VD18. *Das Verzeichnis Deutscher Drucke des 18. Jahrhunderts* <https://kxp.k10plus.de> [accessed 26 April 2022].
Worldcat <https://www.worldcat.org> [accessed 23 April 2022].

Card catalogues

A-MB; A-Wgm; A-Wn; B-Bc; D-B; D-Dl; D-Eu; D-HAmi; D-Hs; D-Ju; D-KA; D-KIl; D-KNu; D-Mbs; D-MHrm; D-MÜs; D-Rtt; D-Sl; D-Wa; DK-Kk; F-Pn; GB-Lcm; GB-Owc; I-Bc; I-BRq; I-BGc; I-CATu; I-Fc; I-FAN; I-Gc; I-Gl; I-La; I-LDEsormani; I-LOcl; I-Ma; I-Mb; I-Mr; I-Ms; I-MAav; I-MAC; I-MC; I-MOe; I-Nc; I-OS; I-Pl; I-PEc; I-PESo; I-PIu; I-PLcon; I-PLn; I-Ra; I-Rama; I-Rc; I-Rdp; I-Rig; I-Rn; I-Rsc; I-Tf; I-Tn; I-Tu; I-PS; I-Vc; I-Vmc; I-Vnm; I-VEc; P-La; P-Lcg; PL-Kj; PL-MO; PL-Ptu; PL-WRzno; RUS-SPsc; S-Skma; SI-Lna;[1] SI-Lsk; SK-KRE; US-Cn; US-LAum; US-NYp; US-SY; US-Wc

---

[1] Although C,S include some copies supposedly stored in SI-Lna, the Head of the Archive confirmed that they do not hold any Metastasian works.

Index Ia.
Chronological Index: by Year

1724, Naples, *Didone*, D. N. Sarro, pr. (1st)	41
1724, Palermo, *Didone*, D. Scarlatti, rvl	43
1724, Rome, *Didone*, D. Scarlatti, pr.	43
1725, Florence, *Didone*	44
1725, Reggio, *Didone*, N. Porpora, pr.	45
1725, Venice, *Didone*, T. G. Albinoni, pr.	43
1726, Crema, *Didone*, T. G. Albinoni, rvl	43
1726, Rome, *Didone*, L. Vinci, pr. (1st)	46
1726, Vienna, *Didone*, L. Vinci, rvl	46
1726, Wrocław, *Didone*, T. G. Albinoni, rvl	43
1727, Livorno, *Didone*	47
1727, Mantua, *Didone*	48
1727, Turin, *Didone*, D. N. Sarro, rvl	41
1728, Syracuse, *Didone*	48
1729, Lucca, *Didone*, L. Vinci, rvl	46
1729, Milan, *Didone*, T. G. Albinoni, rvl	43
1729, Vienna, *Didone*	48
1730, Bologna, *Artaserse*, J. A. Hasse?, rvl	197
1730, Florence, *Artaserse*, L. Vinci, rvl	189
1730, Genoa, *Artaserse*, J. A. Hasse, rvl	197
1730, Linz?, *Didone*, T. G. Albinoni, rvl	44
1730, Lucca, *Artaserse*, J. A. Hasse, rvl	197
1730, Pesaro, *Didone*, T. G. Albinoni, rvl	44
1730, Rome, *Alessandro*, L. Vinci, pr.	111
1730, Rome, *Artaserse*, L. Vinci, pr.	189
1730, Turin, *Artaserse*, J. A. Hasse, rvl	197
1730, Venice, *Artaserse*, J. A. Hasse, pr. (1st)	197
1730, Venice, *Didone*, D. N. Sarro, pr. (2nd)	41
1730, Vienna, *Artaserse*, L. Vinci, rvl	189
1731, Dresden, *Alessandro*, J. A. Hasse, pr.	119
1731, Fano, *Artaserse*, L. Vinci, rvl	189
1731, Ferrara, *Artaserse*, L. Vinci, rvl	189
1731, Hamburg, *Didone* (Ger.), N. Porpora, rvl	45
1731, Kremsier, *Artaserse* (Ger.), J. A. Hasse, rvl	198
1731, Livorno, *Alessandro*, L. Vinci, past.	111
1731, Livorno, *Artaserse*, L. Vinci, rvl	189
1731, London, *Alessandro*, G. F. Händel, pr. (1st)	116
1731, London, *Alessandro*, G. F. Händel, pr. (2nd)	116
1731, Milan, *Alessandro*, L. A. Predieri, pr.	115
1731, Milan, *Artaserse*, J. A. Hasse, rvl	198
1731, Naples, *Artaserse*, L. Vinci, rvl	190
1731, Pesaro, *Artaserse*, L. Vinci, rvl	189
1731, Prague, *Didone*, T. G. Albinoni, rvl	44
1731, Rome, *Artaserse*, L. Vinci, rvl	189
1731, Turin, *Alessandro*, N. Porpora, pr.	114
1731, Vienna, *Alessandro*, N. Porpora, past.	115
1732, Brunswick, *Alessandro*, G. F. Händel, rvl	116
1732, Florence, *Alessandro*, L. Vinci, past.	111
1732, Genoa, *Alessandro*, L. A. Predieri, rvl	115
1732, Hamburg, *Alessandro*, J. A. Hasse + G. P. Telemann, rvl	116
1732, Milan, *Alessandro*, J. A. Hasse, rvl	119
1732, Naples, *Alessandro*, F. Mancini, pr.	127
1732, Perugia, *Artaserse*, L. Vinci, rvl	190
1732, Rome, *Didone*, N. Porpora, N. Broschi, E. Duni, M. Fini, past.	48
1732, Venice, *Alessandro*, G. B. Pescetti, pr.	126
1732, Vienna, *Adriano*, A. Caldara, pr.	271
1733, Brescia, *Alessandro*, L. Vinci, rvl	111
1733, Camerino *Artaserse*, L. Vinci, rvl	190
1733, Ferrara, *Didone*, T. G. Albinoni, rvl	44
1733, Holešov, *Artaserse*, E. Bambini, pr.	208
1733, Messina, *Didone*	49
1733, Naples, *Artaserse*, L. Vinci, rvl	190
1733, Palermo, *Alessandro*	127
1733, Reggio Emilia, *Alessandro*, L. Vinci, rvl	111
1733, Siena, *Artaserse*	208
1733, Venice, *Adriano*, G. Giacomelli, pr.	272
1733, Verona, *Artaserse*, J. A. Hasse, rvl	198
1733, Vienna, *Demofoonte*, A. Caldara, pr.	315
1733, Wrocław, *Artaserse*, A. Bioni, pr.?	208
1734, Bologna, *Alessandro*, G. M. Schiassi, pr. (1st)	128
1734, Brno, *Didone*, D. N. Sarro, rvl	41
1734, Brunswick, *Didone*, N. Porpora, rvl	45
1734, Florence, *Adriano*	273
1734, Genoa, *Adriano*, P. G. Sandoni, pr.	273
1734, Jesi, *Alessandro*, G. M. Schiassi, rvl	128

SC | Index Ia. Chronological Index: by Year

1734, London, *Artaserse*, G. F. Händel and others, past. (x2)	209
1734, London, *Artaserse*, J. A. Hasse and others, past.	210
1734, Naples, *Adriano*, G. B. Pergolesi, pr.	273
1734, Perugia, *Artaserse*, L. Vinci, rvl	190
1734, Perugia, *Didone*, L. Vinci, rvl	46
1734, Pisa, *Artaserse*, G. Giacomelli, pr.	210
1734, Prague, *Alessandro*, A. Bioni, rvl	128
1734, Urbino, *Alessandro*, L. Vinci, rvl	111
1734, Valencia, *Artaserse*	210
1734, Venice, *Artaserse*, J. A. Hasse, rvl	198
1734, Vyškov, *Alessandro*, L. Vinci, rvl	111
1734, Wrocław, *Alessandro*, A. Bioni, pr.	128
1735, Bologna, *Didone*, G. M. Schiassi, pr.	49
1735, Florence, *Didone*	49
1735, Genoa, *Demofoonte*, P. V. Chiocchetti, pr.	318
1735, La Valletta, *Artaserse*, J. A. Hasse, rvl	198
1735, London, *Adriano*, F. M. Veracini, pr.	275
1735, London, *Artaserse*, J. A. Hasse and others, past. (x3)	210
1735, Munich, *Alessandro*, L. Vinci and others, rvl	111
1735, Naples, *Demofoonte*, F. Mancini, D. N. Sarro, L. Leo, pr.	316
1735, Pisa, *Alessandro*, various	129
1735, Rome, *Demofoonte*, F. Ciampi, pr.	318
1735, Venice, *Adriano*	276
1735, Venice, *Demofoonte*, G. M. Schiassi, pr.	316
1735, Vyškov *Demofoonte*, G. M. Schiassi, rvl	316
1736, Caltagirone, *Adriano*	278
1736, Jaroměřice, *Didone*, L. Vinci, rvl	46
1736, Hamburg, *Alessandro*, J. A. Hasse + G. P. Telemann, rvl	116
1736, Lisbon, *Alessandro*, G. M. Schiassi, pr. (2nd)	128
1736, London, *Adriano*, F. M. Veracini, rvl (x2)	275
1736, London, *Alessandro*, G. F. Händel, pr. (3rd)	116
1736, London, *Artaserse*, J. A. Hasse and others, past. (x3)	210
1736, Milan, *Adriano*, A. Bernasconi, pr. (1st)	276
1736, Naples, *Alessandro*, J. A. Hasse, rvl	119
1736, Parma, *Alessandro*, L. Vinci, rvl	112
1736, Prato, *Alessandro*, E. R. Duni, pr.	129
1736, Rome, *Adriano*, E. R. Duni, pr.	278
1736, Venice, *Alessandro*, J. A. Hasse, rvl	119
1737, Brunswick, *Adriano*, A. Caldara, rvl	271
1737, Brunswick, *Artaserse*, G. A. Paganelli, pr.	212
1737, Brunswick, *Artaserse*, G. A. Paganelli, rvl	212
1737, Ferrara, *Alessandro*, J. A. Hasse, rvl	119
1737, Graz, *Didone*, P. Scalabrini and others, pr.	50
1737, Jaroměřice, *Didone*, L. Vinci, rvl	46
1737, Lisbon, *Artaserse*, G. M. Schiassi, pr.	213
1737, Lisbon, *Demofoonte*, G. M. Schiassi, rvl	316
1737, Livorno, *Demofoonte*, various, past.	318
1737, London, *Demofoonte*, E. R. Duni, pr.	318
1737, London, *Didone*, Vinci, Händel and others, past., pr.	51
1737, Mantua, *Adriano*, G. Porta, pr.	278
1737, Munich, *Adriano*, G. B. Ferrandini, pr.	278
1737, Munich, *Demofoonte*, G. B. Ferrandini, pr.	318
1737, Padua, *Alessandro*, G. A. Pampani, pr.	129
1737, Parma, *Artaserse*, F. Poncini Zilioli, pr.	212
1737, Stuttgart, *Adriano*, A. Bernasconi, rvl	276
1737, Treviso, *Adriano*, G. Porta, rvl	278
1737, Vyškov, *Adriano*, J. A. Hasse, pr.	279
1738, Bayreuth, *Didone*, G. A. Paganelli, pr.	52
1738, Bergamo, *Artaserse*, J. A. Hasse, rvl	198
1738, Graz, *Alessandro*, J. A. Hasse, rvl	120
1738, Graz, *Artaserse*, P. Scalabrini and others	214
1738, Klagenfurt, *Artaserse*, J. A. Hasse, rvl	198
1738, Jaroměřice, *Demofoonte*, G. F. Brivio, rvl	320
1738, Livorno, *Artaserse*, D. Zamparelli and other, pr.	215
1738, Madrid, *Alessandro*, F. Corselli, pr.	133
1738, Madrid, *Alessandro*, F. Corselli, rvl (x2)	133
1738, Madrid, *Artaserse*, J. A. Hasse, L. Vinci, past.	198
1738, Madrid, *Demofoonte*, G. M. Schiassi, rvl	316
1738, Mantua, *Alessandro*, B. Galuppi, pr. (1st)	129
1738, Naples, *Artaserse*, L. Vinci (+ L. Leo), rvl	190
1738, Padua, *Artaserse*, G. Brivio, pr. (1st)	215
1738, Piacenza, *Demofoonte*, G. B. Lampugnani, pr.	319
1738, Rimini, *Alessandro*, various	134
1738, Rome, *Artaserse*, L. Vinci, rvl	190
1738, St Petersburg, *Artaserse*, F. Araia, pr.	213
1738, St Petersburg, *Artaserse*, F. Araia, rvl	213
1738, Treviso, *Artaserse*, J. A. Hasse, rvl	198
1738, Turin, *Demofoonte*, G. F. Brivio, pr.	319
1738, Venice, *Alessandro*, J. A. Hasse, pr.	120
1738, Venice, *Demofoonte*, G. Latilla, pr.	319
1738, Vicenza, *Artaserse*, J. A. Hasse, rvl	198
1739, Alessandria, *Demofoonte*, G. Reina, pr.	320
1739, Brunswick, *Didone*, G. Paganelli, rvl	52
1739, Graz, *Demofoonte*, various, past.	320
1739, Klagenfurt, *Alessandro*, J. A. Hasse, rvl	120
1739, Milan, *Didone*, G. F. Brivio or E. R. Duni, pr.	52
1739, Modena, *Artaserse*, J. A. Hasse, rvl	198
1739, Munich, *Artaserse*, G. B. Ferrandini, G. Porta, pr.	216
1739, Naples, *Adriano*, G. A. Ristori, pr.	281
1739, Padua, *Didone*, G. B. Lampugnani, pr. (1st)	52
1739, Rome, *Adriano*, A. Caldara, rvl	271
1739, Vicenza, *Alessandro*, J. A. Hasse	120
1739, Vienna, *Artaserse*	216

SC | Index Ia. Chronological Index: by Year

1740, Catania, *Artaserse*	216
1740, Dresden, *Artaserse*, J. A. Hasse, pr. (2nd)	198
1740, Florence, *Alessandro*, various, past.	134
1740, Florence, *Artaserse*, L. Vinci, rvl	190
1740, Genoa, *Artaserse*, J. A. Hasse, rvl	198
1740, Lisbon, *Alessandro*, A. P. Fabbri, pr.	134
1740, Ljubljana, *Artaserse*, J. A. Hasse, rvl	198
1740, Lucca, *Alessandro*, L. Vinci, rvl	112
1740, Lucca, *Didone*, past.	54
1740, Macerata, *Artaserse*, L. Vinci, rvl	190
1740, Naples, *Adriano*, M. Caballone?, pr.	285
1740, Naples/Palermo, *Alessandro*, M. Caballone, pr.	134
1740, Siena, *Adriano*	281
1740, Turin, *Adriano*, B. Galuppi, pr. (1st)	281
1740, Venice, *Adriano*, G. A. Giai, pr.	284
1740, Verona, *Alessandro*, J. A. Hasse, rvl	120
1740, Vicenza, *Adriano*, G. B. Lampugnani, pr.	284
1749, Vienna, *Didone*, various[NP]	54
1741, Arezzo, *Didone*, D. N. Sarro, rvl	41
1741, Bassano, *Artaserse*, J. A. Hasse, rvl	199
1741, Bratislava, *Alessandro*, J. A. Hasse, rvl	120
1741, Brescia, *Adriano*, P. Giaino, pr.	285
1741, Brunswick, *Demofoonte*, G. Verocai, rvl	322
1741, Catania, *Artaserse*, rvl	216
1741, Erlangen, *Alessandro*	134
1741, Ferrara, *Adriano*, various	285
1741, Florence, *Demofoonte*, G. Verocai, pr.	322
1741, Graz, *Didone*, P. Scalabrini and others	50
1741, Lisbon, *Didone*, R. di Capua, pr.	58
1741, Lucca, *Demofoonte*, L. Vinci, pr.	321
1741, Modena, *Alessandro*, P. Pulli, pr.	134
1741, Modena, *Didone*, B. Galuppi, pr. (1st)	54
1741, Naples, *Demofoonte*, L. Leo, pr.	322
1741, Rome, *Demofoonte*, A. Bernasconi, pr. (1st)	321
1741, Strasbourg, *Didone*, P. Scalabrini and others	50
1741, Turin, *Artaserse*, G. Arena, pr.	217
1741, Venice, *Didone*, A. Bernasconi, pr. (1st)	57
1741, Verona, *Artaserse*, P. Chiarini, pr.	217
1741, Vienna, *Didone*, various	54
1741, Wrocław, *Artaserse*, P. Scalabrini, rvl	214
1742, Alessandria, *Didone*, G. B. Lampugnani, rvl	52
1742, Brunswick, *Demofoonte*, G. Verocai, rvl	322
1742, Città di Castello, *Alessandro*, R. di Capua, pr.	135
1742, Dresden, *Didone*, J. A. Hasse, pr.	59
1742, Genoa, *Artaserse*, P. Chiarini, rvl	217
1742, London, *Artaserse*, G. Brivio, pr. (2nd)	215
1742, Ljubljana, *Didone*, P. Scalabrini and others, rvl	50
1742, Milan, *Alessandro*, G. F. Brivio, pr.	134
1742, Milan, *Artaserse*, C. W. Gluck, pr.	218
1742, Milan, *Demofoonte*	323
1742, Palermo, *Didone*	59
1742, Parma, *Artaserse*, J. A. Hasse and others	199
1742, Rome, *Demofoonte*, L. Leo, rvl	322
1742, Venice, *Artaserse*, G. A. Paganelli and others, pr. (2nd)	212
1742, s.l., *Adriano*, N. B. Logroscino, pr.	285
1743, Berlin, *Artaserse*, C. H. Graun, pr.	218
1743, Cesena, *Didone*, A. Bernasconi, rvl	57
1743, Dresden, *Didone*, J. A. Hasse, rvl	59
1743, Genoa, *Alessandro*, F. A. Uttini or Duni?, pr.	136
1743, Hamburg, *Artaserse*, P. Scalabrini and others, rvl	214
1743, Livorno, *Alessandro*	135
1743, London, *Alessandro*, G. F. Händel (+ G. B. Lampugnani), rvl	116
1743, Milan, *Demofoonte*, C. W. Gluck, pr.	323
1743, Naples, *Alessandro*, D. N. Sarro, pr.	135
1743, Naples, *Artaserse*, L. Vinci (+ G. Manna), rvl	190
1743, Padua, *Demofoonte*, N. Jommelli, pr. (1st)	325
1743, Palermo, *Artaserse*, L. Vinci, rvl	190
1743, Reggio Emilia, *Demofoonte*, C. W. Gluck (+ F. Maggiore), rvl	323
1743, Rimini, *Demofoonte*, various, past.?	325
1743, St Petersburg, *Alessandro*, F. Araia, pr.	136
1743, Venice, *Alessandro*, J. A. Hasse, rvl	120
1743, Vienna, *Adriano*	285
1744, Berlin, *Alessandro*, C. H. Graun, pr.	141
1744, Berlin, *Artaserse*, C. H. Graun, rvl	218
1744, Bologna, *Demofoonte*, C. W. Gluck (and others), rvl	323
1744, Ferrara, *Alessandro*, N. Jommelli, pr. (1st)	137
1744, Florence, *Alessandro*, J. A. Hasse, rvl	120
1744, Florence, *Artaserse*, E. R. Duni, pr.	221
1744, Genoa, *Alessandro*, D. Perez, pr. (1st)	138
1744, Hamburg, *Didone*, P. Scalabrini and others, rvl	50
1744, Naples, *Didone*, J. A. Hasse, rev.	59
1744, Prague, *Artaserse*, P. Scalabrini and others, rvl	214
1744, Venice, *Artaserse*, D. Terradellas, pr.	221
1744, Vienna, *Demofoonte*, C. W. Gluck, rvl	323
1745, Bologna, *Artaserse*, J. A. Hasse, rvl	199
1745, Bologna, *Didone*	64
1745, Brunswick, *Adriano*, G. Verocai, pr.	285
1745, Brunswick, *Artaserse*, C. H. Graun, rvl	218
1745, Crema, *Didone*, G. B. Lampugnani, rvl	52
1745, Fano, *Didone*, A. Aurisicchio, pr.	64
1745, Faenza, *Alessandro*, L. Vinci, rvl	112
1745, Ferrara, *Artaserse*, L. Vinci (+ J. A. Hasse), rvl	190
1745, Ferrara, *Demofoonte*, C. W. Gluck, rvl	323
1745, Gorizia, *Adriano*	285
1745, Mantua, *Didone*, various, past.?	64

397

SC | Index Ia. Chronological Index: by Year

1745, Parma, *Didone*, N. Porpora, rvl	45
1745, Turin, *Alessandro*, C. W. Gluck, pr.	142
1745, Verona, *Alessandro*, P. Chiarini	142
1746, Berlin, *Adriano*, C. H. Graun, pr.	286
1746, Berlin, *Demofoonte*, C. H. Graun, pr.	330
1746, Brescia, *Alessandro*, P. Pellegrini, pr.	142
1746, Dresden, *Artaserse*, P. Scalabrini and others, rvl	214
1746, Florence, *Adriano*, G. Abos, pr.	286
1746, Florence, *Demofoonte*	331
1746, Genoa, *Alessandro*, J. A. Hasse (x2)	120
1746, Hamburg, *Artaserse*, P. Scalabrini and others, rvl	214
1746, Hamburg, *Didone*, P. Scalabrini and others, rvl	50
1746, Livorno, *Adriano*	288
1746, London, *Alessandro*, G. B. Lampugnani and others, pr.	142
1746, Palermo, *Alessandro*	143
1746, Perugia, *Adriano*	288
1746, Pesaro, *Alessandro*, J. A. Hasse, rvl	120
1746, Venice, *Artaserse*, G. Abos, pr.	222
1746, Vienna, *Alessandro*, J. A. Hasse, rvl (x2)	120
1746, Vienna, *Artaserse*, A. Bernasconi, pr. (1st)	223
1747, Ancona, *Alessandro*, G. Abos, pr.	143
1747, Dresden, *Didone*, P. Scalabrini and others, rvl	50
1747, Hamburg, *Didone*, P. Scalabrini and others, rvl	50
1747, Leipzig, *Didone*, P. Scalabrini and others, rvl	50
1747, Lucca, *Artaserse*, G. Scarlatti, pr. (1st)	224
1747, Milan, *Demofoonte*, C. W. Gluck, rvl	323
1747, Naples, *Adriano*, G. Latilla, pr.	288
1747, Palermo, *Artaserse*, V. L. Ciampi, pr.	224
1747, Pavia, *Demofoonte*, G. F. Brivio, rvl	320
1747, Pistoia, *Artaserse*, L. Vinci, rvl	190
1747, Ravenna, *Artaserse*	223
1747, Rome, *Didone*, N. Jommelli, pr. (1st)	64
1747, Trento, *Artaserse*, F. Maggiore, pr.	223
1747, Venice, *Didone*, A. Adolfati, pr.	67
1747–1748, NA, *Demofoonte*, J. C. Smith, pr.	332
1748, Bayreuth, *Artaserse*, J. A. Hasse, rvl	199
1748, Bonn, *Artaserse*, F. Zoppis, pr.	226
1748, Brescia, *Didone*, P. Chiarini, pr.	68
1748, Copenhagen, *Didone*, P. Scalabrini and others, rvl	50
1748, Dresden, *Demofoonte*, J. A. Hasse, pr. (1st)	332
1748, Florence, *Artaserse*, D. Perez, pr. (1st)	225
1748, Genoa, *Didone*	68
1748, London, *Alessandro*, G. F. Händel (+ G. B. Lampugnani), rvl (x2)	116
1748, London, *Didone*, J. A. Hasse, rvl	59
1748, Palermo, *Demofoonte*	337
1748, Piacenza, *Artaserse*, G. Carcani, pr.	224
1748, Prague, *Artaserse*, various (past.)	226
1748, Venice, *Adriano*, V. L. Ciampi, pr.	288
1748, Venice, *Didone*, F. Bertoni, pr.	68
1748, Vienna, *Alessandro*, G. C. Wagenseil, pr.	144
1749, Alessandria, *Artaserse*	233
1749, Copenhagen, *Adriano*, P. Scalabrini, pr.	289
1749, Copenhagen, *Alessandro*, P. Scalabrini, pr.	144
1749, Copenhagen, *Artaserse*, P. Scalabrini and others, rvl	214
1749, Copenhagen, *Demofoonte*, various, past.?	337
1749, Cremona, *Artaserse*, P. Chiarini, rvl	217
1749, Livorno, *Artaserse*	227
1749, Madrid, *Artaserse*, G. B. Mele and others, past.?	227
1749, Madrid, *Artaserse*, G. B. Mele and others, rvl	227
1749, Naples, *Alessandro*, D. Perez, rvl	138
1749, Naples, *Artaserse*, D. Perez, rvl	225
1749, Rome, *Artaserse*, N. Jommelli, pr. (1st)	231
1749, Venice, *Demofoonte*, J. A. Hasse, pr. (2nd)	332
1749, Vienna, *Artaserse*, B. Galuppi, pr. (1st)	227
1749, Vienna, *Didone*, N. Jommelli, pr. (2nd)	64
1749, s.l., *Artaserse*, J. C. Smith, pr.	233
1750, Barcelona, *Alessandro*, G. Scolari, rvl	145
1750, Brunswick, *Adriano*, I. Fiorillo, pr.	290
1750, Brunswick, *Demofoonte*, I. Fiorillo, pr.	340
1750, Cagliari, *Artaserse*, G. Bollano?, pr.	235
1750, Ferrara, *Demofoonte*, F. A. B. Uttini, pr.	341
1750, London, *Adriano*, V. L. Ciampi, rvl	288
1750, Lucca, *Alessandro*, G. Abos, rvl	143
1750, Madrid, *Artaserse*, G. B. Mele and others, rvl	227
1750, Madrid, *Demofoonte*, B. Galuppi (+ G. B. Mele), pr.	337
1750, Madrid, *Demofoonte*, B. Galuppi (+ G. B. Mele), rvl	338
1750, Mannheim, *Demofoonte*, J. A. Hasse, rvl	332
1750, Milan, *Artaserse*, G. B. Lampugnani, pr.	233
1750, Naples, *Adriano*, B. Galuppi, rvl	281
1750, Naples, *Demofoonte*, J. A. Hasse, rvl	332
1750, Pisa, *Artaserse*, L. Vinci, rvl	190
1750, Prague, *Alessandro*, G. M. Rutini, pr.	144
1750, Reggio Emilia, *Adriano*, G. B. Pescetti, pr.	289
1750, Sassuolo, *Alessandro*, B. Galuppi	112
1750, Sassuolo, *Artaserse*, J. A. Hasse, rvl	227
1750, Siena, *Adriano*, G. B. Pescetti, rvl	289
1750, Strasbourg, *Artaserse*	235
1750, Stuttgart, *Artaserse*, C. H. Graun, rvl	218
1750, Turin, *Didone*, D. M. B. Terradellas, pr.	69
1750, Venice, *Artaserse*, A. G. Pampani, pr. (1st)	234
1750, Vicenza, *Alessandro*, G. Scolari, pr.	145
1751, Barcelona, *Demofoonte*, B. Galuppi (+ G. B. Mele), rvl	338

SC | Index Ia. Chronological Index: by Year

1750, Naples, *Adriano*, B. Galuppi, rvl	281
1751, Brunswick, *Artaserse*, I. Fiorillo, rvl	235
1751, Brunswick, *Didone*, I. Fiorillo, pr.	70
1751, Brunswick, *Demofoonte*, I. Fiorillo, rvl	340
1751, Genoa, *Adriano*, A. Adolfati, pr.	290
1751, Genoa, *Didone*, D. Perez, pr.	70
1751, Mannheim, *Artaserse*, N. Jommelli, rev.	231
1751, Madrid, *Demofoonte*, B. Galuppi (+ G. B. Mele), rvl	338
1751, Milan, *Adriano*, A. G. Pampani, pr.	290
1751, Padua, *Artaserse*, B. Galuppi, pr. (2nd)	227
1751, Palermo, *Demofoonte*, L. Santini, pr.	341
1751, Stuttgart, *Artaserse*, C. H. Graun, rvl	218
1751, Stuttgart, *Didone*, N. Jommelli, rvl	65
1751, Venice, *Didone*, G. Manna, pr.	69
1751, Verona, *Artaserse*, D. dal Barba and others, pr.	235
1752, Alessandria, *Alessandro*, G. Calderara, pr.	146
1752, Barcelona, *Didone*, G. Scolari, pr.	72
1752, Brunswick, *Alessandro*, I. Fiorillo, pr.	146
1752, Cremona, *Adriano*	291
1752, Cremona, *Demofoonte*, G. F. Brivio, rvl	320
1752, Dresden, *Adriano*, J. A. Hasse, pr.	279
1752, Dresden, *Didone*, J. A. Hasse, rvl	59
1752, Florence, *Alessandro*	146
1752, Forlì, *Artaserse*, G. B. Ferrandini, G. Porta, rvl	216
1752, Lisbon, *Demofoonte*, D. Perez, pr.	341
1752, Livorno, *Demofoonte*	341
1752, Livorno, *Didone*, F. Poncini Zilioli, rvl	72
1752, Lucca, *Adriano*, G. Scarlatti, rvl	291
1752, Madrid, *Demofoonte*, B. Galuppi (+ G. B. Mele), rvl (x2)	338
1752, Madrid, *Didone*, B. Galuppi, rev.	54
1752, Madrid, *Didone*, B. Galuppi, rvl	55
1752, Milan, *Alessandro*, D. Perez, rvl	138
1752, Milan, *Artaserse*, G. B. Pescetti, pr.	236
1752, Reggio Emilia, *Didone*, D. Perez, rvl	70
1752, Rome, *Adriano*, N. Jommelli, pr.	292
1752, Stuttgart, *Alessandro*, B. Galuppi, pr.	129
1752, Venice, *Adriano*, G. Scarlatti, pr.	291
1752, Vienna, *Didone*, G. Bonno, pr.	73
1753, Barcelona, *Didone*, G. Scolari, rvl	73
1753, Berlin, *Didone*, J. A. Hasse, rvl	59
1753, Bologna, *Adriano*, M. Valentini, pr.	292
1753, Bologna, *Didone*, A. M. Mazzoni, pr.	73
1753, Crema, *Adriano*, G. Cocchi, pr.	293
1753, Florence, *Didone*, B. Galuppi or G. M. Orlandini?, pr.	55
1753, Graz, *Artaserse*, G. Maggiore and others, rvl	223
1753, Lisbon, *Demofoonte* (Port.)	342
1753, Lisbon, *Didone*, D. Perez, rvl	70
1753, Livorno, *Artaserse*	236
1753, Madrid, *Didone*, B. Galuppi, rvl	55
1753, Mantua, *Artaserse*, B. Galuppi, rvl	227
1753, Milan, *Demofoonte*, N. Jommelli, pr. (2nd)	326
1753, Naples, *Didone*, G. B. Lampugnani, pr. (2nd)	52
1753, Paris–Versailles, *Didone*, J. A. Hasse, rvl	59
1753, Pavia, *Didone*	74
1753, Puerto de Santa María, *Alessandro*, G. Scolari, rvl	145
1753, Reggio Emilia, *Alessandro*, G. Scarlatti, pr.	146
1753, Venice, *Alessandro*, G. Latilla and others, pr.	146
1754, Barcelona, *Artaserse*, G. B. Ferrandini + G. Porta, rvl	216
1754, Berlin, *Alessandro*, J. F. Agricola, pr.	147
1754, Bologna, *Artaserse*	237
1754, Brescia, *Didone*, G. B. Lampugnani, rvl	52
1754, Lisbon, *Adriano*, D. Perez, pr.	293
1754, Lisbon, *Artaserse*, D. Perez, pr. (2nd)	225
1754, Livorno, *Adriano*, G. Scarlatti, rvl	291
1754, Lodi, *Demofoonte*, N. Jommelli, rvl	326
1754, London, *Artaserse*, J. A. Hasse, rvl	199
1754, London, *Didone*, V. L. Ciampi, pr.	74
1754, London, *Didone*, V. L. Ciampi, rvl	74
1754, Lucca, *Demofoonte*, G. Cocchi, rvl	343
1754, Madrid, *Didone*, B. Galuppi, rvl (x2)	55
1754, Naples, *Adriano*, N. Conforto, pr.	294
1754, Naples, *Alessandro*, B. Galuppi, rvl	129
1754, Parma, *Artaserse*, L. Vinci, rvl	190
1754, Parma, *Demofoonte*, A. Mazzoni, pr.	342
1754, Pavia, *Adriano*, A. G. Pampani, rvl	290
1754, Turin, *Demofoonte*, G. Manna, pr.	342
1754, Venice, *Adriano*, G. Scolari, pr.	294
1754, Venice, *Artaserse*, B. Galuppi and others, rvl	227
1754, Venice, *Demofoonte*, G. Cocchi, pr.	343
1754, Verona, *Alessandro*, J. A. Hasse, rvl	120
1754, Vicenza, *Demofoonte*, J. A. Hasse, rvl	332
1755, Amsterdam, *Alessandro*	148
1755, Bergamo, *Artaserse*, G. B. Pescetti, rvl	236
1755, Copenhagen, *Demofoonte*, G. Sarti, pr. (1st)	344
1755, Dresden, *Artaserse*	238
1755, Florence, *Demofoonte*	344
1755, Lisbon, *Alessandro*, D. Perez, pr. (2nd)	138
1755, London, *Demofoonte*, various, past.	345
1755, Lübeck, *Artaserse*, J. A. Hasse and others (past.)	199
1755, Madrid, *Demofoonte*, B. Galuppi (+ G. B. Mele), rvl (x2)	338
1755, Madrid, *Didone*, B. Galuppi, rvl (x3)	55
1755, Mantua, *Didone*, D. Perez, rvl	70
1755, Milan, *Didone*, G. A. Fioroni, pr.	74
1755, Munich, *Adriano*, A. Bernasconi, pr. (2nd)	276

SC | Index Ia. Chronological Index: by Year

1755, Munich, *Alessandro*, B. Galuppi, rvl	130
1755, Naples, *Adriano*, J. A. Hasse, rvl	279
1755, Parma, *Alessandro*, B. Galuppi, rvl	129
1755, Reggio Emilia, *Artaserse*, G. Cocchi, pr.	237
1755, St Petersburg, *Alessandro*, F. Araia, rvl	136
1755, Treviso, *Artaserse*, B. Galuppi, rvl	228
1755, Venice, *Alessandro*, B. Galuppi, pr. (2nd)	129
1755, Verona, *Didone*	75
1756, Bologna, *Demofoonte*, B. Galuppi (+ G. B. Mele), rvl	338
1756, Brescia, *Alessandro*, B. Galuppi, rvl	130
1756, Brescia, *Artaserse*, B. Galuppi, rvl	228
1756, Cremona, *Didone*, P. Chiarini, rvl	68
1756, Florence, *Alessandro*, B. Galuppi, rvl	130
1756, Lodi, *Alessandro*, B. Galuppi, rvl	130
1756, London, *Alessandro*, various, past.	148
1756, Munich, *Didone*, A. Bernasconi, pr. (2nd)	58
1756, Pavia, *Alessandro*, D. Perez, rvl	138
1756, Pisa, *Alessandro*, N. Conforto, pr.	148
1756, Stuttgart, *Artaserse*, N. Jommelli, pr. (2nd)	231
1756, Venice, *Artaserse*, A. G. Pampani, pr. (2nd)	234
1756, Vicenza, *Artaserse*, B. Galuppi, rvl	228
1757, Faenza, *Artaserse*, B. Galuppi, rvl	228
1757, Faenza, *Didone*, D. Perez, rvl	70
1757, Ferrara, *Artaserse*, B. Galuppi, rvl	228
1757, Florence, *Artaserse*, various	238
1757, Lucca, *Artaserse*, B. Galuppi, rvl	228
1757, Madrid, *Adriano*, N. Conforto, rev.	294
1757, Milan, *Artaserse*, Q. Gasparini, pr.	238
1757, Pavia, *Artaserse*, G. Scolari, pr.	238
1757, Pistoia, *Demofoonte*, G. Cocchi, rvl	343
1757, Rome, *Demofoonte*, A. G. Pampani, pr.	346
1757, Stockholm, *Adriano*, F. A. B. Uttini, pr.	295
1757, Venice, *Adriano*, G. F Brusa, pr.	295
1757, Venice, *Didone*, T. Traetta, pr. (1st)	75
1757, Verona, *Demofoonte*	346
1757, Vicenza, *Alessandro*, B. Galuppi, rvl	130
1758, Brescia, *Artaserse*, B. Galuppi, rvl	228
1758, Genoa, *Alessandro*, G. Sciroli, pr.	153
1758, Livorno, *Adriano*, B. Galuppi, pr. (2nd)	281
1758, Madrid, *Adriano*, N. Conforto, rvl	294
1758, Madrid, *Alessandro nell'Indie*[NP]	153
1758, Mantua, *Demofoonte*, T. Traetta, pr.	347
1758, Naples, *Demofoonte*, J. A. Hasse, pr. (3rd)	332
1758, Padua, *Demofoonte*, B. Galuppi, pr. (2nd)	338
1758, Pisa, *Artaserse*	239
1758, Rome, *Adriano*, R. di Capua, pr.	296
1758, Rome, *Alessandro*, N. Piccinni, pr. (1st)	149
1758, Siena, *Demofoonte*, P. Vinci, pr.	347
1758, Stockholm, *Artaserse*, F. A. B. Uttini, pr.	239
1758, St Petersburg, *Didone*, F. Zoppis, pr.	76
1758, Venice, *Artaserse*, G. Scolari, rvl	238
1759, Cartagena, *Artaserse*	239
1759, Florence, *Didone*, P. A. Auletta, pr.	77
1759, Lucca, *Alessandro*, J. A. Hasse, rvl	120
1759, Milan, *Alessandro*, I. Holzbauer, pr.	153
1759, Milan, *Demofoonte*, A. Ferradini, pr.	348
1759, Naples, *Adriano*, B. Galuppi, rvl	281
1759, Padua, *Alessandro*, B. Galuppi, rvl	130
1759, Pavia, *Didone*, T. Traetta, rvl	75
1759, Pesaro, *Demofoonte*, T. Traetta, rvl	347
1759, Pisa, *Adriano*, G. G. Brunetti, pr.	297
1759, Rimini, *Demofoonte*, P. Vinci, rvl	347
1759, Salzburg, *Demofoonte*, J. E. Eberlin, pr.	349
1759, Siena, *Didone*, G. Brunetti, pr.	77
1759, Stockholm, *Demofoonte*, F. A. B. Uttini, rvl	341
1759, St Petersburg, *Alessandro*, F. Araia, rvl	136
1759, Turin, *Adriano*, G. B. Borghi, pr.	296
1759, Venice, *Alessandro*, G. Scolari, rvl	145
1759, Venice, *Demofoonte*, various	348
1759, Verona, *Artaserse*, B. Galuppi, rvl	228
1759, Warsaw, *Demofoonte*, J. A. Hasse, rvl	332
1760, Bologna, *Alessandro*, unknown	154
1760, Catania, *Demofoonte*, J. A. Hasse, rvl	332
1760, Copenhagen, *Artaserse*, G. Sarti, pr.	240
1760, Livorno, *Artaserse*, D. Zamparelli and other, rvl	215
1760, Lucca, *Didone*, A. Ferradini, pr.	77
1760, Munich, *Didone*, A. Bernasconi, rvl	58
1760, Naples, *Artaserse*, J. A. Hasse, pr. (3rd)	199
1760, Pavia, *Adriano*, various	297
1760, Prague, *Adriano*, G. Scarlatti, rvl	291
1760, Prague, *Alessandro*, B. Galuppi, rvl	130
1760, Prague, *Demofoonte*, B. Galuppi, rvl	338
1760, Stuttgart, *Alessandro*, N. Jommelli, pr. (2nd)	137
1760, Venice, *Adriano*, B. Galuppi, pr. (3rd)	281
1760, Venice, *Adriano*, A. M. Mazzoni, pr.	297
1760, Verona, *Adriano*, various	297
1760, Verona, *Didone*, various, past.?	77
1760, Warsaw, *Artaserse*, J. A. Hasse, rvl	199
1760, s.l., *Demofoonte*, G. Brunetti, pr.	349
1761, Bratislava, *Artaserse*, J. A. Hasse	199
1761, Copenhagen, *Alessandro*, G. Sarti, pr. (1st)	154
1761, Florence, *Adriano*	297
1761, London, *Alessandro*, G. Cocchi and others, past.	155
1761, London, *Didone*, D. Perez, rvl	70
1761, Palermo, *Adriano*, B. Galuppi, rvl	281
1761, Prague, *Artaserse*	241
1761, Prague, *Didone*, A. M. Mazzoni, rvl	73
1761, Reggio Emilia, *Demofoonte*, N. Piccinni, pr.	349

SC | Index Ia. Chronological Index: by Year

1761, Senigallia, *Demofoonte*, A. Boroni (and others), pr. 350
1761, Treviso, *Demofoonte*, A. Boroni (and others), rvl 350
1761, Turin, *Artaserse*, J. C. Bach, pr. 240
1761, Venice, *Artaserse*, B. Galuppi, rvl 228
1761, Verona, *Alessandro*, D. dal Barba, pr. 154
1762, Barcelona, *Alessandro*, G. Scolari, rvl 145
1762, Brunswick, *Adriano*, J. G. Schwanenberger, pr. 298
1762, Brunswick, *Adriano*, J. G. Schwanenberger, rvl 298
1762, Catania, *Artaserse*, unknown
1762, Copenhagen, *Didone*, G. Sarti, pr. (1st) 78
1762, Florence, *Alessandro*, B. Galuppi, rvl 130
1762, Florence, *Demofoonte*, various, past.? 350
1762, London, *Artaserse* (En.), T. A. Arne, pr. 241
1762, Montepulciano, *Artaserse*, various 243
1762, Naples, *Alessandro*, J. C. Bach, pr. 156
1762, Naples, *Artaserse*, J. A. Hasse, rvl 199
1762, Naples, *Demofoonte*, N. Piccinni, rvl 349
1762, Palermo, *Alessandro*, N. Piccinni, rvl 149
1762, Reggio Emilia, *Alessandro*, T. Traetta, pr. 158
1762, Rome, *Artaserse*, N. Piccinni, pr. (1st) 241
1762, Venice, *Artaserse*, G. di Majo, pr. 241
1762, Vicenza, *Demofoonte*, A. Boroni (and others), rvl 350
1763, Barcelona, *Adriano*, G. Sciroli, pr. 299
1763, Barcelona, *Artaserse*, N. Piccinni and others 241
1763, Barcelona, *Demofoonte*, B. Galuppi, rvl 338
1763, Barcelona, *Didone*, G. Scolari, rvl 73
1763, Ferrara, *Adriano* 298
1763, Ferrara, *Didone*, G. Scolari, rvl 73
1763, Foligno, *Artaserse*, N. Piccinni, rvl 241
1763, Lodi, *Alessandro*, J. C. Bach, rvl 156
1763, Milan, *Adriano*, G. Colla, pr. 298
1763, Milan, *Didone*, T. Traetta, pr. (2nd) 75
1763, Munich, *Artaserse*, A. Bernasconi, pr. (2nd) 223
1763, Palermo, *Didone*, G. B. Lampugnani, rvl 53
1763, Pisa, *Alessandro*, G. G. Brunetti, pr. 158
1763, Prague, *Demofoonte*, various, past. 352
1763, Rome, *Artaserse*, N. Jommelli, rvl 231
1763, Rome, *Demofoonte*, G. di Majo, pr. 350
1763, Stuttgart, *Didone*, N. Jommelli, pr. (3rd) 65
1763, Udine, *Adriano*, B. Galuppi, rvl 282
1763, Venice, *Alessandro*, A. Sacchini, pr. (1st) 158
1763, Vienna, *Artaserse*, G. Scarlatti, pr. (2nd) 224
1764, Bologna, *Alessandro*, G. Sciroli, rvl 153
1764, Cádiz, *Alessandro*, D. Perez and others 138
1764, Cádiz, *Demofoonte*, B. Galuppi, rvl 338
1764, London, *Alessandro*, G. Cocchi and others, past. 155
1764, Lucca, *Adriano*, C. G. Concialini and others, pr. 299

1764, Naples, *Didone*, T. Traetta, pr. (3rd) 75
1764, Prague, *Alessandro*, D. Fischietti, pr. 162
1764, Salzburg, *Adriano*, A. Caldara, rvl 271
1764, Stuttgart, *Demofoonte*, N. Jommelli, pr. (3rd) 326
1764, Venice, *Demofoonte*, A. G. Pampani, rvl 346
1764, Venice, *Didone*, B. Galuppi, pr. (2nd) 55
1764, Verona, *Alessandro*, various 162
1764, s.l., *Adriano*, M. Wimmer, pr. 299
1765, Brunswick, *Didone*, J. G. Schwanenberger, pr. 80
1765, Ferrara, *Artaserse*, J. A. Hasse, rvl 199
1765, Genoa, *Artaserse*, various (incl. G. Colla?) 244
1765, Kassel, *Artaserse*, I. Fiorillo, rev. 235
1765, La Valletta, *Demofoonte*, J. A. Hasse, rvl 332
1765, Lisbon, *Didone*, D. Perez, rvl 70
1765, Lodi, *Artaserse*, G. Sartori, pr. 244
1765, London, *Adriano*, J. C. Bach, pr. 299
1765, London, *Demofoonte*, M. Vento, pr. 352
1765, Lucca, *Demofoonte*, various, past.? 353
1765, Ludwigsburgt, *Demofoonte*, N. Jommelli, rvl 326
1765, Naples, *Adriano*, G. di Majo, pr. 300
1766, Cremona, *Artaserse*, G. B. Lampugnani, rvl 233
1766, Ferrara, *Demofoonte*, various, past.? 353
1766, Livorno, *Didone*, F. Zannetti, pr. 80
1766, London, *Artaserse*, J. A. Hasse, rvl 199
1766, London, *Demofoonte*, M. Vento, rvl 352
1766, Lucca, *Alessandro*, various 162
1766, Mannheim, *Alessandro*, G. di Majo, pr. 162
1766, Munich, *Demofoonte*, A. Bernasconi, rev. 321
1766, Padua, *Alessandro*, G. Sarti, rvl 154
1766, St Petersburg, *Didone*, B. Galuppi, rvl 55
1766, Treviso, *Demofoonte*, P. A. Guglielmi, pr. 353
1766, Turin, *Alessandro*, A. Sacchini, rvl 158
1766, Venice, *Adriano*, P. A. Guglielmi, pr. 300
1766, Venice, *Artaserse*, G. Ponzo, pr. 244
1767, Barcelona, *Alessandro*, G. Scolari, rvl 145
1767, Barcelona, *Didone* 81
1767, Livorno, *Adriano*, G. Scarlatti, rvl 291
1767, Mannheim, *Alessandro*, G. di Majo, rvl 162
1767, Naples, *Alessandro*, G. di Majo, rvl 162
1767, Palma de Mallorca, *Artaserse* 244
1767, Palma de Mallorca, *Demofoonte*, B. Galuppi, rvl 338
1767, Pavia, *Didone* 81
1767, Prague, *Artaserse*, A. Boroni, pr. 245
1768, Cádiz, *Didone* 82
1768, Cremona, *Alessandro*, past. 163
1768, Eichstätt, *Adriano*, H. Mango, pr. 301
1768, Florence, *Alessandro*, J. G. Naumann, pr. 164
1768, Kassel, *Didone* 82
1768, Lisbon, *Artaserse*, G. Scolari, rvl 238
1768, Mannheim, *Adriano*, I. H163olzbauer, pr. 301

401

SC | Index Ia. Chronological Index: by Year

1768, Mantua, *Alessandro*, L. Gatti, pr.	163
1768, Mantua, *Artaserse*, various	246
1768, Naples, *Alessandro*, A. Sacchini, pr. (2nd)	159
1768, Naples, *Artaserse*, N. Piccinni, pr. (2nd)	242
1768, Palermo, *Demofoonte*, B. Galuppi, rvl	338
1768, Prague, *Didone*, A. Boroni, pr.	81
1768, Rome, *Artaserse*, A. Sacchini, pr.	245
1769, Alessandria, *Adriano*, M. de Vincenti, pr.	302
1769, Genoa, *Adriano*, various	302
1769, Genoa, *Alessandro*, F. Bertoni, pr. (1st)	164
1769, Mannheim, *Adriano*, I. Holzbauer, rvl (x2)	301
1769, Naples, *Adriano*, C. I. Monza, pr.	302
1769, Prague, *Alessandro*, J. A. Koželuh, pr.	165
1769, Rome, *Adriano*, G. F. di Majo, rvl	300
1769, Valencia, *Artaserse*, A. Sacchini, rvl	245
1769, Valencia, *Demofoonte*	355
1769, Venice, *Demofoonte*, J. Mysliveček, pr. (1st)	353
1770, Berlin, *Didone*, J. A. Hasse, rvl	59
1770, Cádiz, *Demofoonte*, A. Bernasconi, rvl	321
1770, Florence, *Artaserse*, various	247
1770, Lucca, *Artaserse*, various	247
1770, Lucca, *Didone*, various	85
1770, Mantua, *Demofoonte*, T. Traetta, rvl	347
1770, Milan, *Didone*, I. Celoniati, pr.	82
1770, Modena, *Adriano*, A. Tozzi, pr.	303
1770, Naples, *Demofoonte*, N. Jommelli, pr. (4th)	326
1770, Naples, *Didone*, B. Galuppi, rvl	55
1770, Naples, *Didone*, G. Insanguine, pr.	85
1770, Pisa, *Artaserse*, various	247
1770, Rome, *Demofoonte*, J. B. Vanhal, pr.	355
1770, Rome, *Didone*, N. Piccinni, pr. (1st)	83
1770, Siena, *Artaserse*, various	247
1770, Venice, *Didone*, G. di Majo, pr.	82
1770, Verona, *Artaserse*, A. Boroni, rvl	245
1771, Bologna, *Demofoonte*, various, past.	356
1771, Copenhagen, *Alessandro*, G. Sarti, rvl	154
1771, Copenhagen, *Demofoonte*, G. Sarti, pr. (2nd)	344
1771, Copenhagen, *Didone*, G. Sarti, rvl	78
1771, Livorno, *Alessandro*, A. Sacchini (+ A. Felici), rvl	159
1771, London, *Artaserse*, M. Vento, pr.	247
1771, Padua, *Adriano*, P. Anfossi, pr.	304
1771, Pavia, *Demofoonte*, various, past.	355
1771, Prague, *Adriano*, A. Sacchini, rvl	303
1771, Venice, *Adriano*, A. Sacchini, pr.	303
1771, Venice, *Alessandro*, F. Bertoni, pr. (2nd)	164
1772, Barcelona, *Demofoonte*	356
1772, Bologna, *Didone*	86
1772, Florence, *Alessandro*, P. Anfossi, rvl	165
1772, Florence, *Didone*, M. Mortellari, pr.	86
1772, Florence, *Didone*	86
1772, London, *Artaserse*, T. Giordani and others, past.	248
1772, Modena, *Artaserse*, G. Paisiello, pr.	247
1772, Naples, *Didone*, B. Galuppi, rvl	55
1772, Naples, *Didone*, G. Insanguine, rvl	85
1772, Porto, *Demofoonte*, D. Perez, rvl	341
1772, Prague, *Demofoonte*, J. A. Koželuh, pr.	356
1772, Rome, *Alessandro*, P. Anfossi, pr.	165
1772, Venice, *Artaserse*, V. Manfredini, pr.	248
1773, Bologna, *Alessandro*, various	167
1773, Florence, *Demofoonte*, P. Anfossi, rvl	356
1773, Livorno, *Demofoonte*, M. S. Berezovskij, pr.	358
1773, London, *Artaserse*, various, rvl	248
1773, Naples, *Adriano*, G. Insanguine, pr.	305
1773, Naples, *Adriano*, J. Mysliveček, pr.	305
1773, Palermo, *Adriano*, various	304
1773, Perugia, *Alessandro*, A. Sacchini, rvl	159
1773, Prague, *Artaserse*, G. Paisiello, rvl	247
1773, Rome, *Demofoonte*, P. Anfossi, pr.	356
1773, Turin, *Didone*, G. Colla, pr.	86
1774, Berlin, *Demofoonte*, C. H. Graun (+ King Friedrich II), rvl	330
1774, Cremona, *Alessandro*, A. Sacchini, rvl	159
1774, Genoa, *Demofoonte*, P. Anfossi and others, rvl	356
1774, London, *Alessandro*, D. Corri, pr.	168
1774, London, *Artaserse*, L. Caruso, pr.	250
1774, London, *Artaserse*, various	248
1774, Macerata, *Demofoonte*, P. Anfossi, rvl	356
1774, Modena, *Alessandro*, G. Paisiello, pr.	167
1774, Modena, *Demofoonte*, P. Anfossi, pr.	356
1774, Naples, *Alessandro*, N. Piccinni, pr. (2nd)	149
1774, Naples, *Artaserse*, J. Mysliveček, pr.	249
1774, Pavia, *Artaserse*, various	249
1774, Rome, *Didone*, P. Anfossi, pr. (1st)	87
1774, Siena, *Alessandro*, G. Sciroli, rvl	153
1774, Valencia, *Alessandro*	168
1774, Verona, *Adriano*, various	306
1775, Cremona, *Didone*, P. Anfossi, rvl	87
1775, Lisbon, *Demofoonte*, N. Jommelli (+ J. Cordeiro da Silva), rev.	326
1775, London, *Didone*, M. Mortellari, V. Rauzzini, A. Sacchini, F. Giardini, past.	89
1775, Lucca, *Didone*, P. Anfossi, rvl	87
1775, Milan, *Alessandro*, C. Monza, pr.	169
1775, Modena, *Adriano*, G. Monti, pr.	306
1775, Naples, *Demofoonte*, J. Mysliveček, pr. (2nd)	353
1775, Venice, *Alessandro*, G. Rust, pr.	169
1775, Venice, *Demofoonte*, G. Paisiello, pr.	358
1775, Venice, *Didone*, P. Anfossi, rvl	87

SC | Index Ia. Chronological Index: by Year

1776, Alessandria, *Demofoonte*, C. I. Monza, pr.	361
1776, Cremona, *Demofoonte*, G. Paisiello, rvl	358
1776, Cremona, *Didone*, P. Anfossi, rvl	87
1776, Crescentino, *Didone*, F. D. Mombelli, pr.	91
1776, Florence, *Adriano*, J. Mysliveček, pr.	305
1776, Forlì, *Artaserse*, F. Bertoni, pr.	251
1776, Forlì, *Demofoonte*, J. Schuster, pr.	360
1776, Genoa, *Adriano*	306
1776, Havana, *Didone*, N. Piccinni, rvl	83
1776, Lisbon, *Alessandro*, N. Jommelli, rev.	137
1776, London, *Demofoonte*, M. Vento, rvl	352
1776, Naples, *Didone*, J. A. Schuster, pr.	89
1776, Perugia, *Demofoonte*, G. Paisiello, rvl	359
1776, Venice, *Artaserse*, G. B. Borghi, pr.	250
1776, Warsaw, *Demofoonte*, J. A. Hasse, rvl	332
1776, Warsaw, *Didone*, P. Anfossi, rvl (x2)	87
1777, Alessandria, *Artaserse*, G. A. Re, pr.	254
1777, Berlin, *Alessandro*, J. A. Hasse, rvl	120
1777, Florence, *Alessandro*, N. Piccinni, rvl	149
1777, Genoa, *Artaserse*, F. Bertoni, rvl	251
1777, Kassel, *Adriano*, J. A. Hasse, rvl	279
1777, Livorno, *Adriano*, various	307
1777, Lucca, *Artaserse*, F. Bertoni, rvl	251
1777, Macerata, *Artaserse*, F. Bertoni, rvl	251
1777, Milan, *Artaserse*, F. Bertoni, rvl	251
1777, Padua, *Adriano*, P. Anfossi, rvl	304
1777, Pavia, *Adriano*, J. Mysliveček, rvl	305
1777, Pavia, *Demofoonte*, J. Schuster, rvl	360
1777, Perugia, *Adriano*, J. Mysliveček, rvl	305
1777, Regensburg, *Artaserse*, T. von Schacht, pr.	254
1777, Rome, *Artaserse*, P. A. Guglielmi, pr.	254
1777, Stuttgart, *Didone*, N. Jommelli, rvl	65
1778, Alessandria, *Alessandro*, M. de Vincenti, pr.	170
1778, Florence, *Didone*, various, past.?	91
1778, Genoa, *Didone*, various, past.?	91
1778, Lodi, *Alessandro*, J. C. Bach, rvl	156
1778, London, *Demofoonte*, F. Bertoni and others, past.	361
1778, Siena, *Alessandro*, M. Mortellari, pr.	170
1778, Stuttgart, *Demofoonte*, N. Jommelli, rvl	326
1778, Valencia, *Artaserse*	255
1778, Venice, *Alessandro*, L. Marescalchi, pr.	169
1778, Venice, *Didone*, P. Anfossi, rvl	87
1778, Verona, *Artaserse*, G. Paisiello, rvl	247
1779, Forlì, *Didone*, B. Ottani, pr.	92
1779, Lodi, *Artaserse*, G. B. Pescetti, rvl	236
1779, London, *Alessandro*, Händel, Piccinni, G. Giordani and others, past.	170
1779, London, *Artaserse*, F. Bertoni, rvl	251
1779, Mannheim, *Didone*, I. Holzbauer, pr.	92
1779, Rome, *Adriano*, G. Sarti, pr.	307
1779, Venice, *Didone*, J. A. Schuster, rvl	89
1779, Verona, *Alessandro*, A. Calegari, pr.	170
1780, Berlin, *Didone*, J. A. Hasse, rvl	59
1780, Bratislava, *Didone*, G. Astarita, pr.	93
1780, Florence, *Artaserse*, L. Caruso, rev.	250
1780, Florence, *Demofoonte*, G. Rust, pr.	363
1780, Genoa, *Alessandro*, F. Alessandri, pr.	171
1780, Kassel, *Didone*	93
1780, Naples, *Didone*, N. Piccinni, rvl	83
1780, Palermo, *Adriano*	308
1780, Palermo, *Didone*, F. Piticchio, pr.	93
1780, Pisa, *Demofoonte*	362
1780, Treviso, *Adriano*, P. Anfossi, rvl	304
1780, Stuttgart, *Didone*, N. Jommelli, rvl	65
1780, Venice, *Adriano*, F. Alessandri, pr.	308
c. 1780, Rio de Janeiro, *Demofoonte*, various, past.	363
c. 1780, s.l., *Artaserse*, A. Ullinger, pr.	255
c. 1780, s.l., *Artaserse*, P. F. Parenti, pr.	255
1781, Genoa, *Demofoonte*, F. Bianchi, pr.	363
1781, Pavia, *Demofoonte*	363
1781, Perugia, *Artaserse*, 363G. Rust, pr.	255
1781, Perugia, *Didone*, F. Zannetti, rvl	80
1781, Regensburg, *Artaserse*, T. Schacht, rvl	254
1781, Rome, *Alessandro*, D. Cimarosa, pr.	172
1781, Siena, *Demofoonte*, L. Vinci, rvl	321
1781, Verona, *Alessandro*, M. de Vincenti	170
1782, Livorno, *Adriano*, L. Cherubini, pr.	308
1782, Livorno, *Artaserse*, G. Rust, rvl	255
1782, Lucca, *Demofoonte*, various (incl. F. Bianchi), past.	364
1782, Lviv, *Artaserse*	256
1782, Padua, *Didone*, G. Sarti, pr. (2nd)	78
1782, Palermo, *Demofoonte*, G. Gazzaniga, pr.	364
1782, Pavia, *Didone*, P. Anfossi, rvl	87
1782, Rome, *Demofoonte*, G. Sarti, pr. (3rd)	344
1782, Stuttgart, *Didone*, N. Jommelli, rvl	65
1782, Treviso, *Artaserse*, F. Zannetti, pr.	256
1782, Turin, *Adriano*, G. Rust, pr.	308
1783, Berlin, *Artaserse*, C. H. Graun, rvl	218
1783, Florence, *Artaserse*, G. Rust, rvl	255
1783, Lucca, *Alessandro*, M. Mortellari, rvl	170
1783, Modena, *Demofoonte*, A. Pio, pr.	364
1783, Munich, *Didone*, A. Prati, pr.	93
1783, Naples, *Artaserse*, F. Alessandri, pr.	256
1783, Padua, *Demofoonte*, F. Alessandri, pr.	364
1783, Paris, *Alessandro* (Fr.), N.-J. L. F. de Méreaux, pr.	172
1783, Paris, *Didone* (Fr.), N. Piccinni, pr. (2nd)	83
1783, Paris, *Didone* (Fr.), N. Piccinni, rvl	83

SC | Index Ia. Chronological Index: by Year

1783, Rome, *Artaserse*, G. Rust, rvl	255
1784, Berlin, *Alessandro*, C. H. Graun, rvl	141
1784, Brunswick, *Didone*, F. Piticchio, rvl	93
1784, Esterháza, *Didone*, G. Sarti, rvl	78
1784, London, *Demofoonte*, various, past.	362
1784, Mannheim, *Didone* (Ger.), I. Holzbauer, rvl	92
1784, Mantua, *Alessandro*, L. Cherubini, pr.	172
1784, St Petersburg, *Didone*, G. Andreozzi, pr.	93
1785, Brescia, *Artaserse*, F. Bertoni, rvl	251
1785, Genoa, *Alessandro*, V. Chiavacci, pr.	173
1785, London, *Artaserse*, various, past.	258
1785, Paris, *Didone* (Fr.), N. Piccinni, rvl	83
1785, Pisa, *Didone*, G. Andreozzi, rvl	93
1785, Treviso, *Artaserse*, F. Bertoni, rvl	251
1785, Trieste, *Alessandro*, F. Bianchi, rvl	173
1785, Turin, *Artaserse*, D. Cimarosa, pr.	257
1785, Venice, *Alessandro*, F. Bianchi, pr.	173
1785, Venice, *Didone*, P. A. Guglielmi, pr.	94
1785, Verona, *Artaserse*, F. Bertoni, rvl	251
1786, Bergamo, *Didone*, various	95
1786, Crema, *Demofoonte*, A. Tarchi, pr.	365
1786, Cremona, *Alessandro*, L. Cherubini, rvl	172
1786, Cremona, *Artaserse*, D. Cimarosa, rvl	257
1786, Florence, *Alessandro*, various + J. A. Hasse, past.	175
1786, Florence, *Didone*, various	95
1786, London, *Didone*, P. Anfossi and others, past.	94
1786, Lucca, *Didone*, G. Sarti, rvl	78
1786, Siena, *Alessandro*, G. Andreozzi and others, pr.	175
1787, Bologna, *Alessandro*, F. Bianchi, rvl	173
1787, Esterháza, *Alessandro*, F. Bianchi, rvl	173
1787, Genoa, *Didone*, G. Sarti, L. Cherubini, P. Anfossi, F. Bianchi, past.	95
1787, Livorno, *Demofoonte*, various, past.	367
1787, London, *Didone*, P. Anfossi and others, past.	94
1787, Lyon, *Didone* (Fr.), N. Piccinni, rvl	83
1787, Mantua, *Demofoonte*, L. Gatti, pr.	366
1787, Modena, *Alessandro*, G. Paisiello, rvl	167
1787, Modena, *Demofoonte*	367
1787, Padua, *Artaserse*, F. Bianchi, pr.	258
1787, Palermo, *Alessandro*, G. Sarti, pr. (2nd)	154
1787, Pavia, *Artaserse*, F. Bertoni, rvl	251
1787, Perugia, *Demofoonte*, G. Sarti, rvl	344
1787, Reggio Emilia, *Demofoonte*, A. Tarchi, rvl	365
1787, Rome, *Alessandro*, L. Caruso, pr. (1st)	176
1787, Siena, *Artaserse*, F. Bianchi, rvl	258
1787, Venice, *Demofoonte*, A. Prati, pr.	366
1787, Verona, *Alessandro*, F. Bianchi, rvl	173
1787, Vicenza, *Didone*, G. Gazzaniga, pr.	96
1788, Cremona, *Artaserse*, F. Bertoni, rvl	251
1788, Florence, *Demofoonte*, various, past.	368
1788, Genoa, *Artaserse*, F. Bertoni, rev	251
1788, Livorno, *Alessandro*, L. Cherubini, rvl	172
1788, Mantua, *Artaserse*, A. Tarchi, pr.	259
1788, Milan, *Alessandro*, A. Tarchi, pr. (1st)	178
1788, Naples, *Didone*, P. Anfossi, pr. (2nd)	87
1788, Paris, *Demofoonte* (Fr.), L. Cherubini, pr.	368
1788, Rome, *Artaserse*, P. Anfossi, pr.	259
1788, Stuttgart, *Adriano*, J. F. Gauss, pr. (Ger.)	309
1788, Turin, *Demofoonte*, G. Pugnani, pr.	367
1788, Venice, *Artaserse*, various	260
1789, Bergamo, *Alessandro*, F. Bianchi, rvl	173
1789, Bologna, *Artaserse*, P. A. Guglielmi, rvl	254
1789, Livorno, *Artaserse*, G. Andreozzi, pr.	262
1789, London, *Alessandro*, A. Tarchi, rvl	178
1789, Naples, *Alessandro*, P. A. Guglielmi, pr.	180
1789, Padua, *Artaserse*, F. Bianchi, rvl	258
1789, Paris, *Demofoonte* (Fr.), J. C. Vogel, pr.	368
1789, Reggio Emilia, *Didone*, G. Andreozzi, rvl	93
1789, Trieste, *Artaserse*, N. A. Zingarelli, pr. (1st)	368
1789, Trieste, *Demofoonte*, N. A. Zingarelli, pr.	368
1789, Venice, *Didone*, G. Gazzaniga, rvl	96
1790, Ancona, *Artaserse*, F. Bertoni, rvl	251
1790, London, *Alessandro*, A. Tarchi, rvl	178
1790, London, *Demofoonte*, V. Federici, pr.	369
1790, Madrid, *Demofoonte*, various (incl. V. Federici), past.	369
1790, Milan, *Adriano*, S. Nasolini, pr.	309
1790, Modena, *Artaserse*, A. Tarchi, rvl	259
1790, Reggio Emilia, *Artaserse*, A. Tarchi, rvl	259
1790, Venice, *Didone*, F. Bertoni, V. Rampini, J. G. Naumann, G. Gazzaniga, past.	96
c. 1790, s.l., *Adriano*, N. A. Zingarelli, pr.	309
c. 1790, s.l., *Alessandro*, N. A. Zingarelli, pr.	181
1791, Bergamo, *Didone*, F. Bertoni, V. Rampini, J. G. Naumann, G. Gazzaniga, past./rvl	96
1791, Livorno, *Alessandro*, A. Tarchi, rev.	178
1791, Livorno, *Demofoonte*, A. Tarchi, rvl	365
1791, Madrid, *Didone*, G. Andreozzi, rvl	93
1791, Padua, *Didone*, various	97
1791, Pavia, *Demofoonte*, A. Tarchi, rvl	365
1791, Rome, *Demofoonte*, various (incl. G. Nicolini), past.?	369
1791, Siena, *Alessandro*, A. Tarchi, rvl	178
1791, Venice, *Alessandro*, L. Caruso, pr. (2nd)	176
1791, Venice, *Demofoonte*, G. Pugnani (and others?), rvl	367
1792, Florence, *Artaserse*, various	262
1792, Genoa, *Demofoonte*	370
1792, Imola, *Artaserse*, F. Bertoni, rvl	251
1792, London, *Didone*, various, past.	97

SC | Index Ia. Chronological Index: by Year

1792, Madrid, *Alessandro*, L. Caruso, rvl	176
1792, Madrid, *Didone*, G. Sarti + G. Paisiello, past.	78
1792, Naples, *Alessandro*, N. Piccinni, rvl	149
1792, Venice, *Alessandro*, F. Bianchi, rvl	173
1792, Warsaw, *Alessandro*, F. Bianchi, rvl	174
1793, Mantua, *Didone*, G. Sarti, rvl	78
1793, Modena, *Demofoonte*, A. Tarchi, rvl	365
1793, Padua, *Didone*, F. Bertoni, V. Rampini, J. G. Naumann, G. Gazzaniga, past./rvl	96
1794, Genoa, *Artaserse*	262
1794, Genoa, *Didone*, G. Gazzaniga, rvl	96
1794, Livorno, *Artaserse*, N. Isouard, pr.	262
1794, Milan, *Artaserse*, N. A. Zingarelli, pr. (2nd)	260
1794, Milan, *Demofoonte*, M. A. Portugal, pr. (1st)	370
1794, Naples, *Didone*, G. Paisiello, rvl	98
1794, Palermo, *Didone*, G. Paisiello, pr.	98
1795, Florence, *Didone*, G. Paisiello, rvl	98
1795, Udine, *Alessandro*, F. Bianchi, rvl	174
1795, Venice, *Artaserse*, G. Nicolini, pr.	263
1795, Venice, *Demofoonte*, various (incl. N. A. Zingarelli), past.	368
1795, Vienna, *Didone*, L. Koželuh, pr.	100
1795, s.l., *Artaserse*, F. Cerracchini, pr.	263
1796, Corfù, *Alessandro*, L. Caruso, rvl	176
1796, St Petersburg, *Didone*, G. Paisiello, rvl	98
1796, Verona, *Didone*, 368G. Paisiello, rvl	98
1798, Porto, *Didone*, S. Marino and others, pr.	100
1798, Turin, *Alessandro*, A. Tarchi, pr. (2nd)	178
1798, Venice, *Adriano*, J. S. Mayr, pr368.	309
1799, Berlin, *Didone*, N. Piccinni, rvl	83
1799, Lisbon, *Didone*, S. Marino and others, rvl	100
1799, London, *Didone*, G. Paisiello, rvl	98
1799, Paris, *Adriano* (Fr.), E. N. Méhul, pr.	310
1799, St Petersburg, *Alessandro*, G. Paisiello, rvl	167
1800, Lisbon, *Alessandro*, L. Caruso, rvl (x2)	176
1800, Livorno, *Alessandro*, P. Gnecco, pr.	181
c. 1800, Livorno/Florence, *Alessandro*, various	181
c. 1800, s.l., *Adriano*, C. Bernardini, pr.	310
1800, Lisbon, *Alessandro*, L. Caruso	176
1801, Lisbon, *Alessandro*, L. Caruso	176
1801, Lisbon, *Artaserse*, D. Cimarosa, rvl	257
1802, Florence, *Alessandro*, A. Tarchi, rvl	178
1803, Lisbon, *Didone*, S. Marino and others, rvl	100
1804, Pavia, *Artaserse*, N. A. Zingarelli, rvl	260
1804, St Petersburg, *Alessandro* (Ger.), S. Neukomm (pr.)	182
1805, Lisbon, *Alessandro*, D. Perez, rvl	138
1806, Lisbon, *Artaserse*, M. A. Portugal, pr.	263
1807, Vienna, *Adriano* (Ger.), J. Weigl (pr.)	310
1808, Berlin, *Didone*, N. Piccinni, rvl	83
1808, Lisbon, *Demofoonte*, M. A. Portugal, pr. (2nd)	370
1808, London, *Didone*, G. Paisiello, rvl	98
1809, Forlì, *Adriano*	310
1809, Padua, *Adriano*, M. A. Portugal, pr.	310
1810, Florence, *Artaserse*, M. A. Portugal, rvl	263
1810, Paris, *Didone*, F. Paër, pr. (1st)	101
1810, Rome, *Didone*, V. Fioravanti, pr.	100
1811, Mannheim, *Alessandro* (Ger.), A. Ritter, pr.	182
1811, Munich, *Demofoonte* (Ger.), P. J. von Lindpaintner, pr.	371
1811, Naples, *Adriano*, V. Migliorucci, pr.	311
1811, Paris, *Didone*, F. Paër, rvl	101
1812, Dresden, *Didone*, F. Paër, rvl	101
1812, Paris, *Didone*, F. Paër, rvl	101
1812, Rio de Janeiro, *Artaserse*, M. A. Portugal, rvl	263
1813, Como, *Adriano*, M. A. Portugal, rvl	310
1813, London, *Artaserse* (En.), H. R. Bishop, pr.	264
1814, London, *Didone*, F. Paër, pr. (2nd)	101
1814, Verona, *Adriano*, M. A. Portugal, rvl	310
1815, Milan, *Adriano*, M. A. Portugal, rvl	310
1817, Florence, *Didone*, F. Paër, rvl	101
1817, Parma, *Artaserse*, M. A. Portugal, rvl	263
1817, Parma, *Didone*, F. Paër, rvl	101
1819, Lisbon, *Demofoonte*, M. A. Portugal, rvl	370
1821, London, *Demofoonte*, C. E. Horn, pr.	371
1821, Palermo, *Adriano*, P. Airoldi, pr.	311
1823, Berlin, *Didone* (Ger.), B. Klein, pr.	108
1823, Livorno, *Didone*, S. Mercadante, rvl	103
1823, Lucca, *Didone*, S. Mercadante, rvl	103
1823, Milan, *Didone*, S. Mercadante, rvl	103
1823, Turin, *Didone*, S. Mercadante, pr. (1st)	103
1824, Dresden, *Didone*, C. G. Reissiger, pr.	108
1824, Genoa, *Didone*, S. Mercadante, rvl	103
1824, Naples, *Alessandro*, G. Pacini, pr.	182
1824, Palermo, *Didone*, S. Mercadante, rvl	103
1824, Vicenza, *Didone*, S. Mercadante, rvl	103
1825, Cremona, *Didone*, S. Mercadante, rvl	103
1825, Florence, *Didone*, S. Mercadante, rvl	103
1825, Mantua, *Didone*, S. Mercadante, rvl	103
1825, Naples, *Didone*, S. Mercadante, pr. (2nd)	103
1826, Barcelona, *Didone*, S. Mercadante, rvl	103
1826, Gorizia, *Didone*, S. Mercadante, rvl	103
1826, Ravenna, *Didone*, S. Mercadante, rvl	103
1826, Udine, *Didone*, S. Mercadante, rvl	103
1826, Venice, *Didone*, S. Mercadante, rvl	103
1826, s.l., *Adriano* (Fr.), F. Mirecki, pr.	311
1827, Lisbon, *Didone*, S. Mercadante, rvl	104
1827, Lisbon, *Alessandro*, G. Pacini, rvl	182
1827, London, *Didone*, S. Mercadante, rvl	104
1827, Milan, *Alessandro*, G. Pacini, rvl	182

1827, Milan, *Didone*, S. Mercadante, rvl	103	1830, Florence, *Didone*, S. Mercadante, rvl	104
1827, Palermo, *Alessandro*, G. Pacini, rvl	182	1831, Barcelona, *Alessandro*, G. Pacini, rvl	182
1827, Venice, *Didone*, S. Mercadante, rvl	104	1832, Brescia, *Didone*, S. Mercadante, rvl	104
1828, Lisbon, *Adriano*, S. Mercadante, pr.	311	1836, Florence, *Demofoonte*, G. M. Sborgi, pr.	371
1828, Lisbon, *Adriano*, S. Mercadante, rvl	311	1840, London, *Artaserse* (En.), C. Lucas, pr.	264
1828, Venice, *Alessandro*, G. Pacini, rvl	182	1850, Berlin, *Artaserse* (Ger.), H. L. E. Dorn, pr.	264
1828, Verona, *Didone*, S. Mercadante, rvl	104	s.d., Rome, *Didone*, A. Boroni, rvl	81
1829, Turin, *Didone*, S. Mercadante, rvl	104	s.d., Venice, *Artaserse*, L. Vinci, rvl	190

Index Ib.
Chronological Index: by Date and Title

Year	Didone abbandonata		Alessandro nell'Indie	Artaserse	Adriano in Siria	Demofoonte
1724						
carn.	Naples, D. N. Sarro (pr., 1st)	41				
s.d.	Rome, D. Scarlatti (pr.)	43				
	Palermo, D. Scarlatti	43				
1725						
carn.	Venice, T. G. Albinoni (pr.)	43				
	Florence, unknown	44				
Apr.	Reggio Emilia, N. Porpora (pr.)	45				
1726						
carn.	Rome, L. Vinci (pr.)	46				
	Vienna, L. Vinci	46				
Sept.	Crema, T. G. Albinoni	43				
Nov.	Wrocław, T. G. Albinoni	43				
1727						
carn.	Livorno, unknown	47				
	Turin, D. N. Sarro	41				
s.d.	Mantua, unknown	48				
1728						
Nov.	Syracuse, unknown	48				
1729						
carn.	Milan, T. G. Albinoni	43				
	Vienna, unknown	48				
s.d.	Lucca, L. Vinci	46				

SC | Index Ib. Chronological Index: by Date and Title

Year	Didone abbandonata		Alessandro nell'Indie		Artaserse		Adriano in Siria		Demofoonte
1730									
carn.	Pesaro, T. G. Albinoni?	44	Rome, L. Vinci (pr.)	111	Rome, L. Vinci (pr.)	189			
					Venice, J. A. Hasse (pr.)	197			
spr.					Genoa, J. A. Hasse	197			
May	Linz, T. G. Albinoni	44							
summ.					Bologna, J. A. Hasse	197			
Aug.					Vienna, J. Vinci	189			
					Florence, L. Vinci	189			
aut.					Turin, J. A. Hasse	197			
					Lucca, J. A. Hasse	197			
Nov.	Venice, D. N. Sarro (pr., 2nd)	41							
1731									
carn.			Livorno, L. Vinci (past.)	111	Milan, J. A. Hasse	198			
			Milan, L. A. Predieri (pr.)	115	Pesaro, L. Vinci	189			
			Turin, N. Porpora (pr.)	114	Fano, L. Vinci	189			
					Livorno, L. Vinci	189			
Feb.			London, G. F. Händel (pr.)	116					
spr.	Prague, T. G. Albinoni	44	Vienna, N. Porpora & others	115	Rome, L. Vinci	189			
summ.									
Sept.			Dresden, J. A. Hasse (pr.)	119	Ferrara, L. Vinci	189			
aut.					Naples, L. Vinci	190			
Nov.	Hamburg, N. Porpora (Ger.)	45	London, G. F. Händel	116					
s.d.					Kremsier, J. A. Hasse (Ger.)	198			
1732									
carn.	Rome, N. Porpora, R. Broschi, E. R. Duni		Florence, L. Vinci (past.)	111	Perugia, L. Vinci	190			
			Venice, G. B. Pescetti (pr.)	126					
			Naples, F. Mancini (pr.)	127					
Feb.		48	Hamburg, G. F. Händel	116					
summ.			Brunswick, G. F. Händel	116					
Nov.			Genoa, L. A. Predieri	115					
s.d.			Milan, J. A. Hasse	119			Vienna, A. Caldara (pr.)		271

408

SC | Index Ib. Chronological Index: by Date and Title

Year	Didone abbandonata	Alessandro nell'Indie	Artaserse	Adriano in Siria	Demofoonte
1733					
carn.	Ferrara, T. G. Albinoni 44	Brescia, L. Vinci	Naples, L. Vinci 111		
	Messina, unknown	Palermo, unknown 49	Verona, J. A. Hasse 127		
		Reggio Emilia, L. Vinci	Camerino, L. Vinci 111		
Jun.			Wrocław, A. Bioni? (pr.) 208	Venice, G. Giacomelli (pr.) 272	
aut.			Holešov, E. Bambini (pr.) 208		
Nov.					Vienna, A. Caldara (pr.) 315
s.d.			Siena, unknown 208		
1734					
carn.	Perugia, L. Vinci	Urbino, L. Vinci 46	Perugia, L. Vinci 111	Florence, unknown 273	
		Wrocław, A. Bioni (pr.)	London, various (past.) 128	Genoa, P. G. Sandoni (pr.) 273	
			Venice, J. A. Hasse 198		
			Pisa, G. Giacomelli (pr.) 210		
Mar.		Bologna, G. M. Schiassi (pr.) 128			
summ.	Brunswick, N. Porpora		London, various (past.) 209		
July		Jesi, G. M. Schiassi 45			
aut.	Brno, D. N. Sarro	Prague, A. Bioni 41	Valencia, unknown 128	Naples, G. B. Pergolesi (pr.) 273	
Oct.			London, J. A. Hasse & others (past.) 128		
s.d.		Vyškov, L. Vinci	111		

409

Year	Didone abbandonata	Alessandro nell'Indie	Artaserse	Adriano in Siria	Demofoonte
1735 carn.	Florence, unknown	49 Munich, L. Vinci & others	111 La Valletta, J. A. Hasse 198		Venice, G. M. Schiassi (pr.) 316 Naples, Sarro/Mancini/Leo 316
Mar. spr. May		Pisa, unknown 129	London, Hasse & others (past.) 210		Rome, F. Ciampi (pr.) 318
Nov. s.d.	Bologna, G. M. Schiassi (pr.) 49		London, Hasse & others (past.) 210	London, F. M. Veracini (pr.) 275 Venice, unknown 276	Genoa, P. V. Chiocchetti (pr.) 318 Vyškov, G. M. Schiassi 316
1736 carn.		Parma, L. Vinci 112 Venice, J. A. Hasse 119 Prato, E. R. Duni (pr.) 129	London, Hasse & others (past.) 210	Milan, A. Bernasconi (pr., 1ª) 276 Rome, E. R. Duni (pr.) 278	
Feb. Mar.			London, Hasse & others (past.) 210	London, F. M. Veracini 275	
May			London, Hasse & others (past.) 210	London, F. M. Veracini 275	
Jun.			London Hasse & others (past.) 210		
aut. Nov. Dec. s.d.	Jaroměřice, L. Vinci	46 Naples, J. A. Hasse 119 London, G. F. Händel 116 Hamburg, G. F. Händel 116 Lisbon, G. M. Schiassi 128		Caltagirone, unknown 278	

SC | Index Ib. Chronological Index: by Date and Title

Year	Didone abbandonata	Alessandro nell'Indie	Artaserse	Adriano in Siria	Demofoonte
1737					
carn.	Graz, Scalabrini & others (pr.) 50	Ferrara, J. A. Hasse	Parma, F. Poncini Zilioli (pr.) 119	Munich, G. B. Ferrandini (pr.) 278	Livorno, various 318
	Jaroměřice, L. Vinci 46		Brunswick, G. Paganelli (pr., 1st) 212	Mantua, G. Porta (pr.) 278	
Apr.	London, Vinci, Händel... 51			Stuttgart, A. Bernasconi 276	
May				Treviso, G. Porta 278	Lisbon, G. M. Schiassi 316
summ.			Brunswick, G. Paganelli 212		London, E. R. Duni (pr.) 318
Oct.					Munich, G. B. Ferrandini (pr.) 318
s.d.		Padua, A. G. Pampani (pr.)	Lisbon, G. M. Schiassi (pr.) 129	Vyškov, J. A. Hasse (pr., 1st) 279	
				Brunswick, A. Caldara 271	
1738					
carn.		Graz, J. A. Hasse	Bergamo, J. A. Hasse 120		Venice, G. Latilla (pr.) 319
		Mantua, B. Galuppi (pr., 1st)			Piacenza, Lampugnani (pr.) 319
		Venice, J. A. Hasse	Klagenfurt, J. A. Hasse 129		
			Naples, L. Vinci & others 120		
			St Petersburg, F. Araia (pr.) 198		Turin, G. F. Brivio (pr.) 319
			Graz, P. Scalabrini & others (pr.) 190		
Jan.					
Apr.			Treviso, J. A. Hasse 213		
			St Petersburg, F. Araia 214		
May	Bayreuth, G. A. Paganelli (pr.) 52	Madrid, F. Corselli (pr.)	198		
spr.			Padua, G. F. Brivio (pr., 1st) 213		
			Livorno, Zamparelli & others (pr.) 215		
Jul.		Madrid, F. Corselli	Rome, L. Vinci 215		
Aug.			190		
Oct.		Madrid, F. Corselli	Vicenza, J. A. Hasse 133		
Dec.			133		
s.d.		Rimini, various	Madrid, Hasse + Vinci 134		Jaroměřice, G. F. Brivio 320
			198		Madrid, Schiassi & others 316

411

SC | Index Ib. Chronological Index: by Date and Title

Year	Didone abbandonata		Alessandro nell'Indie		Artaserse		Adriano in Siria		Demofoonte	
1739										
carn.	Milan, E. R. Duni/G. F. Brivio	52	Klagenfurt, J. A. Hasse		Modena, J. A. Hasse	120	Rome, A. Caldara	198	Graz, various	320
Fair			Vicenza, unknown			120				
Aug.	Padua, G. B. Lampugnani (pr.)	52								
Oct.					Munich, Ferrandini & others (pr.)		Naples, G. A. Ristori (pr.)	216	Alessandria, G. Reina (pr.)	320
Dec.						216		216		
s.d.	Brunswick, G. A. Paganelli	52			Vienna, unknown					
1740										
carn.			Lucca, L. Vinci		Florence, L. Vinci	112	Siena, unknown	190		281
			Verona, J. A. Hasse		Catania, unknown	120	Turin, B. Galuppi (pr., 1st)	216		281
					Ljubljana, J. A. Hasse	198				
					Macerata, L. Vinci	190				
			Lisbon, A. P. Fabbri (pr.)			134				
			Florence, various (past.)			134				
May	Vienna, various^{NP}	54								284
spr.					Genoa, J. A. Hasse	198	Venice, G. A. Giai (pr.)			
Aug.	Lucca, various (past.)	54					Vicenza, Lampugnani (pr.)	284		
Sept.					Dresden, J. A. Hasse (pr., 2nd)	198				
aut.										285
s.d.			Nap./Palermo, Caballone (pr.)	134			Naples, M. Caballone			
1741										
carn.	Modena, B. Galuppi (pr., 1st)	54			Bassano, unknown	199	Brescia, P. Giaino (pr.)	217	Lucca, L. Vinci (pr.)	321
	Graz, P. Scalabrini & others	50			Verona, P. Chiarini (pr.)			216	Rome, A. Bernasconi (pr., 1st)	321
					Catania, unknown		Ferrara, unknown	217		
	Venice, A. Bernasconi (pr., 1st)	57	Modena, P. Pulli (pr.)		Turin, G. Arena (pr.)	134				
Jun.			Bratislava, J. A. Hasse			120			Florence, G. Verocai (pr.)	322
summ.									Brunswick, G. Verocai	322
Oct.	Arezzo, D. N. Sarro	41								
Dec.									Naples, L. Leo (pr.)	322
s.d.	Lisbon, R. di Capua (pr.)	58	Erlangen, unknown		Wrocław, P. Scalabrini	134		214		
	Strasbourg, Scalabrini & others	50								
	Vienna, various	54								

SC | Index Ib. Chronological Index: by Date and Title

Year	Didone abbandonata	Alessandro nell'Indie	Artaserse	Adriano in Siria	Demofoonte
1742 carn.	Ljubljana, Scalabrini & others 50	Milan, G. F. Brivio (pr.) 134	Milan, C. W. Gluck (pr.) 218		Brunswick, G. Verocai 322
			Genoa, P. Chiarini 217		Rome, L. Leo 322
Asc.	Alessandria, G. B. Lampugnani 52		Parma, J. A. Hasse & others 199		
May			Venice, Paganelli & others (pr.) 212		
summ.	Palermo, unknown 59				Milan, unknown 323
aut.	Dresden, J. A. Hasse (pr.) 59				
Oct.			London, Brivio & others 215		
Dec.					
s.d.		C. di Castello, R. Capua (pr.) 135		s.l., N. B. Logroscino (pr.) 285	
1743 carn.		Livorno, unknown 135	Palermo, L. Vinci 190		Milan, C. W. Gluck (pr.) 323
		Venice, J. A. Hasse 120			
		Naples, D. N. Sarro (pr.) 135			
spr.	Dresden, J. A. Hasse 59				Rimini, various 325
	Cesena, A. Bernasconi 57				Reggio Emilia, C. W. Gluck 323
May					
Jun.					Padua, N. Jommelli (pr.,1st) 325
Nov.			Naples, L. Vinci + G. Manna 190		
		London, G. F. Händel 116	Hamburg, P. Scalabrini & others 214		
Dec.		Genoa, Urtini or Duni (pr.) 136	Berlin, C. H. Graun (pr.) 218		
s.d.		St Petersburg, F. Araia (pr.) 136		Vienna, unknown 285	
1744 carn.	Naples, J. A. Hasse 59	Florence, J. A. Hasse 120	Prague, P. Scalabrini & others 214		Bologna, C. W. Gluck & others 323
		Ferrara, N. Jommelli (pr.,1st) 137			
Jul.		Genoa, D. Perez (pr.,1st) 138	Florence, E. R. Duni (pr.) 221		
Aug.			Venice, D. Terradellas (pr.) 221		
Oct.	Hamburg, Scalabrini & others 50		Berlin, C. H. Graun 218		
Dec.		Berlin, C. H. Graun (pr.) 141			Vienna, C. W. Gluck 323

SC | Index Ib. Chronological Index: by Date and Title

Year	Didone abbandonata	Alessandro nell'Indie	Artaserse	Adriano in Siria	Demofoonte
1745					
carn.	Parma, N. Porpora 45	Turin, C. W. Gluck (pr.) 142	Brunswick, C. H. Graun 218	Gorizia, unknown 285	Ferrara, C. W. Gluck 323
	Mantua, various 64	Verona, P. Chiarini (pr.) 142		Brunswick, G. Verocai (pr.) 285	
spr.	Fano, Aurisicchio & others (pr.) 64		Ferrara, L. Vinci + J. A. Hasse 190		
Jul.	Bologna, various 64		Bologna, J. A. Hasse 199		
s.d.	Crema, G. B. Lampugnani 52	Faenza, L. Vinci 112			
1746					
carn.		Brescia, P. Pellegrini (pr.) 142		Florence, G. Abos (pr.) 286	
		Pesaro, J. A. Hasse 120		Berlin, C. H. Graun (pr.) 286	
		Genoa, J. A. Hasse 120	Venice, G. Abos (pr.) 222	Livorno, unknown 288	
		London, J. B. Lampugnani (pr.) 142		Perugia, unknown 288	Berlin, C. H. Graun (pr.) 330
Apr.		Vienna, J. A. Hasse (?) 120	Dresden, P. Scalabrini & others 214		
Aug.		Genoa, J. A. Hasse 120			
Sept.					
aut.					
Oct.			Vienna, A. Bernasconi (pr., 1st) 223		Florence, unknown 331
			Hamburg, P. Scalabrini & others 214		
Nov.	Hamburg, Scalabrini & others 50	Vienna, J. A. Hasse 120			
Dec.		Palermo, unknown 143			
s.d.					

414

SC | Index Ib. Chronological Index: by Date and Title

Year	Didone abbandonata		Alessandro nell'Indie		Artaserse		Adriano in Siria		Demofoonte	
1747										
carn.	Rome, N. Jommelli (pr.,1st)	64			Pistoia, L. Vinci	190			Pavia, G. F. Brivio	320
	Venice, A. Adolfati (pr.)	67								
spr.					Ravenna, unknown	223				
May									Milan, C. W. Gluck	323
Jun.	Dresden, Scalabrini & others	50			Trento, F. Maggiore (pr.)	223				
Jul.			Ancona, G. Abos (pr.)	143	Lucca, G. Scarlatti (pr., 1st)	224				
Aug.	Leipzig, Scalabrini & others	50								
Mich.	Hamburg, Scalabrini & others	50								
Nov.										
Dec.							Naples, G. Latilla (pr.)	288		
s.d.					Palermo, V. L. Ciampi (pr.)	224				
1747–1748										
s.d.									s.l., J. C. Smith (pr.)	332
1748										
carn.	Venice, F. Bertoni (pr.)	68			Piacenza, G. Carcani (pr.)	224	Venice, V. L. Ciampi (pr.)	288		
	Genoa, unknown	68								
Feb.			London, G. F. Händel	116					Dresden, J. A. Hasse (pr., 1st)	332
Mar.			London, G. F. Händel	116						
Aug.	London, J. A. Hasse & others	59								
Sept.			Vienna, G. C. Wagenseil	144						
aut.	Brescia, P. Chiarini (pr.)	68			Bayreuth, J. A. Hasse	199				
					Florence, D. Perez (pr., 1st)	225				
					Prague, various (past.)	226				
	Copenhagen, P. Scalabrini & others				Bonn, F. Zoppis (pr.)	226				
s.d.		50							Palermo, unknown	337

Index Ib. Chronological Index: by Date and Title

Year	Didone abbandonata	Alessandro nell'Indie	Artaserse	Adriano in Siria	Demofoonte
1749 carn.			Cremona, P. Chiarini 217		Venice, J. A. Hasse (pr., 2nd) 332
			Livorno, unknown 227		
			Madrid, G.B. Mele & others (pr.) 227		
			Naples, D. Perez 225		
			Vienna, B. Galuppi (pr., 1st) 227		
			Copenhagen, Scalabrini & others 214		
Jun.	Vienna, N. Jommelli (pr., 2nd) 64		Rome, N. Jommelli (pr., 1st) 231		
Nov.			Madrid, G. B. Mele & others 227		
Dec.		Naples, D. Perez 138			
s.d.		Copenhagen, Scalabrini (pr.) 144	Alessandria, unknown 233	Copenhagen, Scalabrini (pr.) 289	Copenhagen, various 337
			s.l., J. C. Smith (pr.) 233		
1750 carn.		Prague, G. M. Rutini (pr.) 144	Milan, G. B. Lampugnani (pr.) 233		Madrid, Galuppi+ Mele (pr., 1st) 337
		Vicenza, G. Scolari (pr.) 145	Pisa, L. Vinci 190		Mannheim, J. A. Hasse 332
	Turin, D. Terradellas (pr.) 69				Naples, Hasse + Latilla 332
Feb.			Venice, A. G. Pampani (pr., 1st) 234	London, V. L. Ciampi (rev.) 288	Madrid, B. Galuppi + Mele 338
May				Reggio Emilia, Pescetti (pr.) 289	
summ.			Cagliari, G. Bollano? (pr.) 235		Brunswick, I. Fiorillo (pr.) 340
Jul.				Siena, G. B. Pescetti 218	
Aug.			Stuttgart, C. H. Graun 143		
aut.		Lucca, G. Abos 143			
		Sassuolo, L. Vinci 112			
Dec.		Barcelona, G. Scolari 145			
s.d.			Madrid, G. B. Mele & others 227	Brunswick, I. Fiorillo (pr.) 227	Ferrara, F. A. B. Uttini (pr.) 341
			Sassuolo, B. Galuppi 227	Naples, B. Galuppi 235	281
			Strasbourg, unknown 235		

SC | Index Ib. Chronological Index: by Date and Title

Year	Didone abbandonata	Alessandro nell'Indie	Artaserse	Adriano in Siria	Demofoonte
1751					
carn.			Sturtgart, C. H. Graun 218	Milan, A. G. Pampani (pr.) 290	Brunswick, I. Fiorillo 340
			Verona, Dal Barba & others (pr.) 235	Genoa, A. Adolfati (pr.) 290	Palermo, L. Santini (pr.) 341
	Venice, G. Manna (pr.) 69				
Feb.			Mannheim, N. Jommelli (rev.) 231		
May					
Jun.			Padua, B. Galuppi (pr., 2nd) 227		Madrid, B. Galuppi + Mele 338
summ.			Brunswick, I. Fiorillo (pr.) 235		Barcelona, B. Galuppi + Mele 338
win.	Brunswick, I. Fiorillo (pr.) 70				
	Genoa, D. Perez (pr.) 70				
s.d.	Sturtgart, N. Jommelli 65				
1752					
carn.	Livorno, F. Poncini Zilioli (pr.) 72		Milan, G. B. Pescetti (pr.) 236	Cremona, unknown 291	Cremona, G. F. Brivio 320
				Dresden, J. A. Hasse (pr., 2nd) 279	Madrid, B. Galuppi + Mele 338
spr.		Milan, D. Perez 138			
Apr.		Florence, unknown 146		Venice, G. Scarlatti (pr.) 291	
May	Reggio Emilia, D. Perez 70				Madrid, B. Galuppi + Mele 338
Aug.	Barcelona, G. Scolari (pr.) 72				
aut.		Sturtgart, B. Galuppi 129		Lucca, G. Scarlatti 291	
Sept.	Madrid, B. Galuppi (rev.) 54				Livorno, unknown 341
Dec.	Madrid, B. Galuppi 55				Lisbon, D. Perez (pr.) 341
	Dresden, J. A. Hasse 59	Alessandria, G. Calderara (pr.) 146	Forlì, Ferrandini & others 216		
s.d.	Vienna, G. Bonno (pr.)NP 73	Brunswick, I. Fiorillo (pr.) 146		Rome, N. Jommelli (pr.) 292	

417

SC | Index Ib. Chronological Index: by Date and Title

Year	Didone abbandonata		Alessandro nell'Indie		Artaserse		Adriano in Siria		Demofoonte	
1753 carn.	Florence, B. Galuppi?	55	Venice, G. Latilla & others	55	Graz, F. Maggiore	146				
	Berlin, J. A. Hasse	59			Mantua, B. Galuppi	223				
	Bologna, A. M. Mazzoni (pr.)	73				227			Milan, N. Jommelli (pr., 2nd)	326
	Lisbon, D. Perez	70								
	Naples, Lampugnani (pr., 2nd)	52								
spr.										
May	Paris–Versailles, J. A. Hasse	59	Reggio Emilia, G. Scarlatti (pr.)	146			Bologna, M. Valentini (pr.)	292		
Aug.	Madrid, B. Galuppi	55								
Oct.	Barcelona, G. Scolari	73								
aut.					Livorno, unknown	236	Crema, unknown	293		
Dec.			Puerto de S. María, G. Scolari	145						
s.d.	Pavia, unknown	74							Lisbon, unknown (Port.)	342
1754 carn.	Brescia, G. B. Lampugnani	52	Berlin, J. F. Agricola (pr.)	147	Parma, L. Vinci	190	Lisbon, D. Perez (pr.)	293	Lodi, N. Jommelli	326
			Verona, J. A. Hasse	120	Venice, B. Galuppi & others	227			Vicenza, J. A. Hasse	332
	London, V. L. Ciampi (pr.)	74	Naples, B. Galuppi	129			Livorno, G. Scarlatti	291		
Apr.	London, V. L. Ciampi	74			London, J. A. Hasse	199	Venice, G. Scolari (pr.)	294	Parma, A. Mazzoni (pr.)	342
spr.	Madrid, B. Galuppi	55							Turin, G. Manna (pr.)	342
May					Bologna, unknown	237				
Jun.					Lisbon, D. Perez (pr., 2nd)	225			Venice, G. Cocchi (pr.)	343
aut.					Barcelona, Ferrandini & others	216				
Nov.							Naples, N. Conforto (pr.)	294	Lucca, G. Cocchi	343
Dec.	Madrid, B. Galuppi	55								
s.d.							Pavia, A. G. Pampani	290		

418

SC | Index Ib. Chronological Index: by Date and Title

Year	Didone abbandonata	Alessandro nell'Indie	Artaserse	Adriano in Siria	Demofoonte
1755					
carn.	Mantua, D. Perez 70		Bergamo, G. B. Pescetti 236		Florence, unknown 344
	Madrid, B. Galuppi 55		Treviso, B. Galuppi 228	Munich, A. Bernasconi (pr., 2nd) 276	Copenhagen, G. Sarti (pr., 1st) 344
	Milan, G. A. Fioroni (pr.) 74	Parma, B. Galuppi 129			
Mar.	Verona, unknown 75	Lisbon, D. Perez (pr., 2nd) 138			
Apr.	Madrid, B. Galuppi 55				
Asc.	Madrid, B. Galuppi 55	Venice, B. Galuppi (pr., 2nd) 129	Reggio Emilia, G. Cocchi (pr.) 237		
Aug.		Amsterdam, unknown 148			
Sept.					Madrid, B. Galuppi + Mele 338
Oct.		Munich, B. Galuppi 130			
Nov.					
Dec.			Lübeck, J. A. Hasse & others 199	Naples, J. A. Hasse 279	London, various (past.) 345
					Madrid, B. Galuppi + Mele 338
s.d.		St Petersburg, F. Araia 136	Dresden, Mei or Peretti? (pr.) 238		
1756					
carn.	Cremona, P. Chiarini 68	Brescia, B. Galuppi 130	Brescia, B. Galuppi 228		
	Munich, A. Bernasconi (pr., 2nd) 58	Lodi, B. Galuppi 130	Venice, A. G. Pampani (pr., 2nd) 234		
May		Pavia, D. Perez 138			
Aug.			Vicenza, B. Galuppi 228		Bologna, B. Galuppi + Mele 338
			Stuttgart, N. Jommelli (pr., 2nd) 231		
Sept.		Florence, B. Galuppi 130			
Dec.		London, various (past.) 148			
s.d.		Pisa, N. Conforto (pr.) 148			

419

SC | Index Ib. Chronological Index: by Date and Title

Year	Didone abbandonata		Alessandro nell'Indie		Artaserse		Adriano in Siria		Demofoonte	
1757										
carn.	Faenza, D. Perez	70			Milan, Q. Gasparini (pr.)	238			Verona, unknown	346
					Florence, various	238				
					Faenza, B. Galuppi	228	Venice, G. F. Brusa (pr.)	295	Rome, A. G. Pampani (pr.)	346
					Ferrara, B. Galuppi	228			Pistoia, G. Cocchi	343
Jul.										
Aug.							Stockholm, Uttini (pr.)	295		
Sept.					Lucca, B. Galuppi	228	Madrid, N. Conforto (rev.)	294		
aut.	Venice, T. Traetta (pr., 1st)	75								
s.d.			Vicenza, B. Galuppi	130	Pavia, G. Scolari (pr.)	238				
1758										
carn.							Rome, R. di Capua (pr.)	296	Siena, P. Vinci (pr.)	347
									Mantua, T. Traetta (pr.)	347
Mar.			Rome, N. Piccinni (pr., 1st)	149						
spr.							Madrid, N. Conforto	294		
Asc.			Genoa, G. Sciroli (pr.)	153	Pisa, various	239	Livorno, B. Galuppi (pr., 2nd)	281		
Jun.					Venice, G. Scolari	238			Padua, B. Galuppi (pr., 2nd)	338
Aug.					Stockholm, F. A. B. Uttini	239				
Nov.	St Petersburg, F. Zoppis (pr.)	76			Brescia, B. Galuppi	228			Naples, J. A. Hasse (pr., 3rd)	332
s.d.			Madrid, unknown[NP]	153						
1759										
carn.	Pavia, T. Traetta	75	Padua, B. Galuppi	130			Turin, G. B. Borghi (pr.)	228	Milan, A. Ferrandini (pr.)	348
	Siena, G. Brunetti (pr.)		Milan, I. Holzbauer (pr.)	153			Pisa, G. G. Brunetti (pr.)		Pesaro, T. Traetta	347
									Venice, various	348
									Rimini, P. Vinci	347
Asc.			Venice, G. Scolari	145						
May										
Jul.					Cartagena, unknown		Naples, B. Galuppi	239		
Aug.	Florence, P. A. Auletta?	77	Lucca, J. A. Hasse	120					Stockholm, F. A. B. Uttini	341
Sept.									Salzburg, J. E. Eberlin (pr.)	349
Oct.									Warsaw, J. A. Hasse	332
s.d.			St Petersburg, F. Araia	136						

SC | Index Ib. Chronological Index: by Date and Title

Year	Didone abbandonata	Alessandro nell'Indie	Artaserse	Adriano in Siria	Demofoonte
1760					
carn.	Munich, A. Bernasconi 58		Livorno, Zamparelli & others 215	Verona, various 297	
	Verona, various 77		Copenhagen, G. Sarti (pr.) 240	Pavia, various 297	
Jan.			Naples, J. A. Hasse (pr.,3rd) 199		
Feb.		Stuttgart, Jommelli (pr.,2nd) 137			
Asc.	Lucca, A. Ferradini (pr.) 77			Venice, A. M. Mazzoni (pr.) 297	
				Venice, B. Galuppi (pr.,3rd) 281	
Aug.		Prague, B. Galuppi 130			
aut.		Bologna, unknown 154	Warsaw, J. A. Hasse 199		
s.d.				Prague, G. Scarlatti 199	Catania, J. A. Hasse 332
					Prague, B. Galuppi 338
					s.l., G. Brunetti (pr.) 349
1761					
carn.	Prague, A. M. Mazzoni 73	Verona, D. dal Barba (pr.) 154	Venice, B. Galuppi 228	Florence, unknown 297	
Mar.	London, D. Perez + B. Galuppi 70		Turin, J. C. Bach (pr.) 240		
May					
Jun.					Reggio Emilia, N. Piccinni (pr.) 349
aut.		Copenhagen, G. Sarti (pr.,1st) 154			Senigallia, A. Boroni & others (pr.) 350
Oct.		London, Cocchi & others (pr.) 155	Prague, unknown 241	Palermo, B. Galuppi 281	
s.d.			Bratislava, J. A. Hasse 199		Treviso, A. Boroni 350

421

Index Ib. Chronological Index: by Date and Title

Year	Didone abbandonata		Alessandro nell'Indie		Artaserse		Adriano in Siria		Demofoonte	
1762										
carn.			Naples, J. C. Bach (pr.)	156	Genoa, Zannetti & other (pr.)	241			Vicenza, various	350
					Venice, G. F. di Majo (pr.)	241				
					Lonon, T. Arne (pr., En.)	241				
					Rome, N. Piccinni (pr.,1st)	241				
Apr.			Florence, B. Galuppi	130						
spr.			Reggio Emilia, T. Traetta (pr.)	158	Montepulciano, various	243				
summ.			Palermo, N. Piccinni	149						
Jul.	Copenhagen, G. Sarti (pr.,1st)	78			Naples, J. A. Hasse	199				
Aug.							Brunswick, Schwanenberger (pr.)	298	Florence, various	350
Sept.			Barcelona, G. Scolari	145			Brunswick, Schwanenberger	298		
Dec.									Naples, N. Piccinni	349
s.d.										
1763										
carn.	Ferrara, G. Scolari	73	Lodi, J. C. Bach	156	Foligno, N. Piccinni	241	Udine, B. Galuppi	282		
	Milan, T. Traetta (pr.,2nd)	75	Pisa, G. G. Brunetti (pr.)	158	Rome, N. Jommelli	231	Milan, G. Colla (pr.)	298		
					Munich, A. Bernasconi (pr.,2nd)	223	Ferrara, unknown	298		
					Barcelona, Piccinni & others	241				
Feb.	Stuttgart, N. Jommelli (pr.,3rd)	65			Vienna, G. Scarlatti (pr.,2nd)	158				
May			Venice, A. Sacchini (pr.,1st)						Rome, G. F. di Majo (pr.)	350
Asc.							Barcelona, G. Sciroli (pr.)	224		
Aug.									Barcelona, B. Galuppi	338
aut.									Prague, various (past.)	352
win.	Palermo, G. B. Lampugnani	53								
Nov.	Barcelona, G. Scolari	73								

422

SC | Index Ib. Chronological Index: by Date and Title

Year	Didone abbandonata	Alessandro nell'Indie	Artaserse	Adriano in Siria	Demofoonte
1764					
carn.	Venice, B. Galuppi (pr., 2nd) 55	Prague, D. Fischietti (pr.) 162			Venice, A. G. Pampani 346
	Naples, T. Traetta (pr., 3rd) 75	Verona, various 162			
Feb.					
Mar.		London, G. Cocchi & others 155			Stuttgart, N. Jommelli (pr., 3rd) 326
spr.		Bologna, G. Sciroli 153			
May					
Aug.				Lucca, Concialini & others (pr.) 299	
s.d.		Cádiz, D. Perez & others 138		Salzburg, A. Caldara 271	Cádiz, B. Galuppi 338
				s.l., M. Wimmer (pr.) 299	
1765					
carn.			Ferrara, J. A. Hasse 199	London, J. C. Bach (pr.) 299	
			Lodi, G. Sartori (pr.) 244		
Feb.				Naples, J. F. di Majo (pr.) 300	
Mar.					Ludwigsburg, N. Jommelli 326
summ.	Lisbon, D. Perez 70		Genoa, various (incl. Colla?) 244		London, M. Vento (pr.) 352
Aug.	Brunswick, Schwanenberger. (pr.) 80				
aut.					La Valletta, J. A. Hasse 332
s.d.			Kassel, I. Fiorillo (rev.) 235		Lucca, various 353
1766					
carn.	Livorno, F. Zannetti (pr.) 80	Turin, A. Sacchini 158	Cremona, G. B. Lampugnani 233	Venice, P. A. Guglielmi (pr.) 300	Ferrara, various 353
			Venice, G. Ponzo (pr.) 244		Munich, A. Bernasconi (rev.) 321
Feb.	St Petersburg, B. Galuppi 55		London, J. A. Hasse 199		
Mar.					
Jun.		Padua, G. Sarti 154			
Aug.		Lucca, various 162			London, M. Vento 352
aut.					
Nov.		Mannheim, G. F. di Majo (pr.) 162			Treviso, P. A. Guglielmi (pr.) 353

423

Year	Didone abbandonata	Alessandro nell'Indie	Artaserse	Adriano in Siria	Demofoonte
1767					
carn.	Pavia, unknown	Mannheim, G. F. di Majo 81	162		
Jul.			Palma de Mallorca, unknown 244		Palma, B. Galuppi 338
Aug.		Barcelona, G. Scolari	145		
Nov.		Naples, G. F. di Majo 81	162 Prague, A. Boroni (pr.) 245	Livorno, G. Scarlatti 291	
s.d.	Barcelona, unknown				
1768					
Jan.			163 Rome, A. Sacchini (pr.) 245	Eichstätt, H. Mango (pr.) 301	
carn.	Prague, A. Boroni (pr.)	Cremona, various 81	Mantua, various 246		
May		Mantua, L. Gatti (pr.)	163 Lisbon, G. Scolari 238		
Nov.	Cádiz, unknown	Naples, A. Sacchini (pr., 2nd) 82	159 Naples, N. Piccinni (pr., 2nd) 242	Mannheim, I. Holzbauer (pr.) 301	Palermo, B. Galuppi 338
win.					
s.d.	Kassel, unknown	Florence, J. G. Naumann (pr.) 82	164		
1769					
Jan.				Mannheim, I. Holzbauer 301	
carn.			Valencia, A. Sacchini 245	Rome, G. F. di Majo 300	Venice, J. Mysliveček (pr.,1st) 353
spr.		Genoa, F. Bertoni (pr.,1st)	164	Genoa, various 302	
Oct.				Alessandria, M. Vincenti (pr.) 302	
Nov.				Naples, C. I. Monza (pr.) 302	Valencia, unknown 355
win.		Prague, J. A. Koželuh (pr.)	165	Mannheim, I. Holzbauer 301	

SC | Index Ib. Chronological Index: by Date and Title

Year	Didone abbandonata		Alessandro nell'Indie		Artaserse		Adriano in Siria		Demofoonte	
1770										
carn.	Berlin, J. A. Hasse	59								
	Milan, I. Celoniati (pr.)	82			Florence, various	247				
	Venice, G. F. di Majo (pr.)	82			Verona, A. Boroni	245				
	Rome, N. Piccinni (pr.)	83								
	Naples, G. Insanguine (pr.)	85					Modena, A. Tozzi (pr.)	303		
spr.					Pisa, various	247				
summ.					Siena, various	247			Mantua, T. Traetta	347
Aug.	Lucca, various	85								
aut.					Lucca, various	247				
Nov.										
s.d.	Naples, B. Galuppi[NP]	55							Naples, N. Jommelli (pr., 4th)	326
									Cádiz, A. Bernasconi	321
									Rome, J. B. Vanhal	355
1771										
carn.			Venice, F. Bertoni (pr., 2nd)	164						
			Livorno, A. Sacchini & others	159						
Jan.					London, M. Vento (pr.)	247			Pavia, various	355
Apr.										
Asc.			Copenhagen, G. Sarti	154					Copenhagen, G. Sarti (pr., 2nd)	344
spr.	Copenhagen, G. Sarti	78					Venice, A. Sacchini (pr.)	303	Bologna, various	356
Jun.							Padua, P. Anfossi (pr.)	304		
aut.							Prague, A. Sacchini	303		

425

SC | Index Ib. Chronological Index: by Date and Title

Year	Didone abbandonata	Alessandro nell'Indie	Artaserse	Adriano in Siria	Demofoonte
1772					
carn.			Modena, G. Paisiello (pr.) 247		Prague, J. A. Koželuh (pr.) 356
			Venice, V. Manfredini (pr.) 248		
Feb.	Bologna, various 86	Rome, P. Anfossi (pr.) 165			
	Naples, G. Insanguine 85				
Apr.	Florence, M. Mortellari (pr.) 86		London, various (past.) 248		Porto, D. Perez 341
Jun.	Florence, unknown 86				
Sept.					
Oct.					
Nov.		Florence, P. Anfossi 165			Barcelona, unknown 356
s.d.	Naples, B. Galuppi 55				
1773					
carn.	Turin, G. Colla (pr.)	Bologna, various 167	Prague, G. Paisiello 247	Palermo, various 304	Rome, P. Anfossi (pr.) 356
		Perugia, A. Sacchini 86		Naples, J. Mysliveček (pr.) 305	Florence, P. Anfossi 356
aut.					
Nov.				Naples, G. Insanguine (pr.) 305	
Dec.			London, various (past.) 248		
s.d.					Livorno, Berezovskij (pr.) 358
1774					
carn.		Cremona, A. Sacchini 159		Verona, various 306	Macerata, P. Anfossi 356
		Modena, G. Paisiello (pr.) 167			Berlin, C. H. Graun 330
		Siena, G. Sciroli 153	Pavia, various 249		Modena, P. Anfossi 356
		Naples, N. Piccinni (pr., 2ⁿᵈ) 149			Genoa, P. Anfossi & others 356
spr.					
May			London, various (past.) 248		
Aug.	Rome, P. Anfossi (pr.,1ˢᵗ) 87		Naples, J. Mysliveček (pr.) 249		
Dec.		London, D. Corri (pr.) 168			
s.d.		Valencia, unknown 168	London, L. Caruso (pr.) 250		

SC | Index Ib. Chronological Index: by Date and Title

Year	Didone abbandonata		Alessandro nell'Indie		Artaserse		Adriano in Siria		Demofoonte	
1775										
Jan.			Milan, C. Monza (pr.)	87					Naples, J. Mysliveček (pr., 2nd)	353
carn.	Cremona, P. Anfossi	87					Modena, G. Monti (pr.)	306	Venice, G. Paisiello (pr.)	358
May										
Asc.	Venice, P. Anfossi	87	Venice, G. Rust (pr.)	87						
Jun.										
aut.	Lucca, P. Anfossi	87								
Nov.	London, various (past.)	89							Lisbon, N. Jommelli (3rd rev.)	326
1776										
carn.	Cremona, P. Anfossi	87			Venice, G. B. Borghi (pr.)	250	Genoa, unknown		Cremona, G. Paisiello	358
	Naples, J. A. Schuster (pr.)	89								
spr.									Perugia, G. Paisiello	359
Jun.									Forlì, J. A. Schuster (pr.)	360
Jul.			Lisbon, N. Jommelli (rev.)	137						
aut.							Florence, J. Mysliveček		Warsaw, J. A. Hasse	332
Oct.	Havana, N. Piccinni	83								
	Crescentino, F. Mombelli (pr.)	91			Forlì, F. Bertoni (pr.)	251			Alessandria, C. I. Monza (pr.)	361
s.d.	Warsaw, P. Anfossi	87							London, M. Vento	352
1777										
carn.	Florence, N. Piccinni				Milan, F. Bertoni	149	Livorno, various	251	Pavia, J. A. Schuster	360
	Stuttgart, N. Jommelli	65	Berlin, J. A. Hasse		Macerata, F. Bertoni	120	Perugia, J. Mysliveček	251		305
spr.					Rome, P. A. Guglielmi (pr.)			254		
Jun.					Genoa, F. Bertoni		Pavia, J. Mysliveček	251		305
aut.							Padua, P. Anfossi	254		304
Oct.					Lucca, F. Bertoni			251		
s.d.					Alessandria, G. A. Re (pr.)		Kassel, J. A. Hasse	254		279
					Regensburg, T. Schacht (pr.)					

427

SC | Index Ib. Chronological Index: by Date and Title

Year	Didone abbandonata	Alessandro nell'Indie	Artaserse	Adriano in Siria	Demofoonte
1778					
carn.		Lodi, J. C. Bach 156	Verona, G. Paisiello 247		Stuttgart, N. Jommelli 326
Jan.	Genoa, various 91				
spr.		Venice, L. Marescalchi (pr.) 169			
Asc.	Venice, P. Anfossi 87				
May		Siena, M. Mortellari (pr.) 170			
Jul.	Florence, various 91	Alessandria, M. de Vincenti (pr.) 170			
Oct.					
Nov.					London, Bertoni & others (past.) 361
s.d.			Valencia, unknown 255		
1779					
carn.		Verona, A. Calegari (pr.) 170	Lodi, G. B. Pescetti 236	Rome, G. Sarti (pr.) 307	
	Venice, J. A. Schuster 89		London, F. Bertoni 251		
spr.	Forlì, B. Ottani (pr.) 92				
Jul.	Mannheim, I. Holzbauer (pr.) 92				
Nov.		London, various (past.) 170			
1780					
carn.	Palermo, F. Piricchio (pr.) 93			Venice, F. Alessandri (pr.) 308	Pisa, unknown 362
	Berlin, J. A. Hasse[NP] 59				
Mar.			Florence, L. Caruso (rev.) 250		
Apr.		Genoa, F. Alessandri (pr.) 65			
spr.	Stuttgart, N. Jommelli 171				Florence, G. Rust (pr.) 363
Oct.				Treviso, P. Anfossi 304	
aut.					
Dec.				Palermo, unknown 308	
s.d.	Bratislava, G. Astarita (pr.) 93		s.l., A. Ullinger (pr.) 255		
	Kassel, unknown 93		s.l., P. F. Parenti (pr.) 255		
	Naples, N. Piccinni 83				
c. 1780					Rio de Janeiro, various 363

SC | Index Ib. Chronological Index: by Date and Title

Year	Didone abbandonata	Alessandro nell'Indie	Artaserse	Adriano in Siria	Demofoonte
1781					
Feb.		Rome, D. Cimarosa (pr.) 172			
spr.					Genoa, Bianchi + Anfossi (pr.) 363
summ.	Perugia, F. Zannetti 80				Pavia, unknown 363
aut.			Perugia, G. Rust (pr.) 255		
s.d.		Verona, M. de Vincenti 170	Regensburg, T. Schacht 254		Siena, L. Vinci 321
1782					
carn.	Pavia, P. Anfossi 87			Turin, G. Rust (pr.)	Palermo, G. Gazzaniga (pr.) 364
spr.				Livorno, L. Cherubini (pr.)	Rome, G. Sarti (pr., 3rd) 344
Jun.	Padua, G. Sarti (pr., 2nd) 78		Livorno, G. Rust 255		
Jul.					
aut.	Stuttgart, N. Jommelli 65		Treviso, F. Zannetti (pr.) 256		Lucca, various (past.) 364
s.d.			Lviv, unknown 256		
1783					
carn.			Florence, G. Rust 255		Modena, A. Pio (pr.) 364
			Berlin, C. H. Graun 218		
			Rome, G. Rust 255		
Jun.		Lucca, M. Mortellari 170			
aut.		Paris, Méreaux (pr., Fr.) 172			Padua, F. Alessandri (pr.) 364
Aug.					
Oct.	Paris, N. Piccinni (pr., 2nd, Fr.) 83		Naples, F. Alessandri (pr.) 256		
Nov.	Munich, A. Prati (pr.) 93				
Dec.	Paris, N. Piccinni (Fr.) 83				
1784					
carn.		Berlin, C. H. Graun 141			
Mar.		Mantua, L. Cherubini (pr.) 172			
May					
Jun.	Mannheim, I. Holzbauer (Ger.) 92				London, Bertoni & others (past.) 362
	Brunswick, F. Piticchio 93				
win.	Esterháza, G. Sarti 78				
s.d.	St Petersburg, Andreozzi (pr.) 93				

429

SC | Index Ib. Chronological Index: by Date and Title

Year	Didone abbandonata		Alessandro nell'Indie		Artaserse		Adriano in Siria	Demofoonte	
1785									
carn.			Genoa, V. Chiavacci (pr.)	173	Turin, D. Cimarosa (pr.)	257			
			Venice, F. Bianchi (pr.)	173					
Feb.	Pisa, G. Andreozzi	93			Brescia, F. Bertoni	251			
Apr.					London, various (past.)	258			
spr.			Trieste, F. Bianchi	173					
aut.					Treviso, F. Bertoni	251			
					Verona, F. Bertoni	251			
s.d.	Paris, N. Piccinni (Fr.)	83							
	Venice, P. A. Guglielmi (pr.)	94							
1786									
carn.			Cremona, L. Cherubini	172	Cremona, D. Cimarosa	257			
Feb.	London, various (past.)	94	Florence, various (past.)	175					
May			Siena, Andreozzi & others? (pr.)	175					
summ.									
Aug.	Lucca, G. Sarti	78							
	Bergamo, various	95							
Sept.									
Oct.	Florence, various	95						Crema, A. Tarchi (pr.)	365
1787									
carn.			Rome, L. Caruso (pr., 1st)	176	Pavia, F. Bertoni	251		Venice, A. Prati (pr.)	366
			Verona, F. Bianchi	173				Perugia, G. Sarti	344
			Modena, G. Paisiello?	167					
Mar.	Genoa, G. Sarti & others	95						Mantua, L. Gatti (pr.)	366
May	London, various (past.)	94						Modena, unknown	367
spr.									
summ.	Vicenza, G. Gazzaniga (pr.)	96			Padua, F. Bianchi (pr.)	258			
Jun.			Bologna, F. Bianchi	173				Reggio Emilia, A. Tarchi	365
Oct.									
aut.								Livorno, various	367
win.			Palermo, G. Sarti (pr., 2nd)	154	Siena, F. Bianchi	258			
s.d.	Lyon, N. Piccinni (Fr.)	83	Esterháza, F. Bianchi	173					

430

SC | Index Ib. Chronological Index: by Date and Title

Year	Didone abbandonata	Alessandro nell'Indie	Artaserse	Adriano in Siria	Demofoonte
1788					
carn.		Milan, A. Tarchi (pr.,1st)	Rome, P. Anfossi (pr.) 178		Turin, G. Pugnani (pr.) 367
spr.			Cremona, F. Bertoni 259		
May	Naples, P. Anfossi (pr.,2nd) 87		Mantua, A. Tarchi (pr.) 251		
aut.		Livorno, L. Cherubini 172			
Oct.			Venice, various (past.) 259		Florence, various 368
Nov.					
Dec.			Genoa, F. Bertoni (rev.) 260		Paris, L. Cherubini (pr., Fr.) 368
s.d.			251	Stuttgart, Gauss (pr., Ger.) 309	
1789					
carn.			Bologna, P. A. Guglielmi 254		
March			Trieste, N. A. Zingarelli (pr.,1st)		
Jun.		London, A. Tarchi 178			
Aug.		Bergamo, F. Bianchi 173			
Sept.			Livorno, G. Andreozzi (pr.) 260		Paris, J. C. Vogel (pr., Fr.) 368
aut.					
Nov.		Naples, P. A. Guglielmi (pr.) 180			
s.d.	Reggio Emilia, G. Andreozzi 93		Padua, F. Bianchi 262		Trieste, N. A. Zingarelli (pr.) 368
	Venice, G. Gazzaniga 96		258		
1790					
carn.				Milan, S. Nasolini (pr.) 309	
Apr.		London, A. Tarchi 178			London, V. Federici (pr.) 369
spr.			Ancona, F. Bertoni 251		
Jun.	Venice, F. Bertoni & others 96		Modena, A. Tarchi 259		
aut.			Reggio Emilia, A. Tarchi 259		
s.d.					Madrid, various 369
c. 1790		s.l., N. A. Zingarelli (lost) 181		s.l., N. A. Zingarelli (pr.) 309	

Year	Didone abbandonata		Alessandro nell'Indie		Artaserse		Adriano in Siria	Demofoonte	
1791									
carn.			Venice, L. Caruso (pr.,2nd)	176				Rome, various	369
								Pavia, A. Tarchi	365
								Venice, G. Pugnani	367
Aug.	Madrid, G. Andreozzi	93							
	Padua, various	97							
	Bergamo, F. Bertoni & others	96							
aut.			Siena, A. Tarchi	178				Livorno, A. Tarchi	365
s.d.			Livorno, A. Tarchi (rev.)	178					
1792									
carn.			Naples, N. Piccinni	149				Genoa, various	370
May	London, various (past)	97							
summ.					Imola, F. Bertoni	251			
Sept.					Florence, various	262			
Nov.			Venice, F. Bianchi	173					
s.d.	Madrid, G. Sarti + G. Paisiello	78	Madrid, L. Caruso	176					
			Warsaw, F. Bianchi	174					
1793									
carn.	Mantua, G. Sarti	78						Modena, A. Tarchi	365
s.d.	Padua, F. Bertoni & others	96							
1794									
carn.	Genoa, G. Gazzaniga	96			Milan, N. A. Zingarelli (pr.,2nd)	260			
					Genoa, unknown	262			
Feb.	Palermo, G. Paisiello (pr.)	98						Milan, M. A. Portugal (pr.,1st)	370
summ.					Livorno, N. Isouard (pr.)	262			
Aug.	Naples, G. Paisiello	98							
Nov.									

SC | Index Ib. Chronological Index: by Date and Title

Year	Didone abbandonata	Alessandro nell'Indie	Artaserse	Adriano in Siria	Demofoonte
1795					
Jul.	Florence, G. Paisiello 98				
Aug.		Udine, F. Bianchi 174			
Nov.			Venice, G. Nicolini (pr.) 263		Venice, N. A. Zingarelli 368
s.d.	Vienna, L. Koželuh (pr.) 100		s.l., F. Ceracchini (pr.) 263		
1796					
carn.	Verona, G. Paisiello 98				
Oct.	St Petersburg, G. Paisiello 98				
s.d.		Corfù, L. Caruso 176			
1797					
1798					
carn.		Turin, A. Tarchi (pr.,2nd) 178			
Asc.				Venice, J. S. Mayr (pr.) 309	
summ.	Porto, S. Marino & others (pr.) 100				
1799					
May	Berlin, N. Piccinni 83				
Jun.	London, G. Paisiello 98			Paris, E.-N. Méhul (pr.,Fr.)[NP] 310	
Sept.		St Petersburg, G. Paisiello 167			
Oct.	Lisbon, S. Marino & others 100				
1800					
Jun.		Lisbon, Caruso + Federici 176			
aut.		Livorno, P. Gnecco (pr.) 181			
Dec.		Lisbon, Caruso + Federici 176			
c. 1800		Livorno/Florence, various 181			
1801					
Jan.		Lisbon, Caruso + Federici 176	Lisbon, D. Cimarosa 257	s.l., C. Bernardini (pr.) 310	
Feb.					
1802					
carn.		Florence, A. Tarchi 178			

433

SC | Index Ib. Chronological Index: by Date and Title

Year	Didone abbandonata	Alessandro nell'Indie	Artaserse	Adriano in Siria	Demofoonte
1803 Dec.	Lisbon, S. Marino & others 100				
1804 carn.		St Peters., Neukomm (pr., Ger.) 182	Pavia, N. A. Zingarelli 260		
Sept.					
1805 win.		Lisbon, D. Perez 138			
1806 aut.			Lisbon, M. A. Portugal (pr.) 263		
1807 s.d.				Vienna, J. Weigl (pr., Ger.) 3130	
1808 Jan.	London, Paisiello + Buonaiuti 98				
Apr.	Berlin, N. Piccinni 83				
Aug.					Lisbon, Portugal (pr., 2nd) 370
1809 spr.				Forlì, unknown 310	
Jun.				Padua, M. A. Portugal (pr.) 310	
1810 Lent			Florence, M. A. Portugal 263		
Jun.	Rome, V. Fioravanti (pr.) 100				
s.d.	Paris, F. Paër (pr., 1st) 101				
1811 Jan.	Paris, F. Paër 101				
Jun.		Mannheim, Ritter (pr., Ger.) 182			
Dec.				Naples, V. Migliorucci (pr.) 311	
s.d.					Munich, Lindpaintner (Ger.) 371
1812 Jan.	Paris, F. Paër 101				
Dec.			Rio de Janeiro, M. A. Portugal 263		
s.d.	Dresden, F. Paër 101				
1813 summ.				Como, M. A. Portugal 310	
Sept.			London, H. Bishop (pr., En.) 264		

SC | Index Ib. Chronological Index: by Date and Title

Year	Didone abbandonata	Alessandro nell'Indie	Artaserse	Adriano in Siria	Demofoonte
1814 Jul. s.d.	London, F. Paër (pr., 2nd) 101			Verona, M. A. Portugal 310	
1815 carn.				Milan, M. A. Portugal 310	
1816					
1817 carn. spr.	Parma, F. Paër 101 Florence, F. Paër 101		Parma, M. A. Portugal 263		
1818					
1819 Apr.					Lisbon, M. A. Portugal 370
1820					
1821 Jun. s.d.				Palermo, M. A. Portugal 311	London, C. E. Horn (pr., En.) 371
1822					
1823 carn. summ. aut. Oct.	Turin, S. Mercadante (pr.,1st) 103 Milan, S. Mercadante 103 Livorno, S. Mercadante 103 Lucca, S. Mercadante 103 Berlin, B. Klein (pr., Ger.) 108				
1824 carn. Jan. summ. Sept. s.d.	Genoa, S. Mercadante 103 Dresden, Reissiger (pr., Ger.) 108 Vicenza, S. Mercadante 103 Palermo, S. Mercadante 103	Naples, G. Pacini (pr.) 182			
1825 carn. spr. Jul. Nov.	Mantua, S. Mercadante 103 Florence, S. Mercadante 103 Naples, S. Mercadante (pr.,2nd) 103 Cremona, S. Mercadante 103				

SC | Index Ib. Chronological Index: by Date and Title

Year	Didone abbandonata		Alessandro nell'Indie		Artaserse		Adriano in Siria		Demofoonte	
1826										
carn.	Ravenna, S. Mercadante	103								
Aug.	Udine, S. Mercadante	103					s.l., F. Mirecki (pr., Fr.)	311		
s.d.	Barcelona, S. Mercadante	103								
	Gorizia, S. Mercadante	103								
	Venice, S. Mercadante	103								
1827										
carn.	Milan, S. Mercadante	103	Milan, G. Pacini	182						
Apr.	Lisbon, S. Mercadante	104								
spr.	Venice, S. Mercadante	104								
Jun.			Lisbon, G. Pacini	182						
Jul.	London, S. Mercadante	104								
Aug.			Palermo, G. Pacini	182						
1828										
carn.	Verona, S. Mercadante	104	Venice, G. Pacini	182						
Feb.							Lisbon, S. Mercadante (pr.)	311		
Sept.							Lisbon, S. Mercadante	311		
1829										
carn.	Turin, S. Mercadante	104								
1830										
spr.	Florence, S. Mercadante	104								
1831										
s.d.			Barcelona, G. Pacini	182						
1832										
Aug.	Brescia, S. Mercadante	104								
1836										
s.d.									Florence, G. M. Sborgi (pr.)	371
1840										
s.d.					London, C. Lucas (pr., En.)	264				
1850										
s.d.					Berlin, H. L. E. Dorn (pr.)	264				
s.d.	Rome, A. Boroni	81			Venice, L. Vinci	190				

Index II.
Index of Names: Composers

Abati, Carlo, *Demofoonte* (arias, 372)
Abos, Girolamo, *Adriano* (1746, 286); *Alessandro* (1747, 143); *Artaserse* (1746, 222)
Adolfati, Andrea, *Adriano* (1751, 290); *Alessandro, Artaserse, Demofoonte* (arias, 184, 213, 372); *Didone* (1747, 67)
Agnesi, Maria Teresa, *Alessandro* (arias, 184)
Agricola, Johann Friedrich, *Alessandro* (1754, 147)
Airoldi, Pietro, *Adriano* (1821, 311)
Alberti, Giuseppe Matteo, *Didone* (arias, 110)
Albinoni, Tomaso Giovanni, *Didone* (1725, 43)
Alessandri, Felice, *Adriano* (1780, 308); *Alessandro* (1780, 171); *Artaserse* (1783, 256); *Demofoonte* (1783, 364)
Andreozzi, Gaetano, *Alessandro* (1786, 175); *Artaserse* (1789, 262); *Didone* (1784, 93)
Anfossi, Pasquale, *Adriano* (1771, 304); *Alessandro* (1772, 165); *Artaserse* (1788, 259); *Demofoonte* (1773, 356); *Didone* (1774, 1788, 87)
Anfossi, Pasquale and others, *Didone* (1786, 94)
Annibali, Domenico, *Didone* (arias, 108)
Aprile, Giuseppe, *Alessandro* (arias, 184)
Araia, Francesco, *Alessandro* (1743, 136); *Artaserse* (1738, 213)
Arena, Giuseppe, *Artaserse* (1741, 217)
Armeni, Gioacchino, *Artaserse* (arias, 264)
Arne, Thomas Augustine, *Artaserse* (1762, En., 241)
Asioli, Bonifacio, *Adriano* (arias, 312)
Astarita, Gennaro, *Adriano, Artaserse* (arias, 312, 264); *Didone* (1780, 93)
Auletta, Pietro Antonio, *Didone* (1759, 77)
Aurisicchio, Antonio, *Alessandro* (arias, 184); *Didone* (1745, 64)
Avondano, Pedro António, *Didone* (arias, 72)
Azzopardi, Francesco, *Artaserse* (arias, 264)

Babbi, Gregorio, *Alessandro* (arias, 184)
Bach, Johann Christian, *Adriano* (1765, 299); *Alessandro* (1762, 156); *Artaserse* (1761, 240); *Demofoonte, Didone* (arias, 372, 108)

Bachschmid, Johann Anton Adam, *Adriano, Demofoonte* (arias, 312, 372)
Bajamonti, Julije, *Artaserse* (arias, 264)
Balduino, Domenico, *Adriano* (arias, 312)
Bambini, Eustachio, *Artaserse* (1733, 208)
Barthélemon, Hyppolyte, *Adriano, Artaserse* (arias, 312, 265)
Beecke, Ignaz von, *Adriano* (arias, 312)
Beltramo, Agostino, *Artaserse* (arias, 265)
Benda, Georg, *Alessandro, Artaserse* (arias, 184, 265)
Berezovskij, Maksim Sozontovič, *Demofoonte* (1773, 358)
Bernardini, Carlo, *Adriano* (c. 1800, 310)
Bernasconi, Andrea, *Adriano* (1736, 1755); *Alessandro* (arias, 185); *Artaserse* (1746, 1763, 223); *Demofoonte* (1741, 1766, 321); *Didone* (1741, 1756, 57)
Bernetti, *Artaserse* (arias, 265)
Bertoni, Ferdinando, *Alessandro* (1769, 1771, 164); *Artaserse* (1776, rev. 1788, 251); *Didone* (1748, 68)
Bertoni, Ferdinando; Mysliveček, Josef; Monza, Carlo; Sarti, Giuseppe, *Demofoonte* (1788, 361)
Bertoni, Ferdinando; Rampini, Vincenzo; Naumann, Johann Gottlieb; Gazzaniga, Giuseppe, *Didone* (1790, 96)
Bianchi, Francesco, *Alessandro* (1785, 173); *Artaserse* (1787, 258); *Demofoonte* (1781, 363)
Bindi, *Didone* (arias, 108)
Bioni, Antonio, *Adriano* (arias, 312); *Alessandro* (1734, 128); *Artaserse* (1733, 208)
Bishop, Henry Rowley, *Artaserse* (1813, En., 264)
Boccherini, Luigi, *Adriano, Artaserse, Demofoonte, Didone* (arias, 312, 265, 372, 108)
Böhme, Johann Gottfried, *Didone* (arias, 108)
Bollano, G., *Artaserse* (1750, 235)
Bonno, Giuseppe, *Adriano, Demofoonte* (arias, 312, 372); *Didone* (1752, 73)
Bononcini, Giovanni, *Adriano* (arias, 312)
Borghi, Giovanni Battista, *Adriano* (1759, 296); *Alessandro* (arias, 185); *Artaserse* (1776, 250); *Didone* (arias, 108)

Index II. Index of Names: Composers

Boroni, Antonio, *Artaserse* (1767, 245); *Demofoonte* (1761, 350); *Didone* (1768, 81)
Brandl, Johann Evangelist, *Demofoonte* (arias, 372)
Bresciani, Giovanni Battista, *Didone* (arias, 108)
Brivio, Giuseppe Ferdinando, *Alessandro* (1742, 134); *Artaserse* (1738, 1742, 215); *Demofoonte* (1738, 319); *Didone* (1739, 52)
Brunetti, Giovan Gualberto, *Adriano* (1759, 297); *Alessandro* (1763, 158); *Artaserse*, *Demofoonte* (arias, 265, 372)
Brunetti, Giuseppe, *Demofoonte* (1760, 349); *Didone* (1759, 77)
Brusa, Giovanni Francesco, *Adriano* (1757, 295)
Bucelli, Orazio, *Didone* (arias, 108)
Buonanni, *Demofoonte* (arias, 372)
Busecchi, Ignazio, *Demofoonte* (arias, 372)

Caballone, Michele, *Adriano* (1740, 285); *Alessandro* (1740, 134)
Caffi, Francesco, *Demofoonte* (arias, 372)
Caldara, Antonio, *Adriano* (1732, 271); *Demofoonte* (1733, 315)
Calderara, Giacinto, *Alessandro* (1752, 146)
Calegari, Antonio, *Alessandro* (1779, 170)
Callenberg, Georg Alexander Heinrich Hermann, *Adriano*, *Alessandro*, *Artaserse* (arias, 312, 185, 265)
Campanile, Giuseppe, *Artaserse* (arias, 265)
Campobasso, Alessandro Vincenzo, *Artaserse* (arias, 265)
Capuzzi, Antonio, *Alessandro*, *Artaserse* (arias, 185, 265)
Carcani, Giuseppe, *Artaserse* (1748, 224)
Caruso, Luigi, *Alessandro* (1787, 1791, 176); *Artaserse* (1774, rev. 1780, 250)
Ceccoli, Tommaso Maria, *Artaserse* (arias, 265)
Celestino, Eligio, *Adriano*, *Alessandro*, *Didone* (arias, 312, 185, 108)
Celoniati, Ignazio, *Didone* (1770, 82)
Ceracchini, Francesco, *Artaserse* (1795, 263)
Cerro, Antonio, *Artaserse* (arias, 265)
Cherubini, Luigi, *Adriano* (1782, 308); *Alessandro* (1784, 172); *Artaserse*, *Demofoonte* (arias, 260, 372); *Demofoonte* (1788, Fr., 368)
Chiarini, Pietro, *Alessandro* (1745, 142); *Artaserse* (1741, 217); *Didone* (1748, 68)
Chiavacci, Vincenzo, *Alessandro* (1785, 173)
Chiocchetti, Pietro Vincenzo, *Demofoonte* (1735, 318)
Ciampi, Francesco, *Demofoonte* (1735, 318)
Ciampi, Vincenzo Legrenzio, *Adriano* (1748, rev. 1750, 288); *Artaserse* (1747, 224); *Didone* (1754, 74)
Cimarosa, Domenico, *Alessandro* (1781, 172); *Artaserse* (1785 + arias, 257, 265); *Didone* (arias, 108)

Cocchi, Gioacchino, *Adriano* (1753, 293); *Alessandro* (1761, past., 155); *Artaserse* (1755, 237); *Demofoonte* (1754, 343)
Colla, Giuseppe, *Adriano* (1763, 298); *Artaserse* (1765?, 244); *Demofoonte* (arias, 372); *Didone* (1773, 86)
Concialini, Carlo Giovanni and others, *Adriano* (1764, 299)
Conforto, Nicola, *Adriano* (1754, rev. 1757, 294); *Alessandro* (1756, 148); *Artaserse*, *Demofoonte* (arias, 265, 372)
Contiero, Giovanni Battista, *Alessandro* (arias, 185)
Coppola, Luigi, *Demofoonte* (arias, 372)
Cornet, Alessandro, *Artaserse* (arias, 265)
Corri, Domenico, *Alessandro* (1774, 168)
Corselli, Francesco, *Alessandro* (1738, 133)
Curcio, Giuseppe Maria, *Artaserse* (arias, 265)

D'Astorga, Emmanuele, *Artaserse* (arias, 265)
Dal Barba, Daniel, *Alessandro* (1761, 154); *Artaserse* (1751, 235)
Dalfiume, Pellegrino, *Demofoonte* (arias, 372)
Danzi, Franz Ignaz, *Adriano*, *Demofoonte* (arias, 312, 372)
De Ficis, Giulio, *Artaserse* (arias, 265)
De Luca, Giambattista, *Adriano* (arias, 312)
De Vincenti, Melchiorre, *Adriano* (1769, 302); *Alessandro* (1778, 170)
Di Capua, Runaldo, *Adriano* (1758, 296); *Alessandro* (1742, 135); *Didone* (1741, 58)
Di Majo, Gianfrancesco, *Adriano* (1765, 300); *Alessandro* (1766, 162); *Artaserse* (1762, 241); *Demofoonte* (1763, 350); *Didone* (1770, 82)
Dittersdorf, Carl Ditters von, *Demofoonte*, *Didone* (arias, 372, 110)
Dorn, Heinrich Ludwig Egmont, *Artaserse* (1850, 264)
Duni, Antonio, *Alessandro* (arias, 185)
Duni, Egidio Romualdo, *Adriano* (1736, 278); *Alessandro* (1736, 1743?, 129, 136); *Artaserse* (1744, 221); *Demofoonte* (1737, 318); *Didone* (1739, 52)

Ebell, Heinrich Carl, *Artaserse* (arias, 265)
Eberlin, Johann Ernst, *Demofoonte* (1759, 349)
Errichelli, Pasquale, *Demofoonte* (arias, 372)
Ettore, Guglielmo, *Artaserse* (arias, 265)

Fabbri, Annibale Pio, *Alessandro* (1740, 134)
Fago, Pasquale, *Adriano* (arias, 312)
Federici, Vincenzo, *Demofoonte* (1790, 369)
Federici, Vincenzo and others, *Demofoonte* (1791, 369)
Feldmayr, Georg, *Adriano*, *Artaserse* (arias, 312, 265)

SC | Index II. Index of Names: Composers

Fenaroli, Fedele, *Artaserse* (arias, 265)
Ferradini, Antonio, *Demofoonte* (1759, 348); *Didone* (1760, 77)
Ferrandini, Giovanni Battista, *Adriano* (1737, 278); *Alessandro* (arias, 185); *Demofoonte* (1737, 318)
Ferrandini, Giovanni Battista +Porta, Giovanni, *Artaserse* (1739, 216)
Fighera, Salvatore, *Adriano*, *Demofoonte* (arias, 312, 372)
Fillembaum, *Demofoonte* (arias, 372)
Fini, Michele, *Alessandro*, *Didone* (arias, 185, 108)
Fioravanti, Valentino, *Alessandro* (arias, 185); *Didone* (1780, 100)
Fiorillo, Ignazio, *Adriano* (1750, 290); *Alessandro* (1752, 146); *Artaserse* (1751, rev. 1765, 235); *Demofoonte* (1750, 340); *Didone* (1751, 70)
Fioroni, Giovanni Andrea, *Didone* (1755, 74)
Fischietti, Domenico, *Alessandro* (1764, 162)
Fortunati, Gian Francesco, *Artaserse* (arias, 265)
Francisconi, Giovanni, *Alessandro* (arias, 185)
Francone, Michele, *Artaserse* (arias, 265)
Friedrich II the Great, *Alessandro* (arias, 185)

Galuppi, Baldassare, *Adriano* (1740, 1758, 281); *Alessandro* (1738, 1755, 129); *Artaserse* (1749, 1751, 227; arias, 197); *Demofoonte* (1750, 1758, 337); *Didone* (1741, rev. 1752, 1764, 54)
Gasparini, Quirino, *Artaserse* (1757, 238)
Gassmann, Florian Leopold, *Adriano* (arias, 312); *Artaserse* (arias, 258)
Gatti, Luigi, *Alessandro* (1768, 163); *Demofoonte* (1787, 366)
Gauss, Jakob Friedrich, *Adriano* (Ger., 1788, 309)
Gazzaniga, Giuseppe, *Alessandro* (arias, 185); *Demofoonte* (1782, 364); *Didone* (1787, 96)
Gherardeschi, Filippo Maria, *Artaserse* (arias, 265)
Gherardi, Gerardo, *Artaserse* (arias, 265)
Giacomelli, Geminiano, *Adriano* (1733, 272); *Artaserse* (1734, 210)
Giai, Giovanni Battista, *Adriano* (1740, 284)
Giaino, Pietro, *Adriano* (1741, 285)
Giardini, Felice, *Alessandro*, *Artaserse* (arias, 155, 266)
Giordani, Giuseppe, *Adriano* (arias, 312)
Giordani, Tommaso, Vento, Mattia, and Hasse, Johann Adolph, *Artaserse* (1772, 248)
Gluck, Christoph Willibald, *Alessandro* (1744, 142); *Artaserse* (1742, 218); *Demofoonte* (1743, 323)
Gnecco, Pietro, *Alessandro* (1800, 181)
Graun, Carl Heinrich, *Adriano* (1746, 286); *Alessandro* (1744, 141); *Artaserse* (1743, 218); *Demofoonte* (1746, 330)

Gresnick, Antoine Frédéric, *Artaserse* (arias, 266)
Guglielmi, Pietro Alessandro, *Adriano* (1766, 300); *Alessandro* (1789, 180); *Artaserse* (1777, 254); *Demofoonte* (1766, 353); *Didone* (1785, 94)

Hamal, Henri, *Demofoonte* (arias, 372)
Händel, Georg Friedrich, *Alessandro* (1731, 1731, 1736, 116)
Händel, Georg Friedrich and others, *Artaserse* (1734, 209)
Hasse, Johann Adolph, *Adriano* (1737, 1752, 279); *Alessandro* (1731, 1736, 1738, 119); *Artaserse* (1730, 1740, 1760, 197); *Demofoonte* (1748, 1749, 1758, 332); *Didone* (1742, 59)
Hasse, Johann Adolph and others, *Artaserse* (1734, 210)
Hasse, Johann Adolph + Vinci, Leonardo, *Artaserse* (1738, 198)
Häusler, Ernst, *Alessandro* (arias, 185)
Haydn, Joseph, *Alessandro* (arias, 175)
Haydn, Michael, *Adriano* (arias, 312)
Hertel, Johann Wilhelm, *Adriano*, *Alessandro*, *Demofoonte*, *Didone* (arias, 312, 185, 372, 108)
Holzbauer, Ignaz, *Adriano* (1768, 301); *Alessandro* (1759, 153); *Didone* (1779, 92)
Höpken, Arvid Niclas von, *Artaserse* (arias, 266)
Horn, Charles Edward, *Demofoonte* (En., 1821, 371)
Hurka, Friedrich Franz, *Alessandro* (arias, 185)

Imbimbo, Emanuele, *Alessandro* (arias, 185)
Insanguine, Giacomo, *Adriano* (1773, 305); *Artaserse* (arias, 266); *Didone* (1770, 85)
Isola, Gaetano, *Adriano* (arias, 312)
Isouard, Nicolas, *Artaserse* (1794, 262)

Jommelli, Niccolò, *Adriano* (1752, 292); *Alessandro* (1744, 1760, rev. 1776, 137); *Artaserse* (1749, rev. 1751, 1756, 231); *Demofoonte* (1743, 1753, 1764, 1770, 325); *Didone* (1747, 1749, 1763, 64)

Klein, Bernhard, *Artaserse* (arias, 266); *Didone* (1823, 108)
Koželuh, Jan Antonin, *Adriano* (arias, 312); *Alessandro* (1769, 165); *Demofoonte* (1772, 356)
Koželuh, Leopold, *Didone* (1795, 100)
Kraus, Benedikt, *Didone* (arias, 109)
Kraus, Joseph Martin, *Adriano*, *Artaserse*, *Demofoonte* (arias, 313, 266, 372)
Kunzen, Adolph Carl, *Adriano* (arias, 313)

SC | Index II. Index of Names: Composers

La Barbiera, Baldassare, *Adriano, Artaserse* (arias, 313, 266)
Lampugnani, Giovanni Battista, *Adriano* (1740, 284); *Alessandro* (1746, 142); *Artaserse* (1750, 233); *Demofoonte* (1738, 319); *Didone* (1739, 1753, 52)
Lanno, *Alessandro* (arias, 185)
Lapis, Santo, *Demofoonte* (arias, 372)
Latilla, Gaetano, *Adriano* (1747, 288); *Alessandro* (1753, 146); *Demofoonte* (1738, 319)
Lemner, Thomas, *Alessandro, Didone* (arias, 185, 109)
Lenzi, Carlo, *Demofoonte* (arias, 372)
Leo, Leonardo, *Adriano* (arias, 313); *Artaserse* (arias, 197); *Demofoonte* (1741, 322)
Leonardi, Silvestro, *Demofoonte* (arias, 372)
Levis, Giovanni Battista, *Artaserse* (arias, 266)
Lindpaintner, Peter Joseph von, *Demofoonte* (Ger., 1811, 371)
Logroscino, Nicola Bonifacio, *Adriano* (1742, 285); *Alessandro* (arias, 185)
López Jiménez, Melchor, *Adriano* (arias, 313)
Lucas, Charles, *Artaserse* (1840, En., 264)
Lucchini, Matteo, *Alessandro* (1734, 128)
Luciani, Domenico, *Alessandro* (arias, 185)
Lustrini, Bartolomeo, *Alessandro* (arias, 185)

Maggiore, Francesco, *Artaserse* (1747, 223); *Demofoonte* (arias, 325)
Mancini, Francesco, *Alessandro* (1732, 127)
Mancini, Francesco; Sarro, Domenico Natale; Leo, Leonardo, *Demofoonte* (1735, 316)
Manfredini, Vincenzo, *Artaserse* (1772, 248)
Mango, Hieronymus, *Adriano* (1768, 301)
Mangold, Wilhelm, *Alessandro* (arias, 185)
Manna, Gennaro, *Artaserse* (arias, 197); *Demofoonte* (1754, 342); *Didone* (1751, 69)
Maraucci, Giacomo, *Adriano, Demofoonte* (arias, 313, 372)
Maraucci, Stefano, *Alessandro* (arias, 185)
Marescalchi, Luigi, *Alessandro* (1778, 169)
Marino, Settimino and others, *Didone* (1798, 100)
Martínez, Marianna von, , *Artaserse* (arias, 185, 266)
Martini, Giovanni Battista, *Alessandro* (arias, 185)
Marziani, Mauro Maria, *Adriano* (arias, 313)
Mayr, Johann Simon, *Adriano* (1798, 309); *Alessandro, Didone* (arias, 185, 109)
Maziotti, Michele, *Adriano* (arias, 313)
Mazzoni, Antonio Maria, *Adriano* (1760, 297); *Alessandro, Artaserse* (arias, 185, 266); *Demofoonte* (1754, 342); *Didone* (1753, 73)
Méhul, Étienne-Nicolas, *Adriano* (1799, Fr., 310)
Mei, Orazio or Peretti, NIccolò, *Artaserse* (1755, 238)

Mele, Giovanni Battista and others, *Artaserse* (1749, 227)
Mercadante, Saverio, *Adriano* (1828, 311); *Demofoonte* (arias, 372); *Didone* (1823, 1825, 103)
Merchi, Giacomo, *Alessandro* (arias, 185)
Méreaux, Nicolas-Jean Le Froid de, *Alessandro* (1783, Fr., 172)
Micheli, Benedetto, *Alessandro* (arias, 185)
Migliorucci, Vincenzo, *Adriano* (1811, 311)
Milani, Matteo, *Adriano* (arias, 313)
Millico, Giuseppe, *Artaserse* (arias, 266)
Mirecki, Franciscek, *Adriano* (1826, Fr., 311)
Mombelli, Francesco Domenico, *Didone* (1776, 91)
Monti, Gaetano, *Adriano* (1775, 306)
Monza, Carlo Ignazio, *Adriano* (1769, 302); *Alessandro* (1775, 169); *Demofoonte* (1776, 361)
Moroni, Filippo, *Artaserse, Didone* (arias, 266, 109)
Mortellari, Michele, *Alessandro* (1778, 170); *Demofoonte* (arias, 373); *Didone* (1772, 86)
Mortellari, Felice; Rauzzini, Venanzio; Sacchini, Antonio; Giardini, Felice, *Didone* (1775, 89)
Mosel, Ignaz Franz von, *Alessandro* (arias, 185)
Mozart, Wolfgang Amadeus, *Artaserse, Demofoonte, Didone* (arias, 266, 373, 109)
Mysliveček, Josef, *Adriano* (1773, 305); *Alessandro* (arias, 185); *Artaserse* (1774, 249); *Demofoonte* (1769, 1775, 353)

Naselli, Diego, *Adriano, Didone* (arias, 313, 109)
Nasolini, Sebastiano, *Adriano* (1790, 309)
Naumann, Johann Gottlieb, *Adriano* (arias, 313); *Alessandro* (1768, 164); *Artaserse* (arias, 266); *Demofoonte* (arias, 373)
Negri, Benedetto, *Didone* (arias, 109)
Neukomm, Sigismund, *Alessandro* (Ger., 1804, 182)
Nicolini, Giuseppe, *Artaserse* (1795, 263)
Nicolini, Giuseppe and others, *Demofoonte* (1791, 369)
Niola, Gennaro, *Demofoonte* (arias, 373)
Notte, Girolamo, *Artaserse* (arias, 266)

Orgitano, Vincenzo, *Artaserse* (arias, 266)
Orlandini, Giuseppe Maria, *Didone* (1753, 55)
Ottani, Bernardo, *Adriano* (arias, 313); *Didone* (1779, 92)

Pacini, Giovanni, *Alessandro* (1824, 182)
Paër, Ferdinando, *Didone* (1780, 1814, 101)
Paganelli, Giuseppe Antonio, *Artaserse* (1737, 1742 and others, 212); *Didone* (1738, 52)
Paisiello, Giovanni, *Alessandro* (1774, 167); *Artaserse* (1772, 247); *Demofoonte* (1775, 358); *Didone* (1794, 98)

Index II. Index of Names: Composers

Palafati, Domenico, *Artaserse* (arias, 197)
Palma, Silvestro, *Alessandro* (arias, 186)
Pampani, Antonio Gaetano, *Adriano* (1751, 290); *Alessandro* (1737, 129); *Artaserse* (1750, 1756, 234); *Demofoonte* (1757, 346)
Panerai, Vincenzo, *Demofoonte* (arias, 373)
Paradies, Pietro Domenico, *Adriano, Alessandro, Demofoonte* (arias, 313, 186, 373)
Parenti, Paolo Francesco, *Artaserse* (c. 1780, 255)
Parolini, Pietro Giovanni, *Demofoonte* (arias, 373)
Pazzaglia, Salvatore, *Artaserse* (arias, 266)
Pellegrini, Pietro, *Alessandro* (1746, 142)
Pellizzari, Benedetto, *Artaserse* (arias, 266)
Pepe, Francesco Cherubino, *Artaserse* (arias, 266)
Perez, Davide, *Adriano* (1754, 293); *Alessandro* (1744, 1755, 138); *Artaserse* (1748, 1754, 225); *Demofoonte* (1752, 341); *Didone* (1751, 70)
Pergolesi, Giovanni Battista, *Adriano* (1734, 273); *Artaserse, Demofoonte* (arias, 266, 373)
Perillo, Salvatore, *Didone* (arias, 109)
Perotti, Giovanni Domenico, *Demofoonte* (arias, 373)
Persichini, Pietro, *Alessandro* (arias, 186)
Pescetti, Giovanni Battista, *Adriano* (1750, 289); *Alessandro* (1732, 126); *Artaserse* (1752, 236)
Piccinni, Niccolò, *Alessandro* (1758, 1774, 149); *Artaserse* (1762, 1768, 241); *Demofoonte* (1761, 349); *Didone* (1770, 1783, Fr., 83)
Pignatelli, Giuseppe, *Demofoonte* (arias, 373)
Pio, Antonio, *Demofoonte* (1783, 364)
Pircker, Johan, *Alessandro* (arias, 186)
Piticchio, Francesco, *Didone* (1780, 93)
Plantade, Charles-Henri, *Didone* (arias, 109)
Platone, Luigi, *Artaserse* (arias, 266)
Pompili, Marcello, *Artaserse* (arias, 266)
Poncini Zilioli, Francesco, *Artaserse* (1737, 212); *Didone* (1752, 72)
Ponzo, Giuseppe, *Artaserse* (1766, 244); *Demofoonte* (arias, 373)
Porpora, Nicola, *Alessandro* (1731, 114); *Didone* (1725, 45)
Porpora, Nicola; Broschi, Riccardo; Duni, Egidio Romualdo; Fini, Michele, *Didone* (1732, 48)
Porta, Giovanni, *Adriano* (1737, 278)
Portugal, Marcos António, *Adriano* (1809, 310); *Artaserse* (1806, 263); *Demofoonte* (1794, 1808, 370)
Prati, Alessio; *Demofoonte* (1787, 366); *Didone* (1783, 93)
Predieri, Luca Antonio, *Alessandro* (1731, 115); *Artaserse* (arias, 266)
Pugnani, Gaetano, *Demofoonte* (1788, 367)
Pulli, Pietro, *Alessandro* (1741, 134)

Quantz, Johann Joachim, *Demofoonte* (arias, 373)
Quilici, Gaetano, *Alessandro* (arias, 186)

Rauzzini, Venanzio, *Adriano* (arias, 313)
Re, Giuseppe Abate, *Artaserse* (1777, 254)
Reggio, Antonino, *Alessandro, Artaserse* (arias, 186, 266)
Reicha, Antoine, *Alessandro* (arias, 186)
Reichardt, Johann Friedrich, *Adriano, Artaserse, Demofoonte, Didone* (arias, 313, 267, 373, 109)
Reina, Giuseppe, *Demofoonte* (1739, 320)
Reissiger, Carl Gottlieb, *Didone* (1824, 108)
Reno, Carlo, *Demofoonte* (arias, 373)
Rickert, Aemilius, *Didone* (arias, 109)
Ristori, Giovanni Alberto, *Adriano* (1739, 281); (arias, 47)
Ritter, Alexander, *Alessandro* (Ger., 1811, 182)
Robuschi, Ferdinando, *Artaserse* (arias, 267)
Rocco, Benett, *Adriano* (arias, 313)
Rust, Giacomo, *Adriano* (1782, 308); *Alessandro* (1775, 169); *Artaserse* (1781, 255); *Demofoonte* (1780, 363)
Rutini, Giovanni Marco, *Alessandro* (1750, 144); *Demofoonte, Didone* (arias, 373, 109)

Sacchini, Antonio, *Adriano* (1771, 303); *Alessandro* (1763, 1768, 158); *Artaserse* (1768, 245); *Demofoonte* (arias, 373)
Sala, Nicola, *Adriano* (arias, 313)
Salieri, Antonio, *Didone* (arias, 109)
Sandoni, Pietro Giuseppe, *Adriano* (1734, 273)
Santarelli, Giuseppe, *Alessandro* (arias, 186)
Santini, Leopoldo, *Demofoonte* (1751, 341)
Sarro, Domenico Natale, *Alessandro* (1743, 135); *Didone* (1724, 1730, 41)
Sarti, Giuseppe, *Adriano* (1779, 307); *Alessandro* (1761, 1787, 154); *Artaserse* (1760, 240); *Demofoonte* (1755, 1771, 1782, 344); *Didone* (1762, 1782, 78)
Sarti, Giuseppe; Cherubini, Luigi; Anfossi, Pasquale; Bianchi, Francesco, *Didone* (1787, 95)
Sartori, Girolamo, *Artaserse* (1765, 244)
Savoja, Paolo, *Artaserse* (arias, 267)
Sbacchi, Guglielmo, *Didone* (arias, 109)
Sborgi, Giuseppe Maria, *Demofoonte* (1836, 371)
Scalabrini, Paolo, *Adriano* (1749, 289); *Alessandro* (1749, 144); *Artaserse* (1738, 214); *Didone* (1737, 50)
Scarlatti, Domenico, *Didone* (1724, 43)
Scarlatti, Giuseppe, *Adriano* (1752, 291); *Alessandro* (1753, 146); *Artaserse* (1747, 1763, 224)
Schacht, Theodor von, *Artaserse* (1777, 254)
Schiassi, Gaetano Maria, *Alessandro* (1734, 1736, 128); *Artaserse* (1737, 213); *Didone* (1735, 49); *Demofoonte* (1735, 316)

SC | Index II. Index of Names: Composers

Schubert, Franz, *Demofoonte* (arias, 373)
Schuster, Joseph Anton, *Demofoonte* (1776, 360); *Didone* (1776, 89)
Schwanenberger, Johann Gottfried, *Adriano* (1762, 298); *Didone* (1765, 80)
Sciroli, Gregorio, *Adriano* (1763, 299); *Alessandro* (1758, 153); *Artaserse* (arias, 267)
Scolari, Gregorio, *Adriano* (1754, 294); *Alessandro* (1750, 145); *Artaserse* (1757, 238); *Didone* (1752, 72)
Sellefco, *Alessandro* (arias, 186)
Sellitto, Giacomo, *Artaserse*, *Demofoonte* (arias, 267, 373)
Selvaggi, Gaspari, *Adriano*, *Didone* (arias, 313, 109)
Seydelmann, Franz, *Artaserse* (arias, 267)
Sickingen, Karl von, *Demofoonte* (arias, 373)
Silva, José Gomes da, *Adriano*, *Artaserse* (arias, 313, 267)
Silverstolpe, Fredik Samuel, *Alessandro* (arias, 186)
Skavronsky, count, *Alessandro*, *Artaserse* (arias, 186, 267)
Smith, John Christopher, *Artaserse* (1749, 233); *Demofoonte* (1747–1748, 332)
Spalletta, Raffaele, *Adriano* (arias, 313)
Sperger, Johannes, *Didone* (arias, 109)
Stuntz, Joseph Hartmann, *Artaserse*, *Didone* (arias, 267, 109)
Süssmayr, Franz Xaver, *Artaserse* (arias, 267)

Tarchi, Angelo, *Alessandro* (1788, rev. 1791, 1798, 178); *Artaserse* (1788, 259); *Demofoonte* (1786, 365); *Didone* (arias, 109)
Terradellas, Domingo Miguel Bernabe, *Artaserse* (1744, 221); *Didone* (1750, 69)
Tozzi, Antonio, *Adriano* (1770, 303)
Traetta, Tommaso, *Alessandro* (1762, 158); *Artaserse* (arias, 267); *Demofoonte* (1758, 347); *Didone* (1757, 1763, 1764, 75)
Trento, Vittorio, *Demofoonte* (arias, 365)
Tulli, Pietro, *Artaserse* (arias, 267)

Uhde, Johann Otto, *Adriano* (arias, 313)
Ullinger, Augustin, *Artaserse* (c. 1780, 255)
Uttini, Francesco Antonio Baldassare, *Adriano* (1757, 295); *Alessandro* (1743, 136); *Artaserse* (1758, 239); *Demofoonte* (1750, 341)

Valente, Saverio, *Alessandro* (arias, 186)
Valentini, Michelangelo, *Adriano* (1753, 292); *Demofoonte* (arias, 373)
Valeri, Gaetano, *Didone* (arias, 109)
Vanhal, Johann Baptist, *Demofoonte* (1770, 355)
Vento, Mattia, *Artaserse* (1771, 247); *Demofoonte* (1765, 352)

Vento, Mattia and others, *Artaserse* (1772, 248)
Veracini, Francesco Maria, *Adriano* (1735, 275)
Vernier, Girolamo, *Alessandro*, *Artaserse*, *Demofoonte* (arias, 186, 267, 373)
Verocai, Giovanni, *Adriano* (1745, 285); *Demofoonte* (1741, 322)
Viani, Francesco, *Alessandro* (arias, 186)
Vinci, Leonardo, *Alessandro* (1730, 111); *Artaserse* (1730, 189); *Demofoonte* (1741, 321); *Didone* (1726, 46)
Vinci, Leonardo + G. F. Händel, *Didone* (1737, 51)
Vinci, Pasquale, *Demofoonte* (1758, 347)
Viotti, Giovanni Battista, *Didone* (arias, 109)
Visconti, *Alessandro* (arias, 186)
Vogel, Johann Christoph, *Demofoonte* (1789, 368)

Wagenseil, Georg Christoph, *Alessandro* (1748, 144); *Artaserse* (arias, 267)
Weigl, Joseph, *Adriano* (Ger., 1807, 310)
Wetzstein, *Alessandro* (arias, 186)
Wimmer, Marian, *Adriano* (1764, 299)
Wiseman, Charles, *Artaserse* (arias, 267)
Wolf, Ernst Wilhelm, *Didone* (arias, 109)
Wranitzky, Paul, *Artaserse* (arias, 267)

Zamparelli, Dionisio, *Adriano* (arias, 313); *Artaserse* (1738, 215)
Zannetti, Francesco, *Artaserse* (1782, 256); *Didone* (1766, 80)
Zannetti, Francesco and other, *Artaserse* (1762, 241)
Zingarelli, Niccolò Antonio, *Adriano* (c. 1790, 309); *Alessandro* (c. 1790, 181); *Artaserse* (1789, 1794, 260); *Didone* (arias, 109)
Zingarelli, Niccolò Antonio and others, *Demofoonte* (1795, 368)
Zonca, Giuseppe, *Adriano* (arias, 313); *Demofoonte* (arias, 373)
Zoppis, Francesco, *Artaserse* (1748, 226), *Demofoonte* (arias, 373), *Didone* (1758, 76)

Unknown composer(s), *Adriano* (1734, 273, 1736, 278, 1740, 281, 1741, 285, 1743, 285, 1745, 285, 1746 (x2), 288, 1752, 291, 1760, 297, 1761, 297, 1763, 298, 1769, 301, 1773, 304, 1774, 306, 1776, 306, 1777, 307, 1780, 308, 1809, 310); *Alessandro* (1733, 127, 1735, 129, 1738, 134, 1740, 134, 1741, 134, 1743, 135, 1746, 143, 1752, 146, 1755, 148, 1756, 148, 1758[NP], 153, 1760, 154, 1764, 162, 1766, 162, 1768, 163, 1773, 167, 1774, 168, 1779, 169, 1786, 175, ca. 1800, 181); *Artaserse* (1733, 208, 1734, 210, 1739, 216, 1740, 216, 1747 , 223, 1748, 226, 1749 (x2), 227, 233, 1750 (x2), 235, 1753, 236, 1754, 237, 1757,

238, 1758, 239, 1759, 239, 1761, 241, 1762, 243, 1765, 244, 1767, 244, 1768, 246, 1770 (x4), 247, 1774, 249, 1778, 255, 1782, 256, 1785, 258, 1788, 260, 1792, 262, 1794, 262); *Demofoonte* (1737, 318, 1739, 321, 1742, 323, 1743, 325, 1746, 331, 1748, 337, 1749, 337, 1752, 341, 1753, 342, 1755 (x2), 344, 345, 1757, 345, 1759, 348, 1762, 350, 1763, 352, 1765, 353, 1769, 355, 1771, 356, 1772, 356, 1780, 362, 1780s, 363, 1781, 363, 1782, 364, 1787 (x2), 366, 367, 1788, 368, 1790, 369, 1791, 369); *Didone* (1725, 44, 1727 (x2), 47–48, 1728, 48, 1729, 48, 1733, 49, 1735, , 1740, 54, 1742 (x2), 54, 59, 1745 (x2), 64, 1748, 68, 1753, 74, 1755, 75, 1760, 77, 1767 (x2), 81, 1768 (x2), 82, 1770, 85, 1772 (x2), 86, 1778 (x2), 91, 1780, 93, 1786 (x2), 95, 1791, 97, 1792, 97)

Index III.
Index of Names: Printers

Academy Press [Academische Schriften, Stamperia dell'Accademia delle Scienze] (Mannheim)
    1766, *Alessandro*, G. di Majo (1st ed.)   162
    1768, *Adriano*, I. Holzbauer (1st ed.)   301
    1769, *Adriano*, I. Holzbauer   301

Albertini (Rimini)
    1743, *Demofoonte*, various   325
    1759, *Demofoonte*, P. Vinci   347

Albizzi, Gaetano (Florence)
    1762, *Artaserse*, various   244

Albizzini, Anton Maria (Florence)
    1740, *Alessandro*, unknown   134
    1741, *Demofoonte*, G. Verocai (1st ed.)   322

Albizziniana, Stamperia (Florence)
    1786, *Didone*, various   95
    1788, *Demofoonte*, various   368
    1792, *Artaserse*, various   262
    1801, *Alessandro*, A. Tarchi   179
    1802, *Alessandro*, A. Tarchi   179

Alessandri, Innocente & Scataglia, Pietro (Venice) – music
    1774, *Alessandro*, G. Paisiello   167
    1775, *Alessandro*, F. Alessandri   171
    1775, *Alessandro*, N. Piccinni   152

Almon, J. (London)
    1786, *Didone*, various   94

Altés, José (Barcelona)
    1767, *Didone*, unknown   81

Amato (Palermo)
    1746, *Alessandro*, unknown   143

Amidei, Fausto (Rome)
    1741, *Demofoonte*, A. Bernasconi (1st ed.)   321
    1749, *Artaserse*, N. Jommelli (1st ed. – 1st ver.)   231
    1757, *Demofoonte*, G. Pampani (1st ed.)   346
    1758, *Adriano*, R. di Capua (1st ed.)   296
    1758, *Alessandro*, N. Piccinni (1st ed.)   149

Andrews, Hugh (London) – music
    1785, *Artaserse*, various   258

Antoine, Vincenzo (Bergamo)
    1786, *Didone*, various   95

Archi (Faenza)
    1757, *Artaserse*, B. Galuppi   228
    1757, *Didone*, D. Perez   71

Artaria (Milan) – music
    1823, *Didone*, S. Mercadante   107

Astorino, Carlo Antonio & Battaglia, Giuseppe (Lodi)
    1763, *Alessandro*, J. C. Bach   156

Avondo, Giacomo Giuseppe (Turin)
    1759, *Adriano*, G. B. Borgui (1st ed.)   296
    1760, *Artaserse*, J. C. Bach (1st ed.)   240

Bacciagaluppi, S. (Warsaw)
    1792, *Alessandro*, F. Bianchi   174

Bailleux, Antoine (Paris) – music
    1779, *Alessandro*, P. Anfossi   166
    1779, *Demofoonte*, G. di Majo   351
    1779, *Demofoonte*, G. Paisiello   360
    1779, *Didone*, P. Anfossi   88
    1780, *Alessandro*, N. Piccinni   152
    1782, *Didone*, G. Sarti   80
    1783, *Demofoonte*, G. Sarti   345

SC | Index III. Index of Names: Printers

1784, *Alessandro*, A. Sacchini	161
1785, *Adriano*, G. Sarti	307
1785, *Artaserse*, G. Rust	256
1786, *Alessandro*, G. Paisiello	167

Balbis, B. (Alessandria)
1749, *Artaserse*, unknown	233

Ballanti, G. & Foschini (Faenza)
1745, *Alessandro*, L. Vinci	113

Barbiani, Antonio (Forlì)
1776, *Demofoonte*, J. Schuster (1st ed.)	360

Barbieri, Giuseppe (Ferrara)
1737, *Alessandro*, J. A. Hasse	121
1741, *Adriano*, various	285
1745, *Artaserse*, L. Vinci	191
1745, *Demofoonte*, C. W. Gluck	324

Barrois, T. son (Milan – Paris)
1820, *Demofoonte*, unknown	371

Bartolomicchi, Giovanni (Rome)
1772, *Alessandro*, P. Anfossi (1st ed.)	165

Bartsch, Christian (Brunswick/Wolfenbüttel)
1732, *Alessandro*, G. F. Händel	117
1734, *Didone*, N. Porpora	45
1737, *Adriano*, A. Caldara	271
1737, *Artaserse*, G. A. Paganelli (1st ed.)	213
1739, *Didone*. G. A. Paganelli	52
1741, *Demofoonte*, G. Verocai	322
1742, *Demofoonte*, G. Verocai	322
1745, *Adriano*, G. Verocai (1st ed.)	285
1745, *Artaserse*, C. H. Graun	219

Bausa, Guillermo (Palma de Mallorca)
1767, *Demofoonte*, B. Galuppi	339

Bazacchi (Piacenza)
1738, *Demofoonte*, G. B. Lampugnani (1st ed.)	319

Benacci, successors of → Sassi, C. M (Bologna)

Bendio, Luigi (Rome)
1779, *Adriano*, G. Sarti (1st ed.)	307

Benedini, Filippo Maria (Lucca)
1747, *Artaserse*, G. Scarlatti (1st ed.)	224
1750, *Alessandro*, G. Abos	143

1752, *Adriano*, G. Scarlatti	291
1754, *Demofoonte*, G. Cocchi	343
1757, *Artaserse*, B. Galuppi	229
1759, *Alessandro*, J. A. Hasse	122
1760, *Didone*, A. Ferradini (1st ed.)	77
1764, *Adriano*, C. G. Concialini and others	299
1765, *Demofoonte*, various	353
1766, *Alessandro*, various	162
1770, *Artaserse*, various	247
1770, *Didone*, various	85
1775, *Didone*, P. Anfossi	88

Benedini, Filippo Maria & Rocchi, Giacomo (Lucca)
1823, *Didone*, S. Mercadante	104

Bennet, Charles (London)
1734, *Artaserse*, various (1st ed.)	210
1735, *Adriano*, F. M. Veracini (1st ed.)	275
1735, *Artaserse*, various	211

Berling, Ernst Heinrich (Copenhagen)
1748, *Didone*, P. Scalabrini	51
1749, *Artaserse*, P. Scalabrini and others	215

Bernabò, Rocco (Rome)
1726, *Didone*, L. Vinci (1st ed.)	46

Berno, Pierantonio (Vicenza)
1750, *Alessandro*, G. Scolari (1st ed.)	145

Bettinelli, Giuseppe (Venice)
1733, Metastasio's works	49, 127, 208, 272, 316

Bianchi, Giovanni Battista (Milan)
1777, *Artaserse*, F. Bertoni	251
1786, *Demofoonte*, A. Tarchi (1st ed.)	365
1788, *Alessandro*, A. Tarchi (1st ed.)	178
1789, *Adriano*, S. Nasolini (1st ed.)	309
1791, *Didone*, various	97
1793, *Artaserse*, N. A. Zingarelli	260
1794, *Demofoonte*, M. A. Portugal (1st ed.)	370

Bianchi & co. (Pavia)
1774, *Artaserse*, various	249

Bigg, George (London)
1778, *Demofoonte*, various	362
1779, *Artaserse*, F. Bertoni	252

Bindi, Francesco (Pisa)
1734, *Alessandro*, unknown	129

SC | Index III. Index of Names: Printers

Birchall, Robert (London) – music
    1808, *Didone*, G. Paisiello — 100
    1815, *Didone*, F. Paër — 102

Bisagni, F. (Catania)
    1728, *Didone*, unknown — 48
    1735, *Artaserse*, J. A. Hasse — 200
    1740, *Artaserse*, unknown — 216
    1760, *Demofoonte*, J. A. Hasse — 333

Bisesti, Pietro (Verona)
    1813, *Adriano*, M. A. Portugal — 311
    1828, *Didone*, S. Mercadante — 106

Bland, J. (London) – music
    1784, *Demofoonte*, various — 362

Bolzani, Giuseppe (Pavia)
    1754, *Adriano*, A. G. Pampani — 290
    1767, *Didone*, unknown — 81
    1771, *Demofoonte*, various — 355
    1777, *Demofoonte*, J. Schuster — 360
    1804, *Artaserse*, N. A. Zingarelli — 261

Bonajuti, Anton (Florence)
    1762, *Alessandro*, B. Galuppi — 131
    1762, *Demofoonte*, various — 350

Bonaria (Cagliari)
    1750, *Artaserse*, G. Bollano? — 235

Bonducciana, Stamperia (Florence)
    1786, *Alessandro*, G. Andreozzi (1st ed.) — 175
    1786, *Alessandro*, various — 175

Bonetti (Siena)
    1750, *Adriano*, G. B. Pescetti — 289

Bonsignori, Francesco (Lucca)
    1777, *Artaserse*, F. Bertoni — 251
    1782, *Demofoonte*, various — 364
    1786, *Didone*, G. Sarti — 78
    1783, *Alessandro*, M. Mortellari — 170

Bordazar, Antonio (Valencia)
    1734, *Artaserse*, unknown — 210

Bracali, A. (Pistoia)
    1757, *Demofoonte*, G. Cocchi — 343

Branchini, F. (Mantua)
    1825, *Didone*, S. Mercadante — 104

Breitfeld (Regensburg)
    1777, *Artaserse*, T. von Schacht (1st ed.) — 255
    1781, *Artaserse*, T. von Schacht — 255

Bremner, Robert (London) – music
    1765, *Demofoonte*, M. Vento — 352
    1772, *Artaserse*, various — 249
    1774, *Alessandro*, D. Corri — 168
    1775, *Didone*, various — 89

Brusi, Antonio (Barcelona)
    1831, *Alessandro*, G. Pacini — 183

Bulhões, José de Aquino (Lisbon)
    1819, *Demofoonte*, M. A. Portugal — 370
    1827, *Alessandro*, G. Pacini — 183
    1827, *Didone*, S. Mercadante — 106
    1828, *Adriano*, S. Mercadante (1st ed.) — 311

Buonarigo, Carlo (Venice)
    1730, *Artaserse*, J. A. Hasse (1st ed.) — 199–200
    1730, *Didone*, D. N. Sarro — 42
    1732, *Alessandro*, G. B. Pescetti (1st ed.) — 126
    1733, *Adriano*, G. Giacomelli (1st ed.) — 272

Burguete, F. (Valencia)
    1769, *Artaserse*, A. Sacchini — 245

Cadell, Thomas (London)
    1774, *Alessandro*, D. Corri (1st ed.) — 168
    1775, *Didone*, various — 89

Campana, Pompeo (Foligno)
    1763, *Artaserse*, N. Piccinni — 242

Campins, Pablo (Barcelona)
    1751, *Demofoonte*, B. Galuppi — 339
    1753, *Didone*, G. Scolari — 73
    1754, *Artaserse*, G. B. Ferrandini and G. Porta — 216

Campitelli, Feliciano & Filippo (Foligno)
    1732, *Artaserse*, L. Vinci — 191

Cannetti, Giovanni Battista (Rome)
    1783, *Artaserse*, G. Rust — 256

Capaci (La Valletta)
    1765, *Demofoonte*, J. A. Hasse — 334

447

SC | Index III. Index of Names: Printers

Capitani, B. (Macerata)
    1777, *Artaserse*, F. Bertoni — 251

Capponi, Lorenzo & Bartolomicchi, Giovanni (Rome)
    1773, *Demofoonte*, P. Anfossi (1st ed.) — 357

Carli, Tommaso Pazzini (Siena)
    1787, *Artaserse*, F. Bianchi — 258
    1791, *Alessandro*, A. Tarchi — 178

Carli (Paris) – music
    1825, *Alessandro*, G. Pacini — 184

Carotti, Giovanni Domenico (Pisa)
    1749, *Artaserse*, unknown — 227
    1758, *Artaserse*, various — 239
    1759, *Adriano*, G. G. Brunetti (1st ed.) — 297
    1763, *Alessandro*, G. G. Brunetti (1st ed.) — 158

Cartolaro a Monte Citorio (Rome)
    1763, *Demofoonte*, G. di Majo (1st ed.) — 350

Casaletti, Arcangelo (Rome)
    1772, *Alessandro*, P. Anfossi (1st ed.) — 165

Casali, Giovanni Battista (Venice)
    1775, *Alessandro*, G. Rust (1st ed.) — 169
    1796, *Alessandro*, L. Caruso — 176
    1828, *Alessandro*, G. Pacini — 183

Casamara, Antonio (Genoa)
    1765, *Artaserse*, various — 244

Chiaramonte & Provenzano (Messina)
    1733, *Didone*, unknown — 49

Chrichley, J. (London)
    1737, *Demofoonte*, E. R. Duni (1st ed.) — 318

Ciché & Gramignani (Palermo)
    1742, *Didone*, unknown — 59

Ciuffetti, Domenico (Lucca)
    1729, *Didone*, L. Vinci — 46
    1730, *Artaserse*, J. A. Hasse — 200
    1740, *Alessandro*, L. Vinci — 113

Colombani, Paolo (Venice)
    1762, *Artaserse*, G. di Majo (1st ed.) — 241
    1764, *Demofoonte*, A. G. Pampani — 347

Comino, Antonio (Venice)
    1761, *Artaserse*, B. Galuppi — 229

Conzatti, Giovanbattista (Padua)
    1738, *Artaserse*, G. F. Brivio (1st ed.) — 215
    1739, *Didone*, G. B. Lampugnani (1st ed.) — 53
    1740, *Adriano*, G. B. Lampugnani (1st ed.) — 284
    1743, *Demofoonte*, N. Jommelli (1st ed.) — 326
    1751, *Artaserse*, B. Galuppi — 228
    1758, *Demofoonte*, B. Galuppi — 339
    1766, *Alessandro*, G. Sarti — 154
    1782, *Didone*, G. Sarti (1st ed. – 2nd ver.) — 78
    1783, *Demofoonte*, F. Alessandri (1st ed.) — 364
    1787, *Artaserse*, F. Bianchi (1st ed.) — 258
    1791, *Didone*, various — 97

Corradi, Lorenzo (Rome)
    1768, *Demofoonte*, A. Sacchini (1st ed.) — 245
    1769, *Adriano*, G. di Majo — 300
    1770, *Didone*, N. Piccinni (1st ed.) — 83

Costantini (Perugia)
    1734, *Artaserse*, L. Vinci — 191
    1734, *Didone*, L. Vinci — 46
    1773, *Alessandro*, A. Sacchini — 159
    1776, *Demofoonte*, G. Paisiello — 359
    1787, *Demofoonte*, G. Sarti — 344

Costantini & Maurizi (Perugia)
    1746, *Adriano*, unknown — 288

Cotta, Christoph Friedrich (Stuttgart)
    1760, *Alessandro*, N. Jommelli (1st ed. – 2nd ver.) — 137
    1763, *Didone*, N. Jommelli (1st ed. – 2nd ver.) — 65
    1764, *Demofoonte*, N. Jommelli (1st ed. – 2nd ver.) — 326
    1765, *Demofoonte*, N. Jommelli — 327
    1777, *Didone*, N. Jommelli — 65
    1778, *Demofoonte*, N. Jommelli — 327
    1780, *Didone*, N. Jommelli — 65
    1782, *Didone*, N. Jommelli — 66

Cotta, Johan Georg (Stuttgart)
    1750, *Artaserse*, C. H. Graun — 219
    1751, *Artaserse*, C. H. Graun — 219
    1751, *Didone*, N. Jommelli — 65
    1752, *Alessandro*, B. Galuppi — 130
    1756, *Artaserse*, N. Jommelli (1st ed. – 2nd ver.) — 231

Crisanti (Palermo)
    1821, *Adriano*, P. Airoldi (1st ed.) — 311

SC | Index III. Index of Names: Printers

D'Affrunti, Pietro (Palermo)
    1794, *Didone*, G. Paisiello   98

D'Almaine, Thomas (London) – music
    1835, *Didone*, S. Mercadante   107

Dale, John (London) – music
    1788, *Demofoonte*, various   362

Dalla Volpe, Lelio (Bologna)
    1731, *Artaserse*, L. Vinci   191

Da Fonseca, Antonio Isidoro (Lisbon)
    1736, *Alessandro*, G. M. Schiassi   128
    1737, *Artaserse*, G. M. Schiassi (1ˢᵗ ed.)   213
    1737, *Demofoonte*, G. M. Schiassi,   316

Davolio, Giuseppe (Reggio Emilia)
    1755, *Artaserse*, G. Cocchi (1ˢᵗ ed.)   237
    1761, *Demofoonte*, N. Piccinni (1ˢᵗ ed.)   349
    1762, *Alessandro*, T. Traetta (1ˢᵗ ed.)   158
    1787, *Demofoonte*, A. Tarchi   365

Davolio, Giuseppe & son (Reggio Emilia)
    1790, *Artaserse*, A. Tarchi   259

De Lormel, P. (Paris)
    1783, *Didone*, N. Jommelli   84

De' Giuli, Giambattista (Jesi)
    1734, *Alessandro*, G. M. Schiassi   128
    1747, *Alessandro*, G. Abos (1ˢᵗ ed.)   143

de' Rossi, Antonio (Rome)
    1736, *Adriano*, E. R. Duni (1ˢᵗ ed.)   278
    1738, *Artaserse*, L. Vinci   191
    1747, *Didone*, N. Jommelli (1ˢᵗ ed.)   65

Decker, Georg Jacob & Hartung, Gottlieb Lebrecht
(Berlin) – music
    1773, *Adriano*, C. H. Graun   287
    1773, *Alessandro*, C. H. Graun   141
    1773, *Demofoonte*, C. H. Graun   331
    1774, *Artaserse*, C. H. Graun   220

Derossi, Onorato (Turin)
    1773, *Didone*, G. Colla (1ˢᵗ ed.)   86
    1782, *Adriano*, G. Rust (1ˢᵗ ed.)   308
    1785, *Artaserse*, D. Cimarosa (1ˢᵗ ed.)   257
    1787, *Demofoonte*,65 G. Pugnani (1ˢᵗ ed.)   367
    1798, *Alessandro*, A. Tarchi (1ˢᵗ ed. – 2ⁿᵈ ver.) 179

1823, *Didone*, S. Mercadante (1ˢᵗ ed.)   104
1829, *Didone*, S. Mercadante   106

Donati, Andrea (Fano)
    1745, *Didone*, A. Aurisicchio (1ˢᵗ ed.)   64

Dova, Carlo (Milan)
    1813, *Adriano*, M. A. Portugal   310
    1815, *Adriano*, M. A. Portugal   311

Dufour, P. (Warsaw)
    1776, *Demofoonte*, J. A. Hasse   334
    1776, *Didone*, P. Anfossi   88

Durand, Clamopin, Grouteau, & co. (Porto)
    1772, *Demofoonte*, D. Perez   341

Ebers, J. (London)
    1827, *Didone*, S. Mercadante   106

Eder, Johann (Vienna)
    1789, *Alessandro*, V. Chiavacci   173

Epiro, Antonino (Palermo)
    1743, *Artaserse*, L. Vinci   191

Escrivano, M. (Madrid)
    1757, *Adriano*, N. Conforto (1ˢᵗ ed.)   294

Espinosa, Manuel (Cádiz)
    1764, *Alessandro*, D. Perez and others   139
    1764, *Demofoonte*, B. Galuppi   339

Espinosa, E. (Cádiz)
    1768, *Didone*, unknown   82

Estienne, J. F. (Kassel)
    1765, *Artaserse*, I. Fiorillo   236
    1768, *Didone*, unknown   82
    1777, *Adriano*, J. A. Hasse   279

Fabbrini, N. (Florence)
    1830, *Didone*, S. Mercadante   106

Fain (Paris)
    1811, *Didone*, F. Paër   101

Falorni, G. V. (Livorno)
    1782, *Adriano*, L. Cherubini (1ˢᵗ ed.)   308
    1782, *Artaserse*, G. Rust   255
    1787, *Demofoonte*, various   367

SC | Index III. Index of Names: Printers

Fanelli, Gaetano (Fano)
    1731, *Artaserse*, L. Vinci   191

Fantechi, Giovanni Paolo & co. (Livorno)
    1752, *Demofoonte*, unknown   341
    1752, *Didone*, Poncini Zilioli (1st ed.)   72
    1759, *Artaserse*, D. Zamparelli and other   216

Fantosini, G. (Florence)
    1810, *Artaserse*, M. A. Portugal   263
    1817, *Didone*, F. Paër   102
    1825, *Didone*, S. Mercadante   105

Felicella, A. (Palermo)
    1733, *Alessandro*, unknown   127

Fenzo, Modesto (Venice)
    1747, *Artaserse*, F. Maggiore   224
    1753, *Alessandro*, G. Latilla and others   146
    1753, *Demofoonte*, J. A. Hasse   333
    1754, *Artaserse*, B. Galuppi   228
    1754, *Demofoonte*, G. Cocchi (1st ed.)   343
    1756, *Alessandro*, B. Galuppi   130
    1756, *Artaserse*, B. Galuppi   228
    1756, *Didone*, T. Traetta (1st ed.)   75
    1757, *Adriano*, G. F. Brusa (1st ed.)   295
    1757, *Alessandro*, B. Galuppi   131
    1757, *Artaserse*, B. Galuppi   228
    1758, *Artaserse*, G. Scolari   238
    1759, *Alessandro*, G. Scolari   145
    1759, *Demofoonte*, various   349
    1760, *Adriano*, B. Galuppi   282
    1760, *Adriano*, A. M. Mazzoni (3701st ed.)   297
    1761, *Demofoonte*, A. Boroni and others (1st ed.)   350
    1762, *Demofoonte*, A. Boroni and others   350
    1769, *Demofoonte*, J. Mysliveček (1st ed.)   354
    1770, *Didone*, G. di Majo (1st ed.)   82
    1771, *Adriano*, A. Sacchini (1st ed339.)   303
    1771, *Alessandro*, F. Bertoni   164
    1772, *Artas68erse290*, V. Manfredini (1st ed.)   248
    1775, *Demofoonte*, G.153 Paisiello (1st ed.)   359
    1775, *Didone*, P. Anfossi   87
    1776, *Artaserse*, G. B. Borghi (1st ed.)   250
    1778, *Alessandro*, L. Marescalchi (1st ed.)   169
    1779, *Didone*, J. Schuster   90
    1780, *Adriano*, F. Alessandri (1st ed.)   308
    1782, *Artaserse*, F. Zannetti (1st ed.)   256
    1785, *Alessandro*, F. Bianchi (1st ed.)   174
    1785, *Artaserse*, F. Bertoni   252
    1787, *Demofoonte*, A. Prati (1st ed.)   366
    1788, *Artaserse*, various   260
    1790, *Didone*, various   96
    1791, *Alessandro*, L. Caruso   176
    1791, *Demofoonte*, G. Pugnani   367
    1792, *Alessandro*, F. Bianchi   174
    1795, *Alessandro*, F. Bianchi   174
    1798, *Adriano*, J. S. Mayr (1st ed.)   309

Ferreira, Pedro (Lisbon)
    1768, *Artaserse*, G. Scolari   239

Ferreira, S. T. (Lisbon)
    1799, *Didone*, S. Marino and others   100
    1800, *Alessandro*, L. Caruso   176
    1801, *Artaserse*, D. Cimarosa   257
    1803, *Didone*, S. Marino and others   100
    1806, *Artaserse*, M. A. Portugal (1st ed.)   263
    1808, *Demofoonte*, M. A. Portugal (1st ed. – 2nd ver.)   370

Ferrer (Palermo)
    1768, *Demofoonte*, B. Galuppi   339
    1773, *Adriano*, various   305

Ferri (Macerata)
    1740, *Artaserse*, L. Vinci   191

Ferri, heirs of Pietro (Rome)
    1741, *Demofoonte*, A. Bernasconi (1st ed.)   321

Flautina, Tipografia (Naples)
    1824, *Alessandro*, G. Pacini (1st ed.)   182
    1825, *Didone*, S. Mercadante (1st ed. – 2nd ver.)   105

Flauto, G. (Naples)
    1759, *Adriano*, B. Galuppi   282
    1760, *Artaserse*, J. A. Hasse   201

Flauto, Vincenzo (Naples)
    1762, *Alessandro*, J. C. Bach (1st ed.)   156
    1762, *Artaserse*, J. A. Hasse   202
    1764, *Didone*, T. Traetta   75
    1783, *Artaserse*, F. Alessandri (1st ed.)   257
    1788, *Didone*, P. Anfossi   88
    1789, *Alessandro*, P. A. Guglielmi (1st ed.)   180
    1792, *Alessandro*, N. Piccinni   149
    1794, *Didone*, G. Paisiello (1st ed.)   98

Fontana, Antonio (Milan)
    1826, *Alessandro*, G. Pacini   182
    1826, *Didone*, S. Mercadante   105

SC | Index III. Index of Names: Printers

Fornari (Ferrara)
    1763, *Adriano*, unknown   298
    1763, *Didone*, G. Scolari   73

Fossati, G. (Venice)
    1764, *Didone*, B. Galuppi   55
    1766, *Adriano*, P. A. Guglielmi (1st ed.)   300
    1766, *Artaserse*, G. Ponzo (1st ed.)   244

Franceschi, G. (Bologna)
    1754, *Artaserse*, G. B. Ferrandini and G. Porta   216

Franchelli, G. (Genoa)
    1734, *Adriano*, P. G. Sandoni (1st ed.)   273
    1735, *Demofoonte*, P. V. Chiocchetti (1st ed.)   318
    1743, *Artaserse*, P. Chiarini (1st ed.)   217
    1748, *Didone*, unknown   68
    1751, *Adriano*, A. Adolfati (1st ed.)   291
    1758, *Alessandro*, G. Sciroli (1st ed.)   153
    1762, *Artaserse*, F. Zannetti and other (1st ed.)   241

Frantechi, G. P. & co. (Livorno)
    1752, *Didone*, F. Poncini Zilioli (1st ed.)   72

Galeazzi, Pietro (Pavia)
    1787, *Artaserse*, F. Bertoni   252
    1791, *Demofoonte*, A. Tarchi   365

Gallici alla fontana (Udine)
    1763, *Adriano*, B. Galuppi   282

Garland, J. (London)
    1785, *Artaserse*, various   258

Gatti, G. S. (Pistoia)
    1733, *Artaserse*, unknown   208
    1740, *Didone*, unknown   54
    1747, *Artaserse*, L. Vinci   192

Gattinara, F. A. (Turin)
    1727, *Didone*, D. N. Sarro   41

Gavelli, N. (Pesaro)
    1729, *Didone*, T. G. Albinoni   44
    1730, *Artaserse*, L. Vinci   191
    1746, *Alessandro*, J. A. Hasse   122

Gavelliana, Stamperia (Pesaro)
    1759, *Demofoonte*, T. Traetta   347

Gayo, B. F. (Lisbon)
    1741, *Didone*, R. di Capua (1st ed.)   58

Generas, Francesc (Barcelona)
    1762, *Alessandro*, G. Scolari   145
    1763, *Adriano*, G. Sciroli (1st ed.)   299
    1763, *Artaserse*, N. Piccinni   242
    1763, *Demofoonte*, B. Galuppi   339
    1763, *Didone*, G. Scolari   73

Geremia, A. (Venice)
    1754, *Adriano*, G. Scolari (1st ed.)   294
    1755, *Alessandro*, B. Galuppi (1st ed.–2nd ver.)   130
    1756, *Artaserse*, A. G. Pampani   234

Gesiniana, Stamperia (Genoa)
    1774, *Demofoonte*, P. Anfossi and others   357
    1776, *Adriano*, unknown   306
    1777, *Artaserse*, F. Bertoni   251
    1778, *Didone*, various   91
    1780, *Alessandro*, F. Alessandri (1st ed.)   171
    1781, *Demofoonte*, F. Bianchi (1st ed.)   363
    1787, *Didone*, various   95
    1788, *Artaserse*, F. Bertoni   252
    1792, *Demofoonte*, unknown   370
    1794, *Artaserse*, various   262

Ghidini, heirs of (Pavia)
    1760, *Adriano*, various   297

Ghislandi, Carlo Giuseppe (Milan)
    1747, *Demofoonte*, G. F. Brivio   320
    1752, *Adriano*, unknown   291
    1753, *Didone*, unknown   74
    1756, *Demofoonte*, N. Jommelli   326
    1756, *Alessandro*, B. Galuppi   130
    1756, *Alessandro*, D. Perez   139
    1759, *Didone*, T. Traetta   75

Giardini, F. de (London) – music
    1755, *Demofoonte*, various   230, 346

Gibert, Carles (Barcelona)
    1767, *Alessandro*, G. Scolari   145

Gillet, J. (London)
    1814, *Didone*, F. Paër   101

Girard, G. (Naples) – music
    s.d., *Didone*, S. Mercadante   107

Giusto, Antonio (Vicenza)
    1787, *Didone*, G. Gazzaniga (1st ed.)   96

SC | Index III. Index of Names: Printers

Godiche, A. H. (Copenhagen)
    1749, *Demofoonte*, various   337
    1755, *Demofoonte*, G. Sarti (1st ed.)   344

González (Madrid)
    1791, *Didone*, G. Andreozzi   94

Griffin, William (London)
    1772, *Artaserse*, various   249
    1773, *Artaserse*, various   249

Guidotti, Domenico & Mellini, Giacomo (Bologna)
    1747, *Artaserse*, unknown   223

Hammond & Cane (London)
    1790, *Alessandro*, A. Tarchi   178
    1790, *Demofoonte*, V. Federici (1st ed.)   369

Hampe, Philip O. (Kassel)
    1780, *Didone*, unknown   93

Hartvig, Andreas (Copenhagen)
    1749, *Adriano*, P. Scalabrini (1st ed.)   289
    1749, *Alessandro*, P. Scalabrini (1st ed.)   144

Haude, Ambros (Berlin)
    1743, *Artaserse*, C. H. Graun (1st ed.)   218
    1744, *Alessandro*, C. H. Graun (1st ed.)   141
    1745, *Adriano*, C. H. Graun (1st ed.)   286
    1745, *Demofoonte*, C. H. Graun (1st ed.)   330

Haude & Spener (Berlin)
    1752, *Didone*, J. A. Hasse   60
    1754, *Alessandro*, J. F. Agricola (1st ed.)   147
    1770, *Didone*, J. A. Hasse   60
    1774, *Demofoonte*, C. H. Graun   330
    1777, *Alessandro*, J. A. Hasse   122
    1783, *Artaserse*, C. H. Graun   219
    1784, *Alessandro*, C. H. Graun   141

Heitz, J. H. (Strasbourg)
    1741, *Didone*, P. Scalabrini and others   51
    1750, *Artaserse*, unknown   235

Hérissant, widow of (Paris)
    1780, Metastasio's works   92, 171, 255, 307, 362

Heugel & co. (Paris) – music
    s.d., *Alessandro*, A. Sacchini   161

Heyinger, Andrea (Vienna)
    1729, *Didone*, unknown   48

Hirnle, Francesco Antonio (Ollomuzio)
    1733, *Artaserse*, E. Bambini (1st ed.)   208

Holland, H. (London) – music
    1790, *Demofoonte*, V. Federici   369

Houston & Hyde (London)
    1784, *Demofoonte*, various   362

Hummel, Johann Julius (Amsterdam) – music
    1760, *Alessandro*, G. Merchi   185

Ibarra, widow of (Madrid)
    1792, *Alessandro*, L. Caruso   176
    1792, *Didone*, G. Sarti   79

Imperial Academy of the Sciences [Accademia Imperiale delle Scienze] (St Petersburg)
    1738, *Artaserse*, F. Araia (1st ed.)   214
    1755, *Alessandro*, F. Araia   136
    1758, *Didone*, F. Zoppis (1st ed.)   76
    1759, *Alessandro*, F. Araia   136
    1766, *Didone*, B. Galuppi   56

Insegna della Scienza (Venice)
    1750, *Artaserse*, A. G. Pampani (1st ed. – 1st ver.)   234

Kamenicky, Leopold Johann (Prague)
    1734, *Alessandro*, A. Bioni   128

Keitel, A. J. (Brunswick)
    1750, *Demofoonte*, I. Fiorillo (1st ed.)   341
    1751, *Artaserse*, I. Fiorillo (1st ed.)   236
    1751, *Demofoonte*, I. Fiorillo   341

Keitel, heirs of A. J. (Brunswick)
    1751, *Didone*, I. Fiorillo (1st ed.)   70
    1752, *Alessandro*, I. Fiorillo (1st ed.)   146

Kelly, M. (London) – music
    1805, *Didone*, G. Paisiello   99

Kleinmayr, Johann Friedrich (Klagenfurt)
    1739, *Alessandro*, J. A. Hasse   121

Kroyss, Franz Anton (Vienna)
    1787, *Alessandro*, F. Bianchi   174

Lami, Antonio & co. (Livorno)
    1788, *Alessandro*, L. Cherubini   172

SC | Index III. Index of Names: Printers

Langiano, Domenico (Naples)
    1747, *Adriano*, G. Latilla (1st ed.)   288
    1749, *Alessandro*, D. Perez   139
    1749, *Artaserse*, D. Perez   225
    1753, *Didone*, G. B. Lampugnani (1st ed. – 2nd ver.)   53
    1754, *Adriano*, N. Conforto (1st ed.)   294
    1754, *Alessandro*, B. Galuppi   130

Lavenu, Lewis Augustus (London) – music
    1814, *Didone*, G. Paisiello   100

Lee, E. (London) – music
    1790, *Didone*, various   94
    1800, *Didone*, N. Piccinni   84

Leone, Pietro (Rome)
    1726, *Didone*, L. Vinci   46
    1730, *Alessandro*, L. Vinci (1st ed.)   112
    1730, *Artaserse*, L. Vinci (1st ed.)   190
    1732, *Adriano*, A. Caldara (1st ed.)   271
    1732, *Didone*, N. Porpora, R. Broschi, E. R. Duni   48
    1733, *Demofoonte*, A. Caldara (1st ed.)   315
    1735, *Demofoonte*, F. Ciampi (1st ed.)   318

Longman, James & Broderip, Francis (London) – music
    1775, *Didone*, various   89
    1780, *Alessandro*, various   171
    1786, *Didone*, various   94
    1789, *Alessandro*, A. Tarchi   179
    1790, *Demofoonte*, V. Federici   369
    1790, *Didone*, various   94
    s.d., *Didone*, N. Piccinni   84

Lonsdale, Christopher (London) – music
    1754, *Didone*, V. L. Ciampi   74
    s.d., *Artaserse*, Hasse and others   211

Lovisa, Domenico (Venice)
    1738, *Artaserse*, J. A. Hasse   200

Mackintosh, William (London)
    1779, *Alessandro*, various   171

Mainardi, Girolamo (Urbino)
    1734, *Alessandro*, L. Vinci   112

Malatesta, Giuseppe Richino (Milan)
    1728, *Didone*, T. G. Albinoni   44
    1730, *Artaserse*, J. A. Hasse   200
    1731, *Alessandro*, L. A. Predieri (1st ed.)   115
    1736, *Adriano*, A. Bernasconi (1st ed. – 1st ver.)   276
    1739, *Didone*, G. F. Brivio or E. R. Duni (1st ed.)   52
    1742, *Alessandro*, G. F. Brivio (1st ed.)   135
    1742, *Artaserse*, C. W. Gluck (1st ed.)   218
    1742, *Demofoonte*, C. W. Gluck (1st ed.)   323
    1742, *Demofoonte*, unknown   323
    1747, *Demofoonte*, C. W. Gluck   324
    1749, *Artaserse*, G. B. Lampugnani (1st ed.)   233
    1751, *Adriano*, A. G. Pampani (1st ed.)   290
    1751, *Artaserse*, G. B. Pescetti (1st ed.)   236
    1752, *Alessandro*, D. Perez   139
    1753, *Demofoonte*, N. Piccinni (1st ed. – 2nd ver.)   326
    1755, *Didone*, G. A. Fioroni (1st ed.)   74
    1756, *Artaserse*, Q. Gasparini (1st ed.)   238
    1759, *Alessandro*, I. Holzbauer (1st ed.)   154
    1759, *Demofoonte*, A. Ferradini (1st ed.)   348
    1763, *Adriano*, G. Colla (1st ed.)   298
    1763, *Didone*, T. Traetta   75

Manfredi, Carlo (Reggio Emilia) – music
    1755, *Artaserse*, G. Cocchi   237

Manini, Lorenzo (Cremona)
    1776, *Demofoonte*, G. Paisiello   359
    1776, *Didone*, P. Anfossi   88
    1786, *Alessandro*, L. Cherubini   172
    1786, *Artaserse*, D. Cimarosa   257
    1788, *Artaserse*, F. Bertoni   252

Marescalchi, Luigi (Venice) – music
    s.d., *Didone*, unknown   110

Marescalchi, Luigi & Canobbio, Carlo (Venice) – music
    1774, *Alessandro*, N. Piccinni

Marescandoli, Francesco (Lucca)
    1731, *Alessandro*, L. Vinci   112
    1731, *Artaserse*, L. Vinci   191
    1737, *Demofoonte*, various   318
    1738, *Artaserse*, D. Zamparelli + unknown (1st ed.)   215
    1741, *Demofoonte*, L. Vinci (1st ed.)   321
    1743, *Alessandro*, unknown   135
    1746, *Adriano*, unknown   288

Martelli, Lorenzo (Bologna)
    1742, *Artaserse*, J. A. Hasse and others   201

Marozzi, Achille (Forlì)
    1779, *Didone*, B. Ottani (1st ed.)   92

Masi, Tommaso & co. (Livorno)
    1771, *Alessandro*, A. Sacchini   159
    1777, *Adriano*, various   307

SC | Index III. Index of Names: Printers

1791, *Alessandro*, A. Tarchi	179
1791, *Demofoonte*, A. Tarchi	366
1794, *Artaserse*, N. Isouard (1st ed.)	262

Minatelli, Cattarino & co. (Venice) – music
1794, *Artaserse*, N. Zingarelli	261

Mojados, Lorenzo Francisco (Madrid)
1749, *Artaserse*, G. B. Mele and others (1st ed.)	227
1750, *Demofoonte*, B. Galuppi (1st ed.)	338
1751, *Demofoonte*, B. Galuppi	338

Mojados, heirs of Lorenzo Francisco (Madrid)
1755, *Demofoonte*, B. Galuppi	339

Monauri, Giulio (Trento)
1747, *Artaserse*, F. Maggiore (1st ed.)	224

Montani, Giovanni (Milan)
1769, *Didone*, I. Celoniati (1st ed.)	82
1775, *Alessandro*, C. Monza (1st ed.)	169

Monte, Giovanni dal (Imola)
1792, *Artaserse*, F. Bertoni	252

Monti (Parma)
1736, *Alessandro*, L. Vinci	113
1737, *Artaserse*, F. Poncini Zilioli (1st ed.)	212
1754, *Artaserse*, L. Vinci	192
1754, *Demofoonte*, A. Mazzoni (1st ed.)	342
1755, *Alessandro*, B. Galuppi	130

Morelli, Francesco (Naples)
1768, *Alessandro*, A. Sacchini (1st ed. – 2nd ver.)	159
1768, *Artaserse*, N. Piccinni (1st ed. – 2nd ver.)	242
1769, *Adriano*, I. Fiorillo (1st ed.)	302
1770, *Demofoonte*, N. Jommelli (1st ed. – 4th ver.)	327
1773, *Adriano*, G. Insanguine (1st ed.)	306
1774, *Alessandro*, N. Piccinni (1st ed. – 2nd ver.)	149
1774, *Artaserse*, J. Mysliveček (1st ed.)	249
1775, *Demofoonte*, J. Mysliveček (1st ed. – 2nd ver.)	354
1776, *Didone*, J. A. Schuster (1st ed.)	89

Mori, Nicolas and E. & Lavenu, Lewis Augustus (London) – music
1825, *Didone*, S. Mercadante	107

Moroni, Marco (Verona)
1778, *Artaserse*, G. Paisiello	248

Murero, Giovanni Battista (Udine)
1745, *Alessandro*, unknown	285

Napier, William (London) – music
1774, *Alessandro*, N. Piccinni	152
1778, *Demofoonte*, various	355, 361, 362
1779, *Artaserse*, F. Bertoni	253
1780, *Alessandro*, various	171

Nicoli-Cristiani, Federico (Brescia)
1825, *Didone*, S. Mercadante	105

Orga, widow of José (Valencia)
1769, *Demofoonte*, unknown	355

Orga, José & Tomás (Valencia)
1774, *Alessandro*, unknown	168
1778, *Artaserse*, unknown	255

Oswald, John (London) – music
1757, *Alessandro*, various	148

Pacini, Antonio (Paris) – music
1823?, *Didone*, S. Mercadante	107
1825, *Alessandro*, G. Pacini	184

Pagani, Giuseppe (Florence)
1732, *Alessandro*, L. Vinci	112

Pagani, Anton Giuseppe (Florence)
1773, *Demofoonte*, P. Anfossi	357
1776, *Adriano*, J. Mysliveček	305
1780, *Artaserse*, L. Caruso (1st ed.)	250
1795, *Didone*, G. Paisiello	98

Pagano (Genoa)
1824, *Didone*, S. Mercadante	104

Pallavicini, Antonio (Lodi)
1779, *Artaserse*, G. B. Pescetti	236

Pall-Mall No. 5
1799, *Didone*, G. Paisiello	98

Paperini, Bernardo (Florence)
1727, *Didone*, unknown	47
1736, *Alessandro*, E. R. Duni? (1st ed.)	129

Parise (Vicenza)
1824, *Didone*, S. Mercadante	104

SC | Index III. Index of Names: Printers

Pasinelli, Angelo (Venice)
    1738, *Artaserse*, J. A. Hasse   200

Pasini, Giuseppe (Brescia)
    1741, *Adriano*, P. Giaino (1st ed.)   285
    1756, *Artaserse*, B. Galuppi   228
    1785, *Artaserse*, F. Bertoni   252

Pavini, Luigi (Venice)
    1747, *Didone*, A. Adolfati (1st ed.)   67
    1748, *Didone*, F. Bertoni (1st ed.)   68

Pazzoni, Alberto (Mantua)
    1737, *Adriano*, G. Porta (1st ed.)   278
    1737, *Didone*, unknown   48

Pazzoni, heirs of Alberto (Mantua)
    1738, *Alessandro*, B. Galuppi (1st ed.)   130
    1745, *Didone*, various   64
    1753, *Artaserse*, B. Galuppi (1st ed.)   228
    1755, *Didone*, D. Perez   71
    1758, *Demofoonte*, T. Traetta (1st ed.)   347
    1768, *Alessandro*, L. Gatti (1st ed.)   163
    1768, *Artaserse*, unknown   246
    1770, *Demofoonte*, T. Traetta   347
    1784, *Alessandro*, L. Cherubini (1st ed.)   172
    1787, *Demofoonte*, L. Gatti (1st ed.)   366
    1788, *Artaserse*, A. Tarchi (1st ed.)   259
    1793, *Didone*, G. Sarti   79

Pianta, Pietro (Brescia)
    1758, *Artaserse*, B. Galuppi   229
    1760, *Adriano*, various   297

Picciotto, Michele (Palermo)
    1780, *Adriano*, unknown   308
    1782, *Demofoonte*, G. Gazzaniga (1st ed.)   364

Pieraccini, Francesco (Pisa)
    1780, *Demofoonte*, unknown   362

Pieri, Cosimo Maria (Florence)
    1735, *Didone*, unknown   49
    1744, *Alessandro*, J. A. Hasse   122
    1744, *Artaserse*, E. R. Duni (1st ed.)   221
    1746, *Adriano*, G. Abos (1st ed.)   286
    1746, *Demofoonte*, unknown   331
    1748, *Artaserse*, D. Perez (1st ed.)   225
    1753, *Didone*, B. Galuppi or G. M. Orlandini?   55
    1755, *Demofoonte*, unknown   344
    1756, *Alessandro*, B. Galuppi   131

Pierron, Nicolas (Mannheim)
    1750, *Demofoonte*, J. A. Hasse   333
    1751, *Artaserse*, N. Jommelli   231

Pillera, J. (Lviv)
    1782, *Artaserse*, unknoen   256

Pirola, Gaetano (Milan)
    1782, *Didone*, P. Anfossi   88

Pisarri, Costantino (Bologna)
    1730, *Artaserse*, J. A. Hasse   200
    1743, *Demofoonte*, C. W. Gluck (+ F. Maggiore)   324

Pisarri, Ferdinando (Bologna)
    1774, *Alessandro*, G. Sciroli   153

Polloni, Pompeo & co. (Pisa)
    1770, *Artaserse*, various   247

Pomatelli, Bernardino (Ferrara)
    1765, *Artaserse*, J. A. Hasse   202

Porro & Bianchi (Pavia)
    1777, *Adriano*, J. Mysliveček   305

Pruscha, Ignaz (Prague)
    1748, *Artaserse*, unknown   226
    1750, *Alessandro*, G. M. Rutini (1st ed.)   144
    1759/60, *Demofoonte*, B. Galuppi   339
    1760, *Adriano*, G. Scarlatti   292
    1760, *Alessandro*, B. Galuppi   131
    1761, *Didone*, A. M. Mazzoni   73

Pruscha, Johanna (Prague)
    1764, *Alessandro*, D. Fischietti (1st ed.)   162
    1768, *Alessandro*, J. A. Koželuh (1st ed.)   165
    1771, *Adriano*, A. Sacchini   303
    1772, *Demofoonte*, J. A. Koželuh (1st ed.)   356
    1773, *Artaserse*, G. Paisiello   248

Puccinelli, brothers (Rome)
    1781, *Alessandro*, D. Cimarosa (1st ed.)   172
    1782, *Demofoonte*, G. Sarti (1st ed. – 3rd ver.)   344

Puccinelli, Crispino (Rome)
    1810, *Didone*, V. Fioravanti (1st ed.)   100

Puccinelli, Gioacchino (Rome)
    1786, *Alessandro*, L. Caruso (1st ed.)   176
    1788, *Artaserse*, P. Anfossi (1st ed.)   259

SC | Index III. Index of Names: Printers

Puccinelli, Ottavio (Rome)
    1763, *Artaserse*, N. Jommelli   232
    1768, *Artaserse*, A. Sacchini (1st ed.)   245

Quercetti, Domenicantonio (Osimo)
    1774, *Demofoonte*, P. Anfossi   357

Quillau, widow of (Paris)
    1755, Metastasio's works   75, 148, 237, 295, 344

Ramanzini, Dionisio (Verona)
    1740, *Alessandro*, J. A. Hasse   121
    1741, *Artaserse*, P. Chiarini (1st ed.)   217
    1745, *Alessandro*, P. Chiarini (1st ed.)   142
    1751, *Artaserse*, D. dal Barba + various (1st ed.)   235
    1757, *Demofoonte*, unknown   346
    1759, *Artaserse*, B. Galuppi   229
    1760, *Didone*, various   77
    1761, *Alessandro*, D. dal Barba (1st ed.)   154
    1764, *Alessandro*, various   162
    1770, *Artaserse*, A. Boroni   245
    1774, *Adriano*, various   306
    1779, *Alessandro*, A. Calegari (1st ed.)   170
    1785, *Artaserse*, F. Bertoni   252
    1787, *Alessandro*, F. Bianchi   174
    1796, *Didone*, G. Paisiello   98

Reichardt, Adam Friedrich (Ljubljana)
    1740, *Artaserse*, J. A. Hasse   201
    1742, *Didone*, P. Scalabrini and others   51

Reynell, Henry (London)
    1784, *Demofoonte*, various   362

Ricchini, Pietro (Cremona)
    1752, *Demofoonte*, G. F. Brivio   320
    1756, *Didone*, P. Chiarini   68

Ricciardi, Cristoforo (Naples)
    1743, *Artaserse*, L. Vinci   191
    1744, *Didone*, J. A. Hasse   60

Ricciardo, Francesco (Naples)
    1724, *Didone*, D. N. Sarro   41
    1738, *Artaserse*, L. Vinci   191

Ricordi (Milan)
    1823, *Didone*, S. Mercadante   107
    1827, *Alessandro*, G. Pacini   184

Riginaldi, Mario (Perugia)
    1781, *Artaserse*, G. Rust (1st ed.)   255
    1781, *Didone*, F. Zannetti   81

Riginaldi, Mario & Tantini, Filippo (Perugia)
    1777, *Adriano*, J. Mysliveček   305

Rioja y Gamboa, Francisco (Puerto de Santa María)
    1753, *Alessandro*, G. Scolari   145

Risaliti, Giovanni (Florence)
    1770, *Artaserse*, various   247
    1772, *Alessandro*, P. Anfossi   166
    1772, *Didone*, M. Mortellari (1st ed.)   86
    1777, *Alessandro*, N. Jommelli   149
    1778, *Didone*, various   92
    1780, *Demofoonte*, G. Rust (1st ed.)   363
    1783, *Artaserse*, G. Rust   256

Rizzi, Vincenzo (Venice)
    1826, *Didone*, S. Mercadante   105
    1827, *Didone*, S. Mercadante   106

Rommerskirchen, heirs of (Bonn)
    1748, *Artaserse*, F. Zoppis (1st ed.)   226

Rossetti, Marino (Venice)
    1725, *Didone*, T. G. Albinoni (1st ed.)   44
    1734, *Artaserse*, J. A. Hasse   200
    1735, *Demofoonte*, G. M. Schiassi (1st ed.)   316
    1736, *Alessandro*, J. A. Hasse   121
    1737, *Adriano*, G. Porta   279
    1738, *Alessandro*, J. A. Hasse   121
    1738, *Demofoonte*, G. Latilla (1st ed.)   319
    1739, *Alessandro*, J. A. Hasse   121
    1740, *Adriano*, G. A. Giai (1st ed.)   284
    1741, *Didone*, A. Bernasconi (1st ed.)   58
    1742, *Artaserse*, G. A. Paganelli   213

Rossi (Bergamo)
    1737, *Artaserse*, J. A. Hasse   200

Rossi, Francesco (Siena)
    1759, *Didone*, G. Brunetti (1st ed.)   77
    1770, *Artaserse*, various   247
    1781, *Demofoonte*, L. Vinci   321

Rossi–Ubaldi (Parma)
    1817, *Artaserse*, M. A. Portugal   264
    1817, *Didone*, F. Paër   101

SC | Index III. Index of Names: Printers

Roullet, Hervé (Paris)
   1783, *Didone*, N. Piccinni (1st ed. – 2nd ver.)   83
   1785, *Didone*, N. Piccinni   84

Roveri, Antonio & Casali, Matteo (Forlì)
   1809, *Adriano*, unknown   310

Roveri, Antonio & sons (Ravenna)
   1825, *Didone*, S. Mercadante   105

Royal print [Stamperia reale] (Rio de Janeiro)
   1812, *Artaserse*, M. A. Portugal   263

Royeriani, heirs of (Bratislava)
   1741, *Alessandro*, J. A. Hasse   121

Rumieri, Andrea (Venice)
   1726, *Didone*, T. G. Albinoni   44

Salaroli, Cristoforo (Parma)
   1745, *Didone*, N. Porpora   45

Salomoni, Generoso (Rome)
   1749, *Artaserse*, N. Jommelli (1st ed. – 1st ver.)   231

Salvoni, Luigi Bernardo (Piacenza)
   1748, *Artaserse*, G. Carcani (1st ed.)   225

Santini, Antonio & co. (Livorno)
   1753, *Artaserse*, unknown   237
   1754, *Adriano*, G. Scarlatti   291
   1758, *Adriano*, B. Galuppi   282

Santini, Giovanni (Bergamo)
   1755, *Artaserse*, G. B. Pescetti   236

Sanz, Antonio (Madrid)
   1738, *Alessandro*, F. Corselli   133

Saracco, Giambattista (Verona)
   1754, *Alessandro*, J. A. Hasse   122
   1755, *Didone*, unknown   75

Sassi, Clemente Maria (Bologna)
   1734, *Alessandro*, G. M. Schiassi (1st ed.)   128
   1743, *Alessandro*, N. Jommelli (1st ed.)   137
   1743, *Didone*, A. Bernasconi   58
   1745, *Artaserse*, J. A. Hasse   201
   1745, *Didone*, unknown   64
   1752, *Didone*, A. M. Mazzoni (1st ed.)   73
   1753, *Adriano*, M. Valentini (1st ed.)   292

   1754, *Artaserse*, unknown   237
   1756, *Demofoonte*, B. Galuppi   339
   1764, *Alessandro*, G. Sciroli   153
   1771, *Demofoonte*, various   356
   1772, *Didone*, various   86
   1773, *Alessandro*, various   167
   1787, *Alessandro*, F. Bianchi   174
   1789, *Artaserse*, P. A. Guglielmi   254
   1792, *Artaserse*, F. Bertoni   252

Schirmers, Johann (Bayreuth)
   1741, *Alessandro*, unknown   134

Schwivkerstschen Verlage (Leipzig)
   1789, *Adriano*, G. Astarita (arias)   312

Scotto, Giovanni Battista (Turin)
   1738, *Demofoonte*, G. F. Brivio (1st ed.)   320

Settari, Giovanni Antonio (Rome)
   1777, *Artaserse*, P. A. Guglielmi (1st ed.)   254

Siess, Joseph (Oldenburg)
   1784, *Didone*, G. Sarti   78

Simene, Saverio di (Camerino)
   1733, *Artaserse*, L. Vinci   191

Simoncelli, Giuseppe (Brescia)
   1832, *Didone*, S. Mercadante   106

Società Tipografica (Livorno)
   1800, *Alessandro*, P. Gnecco (1st ed.)   181

Società Tipografica (Palermo)
   1824, *Didone*, S. Mercadante   104
   1827, *Alessandro*, G. Pacini   183

Soliani, Bartolomeo (Modena)
   1739, *Artaserse*, J. A. Hasse   201
   1750, *Alessandro*, L. Vinci   113
   1750, *Artaserse*, unknown   228

Soliani, heirs of Bartolomeo (Modena)
   1770, *Adriano*, C. I. Monza (1st ed.)   303
   1772, *Artaserse*, G. Paisiello (1st ed.)   247
   1774, *Alessandro*, G. Paisiello (1st ed.)   167
   1774, *Demofoonte*, P. Anfossi   357
   1775, *Adriano*, G. Monti (1st ed.)   306
   1783, *Demofoonte*, A. Pio (1st ed.)   364

SC | Index III. Index of Names: Printers

1787, *Alessandro*, G. Paisiello — 167
1793, *Demofoonte*, A. Tarchi — 366

Solli (Palermo)
  1787, *Alessandro*, G. Sarti — 155

Spiering, Johann Heinrich (Hamburg)
  1743, *Artaserse*, P. Scalabrini and others — 214
  1744, *Didone*, P. Scalabrini and others — 51
  1746, *Artaserse*, P. Scalabrini and others — 214
  1746, *Didone*, P. Scalabrini and others — 51

Stamparia Nova (Venice)
  1733, *Didone*, T. G. Albinoni — 44

Stamperia del Pubblico (Siena)
  1757, *Demofoonte*, P. Vinci (1st ed.) — 347

Stamperia di Corte (Salzburg)
  1759, *Demofoonte*, J. E. Eberlin (1st ed.) — 349
  1764, *Adriano*, unknown — 272

Stamperia di Corte (Stockholm)
  1757, *Adriano*, F. A. B. Uttini (1st ed.) — 295

Stamperia di S. Tommaso dAquino (Bologna)
  1735, *Didone*, G. M. Schiassi (1st ed.) — 50
  1738, *Alessandro*, various — 134

Stamperia Gioaquiniana (Lisbon)
  1740, *Alessandro*, A. P. Fabbri (1st ed.) — 134

Stamperia Governiale [Stamperia dell... Governo] (Trieste)
  1785, *Alessandro*, F. Bianchi — 174
  1789, *Artaserse*, N. Zingarelli (1st ed.) — 260

Stamperia Reale (Lisbon)
  1775, *Demofoonte*, N. Jommelli — 327
  1776, *Alessandro*, N. Jommelli — 137

Stamperia Reale (Turin)
  1757, Metastasio's works — 75, 149, 238, 295, 346
  1766, *Alessandro*, A. Sacchini — 159

Stamperia Regia (Lodi)
  1778, *Alessandro*, J. C. Bach — 156

Stamperia dirimpetto all'Oratorio di S. Filippo Neri (Florence)
  1757, *Artaserse*, various — 238

1759, *Didone*, P. A. Auletta (1st ed.) — 77
1761, *Adriano*, unknown — 298

Stecchi, Giovanni Battista (Florence)
  1752, *Alessandro*, unknown — 146
  1768, *Alessandro*, J. G. Naumann (1st ed.) — 164

Stecchi, Giovanni Battista & Pagani, Anton Giuseppe (Florence)
  1772, *Didone*, unknown — 86

Stössel, Johann Konrad Dresden)
  1731, *Alessandro*, J. A. Hasse (1st ed.) — 121

Stössel, widow of (Dresden)
  1740, *Artaserse*, J. A. Hasse (1st ed. – 2nd ed.) — 201
  1742, *Didone*, J. A. Hasse (1st ed.) — 60
  1743, *Didone*, J. A. Hasse — 60
  1752, *Adriano*, J. A. Hasse (1st ed. – 2nd ver.) — 279
  1752, *Didone*, J. A. Hasse — 60

Stössel, widow of & Krause, J. K. (Dresden)
  1755, *Artaserse*, unknown — 238

Straussin, Elisabetta (Eichstätt)
  1768, *Adriano*, H. Mango (1st ed.) — 301

Stromer, Philipp Ludwig (Hamburg)
  1732, *Alessandro*, G. F. Händel — 117

Svare, Lars Nielsen (Copenhagen)
  1761, *Alessandro*, G. Sarti (1st ed.) — 154
  1762, *Didone*, G. Sarti (1st ed.) — 78
  1771, *Demofoonte*, G. Sarti (1st ed. – 2nd ver.) — 344

Swoboda, Johann Maximilian (Brno)
  1731, *Artaserse*, J. A. Hasse — 200
  1734, *Alessandro*, L. Vinci — 112
  1734, *Didone*, D. N. Sarro — 42
  1735, *Demofoonte*, G. M. Schiassi — 316

Swobodiana, Barbam (Brno)
  1737, *Adriano*, J. A. Hasse (1st ed.) — 279

Sylviana, Stamperia (Lisbon)
  1752, *Demofoonte*, D. Perez (1st ed.) — 341
  1753, *Didone*, D. Perez — 71
  1754, *Adriano*, D. Perez (1st ed.) — 293
  1754, *Artaserse*, D. Perez (1st ed. – 2nd ver.) — 225
  1755, *Alessandro*, D. Perez (1st ed. – 2nd ver.) — 139

SC | Index III. Index of Names: Printers

Tagliabò & Mangrini (Turin) – music
   1830, *Didone*, S. Mercadante   107

Tamburini, Cesare (Milan)
   1823, *Didone*, S. Mercadante   104

Tarigo, Bernardo (Genoa)
   1769, *Adriano*, various   302

Teruel, Francisco (Murcia)
   1759, *Artaserse*, unknown   239

Thuille, Joseph Franz (Munich)
   1763, *Artaserse*, A. Bernasconi (1st ed. – 2nd ver.)   223
   1766, *Demofoonte*, A. Bernasconi   321

Torner, José (Barcelona)
   1826, *Didone*, S. Mercadante   105

Torri, Francesco (Modena)
   1741, *Alessandro*, P. Pulli (1st ed.)   134
   1741, *Didone*, B. Galuppi   55
   1753, *Alessandro*, G. Scarlatti   147

Toscano, Antonino (Palermo)
   1761, *Adriano*, B. Galuppi   282
   1762, *Alessandro*, N. Piccinni   149
   1763, *Didone*, G. B. Lampugnani   53

Trabatti, heirs of Nicola (Lodi)
   1765, *Artaserse* G. Sartori (1st ed.)   244

Trento, Giulio (Treviso)
   1766, *Demofoonte*, P. A. Guglielmi   353

Turlino, Giacomo (Brescia)
   1733, *Alessandro*, L. Vinci   112
   1745, *Didone*, G. B. Lampugnani   53
   1749, *Artaserse*, P. Chiarini   217

Tyrrell, W. H. (Dublin)
   1800, *Didone*, G. Paisiello   98
   1808, *Didone*, G. Paisiello   99

Valenza, Francesco (Palermo)
   1748, *Demofoonte*, various   337

Valetta, Giovanni Battista. (Turin)
   1730, *Artaserse*, J. A. Hasse   200
   1731, *Alessandro*, N. Porpora (1st ed.)   115

Vallarsi, Jacopo (Verona)
   1733, *Artaserse*, J. A. Hasse   200

Valvasense, Stamperia (Venice)
   1763, *Alessandro*, A. Sacchini (1st ed.)   159
   1795, *Artaserse*, G. Nicolini (1st ed.)   263
   1795, *Demofoonte*, various   368

Van Ghelen, Johannes Peter (Vienna)
   1732, *Adriano*, A. Caldara (1st ed.)   271
   1733, *Demofoonte*, A. Caldara (1st ed.)   315
   1736, *Didone*, L. Vinci   46
   1738, *Demofoonte*, G. F. Brivio   320
   1739, *Artaserse*, unknown   216
   1740, *Didone*, various   54
   1741, *Didone*, various   54
   1743, *Adriano*, unknown   285
   1746, *Alessandro*, J. A. Hasse   122
   1746, *Artaserse*, A. Bernasconi (1st ed.)   223
   1748, *Alessandro*, G. C. Wagenseil   144
   1749, *Artaserse*, B. Galuppi (1st ed.)   228
   1749, *Didone*, N. Jommelli (1st ed.)   65
   1763, *Artaserse*, G. Scarlatti   224

Vedrotti, Ippolito (Reggio Emilia)
   1725, *Didone*, N. Porpora (1st ed.)   45
   1733, *Alessandro*, L. Vinci   112
   1743, *Demofoonte*, C. W. Gluck   324
   1750, *Adriano*, G. B. Pescetti (1st ed.)   289

Vedrotti, Ippolito & Davolio, Giuseppe (Reggio Emilia)
   1752, *Didone*, D. Perez   71
   1753, *Alessandro*, G. Scarlatti (1st ed.)   146

Vendrame Liberale (Udine)
   1826, *Didone*, S. Mercadante   105

Vendrami (Udine)
   1826, *Didone*, S. Mercadante   105

Vendramino, Marco (Brescia)
   1746, *Alessandro*, P. Pellegrini (1st ed.)   142
   1748, *Didone*, P. Chiarini (1st ed.)   68
   1754, *Didone*, G. B. Lampugnani   53

Verdi, Domenico Ambrogio (Florence)
   1725, *Didone*, unknown   45
   1730, *Artaserse*, L. Vinci   190
   1734, *Adriano*, unknown   273

SC | Index III. Index of Names: Printers

Vidali, brothers (Padua)
   1759, *Alessandro*, B. Galuppi — 131

Vignozzi (Livorno)
   1823, *Didone*, S. Mercadante — 104

Vimercati, Antonio (Don't break start of blockAlessandria)
   1739, *Demofoonte*, G. Reina (1st ed.) — 320
   1742, *Didone*, G. B. Lampugnani — 53

Vimercati, Ignazio (Alessandria)
   1769, *Adriano*, M. de Vicenti (1st ed.) — 302
   1776, *Demofoonte*, C. I. Monza (1st ed.) — 361
   1777, *Artaserse*, G. A. Re (1st ed.) — 254
   1778, *Alessandro*, M. de Vicenti (1st ed.) — 170

Viviani, Pietro Gaetano (Florence)
   1740, *Adriano*, unknown — 281

Vötter, Johann Jacob (Munich)
   1735, *Alessandro*, L. Vinci (x2) — 112
   1737, *Adriano*, G. B. Ferrandini (1st ed.) — 278
   1737, *Demofoonte*, G. B. Ferrandini (1st ed.) — 318
   1739, *Artaserse*, G. B. Ferrandini (1st ed.) — 216
   1755, *Adriano*, A. Bernasconi (1st ed. – 2nd ver.) — 277
   1755, *Alessandro*, B. Galuppi — 130
   1756, *Didone*, A. Bernasconi — 58
   1760, *Didone*, A. Bernasconi — 58

Walsh, John (London) – music
   1731, *Alessandro*, G. F. Händel — 119
   1734, *Artaserse*, G. F. Händel/L. Vinci — 209
   1734, *Artaserse*, various — 211
   1735, *Alessandro*, G. F. Händel — 118
   1736, *Adriano*, F. M. Veracini — 276
   1737, *Artaserse*, various — 211
   1739, *Adriano*, F. M. Veracini — 276
   1746, *Alessandro*, G. B. Lampugnani — 143
   1746, *Alessandro*, J. A. Hasse — 143
   1746, *Didone*, B. Galuppi — 56
   1750, *Adriano*, V. L. Ciampi — 289
   1754, *Didone*, V. L. Ciampi — 74
   1755, *Demofoonte*, various — 346
   1761, *Alessandro*, G. Cocchi + various — 155
   1761, *Didone*, D. Perez — 72
   s.d., *Artaserse*, D. Terradellas — 222

Wayland, L. (London)
   1789, *Alessandro*, A. Tarchi — 178

Welcker, Peter (London) – music
   1765, *Adriano*, J. C. Bach — 300
   1772, *Artaserse*, various — 249

Wessely, Albert Wilhelm (Prague)
   1731, *Didone*, T. G. Albinoni — 44

Widmanstadj, heirs of (Graz)
   1737, *Didone*, P. Scalabrini and others (1st ed.) — 50
   1738, *Alessandro*, J. A. Hasse — 121
   1738, *Artaserse*, P. Scalabrini and others (1st ed.) — 214
   1739, *Demofoonte*, various — 320
   1753, *Artaserse*, F. Maggiore (1st ed.) — 224

Wood, Thomas (London)
   1731, *Alessandro*, G. F. Händel (1st ed.) — 117
   1733, *Artaserse*, G. F. Händel + various (1st ed.) — 209
   1736, *Alessandro*, G. F. Händel — 117
   1737, *Didone*, L. Vinci (1st ed.) — 52
   1742, *Artaserse*, G. F. Brivio — 215

Woodfall, George (London)
   1748, *Didone*, J. A. Hasse (lib. + music) — 60, 63
   1750, *Adriano*, V. L. Ciampi — 288
   1754, *Artaserse*, J. A. Hasse — 201
   1754, *Didone*, V. L. Ciampi (1st ed.) — 74
   1755, *Demofoonte*, various — 346
   1756, *Alessandro*, various — 148
   1761, *Alessandro*, G. Cocchi + various (1st ed.) — 155
   1761, *Didone*, D. Perez — 71
   1764, *Alessandro*, G. Cocchi + various — 155
   1765, *Adriano*, J. C. Bach (1st ed.) — 299
   1765, *Demofoonte*, M. Vento (1st ed.) — 352
   1766, *Artaserse*, J. A. Hasse — 202
   1766, *Demofoonte*, M. Vento — 352
   1776, *Demofoonte*, M. Vento — 352

Zappata, Pietro Giuseppe & son (Turin)
   1740, *Adriano*, B. Galuppi (1st ed.) — 282
   1741, *Artaserse*, G. Arena (1st ed.) — 217
   1745, *Alessandro*, C. W. Gluck (1st ed.) — 142
   1750, *Didone*, D. M. B. Terradellas (1st ed.) — 69

Zappata, Pietro Giuseppe & Avondo, Giacomo Giuseppe (Turin)
   1754, *Demofoonte*, G. Manna (1st ed.) — 343

Zatta, Antonio (Venice) – music
   s.d., *Adriano*, G. Astarita — 312
   s.d., *Didone*, F. Bianchi — 95

Zatta, Antonio & sons (Venice) – music
    s.d., *Demofoonte*, G. Paisiello   360

Zempel, Giovanni & Mei, G. de (Rome)
    1730, *Alessandro*, L. Vinci (1st ed.)   112
    1730, *Artaserse*, L. Vinci (1st ed.)   190

Zerbini, Giovanni (Modena)
    1787, *Demofoonte*, unknown   367

Zotti, Romualdo (London)
    1808, *Didone*, G. Paisiello   99

Index IV. Theatres

Alessandria

Teatro Nuovo [T. di Alessandria]
    1776, *Demofoonte*, C. I. Monza (pr.)   361
    1777, *Artaserse*, G. A. Re (pr.)   254
    1778, *Alessandro*, M. de Vicenti (pr.)   170

Teatro Solerio
    1739, *Demofoonte*, G. Reina (pr.)   320
    1742, *Didone*, G. B. Lampugnani   52
    1769, *Adriano*, M. de Vicenti (pr.)   302

Unknown theatre
    1749, *Artaserse*, unknown   233
    1752, *Alessandro*, A. Calderara (pr.)   146

Amsterdam

Theatre [T. di Amstellodama]
    1755, *Alessandro*, unknown   148

Ancona

Teatro della Fenice
    1747, *Alessandro*, G. Abos (pr.)   143
    1790, *Artaserse*, F. Bertoni   251

Arezzo

Teatro Nuovo
    1741, *Didone*, D. N. Sarro   41

Barcelona

Teatre de la Santa Creu [T. di Barcelona]
    1750, *Alessandro*, G. Scolari   145
    1751, *Demofoonte*, B. Galuppi   338
    1752, *Didone*, G. Scolari (pr.)   72
    1753, *Didone*, G. Scolari   73
    1754, *Artaserse*, G. B. Ferrandini; G. Porta   216
    1762, *Alessandro*, G. Scolari   145
    1763, *Adriano*, G. Sciroli (pr.)   299
    1763, *Artaserse*, N. Piccinni and others   241
    1763, *Demofoonte*, B. Galuppi   338
    1763, *Didone*, G. Scolari   73
    1767, *Alessandro*, G. Scolari   145
    1767, *Didone*, unknown   81
    1772, *Demofoonte*, unknown   356
    1826, *Didone*, S. Mercadante   103
    1831, *Alessandro*, G. Pacini   182

Bassano del Grappa

Teatro Nuovo
    1741, *Artaserse*, J. A. Hasse   199

Bayreuth

Court theatre [Markgräfliches Opernhaus]
    1738, *Didone*, G. A. Paganelli (pr.)   52
    1748, *Artaserse*, J. A. Hasse   199

Bergamo

Teatro Riccardi
    1786, *Didone*, various   95
    1791, *Didone*, various   96

Teatro di Bergamo
    1738, *Artaserse*, J. A. Hasse   198
    1755, *Artaserse*, G. B. Pescetti   236

Unknown theatre
    1789, *Alessandro*, F. Bianchi   173

Berlin

Court theatre [T. Regio]
    1743, *Artaserse*, C. H. Graun (pr.)   218
    1744, *Alessandro*, C. H. Graun (pr.)   141

1744, *Artaserse*, C. H. Graun 218
1746, *Adriano*, C. H. Graun (pr.) 286
1746, *Demofoonte*, C. H. Graun (pr.) 330
1753, *Didone*, J. A. Hasse 59
1754, *Alessandro*, J. F. Agricola (pr.) 147
1770, *Didone*, J. A. Hasse 59
1774, *Demofoonte*, C. H. Graun 330
1777, *Alessandro*, J. A. Hasse 120
1783, *Artaserse*, C. H. Graun 218
1784, *Alessandro*, C. H. Graun 141
1799, *Didone*, N. Piccinni 83
1808, *Didone*, N. Piccinni 83

Unknown theatre
    1780, *Didone*, J. A. Hasse[NP] 59
    1826, *Didone* (pr.), B. Klein (pr.) 108
    1850, *Artaserse* (Ger.), H. L. E. Dorn (pr.) 264

Bologna

Nuovo Teatro Pubblico
    1772, *Didone*, various 86

Teatro Formagliari
    1734, *Alessandro*, G. M. Schiassi (pr.) 128
    1735, *Didone*, G. M. Schiassi 49
    1745, *Artaserse*, J. A. Hasse 199
    1745, *Didone*, unknown? 64
    1753, *Adriano*, M. Valentini (pr.) 292
    1753, *Didone*, A. M. Mazzoni (pr.) 73
    1754, *Artaserse*, unknown 237
    1756, *Demofoonte*, B. Galuppi 338
    1760, *Alessandro*, unknown 154
    1771, *Demofoonte*, various 356
    1773, *Alessandro*, unknown 167

Teatro Malvezzi
    1730, *Artaserse*, J. A. Hasse 197

Teatro Marsigli Rossi
    1744, *Demofoonte*, C. W. Gluck 323

Teatro Pubblico
    1764, *Alessandro*, G. Sciroli? 153

Teatro Zagnoni
    1787, *Alessandro*, F. Bianchi 173
    1789, *Artaserse*, P. A. Guglielmi 254

Bonn

Poppelsdorf Castle, Theatre of the
    1748, *Artaserse*, F. Zoppis (pr.) 226

Bratislava

Teatro Nuovo
    1741, *Alessandro*, J. A. Hasse 120

Unknown theatre
    1761, *Artaserse*, J. A. Hasse 199
    1780, *Didone*, G. Astarita (pr.) 93

Brescia

Teatro degli Erranti [T. dell' Accademia degli Erranti; T. di Brescia]
    1733, *Alessandro*, L. Vinci 111
    1741, *Adriano*, P. Giaino (pr.) 285
    1746, *Alessandro*, P. Pellegrini (pr.) 142
    1748, *Didone*, P. Chiarini (pr.) 68
    1754, *Didone*, G. B. Lampugnani 52
    1756, *Alessandro*, B. Galuppi 130
    1756, *Artaserse*, B. Galuppi 228
    1758, *Artaserse*, B. Galuppi 228
    1785, *Artaserse*, F. Bertoni 251

Teatro Grande
    1832, *Didone*, S. Mercadante 104

Brno

Teatro della Taverna
    1734, *Didone*, D. N. Sarro 41

Brunswick

Teatro Ducale [Grossen Braunschweigischen Theatre; T. di Braunsviga; T. Grande]
    1732, *Alessandro*, G. F. Händel 116
    1734, *Didone*, N. Porpora 45
    1737, *Adriano*, A. Caldara 271
    1737, *Artaserse*, G. A. Paganelli (pr.) 212
    1737, *Artaserse*, G. A. Paganelli and others 212
    1739, *Didone*, G. A. Paganelli 52
    1741, *Demofoonte*, G. Verocai 322
    1742, *Demofoonte*, G. Verocai 322
    1745, *Adriano*, G. Verocai (pr.) 285
    1745, *Artaserse*, C. H. Graun 218
    1750, *Adriano*, I. Fiorillo (pr.) 290

SC | Index IV. Theatres

1750, *Demofoonte*, I. Fiorillo (pr.) — 340
1751, *Artaserse*, I. Fiorillo (pr.) — 235
1751, *Demofoonte*, I. Fiorillo — 340
1751, *Didone*, I. Fiorillo (pr.) — 70
1752, *Alessandro*, I. Fiorillo (pr.) — 146
1762, *Adriano*, J. G. Schwanenberger (pr.) — 298
1762, *Adriano*, J. G. Schwanenberger — 298
1765, *Didone*, J. G. Schwanenberger (pr.) — 80
1784, *Didone*, F. Piticchio — 93

Cádiz

Teatro Italiano
    1764, *Alessandro*, D. Perez and others — 138
    1764, *Demofoonte*, B. Galuppi — 338
    1768, *Didone*, unknown — 82
    1770, *Demofoonte*, A. Bernasconi — 321

Cagliari

Teatro di Cagliari
    1750, *Artaserse*, G. Bollano? — 235

Caltagirone

Teatro di S. Francesco
    1736, *Adriano*, unknown — 278

Camerino

Teatro di Camerino [T. Pubblico]
    1733, *Artaserse*, L. Vinci — 190

Cartagena

Teatro de Cartagena
    1759, *Artaserse*, unknown — 239

Catania

Teatro dell'Alma Università delli Studi
    1740, *Artaserse*, unknown — 216
    1741, *Artaserse*, unknown — 216

Unknown theatre
    1760, *Demofoonte*, J. A. Hasse — 332

Cesena

Teatro Spada [T. del Palazzo Spada]
    1743, *Didone*, A. Bernasconi — 57

Città di Castello

Unknown theatre
    1742, *Alessandro*, R. di Capua (pr.) — 135

Como

Nuovo Teatro
    1813, *Adriano*, M. A. Portugal — 310

Copenhagen

Court theatre – Charlottenborg Palace [T. di Corte]
    1748, *Didone*, P. Scalabrini — 50
    1749, *Adriano*, P. Scalabrini (pr.) — 289
    1749, *Alessandro*, P. Scalabrini (pr.) — 144
    1749, *Artaserse*, P. Scalabrini and others — 214
    1749, *Demofoonte*, unknown — 337

Royal Danish Theatre [Regio T. Danese; T. Regio Danese; T. Regio di Copenaga; Theatre on Kongens Nytorv]
    1755, *Demofoonte*, G. Sarti (pr.) — 344
    1760, *Artaserse*, G. Sarti (pr.) — 240
    1761, *Alessandro*, G. Sarti (pr.) — 154
    1762, *Didone*, G. Sarti (pr.) — 78
    1771, *Alessandro*, G. Sarti — 154
    1771, *Demofoonte*, G. Sarti (2nd ver. – pr.) — 344
    1771, *Didone*, G. Sarti — 78

Corfù

Teatro di S. Giacomo
    1796, *Alessandro*, L. Caruso — 176

Crema

Teatro di Crema [T. Nuovo]
    1726, *Didone*, T. G. Albinoni — 43
    1745, *Didone*, G. B. Lampugnani — 52
    1753, *Adriano*, G. Cocchi (pr.) — 293
    1786, *Demofoonte*, A. Tarchi (pr.) — 365

Cremona

Private theatre [T. ... d'alcuni Particolari; T. ... di un nobile]
    1749, *Artaserse*, P. Chiarini — 217
    1752, *Demofoonte*, G. F. Brivio — 320
    1756, *Didone*, P. Chiarini — 68

SC | Index IV. Theatres

Teatro Nazari (1747–1784)
    1752, *Adriano*, unknown   291
    1766, *Artaserse*, G. B. Lampugnani   233
    1768, *Alessandro*, various (past.)   163
    1774, *Alessandro*, A. Sacchini   159
    1775, *Didone*, P. Anfossi   87
    1776, *Demofoonte*, G. Paisiello   358
    1776, *Didone*, P. Anfossi   87

→ *becomes*

Teatro dell'Associazione [T. della Nobile Associazione; T. della Società] (1785–1806)
    1786, *Alessandro*, L. Cherubini   172
    1786, *Artaserse*, D. Cimarosa   257
    1788, *Artaserse*, F. Bertoni   251

→ *becomes*

Teatro della Concordia (1806–)
    1825, *Didone*, S. Mercadante   103

Crescentino

Unknown theatre
    1776, *Didone*, D. F. Mombelli (pr.)   91

Dresden

Court theatre [Regio Elettoral T.; Regio T. alla Corte; T. di Corte; T. Elettorale]
    1731, *Alessandro*, J. A. Hasse (pr.)   119
    1740, *Artaserse*, J. A. Hasse (2nd ver. – pr.)   198
    1743, *Didone*, J. A. Hasse   59
    1748, *Demofoonte*, J. A. Hasse (pr.)   332
    1752, *Adriano*, J. A. Hasse (2nd ver. – pr.)   279
    1752, *Didone*, J. A. Hasse   59

Court theatre – Hubertusburg
    1742, *Didone*, J. 50A. Hasse (pr.)59

Nuovo Teatro Privilegiato [Kleines Hoftheater; Nuovo Real T. Privilegiato; Nuovo T.; Opernhaus am Zwinger]
    1746, *Artaserse*, P. Scalabrini and others   214
    1747, *Didone*, P. Scalabrini and others   50
    1755, *Artaserse*, unknown?   238

Royal theatre [Real teatro]
    1812, *Didone*, F. Paër   101
    1824, *Didone*, C. G. Reissiger (pr.)   108

Eichstätt

Court theatre
    1768, *Adriano*, H. Mango (pr.)   301

Erlangen

Unknown theatre (Court theatre?)
    1741, *Alessandro*, unknown   134

Esterháza

Court theatre [T. del Principe; T. d'Esterhazy; T. di Corte]
    1784, *Didone*, G. Sarti   78
    1787, *Alessandro*, F. Bianchi   173

Faenza

Teatro dei Remoti [T. degli Accademici Remoti; T. dell'Accademia dei Remoti; T. Pubblico dei Remoti]
    1745, *Alessandro*, L. Vinci   112
    1757, *Artaserse*, B. Galuppi   228
    1757, *Didone*, D. Perez   70

Fontainebleau → see Paris

Fano

Teatro della Fortuna
    1731, *Artaserse*, L. Vinci   189
    1745, *Didone*, A. Aurisicchio (pr.)   64

Ferrara

Teatro Bonacossi da S. Stefano [T. Bonacossi; T. da San Stefano]
    1731, *Artaserse*, L. Vinci   189
    1733, *Didone*, T. G. Albinoni   44
    1737, *Alessandro*, J. A. Hasse   119
    1741, *Adriano*, unknown   285
    1744, *Alessandro*, N. Jommelli (pr.)   137
    1745, *Artaserse*, L. Vinci   190
    1745, *Demofoonte*, C. W. Gluck   323
    1750, *Demofoonte*, F. A. B. Uttini (pr.)?   341
    1757, *Artaserse*, B. Galuppi   228
    1763, *Adriano*, unknown   298
    1763, *Didone*, G. Scolari   73
    1765, *Artaserse*, J. A. Hasse   199
    1766, *Demofoonte*, various   353

SC | Index IV. Theatres

Florence

Teatro Alfieri
    1830, *Didone*, S. Mercadante   104

Teatro degli Intrepidi [Regio T. degl'Intrepidi detto della Palla a corda]
    1780, *Artaserse*, L. Caruso   250
    1786, *Alessandro*, unknown + J. A. Hasse   175

Teatro dei Risoluti [Real T. dei Risoluti; T. in Via S. Maria]
    1772, *Didone*, unknown   86
    1795, *Didone*, G. Paisiello   98

Teatro del Cocomero [T. di Via del Cocomero]
    1730, *Artaserse*, L. Vinci   189
    1732, *Alessandro*, L. Vinci   111
    1740, *Artaserse*, L. Vinci   190
    1741, *Demofoonte*, G. Verocai (pr.)   322
    1752, *Alessandro*, unknown   146
    1768, *Alessandro*, J. G. Naumann (pr.)   164
    1773, *Demofoonte*, P. Anfossi   356
    1776, *Adriano*, J. Mysliveček   305

Teatro della Pergola [T. di Via della Pergola; Regio T. di Via della Pergola]
    1725, *Didone*, unknown   44
    1734, *Adriano*, unknown   273
    1735, *Didone*, unknown   49
    1740, *Alessandro*, various (past.)   134
    1744, *Alessandro*, J. A. Hasse   120
    1744, *Artaserse*, E. R. Duni (pr.)   221
    1746, *Adriano*, G. Abos (pr.)   286
    1746, *Demofoonte*, unknown   331
    1748, *Artaserse*, D. Perez (pr.)   225
    1753, *Didone*, B. Galuppi or G. M. Orlandini?   55
    1755, *Demofoonte*, unknown   344
    1756, *Alessandro*, B. Galuppi   130
    1757, *Artaserse*, unknown   238
    1759, *Didone*, P. A. Auletta (pr.)   77
    1761, *Adriano*, unknown   297
    1762, *Alessandro*, B. Galuppi   130
    1762, *Demofoonte*, various   350
    1770, *Artaserse*, various   247
    1772, *Alessandro*, P. Anfossi   165
    1772, *Didone*, M. Mortellari (pr.)   86
    1777, *Alessandro*, N. Piccinni   149
    1778, *Didone*, various   91
    1780, *Demofoonte*, G. Rust (pr.)   363
    1783, *Artaserse*, G. Rust   255
    1786, *Didone*, various   95
    1788, *Demofoonte*, various   368
    1792, *Artaserse*, various   262
    1802, *Alessandro*, A. Tarchi   178
    1810, *Artaserse*, M. A. Portugal   263
    1817, *Didone*, F. Paër   101
    1825, *Didone*, S. Mercadante   103

Teatro Pagliano
    1836, *Demofoonte*, Sborgi (pr.)   371

Foligno

Teatro dell'Aquila
    1763, *Artaserse*, N. Piccinni   241

Forlì

Teatro Pubblico [Nuovo T. Pubblico; T. Comunale; T. della Communità; T. del Pubblico]
    1752, *Artaserse*, G. B. Ferrandini; G. Porta   216
    1766, *Demofoonte*, J. A. Schuster (pr.)   360
    1776, *Artaserse*, F. Bertoni (pr.)   251
    1779, *Didone*, B. Ottani (pr.)   92
    1809, *Adriano*, unknown   310

Genoa

Teatro da S. Agostino
    1730, *Artaserse*, J. A. Hasse?   197
    1734, *Adriano*, P. G. Sandoni (pr.)   273
    1742, *Artaserse*, P. Chiarini   217
    1743, *Alessandro*, F. A. B. Uttini? (pr.)   136
    1746, *Alessandro*, J. A. Hasse (x2)   120
    1758, *Alessandro*, G. Sciroli? (pr.)   153
    1762, *Artaserse*, F. Zannetti and other (pr.)   241
    1765, *Artaserse*, various (incl. G. Colla?)   244
    1774, *Demofoonte*, P. Anfossi and others   356
    1776, *Adriano*, unknown   306
    1777, *Artaserse*, F. Bertoni   251
    1778, *Didone*, various   91
    1780, *Alessandro*, F. Alessandri (pr.)   171
    1781, *Demofoonte*, F. Bianchi (pr.)   363
    1785, *Alessandro*, V. Chiavacci (pr.)   173
    1787, *Didone*, various   95
    1788, *Artaserse*, F. Bertoni (rev. ver.)   251
    1792, *Demofoonte*, unknown   370
    1794, *Artaserse*, unknown   262
    1794, *Didone*, G. Gazzaniga   96
    1824, *Didone*, S. Mercadante   103

SC | Index IV. Theatres

Teatro del Falcone
    1732, *Alessandro*, L. A. Predieri?   115
    1735, *Demofoonte*, P. V. Chiocchetti (pr.)   318
    1740, *Artaserse*, J. A. Hasse   198
    1744, *Alessandro*, D. Perez (pr.)   138
    1748, *Didone*, unknown   68
    1751, *Adriano*, A. Adolfati (pr.)   290
    1769, *Adriano*, unknown   302
    1769, *Alessandro*, F. Bertoni (pr.)   164

Gorizia

Teatro di Gorizia
    1826, *Didone*, S. Mercadante   103

Unknown theatre
    1745, *Adriano*, unknown   285

Graz

Theater am Tummel-Platz [T. al Tummel-Plaz]
    1737, *Didone*, P. Scalabrini and others (pr.)   50
    1738, *Alessandro*, J. A. Hasse (pr.)   120
    1738, *Artaserse*, P. Scalabrini and others   214
    1739, *Demofoonte*, unknown   320
    1741, *Didone*, P. Scalabrini and others   50
    1753, *Artaserse*, F. Maggiore   223

Hamburg

Oper am Gänsemarkt [Hamburgischen Schau-Platz; T. di Amburgo; Theater am Gänsemarkt]
    1731, *Didone* (Ger.), N. Porpora   45
    1732, *Alessandro*, G. F. Händel + G. P. Telemann   116
    1736, *Alessandro*, G. F. Händel + G. P. Telemann   116
    1743, *Artaserse*, P. Scalabrini and others (pr.)   214
    1744, *Didone*, P. Scalabrini   50
    1746, *Artaserse*, P. Scalabrini and others   214
    1746, *Didone*, P. Scalabrini and others   50
    1747, *Didone*, P. Scalabrini and others   50

Havana

Teatro Coliseo
    1776, *Didone*, N. Piccinni   83

Holešov

Rottal Theatre [T. Rottal]
    1733, *Artaserse*, E. Bambini (pr.)   208

Imola

Teatro dei Cavalieri [T. dei Cavalieri Associati]
    1792, *Artaserse*, F. Bertoni   251

Jaroměřice

Questenberg Castle, Theatre at
    1736, *Didone*, L. Vinci   46
    1737, *Didone*, L. Vinci   46
    1738, *Demofoonte*, G. F. Brivio and others?   320

Jesi

Teatro di Jesi
    1734, *Alessandro*, G. M. Jesi   128

Kassel

Theatre [T. in Cassel]
    1765, *Artaserse*, I. Fiorillo   235
    1768, *Didone*, unknown   82
    1777, *Adriano*, J. A. Hasse   279
    1780, *Didone*, unknown   93

Klagenfurt

Unknown theatre
    1738, *Artaserse*, J. A. Hasse   198
    1739, *Alessandro*, J. A. Hasse?   120

Kremsier

Unknown theatre
    1731, *Artaserse*, J. A. Hasse   198

La Valletta

Teatro Manoel [Teatro della città]
    1735, *Artaserse*, J. A. Hasse   198
    1765, *Demofoonte*, J. A. Hasse   332

Leipzig

City hall theatre
    1747, *Didone*, P. Scalabrini and others   50

Linz

Teatro Arciducale
    1730?, *Didone*, T. G. Albinoni   44

SC | Index IV. Theatres

Lisbon

Academy on the Trinità Square [Salla dell'Accademia; Sala dell'Accademia alla Piazza della Trinità; Teatro alla Trinità]
    1736, *Alessandro*, G. M. Schiassi (2nd ver. – pr.)   128
    1737, *Artaserse*, G. M. Schiassi (pr.)   213
    1737, *Demofoonte*, G. M. Schiassi   316

Court theatre – Palácio da Ajuda [Gran Teatro di Corte; Real Teatro dell'Ajuda; Real Teatro di Corte; Teatro dell'Ajuda; Teatro di Corte]
    1752, *Demofoonte*, D. Perez (pr.)   341
    1754, *Artaserse*, D. Perez (2nd ver. – pr.)   225
    1775, *Demofoonte*, N. Jommelli (3rd rev. ver.)   326
    1776, *Alessandro*, N. Jommelli (rev. ver.)   137

Court theatre – Palácio de Salvaterra de Magos [Real Teatro de Salvaterra; Teatro Reale di Salvaterra; Villa de Salvaterra]
    1753, *Didone*, D. Perez   70
    1754, *Adriano*, D. Perez (pr.)   293

Nossa Senhora do Cabo
    1753, *Demofoonte* (Port.), unknown   342

Royal theatre – Teatro do Tejo [Gran Teatro nuovamente eretto alla real corte]
    1755, *Alessandro*, D. Perez (2nd ver. – pr.)   138

Teatro de Rua dos Condes [Teatro della Rua dos Condes; Teatro Nuovo della Rua dos Condes]
    1740, *Alessandro*, A. P. Fabbri (pr.)   134
    1741, *Didone*, R. di Capua (pr.)   58
    1768, *Artaserse*, G. Scolari   238

Teatro do Bairro Alto
    1765, *Didone*, D. Perez   70

Teatro de São Carlos [Regio Teatro de San Carlos; Regio Teatro di S. Carlo; Teatro di S. Carlo; Teatro Nacional de São Carlos]
    1799, *Didone*, S. Marino and others   100
    1800, *Alessandro*, L. Caruso (x2)   176
    1805, *Alessandro*, D. Perez   138
    1801, *Alessandro*, L. Caruso   176
    1801, *Artaserse*, D. Cimarosa   257
    1803, *Didone*, S. Marino and others   100
    1806, *Artaserse*, M. A. Portugal (pr.)   263
    1808, *Demofoonte*, M. A. Portugal (2nd ver. – pr.)   370
    1819, *Demofoonte*, M. A. Portugal   370
    1827, *Alessandro*, G. Pacini   182
    1827, *Didone*, S. Mercadante   104
    1828, *Adriano*, S. Mercadante (pr. + rvl)   311

Livorno

Teatro da S. Sebastiano [T. a S. Sebastiano; T. Bonfigli da S. Sebastiano; T. di Livorno; T. di Livorno a S. Sebastiano; T. in Via Remota; T. Pubblico a S. Sebastiano]
    1727, *Didone*, unknown   47
    1731, *Alessandro*, L. Vinci and others   111
    1731, *Artaserse*, L. Vinci   189
    1737, *Demofoonte*, various   318
    1738, *Artaserse*, D. Zamparelli and other (pr.)   215
    1743, *Alessandro*, unknown   135
    1746, *Adriano*, unknown   288
    1749, *Artaserse*, unknown   227
    1752, *Demofoonte*, unknown   341
    1752, *Didone*, F. Poncini Zilioli (pr.)   72
    1753, *Artaserse*, unknown   236
    1754, *Adriano*, G. Scarlatti   291
    1758, *Adriano*, B. Galuppi (2nd ver. – pr.)   281
    1760, *Artaserse*, D. Zamparelli and other   215
    1766, *Didone*, F. Zannetti (pr.)   80
    1767, *Adriano*, G. Scarlatti   291
    1771, *Alessandro*, A. Sacchini   159
    1773, *Demofoonte*, M. S. Berezovskij (pr.)   358
    1777, *Adriano*, unknown   307

Teatro degli Armeni
    1782, *Adriano*, L. Cherubini (pr.)   308
    1782, *Artaserse*, G. Rust   255
    1787, *Demofoonte*, various   367
    1788, *Alessandro*, L. Cherubini   172
    1789, *Artaserse*, G. Andreozzi (pr.)   262

→ *becomes*

Teatro degli Avvalorati [Regio T. dell'Accademia degli Avvalorati; Regio T. degl'… signori Accademici Avvalorati; T. degli Accademici Avvalorati]
    1791, *Alessandro*, A. Tarchi (rev. ver.)   178
    1791, *Demofoonte*, A. Tarchi   365
    1794, *Artaserse*, N. Isouard   262
    1800, *Alessandro*, P. Gnecco (pr.)   181
    1823, *Didone*, S. Mercadante   103

Ljubljana

Palazzo Provinciale
- 1740, *Artaserse*, J. A. Hasse — 198
- 1742, *Didone*, P. Scalabrini — 50

Lodi

Teatro di Lodi
- 1754, *Demofoonte*, N. Jommelli — 326
- 1756, *Alessandro*, B. Galuppi — 130
- 1763, *Alessandro*, J. C. Bach — 156
- 1765, *Artaserse*, G. Sartori (pr.) — 244
- 1778, *Alessandro*, J. C. Bach — 156
- 1779, *Artaserse*, G. B. Pescetti — 236

London

Covent Garden, Royal Opera House [Theatre-Royal in Covent Garden]
- 1736, *Alessandro*, G. F. Händel — 116
- 1737, *Didone*, L. Vinci, Händel and others (past.) — 51
- 1762, *Artaserse* (En.), T. A. Arne (pr.) — 241
- 1813, *Artaserse* (En.), H. R. Bishop — 264

Harmonical Meeting, Soho Square
- 1771, *Artaserse*, M. Vento (pr.) — 247

King's Theatre in the Haymarket [T. di S.M.B.; T. Reale/Regio T. di Hay-Market]
- 1731, *Alessandro*, G. F. Händel (pr.) — 116
- 1734, *Artaserse*, G. F. Händel and others (x2) — 209
- 1734, *Artaserse*, various — 210
- 1735, *Adriano*, F. M. Veracini (pr.) — 275
- 1735, *Artaserse*, various (x3) — 210
- 1736, *Adriano*, F. M. Veracini (x2) — 275
- 1736, *Artaserse*, various (x3) — 210
- 1737, *Demofoonte*, E. R. Duni (pr.) — 318
- 1742, *Artaserse*, G. F. Brivio (2nd ver. – pr.) — 215
- 1743, *Alessandro*, G. F. Händel (+ G. B. Lampugnani) — 116
- 1746, *Alessandro*, G. B. Lampugnani and others (pr.) — 142
- 1748, *Alessandro*, G. F. Händel (+ G. B. Lampugnani) (x2) — 116
- 1748, *Didone*, J. A. Hasse — 59
- 1750, *Adriano*, V. L. Ciampi (rev. ver. – pr.) — 288
- 1754, *Artaserse*, J. A. Hasse — 199
- 1754, *Didone*, V. L. Ciampi (pr.) — 74
- 1754, *Didone*, V. L. Ciampi — 74
- 1755, *Demofoonte*, various — 345
- 1756, *Alessandro*, various — 148
- 1761, *Alessandro*, G. Cocchi and others — 155
- 1761, *Didone*, D. Perez — 70
- 1764, *Alessandro*, G. Cocchi and others — 155
- 1765, *Adriano*, J. C. Bach (pr.) — 299
- 1765, *Demofoonte*, M. Vento (pr.) — 352
- 1766, *Artaserse*, J. A. Hasse — 199
- 1766, *Demofoonte*, M. Vento (x2) — 352
- 1772, *Artaserse*, various — 248
- 1773, *Artaserse*, various — 248
- 1774, *Alessandro*, D. Corri (pr.) — 168
- 1774, *Artaserse*, L. Caruso? — 250
- 1775, *Didone*, various — 89
- 1776, *Demofoonte*, M. Vento — 352
- 1778, *Demofoonte*, various — 361
- 1779, *Alessandro*, various — 170
- 1779, *Artaserse*, F. Bertoni — 251
- 1784, *Demofoonte*, various — 362
- 1785, *Artaserse*, various — 258
- 1786, *Didone*, various — 94
- 1787, *Didone*, various — 94
- 1789, *Alessandro*, A. Tarchi — 178
- 1790, *Alessandro*, A. Tarchi — 178
- 1790, *Demofoonte*, V. Federici (pr.) — 369
- 1792, *Didone*, various — 97
- 1799, *Didone*, G. Paisiello — 98
- 1808, *Didone*, G. Paisiello — 98
- 1814, *Didone*, F. Paër (2nd ver. – pr.) — 101
- 1827, *Didone*, S. Mercadante — 104

Theatre Royal Drury Lane
- 1821, *Demofoonte*, C. E. Horn (pr.) — 371

Unknown theatre
- 1774, *Artaserse*, T. Giordani and others — 248
- 1840, *Artaserse* (En.), C. Lucas (pr.) — 264

Lübeck

Unknown theatre
- 1755, *Artaserse*, J. A. Hasse and others (past.) — 199

Lucca

Teatro del Giglio
- 1823, *Didone*, S. Mercadante — 103

Teatro Pubblico [T. di Lucca]
- 1729, *Didone*, L. Vinci — 46
- 1730, *Artaserse*, J. A. Hasse — 197
- 1740, *Alessandro*, L. Vinci — 112

SC | Index IV. Theatres

1740, *Didone*, various (past.)	54
1741, *Demofoonte*, L. Vinci (pr.)	321
1747, *Artaserse*, G. Scarlatti (pr.)	224
1750, *Alessandro*, G. Abos	143
1752, *Adriano*, G. Scarlatti	291
1754, *Demofoonte*, G. Cocchi	343
1757, *Artaserse*, B. Galuppi	228
1759, *Alessandro*, J. A. Hasse	120
1760, *Didone*, A. Ferradini (pr.)	77
1764, *Adriano*, C. G. Concialini and others (pr.)	299
1765, *Demofoonte*, various	353
1766, *Alessandro*, unknown	162
1770, *Artaserse*, various	247
1770, *Didone*, various	85
1775, *Didone*, P. Anfossi	87
1777, *Artaserse*, F. Bertoni	251
1782, *Demofoonte*, various	364
1783, *Alessandro*, M. Mortellari	170
1786, *Didone*, G. Sarti	78

Ludwigsburg → see Stuttgart

Lviv

1782, *Artaserse*, unknown	256

Lyon

Theatre

1787, *Didone* (Fr.), N. Piccinni	83

Macerata

Teatro di Macerata

1740, *Artaserse*, L. Vinci	190

Teatro dei Nobili [T. Nuovo]

1774, *Demofoonte*, P. Anfossi	356
1777, *Artaserse*, F. Bertoni	251

Madrid

Court theatre – Teatro del Buen Retiro

1738, *Alessandro*, F. Corselli (pr., x3)	133
1749, *Artaserse*, G. B Mele and others (pr., x2)	227
1750, *Artaserse*, G. B. Mele and others	227
1750, *Demofoonte*, B. Galuppi (pr., x2)	337–338
1751, *Demofoonte*, B. Galuppi	338
1752, *Demofoonte*, B. Galuppi (x2)	338
1752, *Didone*, B. Galuppi (rev. version – pr., x2)	54
1753, *Didone*, B. Galuppi	55
1754, *Didone*, B. Galuppi (x2)	55
1755, *Demofoonte*, B. Galuppi (x2)	338
1755, *Didone*, B. Galuppi (x3)	55
1757, *Adriano*, N. Conforto (rev. ver. – pr.)	294
1758, *Alessandro*, unknown[NP]	153
1758, *Adriano*, N. Conforto	294

Teatro de los Caños del Peral

1738, *Artaserse*, J. A. Hasse + L. Vinci	198
1738, *Demofoonte*, G. M. Schiassi and others	316
1791, *Didone*, G. Andreozzi	93
1792, *Alessandro*, L. Caruso	176
1792, *Didone*, G. Sarti + G. Paisiello	78

Unknown theatre

1790, *Demofoonte*, various	369

Mannheim

Court theatre [Corte Elettorale Palatina; T. di Corte]

1750, *Demofoonte*, J. A. Hasse	332
1751, *Artaserse*, N. Jommelli (rev. version)	231
1766, *Alessandro*, G. di Majo (pr.)	162
1767, *Alessandro*, G. di Majo	162
1768, *Adriano*, I. Holzbauer (pr.)	301
1769, *Adriano*, I. Holzbauer (x2)	301
1779, *Didone*, I. Holzbauer (pr.)	92
1784, *Didone* (Ger.), I. Holzbauer	92
1811, *Alessandro* (Ger.), A. Ritter, pr.	182

Mantua

Teatro Regio Ducale [Regio Ducal Teatro; T. Nuovo]

1745, *Didone*, unknown	64
1784, *Alessandro*, L. Cherubini (pr.)	172
1787, *Demofoonte*, L. Gatti (pr.)	366
1788, *Artaserse*, A. Tarchi (pr.)	259

Teatro Nuovo della Società

1825, *Didone*, S. Mercadante	103

Teatro Arciducale [T. Vecchio; Regio Ducal T. Vecchio]

1727, *Didone*, unknown	48
1737, *Adriano*, G. Porta (pr.)	278
1738, *Alessandro*, B. Galuppi (pr.)	129
1753, *Artaserse*, B. Galuppi	227
1755, *Didone*, D. Perez	70
1758, *Demofoonte*, T. Traetta (pr.)	347
1768, *Alessandro*, L. Gatti (pr.)	163
1768, *Artaserse*, various	246
1770, *Demofoonte*, T. Traetta	347
1793, *Didone*, G. Sarti	78

471

SC | Index IV. Theatres

Messina

Teatro della Monizione [T. di Messina]
    1733, *Didone*, unknown   49

Milan

Teatro alla Scala [T. Scala]
    1788, *Alessandro*, A. Tarchi (pr.)   178
    1790, *Adriano*, S. Nasolini (pr.)   309
    1794, *Artaserse*, N. A. Zingarelli (2nd ver. – pr.)   260
    1794, *Demofoonte*, M. A. Portugal (pr.)   370
    1827, *Alessandro*, G. Pacini   182
    1827, *Didone*, S. Mercadante   103

Teatro Interinale
    1777, *Artaserse*, F. Bertoni   251

Teatro Re in Salvatore
    1815, *Adriano*, M. A. Portugal   310
    1823, *Didone*, S. Mercadante   103

Teatro Regio Ducale [Regio Ducal T.; T. Ducale]
    1729, *Didone*, T. G. Albinoni   43
    1731, *Alessandro*, L. A. Predieri (pr.)   115
    1731, *Artaserse*, J. A. Hasse   198
    1732, *Alessandro*, J. A. Hasse   119
    1736, *Adriano*, A. Bernasconi (1st ver. – pr.)   276
    1739, *Didone*, G. F. Brivio or E. R. Duni (pr.)   52
    1742, *Alessandro*, G. F. Brivio (pr.)   134
    1742, *Artaserse*, C. W. Gluck (pr.)   218
    1742, *Demofoonte*, unknown   323
    1743, *Demofoonte*, C. W. Gluck (pr.)   323
    1747, *Demofoonte*, C. W. Gluck   323
    1750, *Artaserse*, G. B. Lampugnani (pr.)   233
    1751, *Adriano*, A. G. Pampani (pr.)   290
    1752, *Alessandro*, D. Perez   138
    1752, *Artaserse*, G. B. Pescetti (pr.)   236
    1753, *Demofoonte*, N. Jommelli (2nd ver. – pr.)   326
    1755, *Didone*, G. A. Fioroni (pr.)   74
    1757, *Artaserse*, Q. Gasparini (pr.)   238
    1759, *Alessandro*, I. Holzbauer (pr.)   153
    1759, *Demofoonte*, A. Ferradini (pr.)   348
    1763, *Adriano*, G. Colla (pr.)   298
    1763, *Didone*, T. Traetta (2nd ver. – pr.)   75
    1770, *Didone*, I. Celoniati (pr.)   82
    1775, *Alessandro*, C. Monza (pr.)   169

Modena

Teatro Ducale [T. di Corte]
    1770, *Adriano*, A. Tozzi (pr.)   303
    1772, *Artaserse*, G. Paisiello (pr.)   247
    1774, *Alessandro*, G. Paisiello   167
    1774, *Demofoonte*, P. Anfossi   356
    1775, *Adriano*, G. Monti (pr.)   306

Teatro Molza
    1739, *Artaserse*, J. A. Hasse   198
    1741, *Alessandro*, P. Pulli (pr.)   134
    1741, *Didone*, B. Galuppi (pr.)   54

Teatro Rangoni [T. Rangone]
    1783, *Demofoonte*, A. Pio (pr.)   364
    1787, *Alessandro*, G. Paisiello   167
    1787, *Demofoonte*, unknown   367
    1790, *Artaserse*, A. Tarchi   259
    1793, *Demofoonte*, A. Tarchi   365

Montepulciano

Teatro Nuovo
    1762, *Artaserse*, various   243

Munich

Court theatre [Hoftheater; T. di Corte; T. di S.A.S.E.; T. Elettorale]
    1735, *Alessandro*, L. Vinci and others   111
    1737, *Adriano*, G. B. Ferrandini (pr.)   278
    1737, *Demofoonte*, G. B. Ferrandini (pr.)   318
    1739, *Artaserse*, G. B. Ferrandini; G. Porta (pr.)   216
    1755, *Adriano*, A. Bernasconi (2nd ver. – pr.)   276
    1755, *Alessandro*, B. Galuppi   130
    1756, *Didone*, A. Bernasconi (2nd ver. – pr.)   58
    1760, *Didone*, A. Bernasconi   58
    1763, *Artaserse*, A. Bernasconi   223
    1766, *Demofoonte*, A. Bernasconi (rev. ver.)   321
    1811, *Demofoonte*, P. J. von Lindpaintner (pr.)   371

Naples

Teatro di S. Bartolomeo
    1724, *Didone*, D. N. Sarro (pr.)   41
    1732, *Alessandro*, F. Mancini (pr.)   127
    1734, *Adriano*, G. B. Pergolesi (pr.)   273
    1735, *Demofoonte*, D. N. Sarro; F. Mancini; L. Leo (pr.)   316
    1736, *Alessandro*, J. A. Hasse   119

SC | Index IV. Theatres

Teatro di S. Carlo [Real T. di S. Carlo]
- 1738, *Artaserse*, L. Vinci — 190
- 1739, *Adriano*, G. A. Ristori (pr.) — 281
- 1741, *Demofoonte*, L. Leo (pr.) — 322
- 1743, *Alessandro*, D. N. Sarro (pr.) — 135
- 1743, *Artaserse*, L. Vinci — 190
- 1744, *Didone*, J. A. Hasse — 59
- 1747, *Adriano*, G. Latilla (pr.) — 288
- 1749, *Alessandro*, D. Perez — 138
- 1749, *Artaserse*, D. Perez — 225
- 1750, *Adriano*, B. Galuppi — 281
- 1750, *Demofoonte*, J. A. Hasse — 332
- 1753, *Didone*, G. B. Lampugnani (2nd ver. – pr.) — 52
- 1754, *Adriano*, N. Conforto (pr.) — 294
- 1755, *Adriano*, J. A. Hasse — 279
- 1754, *Alessandro*, B. Galuppi — 129
- 1758, *Demofoonte*, J. A. Hasse (3rd ver. – pr.) — 332
- 1759, *Adriano* B. Galuppi (3rd ver. – pr.) — 281
- 1760, *Artaserse*, J. A. Hasse (3rd ver. – pr.) — 199
- 1762, *Alessandro*, J. C. Bach (pr.) — 156
- 1762, *Artaserse*, J. A. Hasse — 199
- 1762, *Demofoonte*, N. Piccinni — 349
- 1764, *Didone*, T. Traetta (3rd ver. – pr.) — 75
- 1765, *Adriano*, G. di Majo (pr.) — 300
- 1767, *Alessandro*, G. di Majo — 162
- 1768, *Alessandro*, A. Sacchini (2nd ver. – pr.) — 159
- 1768, *Artaserse*, N. Piccinni (2nd ver. – pr.) — 242
- 1769, *Adriano*, C. I. Monza (pr.) — 302
- 1770, *Demofoonte*, N. Jommelli (4th ver.) — 326
- 1770, *Didone*, G. Insanguine (pr.) — 85
- 1772, *Didone*, B. Galuppi — 55
- 1772, *Didone*, G. Insanguine — 85
- 1773, *Adriano*, G. Insanguine (pr.) — 305
- 1773, *Adriano*, J. Mysliveček (pr.) — 305
- 1774, *Alessandro*, N. Piccinni (2nd ver. – pr.) — 149
- 1774, *Artaserse*, J. Mysliveček (2nd ver. – pr.) — 249
- 1775, *Demofoonte*, J. Mysliveček (pr.) — 353
- 1776, *Didone*, J. A. Schuster (pr.) — 89
- 1780, *Didone*, N. Piccinni — 83
- 1783, *Artaserse*, F. Alessandri (pr.) — 256
- 1788, *Didone*, P. Anfossi (2nd ver. – pr.) — 87
- 1789, *Alessandro*, P. A. Guglielmi (pr.) — 180
- 1792, *Alessandro*, N. Piccinni — 149
- 1794, *Didone*, G. Paisiello (pr.) — 98
- 1824, *Alessandro*, G. Pacini (pr.) — 182
- 1825, *Didone*, S. Mercadante (2nd ver. – pr.) — 103

Unknown theatre
- 1731, *Artaserse*, L. Vinci — 190
- 1733, *Artaserse*, L. Vinci — 190

- 1740, *Adriano*, M. Caballone? (pr.) — 285
- 1770, *Didone*, B. Galuppi[NP] — 55
- 1811, *Adriano*, V. Migliorucci? (pr.) — 311

Oranienbaum → see St. Petersburg

Padua

Teatro Nuovo
- 1751, *Artaserse*, B. Galuppi (2nd ver. – pr.) — 227
- 1758, *Demofoonte*, B. Galuppi (2nd ver. – pr.) — 338
- 1766, *Alessandro*, G. Sarti — 154
- 1771, *Adriano*, P. Anfossi (pr.) — 304
- 1777, *Adriano*, P. Anfossi — 304
- 1782, *Didone*, G. Sarti (2nd ver. – pr.) — 78
- 1783, *Demofoonte*, F. Alessandri (pr.) — 364
- 1787, *Artaserse*, F. Bianchi (pr.) — 258
- 1789, *Artaserse*, F. Bianchi — 258
- 1791, *Didone*, various — 97
- 1793, *Didone*, various — 96
- 1809, *Adriano*, M. A. Portugal (pr.) — 310

Teatro Obizzi
- 1737, *Alessandro*, A. G. Pampani (pr.) — 129
- 1738, *Artaserse*, G. F. Brivio (pr.) — 215
- 1739, *Didone*, G. B. Lampugnani (pr.) — 52
- 1743, *Demofoonte*, N. Jommelli (pr.) — 325
- 1759, *Alessandro*, B. Galuppi — 130

Palermo

Teatro Carolino
- 1821, *Adriano*, P. Airoldi (pr.) — 311
- 1824, *Didone*, S. Mercadante — 103
- 1827, *Alessandro*, G. Pacini — 182

Teatro de' Valguarneri marchesi di S. Lucia
- 1748, *Demofoonte*, unknown — 337

Teatro di Santa Cecilia
- 1724, *Didone*, D. Scarlatti — 43
- 1733, *Alessandro*, unknown — 127
- 1742, *Didone*, unknown — 59
- 1743, *Artaserse*, L. Vinci — 190
- 1747, *Artaserse*, V. L. Ciampi (pr.) — 224
- 1751, *Demofoonte*, L. Santini (pr.) — 341
- 1761, *Adriano*, B. Galuppi — 281
- 1762, *Alessandro*, N. Piccinni — 149
- 1763, *Didone*, G. B. Lampugnani — 53
- 1768, *Demofoonte*, B. Galuppi — 338
- 1773, *Adriano*, unknown — 304

1780, *Adriano*, unknown	308	
1780, *Didone*, F. Piticchio (pr.)	93	
1782, *Demofoonte*, G. Gazzaniga (pr.)	364	
1787, *Alessandro*, G. Arti (2nd ver. – pr.)	154	
1794, *Didone*, G. Paisiello	98	

Unknown theatre
    1746, *Alessandro*, unknown   134, 143

Palma de Mallorca

Teatro de Palma
    1767, *Artaserse*, unknown   244
    1767, *Demofoonte*, B. Galuppi   338

Paris

Académie Royale de Musique, Théâtre de l'
    1783, *Alessandro* (Fr.), N.-J. … de Méreaux (pr.)   172
    1783, *Didone* (Fr.), N. Piccinni   83
    1785, *Didone* (Fr.), N. Piccinni   83

Court theatre – Palace de Fontainebleau
    1783, *Didone* (Fr.), N. Piccinni (2nd ver. – pr.)   83

Court theatre – Palace de Versailles
    1753, *Didone*, J. A. Hasse   59

Opéra
    1788, *Demofoonte*, L. Cherubini (Fr., pr.)   368
    1789, *Demofoonte*, J. C. Vogel (Fr., pr.)   368

Tuileries
    1810, *Didone*, F. Paër (pr.)   101
    1811, *Didone*, F. Paër   101
    1812, *Didone*, F. Paër   101

Unknown theatre
    1799, *Adriano* (Fr.), É.-N. Méhul (pr.)[NP]   310

Parma

Teatro Ducale [Nuovo Imperial T.; Regio T. Ducale]
    1736, *Alessandro*, L. Vinci   112
    1737, *Artaserse*, F. Poncini Zilioli (pr.)   212
    1742, *Artaserse*, J. A. Hasse and others   199
    1745, *Didone*, N. Porpora   45
    1754, *Artaserse*, L. Vinci   190
    1754, *Demofoonte*, A. Mazzoni (pr.)   342
    1755, *Alessandro*, B. Galuppi   129

1817, *Artaserse*, M. A. Portugal   263
1817, *Didone*, F. Paër   101

Pavia

Teatro dei Quattro Cavalieri Associati [T. Nuovo]
    1774, *Artaserse*, various   249
    1777, *Adriano*, J. Mysliveček   305
    1777, *Demofoonte*, J. A. Schuster   360
    1781, *Demofoonte*, unknown   363
    1782, *Didone*, P. Anfossi   87
    1787, *Artaserse*, F. Bertoni   251
    1791, *Demofoonte*, A. Tarchi   365
    1804, *Artaserse*, N. A. Zingarelli   260

Teatro Omodeo
    1747, *Demofoonte*, G. F. Brivio   320
    1753, *Didone*, unknown   74
    1754, *Adriano*, A. G. Pampani   290
    1756, *Alessandro*, D. Perez   138
    1757, *Artaserse*, G. Scolari (pr.)?   238
    1759, *Didone*, T. Traetta   75
    1760, *Adriano*, unknown   297
    1767, *Didone*, unknown   81
    1771, *Demofoonte*, various   355

Perugia

Teatro Civico del Verzaro
    1781, *Artaserse*, G. Rust (pr.)   255
    1781, *Didone*, F. Zannetti   80
    1787, *Demofoonte*, G. Sarti   344

Teatro del Pavone [T. dei Nobili del Casino]
    1732, *Artaserse*, L. Vinci   190
    1734, *Artaserse*, L. Vinci   190
    1734, *Didone*, L. Vinci   46
    1746, *Adriano*, unknown   288
    1773, *Alessandro*, A. Sacchini   159
    1776, *Demofoonte*, G. Paisiello   359
    1777, *Adriano*, J. Mysliveček   305

Pesaro

Teatro del Sole [T. Pubblico]
    1730, *Didone*, T. G. Albinoni   44
    1731, *Artaserse*, L. Vinci   189
    1746, *Alessandro*, J. A. Hasse   120
    1759, *Demofoonte*, T. Traetta   347

SC | Index IV. Theatres

Piacenza

Teatro Ducale
    1738, *Demofoonte*, G. B. Lampugnani (pr.) — 319
    1748, *Artaserse*, G. Carcani (pr.) — 224

Pisa

Teatro Prini
    1780, *Demofoonte*, unknown — 362
    1785, *Didone*, G. Andreozzi — 93

Teatro Pubblico
    1734, *Artaserse*, G. Giacomelli (pr.) — 210
    1735, *Alessandro*, unknown — 129
    1750, *Artaserse*, L. Vinci — 190
    1756, *Alessandro*, N. Conforto (pr.) — 148
    1758, *Artaserse*, various — 239
    1759, *Adriano*, G. G. Brunetti (pr.) — 297
    1763, *Alessandro*, G. G. Brunetti (pr.) — 158
    1770, *Artaserse*, various — 247

Pistoia

Teatro dei Risvegliati [T. dell'Accademia del Risvegliati]
    1747, *Artaserse*, L. Vinci — 190
    1757, *Demofoonte*, G. Cocchi — 343

Porto

Theatre
    1772, *Demofoonte*, D. Perez — 341

Teatro de São João
    1798, *Didone*, S. Marino and others (pr.) — 100

Prague

Teatro Nuovo [T. di Praga]
    1744, *Artaserse*, P. Scalabrini and others — 214
    1748, *Artaserse*, various (past.) — 226
    1750, *Alessandro*, G. M. Rutini (pr.) — 144
    1760, *Adriano*, G. Scarlatti — 291
    1760, *Alessandro*, B. Galuppi — 130
    1760, *Demofoonte*, B. Galuppi — 338
    1761, *Artaserse*, unknown — 241
    1761, *Didone*, A. M. Mazzoni — 73
    1763, *Demofoonte*, various — 352
    1764, *Alessandro*, D. Fischietti (pr.) — 162
    1767, *Artaserse*, A. Boroni — 245

Teatro Regio [T. Reale]
    1768, *Didone*, A. Boroni (pr.) — 81
    1769, *Alessandro*, J. A. Koželuh (pr.) — 165
    1771, *Adriano*, A. Sacchini — 303
    1772, *Demofoonte*, J. A. Koželuh (pr.) — 356
    1773, *Artaserse*, G. Paisiello — 247

Theatre in Malá Strana [Teatro della Città Piccola]
    1734, *Alessandro*, A. Bioni — 128

Teatro Spork
    1731, *Didone*, T. G. Albinoni? — 44

Prato

Teatro Pubblico
    1736, *Alessandro*, E. R. Duni? — 129

Puerto de Santa María

Unknown theatre
    1753, *Alessandro*, Scolari — 145

Ravenna

Teatro Comunale
    1826, *Didone*, S. Mercadante — 103

Teatro Pubblico
    1747, *Artaserse*, unknown — 223

Regensburg

Theatre [Teatro di Ratisbona]
    1777, *Artaserse*, T. von Schacht (pr.) — 254
    1781, *Artaserse*, T. von Schacht — 254

Reggio Emilia

Teatro Pubblico [Nuovo T.; T. Comunale; T. della Comunità; T. dell'illustrissimo publico; T. di Regio]
    1725, *Didone*, N. Porpora (pr.) — 45
    1733, *Alessandro*, L. Vinci — 111
    1743, *Demofoonte*, C. W. Gluck — 323
    1750, *Adriano*, G. B. Pescetti (pr.) — 289
    1752, *Didone*, D. Perez — 70
    1753, *Alessandro*, G. Scarlatti (pr.) — 146
    1755, *Artaserse*, G. Cocchi (pr.) — 237
    1761, *Demofoonte*, N. Piccinni — 349
    1762, *Alessandro*, T. Traetta (pr.) — 158
    1787, *Demofoonte*, A. Tarchi — 365

1789, *Didone*, G. Andreozzi	93		1774, *Didone*, P. Anfossi (pr.)	87
1790, *Artaserse*, A. Tarchi	259		1777, *Artaserse*, P. A. Guglielmi (pr.)	254

Rimini

Teatro Pubblico [T. di Rimini]
- 1738, *Alessandro*, unknown — 134
- 1743, *Demofoonte*, various — 325
- 1759, *Demofoonte*, P. Vinci — 347

Rio de Janeiro

Court theatre [T. della Corte]
- 1812, *Artaserse*, M. A. Portugal — 263

Unknown theatre
- c. 1780, *Demofoonte*, various — 363

Rome

Teatro delle Dame [T. Alibert]
- 1726, *Didone*, L. Vinci (pr.) — 46
- 1730, *Alessandro*, L. Vinci (pr.) — 111
- 1730, *Artaserse*, L. Vinci (pr.) — 189
- 1731, *Artaserse*, L. Vinci — 189
- 1732, *Didone*, N. Porpora; R. Broschi; E. R. Duni (pr.) — 48
- 1738, *Artaserse*, L. Vinci — 190
- 1741, *Demofoonte*, A. Bernasconi (pr.) — 321
- 1752, *Adriano*, N. Jommelli (pr.) — 292
- 1757, *Demofoonte*, A. G. Pampani (pr.) — 346
- 1769, *Adriano*, G. di Majo — 300
- 1787, *Alessandro*, L. Caruso (pr.) — 176
- 1788, *Artaserse*, P. Anfossi (pr.) — 259
- 1791, *Demofoonte*, various — 369

Teatro di Torre Argentina [T. a Torre Argentina; T. Argentina]
- 1739, *Adriano*, A. Caldara — 271
- 1742, *Demofoonte*, L. Leo — 322
- 1747, *Didone*, N. Jommelli (pr.) — 64
- 1749, *Artaserse*, N. Jommelli (pr.) — 231
- 1758, *Alessandro*, N. Piccinni (pr.) — 149
- 1758, *Adriano*, R. di Capua (pr.) — 296
- 1762, *Artaserse*, N. Piccinni (pr.) — 241
- 1763, *Artaserse*, N. Jommelli — 231
- 1763, *Demofoonte*, G. di Majo (pr.) — 350
- 1768, *Artaserse*, A. Sacchini (pr.) — 245
- 1770, *Didone*, N. Piccinni (pr.) — 83
- 1772, *Alessandro*, P. Anfossi (pr.) — 165
- 1773, *Demofoonte*, P. Anfossi (pr.) — 356

1774, *Didone*, P. Anfossi (pr.) — 87
1777, *Artaserse*, P. A. Guglielmi (pr.) — 254
1779, *Adriano*, G. Sarti (pr.) — 307
1781, *Alessandro*, D. Cimarosa (pr.) — 172
1782, *Demofoonte*, G. Sarti (3rd ver. – pr.) — 344
1783, *Artaserse*, G. Rust — 255
s.d., *Didone*, A. Boroni — 81

Teatro di Tordinona
- 1735, *Demofoonte*, F. Ciampi (pr.) — 318
- 1736, *Adriano*, E. R. Duni (pr.) — 278

Teatro Valle
- 1810, *Didone*, V. Fioravanti (pr.) — 100

Unknown theatre
- 1724, *Didone*, D. Scarlatti — 43
- 1770, *Demofoonte*, J. B. Vanhal (pr.) — 355

Salzburg

Court theatre [T. di Corte]
- 1759, *Demofoonte*, J. E. Eberlin (pr.) — 349
- 1764, *Adriano*, A. Caldara — 271

Sassuolo

Teatro Pubblico
- 1750, *Alessandro*, L. Vinci — 112
- 1750, *Artaserse*, J. A. Hasse — 227

Senigallia

Teatro di Senigallia
- 1761, *Demofoonte*, A. Boroni and others (pr.) — 350

Siena

Teatro degli Intronati [T. della Academia dei Intronati; T. della Academia Intronata]
- 1733, *Artaserse*, unknown — 208
- 1750, *Adriano*, G. B. Pescetti — 289
- 1758, *Demofoonte*, P. Vinci (pr.) — 347
- 1759, *Didone*, G. Brunetti (pr.) — 77
- 1770, *Artaserse*, various — 247
- 1774, *Alessandro*, G. Sciroli? — 153
- 1778, *Alessandro*, M. Mortellari (pr.) — 170
- 1781, *Demofoonte*, L. Vinci — 321
- 1786, *Alessandro*, G. Andreozzi and others (pr.) — 175
- 1787, *Artaserse*, F. Bianchi — 258
- 1791, *Alessandro*, A. Tarchi — 178

SC | Index IV. Theatres

Teatro Grande
    1740, *Adriano*, unknown   281

Stockholm

Royal Theatre – Drottningholm Palace
    1757, *Adriano*, F. A. B. Uttini (pr.)   295
    1758, *Artaserse*, F. A. B. Uttini (pr.)   239
    1759, *Demofoonte*, F. A. B. Uttini   341

St Petersburg

Court theatre – Oranienbaum, Summer Palace
    1743, *Alessandro*, F. Araia (pr.)   136
    1759, *Alessandro*, F. Araia   136

Court theatre – Winter Palace [T. di Corte; T. Imperiale]
    1738, *Artaserse*, F. Araia (pr.)   213
    1738, *Artaserse*, F. Araia   213
    1755, *Alessandro*, F. Araia   136
    1758, *Didone*, F. Zoppis (pr.)   76
    1766, *Didone*, B. Galuppi   55
    1784, *Didone*, G. Andreozzi   93

Deutsches Theater
    1804, *Alessandro* (Ger.), S. Neukomm (pr.)   182

Teatro Hermitage
    1796, *Didone*, G. Paisiello   98
    1799, *Alessandro*, G. Paisiello   167

Strasbourg

Unknown theatre
    1741, *Didone*, P. Scalabrini and others   50
    1750, *Artaserse*, unknown   235

Stuttgart

Teatro Ducale
    1737, *Adriano*, A. Bernasconi   276
    1750, Artaserse, C. H. Graun   218
    1751, *Artaserse*, C. H. Graun   218
    1751, *Didone*, N. Jommelli   65
    1752, *Alessandro*, B. Galuppi   129
    1756, *Artaserse*, N. Jommelli (2nd ver. – pr.)   231
    1760, *Alessandro*, N. Jommelli (2nd ver. – pr.)   137
    1763, *Didone*, N. Jommelli (3rd ver. – pr.)   65
    1764, *Demofoonte*, N. Jommelli (3rd ver. – pr.)   326
    1777, *Didone*, N. Jommelli   65
    1778, *Demofoonte*, N. Jommelli   326
    1780, *Didone*, N. Jommelli   65
    1782, *Didone*, N. Jommelli   65

Teatro Ducale – Ludwigsburg
    1765, *Demofoonte*, N. Jommelli   326

Unknown theatre
    1788, *Adriano* (Ger.), J. F. Gauss (pr.)   309

Syracuse

Casa Senatoria
    1728, *Didone*, unknown   48

Trento

Teatro Nuovo
    1747, *Artaserse*, F. Maggiore (pr.)   223

Treviso

Teatro Dolfin
    1737, *Adriano*, G. Porta   278
    1738, *Artaserse*, J. A. Hasse   198
    1755, *Artaserse*, B. Galuppi   228
    1761, *Demofoonte*, A. Boroni and others   350

Teatro Onigo
    1766, *Demofoonte*, P. A. Guglielmi (pr.)   353
    1780, *Adriano*, P. Anfossi   304
    1782, *Artaserse*, F. Zannetti (pr.)   256
    1785, *Artaserse*, F. Bertoni   251

Trieste

Teatro Regio
    1785, *Alessandro*, F. Bianchi   173
    1789, *Artaserse*, N. A. Zingarelli (pr.)   260
    1789, *Demofoonte*, N. A. Zingarelli (pr.)   368

Turin

Teatro Regio
    1727, *Didone*, D. N. Sarro   41
    1731, *Alessandro*, N. Porpora (pr.)   114
    1738, *Demofoonte*, G. F. Brivio (pr.)   319
    1740, *Adriano*, B. Galuppi (1st ver. – pr.)   281
    1741, *Artaserse*, G. Arena (pr.)   217
    1745, *Alessandro*, C. W. Gluck (pr.)   142
    1750, *Didone*, D. M. B. Terradellas (pr.)   69

SC | Index IV. Theatres

1754, *Demofoonte*, G. Manna (pr.)	342
1759, *Adriano*, G. B. Borghi (pr.)	296
1761, *Artaserse*, J. C. Bach (pr.)	240
1766, *Alessandro*, A. Sacchini	158
1773, *Didone*, G. Colla (pr.)	86
1782, *Adriano*, G. Rust (pr.)	308
1785, *Artaserse*, D. Cimarosa (pr.)	257
1788, *Demofoonte*, G. Pampani (pr.)	367
1798, *Alessandro*, A. Tarchi (2nd ver. – pr.)	178
1823, *Didone*, S. Mercadante (pr.)	103
1829, *Didone*, S. Mercadante	104

Teatro Carignano
1730, *Artaserse*, J. A. Hasse	197

Udine

Teatro della Nobile Società
1826, *Didone*, S. Mercadante	103

Teatro della Racchetta
1763, *Adriano*, B. Galuppi	282

Teatro Nuovo
1795, *Alessandro*, F. Bianchi	174

Urbino

Teatro Pascolini
1734, *Alessandro*, L. Vinci	111

Valencia

Palace of the dukes of Gandia, Theatre in the
1769, *Artaserse*, A. Sacchini	245
1769, *Demofoonte*, unknown	355

Palacio Real
1734, *Artaserse*, unknown	210

Theatre
1774, *Alessandro*, unknown	168
1778, *Artaserse*, unknown	255

Venice

Teatro dei Dilettanti [Teatro dell'Accademia dei Dilettanti]
1754, *Artaserse*, B. Galuppi and others	227

Teatro di S. Girolamo [Palazzo Labia]
1747, *Didone*, A. Adolfati (pr.)	67
1748, *Didone*, F. Bertoni (pr.)	68

Teatro Grimani di S. Benedetto
1756, *Artaserse*, A. G. Pampani (2nd ver. – pr.)	234
1757, *Adriano*, G. F. Brusa (pr.)	295
1759, *Demofoonte*, various	348
1761, *Artaserse*, B. Galuppi	228
1762, *Artaserse*, G. di Majo (pr.)	241
1764, *Didone*, B. Galuppi	55
1766, *Adriano*, P. A. Guglielmi (pr.)	300
1766, *Artaserse*, G. Ponzo (pr.)	244
1769, *Demofoonte*, J. Mysliveček (pr.)	353
1770, *Didone*, G. di Majo (pr.)	82
1771, *Adriano*, A. Sacchini (pr.)	303
1771, *Alessandro*, F. Bertoni	164
1772, *Artaserse*, V. Manfredini (pr.)	248
1775, *Demofoonte*, G. Paisiello (pr.)	358
1776, *Artaserse*, G. B. Borghi (pr.)	250
1778, *Alessandro*, L. Marescalchi (pr.)	169
1779, *Didone*, J. A. Schuster	89
1780, *Adriano*, F. Alessandri (pr.)	308
1785, *Alessandro*, F. Bianchi (pr.)	173
1787, *Demofoonte*, A. Prati (pr.)	366
1791, *Demofoonte*, G. Pugnani	367

→ <u>becomes</u>

Teatro Vernier in S. Benedetto [T. in S. Benedetto]
1798, *Adriano*, J. S. Mayr (pr.)	309
1827, *Didone*, S. Mercadante	104

Teatro Grimani di S. Giovanni Grisostomo
1730, *Artaserse*, J. A. Hasse (pr.)	197
1730, *Didone*, D. N. Sarro (2nd ver. – pr.)	41
1733, *Adriano*, G. Giacomelli (pr.)	272
1734, *Artaserse*, J. A. Hasse	198
1735, *Demofoonte*, G. M Schiassi (pr.)	316
1736, *Alessandro*, J. A. Hasse (2nd ver. – pr.)	119
1738, *Alessandro*, J. A. Hasse (3rd ver. – pr.)	120
1738, *Demofoonte*, G. Latilla (pr.)	319
1740, *Adriano*, A. Giai (pr.)	284
1741, *Didone*, A. Bernasconi (pr.)	57
1743, *Alessandro*, J. A. Hasse	120
1744, *Artaserse*, D. Terradellas (pr.)	221
1746, *Artaserse*, G. Abos (pr.)	222
1749, *Demofoonte*, J. A. Hasse (2nd ver. – pr.)	332
1750, *Artaserse*, A. G. Pampani (pr.)	234
1751, *Didone*, G. Manna (pr.)	69

Index IV. Theatres

    1789, *Didone*, G. Gazzaniga — 96
    s.d., *Artaserse*, L. Vinci — 190

Teatro Grimani di S. Samuele
    1754, *Adriano*, G. Scolari (pr.) — 294
    1755, *Alessandro*, B. Galuppi (2nd ver. – pr.) — 129
    1760, *Adriano*, A. M. Mazzoni (pr.) — 297
    1775, *Alessandro*, G. Rust (pr.) — 169
    1788, *Artaserse*, various — 260
    1790, *Didone*, various — 96
    1791, *Alessandro*, L. Caruso (2nd ver. – pr.) — 176

Teatro Giustiniani di S. Moisè
    1757, *Didone*, T. Traetta (pr.) — 75
    1775, *Didone*, P. Anfossi — 87
    1778, *Didone*, P. Anfossi — 87

Teatro La Fenice
    1792, *Alessandro*, F. Bianchi — 173
    1795, *Artaserse*, G. Nicolini (pr.) — 263
    1795, *Demofoonte*, various — 368
    1828, *Alessandro*, G. Pacini — 182

Teatro Sant'Angelo
    1732, *Alessandro*, G. B. Pescetti (pr.) — 126

Teatro Tron di S. Cassiano
    1725, *Didone*, T. G. Albinoni (pr.) — 43
    1748, *Adriano*, V. L. Ciampi (pr.) — 288
    1752, *Adriano*, G. Scarlatti (pr.) — 291
    1753, *Alessandro*, G. Latilla and others (pr.) — 146
    1764, *Demofoonte*, A. G. Pampani — 346

Teatro Vendramin di S. Salvatore
    1742, *Artaserse*, G. A. Paganelli (2nd ver. – pr.) — 212
    1754, *Demofoonte*, G. Cocchi (pr.) — 343
    1758, *Artaserse*, G. Scolari — 238
    1759, *Alessandro*, G. Scolari — 145
    1760, *Adriano*, B. Galuppi — 281
    1763, *Alessandro*, A. Sacchini (pr.) — 158

Unknown theatre
    1735?, *Adriano*, unknown — 276
    1785, *Didone*, P. A. Guglielmi (pr.) — 94
    1826, *Didone*, S. Mercadante — 103

Verona

Teatro dietro alla Reina
    1751, *Artaserse*, D. del Barba and others (pr.) — 235

Teatro Filarmonico [Accademia Filarmonica]
    1733, *Artaserse*, J. A. Hasse — 198
    1740, *Alessandro*, J. A. Hasse — 120
    1741, *Artaserse*, P. Chiarini (pr.) — 217
    1745, *Alessandro*, P. Chiarini (pr.) — 142
    1754, *Alessandro*, J. A. Hasse — 120
    1755, *Didone*, unknown — 75
    1757, *Demofoonte*, unknown — 346
    1759, *Artaserse*, B. Galuppi — 228
    1760, *Adriano*, various — 297
    1760, *Didone*, various — 77
    1761, *Alessandro*, D. dal Barba (pr.) — 154
    1764, *Alessandro*, unknown — 162
    1770, *Artaserse*, A. Boroni — 245
    1774, *Adriano*, unknown — 306
    1778, *Artaserse*, G. Paisiello — 247
    1779, *Alessandro*, A. Calegari (pr.) — 170
    1785, *Artaserse*, F. Bertoni — 251
    1787, *Alessandro*, F. Bianchi — 173
    1796, *Didone*, G. Paisiello — 98
    1814, *Adriano*, M. A. Portugal — 310
    1828, *Didone*, S. Mercadante — 104

Unknown theatre
    1781, *Alessandro*, M. de Vicenti — 170

Vicenza

Teatro delle Grazie
    1740, *Adriano*, G. B. Lampugnani (pr.) — 284
    1754, *Demofoonte*, J. A. Hasse — 332
    1756, *Artaserse*, B. Galuppi — 228
    1757, *Alessandro*, B. Galuppi — 130
    1762, *Demofoonte*, A. Boroni and others? — 350

Teatro di Piazza
    1738, *Artaserse*, J. A. Hasse — 198
    1739, *Alessandro*, J. A. Hasse — 120
    1750, *Alessandro*, G. Scolari (pr.) — 145

Teatro Eretenio [T. Nuovo]
    1787, *Didone*, G. Gazzaniga (pr.) — 96
    1824, *Didone*, S. Mercadante — 103

Vienna

Burgtheater [Altes Burgtheater, Theater nächst der Burg]
    1744, *Demofoonte*, C. W. Gluck — 323
    1746, *Alessandro*, J. A. Hasse (?) — 120

SC | Index IV. Theatres

Court theatre [Großes Hoftheater, T. di Corte]
    1732, *Adriano*, A. Caldara (pr.) — 271
    1733, *Demofoonte*, A. Caldara (pr.) — 315
    1807, *Adriano* (Ger.), J. Weigl (pr.) — 310

Kleines Hoftheater
    1726, *Didone*, L. Vinci — 46

Teatro Privilegiato [Theater am Kärntnertor]
    1729, *Didone*, unknown — 48
    1730, *Artaserse*, L. Vinci — 189
    1731, *Alessandro*, N. Porpora — 115
    1739, *Artaserse*, unknown — 216
    1740, *Didone*, various — 54
    1741, *Didone*, various — 54
    1743, *Adriano*, unknown — 285
    1746, *Alessandro*, J. A. Hasse — 120
    1746, *Artaserse*, A. Bernasconi (pr.)? — 223
    1748, *Alessandro*, G. C. Wagenseil (pr.) — 144
    1749, *Artaserse*, B. Galuppi (pr.) — 227
    1749, *Didone*, N. Jommelli (2nd ver. – pr.) — 64
    1752, *Didone*, G. Bonno[NP] — 73
    1763, *Artaserse*, G. Scarlatti (2nd ver. – pr.) — 224
    1795, *Didone*, L. Koželuh (pr. – lost) — 100

Vyškov

Theatre
    1734, *Alessandro*, L. Vinci — 111
    1735, *Demofoonte*, G. M. Schiassi — 316
    1737, *Adriano*, J. A. Hasse — 279

Warsaw

Radziwiłł palace, Theatre in
    1776, *Didone*, P. Anfossi — 87

Royal Theatre [T. Reale; T. Regio]
    1759, *Demofoonte*, J. A. Hasse — 332
    1760, *Artaserse*, J. A. Hasse — 199

Theatre [T. di Varsavia]
    1776, *Demofoonte*, J. A. Hasse — 32
    1776, *Didone*, P. Anfossi — 87

Teatro Nazionale
    1792, *Alessandro*, F. Bianchi — 174

Wrocław

Teatro Ballhaus [T. di Breslavia; Theatro zu Breslau]
    1726, *Didone*, T. G. Albinoni — 43
    1733, *Artaserse*, A. Bioni? (pr.) — 208
    1734, *Alessandro*, A. Bioni (pr.) — 128
    1741, *Artaserse*, P. Scalabrini and others — 214

Unknown city

    1742?, *Demofoonte*, N. B. Logroscino? (pr.) — 285
    1747–1748, *Demofoonte*, J. C. Smith (pr.) — 332
    1749, *Artaserse*, J. C. Smith (pr.) — 233
    1760, *Demofoonte*, G. Brunetti (pr.) — 349
    1764, *Adriano*, M. Wimmer (pr.) — 299
    1780s, *Artaserse*, P. F. Parenti (pr.) — 255
    c. 1790, *Alessandro*, N. A. Zingarelli (pr.) — 181
    c. 1790, *Adriano*, N. A. Zingarelli (pr.) — 309
    c. 1800, *Adriano*, C. Bernardini (pr.) — 310
    1795, *Artaserse*, F. Ceracchini (pr.) — 263
    1826, *Adriano* (Fr.), F. Mirecki (pr.) — 311